11C1P

ELEVEN CHARLIE ONE PAPA

JAMES M. MALLEN

AuthorHouse™
1663 Liberty Drive
Bloomington, IN 47403
www.authorhouse.com
Phone: 1-800-839-8640

Published by AuthorHouse 09/05/2012

ISBN: 978-1-4772-6599-4 (sc)
ISBN: 978-1-4772-6600-7 (e)

Library of Congress Control Number: 2012916288

Republic of Viet Nam
July 1966 to July 1967

Weapons Platoon
Alpha Company
4th Battalion
503rd Airborne Infantry Regiment
173rd Airborne Brigade (Separate)

CONTENTS

Preface

This book has not been edited. It has not been edited for continuity, interest, or marketability. It has not been edited to make it more enjoyable or entertaining. It is simply a description of a year in Viet Nam, on the ground, straight out, full on. If you are looking for some intellectualized or romanticized or patriotic or sanitized version of war then this book is not for you.

If you want to know the details of what life was like for an Infantryman in a combat zone, what this Country requires of a combat soldier and what any Country requires of human beings, in the war of ideas, then read further. Kings, Presidents, Prime Ministers, and Politicians think that their ideas require War but they never personally suffer the consequences of their ideas, as opposed to a combat soldier. At worse, they lose their jobs while their combat soldiers are killed, murdered, maimed, wounded, sometimes horribly, physically and or mentally, usually, sometimes in ways that the average citizen simply cannot possibly imagine or comprehend, and it seems, do not want to consider in all of its horrible forms and ramifications. A President or Prime minister along with their Senate usually decide to wage war without any possible comprehension of what that decision will mean to the men and their families who will bear the cost and burden of the battle.

Sometimes, leaders of countries declare that the actions of another Country or People are not acceptable, and therefore to "right that wrong", Soldiers will be sent to correct the situation. The leaders of those countries will never bear the horrible consequences of "righting a wrong". That is left to the men and women in uniform and their families who will suffer insufferable consequences because some Senator in a an impeccably tailored and meticulously clean three piece suit seeks reelection for his own personal gain.

Before you say, "Lets go kick their ass", Why don't **you,** personally, go and kick their ass. To any politician who has not served in combat, I say, You have no idea of what you ask of the combat soldiers and their families. To those politicians who have served in combat, the damned very, very few that there are, I say if you support a war only because it helps your quest for re-election, against what you know, it will probably result in your eternal damnation. It has certainly resulted in Hell on Earth for hundreds of thousands of combat soldiers and their families"

And, to those millions of people who think that "righting a wrong" is worth fighting, I simply say, "What are **You** going to do about it, other than requiring someone else to suffer unimaginable horrors and unendurable pain and unrelenting torture, requiring their families to suffer insufferable hardships and heartache, for many, many years so that You can say, "Well, it had to be done, it was right that We had done it." We didn't do it. The leadership of this Country, and its Citizens, required a very small percentage of its Citizens to assume a burden that was unspeakably unbearable, far beyond the imagination of a normal human being, a burden of horror and pain and suffering that a Citizen, in his right mind, cannot comprehend, an unimaginable, interminable torture that the Citizens of a good country imposed upon their own sons and grandsons.

Declared war is war declared on ones own citizens. I hope that this book testifies to the absolute horrors that a Country demanded to be suffered upon its own sons and daughters.

Some men had "other priorities", like Dick Cheney, to avoid military service. There were tens or hundreds of thousands of young men who "Beat the Draft" by moving to Canada. My statement to those of you who followed that path, supported now by history, is that: although your effeminate friends and cowardly associates tried to justify your choices, there were hundreds of thousands of Men and Women who answered their Nations call and you, forty years later, as History reports, were just a bunch of cowardly misfits, a disgrace to your families, to your Country and to yourselves. You saved your asses, but at what cost to your psyches, personalities, your manhood, your honor and your personal accountability before God as a human being?

James Jones, author of "From Here to Eternity" said of World War II:

> **"It was an event so powerful in the lives of those who experienced it that they spent the rest of their lives walking backwards looking at it."**

From a perspective of forty years after Viet Nam I can see that that was the reality of surviving Viet Nam veterans. May God bless and help every one of them and their families.

If you're still with me. If you want to know what life was like "On the Ground" for an American Infantryman in Viet Nam, then grab your bug juice and "RUCK UP". We're goin' in amongst them.

Chapter 1
BEGINNING

When a Country declares war on another Country, it declares war on its own Soldiers.

Unknown

The interior of the commercial jet was very warm, almost hot. It must have been sitting on the tarmac for an hour or so without power, but it still had a slight, vague coldness and smell of air-conditioning. The sight of very comfortable seats made me even happier than I had been. I walked forward down the aisle, towards a Sergeant who was in charge of the seating. With exaggerated waving of his arms and shouting, which could not be understood above the roar of the engines, he pointed his fingers at the first man in line, in turn, and then pointed to a seat.

Somehow, the men in front of me discerned what he meant and everyone were seated in the aircraft very quickly and efficiently. When it came to be my turn, the Sergeant deliberately walked towards the back of the plane, bypassing about 10 empty rows, and pointed to an empty seat, directing me to sit in an aisle seat next to a person who was mid-seated. I gladly fell into that seat. Then the Sergeant backpedaled quickly, wildly gesticulating, directing people to sit up forward again.

I was only vaguely aware that there was another guy already seated in the middle of the 3-seat cluster on the starboard side of the plane but I did wonder why he was sitting so completely out of proper loading order, and why I was selected to sit so completely out of order next to him. He seemed to be almost desperately intent on finding something that he had dropped or lost. He was searching the floor down by his feet, to his left and right, below his seat and then, half standing, at the row behind him. Why was that guy there, and why did the Sergeant pick me to sit beside him? I still don't know why.

The Sergeant in charge was seating men into every seat in a very methodical manner, from front to back. He was filling seats ten rows in front of me so I assumed that he had made a mistake and I tried to catch his attention. I waved my hand and stared directly at him, trying to convey that obviously I had been placed out of order. I certainly didn't want some sort of administrative error to interfere with me leaving Viet Nam or to cause problems upon entering the USA.

I thought that my seating order might have been mixed up somehow because the loading order and seating manifest that we had been assigned was very specific. The seating Sergeant finally looked directly at me, as if to say that he was very aware of the situation, but then he suddenly looked downwards, avoiding my questioning gaze, and continued assigning men into their seats. When he reached my row, he deliberately did not assign anyone to sit at the empty window seat next to me. Why in the world I wondered, would that Sergeant leave that seat unoccupied when obviously there were enough men in line to fill every single seat. That meant that someone who was scheduled to leave on that plane would have to be left behind. In fact, during the flight, I noticed that every seat was occupied except for the window seat in my row.

The guy beside me suddenly looked directly at me, with a look of desperation and horror. One look into his eyes and it was obvious that there was something terribly wrong. After about ten seconds he stated, to no one in particular, that "The Viet Cong are very close!" He looked out of the window to his right and then frantically looked towards the back of the plane, then violently turned around looking towards the front of the plane, then very quickly twisted his body and half raised up out of his seat to look at the floor that was directly behind his seat.

He desperately tried to shout out a warning to everyone on board: "We're all going to die!, We're all going to die!" many times over but the sound level was scarcely more than a whisper, only I could make out what he was saying. Basically, I guess, he was so horrified and terrified that he couldn't shout or scream much above the sound level of a ghastly, hoarse whisper.

I looked again at the Sergeant and he just returned my look. He was very aware of the situation, and I slowly began to realize that he had deliberately put me next to this guy to see what I might be able to do with the situation. Maybe the decorations that I wore on my uniform, my Combat Infantryman's badge, 173rd Airborne Brigade combat patch and paratroopers wings made him select me to see what could be done with that guy. I figured that that guy must have seen much more combat than I had and was now suddenly sensing danger where there was none. I assumed that now that he was so close to going home that he was hyper-sensitized to possible dangers, especially due to what he must have experienced during his tour of duty. I thought that that guy must be having a psychotic breakdown or was very close to it.

I wanted to help him because he was obviously in extreme distress but I was no psychiatrist. The only thing that I could do was to try to try to talk that panic-stricken guy down and so I tried to begin a conversation with him, to try to take his mind off of his fears or to divert his attention. Actually, for the first half minute that guy had me going and I thought that there really was some danger close by, but I knew from experience how men usually react in a dangerous situation and there was no other shouts or sudden movements from the others on the plane. Plus, there were aircraft personnel on the ground. If there really was some enemy activity close to the aircraft then they would certainly have seen it and acted appropriately.

After we talked for a minute, he said that he was wigged out because of "Those big explosions!" last night. I told him that that was just our huge artillery at Long Bien firing fifteen miles away and not even in our general direction. Then he said that there were VC outside of the plane and that there was a bomb aboard. Something about what he said just didn't ring true. We spoke for a few minutes more and I asked him what unit he had served in and he told me some meaningless letters and numbers, designating a Unit that I didn't recognize at all. I asked him what his MOS (Military Occupational Specialty) was and he told me something that I didn't apprehend at all. Finally I asked him what, exactly, he had been doing for the last year in Viet Nam. He replied that he had been a Navy bartender at an officers club in Saigon. He told me that, horror of horrors, one night a Vietnamese prostitute went into his club and had actually stabbed him in the forearm with a fingernail file!

That information was beyond comprehension to me. I suddenly realized that there were American military personnel in Viet Nam who were not infantry, artillery, armor or combat aircraft personnel. I suddenly thought: "Does this guy have any idea of what it is like out there in the jungle?, on combat operations?" The guy had settled down a bit by that time, which was good, but he had regained part of the force of a normal voice and his remarks about VC outside of the plane and his repeating, again and again, that we were all going to die was having an effect on a number of passengers on the plane. I looked around and noticed that there were ten or fifteen people close by who could hear his warnings and they were getting very jittery and were looking at me and the guy beside me with growing alarm.

Within a minute or so the psychotic next to me was again ramping up his act, now he was half way out of his seat, yelling and carrying on. I didn't know what to do, but I knew for a fact that that act was not going to mess up my transcontinental airplane trip home. That act was not going to continue for the next six hours of the duration of this leg of the trip. I looked over at him and said "SHUT UP! You F . . . .". The effect on him was instantaneous.

I didn't even finish the word that began with "F" because at that point, his head twisted to face to the front faster than I would have thought was humanly possible, his body seemed to have been frozen solid instantly. He stayed that way for about five minutes, not moving at all and not uttering another word. Eventually I looked over at him to see if he was still alive. The thought struck me that I hoped that I hadn't killed him. If a man can die of fright or shock then that guy was a prime candidate for death. Luckily, I could just barely discern that he was breathing.

I exited my seat to use the rear rest room. Now there were some rumblings among the close by passengers about how I had been too abrupt with him, how I had maltreated him. Three of them, in a row close by, stated to me very forcefully and menacingly that I should leave that guy alone. They said: "that guy has probably seen so much combat that he has gone over the edge". Now I am going to have to fight those three guys I thought. I wasn't looking forward to it, but I was game for it. I yelled to them: "Hey, that guy spent the last year as a Navy bartender at an officers club in Saigon." One of them said: "How the hell do you know that?". I told them: "because that's what he told me", and I just continued walking. Apparently that statement changed everything because as was returning to my seat one of them suddenly turned around and spotted me, staring directly and intently at me. "OK, lets go!", I thought. "I was happy and calm but if you guys want to play it this way, then there is suddenly going to be some extreme violence on this plane that most of the passengers have never experienced". As I approached that group of three, they said things like: "Yeah, good for you!" and "That guy had to be put down!" and "Someone had to do something, Thanks a lot!" Men around them shook their heads and smiled in approval.

I settled in my seat and thought back to how I had arrived at this day and place. On January 4, 1966 I joined the Army. I joined, because I was going to be drafted anyways (I got my draft notice 6 weeks after I joined) and I figured that if I voluntarily joined, that the Army would look out for my interests, would treat me differently than if I was just drafted, that they would consider my scores on the aptitude tests and IQ tests, and place me in a job and occupation to which I was suited. That was an incorrect assumption.

I had no idea of what to do with my life. I figured that the aptitude tests would point out what career and education that I should follow. I had scored exceptionally high on all of the Army aptitude tests and IQ tests except for infantry, but Infantrymen were in short supply and that was what the Army determined would be my lot in life, a decision over which I had no control and one which would profoundly affect the rest of my life.

Basic training for 8 weeks was followed by advanced airborne infantry training for another 6 weeks and then 4 weeks of Jump school (to become a paratrooper, airborne qualified). On the last day of Jump school, everyone received their individual orders as to where next they should report for duty. Some guys were assigned to Germany or Korea or somewhere in the US, but 95% of us, including me, received orders to report to Viet Nam. We did not know to which unit we would be ultimately assigned. The orders just said to report to Fort Dix, New Jersey for transportation to Viet Nam and then temporary assignment to a Replacement Company once we arrived in Viet Nam.

We had been promised a 30-day leave, but the orders only allowed for 22 days. Most guys stated that they would take the 30 days and the Army could discipline them later if they wished. The feeling and logic was "What are they going to do? Send us to Viet Nam?"

However, almost everyone reported on time, or within a day or two. At the time, there was an airline strike and most flights were cancelled. When I arrived at the airport, I had a reservation but reservations were not being honored. My father spoke with an airline ticket agent and explained that I was active duty Armed Forces and had orders to report later that day. I was given priority boarding and assigned a seat on the next flight, about 15 minutes later.

There were probably many other people there that dearly wished to get on that flight, I was the last person who wanted to get to my destination. I shook my fathers hand and kissed my mother and girlfriend goodbye. I thought that the probability of ever seeing them again to be about 5 percent, including the fact that when and if I did see them, I may well be missing limbs or blinded or head shot. My age was 19 years and 2 months old. I was an airborne infantryman, going into combat in Viet Nam. I figured that the probability of returning alive and uninjured was extremely low, which proved to be accurate.

We were at Fort Dix for about 5 days when we were ordered to get all of our gear and get onto a bus. My mother had asked me to call her when I was actually leaving. Luckily, there was a phone booth nearby so I could call her. Basically, this was it, this was the final warning or confirmation that I was leaving. The conversation could only last 2 minutes before the busses arrived. My mother was very upset. I thought that this was as bad as things can get. This is like a man calling his family to tell them that, yes, he was finally actually in the gas chamber and they would be dropping the gas pellets any minute now, but I tried to sound upbeat, I told my mother that everything would be all right, don't worry about me.

Chapter 2
IN COUNTRY

Cardboard House

We went to Viet Nam via a chartered commercial jet airliner. There were stewardesses and free drinks and movies. Just like going on vacation. But the flight took an extraordinarily long time, maybe 18 hours or more, and every time that we landed to refuel we were never allowed to disembark the plane.

We landed for refueling and changing crews in California, Hawaii, and Okinawa before finally arriving. At each stop of the plane, the stewardesses seemed to decrease in appearance and increase in seriousness. I thought that perhaps it was just my interpretation but other passengers increasingly expressed the same interpretation.

On our final approach to Viet Nam, I strained to look out of the window.The scenery below us seemed surreal.The exceptionally green colors against the extremely stark and barren stretches of brown soil and concrete of the airfield was something that I had never seen. I had a feeling of utter awe and utter dread. But it was all happening now. There was nothing that I could do to get out of it, so I steeled myself for the beginning of a great adventure.

We had left Fort Dix, New Jersey in July and I had been trained at the Airborne Advanced Infantry school and Jump school in Georgia for the previous months in May and June so when I walked down the gangplank of the plane the heat and humidity of Viet Nam was not so much of a shock as others would feel upon coming in the winter, but it was still worse than the American South. We loaded up on busses for a trip from the airport to the Replacement Company in Long Bien, about a 30-minute ride from the airport in Saigon.

The busses had a heavy-duty screen over each glass-less window and over that metal bars. Someone asked aloud what the screens are for and someone replied, "To keep the enemy from throwing grenades into the bus". Some people laughed. I realized that that was in fact the only possible reason.

The road, for the most part, was a wide, modern superhighway, the only one in the country but only about 10 miles long. It was built specifically and only for military re-supply from the Saigon airport to the main Army depot in Long Bien.

After exiting the superhighway, we continued on a narrow two-lane dirt road that traveled past civilian areas. My senses, and psyche were assaulted at the things that I was witnessing, sights and sounds and smells that were completely foreign, shocking and terrible. For more than a few moments I seriously questioned whether I had in fact been killed on the airplane or maybe blown up by a bomb and was now dead because this seemed to be some corner of Hell.

There was an overwhelming smell of diesel fuel from all of the military trucks using the road. The air that I was breathing seemed to have a distinctly oily feel, something that must be very unhealthy to breathe. The very heavy smell of diesel smoke still did not hide the sickly sweet odor of decaying garbage along with a distinct element of human and animal waste, trampled jungle vegetation, rotting fruits on the ground and of strange foods being cooked by the civilians that lived along the road. In the hot, heavy humid air it was an assault upon ones lungs and nose that I could have never imagined in my previous life.

The civilians wore strange clothing that were mostly filthy and tattered. Many of them wore strange conical straw hats and were waiting around, stooping, with their buttocks an inch off of the ground in a posture that I didn't think was humanly possible. The children ran around naked, or, if they wore anything, it was a colored t-shirt that was beyond filthy. From what I could see, all of the old women living there had teeth that were stained a midnight black. I learned later that was from them chewing on betel nuts (a very mild drug).

The houses were made of crooked old branches and discarded randomly sized pieces of old cardboard. The floors were of dirt. There was obviously no electricity or running water. In the center of those hovels were old black pots on old worn out bricks with a little sort of camp fire of smoking sticks. The smoke filled the houses and wafted through adjacent houses, although they could not really be called houses at all, in fact these dwellings really couldn't be called hovels. How any human being could be reduced to living in that squalor was beyond my understanding. The poverty and living conditions of these people were far and away worse than anything I could have ever imagined in my wildest nightmares.

Chapter 3
REPLACEMENT COMPANY

"Mankind must put an end to war, or war will put an end to mankind."

John F. Kennedy

Most people, upon entering the Country, were assigned to a Replacement Company. That was just an outfit that sorted out everyone coming into the Country, probably with most people already assigned to a specific outfit. At the replacement Company, after a few days, most of the guys were given their orders to report to their respective Units. Everyday, more people arrived, and more of the guys in my original airplane group were given their orders and were transported to their assigned outfits. After about a week, everyone from my group had received their orders and moved on, except for me.

Living conditions at this camp were relatively primitive and the only hot water that was available for shaving had to be prepared each day. If they had gravity fed cold water showers available I never saw any of them during my stay. Water was placed into a 40-gallon trash can and then a contraption was placed into the water. Gasoline dripped from a very small spigot, was set afire with a book of matches thrown into the dripping gasoline and then with a loud "whoosh" and rush of air, the minor explosion of the gasoline and gasoline vapors would start to burn and then that contraption would heat the water. Many times it took five or ten attempts to set it ablaze, each of which entailed a serious threat of blowing up in the face of the operator.

One day, a Sergeant asked me if I would be willing to get that contraption going every morning. He said that if I agreed to do that, then I would not be put on any other duty (KP or guard duty), I readily agreed. Early every morning I would go directly to the can and fill it with water and fill the contraption with gasoline. Then I would turn on the spigot for the gasoline, adjust the rate at which the drops fell, and then threw in a match or a lighted piece of newspaper. It would almost always take several attempts to light it and by that time there was too much gasoline and vapors in the contraption so it would suddenly light up with a sudden explosion of flame. The principle was to turn on the gasoline, light a match or burning newspaper, throw it into the contraption and then run for your life away from it. If it did not light off, then give it more gas, repeat the procedure, and then run even more quickly away from it while trying to light it up. When it fired up, you would have to run back to it and adjust downwards the rate of fuel to fire. It could, and frequently did, suddenly flame up into your face, the results of which could be horrific. I was afraid of that contraption, with very good reason.

Everyday I would stand in formation in the morning, and everyday men were given orders, but for some reason, I would not be called. After almost 3 weeks, I was still there and I thought that the Army had lost my records, which would be all right with me. Maybe my name had been taken off of the duty list because of my morning detail, maybe it was lost due to my mothers prayers. Perhaps, I thought, I could just stay here, every day going by counting against my 365 days of required duty.

One night I decided to take a walk around the compound a little. There was no one else about and it was very quiet. Suddenly I heard a very loud scream, truly a terrifying and bloodcurdling scream that seemed to come from the perimeter of the compound or maybe a tent close by. I stood there frozen for a while, in the middle of the dirt street, acutely aware that I was unarmed. There was no other soul around and there was nothing to use for cover. I stood motionless for a couple of minutes but did not hear anyone talking or anyone moving about. I don't know if it was someone having a nightmare or a sentry being knifed on the perimeter or exactly what it was, but I considered it a very bad omen.

A week or so later, after tending to my morning duties, I returned to my tent. There was no one else in the tent, in fact there seemed to be almost no one left in the camp so out of boredom I decided to just take a walk around the camp. A lone Sergeant who was also walking about seemed quite taken aback to see me, or actually anyone else, in this camp, and asked me what I was doing and where were my orders. I told him that I had not as yet received orders. He asked me how long I had been there and when I answered 3 weeks, he became visibly upset and angry. He went directly to the administration tent. The next day I received orders to report to the 173rd Airborne Brigade in Bien Hoa, about a 30-minute ride truck ride away.

Four other soldiers had reported to the replacement company the day before and were immediately assigned to the 173rd Airborne. So the next day all of us loaded onto a truck for transport to the 173rd base camp. When we arrived at base camp there were very few men around. The Company was in the field, the entire battalion was in the field on an operation.

We had not yet been issued any equipment and certainly no weapons and most of us felt rather vulnerable since it seemed that the post was very lightly guarded and there were many Vietnamese civilian workers on the base, all of them involved in heavy construction labor and possibly, we thought, enemy infiltrators.

About the only person from the Company who was at base camp and not in the field was the supply Sergeant. In fact, he was the highest ranking person in the Company that was in base camp (Staff Sergeant E-6). He was a friendly guy and we talked with him to try to get an idea of what it was like in the bush but he really didn't personally spend any time with the infantry so he couldn't really give us an accurate description of what it was like to be on an operation.

Later that day, as the sun was going down, we saw some Vietnamese civilian workers and beckoned them over. Through sign language, we tried to determine if there were any Viet Cong in the area, and, since we had not been issued any weapons so far, we tried to ascertain if we could buy some weapons from them. The translation didn't go over very well, although the Vietnamese civilians seemed to be very friendly, but suffice it to say, we could not procure any illegal weapons from them.

Chapter 4
THE FARM

Chinook with water trailer

About three days later the supply Sergeant called us to the supply shack (a Quonset hut) where we were issued weapons and what seemed to be huge amounts of miscellaneous equipment. Then we returned to our hooch to sort out all of the gear and get our act together.

In addition to our combat fatigue clothing and jungle boots and a towel, the equipment consisted of:

A. A steel helmet with a standard chin strap consisting of a half-inch wide heavy duty cloth strap that went under the chin, designed to tend to keep the helmet on ones head while bending over or running. In an Airborne unit, there was also a "paratrooper" type strap that fitted around the chin, designed to keep the helmet in place when "crash landing" onto the ground on a parachute assault. Inside the steel helmet was a separate, thin fiberglass helmet liner. Also issued was a green cloth camouflage cover that was held in place by a thick green loop of elastic.

B. Load-bearing gear (lbg), which consisted of a two inch wide pair of suspenders that were extraordinarily heavy duty, nothing remotely like suspenders that one might find in civilian life. The suspenders attached to a wide, very heavy duty canvas cloth belt (which had many brass grommeted perforations designed to hold many different pieces of various gear such as ammo pouches). Many different items could be attached to the belt, the weight of which would mostly be supported by the suspenders.

C. Two canteens. They were ruggedly built of a hard, dark green plastic with a screw top. Each held one quart of water. That was placed into a stainless steel cup that perfectly fit around the lower part of the canteen with a capacity of perhaps sixteen ounces. It had a folding handle for storage purposes. Those two elements were placed into a canteen cover, a thick piece of canvas with a fuzzy cotton fabric bonded to the inside of it. The canvas canteen cover was designed so that if the outside fabric become water-logged from time to time from river crossings or monsoonal downpours it might provide a cooling effect to the water in the canteen due to the cooling effects from evaporation. It also provided some protection from abrasion to the canteen and had a crooked metal piece that was used to attach it to the belt.

D. A rubberized poncho which was essentially a four foot square of fabric with a built in hood in the middle of it, designed to serve as basically a rain coat.

E. An entrenching tool (basically a two foot long hard wood rounded shaft at the end of which was a shovel and something that could be used as a pick on hard ground. The shovel and pick could be folded back upon the handle which made it a bit less unwieldy to carry.

F. A bayonet with scabbard.

G. Nine boxes of C-rations.

H. Many thin cardboard boxes, each containing twenty rounds of rifle ammunition along with eight black metal magazines.

I. Grenades. Each was contained in a hard black cardboard cylinder. I didn't even know what they were until I peeled off the duct tape that kept the two halves of the cylinder together and dumped the contents onto the bunk. Some contained high explosive (HE) grenades, others had smoke grenades. I would eventually learn to decipher the markings on the containers to discern which type of grenade was contained within.

J. Rucksack, or backpack if you will, which was used to carry most equipment other than the very essential things. In all of my training thus far, I had never even seen a rucksack.

K. M-16 Rifle

Emptying the rifle ammo onto my bunk, I picked up the bullets, one by one, and loaded them into the metal magazines that would actually be fed into the weapon. It was a slow and boring process until I had finished loading 10 magazines with 200 rounds total. I felt a rush of anticipation and excitement along with a sense of danger, realizing that

I actually had live ammo and was loading it so that it would be available for whatever adventures lay ahead of us.

Three magazines were placed into each of the three ammo pouches and attached to the belt of the LBG. Then I added to the belt a hanging bayonet with scabbard, the entrenching tool and two canteens. All of those components had crooked metal hangers designed to be easily attached and detached to and from the belt but also designed to not detach by accident. The ammo pouches had a snap loop on each side of it to which I attached my HE (High Explosive) and smoke grenades. I stuffed all of my other gear into the rucksack and then stood and looked down at the bunk bed, its very tight green woolen blanket the background for the LBG with its attached ammo and explosives, the rucksack, the helmet and the M-16 rifle lying on my bunk. I thought: "Yes, this is very, very real!!".

A couple of troopers walked through the door to the hooch. They obviously knew that we were "cherries", extremely low ranked troops with no experience in a war zone. I think that they knew that because our combat fatigue uniforms were brand new, along with our jungle boots. They noticed our fully loaded up LBG and rucksacks. They advised us, in wise, knowing terms, to take only what was absolutely necessary. Good advise, except none of the new guys had any idea what was or was not absolutely necessary, so all of us took all of the gear that had been issued to us out to the field.

An hour later myself and another two replacement soldiers loaded onto a helicopter that would take us and other supplies out to the field to join up with the Company, already on

combat operations. We landed at a forward Battalion Supply Operations Point (BSOP) and spent the night there. That was an area that just contained a few large tents with large quantities of ammunition, C-rations and some clothing and extra medical supplies. It was located relatively close to the main operating force so that those emergency supplies could be rushed to where they may be desperately needed. There was almost no security to protect us, no guarded perimeter at all. There seemed to be only two or three soldiers assigned to the area. They were out in the middle of nowhere with practically no protection against an enemy assault. Three soldiers, with a relatively huge amount of supplies (by Viet Cong standards), left to fend for themselves in the middle of enemy territory. I was still basically a raw recruit, but I thought that that situation just didn't seem right.

The supply sergeant, already on the ground, seemed for some reason to be very happy to see the three of us, later I guessed why. At least we were three bodies that could supply some additional defense to his position.

That was the first night in the bush for me and the other untested soldiers. That tiny supply post was really a rear area, out of the area of the ongoing combat operation of the Battalion to a great extent but certainly in the middle of the jungle and most certainly subject to enemy attack.

Myself and another guy got together and joined our poncho halves together to make a makeshift pup tent with a few pieces of saplings as the main support and then we just slept on the ground. That day didn't involve much physical effort at all but I was extremely, extremely tired, probably due to dehydration and the psychological anxiety and worry as to what we were in for the next day.

In the morning we again loaded onto a helicopter to actually join up with the Company. As we approached the area where the Company had been set up for a few days, still at an altitude of about a thousand feet, we noticed another helicopter on the ground, its rotor seemingly rotating at maximum speed, apparently ready to ascend. The crew chief of our chopper yelled at the top of his lungs, so that we could hear him over the roar of our own aircraft, that we would land a few hundred yards away from the chopper on the ground.

As we approached, the chopper on the ground began to lift off. It rose about fifty feet into the air, straight up vertically. I looked away for a few seconds and when I looked back, that chopper was back on the ground. How the heck did that chopper land back onto the ground so quickly, I thought, and why would it have landed back to earth at all? Plus, it didn't quite look right. Subtly, it seemed that the airframe was ever so slightly twisted, maybe it was just my mis-interpretation of what I was looking at, or maybe it was some kind of optical illusion. Later I figured out that it didn't quite look right because it skids were collapsed from its crash landing. But then I noticed that there was white smoke coming up from it, quite a bit. I don't know, what did I know about helicopters, but some thing or things just didn't seem right at a basic, primal level of my brain.

I later learned that, obviously, that chopper had crashed. It had had risen from the ground about fifty or a hundred feet high and then crashed back to earth killing most of the men in it and seriously injuring any other passengers and crew. I hadn't even joined the unit yet, I was three minutes from actually joining them on the ground, and already I had witnessed a situation where two or three men had been killed and others terribly injured. I later learned that one of the dead was an E-8 Master Sergeant who was returning to the US because he had completed a full twenty years of service and was to retire in a few days.

I had a full complement of gear and struggled mightily to carry it for two hundred feet or so over to the squad to which I was assigned. The Company had already beaten the bush for three days on its latest operation and was now bivouacked for the last day or two at that area, using it as a type of base of operations while the platoons and squads searched the surrounding area.

I met the guys in my squad. This was the Heavy Weapons Platoon of Alpha Company, Fourth Battalion, 503rd Airborne Infantry Regiment, 173rd Airborne Brigade (Separate). Many of them seemed very aloof, certainly unimpressed with the arrival of soldiers with only six months of training, much of which would prove to be of very little use in the fighting of Viet Nam.

After a while, the squad Sergeant told everyone to clean their weapons. I tried to break down my M-16 rifle but I forgot how to initially open it, since in training I had had only a quick and vague "familiarization" course with that weapon months before. I was a mortarman and as such, according to World War II standards, normally would only have a .45 caliper pistol as a personal weapon, not a rifle. This was a new war, with new ways of fighting, but the Army still relied on standards that had been established twenty-five years previously.

In training, while other infantrymen were learning about various light weapons infantry weapons and tactics, I had been learning how to operate a mortar. I said to a couple of guys in the squad, while holding out my M-16, "Hey, how do you open this thing now?" They were flabbergasted, horrified and disgusted. They said amongst themselves "What the heck kind of people are they sending us as replacements?" "They don't even know how to clean or dis-assemble even an M-16!" That was true enough. I knew how to load the weapon and fire it. I remembered how to disassemble it and clean it save for the fact that I couldn't remember the very first step in doing so. Those guys had probably already dis-assembled and cleaned their weapon hundreds of times during training, I had done it once before. Grudgingly, they showed me how to initially open the weapon, I was OK after that, but suspected that there were many tricks of the trade of which I was completely unaware of.

Later, the squad Sergeant told me to dig a fighting position for myself. In World War I soldiers dug "fox holes" which were cylindrically shaped holes designed for one man. In Viet Nam we dug "fighting positions", a rectangular hole dug into the earth about four feet long, two feet wide and four feet deep, designed to accommodate two soldiers.

I got my entrenching tool (a folding shovel) from my LBG and began my work but it progressed very slowly. Due to my technique, as hard as I worked, it was still very inefficient. Hey, to dig a hole you get your shovel and start to remove dirt, very simple, or so I thought. I really did not know at all how to efficiently dig a hole, especially using that tool. Again, my associates in the squad were disgusted and dismayed but one of them came to me and said "Didn't they even show you in training how to dig a hole?", my answer was "I guess not" which was obviously and painfully true. Then he demonstrated the proper technique. It would have taken me days to dig that position my way, but after a little instruction, it could be dug in ninety minutes or so. However, regardless of the efficiency and time saved using the proper technique, the effort of digging that hole, in hard earth, and in the blazing sun and horribly oppressive humidity, left me beyond exhausted.

I thought that, if I was not taught to properly clean, or even to open a basic weapon or dig a hole properly, then what else was missing in my Army education. The answer, I later discovered, was that I was totally unprepared and unschooled in what would be required. I was a third grader amongst high school graduates. If you lived long enough, you might get the equivalent of a Phd in infantry fighting but it was all on the job training and your Phd sash and gown was certainly not bulletproof. No one in the Company, regardless of their experience on or off the battlefield, had sufficient experience or knowledge that could have ever really prepared them for the situations and things that they would encountered later.

The "veterans" knew from experience to twist up the hood on the poncho tightly four or five times and then tie it securely with a piece of string, usually scavenged from a sand bag so that no water could leak through, basically making it a square plastic leak proof sheet. They would then stretch out a poncho and place wooden stakes, chopped from the surrounding saplings in the jungle, about a foot away from the corners of the poncho. Then they would pound the wooden stakes into the earth using their folded up entrenching tools as a hammer and then stretch out the poncho, horizontally, adjusting it as tightly flat as possible using the string, to try to keep out the rain from cruelly and coldly affecting the soldiers seeking shelter underneath it.

The poncho would be set up very close to the ground so as to be the least conspicuous to enemy detection or fire, about fifteen inches off of the ground. Properly constructed, as a soldier slept underneath it, his breath rebounded onto his face. I was horrified that these soldiers had learned how to effectively set up a shelter whereupon me and my cherry associates has set up some kind of a ridiculous boy scout pup tent the night before.

Obviously, those guys knew much more about combat operations than I did and I figured that that lack of knowledge on my part would cost me my life. The fact of the matter is that war games at Fort Campbell for two or three years or more for these guys had taught them a lot, but not nearly enough what they would learn, the hard way, through experience in the jungles of Viet Nam.

The weather was heavily overcast and cloudy, not overly hot but certainly oppressively humid. Still the sudden dropping from the sky of fat warm raindrops was a surprise, it very quickly turned into a downpour. I was going to set up my poncho, joined with another soldiers poncho a sort of pup tent, as we had been instructed in previous training. I yelled out, to no one in particular, to join their poncho with mine but received no reply.

Anyways, I had no sticks to use for stakes and would have had to travel across the flat farmland, into the jungle at the edge, to secure some. I could have just put my poncho on and sat on the ground, but I had no idea of how long the rain would last and in any event I would end up completely sodden from the rain and mud running under my rump. I figured that I would get soaking wet and filthy dirty from the mud anyways, so I just sat on the ground while the rain poured down, while my associates stared at me from their shelters like I was crazy. I suppose that they were convinced that I was totally ignorant and totally stupid and probably fairly crazy as well. I figured that during my tour that I would be out in the rain and mud a lot, so I may as well get used to it now. I also figured that their impression of me was probably spot on, but I didn't know any better.

All of those guys had known each other for a year or more and all came to Viet Nam as a unit via a thirty day ship ride on the USS Pope. They came from Ft. Campbell, from the 1st Battalion, 501st Airborne Infantry Regiment of the 101st Airborne division, The original "Geronimo" battalion, the oldest Airborne Battalion in the Army. Now they were the 4th Battalion, 503rd Airborne Infantry Regiment of the 173rd Airborne Brigade (Separate), which was the newest Airborne Battalion in the Army.

The designation of the 173rd which was (Separate) referred to the fact that this Brigade was by itself, not part of a Division and if we needed any equipment or resources that would normally be available to an Army Division, we would simply have to do without it or try to borrow it from other units.

The entire Company was bivouacked on a farmland that was certainly not flat, it just followed the natural rolling terrain of a farm that was hacked out of the jungle centuries ago. The 173rd may have been sending out patrols into the jungle from this sort of base camp, but I'm not sure. My platoon was not going on patrols. We had the 81mm mortars so we stayed in one place in case the patrols needed our support. Soon I was put on a rotation where everyone in the squad spent two hours at a time at the perimeter of the encampment, standing in fighting positions that had been dug, and perhaps four hours off duty and then two hours of immediate standing by to fire the mortars. Actually, anyone and everyone who was "off duty" were conditioned to quickly respond to any shouted order of : "fire mission!".

Our job was simple guard duty (sit or stand in the fighting positions and watch for enemy activity to our front and standby for fire missions to support patrols out in the surrounding bush). The farmland was absolutely void of any live vegetation. It was generally flat but had very many small rises and slopes and was obviously worked just by hand. It was strewn with large black volcanic rocks that were about the size of basketballs. The stones were relatively light for their size, I guess because they were filled with voids due to volcanic gasses. The stones were sort of a blackish chocolate color, their surface had many circular imperfections where the gas had made its way to the surface in the form of bubbles before the rock solidified. They lay on a ground that was a medium brown color, a sort of light dusty ground that was perhaps an half in thick until encountering a hard black volcanic stone base. The boulders where everywhere, Maybe four generations of farmers had tried to clear those boulders, and had done a good job of it, but there were just thousands and thousands of them still remaining.

Later I noticed that there were little lines on the ground that traveled all over the land. They looked as if someone had taken their finger, pressed down hard, and drawn a line on the ground. However, if you took your finger and tried to draw a line, it could not be done because the dirt had a very hard crust to it. These lines, I later determined, were probably made by ants, millions, probably billions, of large ants, all traveling the same paths, for who knows how many hundreds or thousands of years that had trodden those paths.

The next day, while on guard duty, a small Vietnamese boy, who was probably about 10 years old, came by selling sodas. They were warm, but were a welcome treat. I tried to speak to the boy but of course neither one of us could understand the other. He seemed to be very friendly and happy. Luckily, I had brought some money to the field, only because I was completely ignorant of the realities out there, but actually it came in handy. I bought a few sodas, at an extremely low price for an American. The boy seemed to be extremely happy.

Later, while walking around, looking around our encampment, I found what looked to be some harvested vines in a big pile, maybe 3 to 5 of them heaped together about 8 feet in diameter. They were straw colored, thin vines all piled up in a heap on the ground. Upon closer inspection they seemed to be peanut vines. They were mostly harvested of peanuts but some peanuts remained which I broke loose and brought over the guys in my squad.

That find made me very happy, to have peanuts which would be a welcome treat and respite from the c-rations, a very welcomed addition to my nutrition. I broke open a peanut and popped it into my mouth and started chewing. I immediately spit it out loudly, thinking perhaps that the VC had somehow poisoned them. Much to the dismay and disgust of my associates, they informed me that any idiot knows that peanuts must be cooked. The country boys insisted that they need not be roasted, indeed that they are best boiled, which they proceeded to do, using as much salt as they could find along with as much water and peanuts that would fit into an old tin can boiled over a make-shift C ration can stove that they could use for a cooking pot.

Later I found a small bush holding many small red peppers. I picked one and took a very small bite from the end and immediately spit it out, with my mouth on fire. I had no idea that any peppers could possibly be that hot, again I thought that the enemy must have poisoned those plants.

At dusk, I was on guard duty, sitting on the ground with my legs dangling into the rectangular fighting position and looking out at the jungle that surrounded the farm, the edge of our protective area, a cleared area about 200 yards away. As I scanned and evaluated the area, I thought that a sniper could be hiding anywhere and that at any moment he could shoot at me or any of the other guys. In fact, I thought that there could be 100 enemy in that jungle maybe more, and that if they attacked we would have a desperate fight on our hands, in fact, there could be 1000 VC in that jungle and at any moment there could be a large scale assault and that I could not really think of any way that we could survive an attack of that size. It also occurred to me that the enemy could have a mortar a mile away and hit us with that and we would have no way of knowing exactly where that gun was and so no way of disabling it.

After a while, I was joined by another guy who was to replace me on guard duty in fifteen minutes or so. I wondered why he didn't take the fifteen minutes to sleep or something. We spoke for a while and I told him of my concerns, hoping that he would tell me of the error of my thinking. After some discussion, in which he confirmed my concerns, I told him that I thought that there was not much hope that I would make it back alive. He fully agreed that, certainly, the probability of survival of anyone in the Company was very low. This guy had been into the jungle already on this operation. He did not tell me exactly how that was, but insinuated that it was much more dangerous and difficult than our current situation. As much as I was worried about our current situation, he indicated that it was very different, and safe and easy compared to a combat patrol.

During the next two days my platoon just sat around, close to the mortars in case they were needed. One of the men in my squad had been humping the baseplate and M79 grenade launcher because he was the "ammo bearer". After he had a few words with my squad Sergeant, I was told that I would be the "assistant ammo bearer", basically the bottom of the social chart in a heavy weapons platoon. I would now be assigned to hump the baseplate and I was told to give my M-16 and ammo to the ammo bearer and he would give me his M-79 grenade launcher. The ammo bearer was very happy to be rid of the M-79 because it was such a slow-fire weapon and also because it required its owner to carry about 70 rounds of heavy ammo for it, which a was a much heavier load that that required for the M-16. He also gave me a US issue .45 automatic pistol with 2 magazines and a shoulder holster that he had personally purchased downtown in Bein hoa. The shoulder holster was an ideal piece of work for the job, but the Army had not as yet recognized its usefulness and therefore did not issue such a piece of equipment. Although the 45 auto was invented in 1911 and had undergone only minor superficial improvements to it since then the Armys standard issue was a belt carried holster.

The shoulder holster strap went over the left shoulder, directly connected to the pistols holster, then continued downwards, ending in a snap loop that was connected to the belt. It also had an attached strap that went around your back and snapped back onto the pistol compartment. The end result was that it held the weapon from going up or down and also from shifting left to right. It was made of heavy, stiff black leather. Crudely made but it certainly was up to the task for which it was made and it was far and away an improvement over what the US government or the Army offered their soldiers at that point.

I figured that he bought it in downtown Bien Hoa from a street vendor. It was just too heavily constructed and unadorned to have come from the States. Of course, here, it didn't have to look nice, it simply had to fulfill its function. I could have gotten an Army issue holster that attached to the web belt and hung below it but the US Government approved issue would have been much less functional. The US government issued holster looked good on a rear-echelon General but the extra time and trouble that would be required to draw the weapon in actual combat made it a good-looking piece of leather that gets people killed in the real world.

The next day we were ordered to ruck up and move out. I strapped on the hellaciously heavy load of my equipment and walked about a thousand feet. My squad Sergeant turned around and asked me where the base plate was. I told him that I had left it back at our departure point. He seemed to be astonished. I told him that obviously, you couldn't require a human being to carry that and his combat load. He told me to go back and get the base plate. I ran back a thousand feet and picked up the base plate. But, or course, no human being could be expected to carry that hunk of iron and carry his combat load of gear.

I picked up the base plate and placed my rucksack on the ground. How, I thought, would my rucksack be reunited with me back in base camp but I figured that they had figured out some sort of organization. I was greatly impressed. I ran the distance to the squad Sergeant with the base plate in my hand. He asked me where my rucksack was. I told him that I had left it where the base plate was. He asked me why I had done that. I simply and honestly told him that since it would be impossible for a human being to carry a fully loaded rucksack and a mortar base plate, that, since a human being could only carry one of the two possibilities, and that he had ordered me to get the base plate, that I had got the base plate but had dropped my rucksack. I asked him how they would know enough to reunite me with my rucksack back in base camp or whether I would just be issued new gear. He seemed to be dumbfounded and ordered me to retrieve my rucksack. I dropped the base plate onto the ground and ran back to retrieve my rucksack.

When I returned to the Sergeant, he ordered me to pick up the base plate and to follow him into the jungle. The pain and suffering was almost unbearable. No one could endure that suffering for more than ten minutes, at the maximum. Then, I sort of laughed to myself. This must be some sort of incitation rite I thought. Obviously, no human being would survive such an inhuman beating. I thought that I would endure it as long as I could. Luckily, we only had to hump about a thousand meters to get to our extraction LZ. At that time I thought that I had more than reached my physical limits and psychological limit of pain. Luckily, I had pushed through. I had gone through the squads initiation rites I thought. I had no idea that that "initiation rite" was the easy introduction to everyday life in the bush for an American Infantryman.

I think that we were loaded onto helicopters and taken back to base camp after another day or two. Back to a base camp that was just canvas cots and primitive latrines and essentially just a canvas tent over your head, but it was much better than out on the farm. Here it was a lot more comfortable and safer. Much safer than a civilian might think that a combat soldier might be used to, but much, much more uncomfortable than most people in the US were used to. Literally it was a hundred times safer than life in the Bush, but still ten thousand times more dangerous than civilian life in the US. We were still subject to the very real possibility of daily mortar and suicide attacks, sniper shots and full on small infantry attacks and sappers intent on killing the command personnel and destroying the aircraft on the ground.

Chapter 5
OPERATION AURORA

The next operation took us only a few miles from our base camp via army convoy trucks. Still, once we had disembarked from the trucks we had to hump a painfully goodly distance.

I really didn't know whether I could keep up the hump. It was indescribably horrible and painful. I realized that I was beyond what I would have expected to be human limits of endurance and pain.

My platoon Sergeant had stopped and was giving encouragement to the men as they filed by in line, seeing how each was doing. I walked past him, head down, doing everything I could to just take one more step before I finally dropped dead.

A minute later he walked up to me and without saying anything and just took the aiming stakes that I was carrying, which weighed probably eight pounds, out of right hand. I looked at him and tried to hand him the baseplate being carried in my other hand but I was much too weak to even lift it an inch upwards. He shot me a glance as if to say, "No way Troop".

I unstrapped my rifle to hold with my now empty hand, glad that I finally had immediate access to it. For most of the day previously my hands were filled with mortar equipment and I was so beaten down by the weight that many times I couldn't even look around for the enemy. I was just a horribly overburdened beast of burden. The constant terrible pain and suffering was simply indescribable, completely unknown and unimaginable in civilian life.

At the end of the hump the mortar platoon set up in the middle of the bivouac area and the Company sent out patrols. Large tents were brought in for our sleeping quarters. Obviously, the Army intended to set up this area as some sort of permanent advance staging area.

After a few hours of digging in, we were called to our mortar for a fire mission. But it turned out to be a mission to just basically register the gun onto specific landmarks. We would fire a few rounds out a mile or so and the forward observer would report exactly where they landed. That information would be given to the fire direction control team and noted on a map so that if mortar fire was required later to support the patrols then hopefully the fire would be more accurate and could be brought to bear faster than without the landmarks.

Given the elevation, deflection and charge, we prepared a few rounds and fired the first one. One of the Sergeants in the Fire Direction Control (FDC) team spoke into the radio "Round out". That alerted the Forward Observer (FO) who was in the bush, to expect the round to land shortly. The mortar round landed and exploded.

The FO called in a correction. Perhaps the round was targeted to land exactly on top of a hill but it did not land exactly on target. The forward observer (FO) would then call by radio a correction, perhaps he might say something like "add 100 yards elevation, adjust fire 50 yards to the right!". (Actually, he would say: "add 100, right 50." The new parameters were computed by the FDC and then settings and adjustments to the mortar were shouted to us. We would make the adjustments to our instruments, level and stable the tube and then fire off as many rounds as the FDC instructed us to do, usually only one round at a time as they tried to zero in onto the target.

The 81 mm mortar is a "crew served weapon". It is a serious piece of weaponry. One well trained man can aim and fire it, but it really runs a lot better with a four man crew. It was subject to malfunctions and problems due to absurdly old ordinance which could and did kill the gun crews That situation was beyond comprehension. We and the infantry around us were being killed because some bureaucrat in Washington D.C. wanted to save a hundred dollars on some kind of spreadsheet so he was sending us ammo that was 27 years old.

The gooks knew that the 81 mm mortars would have a serious effect on their attacks. Their primary goal, which I learned about a lot later, was to attack the Americans with a full-on hard core infantry assault, preferably at night so that the US wouldn't have good artillery or air support. Their primary objective was to take out the 81mm mortar gun crews first, regardless of their cost in wounded and dead. They knew that with the 81mm crews in action, their attack would most likely result in disaster for them.

I dropped the next round into the tube, but instead of the round leaving the tube with a deafening blast, there was just a was a sick, popping sound. The round was weakly shot out of the tube, up perhaps

150 feet high and landed 100 yards away, right outside of a tent containing eight men. Very luckily it did not explode. That's what is called a "short round". Many people are killed by such rounds, most of them are friendly forces. Maybe the charges are wet, maybe the initial round is old and weak or the coordinates are wrong, the firing pin is used up, the round is old and defective, it doesn't matter to the gun crew and the soldiers on the ground, the bottom line is that we could not deliver accurate fire on the enemies position and at the same time we have a high probability of being killed by our own old, mal-functioning weapons and ammo.

I went over and into the tent and told the men there what happened and told them to evacuate the area because the short round had landed very close to their position. It hadn't exploded but it could explode at any second. (it was only about 2 feet from the tent). They looked at me in a very bored manner and continued their game of cards. I thought that either these men were very, very brave or they were immune to the danger. Perhaps they knew that they all would not survive this tour of duty anyways, so a mortar round that landed two feet from them didn't seem to affect them at all.

The unexploded round was eventually picked up and moved, at great peril to those men doing so. Our fire mission was over so I wandered around a bit and joined a group of eight soldiers in a tent. They were in the process of cleaning their weapons. One of the group had his .45 caliber automatic pistol in his hand and was waving it around. He was playing with it, twirling it around his finger etc. and in the process sweeping the barrel and its line of fire across everyone in the tent.

I yelled at him, in no uncertain terms to "put that thing down!". I was about to grab his gun and slap him across the face violently (his lack of safety most certainly called for such a response) but then others in the tent began to yell at him, demanding that he watch where he pointed that thing. He then proceeded to attempt to clean the weapon. He slid back the receiver seven times, each time ejecting a bullet onto the ground. Then, without ejecting the magazine or checking whether it was truly empty of rounds, he pulled the trigger, luckily he was pointing it at the calf of his own leg.

An Army .45 has seven rounds in its magazine. However, one can have a round alreadt loaded into the barrel therefore making eight rounds available. He shucked out seven rounds but didn't realize that he still had one more round available to be fired. He pulled the trigger, standard operating procedure so that he could then dis-assemble and clean his weapon. But the weapon still had one round loaded into it. The noise of the discharge was extraordinarily loud in the enclosed tent. I thought that a mortar round or grenade had landed very close by. The shooter sat on the ground, holding his calf very tightly with both hands and grimacing strongly, rocking back and forth with his face a beet red color yet not uttering a sound. The bullet had hit his calf bone but had then, inexplicitly, had changed direction 180 degrees and traveled fourteen inches along the bone up towards his knee. I don't think that it broke any bones, it just horribly tore up his muscles and tendons. Of course, I don't think that it made his calf bone any healthier by any means.

You could see where the bullet had traveled up his shinbone because it looked like he had a steel rod about a half an inch in diameter under his skin, along side of his shin, for almost the length of his calf, starting about two inches above his ankle and terminating about two inches from his kneecap.

People quickly recognized that that guy had just shot himself in the leg. Some guys started yelling "Medic, Medic!" After a minute, the gunshot guy said "Shut up!" Someone said "Don't you think that you need a medic?" and he said, "I am the medic!".

Eventually, another medic showed up and administrated advanced first aid. A lieutenant from headquarters came out by helicopter about an hour later to investigate the incident. I guess he wanted to know whether the shooter did it deliberately or not and he seemed to strongly suspect that one of us in the tent had maybe shot him. The lieutenant specifically interrogated me because I was a witness. I did the shooter a favor and told the Lieutenant that I thought that the shooter was just a reckless idiot (which was doing him a favor because the Lieutenant wanted to charge him with deliberate infliction of harm so as to avoid his duty). Who knows what really happened. The shooter was very seriously injured, perhaps permanently. I later heard that he was in the hospital and incapacitated for two months. Still, that was a lot better than beating the bush.

My squad was sitting on the ground the next day, just shooting the bull, talking about anything and nothing. My squad Sergeant suddenly appeared, carrying a new pair of boots that he had somehow obtained. He said: "Mallen! Take off those boots and throw them away! Put these on!" as he quickly threw them to me. I had been issued jungle boots but they did not have a reinforcing slash of fabric across the ankle as all of the other boots had. After about seven days in the bush my ankles had worn through and were sticking out of those now raggedy looking boots.

I wondered just what type of equipment we were being issued, that wouldn't last for ten days in the field. The boots that I was initially issued were undoubtedly the first generation of boots, now I had been given the second generation of boots. They were substantially better. The new, improved boots also had a special piece of metal built into the sole that was supposed to protect against metal spikes and punji stakes.

I wondered how effective they were. The black leather part of the boot was supposed to be some kind of advanced technology quick drying leather. Above the black leather part of the boot, which covered about what a shoe might, the boot was made of a heavy green cloth. Near the bottom of the boot was a brass element that was perforated many times. I guess it was to drain out any water if we had to cross any creeks. The only socks we were ever issued were made of very heavy wool socks, probably from the WW2 era that were designed for extreme winter wear.

The next day we went out on patrol. The area was not very overgrown at all and there were some rubber trees around us. I left most of my gear on the ground and carried only mostly my LBG. It was a very heavy hump, ball-busting. We returned to our little sort of base camp later that afternoon. We settled in for the night, I had an early perimeter guard duty that night and didn't have to pull a second shift so I went to sleep early and slept all night. I thought that it was the middle of the night when I was rudely awakened by the sounds of gunfire. I jumped up inside my poncho hooch , noticing that it was full sunlight in the morning. The boys on the line six feet away were obviously fighting for their lives since it sounded like everyone was shooting with M16s and M79s and M60 machine guns and throwing hand grenades.

I was very confused and looked around my hooch for my weapon but the M79 and rucksack was outside of my hootch. I grabbed my .45, cocked it , and jumped outside on my hands and knees looking around as to what was going on. There was a Sergeant close by and he looked at me with a bored expression on his face. I yelled at him, desperately questioning what was happening, when all fire suddenly stopped, as quickly as it had started. I was just there, on my hands and knees, with my heart beating wildly, thinking that we were being overrun by a Battalion size force. The squad sergeant said, "Its just a mad minute". I asked him what that could be. He said "You know, where, in the morning, at a given time and signal, everyone on the perimeter fired into the jungle, just in case there were any VC who had sneaked up during the night are now waiting to ambush us as we move out". I had never heard of such a thing. Such a thing almost never happened to me again.

We soon moved out on the operations patrol for another couple of days. Nothing out of the ordinary. Probably took casualties from VC 60mm mortar attacks and snipers. Probably just suffered horribly from carrying our equipment, probably endured the pain and suffering from malaria and dysentery. Just endured the constant danger from a hundred types of very real possible killing and maiming situations.

Somehow, we made it back to base camp in Bien Hoa.

Chapter 6

OPERATION TOLEDO

Above all, Vietnam was a war that asked everything of a few and nothing of most in America.

Myra MacPherson

All Gave Some, Some Gave All

"Agony of War"

It was M-minute of H-hour to begin a new operation and we got the word to bring all of our gear out to the Company street.

That "street" was just the bare ground in front of our hoochs. Some soldiers made three separate trips to carry all of their equipment outside because each load was so heavy. The problem was that even though it was difficult and painful to carry one load fifty feet outside, those guys would be carrying all of their load, all day, usually everyday of an operation. It would very nearly kill them, the suffering would be horrendous.

They knew that the suffering would be unimaginable but no one complained, no one even mentioned it. To me, it was as if all of those guys knew that they were going to have five teeth extracted, without Novocain, and the operation would be done very, very slowly over a period of hours and days yet they simply didn't complain about it, they didn't even mention it. I was greatly impressed. What type of men are these I thought.

A combat load of gear, that would be carried all day, in extreme heat and horrible humidity, for days on end, is something that must be personally experienced to be appreciated, to be fully understood. There are no words that could possibly convey an understanding of the pain and suffering that went along with it. It was way beyond the comprehension of a civilian. A civilian, indeed any normal human being, could never have imagined the absolute brutality, savagery and horribleness of it, the suffering and pain of it.

Everyone's load was different, depending on his primary task and what he needed and what he wanted and what he was willing to carry in addition to his mandatory load of weapons and ammunition.

What each soldier chose to attach to the belt was mostly a personal decision. One could decide to attach a certain item to his belt, or attach it to the outside of his rucksack or put it into his rucksack, or carry into his shirt pocket or into the front or rear pants pockets of his trousers or the cargo pockets on the thighs of his pants on put into a bandolier or somehow attach it to a bandolier.

Upon my landing in Viet Nam I had been issued a rucksack that was not new but in good shape. There were obvious signs of severe use around the corners of the nylon compartments. The dark green paint on the aluminum frame had been worn away or rubbed away or blasted away in several places so that the aluminums color was evident, although that metal contained dirt that had been pounded into it during previous operations. That rucksack now contained another fifty rounds of M79 ammo (inside a spare sandbag), food, shaving gear and poncho.

We carried gas masks at all times, in its own carrier, usually attached at the waist and around the leg, sort of worn like it was an old Peacemaker from an old Western film. That way it was immediately available for use but it usually caught vines and thorns while humping the bush so some guys attached it to their rucksacks or even carried them inside their rucksacks. Gas masks were mandatory combat equipment that had to be taken on all operations.

I put on my .45 caliber automatic pistol, carried in a shoulder holster under the left arm (so as to better grab it quickly with the right hand). Then put on the Load Bearing Equipment (LBE) with attached ammo pouches, grenades, canteens and entrenching tool. Then I slung over my shoulder two bandoliers of M79 ammo. A bandolier was a soft cloth Army green thing with compartments in the middle and cloth straps on both sides of that. It could be tied/adjusted to a wide range of circumferences but most people adjusted it so that it could be worn around the neck on the right side and have the containers hanging down over the left side of the chest. That made the rounds immediately accessible but I never liked the idea of carrying high-explosives directly in contact with my chest, inches from my heart and directly under my neck and chin. If they were hit with bullets or shrapnel or bits of napalm I didn't know if they would explode or not. Hell, I thought, if they do explode I will never have time to analyze the wisdom or engineering theories behind the idea in the millionth of a second between detonation and my death.

Each bandolier had three separate compartments, each one having a covering that had a snap on it so that rounds wouldn't usually fall out under normal circumstances, and each compartment had a white plastic "cup" inside that held rounds more securely and protected them somewhat from abuse. They had bandoliers for M79's rounds and others for magazines of M-16 ammo.

In one of my bandoliers I had placed only high explosive rounds. In the other was three HE rounds and three shotgun rounds, each containing about twenty very large ball bearings. No, these shotgun rounds do not fit into any other type of shotgun made on Earth, not even close. They essentially turned the M-79 into the most absurdly powerful shotgun, by far, in the world. The problem was that the effective range was probably only about a hundred feet. When you have to fire shotgun rounds from an M-79 then you really should have a bayonet between your teeth and your entrenching tool within arms reach because things are probably going to get very ugly and up close and personal within seconds.

At that time I was the ammo bearer on the mortar squad so I carried the baseplate for the mortar (48 pounds) Later, we were issued a baseplate that broke down into an inner ring and a larger outer ring so it could be distributed between two men to carry, or sometimes we just carried the smaller inner ring.

Total weight for all equipment was probably a hundred and twenty pounds minimum, that was for one man. On later operations I would carry that load and an additional two or three mortar rounds at an average weight of twelve pounds each. It was a man-killing load, an absolutely insufferable load, a seemingly impossible load for a human to carry. It could be humped, and it was humped, for miles every day, all day, but the amount of struggle, the level of effort and the pain and suffering far surpassed anything that I could have previously imagined was humanly possible.

The mortar consisted of A. the barrel at 28 pounds that was held upright by the B. bipod which weighs 40 pounds. The bottom of the barrel was placed into a C. baseplate (48 pounds) which distributed the blasting force over a larger area so that the barrel wouldn't bury itself 8 feet into the ground due to its recoil power. The mortar crew carried those components in addition to their combat gear.

There was also the sight, usually carried in an old metal ammo box to protect its glass lens, at about 8 pounds, which consisted of two knobs with numbers on them and two built-in bubble levels and a sighting device. There was also the aiming stakes, 2 poles painted alternatively red and white in vertical sections about six feet tall but could be broken down into 2 pieces each for easier transport. This operation was not going to be like some high school football team doing pushups in the hot sun. This operation, and most others would be into new dimensions of pain and struggle, we would be into an unimaginable realm of suffering and torment.

The barrel was usually carried on the shoulder, the bipod was carried with the legs sort of hung down in front of the body, with its heaviest part resting on the shoulder. The baseplate had a handle on it which was a thick piece of manila type rope with a metal pipe in the middle. It was carried with one hand.

I hoisted my rucksack in one hand and carried it out onto the street and then returned to the tent to get the baseplate and carry that outside. Lastly I returned to the hooch to get my M-79 grenade launcher, my main and principle defensive/offensive weapon for individual combat and then checked that I had all of my gear.

The M-79 was a strange looking gun. It had a wooden stock and a huge metal barrel about two inches in diameter and only about 18 inches long. On the top of it was a metal lever that looked like it came from a 16th century weapon. When that lever was pushed sideways, the barrel would break open, away from the stock but still attached at the bottom. It sort of looked like a cross between a 17th century blunderbuss and a sawed-off shotgun designed for killing dinosaurs. It fired two types of rounds. The first was a shotgun round with about 20 double odd buck sized shotgun ball bearing pellets, in a round that was 4 inches long and 2 inches thick, a sort of super shotgun shell.

The other type of round was HE or high explosive. This round looked like a giant bullet but its projectile was not solid brass and lead but a round that contained an explosive that upon landing would produce 600 white hot tiny bits of titanium traveling at super-sonic speed. It was a very effective weapon, its main drawback being that you could only fire one round at a time, then you had to push the lever, break open the barrel, extract the previous round casing, put in another round, close the barrel, aim the weapon, switch off the safety and then pull the trigger. Because it was so slow to fire between rounds, all M-79 grenadiers carried .45 automatic pistols for combat up close and personal.

The M-79 also had a very odd aiming mechanism. For very short distances you sighted through a slot that was half-ways up the weapon and a thin metal projection at the end of the barrel. To aim at anything over 100 yards, there was a rectangular device that was flipped up and a sliding mechanism that was moved up or down depending on the range to the target. That procedure for aiming required you to guess the range to the target. The maximum distance of an M-79 HE round was about 400 yards and at that distance the weapon would be pointing upwards at a 45-degree angle. The rate of travel of the HE round was very slow, many times you could actually see the round travel through the air.

Fortunately, the weapon was extremely well balanced and after firing a few rounds many men could bring very accurate fire upon a target just by a sense of balance and feel. There was always the choice of which round to keep in the chamber when on an operation. While going through heavy jungle a shotgun round was best because you couldn't see beyond ten feet anyways. If crossing a rice paddy, the high explosive round would be a good choice because chances are that the enemy would fire at you from a hundred yards away, at the edge of the jungle.

We loaded onto trucks at the base camp to begin the operation. We rode for about fifteen minutes just to reach the main gate of the huge base camp/airbase area then turned right and proceeded down the main street of Bien Hoa, past a nice looking light tan colored building with red flowered vines all over the property. There was a little sign in front of it, the gist of which, printed in Vietnamese and English, was that it was a mental hospital.

For some reason I thought that it was unusual that people who lived in this country might have mental problems and also noted that the building was much nicer than the shacks and hovels that most of the people occupied in utter destitution. I thought, the people who are living in that place must have a nice life, nice and peaceful. I guess that is what you need if you are crazy. I would pass by that institution several other times during my stay in Viet Nam, going out and coming back from operations and came to appreciate how soft and gentle and easy I imagined life was in there, as we went out into a living nightmare, a world that those inhabitants probably never imagined existed, or maybe some of them had seen it, up close and personal, and that's why they were there.

We had been ordered not to load ammo into our weapons because they didn't want any accidents as we rode through friendly areas but now that we were entering the countryside we were ordered to "lock and load", that is to lock a magazine into your weapon and load the first round into the chamber. After that, a flick of the safety on the weapon and it was just a trigger pull away from firing. I had an M-79 grenade launcher and loaded in a full sized shotgun round then pulled my .45 automatic from its shoulder holster, held it out at arms length and pulled back the slide to load in the first round.There was suddenly some commotion and guys started yelling at me, saying that I had pointed the gun at them when I loaded it. I probably did, I tried to point it off to the side of the road, but just as I let go of the slide, the truck rocked sideways and my muzzle shifted, directly pointing at about five men on my side of the truck. I was a new replacement anyways, so they probably thought that I didn't know what I was doing, and they were mostly correct.

This was the first operation where I would actually walk in the woods for any sizable distance through the jungle.To hump 120 pounds all day, with the heat index at a murderous high was beyond what words can describe. It was an extraordinary torture, all day, relieved only by brief hesitations in the line of march where you might sit on the ground for a few seconds or minutes, only then to struggle mightily to stand again and continue the march. Many men looked as if they had fallen into a river because every inch of their uniforms were soaked with sweat.

We rolled up our sleeves to afford some small measure of cooling but it seemed that every vine and bush and tree in Viet Nam, even the grass, has some sort of thorn or spike growing on it or some razor edge to it and our arms were continuously slashed and cut and torn. If you snagged yourself on a vine and had five big thorns piercing your arm, you could perhaps back up and try to extract them, slowly, but many times, you were trying to keep up with the guy in front of you so you just shoved your arm forward with all of your might, tearing away from the thorns by ripping them out of your skin resulting in a bright red string of bleeding wounds. It did not take too long on an operation for my arms to be a filthy dirty mass of hair, dirt, sweat, shredded little pieces of leaves, pieces of thorns and old insecticide mixed with a good amount of blood that was rubbed into many, many open wounds.

We had been humping the bush for several days, each man blindly following the man in front of him in single files the size of a platoon or two, each line making its way, roughly parallel to the other platoons in the Company so as to cover more area than a single column but with each platoon assuming much more danger that would a Company line of march.

It was medium jungle with mostly indirect lighting from the sky because of the heavy leaf cover of very tall trees. On the ground were trees and bushes and vines of many different types so that in general a person could only see perhaps twenty feet in any direction.The ground was covered with fallen, chocolate covered leaves in a state of damp decay. The general effect was that we were in a world of a hundred shades of green completely surrounding us and above us. You almost never could see the blue sky, or more that a few feet of it because of all the heavy foliage of the leaves of the tall trees above us.

We came upon a huge grey smooth set of mostly attached rock in the middle of the jungle, perhaps 18 feet high and 150 feet long. The pointman had already crossed on top of this rock, so the remaining line of men would follow. There was a place where we could relatively easily climb to the top of that outcropping of rock but I was concerned how we were going to get down from it. I strongly hoped that we would not have to retrace our steps or have to go to extraordinary lengths to somehow get off of it and around it.

How could this very smooth formation of rock could ever exist out here in the middle of nowhere. I figured that this must have been in the middle of a river four hundred million years ago, but there wasn't any water flowing anywhere around now.

I didn't know very much, but while crossing that rock I had a very bad feeling. This would be a perfect place for an enemy sniper or machine gun to fire upon us since we had no cover at all and would be perfectly exposed. I shuttered to think what would happen if a mortar round landed on that solid mass of rock, the earth would not absorb any of the explosive force. A mortar round would shatter homicidally on that solid rock and anyone close by would be killed or maimed by the concussion of the round and the resulting blown out pieces of rock, it kill or wound anybody close to it, blowing them to pieces.

The line of march continued and I finally climbed down from that rock, it wasn't nearly as difficult that I expected it to be. There was a place where the rock sloped down gently. I finally got off of that rock and had moved about 80 feet away when the line of march suddenly stopped. There was undoubtedly a delay at the front of the line for some reason. I could see that there were still men on the rock because of the line of march and was glad that I was not one of them. It was impossible to know just how many men were still in that general area but I hoped that there weren't many of them because I thought, in my cherrified, unknowing way, that that was not a good place for them to be for any length of time.

The line had been stopped for a few minutes and soldiers who were close to me in line seemed to gravitate towards each other and I joined them, which was completely against policy, we should have maintained a distance between ourselves of the standard fifteen meters.

Those guys were talking, probably about what time it was or speculating why we had stopped when in the mid-sentence of a soldier speaking, there was a sharp, somewhat muted sound about 100 feet away. I was wondering how the line of men had wound around way over from where the sound had originated. I assumed that the sound had come from our own troopers, but it seemed to have come from high up, up in the trees and there was something decidedly foreign about that sound.

Then someone strongly whispered "Sniper!" I wasn't sure if that sound had been from a sniper or not, but decided to yield to the experience of another person (although that other person, at that time, probably did not have any more experience with snipers then I had). That offensive fire seemed to have been directed at the large rock. It was practically impossible to determine with any certainty at all as to where the fire was coming from, but it was certainly coming at us. I could almost tell that the fire was coming from the west but that was a 90 degree estimate of it, certainly not enough to return accurate fire.

The group that I had been in had just been standing around, completely ignoring any principles of tactical security and we were completely caught by surprise. We were just standing there, still, confused, shocked and struck with fear by this first encounter with enemy gunfire.

We should have fallen immediately onto the ground and sought out any cover behind trees or at least tried to conceal ourselves within the bushes. But, there was a strange fascination with the sights and sounds around us, an unreality, a surrealistic interpretation of reality where the underlying, unconscious realization was that you were probably going to be killed or horribly wounded within seconds.

The sound of gunfire aimed at you or in your general direction is very distinct from the sounds of the rifle range back home. There were several moments, for me at least, where my brain and soul realized, and then contemplated, the nearness of the end of my life. The thought went through my brain that my life may very well end before I could even finish the thought.

There were several further shots by the sniper and we were still standing, looking around, in a circular group, having no idea what to do, when an enemy mortar crew hidden somewhere far into the jungle started to drop rounds onto us.

They fired three rounds very quickly. I heaed the screeching of the rounds coming down. That screeching lasted less than a second before the explosions were heard, a sure sign that they were landing very close. One of the rounds screeched in quickly but did not explode, another one seemed to have exploded directly on the rock, with a horrible sound. The next round had absolutely no warning screeching sound to it at all. It simply came in very, very close and exploded.

It simply caught us in the mid-sentence of a thought. I had been looking to my right and saw the leaves of a bush violently blown off with a hurricane of shredded vegetation blown directly into the face and the front of the body of a soldier standing six feet from me, the other soldiers were buffeted with the blast and shredded leaves and branches. It had exploded two feet sideways and six inches in front of my boot. A good sized explosion that left a crater two feet wide and six inches deep. A 60mm gook mortar round I figured. Not a nuclear weapon but one that, by any measure of the imagination, should have killed or maimed everyone in my group.

By some miracle, only one guy in my group of four was hit by the shrapnel. The wounded man was only very slightly injured by a small piece that lodged in his neck, about an eighth of an inch from his jugular vein. He had obviously been punctured by something but it was buried beneath the skin. A medic examined him. Although the outwards appearance of the wound seemed to be trivial, the medic seemed to be very concerned about it and he contacted a doctor back at base camp via radio. That was a very unusual happening. It was decided that the wounded soldier should be flown out on the next available medivac chopper because any movement from him could cause the piece of shrapnel to enter into his blood system or sever his main neck artery. Another man in my platoon was wounded in the calf by shrapnel from a mortar round that had hit further down the line from me.

The mortar round that had landed on the rock resulted in threre causalities. Two men seriously injured and one man, a guy that I knew, had been killed, a guy named Corfman. { I learned many years later that he was married and had an infant daughter. He had just recently received a "Dear John" letter. His fatal wound was a piece of mortar shrapnel through the heart. }

The enemy sniper and mortar fired suddenly stopped, and word came down the line to move out, to start moving forwards towards our objective for the night.

That was a good decision I thought because the gooks obviously had us zeroed in with their mortars. Why they ever stopped firing I will never know. Perhaps they had run out of ammunition, perhaps they were waiting for more ammo to be brought up to the gun crew from their ammo bearers. If they had fired another ten or twenty rounds they would have certainly inflicted many causalities upon us.

Maybe they thought that we soon would roughly determine where they were and would then pound them with medium and heavy mortars, artillery, helicopter gunships and airstrikes. When they had fired on us we could faintly hear the "pop" noise of the round leaving the tube. They were not very close but not very far away either. They obviously had the large rock formation registered in. They had probably fired rounds upon it previously, maybe years previously, and had a notebook of the elevation, deflection and charge for their mortars to hit that target. Much later, I realized that the sniper was probably not only trying to kill us individually but also radioing in our position to the enemy mortar crews.

One of the soldiers close to me started to complain loudly of a headache. He hung his head, looking at the ground and walked around with a certain attitude, one that a person might expect of a person who had just broken his finger and was in agony and reaching out for some desperately needed help. I thought that it was absurd for him to complain of such a condition considering the casualties that we had just taken but he was very serious and I finally told him, in exasperation, to go to a medic and get an aspirin.

I asked about the causalities, and how they were going to be evacuated, but the line was already moving. I was told to just shut up and move out. I wondered for a long time how the casualties were evacuated.

{ Many years later I saw a now very famous photograph named "DeathWatch", also known as "The Agony of War". It is a picture of a soldier scanning the sky, looking for a helicopter, another soldier is pictured sullenly gazing down at the ground at Corfmans body, all wrapped up in a poncho, waiting to go home to his funeral. He was the first fatal casualty of the 4th battalion. That famous photo is usually accompanied by the saying "All gave some, Some gave all". }

The guy looking up at the sky, searching for a Medi-evac helicopter is a guy named Reichman. He was the radio-telephone operator (RTO) for the battalion commander and a friend of mine. He had served a six year tour of duty with the French Foreign Legion before joining the 173rd Airborne in Viet Nam. The soldier solemnly looking at the body on the ground was Corfmans squad Sergeant. { I found out much later that he was Killed In Action on a second tour of duty in Viet Nam with the Special Forces. }

We continued the hump for the rest of the afternoon, always wondering if and when we would again take sniper or mortar fire in addition to the other things.

The next morning, the guy with the headache was complaining loudly again about how much his head hurt. He again asked me what he should do. I told him to go to the medic and get an aspirin and to shut up. He walked back to his little tent, picked up his weapon and helmet and then let out a loud expression. He closely examined his helmet then told everyone to look at it. He brought it over to me and I could see a bullet hole in one side of the helmet where the bullet went in, and another hole on the other side of the helmet where the bullet went out.

What happened was that a snipers bullet had entered one side of the helmet, smashed against the thin, inner fiberglass liner (and his head), probably fracturing his skull in several places and causing serious brain damage. It then must have traveled over the top of the helmet, and exited on the exact opposite side of the helmet. It was exactly as if someone had set up just the steel helmet on a sand bag bunker and put a round straight through it.

The thin fiberglass inner helmet within the steel helmet had saved him. I would see him 8 months later, ready to go home, holding that helmet by its strap like an extremely valuable souvenir that he most certainly did not want to lose. I realized why he had had a "headache".

At the end of each day, we would establish a night defensive position. After humping 120 pounds of gear all day, we had to dig 2man-fighting positions for the night. That consisted of two men digging a hole about 6 feet long, 3 feet wide and about 5 feet deep. Then we chopped down a number of small trees and made a sort of framework roof, filled many sandbags with dirt and placed them onto the roof for overhead cover. Then everyone stood guard duty for an hour or so while the sun set.

After that, for most soldiers, one of the two man groups could go to sleep for 2 hours, only to be awakened so that he could stand another 2 hours of guard duty, get two more hours of sleep and then be awakened for more guard duty. So it went throughout the night. A person might get 4 hours of sleep, 2 hours at a time, and then, everyone was on guard duty for an hour or so, beginning before dawn. Of course if the enemy mortared us at night or tried to probe our perimeter all bets were off for anyone sleeping.

While on guard in the middle of the night it was usually completely quiet. You might think that the jungle would be filled with noises at night but that is not the case at all, Hollywood movies aside, the jungle is deathly quiet. I think that the animals of the jungle detected 100 very large creatures (us) and wanted nothing other than to get as far away from us as possible. Many times, there would be absolutely no light whatsoever. Even if there was any light from the moon, it mostly did not filter down through the jungled treetops to the ground. It was so dark that you literally could not see your hand in front of your face. You could hold up your hand a foot in front of your face and hold up three fingers. Then you could ask yourself "how many fingers do you see?" The answer most times was "zero". It was somehow beyond pitch black zero, and that was with three hours of darkness so that your night vision was at its maximum.

Sometimes, while on guard duty, I would hold my eyelids open to make sure that they actually were open because the only thing you could see was total blackness ...., in total silence. I couldn't be sure be if my eyelids were open or shut. The blackness was absolute.

I fell asleep several times while on guard duty during my tour of duty. I would guess that most of the other men did too at some time or another, it was basically impossible not to do so sometimes. The combination of days and days of unimaginable and indescribable heavy physical labor, severe dehydration, mal-nourishment and continuous sleep deprivation obviously had to have an effect on any human being, no matter how hardcore. Olympic athlete or hard, hardcore trooper, the human body can sustain much more abuse than most people can imagine, beyond anything remotely imaginable in civilian life. But after awhile no matter how hardcore a soldier might be, the human body can sustain only so much abuse after which it will begin to shut down.

After 2 hours of guard duty, in total blackness, our night vision would be perfect, literally capable of detecting light that was one ten thousandth as bright as a person without developed night vision. Even with a night vision scope so developed, it was so abysmally dark that it made no difference. It was just so perfectly and completely dark that fully developed night vision really made no difference. If the enemy attacked or probed the perimeter, even with perfectly developed night vision we would never see them. Then, when the fighting began, whether it began with a single shot from a pistol, the explosion of a hand grenade, the detonation of a claymore mine, the "pop" of a trip-wired light flare or the muzzle flash from your own M-16, the resulting light would have instantly ruined everyone's hours long developed perfect night vision. I realized at a gut level that I was completely blind.

When I was relieved of guard duty, I orientated myself perpendicular to the fighting position and crawled on my hands and knees, hoping that I wouldn't crawl beyond the limit of the opposite end of the perimeter and then be shot by the Americans on guard.

My eyes were wide open as I laid down but it was still as pitch black dark as a coffin buried 6 feet underground in the middle of pitch black jungle on a moonless night. I wasn't entirely sure that I hadn't been hit in the head by a sniper and my optic nerves hadn't been completely severed or hit in the brain and the area that analyzes light hadn't been completely destroyed. There was just a complete, absolute absence of light, light of any kind. I thought of striking a match, just to see if my eyes were working, but that would have lit up the area for a second and invited any snipers to hit me or my friends. I would have really liked to know whether I was completely and permanently blind. By snapping my fingers ever so slightly right directly against my ears I determined that I was not completely deaf but I couldn't be sure of it. The situation was of complete, total blackness and complete, total silence.

Breakfast consisted of whatever you had brought with you. Usually I had coffee from a packet that came with the C-rations. The packet was mixed with my precious water, that had probably come out of a stream that we had crossed the day before. Sometimes I might eat a can of cold C-rations but that was a very rare situation. I considered myself very lucky if I had so much as a small piece of bread with a little jelly on it. For lunch I might have a candy bar and for supper I might have a can of C-rations, probably less than 1000 calories a day. Many times we did not even have that much food, our world record was four days without any food whatsoever. Sometimes I would dip into my precious stash of candy bars that my mother would mail to me from time to time but I would have exhausted my supply after a few days on an operation.

We humped the bush for another few days and then one evening we had set up our night position as usual. The perimeter was small that night, perhaps only 100 feet wide. It had been raining for the last hour so everyone was completely soaked. The mortar platoon was set up in the middle of the perimeter. The theory behind that setup is that if we are attacked at night, the mortar platoon could bring the gun into action to defend the entire perimeter. That night it was decided that we would fire a few rounds to "register" the gun, to make sure that our settings (elevation and deflection) were accurate, but this time, we would register a round at 100 feet away.

A hundred feet away is at the edge of the "casualty radius", the radius in which a mortar round will achieve 50% killed or wounded. We then set up the gun to fire as close as was possible with the weapon without killing the mortar crew or the men on the defensive perimeter. Another gun crew was chosen to fire the round and I just stayed in my hooch, out of the rain, but completely drenched. I knew that I would be wet throughout the night, and it was starting to get cold.

The fire direction control team issued its directions. The mortar crew made the appropriate adjustments and I then heard the round sliding down the tube. Instead of a loud blast or at least a solid "pop" sound there was a very dull thud of a sound and someone yelled "Short round!" I jumped out of the hooch, ran as fast as possible and jumped into the nearest foxhole that was not occupied, about 30 meters from the gun. I think that the round may had already landed before I reached the foxhole. A guy came running over and yelled "That's my hole, get out!" I realized that the round would be landing in a split second, if it hadn't already landed, so I ignored him and ducked down in the hole. The round landed about 10 feet away but did not explode. I climbed out of the hole and was horrified to see that it was a white phosphorous round. If that had exploded twenty of us would have been killed and/or burned horribly.

The guy into whose hole I had jumped was equally horrified that I had taken an action that could have resulted in his death. He told me in no uncertain terms that that was his hole and, in the case of emergency, I should go into my own self-dug hole. I agreed with him completely and apologized. He was of course absolutely right. I checked the gun and noticed that the tube was virtually completely vertical. A fired round then would seem to go straight up and come straight down. The fire direction control Sergeant assured me that, no, the round should land 100 feet away. We were setting up and firing the gun under circumstances that would result in court martial for the instructors back in the States, and with good reason.

The active gun crew were going to fire another round, so I returned to my hooch. There was then another dull thud, another cry of "Short round", and again, I jumped out of my hootch and scrabbled across the ground sideways like a crazed monkey, trying to keep a low profile and dived into the nearest hole which was the one that I previously used which caused quite of bit of consternation for the owner of that hole again.

About 10 minutes later I heard someone yelling "Clear the area!" and when I looked around everyone was running very quickly. I realized that I didn't have time to run so I just laid on the ground, my head facing away from the gun, my arms covering my head. It had been another short round, this time a high explosive type, it landed about 50 or 60 meters from me but about one meter from a hooch containing two men I think. That round failed to explode although it was certainly far enough from the gun that its safetys should have been disengaged and it should have exploded. It was not only a short round but a dud as well.

My gun crew was then ordered to set up and fire a registration round. Our first round was on target, landing very close to us. The second and third rounds were short rounds again, again being of no threat to the enemy, but seriously jeopardizing out own troops.

The mortar rounds have a safety device built into it so that if it is not ejected from the barrel at a certain velocity, it should not explode. However, every short round has the substantial possibility of killing the gun crew or others in the Company, and every short round is taken to be deadly serious. Even if the round does not explode, it certainly may explode when it is picked up or otherwise handled, a short unexploded rounded is quite capable of self exploding for no reason at all from the next 70 seconds to the next 70 years. In fact, the older that they get the more dangerous they are, although a "dud" is extremely dangerous within the hour in which it was fired.

Most of the ammo that we had been humping on this whole operation was defective, it was probably World War II vintage. After this operation there would be a major investigation and a congressional inquiry as to why we had been issued ammo that was so obviously defective. I do not know the result of that inquiry.

How in the world did front-line, elite combat troops end up with completely defective ammunition? Ammunition that could not hurt the enemy, but could certainly kill friendly troops? And why did we have to break our backs humping useless metal? What's the answer? I don't know.

As Airborne troops, we were usually given the best and newest equipment. We were the first to be issued M-16s for example. However, most other things were second rate or worse. The defective mortar ammo is one example. We were issued, eventually, the latest "lurp" food rations but much of the time we were issued rations that were 20 years old and many times we were not even issued enough food. Food that has been in a can for the last twenty years. Actually the old stuff was pretty good. We had new "jungle" boots but World War II Russian winter infantry socks. We basically operated in a unit that was severely dehydrated and mal-nourished with bad food. I thought that if the American people knew of that situation that they would, with good reason, be outraged.

We had space age Starlight scopes but not enough batteries to operate them. We had the latest hand-grenades but also were forced to use old "pineapple" grenades that were manufactured 25 years previous and could never be trusted to work. We had ammunition that was twenty years old, it didn't work very well if at all.

I went back to my hooch and took a letter out of my rucksack that I had not read. I figured that I better read it because it's going to get very wet out here and its liable to ruin any letters. The letter was from my father. He had sent me an article that was in the newspaper. The article did not mention my unit at all. I am completely surprised that he sent it to me. My father had no idea that it was about my Company. I have no idea of who wrote it, but it names men in my Company and especially in my Platoon. The newspaper read as this:

Rest for Weary 5-MINUTE BREAK: Viet Style

PHUOC LE, Vietnam—

They have a sort of coffee break in the Vietnamese war, except there is seldom time for coffee.

The breaks came infrequently for U.S. paratroopers searching for the enemy in the steamy jungles of Phuoc Tuy province east of Saigon.

When the company commander passed the word down to the platoons for a five-minute break, Pfc. Larry Thompson of Los Angeles sat down and drank thirstily from his water bottle. Soldiers have little time to boil coffee.

Sgt. Adolph J. Breecher of Saginaw Mich. downed the 40 pound pack he'd been carrying all morning and lit a cigarette.

Squatting on the damp jungle floor, Spec. 4 Denis P. Elwell of Secaucus, N.J. used the few minutes of respite to peer down the barrel of his rifle to see how much dust and moisture had accumulated. He swabbed it out.

The old pro of the outfit, Sgt. Maj. Robert O. Cruz of Clarkville, Tenn., stood against a tree, the sweat streaming down his clean-shaven face. He had shaved every morning for 12 days as the soldiers carved their way through Phuoc Tuy.

Few of the men talked. Sgt. Homer O. Poorman of Buckeye Lake, Ohio, a drop of sweat on his nose, looked into the distance. Was he thinking of his wife and kids back home, the dangers that lay ahead for his squad, the men who had been killed in the past weeks?

Pfc. Eugene Cabbagestalk of Pittsburgh, his hand brushing his brow, smiled across at a buddy lying prostrate on the ground. Weary, on the verge of heat prostration, legs and arms cut with twigs and brambles, his buddy had kept plugging on, forcing himself to keep going on the endless patrol.

The company commander whispered the order to get moving again. There would be more breaks later on, between this one and the next there might be the enemy and war.

Four notes about that article:

1. It gives a very vague <u>hint</u> of what it was like

2. 40 pound pack mentioned was more like 100 pounds

3. Sergeant Poorman was in my Platoon. Some people referred to him by his initials "HOP" for Homer Oscar Poorman. He was a very nice person. He would be drastically wounded before he completed his tour of duty and medically evacuated out of the Republic of Viet Nam.

4. Eugene Cabbagestalk was a friend of mine. He would lose his life in that terrible Country. The cause of death noted as "accidental homicide".

Somehow, and sometime and some way, I don't remember, we returned to Base Camp.

Chapter 7
BASE CAMP A

We returned to base camp in Bien Hoa. We took a shower, and got new clothes. The supply Sergeant made us sign forms that declared that we needed new clothes and should not be made to pay for them out of our paychecks due to "combat loss". I liked the sound of that, maybe because now there were official records that we had been in combat, or maybe I liked the idea of getting something for free for my troubles. Of course I would have been outraged if I had to pay for them. Everyone needed new clothing but not because they had spilled milk on them while eating breakfast at Stateside restaurant.

A few guys were taking their new fatigue shirts to a tailor on base to sew on patches and I asked them to take mine as well. When they returned, my shirt had the parachute wings sewn on and on the left shoulder was the patch of the 173rd airborne brigade, a white wing carrying a red bayonet on a blue background. Above it was a tab with the word "Airborne" on it. That patch signified that I was an active, assigned member of the 173rd Airborne Brigade. I liked that, I liked that a lot, but I thought that noone that I knew back in the World would ever see that. Would ever see me, alive, wearing that decoration. I assumed, with very good reason, that I would never make it out of this country alive. I had come through several close calls. I had come through many situations where some of them could only be explained as a miracle. But, I had a bad feeling that I was to see many even more desperate situations, and I would be proven correct.

Other units wore subdued patches, that is, patches that are just black and green, a type of camouflage, but the 173rd proudly and defiantly wore our unit patches in full color. It was proud and defiant but also dangerous. I wondered what type of a good target that little white wing would make on a dark night out in the bush but then thought that a VC sneaking up on our position at night might be a little put off by seeing 10 or 20 small white wings carrying a bayonet floating in the darkness of the forest.

The hoches at base camp were just large tents that held perhaps twenty men, mostly each tent assigned to a specific platoon. There was a concrete slab floor and walls made of 2x4's covered with screen. A large canvas tent was put over that frame and held up with large upright poles inside the hooch. The tent walls were then rolled up. The outside walls had sheets of corrugated metal slanting outwards so that the effect was screened walls to keep out insects, the corrugated metal to keep out most of the rain while allowing maximum air circulation, with the canvas tent roof providing shade. Inside it was very hot during the day, and the corrugated metal did not keep all of the rain out, but it was 100 times better than what we had in the bush. Our bunks were just simple, fold-up canvas cots, nothing like a regular bed but a lot better than sleeping on the ground.

The restroom was a 6-man outhouse two hundred feet up the road, of course with no privacy whatsoever. It had a metal roof and wooden slats about 5 inches wide slanting outwards to keep out the direct sunshine yet allow air circulation. There was screening material around all of the walls and the toilet consisted of 6 round holes cut into a wide plank, sort of like sitting on a bus bench, defecating while four others beside you did the same. The urinal was a 4-inch diameter pipe sticking three feet out of the ground at an angle, completely out in the open, beside the outhouse. The accumulations of the outhouse fell into a number of 55 gallon drums that had been cut in half and each day, the drums were dragged out, diesel fuel poured into it and set afire. The result was a very smoky and smelly fire from an absolutely disgusting mass of toilet paper and human waste. Luckily I only had to pull latrine duty twice. It was not a good detail.

We only had two nights and one day before we would start the next operation. The base camp had a mess hall which we all took full advantage of. The food however was typical Army food which was terrible. I liked the bread though, high in carbohydrates and calories, which seemed to have caraway seeds in it. I thought that that was good. It must be some sort of rye bread. I love rye bread. But the bread didn't taste like rye bread, just bland.

I picked one of the caraway seeds out of a slice, inspecting it closely. I thought that probably the seeds had dried out and therefore had no flavor. Upon very close inspection, I saw that they were not seeds at all but were in fact cooked insects that had been in the flour. I and the men at my table were outraged. We took our complaint directly to the head cook who told us that in Viet Nam, they had to buy some supplies locally and it was impossible to keep the bugs out of the flour. He told us that every native Viet Nameese just accepted the fact of bugs in bread was just an expected way of life. I returned to my table, picking up another bread on the way. Knowing now that they were bugs, I sat down and ate it. I was vaguely aware, almost sub-consciously, that my body desperately needed the nutrition. The mess hall had only powdered milk mixed with water, a particularly un-appitizing substance that had no relationship with fresh milk whatsoever. For the entire tour of duty I would never have fresh milk although me and my fellow soldiers would desperately need good protein like that.

The company commander brought in a trailer load of iced beer and soda and we drank our fill and then some more. They brought out the hot dogs and hamburgers and steaks and cooked them over a large barbeque. We sat around and ate and drank our beer and soda and had shots of liquor and felt safe. The idea that I would be back in the bush tomorrow seemed like some horrible nightmare that I hoped that I would awaken from.

Chapter 8
THE HOSPITAL

String of Helicopters from above

The next day, early, before even the mess hall had opened, we moved our gear out from the hooches and onto the company street. This was the real deal and a missed breakfast was nothing to be concerned about. I guess that we missed having a "Breakfast of Champions" but this was not an Olympian event, it was much worse. We were not going to have a full breakfast and then get a muscle massage and then go out and throw the discus. We were not going out to run a hundred yards after years of coaching and resting and eating well. We were not going out to lift a heavy weight, one time, above our heads after years of training and scientifically proven nutritional meals. We were going out on an operation that would make an Olympian balk and back away. We were going out to do things that an Olympian would consider impossible. We were going out to do things that every coach would forbid, knowing that the end result would be ruination of a bodies strength and spirit. But that was what we would do. Most good American citizens had no idea, none whatsoever, of what their leaders demanded of their sons and grandsons and daughters.

Every combat Infantryman would be called upon to do and endure feats of superhuman strength, every day, and the only way that they could do it would be with extraordinary human pain and suffering. This Company of men would go out and do things where the phase "no pain, no gain" was a motto for little girls. Those men would endure pain that was beyond their wildest imaginations and would know, at least sub-consciously, that there would be no gain, only destruction of their bodys. It would do things to their minds as well.

A convoy of trucks soon arrived and we were driven to a section of the air base where there were about ten helicopters awaiting us. The choppers would need about three round trips to deliver the entire Company. That was be my second helicopter ride. On the first ride, I had stayed completely inside the chopper, sitting on the floor, but they were only transporting three troopers so there was plenty of room but that's not the way it's done for an infantry assault.

There were three men on each side of the chopper, sitting on the edge with their legs dangling into the air. There were no safety belts or anything to keep one from just falling out. As we were riding at about 1000 feet, the pilot suddenly banked the chopper and I felt myself falling out. Instinctively, I reached out with both arms and struck the backs of the two men to either side of me. The effect of that maneuver would be to either keep me inside the chopper, or me taking the other two men out of the aircraft with me. It was an instinctive thing. It would have been difficult, now that I think of it, to have slid 600 pounds of men and equipment a foot across the floor of the helicopter and out into thin air, but I didn't know that at the time. I did not fall. I immediately leaned back as far as I could onto my rucksack, changing my center of gravity and using the weight of the rucksack to help keep me inside. The two men on either side of me gave me a glance that did not seem friendly at all, but they didn't say anything.

We eventually rose to about two to three thousand feet high. The landscape below was just a jumbled sea of different green colors. If I leaned forward a bit, I could sometimes see the other choppers in the stick in front of us or behind us. Once in a while, a small helicopter would come by at full speed with no one in it except for the pilots and door gunners. Those were the gun ships, laden fully with ammo and the crew just bursting with the anticipation of raining 6000 rounds per minute on an enemy targeting the main stick of assault choppers.

Coming down into the landing zone was always a time of high excitement and concern. It could be a walk in the park with no troubles at all or something very, very much different. This time there was no troubles at the LZ (landing zone). The stick of choppers set down and we disembarked at full speed and moved into the tree line and set up a perimeter. That first stick had already lifted off. We stayed at high alert, anxiously awaiting the return of the choppers and the rest of the Company.

Eventually the choppers returned with their human cargo, setting down very quickly with troopers jumping off of the choppers and running towards us to reinforce our defensive line. I noticed that those troopers had an extremely grim and determined look to them and I suddenly realized that that was probably how we looked when we first landed. The weight of their gear bogged them down considerably but they seemed to be exerting their maximum energy in trying to get to their assigned positions on the landing zone as quickly as possible. Everyone has an assigned location at the landing zone, that way the Commanders would know exactly where friendly forces are located and could direct artillery or aircraft fire to support them if it was needed. All of those men anticipated a direct enemy attack, just waiting for the sounds and sights of the killing to begin.

When all were assembled we set off on our mission. That day our mission was to capture a VC hospital hidden in the jungle. We humped for about two hours when word was passed down the line that we were very close to our objective. A few minutes later, the word was passed down that there were booby traps ahead.

As we got closer, the man in front of me turned around and pointed to the front of him and off to the left. After a few seconds I realized that he was pointing at a punji pit. It was about two feet square and about 3 feet deep. At the bottom was a bunch of sharpened bamboo stakes. I recalled from advanced infantry training that they had mentioned that the punji stakes are usually smeared with feces to make it a particularly nasty blood-infected wound. Usually the sharpened stake has a sort of fish hook cut into it so that it became a particularly nasty thing from which a soldier would have to try to extricate himself. Sometimes the stakes are made of iron and cut and curved like fishhooks so that when a soldiers leg and foot was impaled on it, it could be almost impossible to free themselves. They could always finally extricate themselves but not at a horrible cost of human suffering and destruction to their bodies. The punji pits were covered with a light framework of thin sticks and then covered with leaves. That punji pit could be seen because the camouflage had deteriorated over time or washed away partly with rain. I moved close to it and turned around to the guy behind me and pointed at it, and then he in turn showed the guy behind him and so on. We encountered about fifteen of them, staggered in place. I worried that there could be several more that were still hidden, undetected by the troopers in front of me until someone, most likely me, discovered it by falling into it.

The landscape now was relatively open. Visibility was about 100 feet and it appeared that we were approaching an area that had once been a plantation or orchard a long time ago. There were a few tall trees with large vines growing on them but mostly there were trees about 15 feet tall and lots of grass about a foot tall and there were many areas of open blue sky.

My section of the line seemed to have walked out of the field of punji pits when the guy in front of me again stopped abruptly and pointed down to his left and then quickly proceeded forwards. I looked but could not see anything. I whispered strongly and hoarsely for him to stop. I got closer to him and asked what he was pointing to. He showed me that there was a field of punji stakes that were about six inches long and inserted into the ground at an angle. In fact, I then saw that we were in the middle of that field. They were hidden among the low growing vines and grass.

They were made of bamboo that had been split into pieces that were half or a quarter of their original diameters. They were about an inch wide and sticking six inches above the ground, sharpened into a point like an arrow at the end. They appeared to have been there for a while because they had changed into a light tan color which blended in with the groundcover of dead vines and leaves. We could just walk gingerly around them, in fact you could step on them carefully and slowly and break them off. Their purpose is such that, when the VC ambushes you or starts shooting, your first impulse is to hit the ground, whereupon you are stabbed five or ten times with bamboo stakes. That was a bad situation because the VC would have set out that field in a place where they planned to ambush a patrol and to make matters worse, I could now actually see the hospital and figured that the shooting would begin at any second.

It was a white one story building made of concrete or something similar. We seemed to be out in the middle of nowhere, it seemed that there were no other houses or farms within miles of it. We cautiously continued forward until the pointman was about 200 feet from it. The guy in front of me again turned around and pointed to his right front. There was a mine, with a yellow top. There had obviously been leaf litter and dirt covering it at one time but now, probably due to monsoonal storms of rain and wind, the tops had been uncovered. Now we proceeded forward, through a minefield of about 40 mines. The procedure was that the point man spotted a mine, stopped, turned around and pointed it out to the man in back of him. That man in turn would wait until the next guy in line approached and then pointed directly at the mine and so it went down the line and mine after mine.

I stared at the twentieth mine and pointed it out to the soldier behind me and then turned around and noticed that the weapons platoon Sergeant, Sgt. Winfrey, was now in front of me but fifteen feet to the left of our line of march. He walked relatively quickly up and down the line, encouraging us to proceed and instructing us to be extremely cautious. He was then also to supervise a large group of men.

He could have stayed in the line of march and have thirty men in front of him look for mines and proceed through the mine field before he did. Now, he was walking through the minefield by himself, taking an extraordinary risk, one taken only to oversee the welfare of his troops at great danger and peril to himself. I realized, right then and there that I had never seen a man of such courage, truly an extraordinary soldier and human being.

Suddenly there appeared an ambulance, going towards the hospital along what I later discovered was a dirt road. It was an old-fashioned station wagon type. The driver passed right by a line of soldiers that I suddenly noticed. I expected him to stop and reverse course but I think that he didn't notice the soldiers until he was in amongst a group of them. That's when I realized that we were assaulting this hospital from a number of different directions, not just the line of march that I was in. No one tried to stop it although some soldiers were within ten feet of it as it passed them. It continued forward and stopped at the hospital. Some Vietnamese took the passenger who was on a stretcher out of the ambulance and carried him into the hospital.

Within minutes we had reached the hospital and had surrounded it. I had been anticipating a serious firefight but there was absolutely no resistance whatsoever. After about 15 minutes some ARVN soldiers and civilians arrived and entered the hospital (doctors, nurses, admin types?, I have no idea). The ARVNs had control of the hospital and the people within it so, after about an hour, we left and began patrolling the surrounding area.

We probably stayed out in the bush for another week on patrols into the surrounding area. One day while on patrol in an area that had a lot of undergrowth. The front of the patrol came to a relatively clear area and the pace of the patrol picked up. We were soon moving very fast, and spreading out more, trying to put the standard operating distance of fifteen meters distance between each man. I was almost running and looked behind me and noticed that the guy in back of me was quite a distance away. I wanted to wait to make certain that he could see me but I had to hurry ahead myself or I would lose track of the guy in front of me. I hurried ahead, then waited, then ran back a little searching for the soldier who was in back of me, sometimes waving to the soldier so as to catch his attention and indicate to him where I was, which was the line of march. I really didn't like waving my arms to attract his attention because I realized that I was also attracting the attention of any enemy in the area but I realized that it could be disastrous to cause the line of march to be broken. Such a situation would isolate a group from the main group and expose the smaller group to attack.

My choice was to lose the line in front of me or stay with the men in back of me. I chose the latter. As they began to catch up with me, a Sergeant that had been in front of me and had now backtracked was now yelling at me. He told me, "Don't worry about the guys in back of you, your job is to maintain the continuity of the line!". He was not happy at all.

He was very disturbed and asked me why I didn't answer him when he was yelling at me before. I told him that I didn't hear him yelling. Then he said something that I didn't understand and I asked him to repeat it. He was very upset now and told me that when we get back to base camp that he was sending me to the medics because obviously there was something wrong with my hearing.

Actually, when he said that, I thought that his manner of speaking had degraded considerably over the last month. I thought that he used to speak clearly but he now sounded like he had a mouthful of marbles. As mad as he was, I thought that he wasn't speaking very loudly. He never sent me to the medics and I thought for a long time that he and the other guys had somehow and for some reason had lost their ability to speak clearly and loudly enough to be understood. I didn't understand it at the time, but of course, the mortar fire from my gun had already done serious and permanent damage to my hearing, I just didn't realize it then. There would be a lot more mortar fire and serious, permanent physical damage to our hearing to come.

Later that day we came to a place where very large trees, maybe three feet in diameter and 120 feet tall that had been knocked down, probably by very large bombs dropped by aircraft. We climbed through the branches and over the trunk that were on the ground. It was extremely difficult to make our way through that tangle of branches and leaves. Eventually I made my way to an area where the base of a tree was and there was not the absurd tangle of branches. Those trees mostly had a smooth bark and no branches for about 30 or 40 feet up the trunk.

We just stayed in one place for a while so I rested my rucksack against one of the trunks. I started to think that this was a very strange place indeed. A hurricane or typhoon or tornado could have never knocked down those huge trees yet here they were, killed and knocked over by unimaginable human produced weapons. A thought slowly crept into my mind. I slowly but surely realized that I would almost certainly never make it out of this country alive or without some sort of horrible lifetime injury. It crossed my mind as to what had I accomplished with my life? Is this how it really ends, horribly tortured for months and months and then killed while I'm still a teenager? My logical brain answered: "yes".

I looked at the unusual bark on the downed trees and thought that maybe somewhere in this jungle was a plant that could cure some sort of disease. Of course, I would never be the person to discover it. I don't have the education, and I'll never get that education because I would never make it out of this place. I started to pick at the bark, it had an extremely thin top layer and then another, darker colored layer below it. For such a very large tree it had an extremely thin, paper thin bark. It also was very smooth, that was probably the only tree or bush or plant that I had ever seen in that country that didn't have thorns or spikes or razor sharp edges and I wondered what protection this tree had from animals. In this state of mind, I decided to peel off a piece of the bark and eat it. Maybe it would have some useful property to it, at least it should provide some element of nutrition and if it was deadly then maybe that would be useful information to someone. I half wished that it would kill me, I was just looking at another eight months of horrible pain and suffering.

Later that day my squad Sergeant came over to me and tried to hand me a bayonet. I have no idea of where he came up with a spare bayonet in the middle of the jungle. Maybe they had just medically evacuated a guy down the line and his equipment was split up among the others. Anyways, up until this time I never had a bayonet, I was never issued one. I told the Sergeant that I didn't want it. It was just extra weight to me. I told him that there was no sense in me having a bayonet because it couldn't be affixed to my M-79 grenade launcher and anyways, because of that, I carried extra ammo for my .45 pistol. He was insistent that I take it, most probably because if I didn't then he would have to carry it. I got pretty mad at him and let him know it but then he was equally mad. In the end, of course, I had to take it.

Chapter 9

RUBBER PLANTATION

We few, we happy few, we band of brothers;
For he to-day that sheds his blood with me
Shall be my brother;

Shakespeare

Rubber Plantation

We had been beating the bush on a new operation for a few days when we got the word that after we set up a perimeter tonight we would then stay there for a day or two. That would be a day of rest, relatively speaking, for my platoon. That evening, my squad sergeant had a quick meeting with us. He said, "Looks like tomorrow we're going for a walk in the woods". The Company's mission would be to send out platoon sized patrols, including my Weapons Platoon, and then return to our present perimeter that night. One platoon would stay behind to guard the site. That meant that we could then leave some equipment behind, like our tents and extra food. We would still be carrying a substantial load but when we returned from patrol we wouldn't have to dig in again.

The plan was for the Company to move out, including the Weapons platoon, for about five hundred meters. At that point, the Weapons platoon would look for a place to set up their gun, someplace where there was a break in the overhead branches through which we could fire our mortar. The other platoons would continue on patrol, with the Weapons platoon set up, ready to support them as needed. We could as well have done the same thing from the "base camp" unless they were going out four or five miles, which I doubted.

We humped a full five hundred meters and I saw several places where we could have stopped and set up our gun, places where the jungle canopy was open so we could fire. However, we bypassed those places and continued to hump. After about a thousand meters, we were ordered to set up, so my team set up the gun and the rest of the platoon provided a circular defensive perimeter around us. I was happy that the first half of the hump was over. Now I could rest for a few hours, unless the other platoons or we were attacked.

After about ten minutes we were ordered to pack up and move out. We humped another five hundred meters and were ordered by radio to set up our gun again, which we did. We were now completely out in the open. In front of us was an overgrown rubber plantation and in back of us was jungle but between the two was a wide open area of foot tall grass, about two hundred feet wide and hundreds of yards long to our left and right. This situation was both good and bad. The good part was that we had a lot of area around us that we could see clearly and had no overhead obstructions. The bad part was that the VC would had an unobstructed view of us and an excellent opportunity to hit us with sniper fire, 60 mm mortars or a full on infantry attack.

After a few minutes, we heard gunfire in the distance and over to our right. I calculated that it must be the Third platoon engaged with the enemy. Then we heard gunfire from the left, the First platoon was now engaged in a separate battle. Then we heard gunfire from the direct front. Now all platoons were engaged, each platoon separated from each other and fighting their own personal battles. We started to unload and unwrap more mortar rounds, expecting a fire mission at any moment. I worried that we might be attacked by a large force and overwhelmed since there were only about twenty five men in my platoon and the enemy would dearly like to take out a mortar platoon because it would make it that much less dangerous for them to take on the other American platoons. Very soon thereafter, we were ordered to pack up and move out.

We had moved from the jungle to an open grassy area and now we were moving at flank speed into a rubber plantation. That was bad because it would limit our range of mortar fire because of the overhead obstruction of the rubber tree branches. I realized that we were being ordered in, not to support the other troops with our mortar, from a thousand feet away, but to engage the enemy directly with small arms. One of the problems was that we were loaded down with the mortar so we couldn't move very fast and now, operating as a separate straight infantry unit, which we had just turned into, I don't think that the Weapons platoon even had an M-60 machine gun.

I was the second to last man in the platoon line, and I had just entered the rubber plantation for about a hundred meters when the VC opened up on us, down the entire line of march. All of us hit the ground immediately of course. We were definitely taking machine gun fire, but it was impossible to determine with any degree of accuracy where exactly the fire was coming from. Some bullets were flying around myself and others close by but it seemed that the major portion of the fire was directed at the front of the line. At the same time, you could hear the other three platoons actively engaged with the enemy. As close as I could determine, the Company was confronted with three crew served machine guns to our left flank, raking and raking and raking the entire line of march of the Weapons platoon and Second platoon that was in front of us. I didn't know at first whether it was enemy machine guns or just three or four enemy soldiers with full automatic AK-47 weapons. After a few minutes I determined that the enemy was hitting us with long bursts of ten, twenty, thirty, forty rounds at a time. Obviously, it was not individual AK-47 soldiers. It had to be crew served machine guns.

I noticed that I had hit the ground very close to a small depression in the ground. It was about six inches deep and about the size of a grave. It probably was an old grave I thought, but it provided an additional six inches of cover so I crawled into it.

Ominously, there was absolutely no return fire from the platoons. I crawled forward a few feet to try to see the source of the fire. I would have crawled more, but then remembered my advanced infantry training. The line of the platoon was directly to my right. If I crawled in front of that line, I am liable to be hit not only from incoming enemy fire but by outgoing friendly fire. I didn't want to crawl into a WWI no mans land where both sides of the conflict would kill you, assuming that you were an enemy.

Some message was being passed down the line, from one man to the next and when it reached me, the message was straightforward and simple "M-79s up front!" I turned and gave the message to the last man in line, but I was the last in line with an M-79 grenade launcher. I had already taken off the rucksack so I jumped up onto my knees and grabbed the sandbag that was attached to the rucksack which contained about twenty loose rounds of shotgun and high explosive M-79 rounds. The sandbag was tied to the rucksack. I figured that I didn't have time to try to untie it so I ripped at it mightily, violently, with my full strength and tore it loose. I grabbed another bandolier of M-79 rounds from my rucksack and put a shotgun round into the weapon. I noticed that the guy behind me had a wild look in his eyes and was staring at me as if he had just gone mad. Others yelled at me to "Get down!" but I was already on my knees and I jumped up with the M-79 in one hand and the sandbag full of rounds in the other and started to run down the line.

The line of march had left most of the men on top of a long elevation, sort of like an earthen dike, about thirty feet wide and six feet tall. The earth then sloped down sharply, towards the enemy. This was a rubber plantation with trees planted about every thirty feet but there was very heavy undergrowth of bushes between the VC and us.

As I ran forward, passing one man after another, they were all hugging the ground and most of them yelled at me to "get down!".

There was steady enemy machine gun fire from two or three guns but they were directing their fire towards the front of our line of march. I don't think that they noticed me right away but I was certainly the best target available. I quickly approached another guy with an M-79 who was trying to be one with the ground, who seemed to be very hesitant to proceed. As he noticed me running with my M-79 and passing him he seemed to begin to rise up. The same thing happened when I passed another M-79 grenadier.

The enemy fire seemed to now concentrate upon the general region where I was. It seemed to be three crew served machine guns, firing almost nonstop. There was an annoying sound in the air, I thought that someone had snapped off a thin, long stick and was hitting the leaves on a tree with it rapidly. I couldn't understand why someone would be doing that. Then I realized that that sound was the sound of bullets zipping past me, at extremely close range, feet or inches from my face. The air was filled with a very acrid smoke and the noise of the gunfire was much louder than one might imagine or what I was used to. Of course now we were in front of enemy machine guns that were trying their best to kill us instead of U.S. soldiers firing at us with blanks on a rifle range back in the States and it sounded very different between rounds going away from you and rounds coming at you. I could see white tracers flashing through the undergrowth and hundreds pf small pieces of leaves were falling everywhere as the bullets flew all around us and past us.

The enemy really poured it onto us and I thought that surely they must stop soon before they melt their barrels or at least had to re-load. I wondered just how much ammo those people could have, surely they must run out very shortly because that had been putting a tremendous amount of fire on us for the last three minutes.

Eventually I reached a gully that was about ten feet deep with steep sides and twenty feet wide. A Sergeant was on the other side, standing behind a tree, and he gestured wildly and shouted for me to get down. I had been running very quickly and the momentum and the fear that the guys at the front of the line were being murdered kept me going. The thought occurred to me to just hit the ground, especially since by this time the enemy gunners had started firing directly at me.

At first one of the enemy gunners had spotted me and started firing in my general direction, then, very quickly the second gunner brought his fire to bear on me and then, very quickly, the third gun started firing in my general direction, although that third gun would have had a hard time seeing me because of the undergrowth. I made a split-second decision to continue on although actually my momentum probably would have plunged me down into the gully even if I decided to hit the ground. I thought that even if I die, each step will bring this M-79 closer to where they will need it. I ran down the near side of the gully and looked to the left. It was a long gully, perhaps a hundred and fifty or two hundred feet long at least. The enemy fire from one of the machine guns seemed to be concentrated directly at me. They seemed to be located almost directly at the end of the gully, perhaps fifty feet to the left in the bush, but with a clear shot at the gully.

I could see white tracers coming directly at me, flying over my head, into the ground, in front of me, behind me, to the left and right of me, seemingly aimed by a desperate enemy at my head and feet and legs and lungs and heart, hitting the ground on the opposite gully and flying directly into the path of my running.

The gook machine gun crews were using tracers. Perhaps one in fifteen or twenty rounds were tracers. Therefore, if a person saw tracer rounds coming at them they were only seeing one in fifteen or twenty rounds that were actually coming at them.

They mostly looked like one to twelve foot foot-long white hot rods of iron as they came at me at fifteen hundred miles per hour. I could have hit the ground but realized that I was totally exposed in that gully. To hit the ground here would mean certain death in a few seconds, but to run forward, directly into a hailstorm of tracers would certainly tear me to pieces a split second later. I had a one in a million chance of surviving that horizontal hailstorm of machine gun bullets if I ran forward but I had an absolutely zero chance if I hit the ground right there. I clenched my teeth and drove on, expecting my life to end immediately, instantly, torn to shreds in some rubber plantation a million miles from my home.

I looked at the Sergeant on top of the gully, who was half standing behind a tree with a strange look on his face and then I glanced at the M-79, as if to tell him, this is the end for me, but here's the M-79, I hope that it helps out the platoon. I pressed on into the storm and up the side of the gully and then hit the dirt while a tornado of machine gun fire continued over my head and all around me.

The Sergeant yelled: "Stay down!!" as did one or two other men and I did stay on the ground for a few seconds. The line of men now made a 90-degree turn to the left, directly facing the enemy. The enemy guns were now firing at me personally, hundreds of rounds directed not just at anyone and everyone, but at me personally. I took that to be a personal insult. I started to low crawl on my stomach as fast as I could but determined that that would be much too slow so I jumped up onto my hands and knees and proceeded forward as fast as I could in that position. The enemy fire continued from the furthest two guns, they probably assumed that I was out, but the closest gun was ominously silent and I figured that those boys were very precisely bringing their gun to bear directly on me while reloading.

I went past about three soldiers, then noticed that the line of men changed 90 degrees to the right again. The elevated plot of land and line of men was exactly as it was when I started but now the enemy was very much closer. There was no return fire at all from Americans. They were all on the ground, behind trees and logs and the enemy mercilessly raked that section of the line with all three machine guns, again firing almost non stop and chewing up the ground and shredding the leaves so quickly and thoroughly and loudly I could not have imagined something like that before.

I decided that I must stand up and run, to get the M-79 up to the front as soon as possible.

The enemy fire seemed to quiet down for a few seconds but then I could see tracers from my left, coming out of the undergrowth and aimed directly at me. The first few bursts went in front of me and high, the next burst was behind me and low, so that the rounds hit the side of the embankment but the enemy had their exact aiming point. The next burst started low, hitting the ground and moving up the embankment as I ran towards it. Now the enemy had me sighted in and I knew that the next burst would be deadly accurate, but still I ran forward. The next burst started low and, seemingly in slow motion, proceeded up the embankment. My mind instantly calculated what was happening. As I ran forward, the bullets were coming up the embankment and the rate of climb of the bullets exactly matched my forward progress so that I realized that I would be hit for sure, my direction of running would exactly intersect the rounds coming up the embankment. My momentum made it impossible to stop in time. Obviously a VC gunner had me expertly in his sights. One round hit very near the top of the embankment, the next about knee level and the next was coming with a final and deadly path that would intersect with my head precisely. Very suddenly, someone very strongly pushed on the middle of my back and pushed me down to the ground while a fusillade of bullets flew overhead and around me.

I spun around to see who had pushed me but there was no one there. I yelled to the two guys that were closest to me "Hey!, you didn't have to push me down!", "Leave me alone!" Although I realized that they had certainly saved my life I didn't like the idea of them man handling me. They looked at me with terror and horror. I suddenly realized that it was impossible for any one of them to have pushed me, they were glued to the ground and were too far away to have done so. Someone had most certainly pushed me to the ground but it would have been impossible for one of them to have done so, but who could it have been? Of course I filed that away as something to figure out later.

Now I again did a low crawl along the line of men. The enemy machine guns were firing slower now, and concentrated again at the front of the line, which I was getting very close to now. They had probably figured that they had certainly taken out any threat that I might have imposed on them. That machine gun had me clearly in its sights and dead to rights and put ten rounds directly on me and I went down very quickly, maybe faster than humanly possible. The VC must have figured that they had killed me for sure because they were concentrating their fire at the front of the line. He must have assumed that he had killed me. Personally, I did not know for sure why I wasn't dead.

Again, I jumped to my hands and knees and scrabbled as fast as I could in that position then, ascertaining that my progress was too slow, a few seconds later I jumped up and ran. As I was running, a Sergeant called out to one of his troopers: "See where that fire is coming from!" I noticed one soldier lying perpendicular to the line of fire, behind a fallen log about six inches high. As I approached him, about six machine gun rounds hit the top of the log, tearing off huge splinters, about a half an inch from that mans head and body, tearing off ragged pieces of wood that would do horrible things to a human beings body. He semi-turned to his Sergeant and yelled something to the effect of: "Screw You!"

The embankment that I was on ended close to that point, terminating where the embankment was only about ten feet wide and sloping gently backwards. There was a break in the embankment, a gap of about eight feet and then the embankment raised up again about four feet wide. A platoon leader (2nd Lieutenant) was hunkered behind that little hill of dirt about five feet tall, with his radioman and another trooper. It was barely wide enough cover for them and that was only because they were turned sideways and some of them were partly behind others. The VC machine was spraying vicious, accurate fire all around the little mound.

I fell down at the end of the main embankment, fully expecting to be torn to pieces from the enemy fire, looking across the unprotected gap,. I really could not believe that I was still alive, still in one piece instead of in thirty pieces strewn over the battlefield. The Lieutenant yelled to me "Use HE!!" (high explosive). I almost yelled back something questioning his intelligence. Of course it called for high explosive, the enemy seemed to be about eighty or a hundred feet directly to our front. I pulled the shotgun round out of the M-79 and put in a high explosive round.

I looked over the mound in front of me and could see the tracers again coming directly at me, apparently the enemy was determined to kill me personally. I jumped forward a bit to sight the enemy. He was on top of another embankment but was twenty feet back from the edge, hidden in the undergrowth. The embankment rose to a height of about fifteen feet.

I put my sight on the very top of the ridge and was about to fire when I thought that I would aim middle ways up of the embankment. It would probably be a wasted shot, but it would register a round for sure and then I could more accurately adjust fire, rather than firing high and not knowing how far off my aim was. I squeezed the trigger and there was a dull pop as the round left the tube, followed a split second later by an explosion that was directly on the top edge of the enemy embankment, a perfect shot. I just had to aim slightly higher to put the round right into their faces.

I slithered backwards a few feet, down its sloping side so that I was not directly exposed to their fire, to eject the spent cartridge and replace it with another HE round from the bandolier. Now it was time to fire again. I knew that I should be able to place deadly accurate fire on their position but I could not plainly see them at all. They were expertly concealed in the undergrowth. The enemy fired and fired and fired, pouring hundreds of more rounds directly above my head and all around me and the three troopers crouched behind the mound beside me. That mound was getting smaller all the time as the enemy rounds tore pieces of it off. The troopers there were surrounded and immersed in a cloud of dust. The VC seemed to have managed to prevent anyone in this platoon from returning even one round with their continuous, almost unbelievable rate of fire but the fight now was so close that I realized that it was impossible to hear any other fire.

I jumped up and forward, fully exposing my head to their fire and took aim. But it now occurred to me that when I pulled that trigger, when I slightly tightened my finger, people are going to die. There were a few seconds of hesitation, a moment where my conscience screamed that I can not kill another human being, I cannot take the life of a person, I cannot deprive a wife of her husband or a sister of her brother or a mother of her son or a child of his father. That I could not deliberately kill a man, even though he certainly tried his best to kill me. But then, I thought that I couldn't allow this enemy to kill my entire platoon. I cannot allow him to continue his rampage. I could not deliberately kill another human being but then I rationalized that the enemy had a chance of living if they took a direct hit from an M-79, although it would be perhaps one in a million chance. I thought, "Couldn't we all just walk away from this situation? Couldn't we retreat and not force the enemies hand?" But no, that's not likely to happen. Anyways, the enemy had been intent upon killing us for the last five minutes, this insanity has to stop I thought and I am just the boy to do it.

I pulled the trigger. The round landed perfectly, just on top of the ridge and back in a little. I knew exactly the direction of the enemy, I was just unsure exactly how far back into the vegetation he was. Of course, he knew exactly where we were, as proven by his deadly accurate fire.

The enemy had instantly stopped firing when I had let loose but as I slid backwards and down to reload, he began his vicious fire directly at me again. Then, in the middle of his fire, I jumped forward and a up a little again, while he desperately tried to kill me and again, when I fired at him, he had a second while the high explosive round was in the air, on its way to its target, to get down under cover and so stopped firing. He could hear, if not see, every time I fired and because of the slow speed of the high explosive grenade, he had time to duck.This went back and forth for a few minutes. I realized that I was taking much more of chance than him. He fired ten to thirty rounds directly at me, for every one round that I put at him. He had a second to continue to blast me and then get under cover when he saw my head exposed over the edge of the embankment and he heard the "pop" of my grenade launcher.

We traded fire like that for a few minutes, him firing a hundred rounds while I reloaded and when I exposed my head for one shot at him he fired many rounds directly and accurately at me. This was an ass-kicking contest where he got to shoot many rounds directly at my exposed face and head while I was in plain sight and I got one chance to shoot at him where he had a seconds worth of advance notice and could get under effective cover before the round exploded near him.

I could see that I was going to lose that bet. This could not go on. If he killed me, he would continue his murderous rampage on my platoon. I thought that it would be bad enough if I was killed, but that would result in the certain killing of the guys in my platoon. Things were happening extremely quickly and with extreme consequences. The smell of gunpowder was very, very heavy in the air. The sounds of gunfire was far beyond anything that I had encountered on the rifle range back in the US. It was an extreme situation, far beyond anything I had ever encountered or been trained for.

I pushed forwards and up again and gave them another round but this time I noticed tracers coming from my left. It must have been the first VC machine gun that I thought had retired from the fight. They were obviously back in action but instead of shooting at the soldiers closest to them they were firing diagonally across the whole line of troopers and directly at me and the platoon leader and the other two troopers. That was really not good because that VC gun team had a good line of sight on the other three men. Now those men were kneeling, practically one behind the other, trying to get cover from two machine guns in different directions.

As I reloaded I suddenly formulated a desperate plan, it was beyond desperate. I sprang forward and up a little and then I jumped up on my knees, in full view of the enemy machine gun. The enemy again poured on his fire, the tracers coming directly at my face, above and below me and all around me. I brought the M-79 to my shoulder and seemed to aim, but did not pull the trigger. I waited a second, while that enemy gunner poured his fire directly at me, in full view and as a perfect target. They knew that I was going to put an HE round onto them and they crouched down in their hole to let it pass, temporarily ceasing fire on us.

Then I lowered the weapon and looked at it, as if I had had a misfire. The enemy must have observed that and thought that that was a colossal mistake on my part, which it probably was. Obviously, they must have thought, that I was a completely incompetent rookie. Now, they must have thought, that they had an easy shot, what kind of absolute rookie would expose himself while trying to deal with a misfire. They tried their utmost to tear my body apart with their fire, hundreds of rounds going past me in a metallic hailstorm, I could feel the heat of the rounds, they were missing me by inches, maybe less.

As the enemy fired round after round directly at me, trying desperately to kill me but the sound of their firing exposed themselves somewhat and I casually brought up my weapon, aiming from the hip and pulled the trigger. The round flew straight and true. While it was in flight the machine gun fire this time did not stop, apparently they didn't realize that I had fired. After all, what kind of completely incompetent rookie would just fire from the hip. They poured their murderous fire onto me with fearsome accuracy, damned and determine to kill me. I did not drop down, that may have alerted them to what I had done. The M-79 sailed straight and true, exploding exactly where I had aimed it.

As I was jumping back down to reload I noticed the Lieutenant who was on his knees behind a mound of dirt staring at me in shock, another trooper just looked at me with his mouth wide open. The lieutenant instantly jumped up, fully exposing his head and upper chest. He leveled his pump shotgun and fired his shotgun as fast as he could pump out rounds, pumping and pulling the trigger until he emptied his weapon. I was amazed at how fast he made that weapon perform. His radioman immediately straightened up, placed his M16 on top of the mound that he had been using for cover and emptied his M-16 on full automatic at the enemy. By that time I had reloaded and jumped forward and fired another HE round directly into the face of the enemy machine gun crew that was a direct threat to us (the other two machine gun nests, for some reason, had ceased fire and had apparently left the area)

There was suddenly an explosion in the trees to my left. Oh no, I thought. The VC are hitting us with mortars now. By this time the other two guys with M-79s had finally reached a point were they were close to the front of the line and one of them had fired a round. The round, however, was aimed very imprecisely and very high, so that it exploded into the tree branches that were directly above the men at the front of the line. It didn't hurt or kill anyone although it certainly could have done so, and someone yelled, "M-79s cease fire!".

I put another HE round into my M-79 and jumped forward to give it to them. A Lieutenant to my left yelled at me: "M-79s Cease fire!" I yelled over to him: "That's someone else! I'm engaging!" But no. He was very insistent that I not fire my M-79. I rolled over onto my back and pulled out the .45 automatic from my shoulder holster, switched off the safety and rolled back on my belly and moved forward, placing the aiming point directly at the enemy, holding it with both hands, resting on the ground and waited for the enemy gun to open up so I could get a more exact idea of his location. But, now there was no fire at all, the other two enemy guns had ceased fire minutes ago, for some unknown reason and the main gun was now silent. About a minute later, another platoon approached us from the right in a flanking maneuver. We yelled at them to get down but they ignored us and continued forward but stopped at the end of our line. They seemed to me to be very nonchalant. They seemed to me to be acting like they were standing in the food line, rather than aligning themselves to assault three machine guns. They themselves had just finished engaging the enemy in a separate action. There was gunfire relatively close by which must have been the other Companys platoon engaging.

At that time there was now gunfire at all near me. The new platoon was going to perform a flanking maneuver and sweep across our line of fire so that the men in my line would have to be very careful about shooting. My platoon Sergeant ordered a guy to go out to where the fire had been coming from and check it out. It was a guy named Mills. He and I entered the Army on the same day and had been together throughout basic and advanced infantry training and jump school and then ended up in the same platoon in Viet Nam. I watched him walk out, beyond our line. He seemed to me to be a man walking up the gallows for his own execution and I fully expected him to be cut down at any moment. I was feeling very bad for him as he walked directly towards where the last enemy machine gun that we engaged was. I thought that we had been through the entire course together for the last ten months and now I was going to have to watch him killed but there was no enemy fire. The VC had retreated back into the undergrowth and rubber trees. I fully expected the other platoon to take ten dead immediately once the first and second enemy machine guns opened up on them in their standing flank attack but the other platoon swept through the area and there was no further enemy contacts. All three enemy machine gun crews had exfiltrated the area.

There of course was a decided change of attitude now among the men. They slowly began to standup and talk among themselves although they continuously scanned to their left and right, not quite believing that the enemy had retreated. It was quiet now. The sound of the gunfire had been much louder than one would have expected, maybe because we were directly in front of the machine guns, taking fire. The smoke and smell and clouds of expended gunpowder began to blow away in the wind and now it was just a quiet nature scene, in a way, in a rubber plantation far, far, away from home.

I sat on the ground, down slope from the edge of the embankment and started to take loose rounds from the sandbag to replace into the bandolier the rounds that had been used up. I wondered why the men around me seemed to be happy. We survived this fight but we may very well all be dead in another ten minutes. We are going to continue this patrol and we still face many months ahead of dangers. I was more glum than happy or relieved.

There appeared a group of four or five men walking towards me who seemed to be very angry and one guy asked me if I had the M-79. I figured that they were going to jump me for hitting them with shrapnel from the round that another guy had fired. I said: "Yeah, I have the 79 but I'm not the guy who hit the tree, anyways, leave him alone, anyone can make a mistake". One guy said, yes they know who he is, you must be the guy that ran from the back of the line and took on those machine guns. I said, yeah, that was me.

I must have run through the Weapons platoon and then through the 1st platoon or maybe the 2nd platoon or maybe both of them because I did not recognize any of those soldiers. One guy said, "Is that him?", another said "Yes", another soldier said "It can't be, he looks human".They approached me very cautiously and one guy reached out and touched me on the shoulder. He exclaimed, "He's real, I touched him!" then another guy reached out very tentatively and touched me and looked at his hand as if he could not believe that he had touched something solid.

I started to ask what they were talking about when another small group of men approached.They all wanted to shake my hand and stated to me and to the others things like "You saved my life man!" "How is it possible?" "How many times were you shot?" "Are you an Angel?" "Are you real?" I thought at first that those guys were kidding me, but their demeanor was extremely serious.Those guys had just endured five minutes of otherwise unbelievable machine gun fire and were in no mood for jokes.They were not kidding me. I was humbled and shocked by their remarks. I couldn't have been prouder if I had received seven Medals of Honor. But to me, I was just trying to save the lives of my friends and fellow soldiers and was damned determined to do it or die trying.

Soon other guys came up to me, some guys that I knew. One guy said that he saw a tracer miss my head by about two feet when I was pushed to the ground, I think it was a lot closer than that. When that was happening, <u>That</u> was when someone seemingly put their hand directly onto the middle of my shoulders and very forcefully and substantially pushed me down to the ground.

Of course you can only see tracer rounds, and they were probably one in ten rounds or one in 20 rounds. One tracer a foot in back of my head meant ten or twenty unseen other bullets were flying around my body and head. One or two of those rounds would have gone directly through the side of my head if someone had not so quickly and forcefully pushed me forward and down. I asked him who pushed me and he said, "No one!, No one was near you!!" I never did find out who pushed me down, but later in my life, when faced with certain death, almost exactly the same thing happened. One of those times someone seemed to grab me by the middle of my back and lift me up, and carry me, away from a death that seemed impossible to avoid. What had saved me this time was an Angel, or the hand of God Himself.There is no other possible explanation for what happened then and the three other times in my life where almost the exact same thing happened, where it was impossible to escape death but somehow I did. Only through Divine intervention.

Glory to God in the highest.

A few other guys came by and shook my hand. One said to his buddies "Man, I've never seen anything like that, that guy was like John Wayne" Others said "Man, that is not like John Wayne. John Wayne never did anything like that, I cannot believe my eyes, I cannot believe what that guy did" Another said "That guy makes John Wayne look like little red riding hood". It was, of course, a miracle. I had survived approximately a thousand rounds of very accurate machine gun fire from three guns, aimed directly and personally at me. A guy said that during this action, he laid on the ground and cursed the Army for putting buttons on his shirt. When I asked him why, he said because they kept him that much higher above the ground and exposed to the fire.

I slowly walked back down the line, back to my original position at the end of the line of march. The soldier that had been in front of me when all of that started was still there. The guy who looked crazed when I first jumped to my knees and ripped off the sandbag full of M-79 rounds to begin my run. He said that he wasn't terribly afraid at first, even though we were taking some fire, until I jumped up and tore the sandbag full of M-79 rounds off of my rucksack and began running. I asked him why that caused him to became terrified, did he think that I was going to be killed? He said "No, not you, but by your actions and the look on your face, I knew for sure that people were now going to start being killed".

After about thirty minutes, when all of the fire from the other platoons had stopped, indicating that the enemy had broken contact, we again moved out on the patrol. The sounds from the other platoons fights had been one sided at first but then there had been the unmistakable sounds of American return fire. At first, there had been the sounds of enemy machine gun and automatic weapons fire, but after a minute or so, there had been the start of American M-16s being brought into action and then the "thump" of American M-79s and then the chatter of American M-60 machine guns slowly but surely rising in crescendo to answer the VC fire and eventually overpower it.

About two hours later a firefight broke out about two hundred yards to the right of our line of march. The sound of the enemy fire was very different from the M-16s. It was very loud, very distinctive, very powerful and very scary. I think it was VC AK-47s. I was all charged up to go and proceeded in that direction, get into the action, get it over with either me killing the enemy or me getting killed, but we were ordered to halt. That fight was with the 2nd platoon and we were ordered to proceed in our original direction. I don't know if we were forming a flanking position for that attack or were supposed to check the story in our area of operation, but as we walked, the firefight slowly died down and after a while I couldn't hear it any more.

I questioned why I was so gung ho to get involved in that new action. I don't know. Maybe it was a delayed reaction to the previous action, maybe it was because my adrenaline level was still on high. Maybe it was because I just wanted to get it over with. My thinking at the time, although unconsciously, was probably something along the lines of "Lets just get it over with. My life is a living nightmare of pain and torture. Lets get it over sooner rather than later. You might say "Hey, stick it out kid" or maybe you might say "Hey kid, things will get better".

I say, Hey, you have no idea whatsoever of the pain that we had to endure. I would say that the pain of carrying my load was insufferable, but that's not exactly true. It was far beyond anything that I could have imagined in my worst nightmares. Death would be a welcome respite. I knew that my death would have

been terrible news to my family, but if they knew of the pain and suffering of the daily walk in the woods that I had to endure every day, they would have been thankful to have learned of my death. Yes, that is how bad it was. I had reached the point that I would have welcomed death, sometimes I even prayed for it. Before I prayed that I might be wounded, not too bad, and sent home. Now I prayed to be killed. This was not some kind of difficult thing to do. This was not some kind of uncomfortable task. This was a kind of torment and torture that is not even remotely known in civilized society. The suffering and pain of the humping our heavy loads in the heat and humidity was unimaginable. The fact that you could very likely be killed or wounded horribly at any second was a secondary consideration.

The other platoons took some casualties that day with one man Killed In Action. We got the word down the line that a radioman had been killed. As my part of the line moved forward there were three soldiers standing around. There was no body but there was a radio and rucksack and LBG on the ground. The line of march stopped temporarily and I was close to that position.

I asked the men there what was going on. They told me that that was where the radioman had been killed and that I was now looking at his equipment. They told me that he had been shot almost perfectly in the middle of his radio which he carried on his back. The radio deflected the bullet away from his spine but was deflected by the internal components of the radio and exited from the top of the radio, out directly into the back of his neck and lower skull. You could clearly see where the bullet had entered and where it had exited.

Later I learned that that rubber plantation probably belonged to the Michelin Company, the one that makes automobile tires etc. For the rest of my life, whenever I saw the brand name Michelin on a tire, the question would flash through my mind was that I wondered if the person owning that tire had even the remotest idea of things that happened in that company's rubber plantations on the other side of the world.

The next morning we had filled in our fighting positions and packed up. There was suddenly some incoming sniper fire at the other end of the perimeter, about a hundred yards from me. No one in my immediate vicinity seemed to be upset or even concerned about it at all. I figured that the boys closest to the sounds of gunfire would handle it but felt sorry for them, imagining them on the ground, searching the trees and forest for a sniper that was probably impossible to see. Just laying there, taking it, with not much to do until they get a better bearing of where the fire was coming from, if they ever did.

We were going to be moving out at any time but I had taken my poncho and placed an end of it over a four foot high stick in the ground with the rest of it placed a foot over my head. I thought that that was an excellent idea because it provided shade from the direct sun that was already getting murderously hot even at eight A.M. When the line moved out I would simply tear it down and stuff it into my rucksack. The word came down the line "Ruck up" (load up with your rucksack and equipment). I had been sitting on my helmet on the ground and I went to stand up. I got about a foot off of the helmet when suddenly I lost my balance and sort of staggered to my right, awkwardly falling onto my buttocks. I thought that that was very strange. Maybe, I thought its my bodys way of telling me, "No more! No more of this torment!, Not this day!"

I picked myself up a bit and sat back on my helmet for half a minute to rest. The line of march was not yet moving so I figured that I could just sit there and then at the last second stand up, throw the poncho into my rucksack and drive on. I sat there for a minute and then for some reason, I had a strong urge to ruck up even though the line of march was not moving.

I had in my hand the strap of my .45 shoulder holster which was strongly attached to the pole holding up the poncho so that I certainly would not fall again. I went to stand up again when someone pushed me strongly sideways and down, knocking me again down to the ground. As I was falling there was a very sharp pain on the top of my shoulder. It felt like a part of my anatomy had snapped, broken in two. What is on top of your shoulder I thought. Muscles, tendons, nerves, blood vessels? I didn't know but it seemed as if all of them had snapped. I wondered what that was about, but I thought that it was just my body violently objecting to the thought of me loading it up with a torturous, beyond insufferable load of abuse for another day. I thought that it's my mind and body telling me not to subject it to further abuse. I thought it strange that my mind would produce such a sharp pain in my shoulder. I thought: "This load of equipment was hurting me before I could even put it on".

I loaded on my rucksack and began the operation with the pain and strain instantly at a brutal level, I knew that it would get much worse. The sharp pain in my shoulder went away after a few minutes. After a few hours of horrible suffering I noticed that there was again a pain on the top of my shoulder. That was of mild interest because the ache in my back from humping a hundred and forty pounds of gear was beyond unbearable, surely over-riding any other little pain. As the march progressed, the pain on my shoulder became more and more intense. I thought that maybe I picked up a twig or thorn under my rucksack straps. It was impossible to check it while walking but I thought that the very next time that I had a chance I would check for thorns. As every minute clicked on the pain rose in amplitude

It took about fifteen minutes before the line stopped, each minute resulting in higher and higher levels of pain. I just wanted to grab a minutes time to stop and check my equipment, to stop that pain, but the hump had continued. When we did finally stop for a bit, I dropped my rucksack and shrugged off my LBG but I couldn't see anything wrong. I felt up around my neck and shoulder but didn't find anything. I just couldn't understand what was causing the sharp pain.

After a few hours the pain in my shoulder reached an extremely intense level, an excruciatingly white hot type of pain. After ten minutes of that I thought that it was a new dimension of torture. Something like being on a rack, in a medieval torture room where you were on the rack, where the torturers were trying to tear your arms and legs apart and then, in the middle of that, they poured oil upon your shoulder and lit it afire.

My mind suddenly snapped, in a way. I suddenly thought that that was a good thing in a way, because I could concentrate on the white-hot pain in my shoulder and that would distract me from the horribly deep agony that racked the muscles and joints in my back. After another five minutes the deep agony of humping the equipment over-rode the white-hot pain in my shoulder. That deep agony overrode the white hot pain but then it gave way to the white hot pain in my shoulder that demanded of me to take notice and stop it. That scenario repeated over and over again for many hours, the white-hot excruciating pain on my shoulder eventually being overpowered by the dull red horribly heavy agony of the load and then switching back and forth every ten or fifteen minutes.

And so it went until we stopped for the night. Actually both pains were continuous but it sort of helped to just concentrate on the pain coming from one source until the other pain became overwhelming and you had to consider that one. It was sort of like a three-hour tooth extraction without anesthesia interrupted only temporarily and intermittently by the pain of someone trying to break your back with iron bars. No, no you say. It couldn't have been that bad. But that description is no exaggeration, I could not believe it myself even while it was happening. Previous to that time I couldn't have imagined that level of suffering and it went on hour after hour all day long, for days and weeks at a time. Simply beyond human imagining. This time the white hot pain was just another dimension of the suffering, on other patrols it would be other things, on top of the basic destruction of ones body humping through the jungle with more than a hundred pounds of weight. What goes through your mind during that ordeal? I don't remember exactly.

The next morning I was heating up a cup of coffee when a guy came up to me from behind and asked me what happened to me. I had no idea what he was talking about. Another guy came up and the first guy said to him "Look at this guy

(meaning me), he's been shot!". I said "That's ridiculous, what are you guys talking about?" The first guy said, "Man, the whole back of your shirt is soaked in blood". I took off my shirt and turned it around and yes, they were right, it was completely soaked in blood, most of it dried black. The lower two inches of the whole circumference of the back of my shirt was bright red and it was dripping drops of blood at an alarming rate. It was horrifying. I thought: "Hollywood couldn't make up this scenario in a horror movie." Now the two guys had a horrified expression on their faces. Why are they horrified I thought. They can't even see the back of my shirt. Maybe they could see the bright red drops of blood quickly falling to the ground I thought. One of them said: "Man, go see the medic right away! "You've been shot!!"

I tried to see the wound that was on top of my shoulder but it was too close to my neck for me to see it. They were appalled by the ghastly appearance of it. One of them finally said, "Man! I can see your shoulder bone!" I said: "What do you mean, my shoulder bone? How do you know it's a bone? One of them said: "because your muscles are completely gone and I see a pure white bone." I thought that that statement was worrisome. How would a regular person know that a bone was bright white. I didn't know that. I asked him: "Oh, what? Do you see a tiny speck of white or something?" He forcefully, and convincingly, said: "Man, You have some very serious damage. I can't believe that you are still standing."

I had no idea what could have caused an injury like that but then suddenly thought back to the morning of the day before. Why, when I tried to stand up and someone seemingly pushed me to the right did my shoulder muscles and tendons and nerves and blood vessels seem like they had been snapped and severed? I normally would have dismissed those soldiers concerns to be of no consequence. Obviously, I thought, I probably had a twig or something that had later cut into my shoulder. However, their report that they could see a pure white bone concerned me, not to mention that I was obviously bleeding out at an alarming rate.

I tracked down a medic and he examined it and asked me when I had been shot. I said that I don't think I have been shot. I was pretty sure that the strap for my shoulder holster, which was under my lbg suspender straps, which was under my rucksack straps, had slowly rubbed its way through my shirt, then through my skin and downwards through my muscles, eventually hitting bone. I asked the medic what he thought of it and he said, "Yeah man, you have been shot!". I told him that I think that it was just the shoulder holster strap rubbing through my shirt and skin, although that had never happened before and never happened again.

He instantly became very angry and said, "I've seen gunshot wounds!!" You've been shot!!". He examined the wound further and said: "You're lucky, it looks like the bullet just barely hit the bone." Then he put a battle dressing, a huge white piece of gauze six inches by four inches by an inch thick on it and told me to carry on.

He asked for my name. For some reason I demanded to know why he wanted to know. He said that he had to report all combat wounds, especially gunshot wounds. I insisted that I had not been shot and refused to give him my name. He walked away in disgust.

It is strange that that shoulder holster never ate its way through my skin before that incident and it never happened afterwards. It's strange that my shirt had an oblong, torn hole about an inch long, burnt at the edges, but the wound was about four inches long. I guessed that the holster strap rubbed through my shirt and then the hole rubbed back and forth for another three inches to make the wound but that is really highly unlikely.

Who knows, maybe I was shot, maybe by that sniper on the previous morning. That would explain the being pushed off-balance and snapping sensation of muscles and tendons on my shoulder, an inch away from my spinal column and back of the brain, and the incredibly novel but intense white-hot pain during the hump that followed, that had never occurred before or after, and the hole in my shirt.

But I was so sure that it must have been the shoulder strap or a twig or thorn, but I never found a twig or thorn. I had concentrated on that as the source of the pain to such an extent when I was humping that day, that even now I still think it was the strap, but that really could not have been the problem. As I write this, I can see that maybe the others were right. What else could have torn apart my muscles, severed my tendons and chipped out a piece of my collar bone, fracturing it in the process. What else could have explained that someone or some supernatural presence could have pushed me out of the way at the last split second so as to avoided my head being knocked off of my body?

A snipers bullet would explain all of those strange happenings. Also, that might explain why it felt like someone pushed me down and off balance on those two occasions early the previous morning, which prevented me from taking a round in the head. Maybe my Guardian Angel again. Obviously something had cut through my muscles and tendons and blood vessels so deeply that my shoulder bone was exposed. Nothing like that had happened before or afterwards. Who knows,

maybe those soldiers and the medic was right. Maybe that sniper reached out and hit me. That theory seems much more likely, given the evidence, than my theory that it was a twig caught under my LBG. I guess I just psychologically refused to accept the fact that that enemy sniper had very nearly taken my head off the previous morning. I also realized that if "someone" hadn't pushed me at the last split second that the second round would have smashed my backbone into ten pieces right at the base of my skull.

I went back to my hootch and tore it down, finished my coffee then loaded up for that days mission. I still put on my shoulder holster with the .45 in it first. My reasoning was that if we got into it, I would drop my rucksack first. Then if we really were into it, I'd drop my LBG if I used up all of the ammo and grenades that it held. That would still leave me with a .45.

The battle dressing on my shoulder was a good thing. It provided padding and there wasn't the white-hot pain of the previous day. Actually, it didn't hurt at all. It was a fluke of a thing, I had humped for many, many days, on many operations with that shoulder holster, and why it wore through me on that day is something that I have never understood, maybe because I someday have to acknowledge that it could only have been a snipers bullet that snapped all of my muscles and tendons and torn a piece out of my shoulder bone. The hump the previous day was worse than most days but not as bad as some to come.

We continued the operation. Two days later I saw the medic again. Obviously I needed my battle dressing changed and I didn't want to use my personal one. The medic checked me and said that I was good to go. I really wanted to get another battle dressing because it actually helped from the pain of the hump. He told me that it wasn't that bad (of course, I suspect that he didn't want to use up any of his medical supplies). We humped for another couple of days. The pain on my shoulder was very much reduced from the previous time but I really wished that it could have been padded. Then we went back to base camp, I forgot how we got there.

Many years later I evaluated that situation. Other troopers had told me that they could see my bone and the medic told me that there was only a small chip taken out of the bone. I suddenly realized that everyone else was right and I was wrong. Obviously I had been shot. Obviously I hadn't gone to a doctor when it happened. Obviously hard core Airborne Infantry in a combat zone endured unimaginable sufferings and pains as a matter of course. A blasted out section of muscles with cut tendons and a nicked and broken collar bone was just something to "deal with". It just added a new dimension of pain on top of the standard, absolutely horribly physical tortures of humping a hundred and forty pounds, all day, in a ninety-five degree heat, with ninety-five percent humidity. That alone was worse than my wildest nightmares, a green scenario of days long suffering that I would have previously imagined to be impossible and literally insufferable.

Chapter 10
DANANG

Firing the Mortar

Back at the base camp, I went to the supply Sergeants hooch to get new clothes. His office and supplies were in a standard Quonset hut constructed completely of corrugated metal sheets over metal ribs.

It was a long, rather thin building, viewed from either end its outline was that of a half-circle. The walls curved upwards from the ground, eventually becoming the roof and then continuing downwards to form the opposite wall. After he issued me a new set of jungle fatigue shirt and pants I asked him for more magazines and ammo for my .45 auto pistol. He said that, according to his records, I had been issued two magazines and according to Army regulations, that was all that I could get. Those regulations were probably from WW2 where a mortarman would be stationed well within a large defensive perimeter or in a forward base camp that was well protected.

I told him, in case he was unaware of it, that we humped the mortars all day through the bush, that we didn't sit around all day with hundreds of troops as a buffer between us and the enemy. Therefore, I argued, I needed more ammo. He seemed to agree but said there was nothing he could do. I pushed my argument with him further and we had a little back and forth discussion but while he was informing me of his reasons I found myself paying less attention to what he said because a plan was slowly forming in my mind.

It was going to be all right if I couldn't persuade him to give me the ammo. I had formulated three possible solutions to my problem. I would either break into this "building" later that night, punch him in the mouth right now and take my supplies, or just come back in a few minutes with my .45 and shoot the numbskull. Option A was probably the safest I thought. Option B may result in my spending some time in jail but I needed a rest anyways. Option C was drastic although it would probably cause him to find a loophole in the regulations the next time someone wanted some combat equipment and as such I could help my fellow troopers I reasoned. My thoughts and intentions were probably unconsciously telegraphed to him because he suddenly, but very reluctantly decided to give me two more magazines. Then he unexpectedly reached under his counter and produced two boxes of .45 ammo. That was another example of where World War II regulations over-ruled Viet Nam realities. I walked out of there thinking that he was only half of a complete ass.

My take on the situation was that he was trying to protect his career, at my and my friends expense. There was no way that that was going to happen. Its easy to say in retrospect that I had no right to shoot and maybe kill a supply Sergeant that was simply following procedures, that is very true. But this was not a Stateside situation. When that supply Sergeant denied me additional ammo, he was possibly sentencing me to death, and maybe also causing the deaths of my friends and fellow troopers. Perhaps, from his perspective, he may get into some sort of trouble if he issued me additional magazines for my weapon but on the other hand I suppose he wouldn't have any trouble in issuing additional body bags.

I couldn't have known it at that time but that supply Sergeant would later make a decision that probably very adversely affected his career but that most likely saved my life, just to do a kindness for a fellow human being.

The fifty rounds that he gave me was less than I wanted, but I was grateful to get them. When he placed the two boxes of them in my hands however I was surprised by their weight. They probably only weighed about four pounds but they were much heavier than I expected, and in the back of my mind I realized that those 4 pounds would feel like 40 pounds after humping them for a few days in the woods. I almost told him that I had made a mistake and that he could have them back, but I realized on some level that as much as those four pounds would kick my but a good one, I would be glad to have them if we ran into a very bad situation.

I went back to the platoon hooch and asked loudly if anyone there had any extra .45 magazines that they wanted to get rid of. A few guys had extra magazines and ammo that they either didn't want or couldn't use because they were carrying M-16s. Obviously, I thought, they had turned in their pistols to the supply Sergeant but had forgotten to turn in their magazines and bullets. As fastidious as that son of a bitch of a supply Sergeant had been with me, I wondered why he hadn't hounded those guys to turn in their magazines and ammo. Then I slowly began to realize that there was probably a lot of material and ammo that was un-accounted for. In the jungle, equipment gets lost or damaged all the time. It is shot up or blown up or burned up or used up all the time. It occurred to me that the magazines and ammo that these men were handing to me were either equipment that they had forgotten to turn in or that that equipment belonged to a wounded soldier that had been med-evaced or, worse still, equipment that had belonged to trooper killed in action.

When everything was added up, I had seven magazines, each of which was loaded with seven rounds. I also had forty-nine loose rounds that I put into one of the ammo pouches on the belt of my load bearing equipment. Now I was happy. I had not been issued a bayonet, I guess because I was carrying the M-79 grenade launcher and there is no place on that weapon to mount a bayonet. My thinking was, if we were in the middle of a battle and the order came down to "fix bayonets!", I could do a lot more with ninety-eight rounds and a .45 than I could with a bayonet in my hand.

Later in the day we were notified that we were going north. A large number of Marines in Da Nang were moving out to support other Marines near the DMZ(DeMilitarized Zone) bordering north and south Viet Nam. We would take over some of their positions. The word was to take all of our equipment, especially clothes, even civilian clothes. They said it would be very cold up there. How could it be cold? I thought. After all this is Viet Nam. But if they are telling us to take all of our civilian clothing then it must be serious. On the other hand, why didn't they issue us extra clothing, maybe even field jackets? I don't know, maybe because we weren't "authorized".

This would be Operation "Winchester". The 4th battalion of the 503rd Airborne Infantry Regiment, 173rd Airborne Brigade (Separate) would be the first Army unit in that area. (It would be a check-off on a list that would, before our tour of duty ended the next year, eventually place my Battalion as the first and perhaps the only unit during the war to conduct combat operations in all four war zones in Viet Nam.)

The next day we were driven in trucks to the airbase and there loaded onto military cargo planes. The aircraft was certainly not a civilian craft with comfortable seats arranged neatly in the cabin. The only place to sit was in canvas cargo webbing hanging along both sides. There wasn't enough seating for all of the soldiers so many of them just sat on the floor. Oh, and there certainly was not any seatbelts or stewardesses. After landing at an airbase in Da Nang, we were taken by truck to a Marine mess hall on the big Marine base located close by. We had to walk about 500 feet and there were a few Marines that had stopped to stare at the long line of Army Paratroopers that had suddenly appeared at their base. We were carrying our full rucksacks plus large duffel bags that contained all of our clothes and other supplies. I don't think that we were carrying the Mortars or any mortar ammo, that would be delivered later, but the weight and bulk of the equipment was a serious struggle to handle. I didn't want to appear to be struggling, not wanting to give the Marines the impression that we were anything less than Airborne, but it was very difficult indeed to maintain a straight face when walking with all of that bulk and weight.

The Company was split up into two separate forces and loaded onto two groups of trucks. We traveled for about ten minutes just to reach the perimeter of the base and then entered onto a civilian road. Da Nang was supposed to be a large city but I couldn't see anything other than rice paddies and a few shacks as we traveled along the road for the next half hour. The city was probably in the opposite direction from which we were traveling. We crossed a deep river gully over a metal bridge and began to see glimpses of sand and the ocean on our right hand side, to the east. A huge range of mountains stretched from our front left as far as the eye could see all the way over to our front right, ending abruptly at the sea. From a distance, the mountains were black, with their topmost areas shrouded in mist and clouds, they formed an ominous specter. The road led directly into the mountain range and we began a very long ascent.

We drove onwards for another thirty minutes or so. The other group of soldiers, consisting of two platoons from my Company and maybe elements of another Company, were in front of us in the convoy. They stopped halfway up the mountain next to a sloping grassy meadow that terminated at the side of the road and offloaded themselves and their equipment to set up an encampment. The trucks in my part of the convoy stopped for ten minutes or so and then squeezed past the parked trucks on the narrow road and continued onwards and upwards.

The further we traveled the more the road twisted and turned and meandered as it followed a tortuous path, ever upwards. Eventually, the trucks were slowed to no more than ten miles per hour, struggling up the inclined road, spewing large clouds of exhaust amid the noise of powerful transmissions downshifting and creaks and groans from the heavy trucks. The drivers fought their machines, as intensely and powerfully as if they were fighting a man. They gripped the large steering wheels with both hands on one side of it, brutally pulling it around with all the strength that they could muster, rising their bodies up out of their seats with the effort. Then they would have to quickly turn the wheel the other way to straighten out while desperately pushing and pulling and kicking the long gear shift levers and foot pedals, jamming on the brakes one second to avoid going over the cliff and mashing the accelerator to the floor the next second, trying to maintain some momentum up the steep grade. Many times the wheels on the right hand side were less than two feet away from the edge of the road, which was the edge of a cliff that dropped away for a thousand feet or more. There were no guardrails.

For most of the road, one side of the road sloped upwards very sharply. Other sections of the road were cut between almost perpendicular walls of solid stone so it was like traveling at the bottom of a narrow trench, all of it was heavily forested with tall jungle trees and dense bushes. Other sections just had the beginning of a sharp cliff to mark the road. The infantrymen riding in the back were violently shaken back and forth and from side to side as the trucks brawled their way ever upwards.

At some point I suddenly realized that traveling that road was an open invitation to an ambush. The enemy could wait until the first couple of trucks came around a hairpin turn and hit them before the following trucks were even aware of what was happening. A few claymore mines placed against the solid rock wall would kill most of the soldiers in the trucks. The remaining infantrymen would then be facing a vertical rock wall twenty feet tall that would be impossible to assault and five feet behind them would be a cliff face that dropped straight down for hundreds of feet. In the meantime, the following trucks would be blocked from going forward past the disabled trucks and a well-emplaced enemy machine guns and a group of snipers hiding in the dense jungle trees along the road behind them would kill every man in the convoy.

Airplane support would be very difficult and dangerous, Artillery would be impossible. A helicopter gunship might well kill more Americans than enemy in the tight confines of the road even if a ship could be raised and be on scene before most of us were killed. The steep sides of the mountain above the vertical rock walls would make an enemy withdrawal from an ambush site difficult I figured, but then, I thought, they wouldn't have to withdraw quickly if they killed all of us outright.

Eventually we reached a summit that was two hundred feet below the top of the mountain on our right and five hundred feet below the top of the mountain on our left. The convoy suddenly stopped and then turned right, onto an incredibly steep dirt road. Two hundred feet up the road the ground suddenly leveled out into a large, flat clearing.

The most striking feature of that site was that it contained many antennas of all manner of shapes and descriptions, many of them very large. Ten or fifteen of them were placed along half of the long and thin, roughly oval shape of the perimeter, standing almost like sentinels, with the actual antennas mounted on frameworks of metal that were from ten feet high to over fifty feet tall. Obviously, this was the site for some very major communications systems.

The entire perimeter was in a thin elliptical shape perhaps five hundred feet long and a hundred feet wide. At the very top of the mountain were the Marines, the Army Airborne contingent occupied the lower end. The position was already prepared. There were ten or so small sandbag huts. They had been constructed by digging a hole about seven feet by seven feet square and about three feet deep. Then sandbags had been filled and stacked to make walls which were about four feet above ground level. A sloping roof made of corrugated metal sheets with a few sandbags thrown on top of them to hold them down in the wind completed the structure. Each hut could accommodate three or four men. There were a few other larger buildings, similarly constructed, which probably contained communication relays and equipment. That area of huts was in the center of a semi-circular inner perimeter.

The perimeter defenses in our section consisted of a trench about three feet deep with a foot of sandbags placed along its outward facing side. That trench connected fighting positions that had been constructed at intervals of about fifty feet. Standing anywhere on that perimeter, the view was of the mountain sloping downwards very steeply. All of the vegetation had been completely cleared for a distance of about fifty feet out from the trenches so that any enemy approach could be easily detected. In that no-mans land, multiple strands of barbed wire had been strung straight out from three inches to a few feet high, supported by branches and iron bars. There were flares set out, some of them attached to separate tripwires, others set up to use the barbed wire as the detonating wire. We were told that there were land mines out there and I saw that there were obviously claymore mines set in place.

We were very high, perhaps six thousand feet above sea level, and we had an extraordinary view all around. To the west were mountains for a few miles that fell away to the ocean where the vista then extended across the water out to the horizon. To the south was the city of Da Nang. We could see the large meadow where the other unit had set up operations, across the road from a huge oil storage tank, I think it said Esso on it. To the west was a commanding view of other mountains that were lower than ours and we could clearly see a very narrow road that wound through the mountain pass a continuation of the road that we had used, the only road through those mountains. The northern view was of the tops of mountains in a sea of green shades that stretched out for miles.

The entire emplacement was designed to only hold perhaps fifty to eighty men. We replaced most of the Marines that had originally been assigned to this site but there was a contingent of less than twenty Marines still remaining. Most of them manned the upper half of the perimeter. We settled in for the night and the next morning were told to go up a little sloping dirt road within the perimeter that led still higher, to the mess hall that was close to the very top of the mountain. I guessed that the reference to a "mess hall" was a joke. I assumed that we were to go up the road a bit and pick up some cases of C-rations, but, instead, there actually was a small building up there. Its walls were just lumber 2 by 4's spaced about three feet apart that supported a roof of corrugated sheet metal. Screen material was attached to the frame from floor to ceiling to try to keep out most of the insects and there was a four foot tall wall of sandbags around the structure to try to keep out most of the shrapnel and gunfire from an enemy attack. The Marines really had their act together here. We went in expecting powdered eggs and cold coffee but they had fresh eggs cooked to order and bacon and fruit cocktail and steaks, good ones, and cooked to order. The cooks told us to eat as much as we wanted. We were completely flabbergasted.

During our stay on top of that mountain some of the soldiers from our group and the other group that was below us on the mountain sometimes sent out patrols into the nearby vicinity and saw action and ambushes on several occasions but my platoon was never sent out.

I guess that was because we had mortars and could clearly support the patrolling squads and also because the site that we were guarding was so valuable that it was required to be protected by a certain complement of guards.The mortars would have been virtually useless if we had humped them on a patrol because the surrounding terrain was so steep that the mortar baseplates probably wouldn't have enough purchase on the ground and the recoil from the first round fired would have sent the whole gun skidding down the slope.

From the small mountain road that we overlooked, one would have to turn off of that road and ascend a very steep dirt road for about a hundred yards to reach our perimeter. At the bottom of that turnoff to our road was a large sandbagged one story building that contained a number of ARVN troops. The perimeter of the area that we were defending was laid out in a long, thin, roughly oval shape. There was a lower section or end of the perimeter and a higher section with the difference being about two hundred feet in elevation. This was going to be a very good mission for my squad, no humping the bush, no operations, good food and plenty of it every day.

We took turns on guard duty around the perimeter but there were plenty of soldiers to man perhaps only fifteen fighting positions so we only had to pull guard duty once during the day and once at night for a total of perhaps six hours a day. Those of us directly responsible for the mortars sometimes did not have to pull guard duty but simply be awake for four hours late at night when we would run outside and drop a round into the mortar, six or eight times a night at random times, to rain down upon the surrounding country side. It was called H&I fire, Harassment and Interdiction fire. It was just to annoy and disrupt any VC that might be in the area. Let them know that Willie boy was in town.

The mountain road was very narrow with a very steep drop-off at one edge and no guard rails or lighting. The Vietnamese used it as a two-way road but one of the first things that our outfit did was to close the road to traffic going one way for about thirty minutes, and then allow only traffic from the opposite direction to proceed for thirty minutes. The road was obviously too narrow to allow trucks to navigate it from both directions at once. It had obviously been built centuries ago to allow two ox carts to pass but certainly was not sufficient for large military traffic, at least not without substantial danger of falling off of the edge of the continuous cliff.

One day, we could hear gunfire, seemingly in the distance but I just happened to be close to the action and looked down to see a jeep askew on the road directly below us, just before the dirt road that led upwards to our perimeter. One soldier was lying on the road, unmoving and another guy trying to protect him, seeking cover behind the jeep and firing into the junglely growth with a .45 auto pistol. A Sergeant jumped behind a.50 caliber machine gun and let loose and another guy jumped behind an M-60 machine gun and let loose about eight hundred rounds over the head of the ambushed men and into the side of the mountain. A group of ARVN ran out of their house, which was less than fifty feet from the action and started firing at the enemy. What seemed like only a very few minutes later a patrol from the other position lower on the mountain came roaring up the road in three trucks and the enemy ambushers broke off their assault. I heard later that the man lying on the road had been killed. I later heard that he was a Marine commander who was scheduled to return home in a few days, coming out to say goodbye to some of his troops, way out here in the bush.

There were reports of other ambushes along that stretch of road, slightly outside of our vision. About a week later, I saw a convoy of about five military vehicles proceeding down the road a good distance from us. I looked away and about thirty seconds later heard a large explosion followed by heavy gunfire. When I looked down I could see about two thousand yards away the lead truck at an odd angle on the road with smoke rising around it. The soldiers in the trucks were quickly jumping off of and exiting the vehicles and seeking cover behind them. There was no place for them to run to or find effective cover, just an extremely steep cliff falling away from the mountain five feet from their backs. I yelled that we should start firing onto the ambush with our mortar and yelled for the fire direction control team to give us coordinates. A Sergeant jumped behind a .50 caliber machine gun on the perimeter and starting firing bursts of fire into the side of the mountain at least a half of a mile away.

Very quickly thereafter commands were shouted to cease fire. It was ARVN troops who had been ambushed. I guess the ARVN had broken part of the ambush and had directly assaulted the enemy and were now onto the side of the mountain. Our .50 caliber fire was falling among friendly troops. A few seconds later we saw about forty ARVN from the building below us start to run out and along the road towards their fellow soldiers being ambushed. There were no vehicles around and we watched while they ran approximately a mile, strung out one behind each other until they arrived at the group of trucks. During that time the tide of battle seemed to have turned. At the beginning of the ambush there was a lot of fire that must have been from the enemy but no return fire that should have a distinctively different sound due the difference in the weapons used by both sides. That situation changed, from much gunfire of one type, to a mixture of fire sounds, to an overpowering crescendo of what must have been ARVN fire. When the ARVN that had run a mile finally arrived at the scene the battle was over and the gunfire had stopped. That ARVN convoy must have taken many killed and wounded in the ambush.

While walking to the mess hall on that hilltop one day, I suddenly heard one shot that seemed to come from within the perimeter, followed immediately by six or eight other shots from M-16s and shotguns. I quickly unholstered my .45, wishing that I had brought my M-79 and waiting to try to determine what was going on. In a few minutes about eight guys emerged from some dense underbrush that was within the perimeter, at the extreme top of the mountain. Four of them carried a long branch around which was draped a huge dead snake. Later they measured it at 8 feet 4 inches long, with a very substantial thickness. They had nearly stepped on it in the bush and shot it. They all seemed pretty happy with their impromptu wild life hunting expedition. I suspected that they were all happy that the snake hadn't bit one or two of them.

Inside the hoochs were bunks made out of 2 by 4s with mosquito netting above it and hanging down on all sides. I awoke one night and yelled out that I saw a snake on top of my netting. But I was very tired and in the almost pitch darkness of the hooch I wasn't absolutely sure of it. Maybe I was dreaming, maybe I was seeing things. I don't think that I was. There was a small candle burning but its light was almost negligible. My squad Sergeant was very upset and jumped out of his bunk and demanded to know where the snake was and demanded to know if I was really sure that I saw it. I said, "Yeah, I saw a snake, a good sized one, right on top of my netting", then fell right asleep, leaving the

Sergeant to worry about it. A few days later, a guy in a nearby hooch shot a cobra that was hiding in a corner of his abode.

Most of the time we just sat around. The Marines had left about fifty copies of National Geographic magazine in my hooch which had been sent to them by some VFW post in the States. I read and re-read them. We simply sat around all day, pulling some very safe guard duty, eating well and most importantly not having to hump a hundred pounds of equipment through a hundred possible ways of being killed or maimed. Some of the men in my Company did it, it must have been even more beyond painful humping those slopes.

On each corner of the hooch, about six inches outside the four corners of the walls were metal stakes about five feet tall the purpose of them being unknown. They were a type of angle iron with holes drilled into them every few inches. Maybe at one time they had been used to stake down a canvas tent roof for the hooch, I don't know but they had obviously been driven deep into the hard earth with a sledgehammer because they were as fixed and rigid and immovable as if they had been driven into five feet of concrete. Maybe they were. One evening there was a light rain. There was a small but persistent leak from the top of the sloping roof that was made of corrugated metal sheets. It had leaked before on many occasions but I decided this time to climb the roof and rearrange some sandbags that had been placed at the top, probably to hold down the metal in the wind and also prevent most of the rain from entering between where the sheets met together at the top.

I realized that I would have to be extra careful or I would slide down and off of the roof , landing heavily on my back, or, much worse still, be impaled by those stakes. I managed to climb the four foot tall bag of sandbags, but it wasn't easy. Then I pressed my chest down upon the metal and tried to work my way upwards. The metal was slippery. I used the outside edges of my boots for some sort of traction but it was very tricky. I'd move up a foot and then slide down a few inches. I was moving the last sandbag, at the top of the roof, stretching ever so gingerly to move the last sandbag an inch, not quite able to reach it well because the roof was so slippery when I felt myself rapidly sliding down the roof. There was nothing to grab but the slick roof and in an act of desperation as my body began to fall off of the roof I wildly contorted my body, hoping to avoid one of those metal stakes towards which I was rapidly sliding. If I wasn't successful, that metal stake was going to impale me at the groin and go up two feet into my body.

I somehow missed it, falling heavily and awkwardly to the ground. I was pretty sure that I had done a 360 degree roll and a somersault in mid air but I wasn't sure. If fact I don't know how I could have avoided that stake. I landed on my feet but then fell over and heavily crashed to the ground. I was trying to compose myself when a guy walked over to me. I was going to ask him if he had seen what had just happened, maybe he could explain why I was not dead, when he exclaimed that what he had just witnessed was truly extraordinary.

He asked if I had been in the Olympics. He really thought that I must be some sort of Olympic high board diver who had climbed onto the roof to practice his dive. He said he had never seen someone twist around so many times and do two somersaults in such a short distance. He was serious. I guess he thought he had just witnessed the dive that, to his reckoning, was the one I made in '64 to win the gold. It was without a doubt a very serious action that very nearly killed me horribly. I thought that of all the ways to be killed over here, being impaled on a metal stake on top of this mountain while trying to fix a leak in the roof is something one would never think of, yet I had come very close to horribly dying. I told him that, no, I wasn't an Olympic diver, I was just trying to avoid being a human Popsicle. He looked at me in disgust. He had just greatly complimented me and I was trying to make a fool out of him. He walked away in disgust. I yelled after him: "No, really, I was just trying not to be killed." He just continued walking. I wanted him to tell me what had happened. I guess I made more than one summersault and 360 degree rotation.

A few days later, at night, we were in our hooch. It would have been pitch dark inside that hooch except that for some reason we two candles going. As the flames flickered and cast shadows I thought that this must be like how people lived in the middle ages. It was eerie but that was our life now. Me and another guy were sitting beside each other on a lower bunk. Another guy named Gore was sitting on a bunk directly in front of us, all of us just pleasantly shooting the bull. Without any warning, Gore suddenly became extremely agitated for a few seconds. He grabbed a bayonet out of its scabbard from the nearest hanging LBG, pulled his arm back in the finest traditions of that movie "Psycho" and lunged directly at us, plunging it directly and mightily between our faces into the sandbagged wall behind us.

Obviously, that trooper had just had some sort of brain aneurysm and had gone completely insane I thought. I jumped up and grabbed him around the neck to try to restrain him, but he still had his hand on the bayonet and stared directly at it. He was strong, very strong, insanely strong I thought. I yelled to the soldier who had been seated next to me to help me. I thought that I might, might, might be able to pull him away from the other soldier but I had no confidence that I would be able to pull that weapon out of his hand without some serious help. But Gore yelled: "Get out of there!!, Let me go!!, Look out!!" I looked behind me for a split second, hoping dearly that perhaps there was some glimmer of hope that the poor trooper was not completely insane but then realizing that if he wasn't insane then what the heck are we dealing with?

There, impaled on the sandbagged wall by the bayonet that Gore refused to let go of, was a still very much alive, huge wriggling centipede. A bug, you say. The cause of panic was a bug? No, that was not a bug. At what point does a scientist, never mind a soldier, classify a creature that looks like a bug, but is fifty times bigger than any bug you had ever seen and obviously capable of inflicting some very serious damage to a humans skin and muscle not become classified as a bug? What do you call such a creature? Certainly "bug" doesn't really describe it.

That thing had a body was about nine inches long and an inch wide. It had about thirty legs, each about an inch and a half long. It had brown legs but the last three quarters of an inch was solid, designed specifically to puncture its prey I would guess. It was black and quickly reduced down to a needle shape, to a very sharp point. Gore told us that if even one of those legs were to stick you that your flesh would rot away from around the wound. I could certainly believe it.

The creature was very much alive even though Gore had stuck him a good one through his body. The American bayonet had been subjected to a hundred years of research. It was a knife that was specifically designed to kill human beings as quickly and efficiently as possible. A horrible thought if you think about it. Yet here was a "bug" that was still very much alive.

The other guy got another bayonet and cut off the creatures' head but still the body wriggled wildly, trying to get away. Gore got his bayonet and between the two soldiers they managed to pry its body away from the wall. Gore took the still wriggling creatures body outside on the end of his bayonet and tossed it away. He came back and said to be careful not to step on it in the middle of the night because its still infected and dangerous. I didn't doubt him for a second and made a mental note to avoid the area where its body had been tossed for the next couple of days. We had already been exposed to jungle rot. The idea of that creature jumping on my neck and injecting biological horrors into my skin with its thirty legs was disconcerting to say the least.

The group of soldiers at the lower position had been sending out patrols and it was decided that they would get some practice in calling in mortar fire onto a target. In the ocean, far below us and beyond a smaller mountain, was an old wrecked, wooden fishing boat that was half exposed somewhat the waves. That was to be the target. Our fire direction control team was given the map coordinates of the target by the soldiers who were learning and practicing and the FDC would call out the fire mission to one of our guns. It was really a very difficult target to hit and must have been extremely difficult to calculate the angle and charge of the mortar because the target was not just so many yards away and at a certain compass heading, but it was probably 5000 feet below the gun. We did this over a period of a few days, with new groups of soldiers calling in the coordinates and adjusting fire after the first round hit.

I realized after a while that when we let fly with a round, it would take about thirty seconds for it to hit the target and if I ran quickly about a hundred yards away from our gun position that I could see the rounds explode when they hit the water. The fire was accurate, landing within twenty yards of the target, which would cover the target with shrapnel, but we could never score a direct hit on that old boat. It really was an impossible target, but, as the old saying goes "Close" really does not apply to anything other than horseshoes and hand grenades, I'd add mortar rounds to that saying.

The view from our position was absolutely spectacular. Many times there were clouds that were actually below us. It was strange to look down upon clouds and still be on land. The ocean to the southeast was a beautiful blue that looked flat from our position. To the north were mountains as far as one could see, all covered in dark green foliage.

The dirt road leading off the main road and up to the top of the mountain where our position was located had to be plowed every week or so because the rain would wash it out all of the time. Sometimes a bulldozer would plow it out and then would continue up to the small mess hall. That little road leading from our major combat positions two hundred feet above the main road was fairly steep. There was little military value to do that extra work of plowing up the extra dirt road up to the mess hall but sometimes a dozer operator would clear the area out of just human compassion, just to make his life harder but to make our lives easier. If a dozer was going that way, up the hill towards the Mess hall, I would jump onto it to catch a little ride of only about three hundred feet.

One morning, a couple of guys and I were walking up towards the Mess Hall. Yeah, it would have been a bit of a problem, a bit of a physical endeavor but nothing to really speak of. We noticed a dozer going by we decided to just jump onto it, something like a Boston boy might due on a winters day, holding onto the back bumper of a passing car, going ten mph down an ice covered street. I jumped up well onto the dozer but then slipped off of the top of it and fell directly onto the moving track. I knew that I would be killed in a few seconds. I tried to roll off of it but the jaggedly rough treads of the dozer held my clothes fixed. I was being driven forwards on top of the treads, within two seconds at most I would be dumped down directly in front of it and ten thousand pounds of iron would run me over.

I was dead, I thought, mangled and chewed up by the threads of the dozer. The dozer operator spotted me out of the corner of his eye, how he ever saw that I don't know, and instantly jammed on the brakes. I rolled heavily off of the thread onto the ground and then rolled away from that mechanical monster. It was a very close one. As I had walked up that slope that morning to get breakfast I knew in the back of my mind that I could be killed by a VC sniper or mortar round or a direct infantry attack but I never thought that morning that I could be mangled and killed by a bulldozer. It was something to think about. Just another example of how easy, and likely, a soldier could be killed in that country.

The time spent on the perimeter on guard duty was fairly uneventful. One day I caught some movement high in the tall trees outside of the perimeter. I unconsciously brought up my weapon to bear. It was a family of three monkeys, two of them very large, black and white in color, monkeys the likes of which I had never seen in a zoo or in a magazine.There seemed to be a father monkey and a mother monkey with a juvenile monkey.They stared at me and I stared at them, each of us staring at each other as if the other group was in a zoo.

One day some engineers were going to knock down some large trees with explosives to clear the perimeter better.They told everyone to get back three hundred feet and take cover. I was on guard duty in a fighting position only a hundred feet away.They wanted me to get back, but I told them that I should stay here on sentry duty.They reluctantly agreed but warned me in no uncertain terms to duck down into my fighting position which had a foot of sandbags above its ground level when it was time for them to set off the explosives.They gave a loud warning with the cry of "fire in the hole!!, fire in the hole!!", and then counted down from a count of ten.

I, of course, stuck my head up so that I could watch the explosion. I figured if there was any problem I could quickly duck down.After all, the objective was to cut through the tree with a ring of explosives not kill everyone nearby. Suddenly the explosion was ignited, and an unbelievable hurricane of bark and broken wood and branches flew past my face, much faster than anyone could have possibly reacted to (C4 explosive explodes at 44,000 feet per second I later learned). I figured again that I was lucky to have not been killed or blinded by the wooden shrapnel. How I wasn't I'll never know.

The Marines had some strange vehicles. One of them sort of looked like a little tank. They were amphibious and didn't have a cannon on them but they did have six recoilless rifle barrels, three on each side.A recoilless rifle round looks like artillery round but the brass cartridge has many holes in it. It is actually a rocket, shooting a projectile that is about four inches in diameter; the whole cartridge is about three feet long and probably weighs fifty pounds or so. It is designed to take out tanks and there is no doubt that any one of its barrels were quite capable of doing its job, if the crew wasn't killed immediately by the enemy. One of those little vehicles would have been subjected to the entire enemy output of fire upon landing on a beach. It was a fearsomely awesome and destructive little piece of military hardware.

I was sitting in a defensive position one dark night, on guard on the perimeter.The air was crisp and clean and the wind was practically still. It was a beautiful night and all was calm. I thought that I heard the slight rumbling of some machinery and turned to see from where it was coming from when all of a sudden there was a tremendous explosion of bright yellow light with a fearsome noise immediately followed by a horrible, horrible sound that just continued for many, many seconds. I spotted a bright red flame traveling through mid air, away from our position and heading over through the valley, towards the next mountain. The Marines were engaging in their own version of H&I fire with that little six barreled rocket launcher.

I don't know about the enemy but it certainly harassed me. Two hundred years ago rockets were used in wars, not so much to do damage because they were then extremely inaccurate. They were used for the noise and flame that they produced, to terrify the enemy. It works very, very well on that basis, it scared and horrified me. It really makes a horrible sound while it is in flight, a much worse sound when it lands close to you.

For the enemy to assault our position would be extremely difficult because of the extreme slope of the mountain. If they made it far enough up the mountain to be close to us, they would have had to cross the no mans land outside of our perimeter, so we had very few attempts to breach the perimeter or infiltrate that site. One night I was on guard duty on the perimeter. There was a four man latrine at the edge of the perimeter, next to a large sandbag house. Pretty fancy really, a small house made of plywood. Just as the sun had set I spotted a Sergeant that I knew walking down towards it, and then entering the latrine.

The wind had been blowing unusually strongly but then began to blow even harder. One of the effects of that was that the noise of any enemy approach would be well hidden by the sound of the wind. Without warning a trip wire flare ignited. It produced a distinctive popping sound when it was first ignited and then a distinctive crackling sound as it burned furiously and produced a bright white light about a hundred and fifty feet from me but I couldn't see anyone around it In the no mans land. It was a surrealistic sight with the white flare blazing, producing a goodly bright light and a large amount of smoke that blew away quickly in the strong wind. Its light flickering like a hugely powerful candle. It must have been attached to one of the strings of barbed wire that were slightly loose because it swung slightly to an fro casting shadows everywhere in the no mans land and producing moving shadows throughout the jungle at its edge. The soldier who was two fighting positions up from me let loose an M-79 high explosive round that exploded next to the flare and the soldier in the very next position to me likewise fired onto the target area with his M-79 but I did not see anything out there so I withheld my fire.

In a situation like that, the M-79s will open up first because they do not have much of a muzzle flash. If needed, men with M-16s would then start firing, the machine guns would fire only if it was absolutely necessary. That's because the enemy wants to identify the machine gun positions and knock them out first to minimize their casualties during the main assault. The machine guns would fire only under desperate situations. The machine guns could easily turn the tide of a battle, but they say that the life expectancy of a machine gun crew, in combat, was about eight seconds because the enemy would, rightfully, exert all of their efforts to kill a machine gun crew as soon as possible. I believe it.

After a minute the flare died out. I thought that maybe it had been an animal that had tripped it off, or maybe even the wind had set off that flare. Things were settling down after a few minutes when suddenly the tripwire flare directly in front of me ignited. That brought an immediate response from the other two positions. The "pop" sound of the two M-79s in quick succession, followed a split second later by the "whump" sounds of high explosive rounds detonating on the barren ground ramped up my attention and adrenaline. I did not see anybody or any animal but I figured that they could have jumped back into the underbrush. It was extremely coincidental for the flares to be tripped so closely in time. It was just too much of a coincidence. Maybe the wind was setting off our trip flares but I figured that the higher probability was the VC setting them off in anticipation of a full on assault. Suddenly another flare ignited.

Enough is enough. I unloaded two HE rounds into the jungle vegetation, aimed about two feet above the slope so that they penetrated into the jungle about ten feet before they exploded so as to give maximum burst range to the shrapnel. Again, the flare continued to burn for a few minutes and then died down. I expected reinforcements from within the perimeter to come out to back us up but no one seemed very much interested or threatened by such activity on the perimeter although it was extremely unusual.

So here was the situation with the poor Sergeant who had been simply minding his own business on a quiet night on Earth down in the latrine. He had gone to the latrine and then a minute later had found himself what seemed to be the beginning of a battle. He was within the causality radius of the M-79 rounds. After the fire died down he gingerly emerged from the latrine and whispered loudly for us to hold our fire. He was shaken, rightfully, by this action that had occurred as close as twenty feet from him. He was a good guy, I heard a few months later that he was killed in action on another operation.

I checked my extra M-79 rounds to make sure they were close by and moved my hand grenades closer and checked the location of my rocket flares located very close but below the sandbags and then settled down for a long night of heightened vigilance until my shift on guard duty ended. It was a cold night and I couldn't quite shake off the heightened anticipation of another enemy probing of our defenses. I figured that the enemy had already tripped three of our flares and would know that they could attack us easier from that area because our main warning devices had been taken out. I was very relieved when another soldier came and took over my watch, but I have to admit that when I returned to my hooch, I awakened my room-mates and told them to prepare their equipment for immediate action. I told them that there was something going on out on the perimeter. I didn't know exactly what it was, but it wasn't good. I spent some time myself in the light of a candle that surely disturbed the sleep of the other guys in the hooch, laying out my extra ammo and placing my grenades and flares out where I could immediately access them, even in the dark. Eventually I laid down in my bunk. Even though I was extremely tired, it took a while before I could finally fall into an uneasy sleep.

After we had been at that location for about a month, some of us were allowed to go to Da Nang to swim in the ocean, shop for candles and things at some shanties along the road and maybe get some beers or drinks at a bar. I was one of the first few men allowed to leave for a few hours of that day, so myself and about five other guys got into the back of a large truck. We brought our weapons with us.

We were driven down the little steep dirt road that was about two hundred feet long then turned right, away from our destination. The driver told us that we were to pick up another guy manning the main checkpoint and then we'd turn around. The windshield of the military truck was pushed down and a guy sitting in the middle of the front seat, a cook, was terrified because he knew that that road was subject to many ambushes. As we drove for a while we encountered a very large truck traveling in the direction opposite to us. It was piled very high with firewood, with some Vietnamese workers sitting atop the pile of wood, probably fifteen feet off of the ground.

Either they or we were not supposed to be on this road at the same time because traffic was supposed to be one way at any certain time period. To pass that truck we both slowed down to a near stop and the truck that I was riding in had to get extremely close to the edge of the cliff to barely allow each other to pass. The wheels of our truck were probably six inches from the edge of a cliff that probably went down a few thousand feet. That set off the cook even more and he ranted and raved that we would all be killed. A few minutes later we approached two more trucks going in the opposite direction and the cook, who had been holding his M-16, pointing it through the open windshield straight ahead, opened fire on the trucks and the men driving and riding on top of those Vietnamese trucks. The trucks continued forward past us while all of us in the back yelled for the cook to cease fire.

The two trucks passed by us. I don't know if anyone of them were hit. I checked behind me to watch them drive on, wondering whether at any moment they might go off of the road and over the cliff as the drivers bled out from the fire they had just taken. They went around a corner an I couldn't see them anymore. Those of us in the back of the truck (there was an open window between the back of the cab and the back of the truck) yelled at the cook. We told him that we cannot be sure that they are the enemy, that you cannot just shoot people because you suspect that they might be the enemy, but the cook would not hear any of that talk and when we encountered another truck he opened fire on that one. The guy beside him on the front seat grabbed the stock of his weapon and deflected his aim but not before he had placed some accurate fire on that truck. He certainly seemed to be determined to kill anyone that he suspected, might, be a threat.

Now some guys were outraged and demanded that the cook hand over his weapon to them but the cook was crazed with fear and refused. A few minutes later, as another Vietnamese truck approached, the cook again took aim. A guy in the back of the truck poked his rifle through the open back window, placing the muzzle of his M-16 directly against the base of the cooks skull. He simply said "When you shoot, I shoot". He was deadly serious. We didn't have any more trouble from the cook for the remaining duration of the ride.

After turning around and descending the mountain to flat land we then passed over a small iron bridge that was painted grey. There was a very small sandbagged building at each end and in front of each was a sandbagged fighting position. There were probably fifteen 173rd soldiers guarding that bridge. That bridge was the only link to the mountain road above. If it was blown up it would have disrupted things seriously for a month. Someone had done a very nice job of painting a large picture of the 173rd insignia in full color on a large overhead beam of the bridge. I wondered what the Marines would think of that when they returned from the DMZ.

Myself and the other few guys arrived at the beach. There were about 50 other guys there, mostly Marines I think. It was a very long, beautiful, white sandy beach named China Beach. There were spiral clam shells scattered around which I thought was sort of exotic, certainly nothing like anything found on the north Atlantic coast of Boston of my youth. We took off our boots and shirts and waded into the water. The water was very warm, just the way that I like it. A hundred feet offshore the water was a beautiful deep blue color but closer in it was a light sandy, green color. There were long rows of large waves coming in. By the time you were waist deep the waves would break a few feet over your head and knock you down, push your face in the sand for a while and then attempt to drag you out to sea if you weren't drowned outright. I thought that the situation was pretty dangerous and after a while I got out of the water. The conditions might be OK for an expert ocean swimmer but not for me. I found out much later that that area had drowned many people, I could certainly understand why.

I walked up to an area that contained a number of little shops. The Vietnamese were selling beer and soda and basically things for the local population. I only had a few dollars with me so I bought a cool coke and then looked around to get some candles for the hooch back on top of the mountain. Some of the guys that rode down in the truck with me, from the 173rd, had apparently gone directly to the nearest bar.

I heard later that they had gotten into an argument with some Marines about the pros and cons of an M-79 versus a Marine "grease gun" (a very short automatic weapon). Probably after many drinks, it was then decided that the argument would be settled by an old-fashioned gunfight on the street in front of the saloon. Two on each side faced off at a hundred feet and it was only the timely arrival of a few Marine officers that had ended that insanity. I had really wanted to buy some local Vietnamese booze, which was the only type available, but I had foolishly squandered my meager funds on candles, which was probably just as well.

Back on top of the mountain, our mission was coming to an end. We were to leave in a few days and I was serving perhaps my last perimeter guard duty at night. A Sergeant came by and said to fire off flares at random during the night. He said that we wanted to get rid of any old flares and would be getting new ones in a few days. After a few hours I noticed that no one else was firing off flares so I decided to get the party started. The flares are really heavy duty, commercial/ military flares that are in fact very powerful rockets. I unscrewed the top of one, placed in onto the bottom of the flare, held it at an angle so that it wouldn't hit the top of the roof of the fighting position and gave it a quick, forceful jab with the heel of my right hand. This would be the first time that I had fired one of those things. Nothing happened. I adjusted the firing mechanism and gave it another try, but nothing. I had been holding the flare with my left hand and jamming the heel of my right hand into the bottom of it but by hitting it it threw off my aim, causing the flare to dip dangerously downwards or upwards. I was afraid that on the next attempt that the flare would launch but hit the top of the sandbagged roof and ricochet onto my lap.

I fiddled with the firing mechanism again and then decided that I would just hold the flare in my right hand and smash the and of it downwards onto the sandbagged wall around the fighting position. That way there I could control better the aim of the business end.

I tried out my theory. There was a blinding flash of light and a loud roar, for a few moments I could't see. There was a powerful smell of chemical smoke and burned hair. I rubbed my hand over my face to see if it was still there and was surprised and relieved that I could still feel a nose and lips. That rocket flare was much more powerful than I had imagined. That particular flare was a red star cluster. The white exhaust of the rocket rose upwards and then exploded three hundred feet above me and out towards the lower mountain.A bright explosion high in the air instantly turned into five bright balls of fire, like a fireworks display.They floated downwards, glowing brightly before burning out after about four seconds.

I decided to set off another one right away, sort of like getting back on the horse that threw you so that you could overcome your initial fright, and picked up a white parachute flare and fired that off. Suddenly, there was all manner of commotion with men within the perimeter running over and jumping into the perimeter trench with all of their weapons.At the same time I could see the outpost below us, away in the distance, start to come alive with people running with flashlights over to their mortars. Someone came over to me and asked what was going on. I said that I was just shooting off flares as instructed. He was beside himself with rage and insisted that no one had ever given me such instructions. I guess that the color and type of flares had a certain significance.A red star flare followed by a white parachute flare signified to the unit below that we had been overrun by the enemy. Things cooled down very quickly and everyone not on guard duty casually returned to their hoochs.A staff Seargent came over to me and angrily questioned why I had shot off the flares. He specifically stated that he didn't believe the story of me having been told to shoot off flares. I simply said: "Do you think that I have nothing better to do except to give away my position in the middle of the night?" He thought for a few moments and then turned and walked away without another word.

Thanksgiving came and we actually had turkey and many of the fixins at the excellent little Marine tented mess hall near the top of the mountain that we occupied. Now the temperature at night was getting actually cold and now I understood why we were told to take all of our clothes with us for this mission, including any civilian clothes.Why in the world the Army didn't give us good winter clothing, knowing full well that we could expect such whether is beyond me. In fact, they did expect such weather and that was why they had asked us to bring all or our civilian clothing with us.The land below was very hot but at the elevation of that tall mountain the air could be very cold.Two weeks after we left there was a picture and story in the Stars and Stripes newspaper because it actually snowed up there.

I dreaded returning back to beating the bush. On the last day, we loaded into trucks and were driven down the narrow mountain road and onwards towards the Marine base. It was a trip of about twenty miles from the base of the mountain. We were traveling slowly and every once in a while the group of trucks that I was riding in would stop for some reason, probably to allow slower trucks behind us to catch up. The scenery was typical Viet Nam with banana and coconut trees but not heavy jungle, at least not along most of the road.

I noticed that we were approaching a very large solid rock outcropping that seemed to be completely out of the normal. There were no other such rocks around. That rock structure was a grey color with brown and black streaks, almost vertically steep, perhaps 150 feet tall, maybe more. Out of force of habit I scanned the rock for anything out of the ordinary, especially snipers, when suddenly I was shocked to see about three soldiers who appeared to be ARVN seeming to be standing in the middle of the structure, about sixty feet up. Then I suddenly realized that what I was seeing was an enormous rock structure that looked like a snowman. On the bottom was an almost round, solid rock about 80 feet in diameter. On top of that one was another round rock, probably 50 feet in diameter and on top of that another rock that was probably 15 feet tall and wide. The ARVNs had a little lookout post on top of the second rock and a more substantial guard post/road block at the bottom. I thought that this must be some sort of a "wonder of the world". It was simply an extremely unusual, natural occurrence, but something that should be mentioned in world travel books.

We proceeded for ten minutes and then turned right onto a thin dirt road, traveled a mile or so to a rickety steel bridge over a stream and then stopped. There were already some soldiers splashing around in the stream and we were told that we could jump in and swim if we wanted to. Something about that situation didn't seem right to me. We were on our way to the Marine base camp and it couldn't be very far away. Lets just get there I thought. Maybe we can get some cold sodas and beers and take a shower. Oh no! They are not going to let us clean up with a shower I thought. If I jump in the water my pants at least are going to get soaked and they will turn into mud from the dust of the road as we continue on. That's OK I reasoned. If I jump in the water then at least I can somewhat clean my body. A layer of fresh mud wouldn't be so bad after that. I ran down to the stream, tearing off my shirt and jumped in before they changed their minds.

We eventually reached the Marine camp and passed through gates and guard positions and barbed wire into a huge area that was almost completely flat and reddish brown, an area with no vegetation whatsoever. We were told that we would stay there overnight and go back to base camp in Bien Hoa in the morning. About thirty minutes after unloading from the trucks we were told to leave our duffel bags in the trucks and then we walked with all of our military gear up to previously dug defensive positions around a section of the camp.

The defensive position to which I and three other troopers were assigned consisted of a three sided wall of sand bags on the ground about a foot high that surrounded a rectangular fighting position that was probably four feet deep. I had a roof made of various pieces of scavenged lumber with corrugated tin sheets overhead. The roof provided some shelter from the sun and rain but of course no protection whatsoever from mortars. Someone had obviously gone to a lot of trouble to dig that position and it seemed to be a relatively permanent position. I wondered why no one had ever taken the trouble to fill sandbags and put them on the overhead cover but then realized that we did not have any empty sandbags so that question would have to be asked by the next occupants. Next to me and three other Airborne soldiers who were in a fighting position was a Marine tank and its crew.

In the late afternoon, myself and a few other guys went over to inspect the tank. The tank crewmen were friendly and gave us a tour of their monstrous machine. Their spokesman told us that the cannon was made by Pontiac (the same company that makes automobiles), the transmission was made by Chrysler and the engine was made by Roll-Roicse, or maybe it was vice-versa. He regaled us with the specifications of the tank, how heavy it was, how fast it could travel, what manner of ordinance it could survive etc. It was impressive.

I told the tank crewmen a story of how, when I was eleven years old, I was playing on an Army tank that was in a scrap yard in the U.S. I had put my left hand into the hinge of the main hatch and pulled it down with my right hand, quickly withdrawing my left hand as it fell. I was a bit too slow and when I jumped down and tried to walk away something held me in place. When I looked up, I saw that my left hand was caught in the hinge and the hatch was closed. It was a scene out of a horror movie, like "The Fly". Bright red blood rivulets streamed down my arm. Standing on a seat and pushing with all of my might with my right arm and placing my head against it and pushing with everything that I had with my legs, I managed to lift the hatch a sixteenth of an inch, enough to pull my left hand out of the hatch. Hospitalization, surgery and permanent disfigurement followed of course. I was eleven years old and the Army had already hurt me. I thought that those tank crewmen would find that story funny. They didn't.

Directly to the front of our position was a large oil or gasoline shiny steel storage tank, a substantial one probably holding more than a hundred thousand gallons, probably a lot more. Near the storage tank two large floodlights lit up the area, illuminating the storage tank very well, and also silhouetting our position and the armored tank extremely well. I realized that that situation was absurd. Why light up such a rich target to be hit by enemy mortars, more importantly, to any enemy approaching from our rear we were backlit clearly. The VC couldn't have asked for better targets.

I had been lying on the ground. When it was my time for guard duty, I stood in the foxhole but that was uncomfortable after an hour or so. I climbed out of the hole and sat on the sandbags on the ground and smoked a cigarette. The tank had been running their engine continuously for the last few hours and that made it impossible to detect any noise of the enemy approaching us. I became extremely tired, for some reason, and decided to lay down on top of the sandbags, so that I could rest a little and not present such a perfect target.

I was beginning to nod off, suddenly being jolted into full consciousness every once in a while. I heard some yelling. A Marine lieutenant was exiting his Jeep, his driver remained in the vehicle. They had driven up to my position but I had not heard the Jeep, nor had I seen them because my position was on top of a little hill, and they had driven up the side of it, out of my direct view. The Lieutenant was outraged that I was asleep and was stomping around yelling. I thought that he couldn't have possibly made himself a better target. He demanded to know how I could possibly be sleeping. I wasn't sure if I was actually asleep or not, but if not, I was close to it. I said that I was just laying down and didn't he think that this position was extremely exposed? I should have maybe been standing in the fighting position, with my head fully exposed, but I had thought that if I laid down on the sandbags I could see as well and maybe the enemy would not be able to discern that it was a body rather than just part of the sandbag wall.

No, he thought that that fighting position was perfectly all right, which was absurd. He said that he was going to report me, and demanded that I finish my guard duty standing up, on the ground, near the tank. He basically told me that if he returned and I was not standing there that he'd have me shot for dereliction of duty. As soon as he left, I got into the foxhole. I could certainly defend not standing up, being a perfect target, to any reasonable person. I couldn't understand why that Lieutenant had demanded that I stand up or why he thought that that position was not extremely vulnerable, but I then slowly realized that that idiot had probably never even gotten his boots dirty in this Country. He was probably an aide to a rear echelon General and had never been in the bush. If he returned and I was not standing in the open as he had ordered me to do, and he made an issue of that to my Company Commander, I was reasonably sure that our Company Commander, knowing the situation, would have dismissed the case, if he didn't actually literally kick that Marine Lieutenants ass. However I was quite worried about that Lieutenants report that he caught me supposedly asleep on guard duty. Falling asleep on guard duty in a war zone was a Capital offense wasn't it?

The next day, I got the word to report to the Company commanders tent. When I arrived there were about ten other men milling around outside the tent. After some brief conversations, we determined that most of us were there because we had been found asleep at our guard station. I found that very hard to believe. I had been very tired, but ten men falling asleep was basically impossible. We all knew very well how serious and dangerous it could be in the bush, and this Marine base, though in a civilian area somewhat, was probably still a relatively dangerous place.

The Company commander suddenly came out of his tent and called off ten names, including mine and told us to stand in formation. He then proceeded to call us all manner of names, while some of us protested our innocence. Then he told us all to get out of his sight. And that was it, no prison time, and no firing squad. I realized many years later that during that whole day, leading up to the sleep incident, we had no water whatsoever. We had been told that the Marines would provide us with water at their base camp but that never happened. Dehydration usually results in extreme fatigue, I guess that might explain the whole thing. That and the fact that that Marine lieutenant was probably trying to embarrass us. I'm surprised that one of us hadn't somehow "awakened" and shot the idiot "by accident".

The next day, we loaded onto cargo planes and flew to Bien Hoa air base and were taken by truck a mile or so to our base camp.

Chapter 11

OPERATION ATLANTIC CITY

Helicopter Pick-up for Assault

After a few days in base camp we were given C-rations, nine packages each, enough for three days. This was going to be a serious hump, so everyone went through their rations and threw away anything that they didn't really need or want. Of course the requirements of humping was probably nine thousand calories a day and we desperately needed nutrition, but most of us would rather throw away a few pounds of food rather than have to carry it. We carried only those things that were absolutely necessary, and the necessities of ammo and military equipment usually weighed more than a hundred pounds. Some might say that carrying another twelve pounds of food wouldn't make much difference but they would be wrong. Every additional ounce of gear seemed like an additional five pounds after humping it for a few days. The bottom line was the question: would you rather eat or suffer? Would you rather be hungry or in more pain than you would be? It was an easy question to answer for most of us.

Pierce, the new guy that had joined us in Da Nang was at the bottom of the social scale within this mortar squad, and as such would have to assume the duties of the ammo bearer.

I had already discussed that matter with my squad Sergeant when we had been on top of that mountain in Da Nang. Pierce was the low man on the totem pole. I would go up a notch. That meant the he, instead of I, would carry the baseplate of the mortar and that he, not I, would have to carry the M-79 grenade launcher and .45 cal automatic pistol.

I really hated to part with that M-79 and really, very much hated to part with the .45 but the difference in weight would be about twelve pounds, mostly because of the extra weight of the M-79 ammo that was a standard load for our outfit, and that made all of the difference in the world. Also, I would now be the assistant gunner which meant that I carried the barrel of the mortar. The barrel weighed about fourteen pounds less than the baseplate and that was a significant factor in my demanding the change of personal weapons and mortar parts.

If we were back in the States, if another man joined the squad, his rank, like Specialist-4 or Sergeant would determine his position within a squad, but out here, in the war zone of Viet Nam, the only thing that mattered was how much time you had in Country, in combat, as to where you were going to fit into an infantry squad, and even then, a significant factor was how much time you had within a particular Unit. A Private First Class (E-3) with three months of combat experience, easily outranked a squad Sergeant (E-5) with six years of active duty but no combat experience as to where they were going to fit into the respective responsibilities of the gun crew.

We assaulted by helicopter into an LZ that could handle only three choppers at a time, with heavy jungle all around. There was no problem with the landing. We all jumped out, bent over at the waist against the down blast hurricane of the rotors roaring overhead, and ran towards the tree line. I used to think that everyone bent over so that the blades of the chopper would not take their heads off, but the blades were actually about seven feet above the ground. We had to bend over to avoid being knocked down by the hurricane force of wind from the rotors. Sometimes the choppers just landed and stayed there for a while, but with a combat assault, where enemy fire could begin at any moment, the pilots actually hovered their choppers above the ground and ran their engines at almost full speed, ready to begin outbound flight immediately. The result was a tremendous downdraft of hurricane force wind that would blow a man down if he stood to his full height. With all of our equipment we were pretty unstable to begin with.

The Company split into two main columns and each proceeded single file into the bush. The vegetation became denser and the point man had to use his machete more and more. Even with him cutting, there were very heavy bushes and vines for the rest of us to push through. The line stopped every three minutes or so and as time went on we stopped for longer and longer periods while the point man tried to cut his way through the heavy undergrowth.

After a while, as I moved further into the jungle I discovered why the line was going so slow. The point man had led us into an area where there was thick, bamboo type vines, growing in all directions and curling back in upon itself, in circles, almost like concertina barbed wire thrown in amongst a tangle of concertina wire but much much thicker. An area of very unusual plants that was who knows how many hundreds of feet wide and, I would learn, how many hundreds of feet long.

There were spirals upon spirals of those vines, all of them intertwined among themselves, about nine feet tall. Those tough, hard vines were about three inches thick and had very many sharp spikes about three inches long and three eights of an inch thick at the base. The last inch and a half of the spikes were brown and came to a needle sharp point. They were extremely strong, if they caught on your equipment you could not just bull yourself forward and just break them off. I bashed it with my rifle butt but it had no effect at all. I wondered why the point man wasn't cutting those things off because they would surely inflict serious puncture wounds on the men following but then realized that there were too many of them and the vines were so close and intermingled and intertwined that a person couldn't get enough room to get a good swing at them with a machete.

So now the entire platoon was in amongst this jungle jumble, each man had to go through a number of contortions with each step, winding and bending separate parts of their bodies to climb over or under or through those vines. At each step they had to be very careful or they would have a three-inch deep puncture wound to their bodies, probably several of them. We made forward progress of probably about two hundred feet per hour but you couldn't really sit down or take the weight off of you. In fact it was even worse than being on open ground because you had nowhere to sit. If you tried to lean some way against a vine, the thorns on it would catch your rucksack and you would have a bad time trying to get off and away from them. After ten minutes of going through I grabbed one of those spikes and bent it downwards powerfully, trying to break it off but it just bent a little bit and my hand slid off of it. Its point raked a deep gash across my palm, cutting it deeply and causing the skin to open up widely. It started to bleed profusely. I noticed that I was leaving a good blood trail behind.

I thought that that was a good thing because it would give the soldiers behind me a show of what would happen to them if they were not very careful. But then I thought that the troopers behind me couldn't know what kind of wound was causing so much blood. Most of the time, when the line halted for a few minutes we were stuck in a very unnatural, contorted position and we were mostly in the full sun. It was extremely brutal. For about two hours we went through those vines, not being able to rest our combat equipment contorting our bodies and loads in strange ways so that the loads were multiplied because of the strange ways that we had to twist our bodies to get through that tangle of thorns and vines. The amount of blood flowing from my hand was surprising. After five or ten minutes it slowed down considerably, probably helped by the amount of dirt and jungle litter that was pushed into the wound with every step that I took.

I thought it would be an excellent place for the VC to hide and if we were ambushed we would be doomed. We would be like monkeys caught in a barbed wire birdcage. It would be impossible to hit the ground, it would be extremely difficult to even aim your rifle in the direction that you wanted because the vines were so thick and close together and it would be impossible to advance forward or to back up or to go to either side at anything more than about ten feet per minute. I would guess that after two hours we had gone maybe a hundred yards, if even that. When we got out of it, there was heavy jungle for another mile or so and then we hit those vines again but they were not quite as bad as the first nor so extensive but traversing them was extremely brutal nonetheless. We humped the rest of the day, encountering more of those vines at times but there was more distance between the stands and they became smaller and less convoluted, and going through them was less and less trouble but traversing the least of them was truly painful and very difficult.

After a few more days of humping we eventually got out of the area where those vines were located and came upon more open jungle. We passed across a little creek at a spot where the width of it suddenly became much wider than rest of the main stream. We stopped about fifteen minutes later at a place where we would be spending the night and I was told to go back to that creek with about fifteen other men to get some water for our canteens and to wash up. The creek was probably about three hundred meters from our night position but I didn't like the idea of a small force of men being out there by ourselves. We set off in a ragtag group with no one in command and spread out. Someone began to suggest that we get into some sort of military order, all the better to cope with an enemy ambush or attack, which we did. Some of those men were very concerned and apprehensive about that little operation, and so was I, but we got to the creek without incident.

It was decided that half of the men would wash themselves and maybe some of their equipment in the creek and the other half would maintain security for them. I was chosen to be on security first. The fresh water pool was surrounded by a little hills of dirt, about fifteen feet taller than the water. I took up a position on top of a little hill above the jungle floor. During training, we had been shown a film where men were in exactly the situation that we were in now. In the film, the men put their weapons down at the edge of a pool and waded in to bathe. The enemy sneaks up on them and shoots all of them before they could scramble to get their weapons. The point was to never be beyond arms reach of your weapon, a point that I followed all of the time, except once.

I noticed that the men bathing and washing their clothes were all beyond an arms reach of their weapons, something that I would try not to do when it was my turn and I realized then that I had to be exceptionally watchful for any enemy approaching. Half of our group was proving security but still, that was not an excuse for the guarded troopers to be lax for their own safety. The water was almost clear, a light brown tea color. I maintained an extremely vigilant watch because I had a feeling that something wasn't quite right about that place. Eventually most of the men in the water finished washing, not without some strong words from the men on security detail to hurry up. One of the men who had finished washing put on his clothes and

LBG, grabbed his weapon and climbed the little hill to relieve me and so then it was my turn to bathe.

I took off my clothes and then put my boots back on and laced them up. I washed up, naked, except for my laced up boots. There was something about that place and situation that for some reason spooked me out. When and if the stuff hit the fan I wanted to have my boots on so that I could maneuver around. Surely it was a ridiculous scene and situation, yet very real and practical. I soaped down my body very quickly, and tried to wash my clothes a little but those clothes could not possibly ever be cleaned. The absurdity of me standing in the water knee deep, naked except for my boots, with my weapon just an arms length away on the edge of the stream was not lost on me. A picture flashed in my mind of me grabbing my weapon and jumping onto the streambed, killing people, while they tried to kill me, completely nude except for soaking wet boots and thought that that would be a picture that someone would always remember. The idea of me laying on the ground, with just my boots on, bleeding and blasted to pieces was another picture that flashed through my mind. Some of the guys decided to spend some extra time in trying to get their clothes clean, but I decided that I had spent enough time in the water so I resumed my security position on top of the little hill.

I decided that that would be a good time to shave my beard. We had to shave every day, they said that shaving every day was good for "esprit de corps". I figured that it just made for a better looking corpse. I opened my rucksack and found it filled to overflowing with a white foamy substance. I didn't know what it was at first, but then realized that my can of shaving cream had discharged its entire contents while I had been humping that day. Everything in my rucksack was covered in foam and it took a considerable amount of time and trouble to try to wipe most of it off of my spare ammo and supplies. I scooped up some of it and put it on my face, then put a new razor blade in the razor. I didn't have a mirror and with the new blade managed to shave but not without cutting my face about fifty times. I didn't realize that I cut myself at all until I noticed that there was blood dripping all over everything. That would be the last time that I ever used shaving cream for the rest of my life.

The operation ended the next day. We returned to base camp via convoy.

Chapter 12

OPERATION LZ STOMP

Full Load on the ground

We were going out onto another operation. There was always a meeting right before any operation, and almost every day while out in the bush, where we were given details of the operation. For this operation we were not given very much information at all.

This was to be a helicopter assault. Our mission was to secure a landing zone and to improve it, that is, to clear out underbrush and chop down trees to make it a very good landing zone for future operations. The helicopter ride only lasted about ten minutes, we were put down only a few miles from our base camp.

While getting arranged on the LZ I could hear some gunfire in the distance. I looked over about a half a mile away and saw a helicopter that looked like it was in serious trouble. Black smoke was pouring from it and it was flying very erratically. I lost sight of it as it descended below the top of the tree line, but I remarked to another guy that I thought that that chopper had just crashed. I thought that maybe our mission would be instantly changed to rescue that chopper crew but then I noticed a helicopter gunship flying at full speed over to that area. Within a few minutes there were four gunships circling in a tight formation around the downed chopper, heads down, like a swarm of angry bees. I thought that the crashed crew, if they had survived the crash, would be safe from attack because no VC wants any part of four flying machines capable of firing twenty-four thousand rounds per minute between them. I just hoped that no one had been injured or killed by the crash. Whether that helicopter crashed due to enemy fire or equipment malfunction I do not know. If it was due to enemy actions, it was too far away to concern me to any serious extent, but it still concerned me.

We started to move out on our primary mission. I guess the chopper rescue would be left to others. We assumed that the area that we were in was safe because it was so close to our base camp and it turned out that it was very safe for the most part, although I think in the future it become a very hot area.

We set up our perimeter and the line platoons sent out short patrols around the landing zone. The landing zone consisted of a large rectangular area about 500 yards long and 100 yards wide. It consisted entirely of large bushes about eight feet tall, very dense and packed closely together. I assumed that it was an old farm that had been overgrown by some type of weeds.

We started to chop down those bushes with machetes. Some men chopped and others gathered up big bunches in their arms and carried them off of the LZ and throw them into several tall piles. There was so much of it that we started to pile it up on the LZ into unmanageable loads. Some troopers were ordered to set fire to them. It was very healthy and leafy but it burned rather well. There may have been some gasoline poured onto it to get it started but once it got started burning it burned rather quickly, producing a huge, very thick cloud of white smoke. We labored at this task for a while when some of the guys with me stated that they smelled marijuana. We walked around a little and saw three guys squatting in the bushes smoking some marijuana. The guys with me asked the other three for some weed. The soldiers with me said that, of course, they never brought weed on an operation but since this area seemed very secure, they would really like to have some now.

The guys who were smoking were adamant in their refusal. After some argument, the guys with the weed said "What are you guys talking about, just get your own!" The guys with me said "Where are we going to get weed out here?" and the other guys replied: "Look around. What do you think all of these bushes are?" The entire field was completely composed of marijuana plants, that's what we had been cutting down and burning for the last couple of hours. Those plants were so dense and thick and tall that our mission was to cut all of it down so as to make a better landing zone for future operations. It was mostly green but there were dried leaves near the bottom and buds among the plants. We were there for a few days and when we left many of the guys had stuffed every bag and container that they had with buds, with the plastic containers of C4 explosive being at a premium for sure. There was no enemy activity at all at this area so it was a very mellow time. Actually it was a relatively mellow time. We were certainly in the woods and there was always the distinct possibility of enemy attack, but when things are put into perspective, it seemed to be a very quiet time. In retrospect, I was on edge most of the time because I realized that that field of marijuana provided excellent concealment for an enemy attack but on a scale of one to ten on an anxiety scale, that operation rated a score value of one, Where the most anxiety producing situation in civilian life would be a rating of one one-hundredth.

I guess that all of us put things into perspective. A situation that would produce panic in civilian life was an easy day in this country. A situation that a civilian would have nightmares about and repeat endlessly to anyone who would listen would be a situation that troopers in this country would consider not worthy of mention, an easy day. Life for an infantryman was ten thousand times harder and scarier and more dangerous than anything that most civilians had ever imagined, and it happened every day.

On the way back to base camp in helicopters, I noticed below me a green rice paddy that had been more than saturated with bomb craters. There were hundreds if not thousands of bomb craters ranging in size from two to twenty feet wide. Every square inch of the paddy, for a square mile at least, had a bomb crater or was well within the casualty radius of the explosives. Many bomb craters lay partly within the crater of another bomb. It looked as if it had been hit with everything from small mortars to eight-inch shells, to thousand pound bombs. I don't know if all that happened in one day or whether it was the result of years of pounding. In any event I certainly wouldn't have wanted to cross that area. I also realized that that rice paddy that had probably been worked for centuries to clear it of jungle and to make it level, would require years of work with heavy machinery to return it to a plantable rice paddy. Viet Nam doesn't have many machines, I never saw even so much as a tractor. I realized, on a deep level, that the farm below me had probably been destroyed forever.

Chapter 13
BIEN HOA TOWN

Outside of our base camp was the little town of Bien Hoa. At its edge was the main entrance to the air base/base camp. There was a large guard gate manned by Air Force MPs. Once a person passed outside of that gate and walked fifteen feet he would be immediately surrounded by hustlers and children offering many things for sale, some of them illegal. A person could buy a package of Marlboros, or any other brand, filter or not, that looked like a brand new pack of cigarettes complete with the unopened outside cellophane wrapper. But inside were twenty perfectly machine rolled cigarettes of 100% marijuana. The street price was one dollar a pack.

The dirt streets of the town, especially at night, was a wild place of confusion with many, many, small motorcycles racing up and down the street, passing a large number of vehicles that were basically a motor scooter that was built onto a vehicle that could hold six or eight Vietnamese. Something like a very small bus attached to a motor scooter, with one wheel in front and two in back. Mixed among that mass of traffic were large military cargo trucks, so that the scene was one of no rules of the road at all, everyone for himself, mixed with an overpowering smell of diesel truck engines smoke and their accompanying clouds of smoke.

The businesses consisted mostly of small shops, made out of corrugated tin sheets made out of old coke cans and beer cans. There were small restaurants and street vendors and small bars, all of them strictly out of an extremely impoverished third world country. Down the side streets were the houses of the residents and some various illegal enterprises. It was a scene of destitution beyond comprehension. The poverty was unimaginable, at first I literally could not believe my eyes. I could not imagine how a country and its people could be in such a state of deprivation and squalor.

We didn't get into town very often, in fact I think I made it into Bien Hoa on only three occasions, because we were always out in the field. The basic technique was to return to base camp and take a shower. Then go to the supply shack and pick up a new set of fatigues, pants at least, and send out your shirt to be washed at some laundry down on the base. Then catch a ride with a military truck over to the Air force base PX, (Post eXchange) and pick up a half a gallon of vodka or gin or whiskey for about $1.65 since there were no taxes and then return to base camp and consume vast quantities.

Then, when the mood was right, catch a ride down to the edge of the base camp and go out among the civilians. The bars were usually filled with Air Force guys who shuffled papers all day and partied all night, they never even got their boots dirty. The guys from the 173rd would walk into a bar and loudly declare it to be an Airborne bar, which gave everyone, except the bar girls, about thirty seconds to evacuate. There were very few objections and those were quickly overruled, with violence, in favor of the 173rd. The population of the town that included any non Army Airborne Infantrymen would be quickly reduced, filled mostly with perhaps a few hundred paratroopers, all drunk and looking for trouble and a good time, knowing in the back of their minds that in a few days they would be back into the bush, back into a green world of horror and horrific pain and suffering.

I found myself in a little bar where I met up with about ten guys from my platoon, including almost everyone in my little squad section of six people. The little bar only had about eight seats at the bar and about six small tables set up on the opposite wall. There were a bunch of Vietnamese girls there, bar girls, who would try to get you to buy them a greatly overpriced drink. I was talking to one of the girls at the bar, communicating as much as two people can who do not understand each others language, and she invited me to sit down with her and a few other girls at a little booth.

I bought them a few drinks and we laughed and joked. That place was probably really a bar on the bottom floor and a bordello on the second floor, manned mostly by the girls on the first floor. I noticed a chubby sergeant who was in my platoon named Smithson or something sitting at the bar and he said to me "Don't go upstairs". I asked him why not?, What was upstairs? But he just repeated his warning. I wasn't sure what he was talking about but I figured he knew something that

I didn't know about that place or maybe he was just warning me not to get involved in pre-marital sex. I didn't know him very well but he seemed like a very nice guy, a bit overweight with a round red face. He was a little older than most of us and was married with two very small children. Anyways I took his advice

Chapter 14

WAR ZONE D

If you can trust yourself when all men doubt you,
But make allowance for their doubting too;

Rudyard Kipling "If"

Scraggly jungle

The next day we loaded up onto large open bed trucks and were driven about twenty miles away. From that location we would load onto choppers for the operational assault. The word was that they did it this way so that any VC spies around the base camp would think that we were going on a local operation (eg. via motor trucks) instead of on an operation that was a much further distance away or deep into an area where there are no roads.

As we exited the gates of Bien Hoa there was the usual heavy vehicle and foot traffic along the road. As we traveled further from the town the traffic steadily diminished until after about fifteen miles into the trip the civilian traffic became extremely light. After a few more miles I suddenly noticed that there was absolutely no civilian traffic on the road.

The entire column of trucks unexpectedly pulled sharply to the extreme right side of the road, running into drainage ditches and smashing down the head high light vegetation lining the road. Orders were shouted to get off of the trucks immediately and proceed at all speed deep into the scrubby jungle to our left. About a hundred feet into the bush we broke into a very long but narrow clearing. That was obviously a main staging area with large amounts of many kinds of supplies and ammo stacked on the ground along with parked tanks and bulldozers and artillery. There was probably eighty to a hundred artillery pieces there with plenty of ammo surrounding each gun. Obviously something very big was planned, and it was, but as we learned later, that would be in support not of this operation but of the next one.

War zone "D" was only a short helicopter ride away from base camp. Every helicopter assault would get the adrenaline going. As we lifted off, we "locked and loaded", that is, we put our magazines of ammo into our weapons, and made sure that they were locked in, and then loaded the first round from the magazine into the barrel of the weapon. We would fly about two thousand high. You never knew what the landing zone would be like. It could be an easy landing with no resistance at all or something much different. This was an easy one. There was no resistance, no enemy fire. We exited the helicopters and ran into the tree line at top speed to set up a perimeter to protect the other choppers that would be landing, standard operating procedure.

The Company set up and stayed around the perimeter for several hours and then sent out platoon-sized patrols. The Heavy Weapons platoon set up our two guns and dug in. Everything was quiet so after a few hours I decided to walk around the edge of the landing zone a little and see what, if anything, was around there. The LZ was a big meadow, maybe it was a farm at one time or a rice paddy, in any event it was covered mostly with green grass about a foot or two tall. There were a few small trees around and I went over to investigate a little grove of about seven trees all growing in a bunch about eight feet in diameter. Something looked very strange about those trees and as I got about six feet away I began to barely make out the situation. Most of the trees had been bent over sharply about six feet up. In the middle was a round piece of log without any bark, about seven feet long and four inches wide with the top of it sharpened into a wide point. The trees surrounding it had been bent down to make a type of spring, to shoot the log straight into the air. Obviously, that was some type of homemade helicopter booby trap.

A chopper would fly over it, close to the ground, attempting to land with a full crew of troops. The prop blast would set off the trap and a forty pound hunk of half telephone pole would be shot into the belly of the aircraft or into the main blades. It was crude but effective. If it worked, the results would be disastrous. I called over a few guys to show it to them. The "spring" trees were held in tension by a system of vines that was attached to a homemade trigger device made of sticks about as thick as a mans forefinger. I pulled the trigger mechanism from the center of the device. It failed to go off. I pulled the triggering device out of the middle of trees and threw it onto the ground and then stomped on it until it was just a mass of broken pieces. Then I roughly tore at the remainder of the contraption, breaking what vines I could, many of them were very tough and I could not break them, I really needed a machete which I did not have. But I certainly disabled that contraption although it took quite a bit of effort to do so. The assault choppers had been very close to that device when they first landed.

Five minutes later, as I was meandering back to my rucksack, a guy called me over to look at a log that was in the middle of the LZ. He asked me if I saw anything unusual about it and I said that it just looked like an old log. He pointed to an area about two inches square along one side of the log. It looked like a small animal may have made it, it was something that a person would never notice. Then he pushed the barrel of his M-16 into the hole and started to enlarge the hole whereupon you could see that it was actually a fighting position, a dug out rectangle about three feet deep. So the enemy rolls the log, climbs down into the fighting position and rolls the log back on top. It was a sniper position and an extremely well concealed, camouflaged and engineered one at that. A sniper could easily hide there and shoot at will and it would be almost impossible to detect him. Even worse, an enemy soldier with a machine gun could wait for a helicopter assault and rake the belly of ten choppers as they settled in for a landing. I saw another similar position along a trail later in the jungle. A person could camp out for days with those positions five feet away and never notice anything amiss or realize that someone could be hiding there although the enemy could observe us through a very small opening and, of course, take us under fire at his convenience.

We moved the next day away from the wide open LZ and into the surrounding woods but not very far, only about three hundred yards, and set up a new perimeter for the night. We were basically in an overgrown rubber plantation. The next morning we heard the buzz of a small airplane. The change in the pitch and loudness of the engine sounded like the plane was performing some sort of acrobatic maneuvers, flying back and forth and around and up and down, the pilot pushing the aircraft to what seemed to be its extreme limit of maneuverability. There was a sort of wide path through the straight lines of planted rubber trees from which I could get a clear view of a small slice of the LZ that we had left earlier that morning. I ran down a bit trying to get a better viewpoint and suddenly saw a small, grey Air Force airplane, something like a two seater, single engine Cessna type plane. It was banking sharply into a turn, flying about fifty feet above the ground. I suddenly spotted a VC in black pajamas running for his life a hundred feet in front of the plane and then he suddenly disappeared, apparently diving into a hole.

The pilot fired off a white phosphorous rocket that overshot the hole and exploded about seventy feet in front of it. Those missiles are supposed to be used only to mark targets, that the pilot used it in that situation indicated to me that he must be outraged. The VC probably took a few shots at the aircraft, I thought. The pitch and roar from the plane changed dramatically as the pilot threw the craft into an extreme climb and turn, coming around again for another shot.

I was excited that perhaps we could get an enemy KIA or capture him and yelled to the guys around me to grab their weapons and we'll go out and get him but a Sergeant squashed that idea immediately. Someone else would get him I guess. I suggested that we hit the VC with mortar fire. It would be an almost impossible shot to drop a round right down that VC's hiding hole, but it might encourage him to surrender, or at least keep him pinned down while other guys approached him. I don't know what happened to that VC. I don't know if anyone was sent out to try to get him. Later, I realized that my idea to just mortar the VC would have required coordination at several levels. First we would have to learn if there were any friendly forces in the area, then we would have to coordinate with the Air Force if for no other reason that we don't shoot down the plane or put a hundred pieces of shrapnel into it as it attacked at such a low altitude.

We were sent out on patrol for the next two days, beating the bush. On one of the stops during the patrol, I was sitting on the ground, half laid back against my rucksack when I noticed something on the ground about sixty feet away to our flank. Another soldier casually walked over to it, took one look, didn't seem interested, and walked back to his original position. I shrugged my ruck and walked towards it, curious as to what it could possibly be. It was something alive, or maybe was alive at one time. It was a flesh colored, pinkish blob without any distinctive outline, about three feet long and a foot and a half wide, seemingly a mass of something twisting and moving and undulating in a very strange way. It must be alive, I thought, but I couldn't figure out what it could possibly be.

My first impression was that it might be a pile of intestines and I quickly looked upwards at the large tree near where it was, in case there was someone or something up there that had been wounded so badly that his intestines had fallen out. As I got closer, it just looked more and more strange until at three feet distance, I still could not venture any guess as to what it could possibly be. I asked the first guy who had seen it what it was and he simply said "pigs". I thought that that was obviously not true, but as I got even closer, I began to think that maybe they are pigs but pigs like I had never seen before. The first guy said that they were probably just born. They were not miniatures of adults, but looked like a life form from another planet and again I asked the first guy if he was sure and he looked at me like I must have never lived in the countryside or on a farm, which was exactly true. There was probably about four or five of the little creatures all in one pile, lying on top of and next to each other in a jumble. They were completely vulnerable, I think that they were blind, having just been born, and they couldn't walk at all. I thought to myself that none of those little pigs are ever going to live in a brick house, the only things in this country were houses made of sticks and straw and cardboard. Then I thought, OK, little pigs, if I see the big bad wolf I'll shoot him for you, then realized that it might be a good idea to rejoin my group right away. There were things in those woods far, far worse and horrible than big, bad wolves.

The next day, we moved again, back towards the original LZ. Our final destination for that day was going to be that LZ where we had originally landed, but we were told that that night we would be occupying a different sector of it, not the section where we had originally set up.

We humped for a few hours and then came upon a small Allied forward supply base. It consisted of just a small number of boxes of ammo and food with a little aircraft landing strip beside it, just bulldozed down dirt. It appeared that the only one guarding or securing the supplies was a supply sergeant. At the edge of the base, in the woods really, lying on the ground was a brown piece of metal, a gun barrel sort of. It shot a round about an inch in diameter and the barrel was about a half inch thick or more so the barrel was about two inches in diameter and about seven feet long. Beside it was a revolver type mechanism, it reminded me of my old toy cowboy pistol that I had as a child, but this revolver looked like it took bullets about an inch wide and a foot long. Stamped on the revolver part was "manufactured by Pontiac", and stamped on the barrel was "made by General Motors" or something like that. It was probably an automatic, 20mm cannon, a modern day super fast Gatling gun firing explosive shells designed for a jet fighter. I don't know what it was doing out in the jungle. I wondered how that thing ever got way out here in the middle of nowhere. The landing strip was just barely enough for a single engine small plane to land or take off. The whole contraption probably weighed over a thousand pounds. I thought, "I hope it works better than my old Pontiac automobile" and then wondered how much that gun brought in profit compared to an automobile. I and my fellow soldiers were making less than three hundred dollars a month.

We stayed at that site for half an hour and then continued our patrol for a few more hours until we finally reached our night position. It was a very large flat area consisting of solidly packed dark brown earth with a very few small bushes and surrounded by heavy jungle. We dug in the fighting positions close to the tree line in a large circle that was about a hundred meters in diameter. On that night every man in my platoon would have to pull two hours on and two hours off guard duty throughout that entire night. That meant a total of four hours of sleep but set up like this: two hours of guard duty, then two hours or sleep, then two hours of guard duty then two hours of sleep or until the sun began to come up whereupon everyone would be on guard duty. Four hours of sleep was woefully insufficient. Broken up into two hour segments made it so much more inhumanly insufficient.

I was beaten down from just the two days of humping the bush and was sleeping very soundly after my first shift of perimeter guard duty, having fallen instantly asleep after retuning to my hooch after my time was up. Slowly and vaguely, I was slightly awakened by some thumping sounds and explosions and vibrations on the ground. I barely opened my eyes and saw large flashes of red-white light in the tree line about two hundred meters away but just closed my eyes and instantly fell back asleep. A minute later I was roused from my sleep by my squad Sergeant. When I opened my eyes he was about a hundred feet away, yelling for me to get up and get into a foxhole. I raised my head from the ground a bit and shouted to him "What's the problem?" He yelled that we were getting mortared. I looked past him and to the left and could see the explosions as the enemy rounds landed about two hundred feet away, exploding on what was probably some soldiers fighting positions on the perimeter and into the tree line close by. I could hear the initial blast of the mortars leaving the tubes so the VC mortar crew must have been very close. I was tired, dead tired, beyond even that. I just barely raised my head and yelled to him "Wake me up when they get closer" then let my head fall and instantly fell asleep. The squad Sergeant apparently didn't like my answer at all because a few seconds later he shook me awake, shouting to get under cover. I barely opened my eyes to see him running back to the cover of the group of foxholes that he had left, two hundred feet from my hooch, across a wide open area that was barren of any vegetation or protection.

I have to give him credit for leaving the safety of his hole to awaken me, he risked his life and I basically told him not to bother me. After a few seconds of mighty effort, shaking my head violently from left to right and up and down, trying to regain some sense of mental alertness and then trying to have a level of mental control to command and demand my body to comply with my wishes, I struggled to my feet, grabbed my weapon, put on my load-bearing equipment and ran towards the foxholes with the rucksack in my arms.

The mortar rounds were landing closer now. The VC gun crews were walking their rounds towards the group of foxholes that was my objective. The rounds were exploding in a line from my left to my right, in a line that was to be almost directly perpendicular to my run. The enemy was putting extremely accurate fire on our perimeter. The explosions were tremendous, red and white light shot up into the air about fifty feet tall in the darkness of the night followed instantly by shockingly powerful explosions. I suspected that the VC must have overrun one of our artillery positions and were hitting us with 105 mm artillery rounds. Then I realized that it must be enemy 82mm mortar fire. My gun crew had an 81mm mortar so the ammo is about the same for both guns. I had never been in the bush with 81s landing, now I was shocked to see how powerful the rounds really are, shocked to realize the power and terror that my gun crew had been serving up upon the enemy. It looked as if it would be very close as to whether I could reach the fighting positions and jump in before the mortar rounds were walked in and put on top of us, shredding the surrounding area with shrapnel.

It was like driving a car at high speed towards a rail road crossing while you see a freight train barreling towards that crossing, traveling from left to right. My internal computer calculated that, at the speed at which the rounds were advancing and my running speed, that I would almost certainly be within the kill zone of the exploding ordinance, if not directly under it, as I reached the foxholes. In a split second I thought that I should just hit the dirt and let the mortar rounds hit the foxholes, then get up and run forward, but that would leave me completely exposed in an area with no cover whatsoever. Although the line of march of the incoming rounds suggested that they would fall a hundred feet from me that could change instantly. If I threw it down, dropped to the ground, seeking that small amount of safety, it might well be the difference between life and death for me, but, I thought, the foxholes may well be under attack from enemy infantry, and the difference of just one extra US trooper could well mean the difference between life and death for many people.

I thought that I was probably safer laying down on the ground in the open than I would be in the fighting positions in front of me that were under direct and accurate mortar attack. The volume and violence of the mortar attack explosions from incoming bombs would drown out any noise of an infantry ground attack against our positions I thought. I had deliberately grabbed up my rucksack, knowing full well that it would slow me down in my rush for "relative" safety but it contained extra ammo, which my fellow troopers might need. When I was about a hundred feet away, the mortaring suddenly ceased and I ran as fast as humanly possible, given the load of weapons, ammo and explosives that I was carrying in my arms until I reached the foxholes and jumped into one of them. The VC did not fire any more rounds. After about another forty-five minutes without taking any incoming fire the hundred percent alert was called off. I walked back to my hooch and caught about thirty minutes of sleep before being awakened for another two hours of perimeter guard duty.

I thought back to when I was a kid and my mother would try to wake me up in the morning. It was extremely difficult to awaken me and my mother would sometimes say in exasperation, "What does it take to wake you up? A bomb?" The fact that, in real life, even a series of bombs hadn't disturbed my sleep at first made me smile. I had been so exhausted that, yes, literally, bombs didn't wake me up. But I was dismayed that my physical health had been so compromised that even close by VC mortar rounds had not awakened me. The fact that this was only the second day of this operation worried me even more. I knew that every day of the operation would make us weaker and more physically abused than the day before it.

The next morning we began beating the bush, walking through the jungle on our combat patrol. Just a few days of beating the bush can really take it out of you. Future missions would be much longer and much more difficult although at that time I couldn't imagine things being more difficult.

Walking through the bush loaded down with as much as a hundred and forty pounds of gear, in ninety eight degree temperatures and extremely high humidity, all day long, is something that cannot be described in words. The pain and suffering was unimaginably inhuman.

Frequently, the line of march would stop but you never knew whether it would stop for five minutes or five seconds. While stopped, you could sit on the ground and take most of the load off of your shoulders and back and body in general, but, arising from that position, just trying to stand with all of that weight was a difficult and painful experience. Therefore, every time you stopped, you had to guess whether you should take the weight off for a while and struggle to get up, or just stand there. If you stood, you could bend over which would relieve some of the pain and strain, or try to lean against a tree and have some of the weight of the rucksack relieved by the tree holding it up by friction with you applying a steady strong pressure with your legs to hold it against the tree. Neither method was very effective. If you chose to stand, you would dearly regret it if the line remained stopped for more than a minute, but it you chose to sit down, you would dearly regret it if you had to stand up and move out ten seconds later. Of course, at all times you had to be on the lookout for enemy troops or snipers or mines or booby traps. If you could sit down it was a physical rest but it was never a psychological rest.

During that day the line of march stopped, and the word was passed back that we would remain in place for a ten minute break, that didn't happen very often at all. We were in a rubber plantation and I decided to investigate one of those trees to see how the rubber latex was obtained. Some of the trees had a small conical cup attached to the tree but most of them did not. Each tree had its bark scored about five feet high, spiraling downwards around the tree to about three feet high. It looked as if, every year perhaps, another spiral was cut into the bark below the initial cut so that it was more of a band of cuts, about a foot wide, circling the tree a few times. Some of the trees exuded a white milky substance so I took my bayonet and made a cut into the bark and instantly the latex began to run. I picked up a bit of it on my fingers. It was very liquid but within a half a minute it began to congeal and became exactly like a thin rubber coating on my fingers. I stuck my bayonet directly into the tree and it began to leak the white latex. I cut into a small branch and a trickle of latex leaked out. I cut a leaf in half and thin line of white latex instantly formed at the cut. With the missing cups and lack of freshly made cuts it appeared that that rubber plantation had not been worked for quite a while. I wondered why a plantation that had required so much work over many years would now be abandoned. I never knew the answer.

My uncle and aunt had sent a cigarette case to me. It was made of plastic and consisted of two parts. A person could put his package of cigarettes into such a container and could be ensured that his smokes would not be crushed. I had to give my relatives a lot of credit for coming up with such a good idea for a present and I thought that it was an excellent gift. However, in practice, it didn't work out too well. The case worked very well in protecting a pack of smokes from being crushed, which is very likely to occur, but the big problem was that when I crossed a stream that was chin high, water would enter the container and thoroughly soak the cigarettes. The stream water simply filled up the protective container and made each cigarette a soggy mess.

Of course, that didn't make them unsmokable, although any civilian or civilized person would have just thrown the pack into the trash, but for an Infantryman, who didn't have the luxury of just going to the corner store and buying another pack, a soaking wet pack of smokes just made them wet and temporarily unsmokable although it also made them a nasty thing to smoke even after they dried out. Actually, without that protective case, I wouldn't have had anything to smoke at all, the entire pack would have disintegrated into a soggy mess and washed away. You just had to wait until the cigarettes dried up, regardless of whether their soggy state was from rain, stream water or sweat. After they dried they would be a disgusting mess of tobacco stained cigarette paper and tobacco that was not in the least helped by the moisture but they still contained nicotine and they would be the only things available most of the time.

All of the men had Zippo lighters. They were reliable and, at least I, carried one on most operations along with a spare can of lighter fluid. Even if a man did not smoke, he needed a lighter to ignite his fuel tablets for heating water for coffee or to heat up his C-Rations or other food rations. There was a major problem with those lighters in that when we crossed a stream or creek, if the Zippo lighter went underwater the lighter fluid soaking the cloth interior of the lighter would be replaced by water, making it completely inoperable. Once it dried completely you could still make it operate, by adding lighter fluid, but essentially, it would not work for twenty four hours after crossing a creek, and, sometimes, we crossed creeks three or more times in a day. Some soldiers carried their Zippo lighters under the heavy rubber bands that held our helmet camouflage cloth but that was no guarantee of dryness at all. In the rainy season, you could be assured of being thoroughly soaked from top to bottom.

Even in the dry season there was no guarantee that the lighter would remain dry. A soldier might be required to cross a deep stream or river where he might be over your head in water at some point. A trooper then just had to hold his breath and hope that he could hold it until he reached shallower waters. A person wouldn't think that there might be a situation where a man couldn't find a spark to light a cigarette or a heat tab, but that was most certainly the situation several times, where no one in the Company had a dry match or functional cigarette lighter.

Sometimes, in the evening, if there were enough men at the night site, if you asked around you could usually, eventually find someone with a dry match or lighter that worked although how anybody managed that on some operations I never discovered for certain. If even one man in a Company could produce fire, then everyone in the Company could eventually attach that fire, but there were many times where such a scenario was impossible. That meant cold coffee, cold C-rations and, if a soldier only had LRRP rations, it meant that he did not eat that day, since such rations required a half-quart of boiling hot water.

Each C-ration came with a sealed plastic bag that contained matches and other things. I would try to keep at least one of those unopened so I would have matches if I really needed them. Once the bag was opened the matches were exposed to the elements and their usefulness might last from five days to five minutes, depending on conditions. Those individual pouches contained matches, gum, a package of four cigarettes, a tiny, tiny roll of toilet paper etc, etc. Yes, they were useful, but they occupied a lot of room in a rucksack and no Infantryman would deem their contents so useful as to justify the bulk of more than two or three of them in a rucksack during combat operations, however "nice" or "civilized" or "useful" they may be.

Being on an operation was usually, I think, a very personal situation for each soldier. To an outside observer the situation might seem to be a bunch of men walking through the forest. To the individual Infantryman, it was very, very different. It was not a five second film piece on the evening news, it was a twenty-four hour a day hard hump, perhaps on a twenty-one day operation, where a soldier could be killed at any moment and/or horribly crippled and maimed for the rest of his life. It was not like you "may" be killed by lightning on a golf course (probability: 1:10,000,000), it was a situation where people WERE killed and horribly maimed all the time in an Infantry Company, probably one in ten men were. People that you personally knew and people who were in situations that you should have been in and somehow missed by the luck of the draw. Many others, most, were sickened or injured but just not so seriously or horribly. Probably every Infantryman was damaged in one way or another, in ways that would affect them for the rest of their lives. That's what this Country asked of its young citizens, demanded of its draftees but it was a burden that was required of only a miniscule percentage of its population, and their families.

During the line of march during combat operations every soldier kept his interval, a space between any two men, so that one enemy bullet could not go though more than one man (one bullet from a high-powered military rifle can easily go through 3 men). That interval was supposed to be fifteen meters (fifty feet) between men, but in reality, that interval usually became much closer so that a trooper wouldn't lose sight of the man in front of him and the man in back of him in the dense underbrush of the jungle. An Infantryman would go for hours and hours, actually, days and days, sometimes weeks, without speaking with another human being.

At dusk, you might get the word that you have the guard duty after Smith and before Jones and then the only human contact you might have is Smith shaking you awake saying "Hey Man, its your turn on guard duty" and those words might be the only words that you spoke to Jones when your turn of guard duty was finished. It might well be the only words spoken to anyone for that day.

The only other human contact that a soldier might hear are the commands and instructions passed up and down the line all day, passed from one man to the next in a whisper. An instruction might originate from a platoon Sergeant at the front of the line or a Lieutenant at the back of the line or from a squad Sergeant in the middle of the line, that was passed up the line and down the line. A typical days messages might be something like this: "close up the interval, pass it back (to the soldier in back of you)", "Squad leaders to the rear, pass it up (to the soldier in front of you)" "Enemy spotted by point (pointman), pass it back" "Ten minute break, clean your weapon, pass it back" "Second platoon, take rear guard, pass it up", "Weapons platoon take right flank, pass it up", "Mines ahead, watch your step, pass it back". "Trip wires ahead, pass it back" "Man down in 3rd platoon, send a medic, pass it up". Some days there were no messages at all and some nights there would be no mission briefing so that a person could go for days without ever hearing a human voice, each man isolated in his own personal world both day and night.

We were beyond exhausted. There was little time for banter and there was no time whatsoever for such nonsense like "Hey, how are those Red Sox doing?" In this absolutely desperate situation, why would anyone care how a sports team was doing anyways? I think, at least on a sub-conscious level, that most of us thought that we would be killed or seriously and permanently wounded. You might have five minutes in the morning to heat some coffee or food before you moved out on patrol. Then all day you'd have to keep your interval so that you were too far away from anyone to chit-chat. Of course, every trooper needed every bit of breath just to manage to struggle with his combat load. Towards evening, when we finally reached our night site I might hear from the squad sergeant: "Mallen!, You and Keating dig in here. Keating! You have the first watch". I suppose a soldier could have some conversation with the soldier he was partnered with to dig a fighting position, but that was difficult work, hard labor that had to be accomplished under time constraints. If the man who was taking a rest while his buddy worked on the position had an opportunity to make small talk to the soldier digging, the working soldier usually didn't have the breath to spare to waste it on idle chatter.

Everybody would be on guard as the sun set and you might be able to manage a few words with your fighting position partner, but chances are you would still be filling up some sandbags for your overhead cover or trying to eat something before the full guard posting half an hour before sunset where a hundred percent of the soldiers were on full alert and guard duty. Once the guard time started, a soldier would be straining to hear any noises coming from his front or sides, it was not the time or place for idle chatter. No, there wasn't much time for the exchange of pleasantries or some lighthearted banter. Every man was an island and every man was king of his island. The problem was that no one ever visited that island. After a while, some of those hermit kings lost the ability to speak as they had before this experience. They would have great difficulties later in trying to fit into a civilian, civilized situation where the conversation was light-hearted. In the bush, most conversation was very brief, exactly to the point and deadly serious.

Those were not happy times. It was not some sort of Boy Scout jamboree. It was not some invigorating hike in the forest that ended each night with cooking hot dogs over a camp fire and telling ghost stories. It was a green hell of suffering and torment, men hunting other men, each group trying to kill the other in as many ways as possible. It was a back breaking, ball busting extraordinary difficult struggle filled with agonizing pain and misery during the day and sleep deprivation and night terrors after sunset. Profound hunger and thirst and sickness and weakness, skin cut and torn and ripped by thorns and defiled by jungle rot sores was the lot of these boy scouts. That was our life every day on our missions. Some days, the routine would be interrupted by someone being killed or horribly maimed but that just stopped the progress through the jungle for a few minutes. Then the wounded would be bandaged and the dead wrapped up in ponchos and the line of soldiers would move out again, suffering horribly with their loads knowing full well that their next step may well end their lives.

There were many times that I thought that my nineteen year old body would have a heart attack. My pulse rate was probably above two hundred and forty beats per minute. Perhaps you may think that that is an impossible heart rate, such a rate would cause a heart attack for sure. But, I assure you, it is accurate. At one time, I deliberately caught up to the soldier in front of me who had a watch and, without saying a word, I grabbed his arm and stared into his watch while counting my pulse. He wasn't happy with the encounter at all and I didn't have the breath to explain to him the reason for my actions. I just wanted to know, for certain, what my pulse rate was during a particularly difficult hump. My breathing rate was probably over a hundred and twenty breaths per minute.

It was truly an agonizing torture with every step. Sometimes I would take a final step and think that I couldn't possibly, humanly, take another. Then I told myself to just take one more step, one more step to drag my load of weapons and ammo forward to help my fellow soldiers before I dropped dead. I really thought that that one more step would be the end of my life, dead due to heat exhaustion or heart failure. When that step didn't end my life I would tell myself to just take one more step, certain that the strain on my body would be fatal for sure. That could continue for quite a while, while every second seemed like two minutes and every fifteen feet like a mile. Just one more step, where the next step seemed impossible. My thoughts and my brain consisted only of the words, "Just one more step" and with every fiber of my being, dredging up any possible last speck of strength, with my brain screaming and demanding of my body to perform a physical feat that was basically humanly impossible. Each step was a superhuman demand on my body, a horrible, excruciatingly painful torture, an existence of unrelenting very extreme pain. Where the limits of pain of which a person might be knowledgeable, were far, far, far exceeded by the reality. Every step required superhuman struggle and unimaginable, incredible anguish. The Mortar men generally humped heavier loads than other Infantrymen, but each mans load in the Company was insufferable. Eventually the line of march would stop for a while, maybe for five minutes or more likely for five seconds when you could collapse to the ground and rest a bit.

It was not just heavy labor, it was in another dimension of strain and strength and determination and hurt and exhaustion and the pain level was beyond anything that I ever could have imagined. How men did it I don't know. I'll bet that if a physiologist studied the weight of our loads and the length of march and the heat and humidity that he would conclude that it was humanly impossible. It was humanly impossible but these men did it and they bore the horribly extreme pain and misery day after day, all day, in a stinking jungle on the other side of the world. I wondered if the people in the United States really had any idea of what these soldiers had to endure?

How could they? I would never have imagined or comprehended the level of pain and desperation and exhaustion and danger and hunger and thirst and sickness and heat and humidity if I hadn't personally experienced it and I couldn't believe it when it was actually happening. Did the people that sent us to war really know what they were subjecting their soldiers to? Did they care? There were hundreds of news reporters in Viet Nam. I never saw a reporter with a line outfit, humping along with the men. I certainly don't blame them. Ten minutes in the bush, humping an Infantryman's load would cause a regular reporter to soil his pants and fall down in a dead faint. It was beyond the description of any words. I assure you, it was much, much worse than I can possibly describe or convey in just words. I did read a magazine article later that said that the mortar crews did something far, far better than anyone else in VietNam, that was to hump absurdly heavy loads.

One day, while humping through the jungle, several weeks if not months worth of thoughts on a certain subject seemed to coalesce into a clear, reasoned, determined plan. I thought that, if I made it back from this operation, I would go directly to the battalion commanders tent and tell him that he's an ass in no uncertain terms. I would tell him that he must think that we are pack mules, and if we were in fact mules no one would load them down like this. I would ask him how often he ever got into the bush, and if so I'd call him on the fact that he probably never carried a full pack. I was determined to do that, I set my mind to do it for sure. What the hell was he going to do about it? Jump up and punch me out? Good, then I could get in a few licks on him before I was overpowered by his Sergeant Major and staff. At least I would have visited upon him one one millionth of the suffering that he visited on his troops in the field for just the last operation. For the next few days I specifically planned my moves for my upcoming encounter with the Battalion commander, planning what to say and how to react. I especially thought about it while I was beating through the bush, suffering horribly.

About eleven am one morning, while on a combat patrol, through the scraggly jungle in the line of march, I had a partial view of the soldier who was about four soldiers in front of me suddenly stopped at a certain point although I had the impression that the line of march had not halted. There was just something about it that was very unusual. I thought that maybe he had spotted something that was dangerous or perhaps he was relieving himself and I thought: "Hey, you better finish up real quick, you are losing sight of the guy in front of you". He stayed there for fifteen or twenty seconds and then moved on. Then I caught sight of the soldier behind him stopping in exactly the same spot as the previous trooper, staying for perhaps thirty seconds and then moving out quickly to catch up with the line of march. Then I noticed that the next man stopped at the exact same spot for a brief time.

I thought that surely there must be something very interesting there and anticipated seeing it for myself. As I got closer to the "choke point" I noticed two men just standing along the line of march, saying something to everyone who passed by. I couldn't believe my eyes as I got closer and saw our Battalion commander and his Sergeant Major, both in full battle gear with full rucksacks, just standing there. Apparently they were giving words of encouragement to each trooper. As I passed the Colonel he said something like "How's it going Troop?" Here was my chance, my prime opportunity to tell him exactly what I thought of him, but all I could do, in answer to his question, was to put my head down and stare at the ground, which seemed to alleviate my load just a little bit, and utter a heavy grunt, driving on, not slowing for a second. Once I realized that it was the Battalion commander standing there, within two seconds I had some brilliant insights. First, I was greatly impressed with the fact that he was actually on the ground, humping with full ruck. Second, the whole intent of my plans to confront him back at base camp was now realized. He could not possibly now be unaware of the suffering and hardships of his troops. No matter how upbeat and glad and proud to meet his Battalion commander in the bush, no matter how hard a soldier might try to appear strong and fit, his appearance betrayed him. Those men were strung out, physically at the end of their ropes. Then I realized that I didn't know anything about the Colonel, I had no idea of his previous military experience but one thing I certainly noticed upon first seeing him was that he wore an embroidered Combat Infantry Mans badge on his shirt. That said many things about him, all of them good.

My thoughts and plans of the last month or so had evaporated in a split second as soon as I spotted the pair. Both of them were clearly over the age of forty, a great, great grandfather in the eyes of nineteen year old Infantrymen. I figured that if that Battalion commander, who could easily justify sitting back in a relatively cushy, perhaps air-conditioned office, would show up in the middle of a full blown operation in the jungle, with full battle gear and rucksack, humping the trail along with his men, in the middle of all of the danger, just to say "hello" to his troops then that was one seriously good commander of men and obviously a soldier that knew what it meant to carry a full combat load under operational conditions. I later learned that that commander was the oldest (forty one years old) Airborne Battalion commander the history of the U.S.Army, more than twice the average age of his troops. He was one extremely tough and rugged and fit soldier to be humping on operations at that age, actually at any age. Now I knew that he had a good idea of the extent of suffering and pain to which he subjected his men. He must have had done it himself. Later I learned that he had a previous tour of duty in Viet Nam with the Special Forces. Later in his career he became Commander of all Army Special Forces

At around four o'clock we stopped our humping for the day and began digging in for the night. My assigned foxhole buddy was Roger Udell Pierce, the man that would assist me in digging a two man fighting position and who would later rotate with me the night guard duty. After we had dug in the main fighting position we then chopped down small trees to make an overhead cover and then filled up sandbags to place over us as a protective cover against possible VC mortar fire.

I was shoveling up some dirt that we had excavated from the hole and Pierce was holding the sandbags open as I filled them. That was very light duty in the scheme of things and it gave us an opportunity to talk. During the discussion, Pierce brought up the subject of tigers. It wasn't the first time that he had mentioned the subject. Pierce seemed to be extremely concerned about tigers and the appropriate response if we were to ever encounter one of the creatures. He had implored me on more than one occasion to never shoot a tiger because, he insisted, that an M-16 round would probably not kill a tiger instantly. If that was the case then the wounded and enraged tiger would then attack and kill the shooter and several men close by him.

I disagreed with him, but actually I wasn't fully convinced at all that what he said wasn't accurate and that my position on the debate was not correct. My final words to him on that subject was that I told him that I would most certainly shoot a tiger if I ever saw one. He asked me, incredulously, why I would ever do such a thing. I told him "So I can get it stuffed for a trophy". He was very disturbed with that answer. That guy seemed to be more worried more about tigers than anything else. I figured he's better off concentrating and worrying about tigers and on whether I'm going to shoot one than on the very many, much more certain dangers that surrounded us every minute of every day in the bush.

Anyways, tigers are extremely skillful hunters. Any tiger would detect our presence ten minutes before we would be close to him. I figured that any tiger that heard the noise and ground tremors caused by a column of twenty heavily loaded men wouldn't know what it was for sure, but would know for certain that it was not his usual prey and, if anything, it was something so much bigger than him that he would go out of his way to avoid it. A healthy tiger is certainly capable of snatching a man and dragging him deep into the jungle within seconds, so swiftly that the mans associates wouldn't have time to react, and there would be no warning. If a tiger was rabid or sick or injured enough to approach our column in such a manner that he could be easily seen he would have to be put down immediately. Such a tiger would not be in such a position just because he is curious, he would be there because he is desperate for a meal, animal or human, and was incapable of hunting in his normal, most very efficient and stealthy manner.

Surely, I thought, a single M-16 round would probably not immediately stop a healthy tiger in its tracks. An animal of that size and demeanor and strength, even if a round from an M-16 had found its heart or brain would not noticeably slow down its enormous ferocity, if anything, it might strengthen and increase its ferocity but, I reasoned, in such a situation I wouldn't be shooting single shots. Having said that, such a situation would call for everyone in the immediate vicinity to make that tiny but profound thumb movement on his weapon to switch from single shot to automatic fire instantly before the trigger was pulled. In truth, I wouldn't be shooting a tiger because he would make a nice trophy in my den, I'd be shooting him because he would be an extreme danger to me and my fellow soldiers. A tiger attack on one soldier would provoke a response of scores of bullets fired, especially if the tiger had a soldier by the throat and was dragging him into the jungle. Such a scenario would be a very bad situation because a fellow soldier would be hesitant to fire into such a situation because he could not be sure of hitting the tiger or the soldier, but yet be horrified to think that a non response would allow a tiger to kill a soldier and then eat him. A very unlikely scenario you might suggest? In fact, it was not that unlikely at all.

Before I ever joined the Army I read of an account of a Life magazine reporter in Viet Nam who was traveling down a dirt road in a vehicle. He recorded an incident where he was approaching a farmer ahead of him, traveling in the opposite direction, who had a cart that was being pulled by a water buffalo. The report stated that a tiger suddenly leaped from the concealing bushes at the side of the road, struck the water buffalo across its throat with its claws and then bounded into the opposite side of the road, concealed by the vegetation on that side of the road. The reporter mentioned that some of the men in his vehicle were armed but the suddenness and shock of the attack had paralyzed them, they didn't even think to bring their weapons to bear upon the scene.

The reporter then described how the tiger then suddenly jumped from his cover on the left hand side of the road and grabbed the mortally wounded buffalo by its throat. Then, with three mighty tugs, pulled the poor animal, that probably weighed in excess of a ton, into the concealing bushes on the right hand side of the road. I thought, if a tiger can do that to a two thousand pound animal, what could he do to a human being? The fact is that I never heard of such a tiger attack occurring in Viet Nam while I was there. I think the reason is that, twenty very heavily loaded American Infantrymen moving through the jungle, under the most quiet situations, probably sounded to a tiger like a dinosaur.

It was now getting close to Christmas and we expected to be in the bush for the next few days at least, a time span that included and went beyond Christmas Eve and Christmas Day. Surprisingly, that evening we were told that the next day we would move to a landing zone and would be evacuated back to base camp. We would be out of the field on the afternoon of Christmas Eve. That was a very much appreciated change of circumstances. The next morning we humped thru the jungle a relatively short distance to an overgrown rubber plantation. Towards the middle of it was an area where a few columns and long rows of trees had either been chopped down to the ground or simply not planted for some unknown reason, which provided a clearing where helicopters could land. The Landing Zone consisted of an area unobstructed by trees about three hundred feet long by about seventy feet wide with just short grass on the ground. It would be a tight fit for the choppers and only about five or so could land at any one time. One flight of five choppers landing as one group would require the entire length of the clearing so it would probably take four flights to evacuate the entire Company back to base camp.

I was happy now. Oh!, I gradually realized that I had been anything but happy for the entire operation. Happiness now seemed to be an emotional state of being that was a strange and very distant memory. We were being spared another two days of beating the bush and we would be back in base camp for Christmas. Oh Man!, what lucky and fortunate beings we were!! I had mentally accepted that we would be in the bush for Christmas but that change of plans would result in us spending Christmas like civilized Christians and not as abused and suffering pack mules, as filthy, hungry, extremely exhausted men living a sub-human life like animals out in the jungle, hunting other men who hunted us at the same time, all of us trying our utmost to kill the enemy in every possible way, not very Christian at all when you think about it.

Yeah!, I suddenly realized that I was a little happy. Then I realized that I had not been happy for quite a long time now. Happy was some emotion that I vaguely remembered, seemingly from a previous life. Of course that was probably because there was nothing to be happy about if you are an Airborne Infantryman on a combat operation in the woods of Viet Nam. I decided that when I got back to base camp, if I ever made it back to base camp in one piece, that I was going to eat my fill of Army food and drink plenty of purified water and then get some booze and dry cigarettes and sleep on a cot in a tent like a human being and not have to worry about losing my foot, my arm, my face, my eyes or my genitals with each step that I took or losing my life to a snipers shot or to an enemy mortar shell that I would never hear or be blinded by a booby trap or lose my right arm to a bullet from an enemies carbine. The possibilities for injuries were extremely numerous, ranging from painful to far beyond horrible and life-changing to life-ending.

We finally reached the LZ that would accept the choppers that my Company was going to use. According to the briefing of my squad Sergeant that morning, my squad was scheduled to get onto the 3rd "stick" or "flight" of choppers. The first stick of five choppers landed and were loaded up with troopers. The choppers began to lift off and fly out of the LZ, each one in its turn, one after another, separated by a only a few seconds. The last helicopter had just begun to lift off when suddenly there was a burst of gunfire from the front left of the LZ. It was clearly an enemy ambush of the choppers. The enemy had set up at the very beginning (northern edge) of the LZ and as the choppers passed over that spot the VC sent up a murderously vigorous fire upon them. All of the choppers managed to get out of the LZ without catastrophic damage to the airships, flying directly past and through the gunfire from the enemy ambush almost directly below their flight path but I'm sure that some or all of the helicopters certainly were pierced by the massive hailstorm of enemy bullets.

For the VC it was like shooting fish in a barrel, with automatic weapons, how any of the choppers managed to fly through such an assault without every passenger killed and the choppers shot down I will never know. Word came down the line a few minutes later that one of the pilots took a gunshot round through his foot. By my best guess, the enemy were about fifty feet beyond the extreme northern edge of the LZ and about eighty feet to the west of the direct line of flight of the choppers. Once the flight of choppers had lifted off of the ground, they were committed to a line of flight that they could not alter due to the surrounding trees, they had to fly straight ahead. The chopper pilots knew that full well what they were flying

through. Apparently the enemy had figured that out because they took full advantage of that fact to extract the maximum amount of casualties among the U.S. forces, ambushing the choppers at the point of their maximum vulnerability. All of the choppers were being forced to fly through a gauntlet of extremely heavy enemy fire from their left flank and very close by.

All of the enemy fire seemed to be located to the left front side of the LZ. I was greatly thankful that they weren't trying to flank us or initiate a lager attack from around our perimeter but I was strongly worried that that would be their next move. I couldn't understand why they had not yet started to hit us with mortars from the surrounding countryside.

There were American soldiers on the other side of the LZ, maybe about a hundred feet from the enemy. Obviously they had been alerted to the enemy presence by the VC's ambush but they didn't return fire immediately. Apparently they were trying to figure out a rough position from which the enemy fire was originating so that they could return fire but obviously the location of fire from the enemy in heavy scrub jungle was something that was very difficult to discern.

The location of the VC was fairly easy for me to discern, being a ways back from the front of the LZ, but to the troopers at the far end of the LZ it would have been very difficult to discern because of the roar of the choppers as they passed almost directly over them. It was also obvious that the VC knew of the Americans presence because once the VC had blasted the last chopper, they immediately began to directly engage that American portion of a platoon with very heavy automatic weapons fire, machine gun fire and rocket propelled grenades. Maybe they had already directly engaged the Americans while they ambushed the choppers, I don't know. I assumed that all of the enemy fire was directed at the choppers but now I realize that a portion of that fire could well have been aimed at the Infantrymen on the ground. My first thoughts were: "What the Hell!" The Americans haven't even fired one shot and the enemy is now engaging them in a vicious, overpowering fight to murder all of them. I thought: "Oh No!" "Have the VC already killed all of the troopers at the far end of the LZ?"

There seemed to be a substantial number of enemy troops in that immediate area, I would roughly guess their number at around twenty judging by the amount of fire that they presented. It could have been substantially more, I just guessed around twenty assuming that they were all firing their weapons on full automatic. It could well have been a full Company of enemy. The VC put up a tremendous amount of rifle, machine gun and RPG fire onto the American Infantry's ground ranks, about forty seconds of extremely withering fire. It certainly kept the heads of any Americans down, if not killing most of them I thought.

Apparently the VC's plan was to suppress the fire from any American opposition so that they could ambush the next flight of helicopters flying out of the LZ. As the enemies fire began to die down, the half platoon of Paratroopers, (I estimate perhaps fifteen Americans) who were close by, quickly ramped up their fire, responding with a very heavy blast of M-16, M-60 and M-79 fire, quickly intensifying in sound and measure, matching and then overwhelming the VC fire.

My platoon was in the middle of the LZ, at its edge, near the trees on the right flank, and I expected to be ordered to move up towards the action but it seemed that the engaging section of the American platoon had been ordered to put the situation under control. I jumped behind a tree to shield my body from any fire that the enemy might throw at us but I couldn't resist peering my head around the tree, trying to see what was going on at the front of the LZ. I couldn't see any Troopers or VC because of the heavy scrub vegetation but I searched the area for about twenty seconds, looking for any VC that might decide to assault the rest of the Company. Then I had a flash of insight. I dropped onto my stomach, assuming a prone position on the ground, facing outwards, ninety degrees eastward. I had suddenly realized that while I was trying to observe the spectacle to my front, the VC might decide to mount an attack in force from our flank.

The LZ itself was devoid of any Troopers. The Company was spread over the full length of the clearing that ran south to north, stationed and aligned along the very eastern and western limits of the LZ so that the LZ itself was barren of any American soldiers.

I stared deeply into the jungle in front of me but could only see about fifteen feet into it because of the heavy bushes. I tried to listen for any sounds of possible enemy movement to my front but it was impossible to hear anything that I could positively identify because of the extremely loud noise to my left due to the ongoing firefight on the ground. Thousands of rounds were being exchanged between the Paratroopers at the edge of the LZ and the engaging enemy VC. The huge noise was something that is never experienced in civilian life. Fire from VC carbines and automatic fire from their AK47 rifles mixed with American M-16 rifles fired on single shot and automatic and an M-60 machine gun mixed with the VC Rocket Propelled grenade (RPG) fire. The extremely deadly and frightening chatter of VC machine gun fire mixed with the sound of answering American M-60 machine guns was terrifying. The noise of the fire was huge but I could still barely pick out the sounds of American M-79 grenade launchers being fired, followed seconds later by their accompanying explosions.

There was occasionally the sound of an American Anti Tank weapon (ATW) being fired and, among the chaos was the sound of pistols being discharged, on both sides of the battle. At the beginning of the battle, it seemed that the amount of the VCs fire overwhelmed the Americans. There was very little return fire from the Americans and I feared that the VC had sprung an ambush on the Americans on the ground and had killed most of them. I suddenly realized that perhaps the VC were very much numerically superior to our force and were going to over-run us, overwhelm us in manpower and firepower. I was very afraid that the VC had a Battalion or more of soldiers out there in the bush, close by, surrounding us and had a well developed plan to attack and kill all of us from predetermined dug in positions and with previous registration points for their mortars. I guessed that the VC had recognized this area as a good landing zone for choppers and had probably dug in and prepared their fighting positions for a time when the Americans would use it. They had apparently had done a good job of it.

The word was passed down the line to keep down, to seek any available cover. I didn't understand why such an order was passed but a minute later a helicopter gun ship came roaring in, very low and very fast, approaching the LZ from the south-east. From a thousand feet from me, the chopper let loose an incredibly loud and very, very scary burst from its Gatling gun. The pilot suddenly stopped firing and two seconds later he flew almost directly overhead. The absolutely enormous power of the aircraft was overwhelming. It was a huge hunk of metal and machinery, very heavy, emanating a shaking, rattling extremely powerful sound from its massive rotor that loudly chopped the air, from its powerful jet engine and especially the otherworldly roar of its Gatling guns on both sides shooting seven thousand machine gun rounds per minute.

The overwhelming mechanical and explosive roar if its guns amongst the scream from its jet engine saturated the humid air and seemed to make the air in my lungs hum and vibrate due to its power. A half-second later, the pilot touched his trigger again and sprayed the enemy with about a thousand rounds from his Gatling gun, assaulting directly towards and then directly over the enemies position. Those Gatling guns scared me and shook me every time I saw them in action because if the pilot made the slightest mistake at that close range he would kill a hundred of us in less than two seconds. As the gunship ceased fire and flew past the VC the enemy blasted the ship and its crew unmercifully. As it flew past the enemy position I could still hear the enemy firing sporadically at the engaged Americans on the ground.

About ten miles away, in preparation for a massive operation that was to commence in two weeks, the US had assembled about a hundred and twenty artillery cannons. They had been sitting around for the last week, doing nothing I would guess, when they were suddenly given a fire mission to support us, every gun ordered to fire. The word came down the line to every Infantryman to lie flat and get under cover as much as possible. Suddenly, there were two nearly simultaneous explosions in the area where the VC were located (registration rounds called in by our forward observers just to mark and adjust the target) followed a minute later by a hundred artillery rounds suddenly exploding in the area, all within a second of each other, an unbelievable and indescribable spectacle of viciousness, way beyond what might be described as awesome power, explosive destruction and deafening noise. Just an unbelievable situation of a hundred rounds, each containing perhaps thirty pounds of high explosive, suddenly impacted upon a small area.

It was a situation that is never remotely close to a situation that could ever be duplicated, or imagined, in civilian life. The unimaginable level of horror and shock and powerfulness of three thousand pounds of explosives and shrapnel delivered onto a very small target very close by is something that is simply beyond the pale of anything that might happen in civilian life, save perhaps by a huge airliner crashing into your back yard pool while you are cooking on the barbeque. I was horrified that such destruction had occurred so close to our troops, but amazed at the accuracy of all of those guns.

A few seconds later there was a loud, low rumbling sound, very strange, ominous, an eerily deathly roaring sound, slightly shaking the air. Obviously that sound emanated from the muzzles of the artillery guns that had fired those rounds from miles away that eventually reached us. It was the sound of the original blasts of the artillery rounds leaving their tubes. The explosions on the ground preceded the sounds of the artillery rounds leaving their tubes because the artillery rounds traveled faster than the speed of sound. The fact that we even heard the sounds of the artillery guns from ten miles away gave testament to the power of all a hundred and twenty guns being fired simultaneously.

A very large, extremely thick cloud of distinctly white smoke and separately, black smoke, covered the enemy position. Part of it swept to the right and across the American half platoon that was directly engaged in the action by the wind. Within seconds, the wind shifted again and brought the smoke over the LZ, directly towards the rest of the Company.

There must have been a cloud of invisible gas preceding the smoke because there was an over-powering smell in the air of the explosives from the artillery rounds, and of what the artillery rounds had destroyed, a trillion, trillion microscopic bits of destroyed vegetation, dirt, human remains, animals and insects and nature, a burnt, chemical smell, so strong and dense that it seared my nostrils severely and caused me to involuntary gasp and stop breathing.

I took a few very labored breaths and thought that perhaps I should put on my gas mask. But, evaluating the approaching solid dense cloud of smoke, I thought that the invisible, extremely toxic gas would pass over us to be replaced by just a cloud of smoke that we could easily deal with. The cloud of smoke approached us very rapidly, an impossibly thick, seemingly almost solid mass that moved along the ground. The smoke was not rising or dissipating, it seemed to be about an inch off of the ground as it moved towards us. Why the smoke was not rising I don't know, perhaps it was because it contained elements that were not ever found in civilian kinds of fire.

I laid flat on the ground and I turned my face away from the wind and pushed my face into the crook of my arm, trying to avoid at least some of the smoke, hoping that it would stay just a few inches above the ground so that I could breathe I hoped that the advancing smoke cloud would not be so viciously harsh as the invisible gas that had proceeded it but I knew that the density of the smoke would be a problem. Even if it stayed very close to the ground, even if it wasn't as poisonous as the gas, it would almost certainly tear up my eyes and reduce visibility to near zero, rendering me unable to see any potential enemy assault.

The cloud came at us, quickly, inexorably, extremely thick. I willed it to go over us or around us but it drove forward, enveloping us in some sort of vaporous death. It quickly enveloped me and my eyelids involuntarily shut, sharply stung and tearing profusely after just a one second dose. I forced my eyes open but the visibility was zero, my world had suddenly become totally white. I could see nothing beyond a few inches, I could not even see my arms or legs. I started coughing and choking violently and my eyes produced a huge volume of tears that I couldn't have imagined possible prior to this. I was suffocating, like I was drowning, and I had no idea of how long the assault of that smoke would last. I tried to hold my breath but my body refused to allow a lung full of that noxious smoke to linger within it. I involuntarily exhaled strongly and then involuntarily inhaled a lungful of atmosphere but the air was not filled with oxygen but with the extremely poisonous and harsh chemicals which my body immediately and involuntarily rejected. I involuntarily exhaled violently, only to involuntarily inhale strongly again and again.

My breathing was no longer under my control and I rolled around on the ground, inside that smoke, tossing and turning from left to right and from top to bottom, my body afflicted with gasps and coughs and extremely violent, brief bouts of inhalation and exhalation that just filled my lungs with more of that smoke and chemicals. I couldn't breath properly at all, every desperate inhalation resulted in filling my lungs with a noxious, intolerable poison, that resulted in me violently expelling the smoke and gas, only to involuntarily inhaling a huge gasp of air, except that the air was horribly poisoned and deadly.

I desperately needed oxygen but the more I breathed, the more of the noxious smoke and gas filled my lungs. It was as if I was drowning, fifty feet below the surface of a white lake of harsh chemicals. I was on the edge of panic, or maybe beyond that, horrified to think that that cloud would not pass by me before I was asphyxiated. Eventually it did pass and I was left on the ground, desperately gasping huge lung fulls of air, feeling as if I had just held my breath for four minutes, depriving my brain of oxygen, which essentially is exactly what had happened, except for the poisonous smoke that I had inhaled, which had probably poisoned my body while depriving me of badly needed oxygen.

Essentially, I and everyone around me, had been deprived of oxygen for four minutes. Anything that we had breathed was an extremely noxious mixture of harmful gasses and smoke, devoid of oxygen. I wondered how much brain damage we had just sustained and how much damage to our lungs and bodies would be life altering. No, it wasn't just a minor inconvenience, I was fairly certain that those noxious fumes and deprivation of oxygen to our brains for so long would result in a life-altering damage to our bodies, lungs and brains. It was a situation that was absolutely horrendous.

I had just begun to recover, wiping away huge amounts of tears from my eyes with the filthy sleeve of my shirt while frantically trying to regain my vision, when three soldiers suddenly shouted "GET DOWN!!" I looked towards the south and spotted two jet attack aircraft approaching the LZ, dark gray against the sky, nose down, pointed directly at the VC below. Within seconds the jets screamed in at full speed, about three hundred feet high, each unleashed two

two hundred and fifty bombs each. The jets instantly veered upwards and to their right side, breaking off their attack run. The four bombs continued falling down and forward for a few seconds, on a path that ended directly onto the VC position, producing a huge explosion that, even though it was four separate bombs, seemed to be one singular explosion.

That, of course, seemed to be overkill for sure, nothing could have survived that onslaught. The smoke cleared from the VC position after about thirty seconds, mercifully the wind direction and updraft had changed, probably due to the heat and explosive energy of the previous bombs. The resultant smoke didn't envelop the troopers on the LZ. Luckily the white smoke from those bombs lifted and dispersed, blowing directly over my squads position but high enough that it didn't affect us. What was interesting was that the smoke from those explosions were totally white in color. Obviously, the initial bombs had burned everything that made a black smoke color.

Incredibly, the enemy again started firing at the soldiers on the ground although the amount of VC fire seemed to be quite diminished from previous levels. The engaged American sections now retaliated viciously and overwhelmingly with automatic fire from M-16s and M-60 machineguns and M-79 grenade fire. I could not comprehend how any VC could have possibly survived that onslaught, but apparently, the VC were extremely well dug in. After a few minutes the enemy fire tapered off and then abruptly stopped, while the Americans continued their most vicious automatic weapon and grenade assault for another thirty seconds. The Americans must be running low on ammunition I thought.

A few minutes later the next stick of choppers approached the LZ from the south, landing without incident. The next group of Paratroopers ran in a crouch towards them, glancing towards their front, anticipating enemy gunfire, and very quickly loaded onto the helicopters. The choppers started to lift off and fly forward and again, almost immediately after they ascended and were flying over the northern edge of the LZ there was heavy enemy automatic fire at the choppers from almost the exact location as the first ambush. The shots at the helicopters were immediately answered by the half platoon of American troopers that were nearest to them on the ground. Even still, the men on the choppers flew right past, right through, about thirty feet above a vicious firefight at ground level, with enemy fire also almost surely directed into the ships flying overhead as well. Why some of the choppers were not shot down I will never know. As the VC were shooting directly into the choppers, the American half platoon were directly and effectively and positively and heroically directly engaged with the VC. The poor door gunners on the choppers didn't seem to be firing. They were unsure where exactly the American forces were and in any event were so close to the enemy underneath them that they couldn't bring their guns to bear on them I thought.

Then the entire sequence began again. The helicopter gun ships roaring in, putting accurate fire directly upon the VC position. Their Gatling guns fire ripping pieces of wood and bark off of the trees, filling the area with dust and huge splinters and shredded vegetation and tens of thousands of pieces of leaves among the tremendous roar of their aircraft and their armament.

Then there was the urgent command coming down the line to seek any available cover followed minutes later by scores and scores of 120mm artillery rounds being fired simultaneously and exploding in an impossible to imagine scenario of noise and shrapnel and death and destruction, and all of that followed up by a jet planes dive-bombing the enemy, hitting them with thousands of pounds of high explosive bombs before executing extreme aerial maneuvers pulling their ships suddenly up and twisting away from the target.

That's the end of that situation I thought. No one could have possibly lived through such an over-kill attack. It was horribly scary, with that explosive power so close to our position, the slightest mistake would have easily and quickly killed all of us, the entire American Company. They have a radio code for calling in air strikes or artillery called "danger close". That was a situation where we called in an air strike or artillery strike very close to friendly forces. This situation was far more dangerous than what "danger close" might imply.

The scream of the jets slowly receded and then there was a complete silence. I wasn't sure if the gun battle on the ground had stopped or whether I had been deafened by the incredible noise of the previous few minutes. After a while I realized that there was no longer contact between the ground forces. The wind had changed direction and speed so that my squad and most of my Company on the LZ was spared the effects of the smoke that time but I think the soldiers on the other side of the LZ weres hit with it.

The next stick of choppers landed, were boarded and started to take off when the enemy, from almost the same position, again started shooting at the choppers. The amount of enemy gunfire was substantial but far less than the first and second assault. The engaged American section on the ground hit them hard and were still engaged when, for the third time, a helicopter gunship came in blazing. Word was passed to get under any cover that could be found and a minute later that area again erupted with 120mm artillery rounds followed a minute later by Air Force jets and their high explosive ordinance put unbelievably close to American forces yet directly put on top of the enemy. How could enemy soldiers possibly survive such an assault I thought. It was impossible for them to have survived the first attack never mind the second. Obviously, the VC had dug in positions twenty years ago for just this possible scenario, apparently they had dug in well.

The choppers again landed and my squad and I ran over to one and hopped on. The pilot was in a big hurry and before we could get ourselves organized the ship lifted off, with the nose pointing downwards for maximum speed along the ground, then suddenly pulled up very fast to gain as much altitude as possible, sacrificing ground speed for height. I looked over to where the half platoon had been that had done most of the fighting but I couldn't spot them. Then I scanned outwards into the jungles trees and bushes for any enemy paying particular attention to the ground almost directly beneath the chopper. While flying past where the VC were located, we were utterly vulnerable with no cover whatsoever, just sitting on the helicopter floor with our weapons pointed towards the ground, terrified that at any moment the ship and ourselves would be raked by automatic weapons fire from the VC on the ground but managing to maintain a deadly resolve to return fire if I spotted their muzzle flashes.

I surely didn't want to get shot in the face or have my insides scrambled by a machine gun round and I surely didn't want the chopper to take a hit and turn this nice cool helicopter ride into a flaming heap of twisted metal on the ground. All I wanted to do was to get out of that jungle and back to base camp. Hell, it was almost Christmas and I wanted to celebrate it like a civilized Christian. That night would be Christmas Eve, wasn't there supposed to be peace on earth? It was supposed to be that but it certainly was not on that little piece of Earth. We flew through the ambush site with my heart beating strongly, desperately searching for the enemy below, but there was no fire from the ground and within five seconds we were away from the most serious threat. The rest of the Company was evacuated from the area without incident. I never learned what exactly became of the soldiers who had directly engaged the enemy, never learned if they had taken causalities. Maybe they had, maybe they had KIAs, I don't know. Maybe since it was Christmas Eve headquarters withheld the bad news. I certainly didn't want to know, not then.

Back at base camp, we showered and put on clean clothes. We sat outside our hoochs on sandbags that surrounded a long pit, maybe fifty feet long by eight feet wide by four feet deep. The purpose of that pit was for the whole platoon to jump into it if we were mortared or to use it as a fighting position if the camp was overrun. We started to clean our weapons when a guy came up with a big round galvanized pan into which he poured about three gallons of gasoline. We started to use the gasoline to clean our weapons, which went very well. That gasoline worked much better than regular gun cleaning fluid and there was plenty of it. One of the guys lit up a cigarette and I remarked to him that it probably wasn't a good idea to smoke so close to the gasoline. A few other guys said that it was perfectly safe, that only the vapors were flammable and the wind was blowing the fumes away from us. I disagreed with that theory and a guy said, "OK, Watch this" and he flipped his lighted cigarette into the pan full of gasoline whereupon it was instantly extinguished. That was all I needed for proof. I lit up a smoke myself and that group of men and I sat around smoking and cleaning our weapons.

Now it was Christmas Eve. I had gone down to the Air Force Base PX (Post Exchange) earlier in the afternoon and bought a carton of cigarettes for one dollar and a half-gallon of Gilbys vodka for $1.15, there were no taxes in Viet Nam, and returned to the base area after hitch-hiking a ride on a passing Army supply truck.

Usually, I would have gone downtown to the village of Bien Hoa but I decided to just stay in base camp this time, eat some hot dogs and hamburgers and drink some beer and soda and to then just go back to the hooch and sit on my cot and drink my vodka. In retrospect, I suspect that I was depressed. Depressed that it was Christmas Eve and that I would probably never see my family again. Depressed because I thought of how much pain and emotional suffering my mother and father and sisters and brothers and friends would go through upon learning of my death in Viet Nam, never mind how much suffering I might have to endure before dying from combat related wounds. It was the beginning of a fundamental change in my psychological makeup and health. I considered it, at the time, to be simply an admission of the horrendous reality of the situation.

The platoons hooch was very quiet. Some men were sitting on the floor in a circular group playing cards and gambling, others sat on their cots, playing their tape recorders softly. I just sat there on my cot and smoked and drank my vodka, speaking to no one, until I fell asleep, a very, very, very long way away from the snowy, safe Christmas Eves of my youth in Boston, filled with goodwill and Peace on Earth.

Early after dawn on Christmas day we had revile, a bugle call from a loudspeaker, the purpose of which was to basically order us to wake up. Very soon thereafter we got the word that there would be a mail call, that postal mail had been received and would be dispersed immediately. At any mail call, all of the men would gather in a large group and a Sergeant, usually, would examine the mail that he had and would call out a name. The identified trooper would raise his hand and call out an acknowledgement. The Sergeant would then hand the specified mans mail to troops closest to him and they would then pass it back, from trooper to trooper, until the designated recipient of the mail received it.

My mother had sent to me a letter or a package on a continuous and frequent basis but on that day I had no mail at all. I knew for sure that at least my family would have sent something to me, especially for Christmas. I concluded that the fact that I didn't receive anything from them was probably due to the inefficiency and delay of the Army postal system. But I did get one package. It was totally unexpected. Inside the substantial outer wrappings of the package was a leather shaving kit, a package about the size of less than a half a loaf of bread, with a zipper on top of it. Inside was some soap and toothpaste and shaving supplies. The kit also contained a letter which stated that it was a gift from the People of Boston (Massachusetts) and that the gift was a token of their care, concern and thankfulness of my service. I was really deeply touched that the People of Boston had thought of me serving in Viet Nam. Humbled and grateful to think that total strangers had gone to the time and trouble and expense of sending me a gift and a letter. It was a useful gift too. I carried it with me until the end of my tour of duty in Viet Nam. I would have really liked to have brought it home with me as a memento, but by the time I left Viet Nam it had a hundred years of wear and tear on it, along with funguses and molds and probably viruses that were unknown to North America so I thought it best toleave it.

On Christmas day we probably had turkey and mashed potatoes and bug infested bread from the mess hall, I think, I'm not sure, because I was probably drunk for the whole day. I just wanted to escape my situation, to shut out the remembrances of what I had witnessed and the absolute horror and suffering of what was probably going to happen to me in the immediate future. Probably, I hung around all day in the platoon hooch, listening to music and drinking my vodka, trying to figure out, through an alcohol induced stupidity, when we would have to next go out to the field again. It could be in a week, it could be in an hour. The more it weighed on my mind, the more alcohol I drank.

Chapter 15

OPERATION CEDAR FALLS
IRON TRIANGLE

If you can force your heart and nerve and sinew
To serve your turn long after they are gone,
And so hold on when there is nothing in you
Except the Will which says to them: "Hold on";

Rudyard Kipling "If"

Tank in heavy undergrowth

The next day, while still in base camp, we got our mission briefing for the next combat operation. It was to be an operation into the heart of what is known as the Iron Triangle, an area bounded by three rivers, close to Saigon. The essence of the briefing was that the VC had owned and operated out of this area since World War II. They were heavily dug in, well supplied, and there were a lot of them. It would be the largest operation of this war so far and we would be operating in concert with four or five other major army divisions and brigades along with ARVN troops and Australians and maybe even some Korean troops.

In the morning, we loaded onto trucks and were driven for a half hour or so until we reached a huge grassy area to our right, maybe it was a rice paddy or plantation or farm at one time. We were assigned a helicopter number, my squad being instructed something like "Get onto the fourteenth chopper in line, counting from the first chopper to land, on the second stick, that is, on the line of choppers which would land immediately after the first formation of helicopters had landed, loaded up with troopers and departed.

Suddenly and unexpectedly, we heard a substantial noise of rumbling aircraft approaching. I was taken aback when I saw thirty helicopters, flying in single file formation, that suddenly appeared above the close tree line. The noise level quickly increased until, as the first chopper flew almost directly over our heads at an altitude of about a hundred feet, it became a hugely powerful sound. Then the next chopper flew over, and the next, and the next, each one being a little lower and emanating successively more sound and fury.

The helicopter landing was a perfectly orchestrated event and a magnificent display of aviator skill. Each chopper in the line was about sixty feet behind and twenty feet above the chopper in front of it. The lead chopper touched down onto the earth and then each succeeding chopper suddenly flared up and landed, executing the exact flying technique that the chopper in front of it had performed a few seconds before. As they passed nearly overhead it felt like we were inside some kind of huge machine that was a hundred feet wide and four hundred feet long. Our humanness was mixed among the unearthly power and sound and hurricane force winds of the rotors, the roar and scream of the choppers jet engines and the general pops, bangs and cracks made by the roaring, shaking, hugely powerful flying machines. The air itself was shaking, pounding. Amid the terrific blasts of wind and the air pressure changes, the noise from their rotors seemed to go right through my body, powerfully shaking and knocking back and forth the air in my lungs, like X-rays, penetrating my internal organs and bones and muscles. As each chopper passed by there was a left door gunner manning his machine gun and pointing it in our direction to add to the danger and confusion of the situation. My brain function was affected, overwhelmed by the enormity of what was happening, the world had suddenly become surreal.

A large group of the soldiers from my Company quickly ran to and loaded onto the line of choppers, each group in turn, as their assigned choppers touched the earth. Each aircraft took off immediately after it was loaded so that the stick of choppers flew off in the same way that they came in, each one in line, lifting off a few seconds after the one in front of it. It was an awesome display of military hardware and extremely precise and coordinated organization and planning and incredible flying prowess.

We would be on the next flight of choppers. While the first stick of choppers were only about a mile away, flying into battle, another thirty choppers arrived onto the ground. We ran into three hurricanes of noise and wind and threw ourselves quickly and violently aboard the choppers. I could see soldiers were still loading onto the choppers at the back of the stick, while the choppers towards the front of the line were already airborne, nose-down, and on their way into battle. I had never seen an operation of that size. This was going to be a huge operation.

We lifted off and flew at an altitude of about a thousand feet, sitting on the floor of the helicopter with our legs dangling out of the chopper without any restraining straps to prevent us from falling out of the choppers if the pilots deemed it necessary to engage in extreme maneuvers or the chopper was suddenly disabled due to enemy ground fire. We then, without any warning, suddenly came into the landing zone. The only advance warning was that the altitude of the chopper suddenly dropped very rapidly and that we were getting very close to the ground. We touched down and immediately evacuated the airship, running towards the tree line surrounding the LZ.

There was no enemy resistance. Those two paragraphs above do not quite describe the actions and my reactions for that twenty minutes of the assault, before the landing. I had been trying to steel myself for what might happen as we approached the LZ and landed. Indeed, I had tried to steel myself for what might happen on our way to the LZ. We could have easily been shot down or torn up from anti-aircraft fire. The assumption that we would reach the LZ, and then deal with problems was an optimistic scenario at best. I imagined helicopters burning on the landing zone and gunships tearing up the area with rockets and minigun fire and smoke and screams and yelling and blood and severed arms and legs and heads and torn apart soldiers and explosions and heavy enemy incoming small arms and machine gun fire and mortars.

I tried to get my mind right, to be prepared for that, and rev up my adrenaline for what might be a nightmarish fight and scenario. All that went through my mind for a while, but then I just sat back and started to enjoy the ride and the view. I thought, if I am going to be killed or blinded or have my legs blown off in ten minutes, I might as well just smell the roses now.

The landing was uneventful. Upon exiting the aircraft, under great anxiety, we ran about two hundred feet and set up ten feet from the tree line that surrounded the LZ. The helicopters took off and the next flight arrived about ten minutes later. We started to dig in. The Company would spend the night here and then the plan was to send patrols, including the Weapons platoon, into the surrounding jungle on the following day. The plan was for the Company's platoons to patrol all of the next day and then return back to the LZ and use it as a perimeter for that night. The bad news was that my platoon had to go out on a combat patrol, the good news was that if we made it back to the LZ that night we wouldn't have to dig new fighting positions because we could use the fighting positions that we would dig today.

After a half hour after dawn the next morning, the soldiers manning the fighting positions on the perimeter went out into the surrounding jungle to pull in their claymore mines and trip wire flares. One of the guys saw something suspicious deeper in the jungle and went to investigate, then came back and called for us to check out what he had seen. There, a hundred yards from our perimeter was a VC base camp. There were square fighting positions dug into the earth, strung out about ten feet from each other, all of them connected by a trench in a roughly oval overall perimeter configuration. It was a real good thing that it was unoccupied when we landed or our uneventful helicopter assault of the previous day could have turned into what I had feared it might be, a catastrophic destruction of our Company, and especially me personally.

Maybe it was occupied at the time but the noise and movement of all of the choppers suddenly appearing out of nowhere caused them to evacuate the area. Who will ever know what the situation was. If the camp was occupied, and we had engaged in our standard maneuver of patrolling into the jungle soon after landing, the dug in VC would have certainly caused some serious American casualties. We would have been fully exposed on the LZ but the enemy would have been firing from strong fighting positions and in force.

We went on patrols into the surrounding jungle for the next few days. Usually, each evening we would receive a briefing from our squad or platoon Sergeant. Details of what was to be done on the next days mission would be provided and any other additional information would be mentioned. Most of the time those briefings lasted less than three minutes. On the second day of patrolling we came to some small houses made of sticks and sheet metal made of pressed soda cans. Inside was quite a bit of rice in many eighty or hundred pound bags. Much, much more rice than any one family could eat in a year. We got the word to just leave it there and some people would come by later and get it and distribute it to other Vietnamese villages.

Under the roof of the shorter part of the building was a warehouse sized quantity of rice in fifty pound bags. The rice was stacked on the ground in a square 30 feet long on each side and about ten feet high. All of the burlap bags that contained the rice had printed on them "US Dept of Agriculture". I wondered if this was rice that had been directly donated to the Vietnamese from the US in a humanitarian gesture had then been passed to or stolen or extorted by the VC or whether it was Vietnamese rice in reused bags. I surely didn't like the idea that this was rice that had been sent by the US and ended up in enemy hands. We had been told that we were likely to encounter large amounts of VC rice and that any such captured rice would be given to the civilians in the surrounding friendly villages. But now our Company and Battalion and other US groups were finding so much rice that we were told that it was impossible to move and redistribute all of it with our available resources.

We were informed via radio that the rice that we had just discovered could not be redistributed to the local, friendly Vietnamese population. However, we certainly couldn't leave it to feed divisions of the enemy. If we couldn't move it, we were to destroy it. But how do you destroy so much food? You can blow it up, but that only scattered much of the rice and anyways, we didn't carry enough C-4 (an explosive) to have done much harm to the massive amounts of rice that we had found. One way to destroy rice, we had been told in our pre combat operation instructions, was to get it wet, that that would set up a mold on the rice that would make it inedible. This was a huge cache and I certainly did not want it to fall back into enemy hands but I only had two canteens of water and didn't want to use any of it for any reason other than to drink it.

We had been advised of other methods to destroy the rice if we didn't have enough explosives or water to render it unusable to the enemy. So I took it upon myself to destroy the rice in another way that we had learned. That technique was the same as that used for trying to cool down red hot mortar tubes in the middle of a desperate battle. I climbed on top of this huge pile of rice, ten feet tall, and, unfortunately in full view of a number of troopers, unbuttoned my pants and wetted it down, spraying urine in the largest and most effective manner that I could manage, spraying about for maximum effect. Some of the guys on the ground looked at me in a very strange way, I guess they had never heard of that technique. Anyways, I was glad to be able to do my part for the war effort. My Company alone captured seventy tons of rice. I later learned that another 200 tons of rice had been captured by other units. The total for all units on this operation was 3700 tons of rice, that's 7.4 million pounds.

While on a patrol the next day, the line of march quickly started to spread out and go very fast. It was very difficult to maintain contact with the man in front and in back of me. The word was passed up the line several times to slow down but that word probably never reached the front because the line had become broken in several places. After about fifteen minutes of almost running we suddenly stopped and tried to regroup. It took a while but eventually the line was completed except for three guys missing. We stayed in one place for about another ten minutes but had to move on. Now there were three guys out there, by themselves. I worried about them, all alone and lost in the jungle, and wondered if we would ever see them again or ever hear of what had become of them.

After a hard hump all day, we staggered into the clearing where we would set up for the night. In that clearing was the three men who had been lost. Luckily, one of those lost men was a Sergeant who had a map and compass and who had remembered the briefing of the night before as to where we would be setting up on that night. With the map and a compass the three men had made it to this clearing even before the main column had done so and they were just sitting around waiting for us. It was a fortuitous ending to an situation to what I feared might result in an MIA (Missing In Action) forensic expedition twenty years later.

The next day we were humping through an area that had medium sized trees and medium underbrush. The line stopped because someone had discovered a tunnel. The word came down that we would stay in place for a little while to investigate the situation. I fell to the ground and crawled out of my rucksack and just sat on the ground resting, very thankful for the respite from the agony of the hump. A guy close to me said that they had found another tunnel about forty feet from my position so I walked over there to take a look. It looked like a water well to me, roughly hewn, obviously dug by hand, about the size of a manhole cover in diameter and about twenty feet deep. There wasn't any water in it and it looked as if, at the bottom, there might be a continuation of it going horizontally. We wondered what the purpose of it was and, if anything, or anyone, was down there. No one wanted to personally discover the answers.

Someone pointed out that the diameter of the tunnel would pretty much preclude bringing an M-16 down there because no one could maneuver an M-16 around the ninety degree bend at the bottom. A flashlight certainly didn't illuminate the bottom sufficiently because the available sunlight at the top of the tunnel overwhelmed the available light at the bottom of tunnel illuminated by our army flashlights. Some people said that someone could go down there with a .45 (caliber automatic pistol). No one wanted to go down there, including me. We got the word that we would be moving out in five minutes and I certainly did not want to pass up this opportunity to capture or destroy some enemy supplies and weapons that could be used to kill Americans or to capture enemy troops but to go down into that tunnel would have been an absolute horror show.

I really did not want to go down into that deep hole in the ground but, for some reason, I decided to do it. I yelled over to our ammo bearer, "Pierce, give me your weapon, I'm going in." He knew immediately what I meant and walked over to me and handed me his .45 from his shoulder holster. I instinctively ejected the magazine from the weapon and pulled back on the slide. That ejected a round from the pistol. I thought "Good!". Pierce had the weapon loaded for bear and ready to fire. I slid each round out of the magazine, checking for dirt or bits of leaves, making sure that the weapon was clean and ready for action before I descended into that situation. I certainly didn't want to be killed because the weapon or rounds misfired due to being dirty. The magazine and the rounds in it were clean, which was very unusual, but I wiped each bullet on my shirt to clean them more. I wanted to verify for myself that everything was operational before I went down into that tunnel. I then put the seven rounds back into the magazine and put the magazine into the pistol and pulled the slide back and released it. That loaded a round into the chamber.

Then I pulled the magazine out of the pistol and inserted another bullet, replacing the one that had just been loaded up, and then pushed the magazine into the pistol. Now I had one round in the chamber of the pistol, ready for immediate action, and seven rounds in the magazine, eight rounds total, and I was fairly satisfied that the weapon would function as designed if I needed it. I was going into a situation where, without exaggeration, my life may well, and probably would, depend on the functioning of that weapon.

My squad Sergeant gave me his flashlight. I laid on the ground at the edge of the hole and then slowly twisted my body around, allowing my legs to drop into the hole while my upper body was still horizontal on the ground. Then I kicked at the sides of the shaft to get some kind of toeholds to support my body. I then very slowly pushed off. The toeholds supported my weight but I pushed powerfully first one and then the other forearms against the wall, forcing my back against the side of the shaft and basically jamming my body into the hole.

I slowly made my way down. My technique, invented as I went, was to remove one boot from its toehold, then very carefully allow my body to slide downwards about twelve inches, so that one knee was bent at almost a ninety degree angle while the other leg dangled into space. With the lower leg I kicked repeatedly and violently into the side of the wall until I had established what I hoped would be a solid footing. Then, taking advantage of the toehold, I lowered my body again and again kicked strongly and violently with the lower boot to establish another toehold. It was sort of like descending a staircase but instead of putting your right foot on a step and then your left foot on a lower step, it was like putting your right foot onto a step and then putting your left foot onto the same step. That process was a lot slower than was theoretically possible but it was a lot safer and allowed me to rest, to a certain degree, whenever I wanted to. After all, the main principle was not to get to the bottom the fastest, but to get to the bottom safely. I could have easily reached the bottom very quickly, especially if I had lost my traction on the walls and dropped twenty feet straight down in a freefall. As I descended, I noticed that there were already some indentations on the wall of the shaft, toeholds made by the enemy who used that tunnel before me, but they were very shallow and seemed to have been eroded, probably by previous heavy rainfall.

On the way down buckets of dry earth were scraped off from the back of my helmet as I strongly pressed my back and head against the walls. The dirt fell onto my neck, into my shirt and onto the skin of my back. It was a sudden extremely uncomfortable sensation, a distraction just when I was concentrating maximally on the task at hand. I thought, I haven't even reached the bottom yet and this hole was already doing extremely unpleasant things to me. I pushed the distraction out of my mind and directed a hundred percent of my concentration, thoughts and strength to the issue at hand.

Finally I reached the bottom and could stand on the ground, it was a very welcome respite from the struggles to get to the bottom, and the fear, where many times I had lost maximal friction against the walls and thought that I would freefall to the bottom of the pit.

Now I could clearly discern that there was a horizontal tunnel, the length of which I could not possibly know. I stood there for a few moments, contemplating my next course of action, when suddenly I realized that if someone was in the horizontal part of the tunnel I should be getting my body torn to pieces from the knees down by enemy gunfire at any moment. It was a "do or die" situation, right now, or maybe it was "do <u>and</u> die". Also, I realized that if the enemy decided to open up on me with an automatic weapon he would cut me down like a chef cutting up a stalk of celery, beginning with my lower legs and proceeding higher up my body as my lower parts were destroyed and my upper body collapsed under gravity.

A part of my brain screamed "Get out of there!!", "Climb back up into the sunlight!", "You're going to be crippled and destroyed and then killed!!" Another, deeper part of my brain, the Airborne part, told me to keep going, to drive on, to face the horrors that might be in that tunnel, and kill it, or be killed. I quickly crouched down and looked into the horizontal part of the tunnel to see what was in store for me if I continued. It was pitch black darkness after the first foot or so. I had to very much contort my body to be able to put my head in first and then get down on my hands and knees. It required such a contortion that I thought at first that it would be impossible to do if a person was more than five feet tall, but eventually I did it, scraping and hacking at the opening with my bayonet and kicking and punching at the earth until I could eventually squeeze my body into the opening. Once in, and on my hands and knees, the dimensions of the horizontal tunnel allowed only an inch or two of space above my back and a few inches of space on each side. Once the tunnel was entered, it was impossible to turn around. I shined the flashlight and thought that I could see the end of the tunnel about thirty feet away but I wasn't sure of that at all, so I crawled slowly forwards to make sure.

I crawled into the tunnel for about twenty feet when I thought I saw something on the floor. As I got closer I saw that it was the skeleton of a large rat or some other animal. He had probably fallen into the tunnel and couldn't get out. Now I began to wonder if I could get out. I crawled a few more feet and saw that the tunnel ended. It was empty of equipment or supplies, and, thankfully, of any enemy soldiers or booby traps. It was impossible to turn around so I started to crawl backwards which required quite a bit of time and trouble.

Finally, finally, I caught a glimpse of ambient sunlight when I was a few feet from the vertical part of the tunnel. After a series of extreme bodily contortions, at the intersection of the horizontal and vertical aspects of the tunnel, I managed to finally stand up. I then began the climb upwards, again kicking strongly at the footholds and trying to wedge myself in the hole with my arms and back in case I slipped. I wondered, if the footholds failed, how I would get out. I figured that if worse came to worse, the guys above could tie their shirts together and make a kind of rope. One thing was very certain I now realized. If someone encountered a problem in one of those tunnels it would take quite a long time to get out of harms way, a certain delay that could not possibly be aided from anyone on the ground above. The delay of a just a few seconds, trying to escape to the sunlight above, could make a huge difference in the life of a soldier. I finally reached the top, executing a particularly precarious maneuver at the last moment to finally extricate myself. I laid on the ground for a full half-minute, legs still dangling into the well, marveling that I was still alive after such an adventure.

We got the word about five minutes later to move out. I thought to myself that we had just had a twenty minute break to rest and I had spent most of it in that tunnel. Well at least I wasn't humping. A short while later we heard the rumble of heavy machinery, the loud clanking of treads and the sound of very powerful engines. I thought that it was tanks but as we go closer to the sound we encountered some bulldozers. The dozers were busy knocking down the jungle to make a small clearing, probably a resupply and medical evacuation landing zone.

We kept walking but not directly through that rough clearing which would have been easier, but at the very edge of it, through the heavy jungle. I fervently hoped that the dozer operators knew of our presence so close by and wouldn't run us over but through all of the noise and confusion and dust and smoke and a heavy rain of falling bits of leaves and bark and vines and trees I couldn't be sure at all.

About ten minutes later we encountered a dirt road. We shifted direction slightly and began to follow it. After a short time we approached a line of bulldozers in front of us, in the process of making that dirt road that we had followed. The first bulldozer in line would knock down the very large and/or wide trees, the next bulldozer would push aside the downed trees and most of the large bushes and small trees on the ground and the third bulldozer would clean up anything left behind, scraping away everything down to bare earth. The dozers had an infantry unit with them, beating the bush in front and in back and on both sides of their line of travel, providing security for the bulldozers and their operators. It was astonishing to see a cleared path through a heavily grown jungle, cleared away completely right before our eyes. What was, a few minutes previous, very heavy jungle, now had a completely cleared and almost level road of mostly very dense red clay earth running right through it that any vehicle could use.

That evening we set up and dug in for the coming night. We were briefed that the purpose of this operation was not only to search and capture or destroy enemy and enemy equipment in this area, but also to improve access via the newly made bulldozed roads so that Allied forces in the future could more easily bring in troops and equipment and keep this area relatively clear of enemy forces.

Before sunset a chopper came in with hot food. I didn't know it at the time but we would be served a hot meal about every third day of this operation. The food was off-loaded in large, army green, aluminum containers each holding perhaps four gallons of food each one containing one specific food. It had obviously been prepared in a mess hall, probably at base camp. Most of it was disgusting fare, the usual in an Army mess hall, but this stuff seemed to be even inferior to that. However, it was much better than the C-rations that we relied upon most of the time. Sometimes, a trooper could get a little extra mashed potatoes or something if there was some food left over after every man was served.

Sometimes there wouldn't be enough food for everyone and in those cases the food was rationed, sometimes where most troopers got a very meager ration and those at the end of the mess line got nothing at all. Under the very best of circumstances, no one ever received enough food to compensate for the calories expended under even the most lightest days of humping.

In most cases we had to depend upon any C-rations that we carried, that was, if we still had any C-rations remaining after several days without a resupply. Most of us did not and therefore we were seriously hungry most of the time. The United States was spending hundreds of millions of dollars per month for this war, increasing the profit margins of selected corporations, but the reality was that the front line troops, most of the time, didn't have enough food to eat, and any food that we did get was generally of very, very inferior quality.

The chopper this time also dropped off some mail and a Care package. The Care package, as we called it, was a medium sized cardboard box with cigarettes, candy, gum, maybe some toothbrushes and razors and soap. The candy was usually a variety of types. Some if it was some kind of chocolate bars marked "tropical". No one liked those because they had a light brown powdery substance on the surface of it. They simply looked like chocolate bars that had sat around for too long in the sun, shriveled and deformed, with an unappetizing film of brown powder which at first taste was revolting. It most certainly didn't look very appetizing and it was a shock to your tongue and taste when you first took a bite of it. I think that the powder was the cocoa in the chocolate that worked its way to the surface when exposed to high temperatures. I didn't care for them at all, but I still got as many as I could. After a few seconds of taking a bite the bitterness subsided substantially. The bitterness interfered strongly with the sweetness of the chocolate and made them the worse chocolate candy bars ever encountered but I desperately craved the calories that my body could obtain from that candy. Most of my fellow soldiers refused to eat those bars but that made all the more for me. I took all that I could get, in fact, what I ate on combat operations was, to a large degree, some sort of candy.

The next day we went out on patrol again and again we encountered tunnels. The soldiers immediately in front of me pointed out two tunnel entrances that were very close to their positions but they couldn't stop to investigate them because the line of march was proceeding. They had pointed them out only as possible sources of attack by the enemy. I had just passed that spot when the word came down the line that we were stopping the hump so as to investigate numerous tunnel entrances in the area. Obviously, the lead element had passed several tunnels and the decision had been made to stop our forward progress to investigate them. That day I would go down two tunnels. I noticed that while crawling along on my hands and knees in the first tunnel, within the extremely confining, claustrophobic limits of it, that the barrel of my .45 pistol would invariably scrape on the ground and become filled with dirt no matter how diligently I tried to prevent that from happening. I knocked the weapon against my opposite hand and against the floor of the tunnel to try to dislodge some of the dirt but that did not work very well.

I, of course, certainly didn't bring down any gun cleaning instruments or supplies. I never thought that I would need such things. I decided to disassemble the weapon, remove the barrel and blow through it to try to remove at least some of the dirt but suddenly realized that that was a bad idea. I realized that I would look pretty foolish, with a bunch of mechanical parts on the ground, twenty feet underground in a tunnel, with a flashlight under one arm, trying to see what I was doing, if a VC suddenly appeared and rolled a grenade towards me or started to fire point-blank into my head. On the other hand, that was not the time or place to have a weapon that might blow up in your hand if you had to use it. I decided to just keep going deeper into the tunnel and see what happened, I'd simply have to take my chances. Also, I thought that if I have to fire this weapon in this enclosed space, although it wouldn't be the greatest of my worries, it would probably do some very serious and permanent damage to my hearing.

It always felt really good to finally climb out of those tunnels. Later in the war the "tunnel rats" were given special vision equipment to see in the dark and weapons with silencers and other goodies but at this time we didn't have any of those. It was balls out. You went into the tunnels without any special advantage. In fact, the VC had all of the advantages. They were completely familiar with the layout of the tunnel system and could easily just wait until an Allied soldier entered a tunnel and roll a grenade like a bowling ball towards him. The mission of the American "tunnel rat" was to go down into the tunnel and kill or capture anyone down there and/or to discover and destroy any hidden supplies. Most of the time, the basic, essential reality of the mission was to kill the VC before they killed you and at that, any VC in the tunnel had an overwhelming and decided advantage.

I saw several troopers go into those tunnels. When they re-emerged they seemed to be very happy and relieved but I noticed that all of them seemed to have been deeply changed and subtlety but certainly psychologically disturbed by the experience. A soldier who went down into a tunnel was sort of like deliberately going into the Cyclops cave, meeting him, and then somehow miraculously escaping from and/or killing the beast. What would be ones emotions? Joy?, release of fear and anxiety? Those words most certainly do not express the emotion that I, and probably most men felt upon completion of such a mission. Those troopers basically walked right up to a dragon, knowing full well that the dragon could, and will, given half a chance, burn every inch of skin off of their bodies and then the troopers valiantly and selfishly and boldly stuck their bayonet into the throat of the beast, and maybe escaped unharmed. Actually, many of those men did not escape unharmed or alive. Truly, those men were the best that America ever produced.

Later in the day we encountered another tunnel. OK! I was the only person willing to go down into it, but only because no one else seemed to be too keen on doing so. I proceeded down into it just as I had on the previous occasions, each an opportunity to freefall to the bottom and suffer horrible injuries. The vertical part of the tunnel seemed to be deeper than usual, perhaps thirty feet deep. I reached the bottom without incident and then crawled into the horizontal part of it for about fifty feet when all of a sudden I heard someone yell "Ohhhhhhh!!!" It strongly rattled me until I realized that that shout had come from my mouth, involuntarily. While crawling through the tunnel, with an extremely weak flashlight, I suddenly realized that there was another tunnel that was horizontal to the one that I was traversing. The sudden, involuntary shout, was an exclamation of how dangerous that situation was. If a VC had been in that tunnel he could have very easily shot me in the head as I passed by, or could have very easily rolled a grenade into my part of the tunnel and then retreated a few feet into his part of the tunnel. The result would have been that he was completely shielded from the blast of the grenade and I would have taken the full destruction of that device. To say the least, it was tricky going down into those tunnels. Any soldier who did has my greatest respect.

The VC knew the layout of the tunnel systems and in most cases could just wait in a side tunnel for a trooper to crawl past or close and then unload on him before he could even bring his weapon to bear, or simply see the flashlights beam and then reach around a corner and throw a hand grenade. It was basically an almost suicide mission. Many very brave troopers willingly accepted the risks, and many very brave troopers lost their lives, or were wounded horribly or lost their vision or hearing and/or their sanity.

The next day I was selected, for some unknown reason, by my squad Sergeant, to ride along with four other guys on top of a tank. The tank would provide security for the bulldozers and the infantry on the ground would provide security for the tank and the dozers. The rest of the guys in my platoon would hump the bush. I would ride on top of the tank and the tank would hump my rucksack, thankfully. The tank would also carry parts of the other mortar platoon sections equipment and most of the mortar ammo that the platoon usually humped.

I and the men riding the tanks were tasked with keeping an eye on the mortar pieces and ammo that would thankfully not have to be manually carried by the soldiers of the Mortar platoon. Our other task was keep an eye out for any enemy threats from our elevated perch on the tanks. Thankfully, I would not have to hump the bush and my squad would not have to hump the 81mm mortar pieces and the platoon would not have to hump its associated, ass-kicking ammo load. Actually our task was to look for enemy threats to the tank, and, secondarily, threats to the infantry. Actually, the main threats to the tanks were buried, huge, unexploded artillery shells, booby trapped to explode when heavy armor passed over them which were impossible to discern.

We were riding for about three hours when suddenly the tank stopped very abruptly with a loud "thunk" that pushed the bodies of the riders violently and unexpectedly forward. It sounded like and felt like we had hit a solid steel bridge abutment. The driver of the tank tried to power over it, its hugely powerful engine now roaring at full power, accompanied by massive clouds of black smoke. But it couldn't be done. Obviously something had gone terribly wrong. We jumped off of the tank and saw that it had hit a termite mound, about three feet wide and about two and a half feet tall. We couldn't believe that it had stopped a tank. We climbed back onto the tank and yelled down into the hatch, telling the driver what the obstruction was. The driver backed up about five feet and charged the mound at full speed, its immensely powerful engines roaring, only to be stopped instantly and completely by the termite mound, the sudden stopping nearly throwing everyone off of the tank. The driver repeated that technique three or four times but finally was forced to admit defeat and back up his tank and drive around it.

We soon came upon a huge stand of bamboo. That bamboo was about a hundred feet tall. Some of the individual stalks were probably six inches thick at the bottom and most of the stalks were intermingled and entwined with each other as they rose up together, especially about forty feet or so above the jungle floor. I thought, that where I grew up in Boston, the next door neighbor had weeds in her yard that looked something like bamboo to a youngster. Back then, I thought that I'd like to go somewhere, sometime in my life, where real bamboo grows. Now I realized that this was much more awesome than I could have ever possibly imagined as a child. The bulldozers were in front of us but I guess that the tank that we were riding on had received orders to go to the right, to just push though the jungle, outside of the area that the dozers were clearing, probably to provide flank security to the dozers.

The tank crew could have gone around the stand of bamboo but choose to just charge straight at it and through it. The tank easily knocked down some smaller strands of bamboo but as it entered the larger grove it abruptly decelerated to a very slow crawl. The treads churned deeply into the ground while gaining only inches forward perhaps every fifteen seconds. The tank tried to push down the main grove of bamboo but the vegetation would not yield an inch forwards progress to the tank beyond a certain point despite the insistence and assault of a forty five ton mechanical monster with a twelve hundred horsepower diesel engine that was emitting an ear deafening roar at full throttle. The bamboo started to bend downwards as the tank actually began to rise vertically, trying to actually climb up it.

At the top, the branches of the individual bamboo plants were very much entangled with each other. As the tank moved forward, extremely slowly, under full power, chewing up the ground under its tremendous treads, moving only a few inches every ten seconds, the bamboo came down all around us and on top of us. It was impossible to push it off of us or away from the tank since essentially, the hugely powerful engine of the tank was pulling it on top of us. The thick, woody shoots of bamboo were pulled down upon us, entwining our bodies and limbs, pulled down over our bodies, crushing us as severely and as surely would thick steel cables. They would surely kill us unless drastic measures were taken immediately.

Some of the guys on top of the tank started to yell for the driver to stop, the loudness and shrillness of their shouts increasing in direct proportion to the killing power of the bamboo that was crushing us. A couple of them took off their helmets which wasn't an easy thing to do at all because of the crushing bamboo that enveloped our bodies. Those few who managed to do so smashed and banged their helmets onto the hatch and body of the tank in a desperate attempt to attract the attention of the tank commander, who was safely locked up inside of the tank. Something worked, because the tank suddenly stopped.

If the tank had gone another five feet forwards, all of us would have been horribly crushed, mangled and/or killed by the six-inch thick bamboo crushing down and around against us. My left thigh had a piece of bamboo on it. My leg was crushed, the bamboo stalk had surely crushed my leg. It was only about two or three inches thick, about the thickness of my thigh bone. Surely, I thought, that that was the end of my leg, it would surely have to be amputated later I thought or it would be traumatically amputated right now because surely all of my muscles and nerves were destroyed.

As the bamboo came pushing and crushing against us, I thought to grab my rucksack and its attached entrenching tool, to chop against the encroaching bamboo, wishing fervently that I had a machete but quickly realizing that even a machete was not up to the job of trying to save us from this thick, very quickly encroaching, woody, crushing onslaught. I thought to get the entrenching tool and use it to chop the bamboo that was now horribly crushing my leg and the legs and chests and heads and bodies of all of the men on the tank, but in the confusion of the huge amount of thick stalks and leaves that was now curling and crushing us upon the tank, it was impossible to figure out where my rucksack was, never mind to find it and then to reach it. Anyway I figured, my rucksack was probably pinned under ten thousand pounds of jungle vegetation.

Thankfully, someone within the tank had heard our cries and the banging of helmets on the steel and stopped the machine. One of the tank crew tried to open the hatch but could only raise it about two inches because of the bamboo crushing down upon us, that was holding it mostly closed. Men on top of the tank frantically shouted to "Stop the tank!!, Stop!, Stop!!!". When the tank stopped its forward motion, several soldiers yelled loudly, "Go back! Very slowly!!" Now that the tank hatch was opened, even a little bit, we could assume that the tank crew could hear our pleas and instructions. As the tank backed up slowly, all of us frantically tried to get off of the tank, to jump off or just fall off of it, onto our heads if necessary, but each one of us were pinned against the metal of the tank and the bamboo. Some were only held by a boot, others were crushed by the bamboo upon their chests and couldn't breath, others were strangled by the crushing force of the bamboo upon their necks. As the tank retreated and the crushingness was reduced, some of the soldiers tried to jump off of the tank, but most of them were held hanging upside down, parts of their bodies still restrained by the bamboo and they then found themselves in a position, upside down, staring directly into the churning tank treads that were now a very few inches from their faces.

That same situation happened again and again. Not to me but to other troopers in my Battalion and Brigade. When the pressure and confinement of the bamboo slackened, some soldiers fell off of the tank and then some of them onto the churning treads. They had avoided the strangulation and/or crushing death upon the tank only to be traded five seconds later to a very possible death of being torn apart and crushed by the threads of the tank.

The tank reversed course, very, very slowly for fifteen feet and the crushed and wounded troopers dropped off of the tank like flies that were hit with a poisonous spray. Some of them were severely injured, their limbs and bodies destroyed by the crush of the heavy wood and thickness and toughness of the heavy jungles bamboo. You wouldn't think that the clash between a stand of bamboo and a twelve hundred horsepower engine and a hundred thousand pounds of hardened steel would be much of a contest, but the fact of the matter was that the jungle very nearly killed everyone on that tank. It seriously wounded two of them, in a thirty second encounter, and very nearly killed all of us who had been riding on top of that monstrous machine.

Like me, all had made a decision to stay on top of the tank when we first saw the bamboo stand, assuming that the tank crew would seek another forward path, a safer one, or be ensured that the tank crew knew what they were doing. Obviously the tank crew thought that they would just simply mow down that stand of bamboo. That was a hugely mistaken assumption on their and our part. The tank crew was securely locked up into their machine and were totally oblivious to what was happening to their passengers riding atop the tank.

The tank crew proceeded forward, with their faces and bodies securely protected within four inches of specialized, hardened armored steel, completely oblivious to the reality and horrors to which their passengers, on top of the tank, were subjected to. The tank commander was unaware of the horrifying and desperate situation of the Infantrymen who were riding on top of his tank. No one riding on the tank had immediate access to a machete. Someone had the idea to take out an entrenching tool and cut at the vines and yelled to us to employ that devise, but no one could reach such a tool in time to use it, such was the overwhelming, overpowering, complete envelopment of the bamboo.

The only thing that saved us was intervention from God Himself. As the tank backed up, very slowly, one man was freed and he grabbed onto some stalks that were crushing the man beside him and tried to push them aside. Other soldiers struggled mightily to try to free their fellow crushed soldiers even as other bamboo was pulled down from the rear that directly threatened their lives, very seriously and powerfully.

It was sort of like pushing someone out of a car at forty miles per hour when the car was engulfed in flames. He might well die from the fall but he would most definitely die if he stayed in the car. While all of that was happening, any soldier who was somewhat freed began to chop at the bamboo with machetes and entrenching tools if they could possibly reach such a tool, most of us could not. Most of the chopping to free trapped soldiers occurred after some of us somehow were freed from the tank and had jumped or fallen off of the tank, in most cases that was because that was the only time that we had an opportunity to reach a rucksack to obtain a cutting weapon. One of the soldiers managed to pull his M-16 free of the bamboos overwhelming net of power and actually began firing his gun into the crushing bamboo, trying to cut it with bullets and therefore prevent it from killing other soldiers aboard the tank. The bamboo was almost certainly going to cripple them permanently, if it didn't kill them, but he directed his firepower to save other soldiers who were only seconds away from death.

Eventually, all of us fell or jumped off of the tank. Everyone of us were damaged and wounded by the crush of the bamboo, some of us much more seriously damaged than others. We sat on the ground for about five minutes trying to get ourselves together and evaluating the situation and trying to recover from the damage that had been done. No one had been killed, in fact it looked as if everyone was basically all right except for the two soldiers who were unable to even walk, due mostly to their crushing lung and chest and neck injuries.

A number of troopers, myself included, thought that things would be OK, in the scheme of things, for now, because we still had the tank to ride on and hopefully we would regain the full use of our limbs after another few hours of riding on this tank rather than humping a load on the ground. The fact of the matter was that the two of the most injured soldiers would have to be med-evaced by helicopter due to their injuries. We remained sitting on the ground while the tank charged at the bamboo a few more times at full throttle and was repeatedly stopped dead in its tracks, even with a fifty foot pathway to try to get up to full speed, the driver pushing his engine to its limit, but the tank simply could not bull its way through.

My crushed leg was beginning to have strange sensations. It had been completely dead to any feelings for a while and I thought the new sensations were maybe blood returning to the limb or nerves returning to the proper size. I could not walk at all, just hobble a few steps. I should call over a medic I thought. Maybe I could be med-evacked out of here, I certainly was not a very effective soldier if I couldn't walk. But to my great amazement I found that after a while that I could walk. Just not very well, but the leg seemed to be getting better.

The tank commander got orders to go around the stand of bamboo and we got orders to get off of the tank and to hump on the ground until we could meet up with the tank again, if we ever met up with that tank again. We pulled our rucksacks down from the tank and began humping with the Infantry. It was horribly, murderously hot in the open sunlight of scraggly jungle and bushes and my crushed left leg seriously hobbled me. The line was going very slow, which was good because I really don't think that I could have kept up with the usual speed of forward motion because I was limping severely and was continuously worried that I might just collapse onto the ground because of my damaged left leg, it was failing me badly. The pain and distress and suffering was absolutely beyond horrible.

After about twenty minutes, we saw the tank again and were ordered to re-board it, with our rucksacks. I'm pretty sure that I would have dropped out of the line of march if I had to hump the rest of the day. That crushing bamboo on top of the tank had done some very serious damage to my left leg but within two days it would be relatively OK. Except that during those next two days the crush injury would cause me very great pain, continuously.

The next day I rode on the tank again. Tanks and bulldozers were used to make roads but also to destroy enemy base camps that we encountered but I don't think that it did much good because each enemy camp could be dug out again in a few days if not within a week with enough manpower. If we encountered an enemy base camp, most of them were really just a nighttime fighting positions for a VC Company or more, the tanks or bulldozers would simply ride over the trenches and fighting positions, and go forward and reverse several times, collapsing the positions and mostly filling them in with dirt.

The next day I rode again but this time atop a bulldozer. It was to be a straight search and destroy mission. We were assigned a tank to back us up should any problems occur. That tank would travel behind us or to our flank, ready to support us if we encountered any serious problems. Of course, I thought that the attached infantry to my bulldozer was assigned the exact same mission should our brother tank and its infantry encounter any serious problems.

In a magazine that I read months later, there was an article that started with:

> **The dry season had come to the Iron Triangle above Saigon and the temperature had reached 115. Since early light company B, of the 173rd's 4th Battalion, had been plodding through the thick growth —acting as security for bulldozers that were clearing out the Red sanctuary. By high noon, January 16, 1967, the sun was beating unmercifully on the perspiring troops.**

That paragraph sort of provides a description of what it was like on the ground, here's a description of what it was like from my perspective as an Infantryman who was there:

After a while, we encountered very heavy underbrush amongst scattered trees that were about twenty feet tall. It was blazingly hot in the full sun as I and two other Infantry soldiers rode along on top of the dozer. As hot as it was, at least we weren't humping our rucksacks and therefore I had a relatively clear and rational mindset to evaluate the scene around me of the Infantrymen on the ground.

As we proceeded, slightly faster than the Infantry beside us, I could clearly see those soldiers who seemed to be on the edge, or beyond, in some cases way beyond, complete and utter exhaustion and heat stroke, immersed in a world of horrible pain and suffering, beating through the bush next to the tank. For about an hour, as I sat on the dozer as it drove through the underbrush, I could clearly see the Infantry, sometimes no more than eight feet from the dozers treads, slogging alongside, baking in the direct sunlight.

I recognized some of them as soldiers from my own platoon. It was a horrible sight, beyond horrible, way beyond horrible. Those men looked as if they were in Hell and were being horribly punished for their sins. But their particular section of Hell seemed to be not quite as hot as a furnaces direct fire, but horribly hot and humid, a uniquely particular type of torture and pain, beyond the scope of a humans endurance or a civilians imagination. I suddenly realized that how they looked was how I and everyone in the Company usually looked most of the time while beating the bush. The suffering was beyond description.

They pushed through a sea of extremely dense bushes with the full sun scorching down upon their bodies. Those men looked to be way beyond the edge of utter desperation and exhaustion and pain and suffering. They were men pushing on under extremely, unbelievably cruel conditions, tormented and tortured with every step. But they pushed on, step after step after step, under conditions that are impossible to describe with words. I stared at them, for a few minutes at a time, horrified at the ghastly sight of men in the deepest throes of wretchedness and agony. They looked like they had died weeks ago and were now on their labors in Hell. Their suffering must have been unimaginably horrible. That description is not a rhetorical flourish, not by any means, words alone cannot describe the unimaginable agony and suffering of those soldiers which was a common day to day, week after week affliction for the common American Infantryman. I thought that if the American public had any slightest idea of what they were requiring of their sons and brothers and fathers that there would be a serious re-evaluation of the entire situation. I thought that at that moment some politician was sitting in an air-conditioned office, after a three martini lunch, and was giving a speech that America had to lead the world. I hope, I really hope that he didn't realize what his words required of soldiers, but he should have known.

About two hours later the line of men stopped as did the bulldozer that we were riding on. The word was passed that the front of the line had encountered booby traps, then the word was that a white phosphorous round booby trap had been tripped and there were injuries. We got the word that they were evacuating casualties. After about ten minutes a bulldozer approached our position from the front of the line, traveling in a direction that was opposite to our line of march.

On board was the operator/driver and two Infantrymen. As the bulldozer approached us, I could see two soldiers sitting bolt upright on the seat. They wore just their uniforms, no load bearing gear or bandoliers nor were they carrying weapons. They weren't even wearing their helmets. All of their equipment and rucksacks, I thought, was probably on the back of the bulldozer. I thought that that was a huge violation of protocol. They had their fore arms and hands held out in front of them, their hands hung limply downwards. As we got closer I noticed that on their arms and hands and faces was a large amount of some sort of white cream that a medic must have administrated, to slow the hellish chemical that, given access to oxygen, would slowly burn its way through their skin and muscles and even their bones.

I realized that those men were beyond being capable of observing protocol. They had been horribly and seriously wounded and the chemical would just even more destroy their bodies without immediate medical help. They were incapable of supporting a fire fight, Hell, they were probably incapable of living for more than the next thirty minutes if they didn't receive very serious professional medical care. Even if they did survive their wounds, I thought, they would still most certainly be seriously scarred, permanently, physically and psychiatrically for the remainder of their lives. What a horrible nightmare I thought their lives would be, for those poor guys, assuming that they would survive their injuries. The extent of their horrible, disfiguring injuries would be with them for the rest of their lives and to my terrifying realization knew that the same could occur to me at any second.

That was very bad. The burning of the white phosphorous would have been slowed down by the ointment but as soon as that cream wore off, it would flare up and burn through their skin deeper and deeper, and into their bones. Those guys were two Paratroopers who had taken a face full and hands full of white phosphorous. Of course nothing else mattered to them. They were probably permanently and completely blinded. I thought that their faces looked weird, probably just dirt I thought at first. But as they passed us I could see that their faces were actually melted, like their faces had been made of wax and placed close to a fireplace. It was beyond horrifying."Maintain, Maintain" I thought,"Don't let it throw you". I guessed that if I was in their place that I wouldn't care much for the niceties of military protocol. I would just realize that I was permanently blinded and that I would look like a monster to everyone in civilian life. Their suffering had ended in this land and they would begin their unique suffering of another kind in the civilized world.

They looked like they were in abject shock, which undoubtedly there were, with a thousand yard stare. They must have thought that their future life would just consist of many, very painful operations, and a lifetime of physical disfigurement but no amount of operations would restore them from their blindness. I thought that either one of those guys could have been me or someone in my squad. I thought that if I was one of those guys, that it would be much better if I was just killed outright and not have to endure another sixty years of abject misery.

I didn't like the fact that I was carrying a WP(white phosphorous) grenade on my belt. My squad Sergeant had received it on a helicopter resupply and had adamantly insisted that I carry it. It was my responsibility, supposedly, as assistant gunner on the mortar crew, to employ it, dropping it down the barrel of the mortar, to destroy the mortar if we were ever to be over-run, thus denying the guns use to the enemy. To my realization and horror however, I realized that an enemy bullet could crack that grenade open that was attached to my LBG and ruin me, to say the least. That grenade could be used defensively, thrown at the enemy, but you would have to have a thirty yard clear opening to throw it or its detonation could easily destroy yourself and others around you, terribly.

The word was passed for the bulldozer to proceed to the front of the line. We worked our way up to where the line made an almost ninety degree turn to the right. From that position, I could see that there were men in the bush, probably the furthest away were about a hundred feet from the turn. There might have been other men deeper into the bush but the foliage was so thick that I couldn't see them. Other guys, close to that turning point, told the driver that they had stumbled into an area filled with an absurd number of bobby traps and mines and that they did not want to try to go any further through that area. We were ordered to get off of the dozer and to take up positions on top of a tank. The soldiers close by told the tank commander that they wanted the tank to crash its way forward, so that it would set off any booby traps and then the infantry could follow in its wake.

The booby traps seemed to be grenades and small mortar rounds so that the tank crew should be OK if they stayed sealed inside the tank with all hatches shut. After a quick discussion amongst the soldiers riding atop the tank, we decided to dismount for this phase of the operation. After all, small mortar rounds that were booby trapped and set off by the threads of the tank would not harm the tank at all because the tank crew was protected by armor that was four to six inches deep. However, such a munition that exploded six feet away from the tank would likely cause all manner of casualties to those soldiers that were riding atop of it.

It sounded like a very good idea to me for the tank to proceed and set off any booby traps but the driver refused to go further. Me and a few other guys on top of the tank told the tank commander in no uncertain terms to proceed forward, to trip the anti-personnel mines and traps that might kill or injure my Infantrymen friends on the ground. In fact our demeanor and language was such that I fully expected to be court-martialed later on for speaking to a superior officer in such a way. But it made no difference to me. I was not going to allow my friends on the ground to be killed because that tank commander was afraid of hearing loud noises.

The tank commander strongly suggested that if there were that many anti-personnel traps and mines then there were probably mines set up for heavy armor (tanks) also. He claimed, probably rightfully so, that the VC were known to pick up un-exploded artillery shells and even five hundred pound bombs and rig them to detonate only under tons of pressure, like from a tank, booby traps that were specifically designed to only kill tanks and their crew rather than waste the huge explosive to kill only a few infantrymen.

I jumped off the tank and spoke to some of the Infantrymen who had been beating the bush. They told me that there were all kinds of booby traps in that area. I asked them how they knew that and they pointed out three booby trap trip wires with their accompanying explosives within twenty feet of me. That very immediate area was forested with bushes that were perhaps three to six feet high and with very long vines, hundreds of them, of various sizes but mostly very thin, snaking along the ground, close to the ground, through the bushes and on top of the bushes. Most vines were intertangled with many other vines. About a hundred feet away were large trees and heavy jungle.

I couldn't see the trip wires around me at first, until one guy pointed his finger at a wire about three feet away. I still couldn't see it, so the guy moved his finger closer and closer to the wire while I moved closer and closer to him to see what he was pointing out. Only when his finger was an inch away from the wire and I was about four feet from his finger, could I finally make out the very thin, dull black wire. Even then I could only see about a foot of the wire as it led off into the morass of underbrush and vines, to the explosives somewhere in there.

The soldiers who were forty feet in front of me were right in the middle of an area that had a huge number of booby traps. It was overkill really. The VC had set up a field of booby traps so close together as to prevent anyone from proceeding through that area. One tenth of that number of booby traps would have stopped an Allied advance in their tracks for a substantial amount of time. I wondered what was so important in that area that the enemy went to such extraordinary extremes to protect it, to keep us away from it. It was some kind of miracle that those guys had already walked through that area and had only taken the two causalities, although they had been horribly injured due to the white phosphorus(WP). The fact that this VC booby-trapped minefield contained not only high explosives but also WP indicated that they meant not only to kill many of us and slow our forward progress but also to demoralize us with horrendous causalities.

A Sergeant pointed out a grenade attached to a trip wire and pulled out his .45 pistol and aimed his weapon at it. I yelled for him to stop!! I told him that if he shot it it will explode. I told him that that would kill him and the guys around him, including me. But he said, "No, the. 45 will break open the grenade but it won't explode". He then proceeded to pull the trigger, hitting the grenade squarely. He was correct. The grenade vanished into pieces into the underbrush from the .45 round but it didn't explode.

We stayed there for about five minutes when suddenly there was an explosion about fifty feet away from me. Everyone froze in place, afraid to make any move at all for fear of setting off another booby trap or mine. I could see some smoke in the area of the explosion. There was an unnatural, absolute silence for about ten seconds. Suddenly, from the direction of the smoke and explosion came an eerie voice of a man calling for help. The voice was strong but there was just something very wrong about it. He cried, "Help me .... Help me .... God help me .... Oh please .... Please .... God help me!!"

I didn't know at first whether a hidden enemy soldier had fragged him with a grenade or he had tripped a booby trap or stepped on a mine but in the ensuing seconds there was no gunfire so I assumed that there were no enemy troops close by. No one wanted to move. No one really could move or do anything to help him immediately because of the extreme danger of detonating another enemy explosive. A couple of soldiers shouted "Don't move!!"

I told myself that I cannot help him. I told myself that if I attempted to go to his aid that I would be killed or maimed by tripping another booby trap. I told myself that if I tripped a booby trap in an attempt to aid him that the booby trap might not only kill or maim me but also kill or wound other soldiers that were close by. But I noticed that there were only a few soldiers between me and the injured man. After a few seconds, I just couldn't stand to listen to his cries for help.

If the explosion was due to a close by VC who had tossed a grenade, I figured that the wounded man would be helpless against another grenade or an enemy burst of gunfire to kill him. But I couldn't help him, no one could help him, at least not right away. It would require many, many minutes for anyone to very slowly make their way to his position through all of the trip wires.

Something came over me. I looked at my rifle for some unknown reason and then at the ground two feet in front of me, unconsciously and involuntarily inhaling a huge amount or air and forcefully exhaling it. Suddenly a voice in my brain shouted: "Do it!" I started to somewhat gallop, half running, half jumping, half leaping through the undergrowth that was about two feet tall. I thought that that was some sort of tactic, some glimmer of logic to this. I figured that if I encountered a trip wire, maybe I would just push it down to the ground, stretching in only six inches, instead of walking or running where if a trip wire caught my boot would it would pull it several feet and then cause it to detonate. Of course, if someone just touched a trip wire, just slightly, pulling it a few inches or less, it would usually detonate instantly. There were panicked shouts of "Stop!!" and "You'll kill us!!" and some other words that didn't register in my brain. I was determined to try to help that man if it was the last thing I ever did on this Earth, and I realized that there was a fifty-fifty chance that it would be the last thing that I ever did.

Finally I reached him, after half a lifetime where I rightfully feared that each step would produce an explosion that tore me into pieces. He was lying on the ground. The earth around him had been swept clean of all vegetation where the explosion occurred, the ground was just bare, packed down brown earth, not even a single leaf in an area about four feet wide and eight feet long. The wounded soldier was lying at the far end of the clearing.

He looked directly at me but I don't know if he even knew I was there. He was mournfully calling for help. He seemed to know that he was beyond help from other soldiers because he now called only to God to help him. I detected some movement about seventy feet away and someone yelled, "Don't touch him!", "Don't touch him at all!!" I wanted to do something, anything, to help him but I suddenly realized that I didn't know what to do or where to begin. I figured that I would leave him alone for the moment and turned my attention to the surrounding jungle, crouching slightly and pointing my weapon outbound, searching for any movement, trying to at least provide some security since this would be a good opportunity for the VC to attack us and especially attack the guy lying helpless on the ground.

I stared at the Paratrooper writhing on his back, lying on the ground but couldn't see any blood. He still had his load bearing gear attached to his body but his rucksack and weapon and helmet were missing, obviously blown away somewhere into the bushes by the explosion. I almost said to him "Hey man, I think you're all right!" I thought that the explosive that he had set off had maybe just scared him badly, maybe it was pure explosive, without any shrapnel, that might explain why I didn't see any blood on him at all.

Then I realized that if it was just pure explosive it could easily have inflicted fatal wounds to his brain and internal organs just by the concussion, also he could have been hit in the back but I could not see if that was the case because he was laying on his back with his legs off of the ground, knees pointing straight into the air, his legs moving as if he was pedaling a bicycle or doing some sort of dance, some kind of dance of death I imagined.Then he started to shake violently, a vicious shivering that wracked his entire body.

Suddenly I saw another soldier about eighty feet away, walking very quickly, given the circumstances. He moved through the very thick undergrowth, about five feet tall and full of vines and booby trapped wires, in a sort of serpentine fashion, trying to detect any trip wires with every bit of concentration that he possessed but with the full intent of reaching the wounded soldier as quickly as possible. I thought that he was remarkably courageous to move at such a speed through such a very dangerous situation. It would have been impossible for him to detect a trip wire if he moved at anything more than a few feet a minute but he did. I think he was the Company medic. It took him only about a minute to reach my position. His bravery was astounding.

When the medic arrived he threw his green nylon medical kit bag onto the ground and tore it open. He kneeled on the ground and put his arm behind the wounded soldiers back, lifting the injured troopers head and shoulders a little off of the ground. I wondered why the Medic wasn't immediately applying medical techniques.The scene reminded me of what it would look like if a mother came upon the dead body of her child, killed violently, knowing that he is dead and just wanting to somehow make him comfortable in death.

By now, the soldiers closest to us were making their way to our area, very, very slowly, examining every inch of ground around and in front of them before each slow and deliberate step. I looked back down at the man on the ground and couldn't believe my eyes.Ten seconds before he looked OK, now he was covered in blood from head to toe, every inch of his clothing saturated with blood, he looked like he had been dipped into a vat of blood. His bare arms looked as if someone had taken a butcher knife and scooped out very many big pieces of flesh, I suspected that the rest of his body looked the same and was afraid that the back of his body was much worse. I couldn't understand why those wounds were not clearly evident when I first reached the man. I suspected that the explosion had caused so many serious wounds that his body didn't know where to first start bleeding.

The Company Medic reached around and grabbed the wounded mans shirt and violently ripped it open. He then started to apply big battle dressings from his kit. He soon ran out of the huge bandages and called for soldiers to throw him their individual battle dressings which every man carries one on his load bearing equipment, primarily for his personal use.

Soldiers started to throw over their individual battle dressings. I pulled out mine from its container that was attached to my LBG belt and held it out to him but the Medic said to me angrily "I don't want yours!". I still don't know why he said that. Other guys started throwing over their battle dressings, not wanting to take any steps or to move their feet at all. The Medic had applied about fifteen huge dressings, then shouted to everyone, "That's enough, no more!" I guess he couldn't use any more medical supplies on just this one case, since the day was young and there may be a need for many more battle dressings in a little while for other soldiers. I thought to myself, "Hey! Here's a guy who needs heroic medical help and supplies. Don't let him die!". But I also realized that we had to conserve the medical supplies if we were to save others as the day went on.

While the medic was working, the guys trying to make their way over towards us finally made it, but kept about six feet away. They could see the wounded man on the ground and all of the blood and it seemed that they did not want to get any closer to that circle of horrors. They stared for about a minute, then they and others started to very slowly and carefully search and clear an area for a path with which to carry the wounded soldier to the dirt road without getting him and others killed by another enemy explosive. When it was almost verified that there were no booby traps in the very immediate area, the wounded guy was picked up and carried to the dirt road and then placed on another bulldozer, carried away from this area and towards an area where a "dust-off" chopper might land. (Note: "dust-off" is a radio code word for a medical evacuation helicopter)

While the officers were still figuring out how the rest of us we were going to extradite ourselves from this area of scores of booby traps and trip wires everywhere, there was suddenly a loud explosion about a hundred feet from me. I thought at first that it was another booby trap that someone had tripped, but then I heard some very short whistles followed immediately by explosions. We were being mortared. If we stayed here we would die, if we tried to run to seek some cover or to get out of this area, even to lie on the ground, many of us would likely be killed by the booby traps. Among the VC's high explosive mortar rounds they dropped a white phosphorous round about a hundred feet away.

In the area of the latest explosions I saw a soldier just running through the bush, without any equipment, not even his helmet, uttering some sounds that were a cross between a yelling and a screaming hellish despair, the words indecipherable, but filled with terror and horror and agony. Smoke was coming from his shirt and from the front of his body and from his face.

From what I could see, most of the left side of his face had been destroyed. There was just three intersecting dark red areas that seemed to have been deeply gouged out, white smoke issuing from the wounds in his flesh, he was being burned to death. He shot a quick glance towards me, and I could see that the other side of his face had big black gouges, deeply burned into the skin and I could see the muscles and bone of his face. His neck and the top of his chest were a deep red, blackish color, horribly destroyed. His shirt looked as if a large section of the front of it had been burned away, the edges of it ragged and black.

It looked as if part of his shirt had been thrown into a fire. Most of his nose was destroyed, what little that was left of it was horribly blackened. He just came running and crashing through the bushes and booby traps, completely unmindful of the dangers, charging ahead, waving his hands up and down on straightened out arms that were outstretched before him, like a completely panicked, horribly, horribly pained, some sort of horribly maimed and tortured Frankenstein in unbearable, horrific pain. He probably was blind, his eyes and nose and face horribly destroyed by that damnable white phosphorous. He ran for about sixty feet, his arms outstretched and his gait like that of a horribly stricken or disabled person, some sort of a Frankenstein in Hell. Then he just suddenly seemed to trip or fall, arms outstretched, and fell face first directly onto the ground. I couldn't see him but it seemed that he didn't move at all or utter another sound after that. More explosions rocked the area as the VC hit our positions with mortars. We were completely helpless and defenseless against their attack because the VC mortar crews were many hundreds of yards away, hidden deep in the surrounding jungle. I don't really remember that part very well, and I cannot remember why the mortaring and sniper fire stopped but I think that an air strike was called onto the enemy mortar positions and they were silenced after about five minutes.

We eventually, slowly and very carefully, backtracked out of that area. I called out to the Infantry to my left that there was a trooper over there who was probably dead, to check it out. They replied that they knew about it and yes, he was definitely dead. I got back on the tank to continue the patrol, but this time the tank took a slightly different direction. At first we just waited there for another fifteen minutes while I wondered what the hold up was. I asked about the guy who had been running with a face full of WP. Wasn't there anyone who was going to check him out? I was told he was already checked out. He was dead for sure, the hold up had nothing to do to the evacuation of his body through the booby trap trip wires. I guess that we were just basically waiting in case other soldiers were killed or wounded trying to evacuate that body, in which case we would provide security for them. Whatever the VC were trying to hide or protect with that absurd amount of booby traps and laid in mortar coordinates, I will never know. The cost of finding out the answer was just too much.

Later that day, me and the crew that were riding atop the tank were given orders to dismount from the tank and so we became straight infantry again. After about twenty minutes we came upon another tunnel. Again no one wanted to go down into it so I volunteered to do the job. I got a flashlight, a .45 automatic hand gun and stuck a bayonet in my pocket. That tunnel was very tricky getting down, the footholds were very poor and I had to strain with almost all of my strength to push my back against one wall and kick viciously, trying to get a foothold. I almost fell straight down three or four times, sometimes falling four feet before managing to stop the fall, each time narrowly averting a plunge that would cripple or kill me.

I finally reached the bottom, breathing hard due to the desperate physical exertions of my decent. My heart was racing wildly from the adrenalin shot into my blood from the three or four serious brushes with death or permanent disablement. Now came the most dangerous part. As I entered the horizontal part of the tunnel the flashlight became very dim and only lasted until I was in about fifteen feet into that part of the tunnel. The flashlight basically quit working, its batteries were almost completely dead. I left the useless flashlight on the ground and pulled out a book of matches from the left breast pocket of my jungle fatigue shirt. I struck one match and crawled forward, holding it until it started to burn my fingers seriously, trying to extend the life of the light from that match to its maximum, then lighting another match from the preceding one at the last possible second.

With all of that fooling around with the matches, I wasn't paying attention to the .45 which I was carrying while crawling on my hands and knees. When I checked it, the barrel was packed with dirt from scraping and dragging it along the floor of the tunnel.

Because of the impaction of the dirt into the barrel of the pistol, the .45 was basically useless and would probably blow up in my hand if I tried to fire it. I dropped that weapon on the ground and pulled out the bayonet from my pocket. As I made my way deeper into the tunnel, I suddenly saw another tunnel intersecting the one I was in at a ninety degree angle. I was only six inches away from it when I spotted it. I suddenly realized that there could have been someone in that tunnel and he could have just shot me in the head as I passed by or thrown a grenade into my part of the tunnel. I turned to the right, into that tunnel, making a searing mental note that I have to keep track of my travels or I'm liable to get lost in that underground labyrinth. It suddenly occurred to me of what this situation really was, I was twenty feet underground and fifty feet away from the entrance, working my way down another tunnel, with a book of matches in one hand and a bayonet in the other, basically unarmed and going along with the light of a weak candle. I thought, I won't even tell the guys above me, outside this tunnel, about this maneuver, I don't think they would believe me anyways. I was just absolutely determined to explore that tunnel for equipment or enemy soldiers.

After crawling another twenty feet I thought that I could make out sounds of digging from above me. I couldn't really tell if it was some sort of whispering or digging or what. When the match burned out I did not relight it but just laid flat on the floor of the tunnel, utterly motionless, listening in the total darkness. It seemed now to be some sort of digging sound. I lit another match and moved closer. What looked like a tunnel going straight up was perhaps a tunnel at one time and had been filled in. I thought that there might be VC above me in another tunnel, digging it out again.

The match burned out. It was cool down there, a dank coolness that was absolutely void of any light. The sound stopped. As I lay there, listening, a feeling came over me suddenly of peace, a feeling of relief. I was lying on the floor of the tunnel with both arms outstretched on the damp earth. There was absolutely no sound. I wasn't sweating, in fact, I was cool. I wasn't humping a backbreaking load, I was unburdened. I wasn't scanning the bushes and treetops for snipers or the ground for booby traps or anticipating an ambush. I wasn't in the full brightness of a brazingly hot sun, in fact this was pitch black darkness. As long as I didn't hear that digging sound and as long as there wasn't methane gas in there and as long as the tunnel didn't collapse then I thought that, finally, I am really safe. I am safer and more comfortable and less anxious than I had ever been on an operation. I stayed there for a few minutes, enjoying that little luxurious vacation, listening intently to see if the digging sound would return.

There were a few very weak scraping sounds. I crawled a few feet further so that my hands were directly over what appeared to be a circular mark on the top of the tunnel where I figured the people above me would be digging out, had probably already dug out and then filled in. That way, I figured that if they started to break through then I would feel the dirt falling on my hands, I didn't want to risk lighting a match because I didn't want them to suddenly see a light below them and drop a grenade on me. There had been no sounds at all for about five minutes. I closed my eyes and enjoyed the comfort of laying on a cool surface, without a hundred pounds or more of a burden, without the constant threat of murder, in total blackness and rejected the idea that the tunnel might collapse and crush and suffocate me and relishing in the thought that I had not as yet set off a booby trap within the tunnel. I think that I fell asleep for a few minutes. It was, I imagined, the sleep only felt of a person in a deep, dark casket.

A loud voice in my brain suddenly shouted "Ok!" "It might be a really good idea to see sunlight again!" I pushed my body backwards, still flat on the ground for a few feet and then got on my hands and knees and crawled my way back until I reached the first tunnel section. I couldn't back around into the first tunnel because the space was so constricted so I rolled onto my side and assumed an almost fetal position and pushed and twisted trying to negotiate the turn, twisting my head unnaturally to the side and backwards trying to get a look at the tunnel that continued past that point at the first possible instant.

Eventually I made the turn and was facing backwards to the main entrance. I lit a match to try to see how much further this tunnel went forwards, to explore another part of the tunnel system. I crawled on my belly forward but it only went another ten feet or so and then dead-ended. I worked my way backwards, unexpectedly striking something hard on the floor and then suddenly remembering that I had left the .45 pistol there. Another thirty seconds of crawling and I had finally reached the vertical shaft of the tunnel, twisting around with difficulty and finally managing to stand. Straight above me was a magnificent circle of blue sky and sunlight. I started my ascent, falling back down several times until finally I felt hands grabbing my shirt and pulling me up and out, into a glorious world of light and living beings.

I told the soldiers close to the tunnel that I think that there is something down there and if anyone has a tear gas grenade that it might be a good idea to throw one in as we leave. I gradually noticed that those men seemed shaken up quite a bit about something, they looked frightened and anxious. I asked them what the problem was, I thought that they had come under attack again while I was below ground. They said that they had been yelling for me for the last five minutes but had heard no response. I had not heard any voices while I was in the tunnel. I guess they figured that I had been killed. If that was the case then one of them would have had to go into the tunnel to try to retrieve my body and deal with what had killed me, apparently none of them had liked that idea at all.

A huge complex of tunnels, some forty feet deep, were found on that operation. Many of those tunnels had multiple openings to the surface. Some were multi-level and contained rooms for storage of weapons and food and living quarters. Some American soldiers, probably combat engineers, were brought into the area along with gasoline engine powered fans. They would find a tunnel and put the fan over the top of the entrance and use a poncho to make an airtight seal between the fan and the edges of the tunnel. Then they would throw tear gas grenades down into the hole and fire up the fan to try to fill the entire tunnel. The tear gas would hopefully force the VC out of the tunnels. One of the soldiers on such duty told me that tear gas grenades were hard to come by but when they ran out of tear gas they would just throw smoke grenades down there. He told me that the teargas grenades made life miserable for the VC but actually the plain smoke grenades would asphyxiate them. The smoke must have been ejected at the other openings but I never saw any of that. Either those other holes were too far away in the jungle to see and/or the tunnel complexes so large that the smoke was easily dissipated by the volume of air inside them. The other combat engineers, I later learned dropped large explosive charges into the tunnels to try to collapse them.

At the end of the day we found ourselves in a small clearing with three artillery pieces already set up there, probably 105mm howitzers. We dug defensive positions as usual but we had arrived at our night lager site earlier than usual and the ground was relatively soft so we finished digging in with about an hour of sunlight left. There was a little mountain about a mile away, probably two thousand feet tall that was plainly visible through the trees that surrounded us because there was not the usual tangle of tall trees and vines. The foliage around us was probably only forty feet tall with ten foot high bushes, the trees spread well apart. The side of the mountain that faced us was very steep. It was heavily covered in vegetation but there was a rocky area on it where it was probably too steep or hard and barren of soil for any plants to take hold and therefore was just a clearly delineated area of bare rock about a hundred feet around in rough diameter.

As the sun was going down, the Lieutenant in charge of the artillery challenged our mortar platoon leader (a new Lieutenant that I had never before met) to a contest. The challenge, and a money bet, was to hit that rocky area the most times out of three shots each. We told our Lieutenant that it was a sucker bet. The mortars are designed to fire in a high arc. You can fire an artillery piece in a high arc also but the artillery pieces can certainly serve as a direct (line of sight) weapon which the mortars can most certainly not do. Nonetheless, our Lieutenant stated with full confidence that his gun crews (My gun crew included) were the best in the Country and that he would accept the bet.

The mortar fire direction control (FDC) team did an excellent and extraordinary job of estimating the range to the target and computing a correction for trying to hit a target that was at an elevation of about a thousand feet above us but the target on the mountain at that point precipitously dropped, almost straight down. The target area was roughly hundred feet in diameter, but as far as the gun was concerned, it was like trying to hit a two foot wide target, something that was simply way outside the envelope of an 81 MM mortar.

Our first round landed almost at the top of the mountain, directly in line with the target but too high. After an adjustment was calculated and the mortar re-aimed, the second round rose high into the air and came very, very close to the bare rock target, yet missed it by ten feet vertically and therefore exploded down the mountain about two hundred feet below the target because of the steepness of the mountain. We fired one more round but it wasn't any closer than the previous one.

Now it was the artillery's turn. They had the target in direct line of sight. I have to give their fire direction control team credit because they had correctly estimated the altitude of the target and computed the almost flat trajectory of the shells perfectly. The command to "Fire!" was shouted and three rounds hit the target dead on, almost simultaneously, one from each of their three guns. Our Lieutenant paid the bet.

I thought that he would then strongly criticize our mortar fire but he seemed, for some reason, to be very pleased with our performance which was in fact very excellent. I think that the artillery Lieutenant really was impressed with our performance, perhaps he knew that we really couldn't hit that target but was impressed as to how close we had come. The problem was that we were using the wrong tool for the job and the characteristics of the mortar simply didn't lend itself well to such a unique target. It was like a contest where one group tried to hit a target fifty feet away and could take the target under direct fire. And the mortar crew could take on enemy fire from the other side of a small mountain. Given the circumstances there was no contest.

About half an hour later I was standing with a small group of other men. A soldier walked by and told us that a tunnel had been discovered about a hundred and fifty feet away. Curious, I walked over towards the entrance to the tunnel. Previously I had noted that there was a rice paddy that was very close by, in fact it almost constituted one side of our defensive position. I noticed a group of perhaps five soldiers who were very close together, a situation that was certainly not Standing Operating Procedure(SOP). As I approached closer to them, I could see that they were surrounding the vertical entrance to an enemy tunnel.

As I approached the tunnel entrance, I thought, I really didn't want to go down into another tunnel. I thought that if they were looking for volunteers to descend into that tunnel then since they had discovered the tunnel, that if they wanted to discover what was down there that strongly then they should go down there themselves and/or seek volunteers from among their own limited ranks.

If my Company, or most my platoon or most much more likely my squad, had discovered a tunnel then maybe we would have asked for volunteers but certainly one of us would have gone down into it to see what it contained.

A few weeks prior to that time I had begun to think that maybe I had reached my limit in pushing my luck with those tunnels. Moreover, I was very concerned that since this particular tunnel was so close to a rice paddy that it might contain methane or some other type of poisonous or explosive gas. Maybe that tunnel should remain unexamined I thought.

I was looking to my left, observing everything that was going on when suddenly there was a very loud explosion directly in front to my direction of travel, a powerful explosion close by that shook the ground. Strangely there wasn't any smoke or dirt flying. "Oh no!" I thought, that tunnel must have just blown up. At first there seemed to be no concern at all among the soldiers relatively close to the explosion, but that quickly changed. Within a time frame of ten seconds or so there was a quickly escalating sense of commotion and concern. The inflection in the soldiers voices and their rapid movements were out of place. It wasn't a panicked situation at all but more of a sense of a very rapidly increasing sense of urgency, a situation where something required immediate attention and action.

It took me a couple of minutes or so to slowly walk over to the tunnel, deliberately approaching the situation with extreme caution, not knowing what I was walking into. I tried to note and analyze every detail of what was going on all around me and what information and orders were being shouted. It also occurred to me that the explosion had alerted any VC in the area to our exact location and we could expect them to commence mortar fire on us and/or begin a direct infantry assault. I had my M-16 rifle and LBG and magazines of ammo and fragmentation grenades. If there was going to be another explosion from that tunnel shaft and I was too close to it, all of my ammunition and the explosives on my belt would detonate, which would kill me at the best, and at the worst would horribly, horribly maim me for life. But, I could be of use here for a direct enemy attack. I'm also sure that that explosion had drawn the attention of every VC sniper within a mile.

I hoped that I might possibly be of some assistance, even though the probability of being horribly wounded or disfigured or permanently maimed and crippled was rapidly increasing every second. I tried to push those thoughts out of my mind. All I knew was that it was likely that American soldiers were badly wounded and I wanted to help in any way that I could.

As I got within fifty feet of the scene at the entrance to the tunnel I noticed a soldier lying on the ground right next to it, face up, completely motionless. Next to him was another soldier lying on the ground on his back who was completely unmoving, whether he was unconscious or dead, I didn't know. There must have been a medic who had been close to the scene. Maybe he had directly witnessed what had happened, in any event he had obviously responded immediately. He was feverishly providing medical aid to the second trooper. My brain registered the fact that the medic was most obviously **not** attending to the first soldier that I had noticed. I guessed, correctly, as I learned later, that he was already dead.

Very nearby there were two other paratroopers, alive at least for the moment, who were most seriously injured, grossly and horribly injured. One was sitting upright on the ground. The other was lying on his back on the dirt, drifting in and out of consciousness with medics feverously attending to them.

I tried to discern who the wounded and dead were. I didn't think that they were from my platoon but they were almost certainly from my Company. But their faces were very black and seemingly covered deeply with dirt because of their close encounter with the explosion.

As I got within ten feet of them a sudden horribleness overcame me. I couldn't recognize their faces, not because they were covered in dirt and blackened by smoke but because their faces were horribly distorted, fundamentally and basically destroyed by the explosion. Their faces seemed to have been "melted" by the explosion and flames, like their living faces were made of wax and a huge blowtorch had been shot directly into their faces, which is essentially exactly what happened to them. Then I realized that their eyes were probably destroyed and that if they survived their injuries, that they would probably be horribly disfigured and permanently blind.

I was absolutely horrified at the extent of their injuries. It was a situation that a civilian in the United States would have an almost infinitesimal chance of seeing in their entire life, yet here was an absolute horror show that occurred all of the time. I realized that this level of horror and pain faced all of us, the Infantrymen, every day. The chance of such horrendous injuries occurring every hundred years was not one in fifty million, as in civilian life, but more like one in twenty, per year, a horrible, terrifying prospect.

As I got closer, I looked at the lapels of their shirts where many soldiers had an embroidered rank sewn onto them. I thought that if I could discern their rank then I might be able to figure out who they were. However, most of the lapels of their shirts, as well as large parts of the upper parts of their shirts, were horribly burned and blackened, large sections of cloth simply no longer existed, burned off by the explosion, the ragged edges of the cloth surrounding it were blackened and burned, something like taking a shirt and throwing it into a bonfire for a few minutes and then pulling it out.

In horror, I could only imagine what it had done to their bodies. The fact suddenly became evident that those soldiers injuries were that the skin and tissue and cartilage and muscles of their faces especially but also their necks and chests were horribly destroyed, indeed blackened and burned, in fact the very bones of their face were destroyed. In a quick mental horror show I thought: "what about their sinuses?, what about their eyes?, what about their vision?, What about their sense of smell and taste?, what about their noses and lips and skin. What about what they are going to look like?, They will look like monsters for the rest of their lives !!!, Blind and deaf and mute and horribly disfigured, if they survived, I thought. This, it occurred to me, was what was happening to American heroes on the ground halfway around the world. This, I thought, was something that a politician in Washington was not telling his constituents. This, I thought, was beyond the imagination of civilians in the U.S., especially those calling for even more war. Maintain!, Maintain! I thought. Figure out what has to be done. Analyze the situation later.

Other soldiers were running desperately toward the scene of this disaster, most significantly three other medics approaching from different directions. In the extremity of the problem, I noticed that most of the medics came running carrying only their medical packs, leaving behind their LBG, leaving behind even their basic weapons. Obviously unconcerned for their own safety and intent only on providing medical assistance to the wounded and dying.

I could hear two or three people at different close locations, within a hundred feet of the disaster, desperately calling on the radio for a "dust off" (emergency medical evacuation by helicopter). I thought that at the operation center that monitored such requests that there might be confusion but then I thought, better for too many choppers to show up than too few, and this was absolutely a situation that called out for and needed immediate and desperate response. These most horribly and drastically wounded troopers on the ground most definitely needed some serious medical assistance as soon as humanly possible, and it was provided by the Cowboys, the helicopter unit attached to the 173rd Airborne, under the most serious and dangerous situations. A group of aviators who seemed to be completely fearless, they would handle situations where any and all other aviators would absolutely refuse.

It happened much sooner than I had predicted and feared. Incoming enemy rifle fire had suddenly began out of the immediate close chaos and it rapidly ramped up. It came from the tree line on the other side of the rice paddy. Most of it was directly and purposively directed at the medics and the wounded. The medics completely ignored the incoming attempts to kill or maim them, working on their patients solely and diligently with a complete and utter disregard for their own lives. The heavy incoming enemy fire "snap, snap, snap" sounds of bullets were very loud and so obviously very close. Small puffs of dirt and dust from the enemy fire crackled all around the medics, very rapidly and very close to them, within feet. The medics completely ignored it. It was a scene of absolutely extraordinary heroism that I could not have possibly imagined or believed possible prior to personally witnessing it.

I ran a bit and dropped to one knee. I was directly in the line of fire. If nothing else maybe I can spare one of the medics a direct hit. I aimed my rifle at the tree line. The VC were putting in a goodly amount of direct fire but I couldn't see any rifle flashes. I considered running closer to them, down to the paddy dike which would provide some cover but over-ruled that because I would be placed directly between the enemy and my fellow soldiers. It would be a situation where I could be shot by either side. Other paratroopers came out of their partially protected dug in fighting positions and ran down to the little dike that bounded the rice paddy, deliberately placing themselves directly between the enemy fire and the medics. They relatively slowly began to return fire, taking their time to note and acquire a target but once they did they put up a wall of small arms and machine gun fire against the VC, who were doing everything in their power to kill wounded Americans laying helplessly on the ground and the medics who tried only to keep them from dying.

I knew full well that such a fate that had befallen onto the wounded could easily and likely happen to me, but I couldn't stand to dwell on it . . . . It would make me crazy and interfere with what I must do to help my squad mates. I'll think about it later and deal with it and get it straight in my mind. However, as much as I tried to push it off until later or to just not deal with it, it weighted heavily on my mind that I would be killed in a horribly painful and lengthy manner, an expectation that was by no means unreasonable for an infantryman in Viet Nam, a fate that I personally witnessed on those poor heroes. However, I quickly threw out such thoughts from my mind.

There seemed to be enough soldiers returning fire. I considered going over and throwing it down behind the paddy dike and shooting back. Obviously the Americans knew that there were soldiers at the dike and probably not shoot them by accident but then I suddenly realized that I should probably go back to my fighting position close to the mortar. We would most likely be getting a fire mission within minutes to suppress the enemy fire on the far side of the rice paddy. There were four medics working on the wounded and a sufficient number of troopers pouring heavy fire onto the enemy at the dike directly in front of the medics. I would be of much more use manning my crew served eighty-one mm mortar. I yelled to the soldiers around the tunnel: "I have to get back to my gun! Are you OK? They indicated that they were and waved me forward.

I turned around and ran back to my fighting position and waited. The enemy fire suddenly quieted down and then stopped. I figured that the VC had withdrawn from the battlefield because they thought, rightfully, that at any minute my mortar crew would put fire directly upon them. Actually, that would have been the best of circumstances for them. I forget exactly what happened, but we undoubtedly called in artillery or helicopter or air strikes on their position, or at least onto the position that they had occupied while trying to kill men who were lying on the ground dying and the medics attending to them. My mortar gun crew never received a fire mission.

In any event, the enemy broke contact. Maybe it was due to the wall of fire that the paratroopers had set up, I don't know, because the enemy had thrown a huge amount of fire back at us. It was an all out contest where upon you looked directly down the barrel of a VC shooting at you directly and accurately with a machine gun while you are doing the same, a shoot out at the OK corral with automatic weapons that fire six hundred bullets per minute each, per soldier.

About an hour later, when things had calmed down for a while, I walked up to the entrance to the tunnel to talk to a few guys who were close by. But as I approached, other soldiers who had walked up in front of me were there asking them questions. Those inquisitive soldiers were being told in no uncertain terms to get the hell away from them, they didn't want to talk about it. It seemed that the soldiers close to the tunnel were outraged at something and were just looking for an excuse to knock out, to quickly and violently beat to the ground those questioning and inquisitive soldiers who quickly walked away.

I hesitated a bit, not wanting to get into a bad situation, but then something told me to walk right up to them and demand information. I had been right there amongst them while most of that situation had happened and I wanted to know more information about it. I had spoken to a few guys standing around near the entrance to the tunnel when all the commotion at first started and they had told me briefly what had happened but I certainly did not know the full situation.

I expected to be treated as the other inquisitive soldiers had been but surprisingly, they recognized me from the initial action, for some unknown reason, and they were happy to see me. They proceeded to tell me the full details. A soldier had gone down into the vertical shaft of the tunnel and then into the horizontal section of it, going out of sight of two or three soldiers who were peering into the vertical shaft. After about a minute the men above ground called to the tunnel rat soldier but he did not answer. A soldier at ground level at the entrance to the tunnel, thought that he smelled some kind of gas, so he put on a gas mask and climbed down the vertical shaft of the tunnel. After he reached the bottom and crawled into the horizontal part of the tunnel, within a few feet he reached the body of the first tunnel rat who was unconscious (or dead).

He grabbed the boots of the first soldier and managed to drag him half ways out of the horizontal shaft when he too suddenly lost consciousness and collapsed. I guess that the gas mask filtered out the swamp gas but the swamp gas displaced the oxygen from the air. I guess that the second soldier, and the first, lost consciousness not from the methane or other gasses but from the lack of breathable oxygen in that atmosphere. The body of the second soldier was clearly visible from above, sort of folded up, his back against the wall of the vertical shaft with his legs scrunched up into the horizontal shaft of the tunnel and the boots of the first soldier clearly visible.

Clearly, this was a disaster unfolding before the eyes of the soldiers who were now looking down into the shaft of the tunnel. A Sergeant and a Lieutenant I think, quickly approached the tunnel yelling very loudly down the shaft to "Wake up!!" and to "Get out of there!!" when there was a sudden explosion, a blast of noise and flame and smoke that shot out of the vertical tunnel. It ruined the two soldiers at the top of the tunnel, destroying their faces and necks with third degree burns and probably fatally burned their lungs but it didn't kill them immediately, at least I don't think that it did. The two of them lay on their backs, probably permanently blinded at the least. I think then that another Lieutenant, obviously an incredibly brave individual, ran over and without hesitation jumped into the pit. Amidst the poisonous and explosive gas that was still there he managed to hoist them to the surface with the assistance of other soldiers at ground level who had tied their shirts together to form a rescue rope.

They acted in a manner that was completely regardless of the horrible dangers of another explosion that would blind them and burn their faces off. I think that the bottom line was five causalities, one dead and four horribly wounded, their faces destroyed and their lungs probably severely damaged and burned. I realized that any one of those guys could have easily been me.

We went out on other patrols for the next few days, finding many enemy bunkers and some small tunnels that had been dug under termite hills. The inside of some of those termite mounds are naturally occurring tunnels that are big enough for a small man to fit into. After setting up for the night we were told that we would be staying there for two days or so.

The next day the mortar crew was told to stay in place while the other Platoons went out on patrols. We were ordered to reinforce the current position by digging a gun pit for the mortar. We dug a circular hole about eight feet wide and a foot deep and then filled up sandbags to go around the perimeter of the pit to a height of about two feet. If we came under attack, the mortar crew would have to leave their fighting positions to man the gun and in that case we would use it as a fighting position, while simultaneously firing the mortar. Actually, the gun pit would be the position of last resort if the camp was overrun.

We also needed an ammo sump, an underground hole in which to store the ammo for the mortar to protect it from being blown up by enemy mortars. There was a termite mound about three feet tall just outside the gun pit and I decided to use that for the ammo sump. This mound looked like it had already taken a direct hit from an artillery round and a quarter of it was missing, sort of like it had been scooped out. I had seen other termite mounds where a very large artillery round had landed five feet away with no damage whatsoever to the mound. I had seen a couple of mounds that had taken direct hits from artillery and had simply split in two. Those mounds were made of some sort of substance that the termites made that was much tougher and harder than concrete. I thought it was a good idea to sort of hollow out the rest of the mound for the ammo sump because it would provide excellent protection for our ammo. It took me all day of very heavy work to chip away at it with the pick part of an entrenching tool. There were several times when I almost gave up on it. I thought that it would be easier and quicker to just abandon that project and dig a hole in the ground for the ammo and then cover it with a roof of logs and sandbags. I kept on though, not wanting to have wasted the substantial amount of work that I had already put into it and knowing that when it was completed it would be much more resistant to enemy mortars than anything else.

The next day, the other platoons went out on patrols while the mortar crew stayed in place. There were several large artillery pieces located within our position. I walked around a bit checking out the artillery and spoke to some of the artillerymen. They showed me a "beehive" round and a couple of "bees" that they contain. The round was loaded with hundreds of small rocket shaped pieces of metal which was designed to be fired point-blank at an assaulting enemy force. I imagined a scene of an enemy platoon literally shredded, their bodies torn into pieces by white-hot nails with tiny rocket fins on them. Quite a horrible weapon I thought.

We fired off a few mortar rounds for registration later that day and I noticed that with just the right angle of the sun and a small charge, you could actually see the mortar rounds fly out towards their target. Most of the time you could not see the rounds because they were traveling at such high speed when blasted out of the tube. Sometimes you could actually see the last, built-in safety device get ejected sideways from the mortar round when it was about 50 feet out of the tube.

The next day, very early, about forty minutes after sunrise, the other platoons were getting ready to go out on patrol into the surrounding area. I was sitting on the ground against the termite mound/ammo sump. While I had been digging it out the day before I had flattened out one side of it so that now that side acted as a back brace. I don't remember exactly what I was doing but I know for sure that I was just minding my own business when, with no warning whatsoever, there was a very loud, sharp noise and a hurricane of dirt, leaves and shrapnel flew past me from both sides and over my head. The VC had sneaked up to our perimeter and detonated one of their own Claymore mines. It must have been placed directly in front of me. A few seconds later they detonated two other Claymores almost simultaneously. I grabbed my weapon and spun around, kneeling behind that termite mound and using it for cover and trying to look towards the sides, out into the jungle, anticipating an attack. The VC decided not to press their advantage. They just set off those Claymores and then blended back into the vegetation. If I hadn't been sitting there with that mound for protection, that first Claymore would have scattered parts of my body for a hundred feet. I suddenly thought back to when I was digging out that mound and how I had on several occasions almost abandoned that project but something told me to just keep going with it.

The other platoons moved out about five minutes later while I stayed behind with the Weapons platoon. I didn't like the idea of being here with three-fourths of the Company gone but at least I wouldn't have to carry a tortuous load all day. We stayed there for another day or two. Then it was back on the move for us again.

The days work started before sunrise with everyone on full alert guard for half an hour before and after sunrise, followed by the hard labor of filling in the fighting positions and emptying the sandbags under the pressure of time. If we worked quickly we might have ten minutes to heat up some coffee, gulp down some C-rations and shave. We got the word that this was going to be a long hump, about four thousand meters. We had to make it to a predestined location about two hours before sunset in order to set up and dig in for the night.

I put on my load bearing gear, which consisted of a wide belt held up by heavy suspenders. Attached to that belt was two canteens of water, three ammo pouches each holding three magazines of nineteen rounds each, four high explosive hand grenades, three smoke grenades, bayonet, battle dressing and entrenching tool. Around my neck was two bandoliers containing three magazines each of ammo that was slung over the shoulder and around the neck. Then I struggled to put on the rucksack, in which there might be another hundred and fifty boxed up rounds of M-16 ammo, shaving kit, poncho, poncho liner, mess kit, butt pack, mosquito netting, food, air mattress and miscellaneous gear. Strapped to my leg, sort of like a holster, with its own separate belt that went around the waist, was a gas mask in its canvas container. Strapped to the rucksack might be two or three mortar rounds, there are different types of differing weights but they are all heavy (ten to about fifteen pounds each). Then I slung my rifle over my shoulder, put on my helmet and picked up the mortars tube with one hand and the aiming stakes with the other. Total weight probably in excess of a hundred and twenty pounds. Just standing in place was a problem. After walking for about ten minutes it becomes an almost unbearable burden and then it gets much worse as the day progresses.

Some of the men, earlier on, had started to tape two M-16 magazines together with electrical tape, one magazine straight up and the other pointing straight down. The idea is that, in a firefight, you would have another magazine immediately available. That sounded like a good idea but the extra magazine added weight to the magazine that was in the weapon and it had a bad effect of sometimes making both of them fall out of the weapon, especially under heavy beating of the bush. The result was, when you were attacked and thought you had almost forty rounds available, you looked down and realized that you only had one bullet in the chamber and no magazines. Each magazine held twenty rounds, but after putting in seventeen rounds it became rather difficult to add any more because the spring in the bottom of the magazine was being squeezed so tightly. From experience, we learned to never put twenty rounds in because the pressure of the spring in the magazine could be strong enough to jamb all of the bullets together which would hold back bullets from entering the chamber. Better eighteen or nineteen rounds that are sure to be of use than twenty rounds that wouldn't work.

We had been issued some tracer rounds, rounds that would glow a bright red color when fired so that you could have a better idea of where your bullets were actually hitting. You could tell a tracer round because the tip of the bullet looked like it had a dab of red paint on it. Actually that "paint" was some chemical that would ignite from the heat of the initial blast out of the rifle barrel. You cannot use all tracer rounds because it causes the barrel to heat up much too fast which might well seize up the barrel and make the rifle stop functioning and/or cause the rifle to blow up in your hands. So in a magazine every third or fourth round would be a tracer. I kept three tracer magazines in a separate ammo pouch so they would be ready at night or if I had to fire into deep vegetation and couldn't determine for sure where my bullets were going. The problem with tracers is that they work both ways. You can see where your rounds are landing but the enemy can clearly mark you as a target.

You walk and walk and walk all day, always stopping and starting. The strain upon your body is incredible, the pain inhuman. It really is torture but it's a torture that you visit upon yourself. No one else is tearing apart your flesh with red-hot tongs but you wonder if that wouldn't be less painful. You cannot drop out. If you are unable to carry on, for some physical reason, your fellow soldiers will have to carry your equipment. As horribly suffering as you would be, you certainly did not want to place even more of a burden on any other men in the Company.

We had been humping all day and I really thought that this would be the day that I would die of a heart attack. I told myself to take just one more step, then after I managed that, I would think to myself, "Just take one more step", and so on it went, second after back-breaking, agonizingly horrible , indescribably painful second. My heart rate must have been well over two hundred beats per minute, my desperate breathing over a hundred breaths per minute. The heat and humidity was horrible and I was completely saturated with sweat over every inch of my body. I was really on the ragged edge of collapsing.

Up the trail about another two hundred yards, the line stopped for a short while. We were walking up a sort of gulch, perhaps it was a creek in the rainy season. It was just thin short grass and bare earth. I looked around for a place to drop to the ground and walked over about ten feet to an embankment that I could use as a back brace as I sat. I was just about to collapse down when I noticed a pair of VC sandals on the ground, good ones, made out of an automobile tire but they looked brand new. It flashed in my mind that they were probably booby-trapped but I was so utterly exhausted I couldn't manage another step. I just turned around and fell heavily, sitting right on top of them. I knew that was a real bad idea. I brushed the thought aside, concentrating only on trying to catch my breath and resting my body that seemed to creak and groan from the abominable strain that I had willed it to endure.

After a few minutes my heart rate seemed to begin returning to near normal. I noticed that my arms were bleeding. Upon closer inspection they seemed to be bleeding from twenty places although it was hard to see some of them because the blood was mostly hidden, covered with black dirt mixed with sweat. I wondered whether I had received those cuts recently or old cuts were breaking open. The intensity and pain of the hump made a wound that was torn harshly by a thorn a very minor inconvience, most of the time not even noticeable. I was going to try to wash off my arms but didn't want to use any drinking water. I figured that I would probably need a few gallons of water anyways. The black mud was a good thing I thought, it seemed to stem the flow of blood. I'll probably cut my arms another thirty times before this day alone is over I thought.

After about five minutes my mind drifted back to the sandals. I thought that I was maybe sitting on a booby-trap that is of the type that when someone steps on it it arms itself and then when the weight is taken off it explodes. I was actually surprised that it had not detonated when I sat on it and realized that pondering its firing mechanism wasn't going to change anything or help the situation at all. A few minutes later we got the word to move out again. The next closest soldier to me was about twenty-five feet away. I hoped that if it did detonate that it wouldn't injure anyone else too seriously. It was time to go and there was simply nothing else to do than to just stand right up and see what happens. I struggled mightily with the weight of my equipment, turning suddenly so that the blast, if it came, might hit me with most of its force in the back, expecting to loose my legs and other things in the next split second, but nothing happened. I was suddenly very much relieved, in fact I felt so good that I thought that maybe I should pick them up for a souvenir but then a deep voice from within said "No!!" Then I realized that they were just in too good a shape, in such an obvious place, not to be booby-trapped. I couldn't dwell on what had just occurred because the pain and strain of the hump had immediately returned.

We humped another five hundred meters, finding ourselves in a very large clearing, the same location from which we had started this operation more than a week ago. I thought that the word was that we were going to spend the night there, exactly in the location that we had previously occupied. I and my squad were now in exactly the place in the layout of the perimeter where we should be so I staggered another fifteen feet off to the side of the line of march and dropped the baseplate, shrugged off my rucksack, dropped my lbg, stripped off my shirt and then just flopped onto the ground spread-eagle, way way beyond exhaustion.

I laid there for about a minute just staring at the sky until some Sergeant came over and asked me in very impolite terms what I thought I was doing. I looked around and saw that the line of march still existed although it had temporarily stopped, everyone still standing in full gear. I told the Sergeant that I thought we were spending the night here and here is exactly the spot where I had been a week before. He ordered me to get up and put on my gear. We would be spending the night about three hundred meters from this exact spot. I guess the other guys thought that I had just finally said to myself what they all wanted to say, which is "Enough is enough!!. I'm not going to be tortured anymore, not even one more step".

We finally stopped and dug in. We set up our gun and a helicopter brought in two more mortars and a load of ammo for them. I got out my camera and took a picture of the scene. It was pretty colorful, with the bright green grass of a meadow against the faded green of uniforms, wooden ammo boxes, the red and white stripes of the aiming stakes against rising clouds of purple smoke all in front of the dark green of the jungle trees surrounding our position. It was one of the best photos that I have ever taken.

The next day we went out on a patrol. The woods were not a true triple-canopy type of jungle where no sunlight reached the jungle floor. Tiny bits of blue sky could be seen through some leaves of the highest trees probably a hundred and twenty feet above our heads. After about an hour of patrolling through that jungle the line of march stopped for a while and I sat down on the ground, relieving my body of its murderous load.

Now we were very close to the edge of a huge area that was relatively open. There was a shaft of sunlight reaching the ground about three feet from me and I put my hand into it. For some strange reason, the heat of the direct sun became unbearable after about fifteen seconds and my arm recoiled involuntarily away from the sharp pain. It felt as if someone had a big magnifying glass and was concentrating the sun onto my skin. I thought that this must be some sort of strange phenomenon so I tried it again, and then again with my other hand with the same result. I wondered, fearfully, how hot it must be out in the full sun on this day. For the next hour we humped along, a few feet into the treeline, near the edge of that area of full sunlight with me dreading that at any minute the line of march would change and we would have to cross that open area and suffer even more from that burning misery. Then we entered heavier and thicker jungle where our progress was slowed and became considerably more difficult because of thin vines that had to be broken by brute force but I was very relieved not to have been subjected to that searing equatorial sun.

We returned for the night and set up in a grassy area filled with small trees about six feet tall, surrounded by heavy jungle. In the morning I was heating up a cup of coffee when there was a bit of a commotion about fifty feet away from me. There was a small sort of campfire over there made of sticks arranged like a teepee. We never made a campfire so that alone was extremely unusual. A bunch of guys were sitting around that fire, most of them half-shouting seemingly urgent commands and instructions to each other. One guy was jumping about excitedly, like he wanted to run away but couldn't decide which way to go. They were all concentrating on a spot on the ground about ten feet directly in front of them. I thought that I saw a snake there, for a split-second, but rejected that thought. Then one of those soldiers walked over to that area of interest, studied the situation for a few seconds and then executed an extraordinarily quick maneuver, scooping up something from the ground and quickly throwing it a few feet away.

The thing suddenly reared up a foot and a half, faced its attacker and flared out its hood. I yelled to those guys, "Watch out! I think it's a cobra!" One of the troopers looked at me and said, "Of course it's a cobra". By now I was standing and could see the snake clearly. The soldier who knew, of course, that it was a cobra walked over to it and somehow grabbed it by its neck with a lightning fast move that indicated little hesitation and no fear whatsoever. He then sliced its throat with a bayonet, cutting off its head and threw the carcass into the fire. I said, "No really, I think that that was a cobra." The other guy said, "Yeah, I know. Here I'll show you" and he lifted the head out of the fire with a long twig and opened its mouth with the blade of his bayonet. The snake had two extremely long fangs, seemingly impossibly long for the snakes head, folded up against the roof of its mouth. It must have been a country boy who caught that snake. He acted like he does it all the time, like he's done it hundreds of times before, like it was nothing much more than a sharp stick to be picked up and tossed to the side of the road. I saw it as just another way to be killed before you even had your morning coffee.

That day we went out on patrol again. The early morning briefing noted that we should be especially mindful of finding any documents. We had humped hard all day and were getting close to the place where we would settle in for the night. We came to an area that was relatively clear, consisting of bushes about four feet high with a lot of hard brown sun-baked dirt. The line of march had come to a halt and word was that we would be stopped for while, I guess because something had been discovered near the front of the line. I put my rucksack on the ground and wandered off to look around and have a smoke.

I spotted a termite mound about sixty feet away that for some reason just didn't look right. I was hesitant to approach it because it was among some bushes and the heavy vegetation behind it would easily conceal any enemy. I walked slowly towards it with my weapon casually sweeping it and the area around and in back of it. As I got closer I could see that it was some type of fighting position. Someone had dug a hole at the face of the termite mound. It was about three feet deep and roughly circular with about a four foot diameter. Half of the hole was outside of the edge of the termite mound and the other half had been dug under and within the mound. It must have required several days of hard work to excavate through the almost concrete hardness of that termite mound but then the enemy would have a position that on three sides and overhead was virtually indestructible. There was a piece of corrugated sheet metal about two feet square on the ground at the bottom of the hole. I couldn't think of any reason that an enemy soldier would be carrying around pieces of sheet metal. Maybe it was to keep his feet out of the water if it rained a lot. Maybe it was to provide some shelter from the rain or sun from the part of the position that was open. I don't know why it was there, but it was something that was extremely unusual.

I realized that this looked like a very likely place to booby trap but I really wanted to check it out for any weapons or VC supplies. I considered laying on the ground and then gingerly reaching down inside the hole and lifting up the sheet metal to see if it was concealing anything but I didn't like the idea of a booby trap blowing up in my face as I was looking directly at it. I considered that it might not be booby-trapped and, for some reason, decided to just jump in and see what happens. If it blows up I figured that I might have a chance to survive, a better chance than taking the charge directly into my face and neck.

I yelled to Pierce, a member of my gun crew, who was standing about thirty feet away that I was going in. I wanted someone to know that it was me so that in the event that it was booby-trapped maybe the Company could save itself half an hour of wondering where Mallen had wandered off to. Pierce shouted franticly to not even go near that thing. I took a couple of half steps closer to the opening, half listening to shouts of "Get away!" and "Don't get any closer" but I had already made up my mind. I took one quick deep breath and jumped in. I landed squarely on the middle of the sheet metal, with both feet together, just like they taught us in jump school, but this time I had my feet and knees together, not to absorb the shock of a parachute landing, but, in case it was booby trapped, it might not take off everything below the waist. There was no immediate explosion and I stayed motionless for a few seconds, waiting to see if anything happened. I thought, "So far, so good, but now what?" I'm already in, I may as well push my luck some more. I decided to pick up the sheet metal and see what, if anything it was hiding.

I was half crouched down, my back against the inside roof made by the termites. I had to contort my body to put one foot onto the dirt floor and place the other foot into the opposite side of the hole so that there was no weight on the sheet metal. I suddenly realized that the detonator of a booby trap could be placed in the surrounding dirt and not necessarily under the sheet metal, but it was already too late to avoid that possibility. I placed my rifle on the ground outside the hole. I don't know why it was in my hands when I jumped in, just force of habit I guess. I reached down and grabbed a corner of the silver metal and violently picked it up and threw it out of the hole, just staring straight ahead, not wanting to see any potential explosive that would split me in two. Again, there was no explosion. I looked down between my legs and saw another square of sheet metal. I knew that I was really pushing my luck, now I had to re-calculate my odds of surviving moving this one. I knew it was all wrong. I knew that I had pushed it way beyond any reasonableness.

I noticed that my body was trembling, my legs shaking. I put it down to the fact that I was standing in a very contorted position. I've already gone this far, I thought. I might as well go, as the Airborne motto goes, "All the Way". I reached down, grabbed that metal and flung it out of the hole, twisting my body to face away from a potential explosion. All was quiet. I looked again to the ground, half expecting to see a grenade but there on the dirt was a wallet and a small book. Again, I took inventory of the situation. If ever something in this hole was to be booby trapped, this wallet and book would be it. I reached down and snatched it up and flung it out of the hole so that it might survive the blast that I half expected to follow at any instant. I then jumped for my life out of the hole landing on my stomach, spread eagle and scrambling away from the edge of the fighting position in case the timer on a grenade was quickly ticking away its few seconds. There was no explosion.

The wallet had no money or papers in it save for a Vietnamese 5-dong coin in the coin compartment, about the size and material of a US nickel. The small book was hand written in Vietnamese. The word had been passed that if we found anything we were to report it immediately. I walked over to a Lieutenant handed him the book and wallet, but I had already put the coin in my pocket as a souvenir. The Lieutenant reported it to someone, who probably immediately reported it to someone else. A short time later the word came down the line that we would be staying here for another thirty minutes.

About twenty minutes later a chopper arrived and a Lieutenant disembarked. He was obviously rear echelon type, someone with a job where he never went into the bush or got dirty. He wore what looked to be brand new starched fatigues and his boots were spit-shined. The most intriguing thing about him, I thought, was that he was clean. He was a freshly showered, pampered human being amongst a gang of filthy ragged soldiers in the middle of a combat operation. He started asking questions to the soldiers close to the helicopter and soon he was headed directly towards me, with the book and wallet in his hand. He wanted to know all about where I found it and when and how.

I pointed out the termite mound. He assumed that it was laying on top of the termite mound and started taking copious notes. He said to me "Didn't you think that it was dangerous to take it off the top of that mound?" I had to tell him about five times that I found it inside the hole before he began to comprehend what I was saying. I told him no, it was inside a fighting position that was dug into and below the mound. I started walking over to it to show him. He got about fifty feet away and stopped. I wondered why he was hesitating, was he afraid to get some dust on his boots?. Then I remembered when I had first approached it, it certainly was with trepidation. I implored him to come a bit closer so that he could see exactly what the situation was. He carried only a .45 in a holster, I told him that I would cover him with my rifle. He approached closer so that he could see the actual layout of the fighting position-half termite mound. He found it impossible to believe that anyone would be foolish enough to reach inside that hole. Again he asked me if I thought that it was dangerous and I explained that it was found hidden underneath two sheets of metal that I had to remove first. He found that explanation beyond the pale of anything he had ever heard of, he couldn't conceive of anyone doing such a thing. In fact, he wouldn't get closer than fifteen of the termite mound. He suddenly seemed to be very happy with my report. When I asked him why he was smiling he patiently explained that that wallet and book must be genuine. He said that the VC sometimes deliberately plant material in obvious places, meant to be found by Allied forces, which contained deliberately falsified information.

Since my captured materials were concealed in a place where no one in their right mind would dare to explore, then they must be the real deal. He told me that the wallet and book were flown directly to Military Intelligence and that after the intelligence officers read five minutes of the book, which was a diary, they had sent him out on an emergency mission to verify the facts surrounding the acquisition of that book. He said that it was a very, very major discovery. I learned later that the VC liked to keep diaries and the capture of one could provide information of major importance as to what that VC and his unit had been doing and where he had been for the last year or more.

The Lieutenant asked me if there was any money in the wallet, or any coins. In one of the few times in my life that I lied, I said no. I thought that he would take the coin and deprive me of my souvenir. They might have been able to make out what the coin was by checking its imprint that it had left in the leather of the coin pouch, that coin had obviously been in that wallet for a long time because it did have an imprint when I first found it. I learned much later that the VC used coins as identification of what unit they were in, mostly depending on the type of coin and its date.

They made a movie later about the Iron Triangle, where we were at that time, where in the opening of the movie they note that parts of the movie are based on the contents of a diary that was discovered during this operation. I wonder if they were talking about my diary. The Lieutenant did say that it seemed to be an extraordinarily important find. We stayed out in the bush for another day and then were taken back to base camp by helicopter.

Chapter 16

BASE CAMP B

We sleep soundly in our beds
because rough men stand ready in the night
to visit violence on those who would do us harm.

Winston Churchill

Full gear, ready to move out, next to Base Camp Hoochs

Back in base camp we went to the supply Sergeants hooch, which was a corrugated sheet metal Quonset hut, to get some new pants. Someone said that they were taking their shirt to a Vietnamese laundry on base. I said that it would be impossible to get them clean but he assured me that they do a pretty good job. He took my shirt and those of about ten other men. I could have received a new shirt but

I wanted to keep that shirt because it had my parachute wings and 173rd insignia already sewn onto it and I didn't know how long we would be in base camp. It might be for only a few hours and it usually took a few days for the Vietnamese tailor on base to get the patches sewn onto a new shirt.

About the first thing that was done, after returning from the field, was to take a shower. The shower area was completely outdoors with a bare open concrete floor about twenty feet by ten feet. There was a type of wall all around that area made up of a band of corrugated sheet metal about two feet off the ground and extending up to about five feet tall. So when you looked at it from the outside, you could see the men inside from their feet to their knees and then again from about their shoulders upwards. There was only wide open sky for a roof.

There were about ten shower heads with strings attached that, when pulled, would discharge the water for as long as it was pulled. The source of the water was a large metal cylinder resting about ten feet high on a wooden platform that was probably filled by a water truck. There was a good amount of water in that tank, but sometimes not enough for a hundred men to all take a shower so everyone had to demonstrate restraint in using the water. The shower really just removed most of the dirt, certainly not all of it. There was dirt embedded in the skin that would require much more than a quick shower to remove. Thankfully the water was not cold. It had probably been sitting in the big tank for days and the sun had warmed it well. Anyways, the outdoor temperature was probably close to a hundred degrees, cold water would have been a welcomed and strange relief.

Someone had arranged for us to have some decent food. Maybe the Battalion or Company commander or Sergeant major or the Company supply Sergeant. I didn't know or care but was just very grateful for it. They brought in a trailer towed behind a jeep that was filled with eighty pound blocks of ice and soda and beer. A lot of the ice had melted but its resulting ice cold water had chilled the contents greatly. They cooked some steaks on a big barbeque and we all ate our fill. Later someone said that they were going to the Air Force PX to get cigarettes and booze and I decided to go along with them. At the PX I saw two Air Force women in uniform. A soldier with me said, "Look, a couple of round eyes." I didn't know what he meant at first but it was a reference to non-Asian women. We had been out for a long time in the bush and of course there were no women around anywhere there. They were to be the last "round eyed" women that I would see for seven months, in fact, they would be almost the last women that I would see of any kind until the end of my tour of duty.

About two hours later we were sitting around at night in our barracks, drinking beer and liquor, some of the guys maybe smoking a little weed and a couple of groups of soldiers playing cards when there was a sharp explosion close by. Some of us ran outside to see what was going on but couldn't see anything out of place. A guy came in about a short time later and told us that a grenade had exploded in the "D" company area. The word was that there was one soldier KIA along with a Vietnamese civilian guard and two other soldiers who lost legs. Rumor later stated that they were playing a game of chicken with a live grenade. Very, very much later I learned that the KIA was a good friend of mine.

That night I was chosen to be on perimeter guard for our main base camp. The area around our base camp was swept by patrols on a regular basis and I considered it to be a safe area. Myself and five other men reported to a Lieutenant who gave us a quick briefing. I had never seen that Lieutenant before and figured that he was either a new replacement or an Officer that was assigned to the rear area and had never been out to the bush. When he was finished talking we walked about three hundred meters from our hooch to the perimeter. That edge of the base camp had a berm where bulldozers had scraped the ground and made a raised, sort of dam, area about ten feet tall, circling the area. There were no fighting positions on the ground but there were towers about thirty feet tall that were separated from each other by about a hundred feet or so.

I climbed up a wooden ladder on one of the towers and reached a small sandbagged fighting position that was built onto the wooden platform. There was corrugated metal on the walls on the left and right with openings like windows cut into them. The back of it was wide open and the front had rows of sandbags less than two feet tall. There was a bench about five feet above the floor where someone could sit and get a good view of the surrounding area, but then he would be an excellent target. There was an overhead roof of sheet metal that was designed only to protect the guards from the noonday sun and any rain.

Looking out to the front, all of the vegetation had been bulldozed, knocked down, burned or removed so there was an unobstructed view out to the edge of the jungle about 700 yards away. I didn't have any way to communicate with anyone, no radio or landline. The Lieutenant in charge had told us that there were no friendly forces in the area at the present time and to fire upon anything suspicious to our front. I sat on a small bench behind the sandbagged wall for about twenty minutes. I wasn't too keen on getting onto the raised bench but after a while I climbed up there. I figured it was fairly safe and gave me an additional six feet of altitude to see around me better.

After about an hour or so, the sun was just setting, it would be totally dark in about five minutes. I was beginning to relax a bit now. There wasn't the constant danger of being in the bush and I was clean and well fed. The sunset seemed to be particularly spectacular and the air was warm and clear and clean. You almost never saw a sunset or sunrise in the bush, you were down too low and immersed in the jungle to get a good view. Now though, there was a huge expanse of open land in front of me.

I was feeling pretty good for a few minutes and realized that I hadn't felt good for a very long time when suddenly I thought that I detected some movement at the edge of the jungle directly to my front. I stared for fifteen seconds and then yelled over to the guys in the guard towers on either side of me, but they didn't seem to hear me. I saw a man emerge from the jungle, and then another man and then another one until there was a line of about ten men directly approaching our perimeter. I wanted to think that they were civilian farmers or something but as they got closer it was obvious that they were a military unit by the way they moved, in a single line, fifty feet apart, in a snakelike forward progression. As they got a bit closer I could barely make out that they all had weapons. The seven hundred yard unobstructed view of them across a barren no mans land would turn into a pitch black dark field in five minutes.

Now the guy in the guard tower to my right yelled something unintelligible to me and pointed to the patrol coming at us. I didn't know how many more were still in the jungle. I yelled back to him, asking if he had a radio or anything. He said he had a landline but it wasn't working. I suggested that he run back to the Company area and get some more men out here on the perimeter. He vigorously nodded his agreement and then slid down the ladder of his watchtower, both hands sliding along the rough handrails, holding his body off of the ground, his feet never touching the ladder. I yelled at him to hurry, because him leaving meant one less man to defend the perimeter.

I was confident that three of us could deal with the immediate threat but I was worried that there were other enemy soldiers hidden in the jungle that might suddenly assault the entire perimeter. The guard ran up the road about two hundred feet, then abruptly stopped, turned around and ran back to his tower, never saying another word. I guess he was in a bit of a panic.

He probably realized that by the time that he reached the Company and alerted them to our problem and they all ran out onto the perimeter and Battalion was alerted which would result in very heavy mortar fire, followed soon afterwards by Brigade heavy artillery would still result in a situation where the base would be defended but all of the perimeter guards would have been killed. His choice to stay with the perimeter guards instead of running back to the safety of the relatively rear area and getting support to us affected me greatly. Here was a soldier who decided to fight it out with us, at extremely great danger, rather than to retreat to the safety of Headquarters Company.

I guess that he figured that he really didn't need to notify Headquarters of our problem. The extreme noise of a full on fire fight along the perimeter would have noticed them that something very bad was happening. He could have gone back into the camp to notify Headquarters what was happening and I would have never blamed him for it. In fact I would have been very happy that he had done so. But no. He turned back to face death with us. What heroism.

The patrol was getting much closer now but there wasn't any more of them coming out of the jungle. By rights, we should have fired on them at seven hundred yards but something told me that they might be friendly forces. It was very dangerous to let them get closer, but I wasn't about to start killing people if it wasn't absolutely necessary, especially on the off chance that they were ARVN or American soldiers. I thought of firing a few warning shots, but something told me that they were not enemy. They made no attempt to conceal their approach but by now the sun had set and it was getting very dark quickly. When they were about three hundred yards away, I realized that my position, high in that tower, was good for spotting people but not too good for defending, it was just one big obvious target sticking up into the nighttime sky.

I grabbed my gear and started down the ladder and went to yell to the guard next to me to do the same but he was already near the bottom of his ladder. When I reached the bottom of the ladder to my tower, I noticed that the guard to my left had already assumed a prone fighting position near the top of the berm. The other guard to my right and I ran up the slope of the berm until we reached the top, falling to the ground heavily, weapons out, taking aim at the approaching column, exposing only our heads and shoulders and letting the berm protect as much of the rest of our bodies as it could. I quickly snapped the grenades off of my lbg belt and placed them beside me and pulled six magazines of ammo out their containers and placed those close by as well, ready for immediate use.

I noticed that the guards to either side of me were doing the same. I snapped the bipod onto my M-16 and took aim, shuffling around on the dirt to find a spot where I could just barely sight them in so that only the top half of my face and the top of my shoulders were exposed to return fire. My clothes, neck and arms were now thoroughly dirty but I dismissed that thought, I would deal with that problem when and if I ever had to do so. The thought occurred to me that a few minutes ago I was happy and contented and safe and clean, and now, on this clear warm summers night, the killing would most likely begin within seconds.

When the point man of the approaching line of men reached about two hundred feet away, myself and another guy simultaneously ordered them to stop, and they did, instantaneously. We shouted out to them, asking them who they were. We didn't shout out a one phase password to which they were supposed to reply in the password of the day. That was nonsense, few people remembered the ever changing passwords of a challenge password and a response password. The pointman that they were from the Second battalion or something. Some of their words were impossible to hear because of the distance between us but their voices were obviously American so we told them to proceed. Only the pointman and two other troopers approached us, the remainder of the column stayed prone on the ground.

I noticed that they were not pointing their weapons directly at us, that would have been a game changer. The person in charge of that patrol was visibly upset and asked us why we challenged him. We told him that we should have fired on him as soon as he came out of the jungle seven hundred yards away and that the only reason that we didn't was because we wanted to be absolutely sure that it was the enemy, and, to let them get closer so as to assure a better killing zone. He was incredulous and said, "Weren't you informed that there was a patrol out there and that we would be returning at exactly 6:30 pm?"

We said: "No. We were instructed to fire on anything that moved". I guess he couldn't quite believe what he was hearing because he asked us that question again and again and received the same answer. He was a bit flustered, probably realizing that he was lucky to still be alive. He didn't ask us why we didn't follow orders, didn't fire on him as soon as he and his team emerged from the tree line, didn't challenge him with a password as they closed in on us. He didn't ask any more questions, he just suddenly stomped off with fire in his eyes, I guess to find the person that was responsible for this snafu. I think that he realized that he missed being killed tonight only because the perimeter guards were not too nervous or too new to military operations, or not too "short" or maybe they had enough time in the field to take instructions from green Lieutenants as merely guidelines and not direct orders. Maybe it was because these veterans had enough common decency, and courage, to not start shooting at people unless it was absolutely necessary.

I thought that pretty soon a Lieutenant would come stomping out to our position, cursing and yelling because <u>we</u> somehow made a mistake. I figured that the leader of that combat patrol would really raise a ruckus over this entire situation and that we on guard duty would somehow be blamed for it. I thought that, yes, we didn't follow orders to fire on anyone in the killing zone, and yes, we hadn't properly challenged them with a password. On the other hand, I thought, its going to be pretty hard to court martial us for NOT killing friendlies. I never saw that Lieutenant again. We were relieved by other guards about three hours later and I went back to the hooch and put my rifle and ammo and grenades and lbg and helmet next to my cot, then went to a little Quonset hut in the Company area that was the Enlisted Mens club. It just had some tables and chairs and a bar that served only beer and soda but at least they were cold. I had a few beers and talked to a few guys for a little while and then went back to the hooch and fell asleep. I was very tired for some reason.

The next morning I got some food at the mess hall and decided to take another shower. This time I had the shower to myself and really washed down very well. After washing off another layer of dirt I noticed the extent of the sores on my arms. There were many but some of them were worthy of notice. All of them were horrible and nothing like I had ever seen or imagined in civilian life. Ten of them were particularly horrible. Very deep, open sores roughly round in shape, about three inches in diameter and about a half an inch deep. They obviously had penetrated the full thickness of skin and had already started to destroy muscle tissue. They did not look good at all. When beating the bush your arms were continuously cut by sharp leaves and stabbed by spikes on trees and torn and ripped open deeply by thorns. I figured that with all of the dirt and insecticide and old blood and sweat and vegetable matter and poisons that this was probably some sort of "jungle rot". Many soldiers in my Company had lesions on their skin but I had observed that no one else seemed to have exactly this malady, or if they did, I had it a lot worse.

I went to the Company medics' tent and showed them the problem. A few of them examined it and said that there was nothing that they could do for it. They were adamant that I not cover the sores with any ointment or bandages. They insisted that the open air would be good for it. They didn't give me any pills or anything. I asked them if they knew what it was and they said "Oh yeah, we know exactly what it is but we can't tell you." I asked them what the hell they were talking about, but they said that they had orders to report such wounds, but not to provide a diagnosis to the soldiers that had it.

Later that day I went to the mess hall for lunch and was standing last in a short line. Four guys in a group came up and stood behind me. I think that they had just arrived in country. After a few minutes of them speaking softly amongst themselves, one of them asked me what was on my skin. I looked down at my arms and with a straight face, simply said "Leprosy". The guy didn't say a word but just turned around and walked a few steps back to his friends. I faced forwards and couldn't hear what was being said by the group behind me but there seemed to be an urgent, whispered conversation taking place. I waited for about a minute, enjoying my little joke, before turning around to tell them that I was just kidding, but when I looked around everyone behind me in line had walked away from the mess hall line.

In fact, many years later, I found that that injury was due to leishmaniasis (due to a certain insect bite), which is frequently mis-diagnosed as leprosy, in other words, it looks exactly like leprosy. Those sores really are nasty looking. Each sore lasts from three days to fifteen months before they heal, leaving behind a permanent disfigurement, and they keep coming back for thirty or more years. A person so affected may have very many such sores. Thirty years of leprosy, I never volunteered for that. Actually, if a combat soldier actually contracted leprosy, at the time, it would be considered a very minor inconvenience compared to other things going on in the bush. Yes, life as a combat Infantryman was not pretty, not pretty at all. The things that a Country asked of its soldiers in a war was far, far beyond their most horrible imaginations. A soundbite from a politician translated into unimaginable suffering for its citizen/soldiers.

Chapter 17

OPERATION BIG SPRINGS

Cannon to right of them,
Cannon to left of them,
Cannon in front of them
Volleyed and thundered;
Stormed at with shot and shell,
Boldly they rode and well,
Into the jaws of Death,
Into the mouth of Hell
Rode the six hundred.

Alfred Tennyson
The Charge of the Light Brigade

Close By Artillery or Air Strikes

The word for the new operation was that it would be fairly close to our base camp, maybe ten or twenty miles away. I thought that that was a good sign. I figured that the area in that part of the country was fairly safe but since it was to be a seventeen day long operation, it was probably going to be a long, miserable dangerous one under the best of circumstances. We loaded onto trucks and went to where the choppers would pick us up at another part of the base camp/airbase. This time we were not going to be carrying the mortars throughout the operation. We were told that we would carry the mortar for the first day or two and then we could hump without that extra weight and firepower but that they might be brought in by chopper later in the mission, or just brought in at night and evacuated in the morning. I was very glad to know that I might get rid of that mortar barrel and cannon rounds that had nearly brought me to my knees in ultra extreme pain and exhaustion on so many occasions. This hump would be arduous, but somewhat not as extremely bad as it could be.

There were only six helicopters in all but the word was that the landing zone that we were going to assault was only large enough for three choppers at a time. I would be on the first stick. That meant that the three choppers in my group would fly in, unload their troops and immediately take off, then a few minutes later the other three choppers would touch down. Then as each group landed, the choppers would immediately return to the air base to pick up more soldiers, and so on until the entire Company was inserted into the landing zone.

It was an unofficial policy in the 173rd Airborne Brigade that if one helicopter landed, all of them would land, regardless of the situation on the ground. If the first flight of helicopters approached a landing zone and were subjected to extremely heavy fire, they could veer off and fly away and then, maybe, depending on the situation, could call in artillery or air strikes or gunships onto the LZ to suppress the enemy fire. But if the very first helicopters actually landed and the troops jumped out and came under enemy fire then you have a situation where six men are fighting against an enemy force that probably greatly outnumbered them.

If that was the case then those six men were doomed if they were left there by themselves. That was exactly the tactic of the enemy, to allow ten or twenty troopers to land and then to kill every one of them while they scared off the rest of the assault force from landing with a witheringly heavy fire from dug in positions, directed at the troopers on the ground primarily but certainly and heavily at the helicopters coming in.

If I was on the second or third flight of an airmobile assault, I wouldn't like going in under extremely heavy fire, with choppers being shot down and men shot up before they even reached the ground. But I could just as likely have been assigned to the first stick of helicopters and I wouldn't want to be among the first troops on the ground in such a situation either. Once there were men on the ground, come Hell or high water, the rest of the Company will air assault onto the landing zone, regardless of the dangers. So, as the saying goes, "Once one chopper goes in, We all go in".

It was a sunny day, the sky a bright light blue color. It was only about nine o'clock in the morning but already very hot and humid while we waited for the choppers to pick us up. After about fifteen minutes of waiting the choppers picked us up. The flight only lasted about fifteen minutes, flying over rice paddies and farms and jungle. Flying in the choppers though was nice and cool with a breeze blowing past us and through the open sides of the airship but I knew that once on the ground it would be another world of hurt. I was on the second chopper of the first stick. We would be in the first group of eighteen troopers inserted on the ground for this air assault. We always had an assigned position to exit within each aircraft. The pilots didn't want men jumping out at random because he had to immediately correct the pitch and yaw of the aircraft as its weight and center of gravity shifted each time a hundred and eighty pound soldier jumped out each side of the helicopter with a hundred and ten pounds of equipment attached to him. The plan was almost always to have pairs of men, one on each side of the chopper, to jump simultaneously, in a pre-planned order. This time I was to be the first pair to exit our aircraft.

Our flight quickly descended towards an area in the jungle below us that had very tall trees on one side of it. As the choppers suddenly descended quickly and then abruptly slowed, a hundred feet from where we were to jump out. I noticed that the area consisted of extremely dense bushes about eight feet tall growing amongst grass about the height of a man. The pilot hovered and my squad Sergeant shouted the order to me to go. I started to push myself up and out but then suddenly froze. We were too high, way too high, probably twelve feet above the ground. I figured that, loaded down with all of my gear,

I'd break my legs and/or my spine jumping from that height. I leaned back and yelled into the cockpit for the pilot to get lower. He was only about three feet away but I don't think that he could hear me above the roar of the prop blast and the pandemonium of the choppers jet engine screaming. The co-pilot had his head twisted around almost backwards, looking at me, and was yelling something but I couldn't understand what he was saying, in fact I couldn't hear his voice at all.

Suddenly there were strange, distinctly metallic sounds that I thought at first were coming from the engine. It sounded like someone was banging on the choppers engine with a big monkey wrench or sledgehammer. I thought that those sounds must be incredibly loud to be heard over the maelstrom of noise that engulfed us. I thought that the engine was tearing itself apart and feared that we were going to uncontrollably crash land. I happened to look out two hundred yards or so to our side at twenty tall palm trees each about eighty feet tall, all in more or less a straight line. From near the top of most of those trees I easily spotted muzzle flashes from enemy soldiers, all of them firing viciously using automatic weapons.

I almost started to laugh because I thought that this must be some sort of joke, some sort of prank. I thought that maybe someone had hung firecrackers high up in the trees and that this was some sort of training exercise (as absurd as that scenario would have been), but feared deep down that that was not the case. I could see white and green tracers coming directly at my ship and spraying the other choppers. That explained everything, our chopper was taking hits from enemy fire.

Now the squad Sergeant and co-pilot were nearly hysterical, gesturing wildly and yelling for me to jump while the pilot just looked behind his seat, staring at me with a look of utter astonishment. But that didn't change my mind. I figured that we wouldn't be any good if we all had broken bones and if that happened the VC would surely swarm over us and we would all be dead within seconds of landing. I yelled again, directly at the pilot as loud as I could and gestured to bring the bird down lower but I don't think that he could hear me, I couldn't even hear my own voice. He just stared at me with the pupils of his eyes about as big as they could possibly be. After about ten seconds of this stand-off, the Sergeant had had enough and jumped out, landing hard and falling heavily onto his chest and face. He staggered to his feet under the shock of the jump and the heavy load that he was carrying and started to move away from the prop blast, towards the enemy, falling to one knee every other step and staggering like a drunken man due to the shock and injuries that he had suffered from the jump.

I don't think that the pilot got any lower, or if he did it was only a couple of feet, but I figured that if that Sergeant survived the jump then maybe I could too, maybe, but I could see that he had obviously been injured. I pushed myself out and caught out of the corner of my eye the other guys in my chopper and the guys in the other two choppers making the leap.

I hit the ground feet first but the weight of my equipment had shifted during the fall and I was very much off balance when I landed, instantly crashing onto my side. I fell onto tall grass and some bushes which absorbed some of the shock of the landing so that no bones were broken but the landing was so violent that I was dizzy and disoriented, probably knocked out for a few seconds, until the blood in my brain could regain its normal flow.

When I came to my senses, I was lying on my side, with my face pushed deeply into the dry grass. It was a heavy, mighty struggle just to stand up straight from the very awkward position that I was in on the ground and to break free of the heavy vegetation. I still cannot understand why noone in my three chopper stick wasn't seriously hurt or killed by that jump. I don't know for sure, maybe they were.

We were, I realized, like targets on a rifle range and I knew instinctively that my only chance to survive was to get out of that killing zone. I took a few steps and suddenly a white curtain seemed to suddenly blot my vision completely. A roaring, whooshing noise that seemed to come from inside my skull blotted out all other sounds and I realized that I was seconds away from passing out. I shook my head violently and willed with all of my strength to regain my senses. I guess that jump had scrambled my brains more than I had initially realized. A couple of more steps and my body just involuntarily collapsed onto the ground. I regained my vision and pushed ahead but every second or third step brought the curtain of white downwards and half of the time I would inexplicably find myself face down on the ground with no realization of how that had happened. After the tenth fall, I decided to just try to go forward on my hands and knees. I realized that my body simply would not work as I commanded it to do. I had to realize that the extreme shock of landing had obviously done some type of severe injury to my nervous and muscle systems and internal organs.

After crawling on my hands and knees for fifty feet I felt better. I quickly tested out my fitness by standing up and running. About ten feet later my hearing started to recover, the loud whooshing sound gradually being replaced by the sounds of enemy gunfire and helicopters rushing out of and into the landing zone. I started to catch up to my squad Sergeant who was in front of me. There was a soldier in front of him, probably from one of the other choppers.

The Sergeant abruptly stopped dead in his tracks and turned around to look at me over his shoulder. He had a stupid expression on his face as if to say, "Whoa, what do we do now?", or maybe it was an expression of someone being pulled into the water by a huge crocodile with an expression of "Is this really happening to me?"

I just looked at him, looked him in the eyes, and then roughly pushed past him. This was no time for discussion. We all knew what we had to do. Obviously we were all going to be killed, at any second, squarely ambushed by a superior force. There was only one thing to do and that was to directly assault, full on into their guns. We had nowhere to run or hide or seek cover. This was a full-blown ambush and the only thing to do was to try to take as many of them with us into death as we could. We could only answer death with death. We ran directly at them, but it seemed that they were concentrating most of their fire over our heads, at the departing and arriving helicopters. I thought that if someone could make it to the tree line there might be a possibility of surviving, the way we were, we were just in a shooting gallery. We ran about a hundred and fifty feet and I shot a glance over my shoulder and noticed that the paratroopers in the second string of helicopters were jumping out and onto the ground.

I really wanted to fire some M-79 grenades at the VC at the top of the tree line but I realized that I had lost situational awareness of what was happening. I didn't want to fire rounds that did not directly hit the tops of the trees which might well then hit friendly forces. At that point, I didn't know where friendly forces were but I thought that if I got close enough to the enemy then I could hit them with shotgun rounds. We got about two hundred feet from the tree line when the firing stopped suddenly and by the time we reached the tree line, the enemy had jumped down and vanished. They probably knew that they would be subjected to something terrible very soon and about a minute later that terror arrived in the form of a helicopter gun ship. It came in low and hard flying almost directly overhead, the roar of its engine and rotors suddenly overwhelmed by the horrifying blast of it Gatling guns as it saturated the trees with machine gun fire. I still cannot understand how it was possible, but I think that of the first eighteen men on the ground, none of them had been shot, but I'm not sure, not sure at all. The VC had every advantage to kill us all and they tried their best to do so. I think that other troopers were killed and wounded.

We pushed further into the jungle a hundred feet past where the enemy had been in the tall palm trees. While we had passed directly underneath those trees I scanned fervently upwards, worried that a VC might still be in one of the trees, fearful that he might shoot me or one of my fellow soldiers but hoping that I could spot one so I could blast him with my shot gun round from below, that should settle him I thought. We stopped and took up firing positions to await the third stick of choppers. The enemy had disappeared into the jungle, terminating their ambush almost as quickly as they had initiated it.

How could they have known that we would land exactly where we did and then to have set up an ambush? The answer that others discovered and was passed down the line, was that we had inadvertently landed almost directly onto the middle of an enemy base camp. The vegetation was so thick and their positions so well camouflaged that the camp couldn't be detected. (The location of the enemy base camp was unknown to our headquarters and the fact that we landed directly on top of them was a pure happenstance). My squad and other men stayed where we were while other soldiers from the other assault helicopters investigated the base camp and their medics tended to the wounded and dying from the initial two sticks. After about fifteen minutes some Medevac choppers arrived on scene and the American injured and dead were loaded onto them.

We formed up and started to move out in single file, into a heavily overgrown jungle of tall trees with eight feet tall bushes on the ground. I tried to push the events of the last twenty minutes out of my head. We had only just started this mission and we had a full day of horrible suffering humping ahead of us, and then days and days of the same torture ahead of us. Maybe I would have been better off if I had taken an enemy round to the head I thought.

The vegetation in many of the areas in which we operated contained vines. There were vines that grew close to the ground that were thinner than a string and only a few feet long but there were other vines that were hundreds of feet long and thicker and tougher. There were sometimes vines that grew a hundred feet apart and sometimes clusters of vines so thick and entwined among others and growing so close together that a man would snag twenty of them on his boot with each step. Sometimes a vine just grew across a single large bush and sometimes they grew on top of many bushes and snaked through them, from one bush to another, so that it seemed that every bush in the jungle was connected with twenty other bushes via the vines. There were sometimes Tarzan like vines two to four inches thick that hung down from near the tops of very tall trees all the way to the ground and there were sometimes tens of thick vines that reached to the tops of the tallest trees like a scene from a nightmarish fairy tale, their crooked arms seeming to strangle the victim tree.

The ground vines were the most troublesome because they had a tendency to trip a person since they were just a few inches off of the ground. We called them "wait a minute vines" because they would catch on our boots and stop us abruptly in our tracks. Then you had to stop and back up a step or two to get free from them. Many times soldiers didn't notice them mixed amongst the litter on the jungle floor or the extremely dense vegetation and would suddenly lose their balance and stagger sideways or unexpectedly find themselves smashing their face into the dirt, tripped up by what looked to be just leaves.

Many times you could just bull your way through, just kick forcefully and break the vine and continue on, but some of the vines were too thick or tough to break and then you were forced to back up a little and work your feet free. Sometimes a forceful kick would break the vine a goodly distance away from your feet. It was sort of like pulling on the middle of a hundred foot long string. Sometimes it will break where you hold it and sometimes break at one of the ends or break anywhere in between. So that sometimes you had broken the vine but were dragging five twenty-foot vines on each boot so you had to eventually stop and try to disentangle yourself.

Sometimes I would be startled by noises in the bushes twenty to eighty feet away. Sometimes I would be suddenly frightened because a number of bushes suddenly moved and I would abruptly crouch down, swinging my weapon to bear on bushes forty feet to my flank because the vine that I had just kicked was snaked through all of the immediate bushes for a hundred feet although, of course, a moving bush fifty feet away could well have been an enemy soldier. The long vines that were strung out from ankle to head high not only impeded our progress but were doubly troublesome because they tended to get caught on our gear, especially on the ammo pouches and grenades on our load bearing gear belts. I realized also that every time you were suddenly slowed down or stopped by what you may think was a bunch of vines could well be a trip wire to an enemy explosive.

Now we were encountering many vines that grew near the ground and amongst the bushes up to five feet high. My squad was probably about in the middle of the line of march so many of the vines had already been broken by the men in front of us but there were still a number of them that caught at our feet and equipment. We could break through many of them with a forceful kick or a determined lunge forward but I had to continually check my feet to see if I was dragging any of them behind me. After about a half an hour of that situation I was again checking my boots and happened to notice my LBG belt. I was instantly horrified and just weakly said to no one in particular "No, No, No, No!" over and over, turning around and around with my arms at my side and my hands limply flapping in some sort of display of utter panic. I thought that I would be torn apart within a couple of seconds. The cause of my distress was a hand grenade still attached to my belt with the spoon missing. I thought for sure that I was about to die and that there was nothing that I could do fast enough to prevent it.

The body of a fragmentation grenade is mostly oblong, merging into a sort of little neck which in turn meets with the rectangular top of the grenade which contains the arming mechanism. The grenades were carried individually with little straps attached to the LBG belt, each strap wrapped around the neck of the grenade and then snapped closed. On a grenade, there is a lever (spoon) that is held in place by a cotter pin that is attached to a ring. You hold the grenade in one hand, forcing the lever tightly against the side of the grenade. Then you pull on the ring which pulls out the cotter pin. As soon as the grenade is thrown the spoon is automatically flung off by a spring, igniting the fuse and four to six seconds later the grenade explodes.

When I saw the grenade on my belt with the spoon missing I assumed that I would be killed within the next two seconds. A few seconds later I was flabbergasted to realize that I was still alive. I fearfully looked closer at the grenade and noticed that most of the spoon was missing but the cotter pin was still in place so the grenade was not yet armed. I eventually deduced that a vine had caught the spoon of the grenade and broken most of it off. I hadn't felt the tug of that vine while I was trying to bull my way through other vines holding me back. That same situation would occur several more times before I left Viet Nam and every time it happened I almost had a heart attack.

Because of that problem, we bent the cotter pins at a ninety degree angle with a little metal can opener. That meant that you wouldn't be pulling out the pin with your teeth like in the movies. In fact, to throw the grenade would require that you bend the cotter pin back so that it is straight with the little can opener or your bayonet. That would require some precious seconds, but the alternative was to have the ring and cotter pin pulled out by branches or huge thorns or vines and then the grenade would explode unexpectedly while still attached to your body, or maybe be pulled completely off of your belt and kill the man behind you as you continued walking away, oblivious to what had happened. No, actual combat was not according to Hollywood depictions, the reality of it is much more horrible than a movie audience would like to see. It was a dangerous, dangerous business where a soldier could be killed by the seemingly most unlikely and unanticipated causes. Its not that they could be killed, they were killed, on a regular basis at a probability of death about a hundred thousand times what civilians might encounter. The danger that a soldier dealt with every day in the field is beyond, way beyond, the imagination of anyone who has never experienced it.

Most of the soldiers in my Company had modern grenades. Those grenades had a smooth thin metal covering that was painted green. Inside is a coil of wire made of some extremely hard metal that had been "nicked" or partially cut into about five hundred sections. When it exploded, other than its metal shell tearing into jagged pieces of shrapnel, it produced five hundred very small white-hot pieces, any one of which being capable of doing horrible things to a human body. A few other men and I had been issued modern grenades but also "pineapple" grenades that were probably WWII vintage. I wondered whether they would work after probably twenty five years in storage. They sort of looked like a pineapple with a very thick metal covering that had been scored into small squares.

Those grenades would break into only about thirty pieces when the grenade exploded but those pieces would be very much larger and heavier than the modern type. The modern grenades were supposed to be more "effective" but the old pineapple grenades were still very deadly and issued a hideous way to die or get wounded. A big problem with using grenades in a heavily wooded area is that if you are not very careful in throwing the grenade, it can bounce off of a tree branch or get hung up in heavy vegetation and kill the man who threw it or those around him.

The entire area in which we were conducting this operation had been designated as a "free fire zone". The type of mission was "search and destroy". That meant that we were to shoot anything or anyone in this area, no questions asked. The Army would usually fly over some area that was known to be controlled and populated with enemy soldiers. Announcements were made by loudspeaker from a helicopter that any civilians would have ten days or so to evacuate the area. The Air Force would fly over and drop tens or hundreds of thousands of leaflets that commanded the non-combatants to leave the area and instructed them where to go. That helped greatly to eliminate civilian casualties but it gave the enemy advance notice of our intentions. They would then have time to evacuate the area themselves or to prepare fighting positions and set up booby traps and plan and emplace ambushes. It prevented many civilian causalities but greatly increased the amount of our military killed or wounded when eventually we went in amongst them.

We beat the bush for the next couple of days without any causalities on either side. The next day while on our combat patrol we came upon a group of about six houses, arranged in a row. Those houses were just one room shacks. The sides were made of bamboo with straw or grass roofs and dirt floors, no door or windows or electricity or running water. If there was any furniture it was just a small table and some chairs, all of which made from crooked sticks. They were on the edge of a small open grassy area that I guessed was some sort of farmland. That little settlement was a distinct anomaly in this region, out in the middle of the country, many miles from their nearest neighbors.

The settlement seemed to be abandoned. Someone told us that some soldiers had found some people in one of those hoochs.The line of march had stopped and word was passed that we would stay there in place for five minutes.There were a few soldiers standing in front of one of the shacks so I went to take a look at what was happening. There wasn't even a door on that hooch. I couldn't see anybody inside at first so I stepped through the opening and saw two soldiers just casually standing around.

I walked towards the back of the hooch to see if what I thought was the situation was in fact accurate. Upon closer inspection I saw a Vietnamese woman sitting on the dirt floor, huddling with her back to the back wall with two very young children, one probably a year old and the other less than three years old.The youngest child was softly crying while the older child seemed as if he didn't know whether to cry or to join into some sort of new game with the strange people who had suddenly arrived.

We had orders to shoot anyone in that area and those people should not have been there at all, they had obviously been warned by helicopter loudspeakers and leaflets. Luckily, the troopers who discovered them weren't nervous, or maybe they were just professional or maybe they had some human decency about them or maybe they were the type that would jeopardize they own lives to try to avoid killing innocent people. Given the warnings to the civilian population, I would not have blamed them for shooting first and asking questions later. In fact those troopers were directly dis-obeying orders Those people had no right to be there, they had been warned seriously and thoroughly to evacuate the area, at great risk to the Americans issuing the warnings.

If the discovering American troops had been fired upon, the survivors probably would have been court marshaled for dereliction of duty, for not have fired upon the Vietnamese immediately, no questions asked.Those guys had everything to lose and nothing to gain by their actions for failing to shoot immediately.They were nothing short of heroes.

The Vietnamese woman on the ground was obviously terrified. She clutched her children desperately.There wasn't a Vietnamese soldier interpreter immediately available. I thought that my presence in her hooch just added one more monster to her nightmare. She had been caught and now there were strange men loaded down with deadly weapons in her house. I figured that she didn't need another person, like me, my presence alone to further add to her terror, if that was possible. I hoped that the situation could be explained to her soon. That she would be told that everything would be all right. On the other hand, I couldn't understand why she had been left in such a situation by her fellow citizens, who had all evacuated the area. Obviously, it seemed, she was no threat to us but she had been left by her neighbors to be killed.

On other operations, we had strict instructions to "Do Not Fire Unless Fired Upon". That order placed major additional dangers upon us, but kept innocent people from being killed. It kept Vietnamese civilians from being killed but seriously ramped up the probability of us being killed. I felt sorry for the woman because she must have been terrorized at the proximity of a group of heavily armed soldiers. None of the soldiers in that small group spoke any Vietnamese so no one said anything to the woman. The men acted very calmly and spoke softly, regarding the woman and her children gently and generally trying to project a non-threatening demeanor.

No one seemed to know exactly what to do. I searched around the hooch with my weapon at the very ready but didn't see an immediate threat (although she could have had a grenade or electrical wire to a claymore to kill us all behind her back). I just didn't want to kill her, certainly not her children, although that may have been an occurrence of unintentional secondary damage if I could possibly avoid it although that mindset could have easily resulted in me and my squad being killed or maimed. After a quick check of her position I decided to leave the hooch, hoping to lower the woman's anxiety a bit. She was scared to death, she didn't need my presence to give her a full heart attack. She and her children were the only people in this area. Apparently everyone else in the area had gotten the word to evacuate a week ago and had done so or maybe they were out in the jungle in their black pajamas and AK-47s waiting for us. I still don't know why she chose to remain and I don't know what became of her and the children but I'm reasonably sure that they were treated kindly while in our custody.

A few minutes later my platoon got the word to move out. We continued humping for a few more hours and came to a creek. The jungle floor abruptly dropped very steeply, almost vertically, down to a creek running swiftly about thirty feet wide. On each side the bank dropped down very steeply about ten feet.

I thought at first that the pointman had happened upon a good place to cross the stream, with a huge tree that had happened to have been blown down in a hurricane or keeled over due to old age but then I thought that this was obviously not due to natural causes. The explanation was the combat engineers had gone ahead of us and blown down a tree with huge amounts of high explosives to afford us a way to cross over of that creek. It occurred to me that the combat engineers had gone way beyond our infantry and accomplished that situation. Did they have Infantry support to protect them or were they simply absolutely courageous men in front of everyone? I don't know. I guess that it was a combination of both situations. I don't know, but I have to give them a lot of credit.

The first forty feet of the tree didn't have any branches. The trunk of the tree was about three feet wide, very circular so that there was a very small area on which to place your boots while you were walking and even that was curved. It was a very tricky thing to cross, especially with so much equipment. We slung our weapons over our shoulders and stretched out our arms to the sides for balance, trying to execute a delicate high-wire act loaded with a hundred pounds of equipment. It was only a fifteen foot drop into the water, but to fall into that rushing water loaded down with equipment and unable to climb the banks would almost guarantee a fatal outcome. I think that everyone made it without falling. In the scheme of things it was just a little deadly game that broke the monotony of the march for a few minutes. In a civilian situation it would have been an almost unimaginable situation.

That night a new guy, freshly "in Country", was flown in by chopper. He helped another guy dig a fighting position and joined all of us on the perimeter for sunset guard duty. About thirty minutes after sunset, when it was already pitch black dark, we got the word to begin the regular shifts of guard duty, so that half of the men could go to sleep. I was in my fighting position on the first guard shift for about five minutes when suddenly there was a shimmering purplish-white light behind me, lighting up a area for about thirty feet in the deep darkness. I had no idea of what it could possibly be at first, then I could see that it was the new guy, on top of a little hill of dirt about five feet tall, trying to cook something with a heat tab. Someone ran over to him and kicked dirt onto the little C-ration stove he was using and then stomped on the entire contraption that he had, including the food or water that he was heating. Someone huskily whispered "What are you doing?" He said he was trying to make hot cocoa. Obviously this new guy was not clear on the concept. That guy had just made himself (and those around him) a perfect target for any enemy that was beyond our perimeter in the dark. How anyone could possibly be so stupid I will never know. Any new replacement was referred to as an "FNG" as in "Did you see what that FNG did last night?" or "Tell that "FNG" to dig in deeper" or "Tell the FNG that he left his weapon over here". "FNG" being an abbreviation for F . . . . New Guy.

We were sometimes issued heating tabs. They came in a package about four inches long and an inch deep in which there were three purple tabs. When lighted with a match they burned for about four minutes with a strong chemical smell. Just heating a large cup of coffee might require two of them. We were never given very many of them, in fact we were never issued enough of them. We would make a stove out of an old C-ration can. We would take our p38 can opener, which is a little piece of metal with a sort of hooked blade that folded out, which worked very well to open cans, once you got the hang of it. We would take the empty small C-ration can and make about twenty cuts near the bottom of it and about twenty cuts near the top. The top would have already been cut off to get at the contents. Then a heat tab was put into it and set afire with a match. Once it ignited, you could put a metal canteen cup with water or a can of C-rations on top of it and it would maybe get kind of warm if you were lucky.

I noticed that some of the men carried on the outside of their rucksacks a plastic bag that was about two feet long and two inches square, filled with some sort of yellow substance. I used to think that it was some sort of chicken bullion or something. One day everyone was out of heat tabs but I noticed one guy boiling a half a quart of water at a rapid boil on top of his C-ration can stove. I asked him how he managed to get it boiling so vigorously and he reached into his bag of "chicken bullion" and pulled out a piece of the substance, it had about the consistency of Play-Doh. He rolled it into a ball about half the size of a golf ball and gave it to me. I asked him what it was and he informed me that it was C-4 explosive.

He said just put it into your stove and light it with a match. I thought that he was joking but he was very serious. To demonstrate, he put it into my stove and put a match to it. It took about five seconds to ignite, but once it did, it burned with a hissing sound and with the intensity of a blowtorch. I put my C-ration can of food on top of the stove and within five seconds it was bubbling out of the can. I pulled that off and put a half-quart of water in a heavy canteen cup on top of the stove and in ten seconds it was boiling vigorously. Yes, this C-4 explosive worked just excellently. The guy who gave it to me said that it will not explode unless ignited with a blasting cap.

We went on another patrol the next day and eventually set up for the night in a large clearing. After digging in and the sunset guard, some of the guys sat around listening to a small transistor radio. There were very few radio stations in VietNam. The Army

broadcast one of them but we were rock and roll guys and the U.S. government station was pretty lame. There was one station that must have emitted a very strong signal because we could pick it up easily on the radio. Sometimes it was the only station that we could hear. It played good songs and had a sweet talking female DJ. That was Hanoi Jane on a communist broadcast station, hidden somewhere in the country. She would play some good songs and then suggest to her listeners that they were probably homesick and missed their girlfriends and they should all just go home, just tell the Army that they just quit. The problem was that you couldn't just quit without some serious time in the brig or a federal prison, followed by a dishonorable discharge. In fact you couldn't even just desert the Army, you were on the other side of the world, how would you get home? She would play a number of good songs and then would have specialized messages for various units. She liked to talk about the 173rd Airborne Brigade and in her soft and sweet voice told us things like that the 173rd Airborne Brigade would meet up with 4th regiment of VC soldiers within a day or so and that we would all be killed or that the area that we were going to patrol the next day was very heavily mined and booby trapped. It all could be very true but most of us just laughed it off and waited to hear some more good tunes. It was a bit disconcerting though to learn that she had the exact map coordinates of our positions in the field and would say things like "your four tanks" won't help you. How she knew our position and resources I don't know.

We were camped that night in the jungle, just at the edge of a relatively large grass clearing near the top of a hill. There was a gentle downwards slope to this clearing so that there was a clear view of a large expanse of countryside and sky to our east. Off in the distance we could hear almost continuous rumbling sounds and could see bright flashs on the ground probably about four miles away. That was B52 aircraft dropping thousand or two thousand bombs into the jungle, trying to shake the ground and collapse the tunnels that were out there. The planes were so high that you could not hear their huge jet engines, you couldn't even see the aircraft. Somewhere out there in the jungle, without any warning, it must have seemed like the end of the world. For some people out there, it was the end of the world.

I had to go to the bathroom. People had been assigned to dig a long narrow trench to use as a community latrine in this Company sized area but I didn't like the idea of squatting in the bush next to other people. I decided to walk out into the middle of the perimeter, which was all short grass and fairly dark now that the sun had set about an hour ago. I dug a hole with my entrenching tool, and just sat on the ground to complete my business. After thirty seconds or so, I could see across from us, about two miles away, dull flashes of gunfire. Then I started to hear soft but distinctive "put put put" sounds all around me. I suddenly put two and two together and realized that the flashs were from a fifty caliber heavy machine gun and the "put put put" sounds were the sounds of the rounds landing in the clearing all around me, some of them very close.

No one here could hear the fifty caliber explosions as the bullets were shot out of the barrel because they were so far away but you could certainly hear those huge bullets slamming into the ground and the trees and whizzing through the air a few feet away from you. There was no cover at all from where I was so I sat there for a half a minute, hoping that they would move their fire away from my position. Then I jumped up, pulled up my pants and ran over to our fighting positions, yelling loudly that we were taking fire. The other guys in my Company were well aware of what was happening and when I ran up to them said that that fire must be coming from another Company of the battalion that had settled in for the night.

They said that our Company commander was trying to make contact with them to order a cease-fire. It turned out that they were just engaging in Harassment and Interdiction (H&I) fire and were unaware that we were located where we were. I had wondered what it would be like to be a VC taking H&I at night, now I had a much better idea of that experience. They had probably fired two hundred rounds or more into our general vicinity but I don't think that anyone was hurt. I had just been minding my own business, in the middle of a heavily defended perimeter under a magnificent sky and I almost had a two foot hole put into my chest by our own forces from two miles away while sitting on the ground going to the bathroom. There were very many ways to be killed over here, none of them were funny.

The next day we resumed our combat patrols. The general area was rice paddies, rubber trees and medium jungle. We passed some round holes in the ground about ten feet deep and thirty feet across. When we stopped for a five-minute break the guy behind me (an absolute cherry) said that it was unbelievable how the VC could dig those holes. I told him that they were the result of two thousand pound bombs from the B52 strikes. He didn't think that that was true but when I asked him how long he thought it would take a person to dig just one of those holes and what purpose they would serve he realized that I was right, but still found it hard to believe that one bomb could do such damage. In World War II such a bomb was called a "block-buster" because just one could destroy a city block.

Later that day the line of march had stopped for a minute or so and then began to move out again. The two men in front of me were standing and I had just managed to stand up when out of nowhere there was suddenly a huge "whooshing" sound that approached us, flying low almost directly overhead and then continued onwards all in less than one second. At first I couldn't imagine what it could be, my best guess was that it seemed to be three enormous things traveling at an incredible speed, sending out shockwaves that seriously shook the air and then almost instantaneously shook the earth itself at my feet. It was just a horribly and unknown powerful expression of power. A few seconds later we could hear some dull explosions in the vicinity of the area towards which those things were traveling.

We quickly realized that it must be our artillery firing, probably from three miles away, with the huge shells traveling directly over us on an almost flat trajectory, on the way to their distant target. They must have been hundred and fifty-five mm shells. Someone put in a radio call to make sure that the artillery guys knew that we were in the vicinity.

Later in the day we could hear whining sounds, getting louder and louder which was artillery coming in from a very high altitude. The rounds travel faster than the speed of sound, so when you hear a whining sound that lasts for a few seconds, the round would explode quite a far distance from you. When the whining sound lasted for only one second, the round would land quite close to you. When a round landed very close, the whining sound would last only a split second before the explosion. They say that you never hear the round that lands on top of you, that kills you, and that is very true, you're killed by the bomb a split second before its signature screaming would be heard.

Later we came upon an area that had been heavily bombed. There were a few craters made by two thousand pound bombs dropped by B52 aircraft and in that same area it looked like maybe ten very large caliber artillery rounds had landed in a relatively small area. The entire area was burned and blackened so maybe a jet had dropped some napalm in there as well. All of the undergrowth had been destroyed completely but the horribly jagged stumps of some large and small trees still remained. Those stumps were not cleanly cut at all but were just leafless poles terminating with ends that had been torn apart, split into scores of pieces, like a tornado or hurricane had torn them apart. Of course the high explosive gasses and shrapnel from the explosives must have been a hundred times the force of a tornado.

Where a large artillery round had landed there was a hole in the ground and five feet around that perimeter the earth was swept clean of leaves. The shrapnel had been thrown upwards at about a forty-five degree angle so that a tree that was ten feet away from the center of the hole would be reduced to a stump that was shattered at about three feet high and a tree that was thirty feet away would be a stump about seven feet tall. Of course, if a person was within a hundred feet of the explosion and lying on the ground, he might not be killed by shrapnel but the concussion of the blast would probably be fatal.

The casualty radius of an 81mm High Explosive mortar round that weighs about ten pounds is about forty feet. I don't know what the casualty radius of a two thousand pound bomb is but it must be a very far distance indeed. When there were B52 strikes, they were not supposed to target an area that was within two miles of friendly troops.

While walking around through this shattered and burned out area I suddenly spotted a small deer. I thought it was a baby deer but I'm not sure. There were deer in Viet Nam that we would see some times that looked like regular deer, brown with white spots, but were much smaller. I think that a full-grown deer in Viet Nam might be less than three feet tall, probably fifty pounds. This small deer was a young one. I'd guess that it only weighed about fifteen pounds. I thought that perhaps it was looking for its mother because there was nothing to eat in this area, any forage that may have existed had been thoroughly and completely burned and destroyed. It seemed totally at ease with our presence, not in the least bit frightened or concerned. I thought that if its mother had been anywhere near this area when it was bombed that she was probably now in about a thousand pieces and scattered all over this area. Its alive and well I thought but without its mother it would be dead within a week, another living creature killed by the incredible violence that it had initially survived.

As we continued on patrol, we came out of the jungle and into an area of rice paddies and then encountered a few wooden buildings, probably part of some type of farm and we went to investigate the situation. It was some kind of farm with a long building that had no side walls, just a roof held up by wooden posts. The building was "L" shaped with one side about a hundred feet long until it changed direction by ninety degrees and continued on for another fifty feet.

There were a few water buffalo close by. The buffalos were disturbed by our presence, they stomped their feet and shook their massive horns. They were not fenced in and they seemed to be very angry. Their eyes seemed to be horribly bloodshot, either that or their eyes were red like some sort of demon I thought.

The lumber composing the roof was very roughly cut but it was a far cry from the traditional walls of crooked sticks and branches found throughout the rest of the country. The building was mostly empty except for what seemed to be some type of hay.

While other men looked around, examining the building, seemingly unconcerned about any immediate threat, save that of a VC popping out of a hidden and covered hole in the ground or a trip-wired grenade or mine, I was very concerned about those animals. I slid the safety off of my weapon, ready to fire instantly if one of those huge animals came charging at us. I would have hated to have killed a farmers very valuable property but I realized that one of those things could kill a bunch of men very quickly if he so wanted. I thought, if it was necessary, maybe I could just wound them so that they might eventually recover from their injuries and the farmer might have use of them some day. Then , but then I realized that those things are going to need a whole lot of killing to stop them if they charged. I slid the selector switch on my rifle to full automatic.

Most people are familiar with photographs of small children atop a water buffalo. The buffalo becomes accustomed to that child, over many months and the child becomes the buffalos master. The buffalo is submissive to the child but otherwise is extremely aggressive to anyone else. I worried that my M-16, although it could throw out some fearsomely devastating projectiles, probably wouldn't be enough to stop one of those massive, heavily muscled animals before it trampled and gored several men. Their horns were massive, they probably weighed between two to three thousand pounds each.

I mentioned to a few soldiers close to me with M-16s that we should keep an eye on those animals and be ready if they came out rampaging at us. I was trying to stir up an interest in those soldiers to watch those animals so that if the buffalos suddenly decided to charge at us there would be more firepower instantly available, other than myself, to stop them. But those soldiers seemed to be very indifferent towards that possible threat and more interested in investigating the buildings. They basically ignored the animals, and me. I guess they saw the buffalos as some sort of harmless cow. I regarded each animal as twenty professional wrestlers in one package, with muscles five times stronger than a humans, with huge horns, and everyone of them looking and acting as if it was homicidally insane.

So now this was a turnabout for me. I was more concerned about those animals than about any other possible enemy threat. Those bulls seemed to settle down after about five minutes. They didn't seem to be so anxious or angry, they weren't stomping and snorting and shaking their heads nearly as much as before, but they seemed to me to have the same or worse look of hate about them. Those beasts just generally seemed to have an evil malevolence about them, in their big bloodshot red eyes and in the way they acted towards us, in their body language, but thankfully, they kept their distance. I don't know what it would take to drop a heavily muscled animal weighing two thousand pounds or more, maybe much more, in its tracks, on a full out charge, but doubted that I held it in my hands. If they charged it would be like shooting a runaway truck from ten feet away. I yelled to the soldiers nearby to keep an eye on those animals. I really didn't think that fifteen bullets to their head would stop them before they killed a few men.

I thought, that that would be a hell of a way to die in this country, gored and trampled by a water buffalo. Also, it occurred to me that even if I did kill one of them, it wouldn't make much of a trophy hanging on a wall. Their huge head and five foot wide horns, hung on a wall, would not give any indication of how threatening their massive and muscled ton and a half bodies could be, and it most certainly could not indicate the absolute and utter hate that they seemed to have in their eyes, nor the deadly threats of their stomping and stamping and snorting as I saw them now. Anyways, how could I hump a dead water buffalos head until the end of the operation?

The animals seemed very edgy but they kept their distance. I pointed my weapon directly at one of them but it had no effect at changing their demeanor. Of course, I thought, that was like pointing a stick at them as far as they were concerned. They gave every indication that they wanted to kill us but for some reason they kept their distance. After a few minutes of watching them closely I decided to move on and investigate the area with the other soldiers.

A few hundred feet away there was a small pond, about thirty feet in diameter, filled with a solid black liquid substance that looked and smelled like it was some kind of dense manure. I thought that it was very strange to have such a pond and that maybe the VC were using it to conceal weapons. I suggested throwing a grenade into the middle of it to see what happened, maybe the explosive would burst a watertight container under that manure, but a Sergeant overruled me. He went to the edge to investigate the substance but he wasn't keen on reaching in and scooping up a cup of it to determine exactly what it was.

There were no enemy or civilians to be found so we pushed on, out into the hot sun and across a rice paddy, basically completely exposed to any enemy fire from the jungles edge. We crossed rice paddies many, many times in Viet Nam but I never liked doing so. In the paddies we were like cardboard targets in the middle of an open rifle range. Enemy snipers concealed in the surrounding jungle could kill us at will while we wouldn't be able to determine exactly where the fire was coming from and the only cover would be to fall behind a paddy dike and into the water filled with human and animal manure.

We returned in the afternoon to the night site that we had left in the morning. That night it was decided that the mortar crew would fire a few rounds to sight in the gun. We would fire out maybe three hundred yards to as close as a hundred feet, just to get reference points. The rounds would land and the forward observers would call in their corrections. They would basically see where the rounds had landed and then adjust fire to land within a hundred yards of where they were. Usually, the fire direction control team would plot on a map where the rounds were landing and from there they could determine where the forward observers were located and also be able to more accurately place our position on a map.

In training in the United States it was easy to determine ones position from a map. All a person had to do was to take a compass reading to several mountain and hilltops in the distance and triangulate it to locate his position on a map. In Viet Nam, out in the jungle, a person did not have the luxury of having a sweeping command of the landscape all around him. In most cases, a person could not see more than ten feet in front of him, much less the outlines of a far away mountain top. There were streams that were marked on the maps and if we found that stream we would have a better idea of where we were but the course of many of those streams changed from season to season. Sometimes a map would show one stream in the area of operation but during the rainy season we might encounter thirty streams in one day so that it would be impossible to ascertain which stream corresponded to the solitary stream on the map. In the dry season, that marked stream might be just a dry overgrown indentation in the ground that few people would recognize as a seasonal stream.

We fired off one round and waited until it landed so that the forward observer could call in his correction. Then we changed the elevation and deflection of the mortar a little, according to the commands from the fire direction control team and I dropped another round into the tube. The round would slide down the tube making a scraping metallic sound for about one second until it hit a firing pin on the bottom of the tube that would set off the explosion that would shoot the round out of the tube. I dropped the round into the tube and heard the metallic sound then bent over and covered my ear with my hand, waiting for the blast to follow, but there was no blast. Now we had trained for this situation and knew that it was not a good situation at all.

The round had not been set off, exploding out of the tube. However, it could be "cooking off". The primer charge had malfunctioned but it could still be smoldering. It could ignite at any moment, setting off the other charges that blast the round out of the tube. We could just turn the gun upside down and dump out the round, but if the round was cooking and then ignited in the middle of that process the round would explode out of the tube with such force and violence that, if pointed up into the air could propel a twelve pound projectile three miles down range. Such a situation happening at the feet of the gun crew would be horrendous. The built in safeties would prevent the round from exploding, but the tremendous force of the propellant charges would send the round ricocheting off of the ground and into the troops in the area. The recoil from the blast would probably throw the gun thirty feet away, tearing the gun out of the hands of the gun crew. The barrel would probably rip an arm off of the assistant gunner and the bipod would tear the gunners body apart. If it was a white phosphorous round, it would split open and the gun crew and anyone within fifty feet of them would see their skin and muscles melt off of their bodies before they finally died. To get a "dud" out of the tube was an extremely dangerous situation. For my part, it was fraught with horrible dread.

The soldiers in the mortar platoon knew full well the significance of the situation and didn't have to be told to back away from the gun. Other soldiers noticed that something bad was happening and they jumped out of their positions and backed away quickly as well.

We began the extraction procedure. The gunner disengaged the barrel from the base plate gingerly and began to very, very slowly tip the bottom of the barrel upwards which pivoted on the bipod so that the open end of the barrel started to point downwards. My job as assistant gunner was to place the edges of my thumbs and forefingers and the web of skin between them over the open end of the tube to stop the round from hitting the ground as it slid out. We had been taught this technique in advanced infantry training. The rational for this technique is that if the round is suddenly ignited and blasts out of the tube then the assistant gunner will only lose parts of his fingers and hands. But now I suddenly realized that this was not a training exercise. If this round cooked off then people were going to be killed. I placed a goodly portion of my hands over the opening of the tube. My reasoning was that I would lose most of both hands if this round cooked off, but that would maybe save my gun crew and myself from death. A Sergeant came over and told us to stop, that he would handle the situation, that he would perform my duties. That was more than fine with me. I stepped away from the gun and backed up about fifty feet away.

The gunner then continued his task, slowly lifting the barrel so that the round would slide towards the mouth of the gun. The round started to scrape the inside of the barrel as it started to slide towards the opening and was then caught by the Sergeant who had demanded to take my place. He very carefully allowed the round to fall another inch or so until he had it fully grasped between his hands and started to extract it from the gun. Before the entire round was out of the tube someone quickly stepped forward and ripped the secondary charges off of the round. The Sergeant now held the round straight out in front of his face, staring at it like he had a live bomb in his hands, which of course he did.

Another soldier walked up to him and carefully took the round out of his hands and delicately walked over past the fighting positions on the perimeter and placed the round on the ground somewhere into the surrounding jungle. It would be detonated with some C4 explosive tomorrow at a safe range. We examined the inside of the tube to see if there was a problem with the firing pin at the bottom of it and discovered a cleaning rag at the bottom of the tube. The problem was just that someone had left a cleaning rag in the gun and that prevented the round from hitting the firing pin.

The next day was another patrol. We were crossing a rice paddy again. The rice paddies had dikes that divided up the paddy into sections about a hundred feet square. Since the dikes were much easier to walk on than the paddies themselves, they were sometimes mined or booby trapped so we mostly walked through the wet part, if we could. Sometimes the paddies were filled with green rice plants, other times, at other seasons, they would not have any rice in them or sometimes they would have very small plants and other times the plants would be dead and brown, depending on the season and whether they were actively farmed or abandoned.

Some paddies were completely dried up, others had only a few inches of water, others had three feet of water in them, it probably depended mostly on the season. If they had any water at all then they also most certainly had mud at the bottom, some of them only a few inches of mud, others more than a foot. Most of the time the paddys had a foot or two of water and three to six inches of mud but some of them could have five feet or more of water and mud. If they were too deep we would be forced to walk on the dikes, but the vast majority of times we walked in the water and mud.

This time, the water was about a foot and a half feet deep and the mud was probably three inches deep.As I walked, I noticed a commotion in the water next to me down in the water, around my boots. It looked like a school of about fifty small fish vigorously swarming and almost jumping out of the water.Although they were very close to the surface I couldn't see them very well because paddy water has zero visibility due to the mud and manure, human and animal, that makes up most of its composition. I wondered what type of fish could live in a rice paddy and was surprised that they were not frightened away as we stomped through. In fact, they seemed positively drawn to my footsteps and swarmed around the top of my boots as I walked. I mentioned to the guy in front of me to check out the fish, there were a bunch of them swarming around him too. He looked at me with surprise and said, "Those are not fish, they're leechs". Then I could barely make out in the dark muddy water, a number of creatures without fins, of a horrible black/purpleish/brown color.

When I reached the end of the paddy there were a few guys stopped, pulling off their shirts and pulling up their pant legs or taking down their pants. I could see that some of the soldiers had been victimized by the little monsters.The leeches were roughly worm shaped, without any fins and with not much difference between their heads and their tails. Some of the leeches were brownish green, about an inch long and only about the thickness of a pencil while others were more than 3 inches long and about an inch wide with a hideous crimson-black color. I quickly realized that the smaller ones were those that had recently tried but failed to attach themselves to the soldiers bodies while the larger ones were those who were grotesquely engorged with blood.

I was surprised and appalled at the amount of blood that those things could suck out of a human body in such a short time. They appeared to have a sheen to them. I don't know whether it was just water or slime. The men were placing lit cigarettes on them to make them let go, others were trying to slowly pull them trying not to pull the creature apart and leave his head and mouth firmly attached, while others tried to pry them off with their bayonets.

On the cuffs of our jungle fatigue pants was a drawstring. This drawstring was pulled tight, to form a seal between the cuff and the boot, expressively for this purpose, to prevent leeches and other insects from getting into your boots or crawling up your leg. I always kept those drawstrings tight. The pants of the jungle fatigues had a button fly with a double layer of cloth and behind the fly was a large flap of cloth that was held in place by one button to provide some measure of protection from bugs and leeches. Even the shirt had a double layer of fabric where it buttoned in some attempt to keep out insects but that was not very effective at all. I didn't feel anything on me so I just continued onwards but I later learned that when the leeches attach themselves to a body that many times a person cannot even feel them, even when they puncture the skin and start to suck blood.

We came out of the paddy and humped for about an hour when we came upon a VC base camp. There were fighting positions connected by trenches and a large pit, about ten by fifteen feet and about four feet deep, that looked like it was used as a kitchen. There was a table with bowls of cooked rice. Apparently we had surprised the VC in the middle of their meal. About two and a half feet below ground level was a square hole that had been dug horizontally into the wall of the pit, like a type of oven, and in it were the remains of a cooking fire. There was a round hole about six inches in diameter going from the top of the oven upwards through the dirt out to ground level. That opening was covered and was part of what looked like a pipe that led away from the cooking area. The VC had dug a small trench beginning at their cooking fire, about five inches deep and about two hundred feet long.

The pipe was covered and hidden by the leaf litter of the jungle floor. I kicked the pipe hard expecting solid resistance but my boot seemed to go right through it. Upon closer inspection I could see that what looked like a pipe was really a half circular trench dug out of the earth about 5 inches deep. The top part of it was made of a lath of interweaved small thin sticks and then covered with leaves and dirt. That was so the VC could have a cooking fire where the smoke would be diverted away from the kitchen, so that if a plane or helicopter flying overhead might fire on the place where the smoke appeared then the attack would be directed two hundred feet away from the real location of the cooking fire.

We stopped there for fifteen minutes to rest and to eat something. I cut open a C-ration can that contained a little piece of bread about the size of a muffin and then opened two little gold colored C-ration cans about the size of a tuna fish can but only about a half as tall. In one can was about two ounces of peanut butter and in the other about two ounces of grape jelly. That would be my lunch, in the scheme of things a fine and bountiful one.

After eating, I decided to investigate that little base camp further. I left my rucksack and picked up my weapon and helmet and started to follow the smoke tunnel until I reached the end of it. I stepped on top of the smoke tunnel and it collapsed under my weight. I then decided that I would walk on top of the entire length of it, back to my original position, and knock it all down. Some of it collapsed by just stepping on it but some parts were resistant and I had to stop and stomp two or three times in one place to collapse a foot of it. As I was stomping the pipe I spotted a tree trunk about three inches in diameter that someone had chopped off with a machete at a steep angle so it formed a very sharp point about four feet high. After about fifty feet of walking and stomping the tunnel suddenly collapsed sideways under my boot and I lost my balance and fell to my right. In the split second as I was falling, I noticed that I was going to fall directly onto that sharpened tree trunk. I tried to grab it and push it out of the way but I wasn't quick enough and I fell heavily onto it with the sharpened point of it pushing directly into my ribs.

I crashed to the ground on my back and instinctively grasped for the part of the tree that had impaled me, wondering whether it had gone all the way through my body but there was nothing there. I was of course very relieved but also dumbfounded as to why I wasn't impaled. I looked around and saw a two foot piece of that tree with the sharpened end lying on the ground. The tree must have been cut many months ago and was dried out and brittle. When I fell on it, it snapped in two and therefore didn't skewer me like a shish-kabob. I had noticed that tree trunk as I approached it and certainly never considered it to be in the least bit dangerous.

How could it possibly hurt someone? Especially since I had had been so knowledgeable of its existence and yet I fell directly upon it and it almost killed me. I continued onwards with my work, being extremely wary of my surroundings. The more I thought of what had just happened the more de-moralized I became. I thought that if I was nearly killed by a stray tree trunk, how much more likely I am to die because of the obvious dangers in a combat zone. The fact of the matter is that I fully expected to die before my tour of duty was ended and the tree trunk incident was just another factor that indicated the inevitability of it. There were just too many things going on to reasonably expect to survive a year in the bush. The primary question in my mind was not if I was going to die here, but only when .... and how.

We pushed on into the bush. It had been raining and the ground was becoming slippery. We came to a place where the ground sloped sharply downwards. There was no vegetation whatsoever for about five feet wide and extended downwards about twenty feet vertically. It was a natural sluiceway for the heavy rain runoff and that probably didn't allow for anything to grow on it. The point man and some of the others had slipped and fallen badly while trying to go down the grade with all of their equipment. The plan now was for each man, as they reached the slope, to sit down on the ground and slide on their backsides and the backs of their rucksacks down the slope for about thirty feet.

All of the men were filthy dirty from being in the bush for so long and sitting in the mud to take breaks when they could. One guy in particular, for some unknown reason, was particularly dirty. His clothes had no green color whatsoever. He was covered from neck to boots with a slightly odd looking, light yellow/brown color of mud. Something about that color was particularly disgusting. He slid down the incline and at the bottom of his slide he stopped so suddenly that he somersaulted head first onto the ground. Now he was even more filthy, which I didn't think was possible. Now his blond hair was saturated with mud and his face and neck and arms were covered in mud completely. I was next to make the slide and almost did a summersault as well when I made a sudden stop at the bottom. After negotiating that slide all of our bodies and clothing and equipment were now utterly and completely covered and saturated in mud.

At this time, most of the men were suffering from dysentery and had almost uncontrollable diarrhea due to the abysmally poor conditions of living and operating out in the jungle. There weren't many opportunities to relieve themselves while desperately trying to keep up the line of march. The incredible exertion probably led to some of them just defecating many times during the day, mostly with their pants on. The dysentery was probably caused by polluted water, probably from runoff from farm animals or wild animals, I don't know. Some men would be hospitalized with hepatitis later. By this time we had become a group of men forced to live like animals. No, that is not accurate, animals did not live as we were forced to do by combat necessities. When we left the United States we left restaurant and home-cooked food and pure water. We left clean clothes and bathrooms and sofas and soft beds. When we left base camp we left behind cold drinks and fresh food and cold showers and clean clothes and relative safety. In the jungle we became filthy from sleeping on the ground and digging fighting positions and hitting the dirt when we were attacked and wading through the filth of rice paddies, going weeks without a shower but we found our fill of filthy creek water and disease. We starved on slave rations of twenty year old cans of food and our bodies were wracked with dehydration, severe sleep deprivation and physical exhaustion and pain beyond description. We didn't find ghosts or hobgoblins in the woods but we found horrors that we couldn't have imagined. It was a world of filth and sweat and blood and slaughter a million miles removed from civilization.

We all had a small, dark brown glass bottle containing purification tablets, which were tiny dark green/brown iodine pills that were dropped into a canteen of water. They were not a hundred per cent effective against all disease organisms. Most of the time our only source of water was creeks that we crossed while out on an operation. I think that one of the problems was that as men started to cross a creek, if one man had dysentery, it would wash off of his clothes and as other men crossed and opened their canteens as they waded waist deep in slow moving water, the water was polluted further by the first guy with dysentery. Even if all of us were healthy to begin with, the water out in the field was probably teeming with diseases and various harmful micro-organisms The unclean water would become disinfected an hour after the pill was dropped into it.

The problem was that for all intents and purposes, it was as if you had dropped your canteen into a sewer and then killed the germs inside the canteen with the iodine but the cap and the opening of the canteen, where a person would place his lips to take a drink, was still befouled. To really clean the cap and the opening of the canteen would require washing it in hot soapy water for five minutes followed by a healthy dose of bleach. That was simply impossible in this combat situation. I would sometimes take each canteen out of its holder, unscrew the cap slightly and then shake the canteen to cause some of the water to spill onto the cap and neck to try to wash off some of the infected water that they had been dipped into. Most of the time that technique was impossible because we didn't have very many opportunities to stop and fool with canteens.

I discovered a technique where I would unloosen the caps slightly for a minute or two every once in a while while humping. That allowed some of the water to slosh out while I was walking. That technique was far less than what was required but it was the only method that we could use. Anyways, the heavy canvas canteen cover would be saturated with polluted water and that could be easily transferred to the opening of the canteen. Even if a person had a canteen that was brand new and sterilized the first time he crossed a waist deep creek the outside of the canteen would be polluted.

There was no miracle medical treatment that would instantly cure dysentery and if a person had it, he would just have to deal with it, making a horrible, extremely painful, and utterly exhausting situation even more inhuman. In civilian life some of those men would be hospitalized, in this life you just drove on. The iodine tablets also imparted an extremely bad taste to the water and I think that some men were remiss in using the iodine for that reason. My mother would send me letters with Kool-aid packages in it. The Kool-aid added a flavor to the water and made it easier to drink but there was still an overwhelmingly putrid taste and smell. I never got dysentery, due mostly to being very fastidious with using the iodine and incredible luck.

We set up for the night and again each two man team would dig a fighting position which might take anywhere from forty minutes to two hours, sometimes more, depending on how hard the dirt was. Then the soldiers would fill about thirty sandbags to go around the position at ground level and to cover the roof that would be made by small tree trunks that had to be sought out and cut down by machete.

The next day we moved out and by early afternoon we came to a stream. It was running very swiftly and had steep banks about eight feet tall. We slid down the nearest slippery bank and each man entered the water with a big splash, trying desperately not to lose his balance and fall down while in the water.

The creek was about fifteen feet wide. I held my weapon over my head and resigned myself to the fact that all of my gear would get soaking wet, including my ammo. As I reached the middle of the creek, I tried to stand on the balls of my feet, but even with that the water was up to my chin. Anybody behind me that was less than five feet ten inches tall would traverse this section with the water over their heads. As I reached the opposite bank, the depth of the water had receded by about a foot. The slope and slipperiness of the bank made it impossible to climb. I couldn't imagine how the first guy in line managed it.

Maybe the guy in back of him gave him a boost up. I tried to climb up but lost my footing and fell off, almost backwards, into the swiftly moving water. As it was, while I was falling I very forcefully bent forward at the waist and landed in a stooping down position and still, the fast flowing water almost knocked me off-balance and down into its deadly current. I fought mightily and desperately to regain my balance because to go down in that water, with all of your gear strapped to you, meant almost certain death by drowning. I think a lot of soldiers died that way in VietNam.

The guy on top of the bank above me, the soldier that I had been following all day, pointed his M-16 at my face and yelled to me to "Grab on." I stretched out my arms as far as possible and was able to get a grip on the very end of the barrel. Then with me pulling with all of my strength and with him struggling mightily to hold on and haul me up, each of us grasping opposite ends of the weapon, I managed to scramble part of the way upwards towards the top of the bank. When my shoulders were level with the high ground I reached around and clawed deeply into the mud with my right hand, franticly trying to keep from falling back down. The fingers of my right hand were four inchs deep into the wet soil but it didn't provide enough traction so I had to pick up my arm and claw again and again, trying to save my life. The soldier on top had slipped and fallen backwards so that now he was laying on his back, in the mud and rain but he was still holding his end of the weapon.

With my full body weight and equipment at the other end he was being pulled towards the edge of the bank. I felt a panic rising within me, fearing that I would fall back into the creek and take the soldier at the other end of the weapon with me. Our eyes met for a second and I hoped that he could read into my look that I was begging for my life. I couldn't really blame him if he released the weapon. He seemed to grasp the rifle stock like he was determined to strangle it, squeezing it with every bit of his strength while smashing the heels of his boots into the mud, trying to stop his slide towards death. I somehow managed to gain another six inches towards him but that had brought him almost to the edge of the bank. He suddenly and unexpectedly released his grip on the weapon with one hand and reached desperately for the back of my rucksack. He then suddenly stood up on his knees, trying to press his full weight into the muddy ground and gave a mighty pull.

Suddenly, I found myself laying on the ground with my legs still dangling downwards towards the creek but with the weight of my body and equipment firmly on the ground. My life had been saved. I don't know whether I even said thank you to the man who had just pulled me from the brink. I only had a few seconds to try to regain my breath and thoughts and when I looked up the soldier who had saved me was gone, probably running to catch up to the line of march.

I suddenly turned around and looked downwards, into the face of the soldier who was in back of me in the line of march. He looked up at me from the creek with an expression of utter exhaustion and desperation. He didn't say a word, but just looked up at me beseechingly, seemingly to say "Please do the impossible. Please save me." I laid on the ground and leaned part of my upper body down into the pit, stretching out my weapon towards him, pointing the muzzle directly at his face. He stood on his toes to reach it and I pulled mightily. He gained a foot or so when I suddenly twisted around and sat on the ground and pulled with both arms. He gained another foot of height and I started to kick viciously and deeply into the ground, trying to use my legs to get away from the edge and pull up perhaps two hundred and fifty pounds of dead weight up further. Somehow, he reached the top and I could grab his rucksack and pull him clear. And so it went down the line, each man in turn mightily and desperately rising from the stream. When I pulled up the guy in back of me, I immediately jumped up and ran forwards to rejoin the line of march. I had to run about two hundred feet and when I finally caught up I was out of breath and beaten down by the weight of my equipment. I had just been on the brink of death but since I passed that ordeal now my lot in life was to continue the torture of humping my insufferable load. I realized that I had barely escaped death a minute ago but that it could reappear again in ten minutes. It could reappear in ten seconds or sooner. The only certainty was being wounded or killed by the enemy or the jungle and/or the endless agony of the march. The line continued onwards, through the heavy vegetation, while I hoped that noone back at the stream bank would accidentally get shot in the face by the guy in front of them, and that noone would loose their balance and drown and that noone would be caught by the VC in that indefensible position, with no cover while in water.

We had regular pockets on our pants and also big pockets on the side of the thighs. At first I thought that those side pockets would come in handy for keeping things that you might need on a moments notice, but if you put grenades into the pocket, they banged against your leg with every step. That was annoying but more importantly, a few grenades bouncing against each other with every step could break off the spoons or dislodge the cotter pins that kept them from exploding. Some Sergeants kept their maps there for quick references during the day but then had to carry the maps over their heads when crossing streams. After a while I realized that the side pockets might be good for some things, but no good in the rainy season when we crossed many streams. They might look good on paper or on a parade ground but in a combat situation in Viet Nam they were practically useless.

The only camouflage clothing that we had was a cloth covering for our helmets that was held in place by a strong elastic band. It was designed to look like leaves but I thought that those leaves might mimic the forests of North Carolina than the tropical vegetation of Viet Nam. Many guys carried a small plastic bottle of insect repellent on their helmets, secured by the band, for easy access. Others carried cigarettes in the same way, to keep them out of the water when crossing streams but that didn't help much when it was raining all day.

I didn't mind getting wet since I was completely saturated with sweat most of the time anyways and the creek crossing might wash some bit of filth off of your boots, or pants, or equipment or even your helmet, depending on how deep the creeks were. If the water was at least waist high then most of our ammunition would be saturated, which wasn't a good thing.

That night I tried to go to sleep but was still completely wet from the multiple creek crossings of the day. I knew that it must be relatively warm, but with the wet clothes it was very uncomfortable and I actually felt cold. In my rucksack was a poncho liner. It was supposed to go under your poncho when you were wearing it, providing a very minimal amount of insulation against the cold. It was the same size as a poncho and had camouflage color and markings. It was probably only a quarter of an inch thick, made of three parts, an inner and outer covering of thin nylon and a middle layer of some sort of polyester filling. I pulled that over my shoulders and wrapped myself like a mummy. Even though that liner was soaking wet, it provided a remarkable amount of warmth, it really made a tremendous difference in that circumstance.

Half way through beating the bush on the next day we unexpectedly stopped and the word was passed down that we were to remain in place, the humping for that day was over. I couldn't understand why we were going to set up for the night amongst the thick trees and bushes but I just sat down on the ground, thankful for the respite. A few minutes later the soldiers in front of me stood up and moved out and I was thoroughly confused as to what was happening but I only walked another fifty feet when I stepped out of the jungle onto a dirt road and was then told to form up with my squad on the other side of the road at a small clearing.

It seemed to me to be a relatively safe place because there were already troops in the area that seemed to be relatively rear-echelon types and there were a few big trucks parked there. I think that there were fighting positions already dug, enough for most of us. I assumed that this location was previously occupied by American troops who had moved on but had been told not to fill in their positions. A few hundred feet away from where my squad settled in was a wide river. We were surrounded by jungle but there was a roughly semi-circular area along the bank of the river that was devoid of all vegetation. Probably it was a place that was regularly flooded by the river. The ground there was smooth with an unusual light brown color, probably hardened mud.

The dirt road led directly into the water so apparently the road was usable only during the dry season although I couldn't imagine that wide river ever being passable by truck.

About an hour after we had settled into our fighting positions we were ordered to pick up all of our equipment and go to the end of the road. Just before the road ended there was a large mound of dirt about twelve feet high and fifty feet wide where the road had been cut through the middle of it. It sloped sharply downwards on the river side of it to meet a small sandy area about a hundred and fifty feet long and eighty feet wide. There were a few large trucks in that vicinity carrying big ten or fifteen man rubber rafts. We formed into a loose group, still carrying our rucksacks, and were informed that we were to be trained in the use of those watercraft.

There was a small group of soldiers standing in front of us and one of them began his lecture. These were military black rubber rafts and it was said that if they took a bullet that the rubber was so thick that it would seal itself. We got some fundamental instructions, then ran around a bit with the rafts over our heads, just to break our backs I guess, then put all of our rucksacks into the rafts and ran around some more. The rafts by themselves were much heavier that they looked. Then we humped the rafts down to a small river and practiced rowing it. Each man had a paddle and put one leg up onto the pontoon and rowed. Of course we were not coordinated at all at first and it was a bit tricky landing the raft and getting into and out of it. I suspected that some of the troopers had never been in a boat in their lives and some of them didn't seem happy about it. I figured that maybe we would be going on water assaults sometime in the future.

We stayed there that night and then continued the operation. After beating the bush for about ten days, we set up in a clearing and artillery pieces were brought in by Chinook helicopter. We would spend the next five days dug in around those guns providing security for them. We had some time to get our act together. I sat down the next day and pulled my spare pair of socks out of my rucksack. The conventional wisdom is to keep your feet dry at all times and change your socks very frequently. The reality is that you cannot bring thirty pairs of socks on an operation and its impossible to keep your feet dry between crossing streams in the wet season or just soaking your boots every day with your own sweat.

The fact is that I left my boots on at all times, even while sleeping. My rational was that if I had to get up in the middle of the night due to an attack, it would not be the time to be fumbling around in the dark to find your boots, put them on and then to lace them up. I would leave my boots on twenty-four hours a day, for up to fifteen days at a time. I would usually put on my boots in base camp the morning of the first day of an operation and not take them off until I returned to base camp at the end of the operation.

I pulled off my boots and socks expecting the worst but my feet looked ok. They were very white and wrinkled and the skin seemed very soft. I noticed that the socks did not even have an unpleasant smell, seemed to have no smell really. The fact is, or course, that there must have been an extremely strong odor, but we were accustomed to it and therefore could not smell those types of smells any more. The only problem that I had was that I noticed an extremely deep jungle rot sore on my Achilles' tendon at the top of my boot line. We received orders to go back to base camp a few days later.

Chapter 18
BASE CAMP C

Helicopter pickup

About fifteen minutes after returning to base camp, a guy who had been outside of the country on emergency leave or something walked into our hooch. He said that he had smelled about the worse smell possible about a half-mile from reaching our hooch and couldn't understand what it could possibly be. He said that that smell was us. He asked us how we could possibly stand the smell. He had his hand over his nose and said that he had to leave because he could not possibly stand that smell for another moment. I and others asked him what smell he was talking about. I certainly didn't smell anything bad, but I did think that it was strange that living in the jungle, on the ground, and not washing or changing clothes or taking a shower for fifteen days would not produce some sort or type of unpleasant odor. The fact was simply that we had grown accustomed to the smell of unwashed bodies and rotten clothing, accustomed to such an extent that we simply were now totally unaware of it.

We almost never knew when we would be going back out on the next operation. We usually, but not always, were given twenty-four hours notice. Nothing had been said so far about restricting us to base so myself and a few other guys decided to go down to the little village outside of the base camp known as Bien Hoa pronounced "Ben Waa". We sat around in the platoon hooch for a while drinking and considered the fact that we had not been issued official passes to authorize us leaving the base and that there was noone around to give us those passes. We decided to go anyways and changed into civilian clothes. About eight of us started walking towards the entrance to the base camp that was probably two miles away. We tried to catch a ride with any passing vehicle, but most were too small to hold eight men and the other large vehicles refused to stop. They probably didn't want to pick up eight drunken paratroopers heading for town to see what kind of trouble they could get into.

A large enclosed truck approached. It was a civilian Vietnamese truck. The base employed quite a few Vietnamese to do construction work. One of the guys that I was with jumped in front of the truck, barring its passage with his body, and indicating with sign language that we needed a ride. The driver readily shook his head up and down in agreement. We went to the back of the truck and opened the pull down gate and pushed aside a canvas curtain. Inside were about fifteen Vietnamese workers who greeted us with big smiles but not a word of English.

AS we rode along we suddenly realized that when we arrived at the main gate that the Military Police would stop the truck and search it. Our plan was to tell the Air Force MPs to take a hike and then to boldly walk, or run, past them and blend into the crowd in town. Most of the Vietnamese in the trucks had the standard Vietnamese straw conical hats that they used to keep the sun off of them while working in the fields. One of the guys indicated to a Vietnamese that he would like to try on his hat, and he willingly and happily complied. Now we had a plan, we could hide amongst the civilian workers and try to pass for civilian workers by wearing their hats and squatting down on our heels as the Vietnamese tend to do. At the main gate, the truck was stopped and two MPs with M-16s opened the back of the truck. They were dumbfounded for a second and then started to laugh their heads off, with half of us wearing Vietnamese hats and most of us squatting unnaturally. They said, "Obviously you guys are 173rd, do any of you have passes?" We said "No, we don't." The MPs just laughed and told the driver to go ahead and reminded us that the gates close at eleven PM.

We split up into various groups, some guys wanted to go to a tailor and have some civilian clothes made, others were off on more illegal adventures and myself and others went into the nearest barroom and started to throw down some beer and hard drinks. After a couple of hours, myself and another guy decided to get something to eat and stopped in a small restaurant to get some Vietnamese food and Coca-Cola's. When we were finished, it was dark outside and we decided to walk around and check out the little town a bit more.

After a while we realized that we were running late, so we hopped onto the back of two small motorcycles and told the drivers to take us to the front gate and we would give them a dollar each. They were extremely happy to do so and we flew up the main dirt street, zigzagging around other traffic at breakneck speed with me almost falling off many times.

The MPs at the gate asked us for our passes and my partner said that we didn't have any. They said, "You guys are 173rd aren't you?" I said, "Yes, how do you know?" They just looked at the ground and shook their heads in disbelief and told us to stand over to the side and they would make the next vehicle take us to our Company area.

The next day we were told that there would be some entertainment, just in our Company area. An American civilian guy had set up a makeshift stage of plywood on which he had placed his speakers and an electric organ. That was the only musical instrument. With him were two black girls from the States, sort of like go-go girls and vocalists. He played some good songs to an audience of only about twenty-five men, many of them black. For some reason the black guys didn't seem too happy. Maybe because there was not any black American women in Viet Nam or maybe they were thinking of their wives or girlfriends back home.

The guy on the organ said that he had organized this tour with his own money and was happy to perform to such a small audience because he knew that troops like us didn't get to see much live entertainment. I thought that that must have cost him a small fortune. He told us that he was the guy who wrote the song "The House of the Rising Sun" but someone else recorded it. He then sang and played an extraordinary rendition of that song. I thought that it was really good to hear that song, played by its author. I really appreciated him and his singers, their generosity and courage and the fact that they seemed to understand our situation. It was the only show that we would ever see. No, we never saw Bob Hope or anyone like that. We were in the bush almost continuously and if there was a big show at the airbase, we would be in the bush miles away providing extra security for the rear echelon supply Sergeants and Air Force clerk-typists on base.

The next day I decided to go back to Bien Hoa town with a few guys. As soon as you stepped fifty feet outside the main gate to the airport/base camp about fifty people immediately surrounded you. Most of them were children begging for coins or candy with the others offering various illegal services and substances. The other guys with me decided to split up and look around town.

I went by myself to explore a bit. I felt a bit naked because I wasn't armed, the authorities would not let us take our weapons among the civilian population of the town. I walked down a side dirt street. You really couldn't call it a street, more a path for water buffalo drawn carts. I ran into a Catholic priest, Vietnamese, who spoke English a little. He was very friendly and he said that he operated an orphanage somewhere in Bien Hoa. He invited me to see his small church but I wanted to get some drinks and some food. He seemed like a nice guy, but actually I was very concerned about wandering off of the main road. As an American, I would be spotted a mile away in the little village and make a good target for any VC in the area, and there were VC in that area. The priest assured me that it was safe, but, I have to admit, I was really afraid to get myself into such a situation.

There were rickshaws on the streets, pulled by men running along the road with their human cargo behind them. I decided that I would like to try that, a ride in a rickshaw, that seemed very exotic, so I tried to talk to one of the rickshaw drivers and gestured that I wanted to go to get something to eat. He was very happy to have a fare and we negotiated a price. He proceeded down the main street and turned onto a side street. We went about three quarters of a mile, getting far from the center of activity. At the end of the road was a white building with a profusion of plants all around it that seemed to have been landscaped. I felt sorry for the poor out of breath driver, he had obviously done some very heavy labor. I paid him our agreed upon price of ten cents and noted that noone should have to work that hard for such little recompense. When we had made the deal, I didn't know how far the restaurant that he suggested would be.

The restaurant building was a hundred times better than most other structures in that town. It was made of some sort of plaster, some sort of a light rose color. It was a restaurant with a bar. The tropical foliage and flowers surrounding it was stunningly beautiful. There was space for about a hundred people but there were only a one or two other customers in there. The waiter spoke some very limited English and I ordered a meal of fried rice with a large assortment of seafood and vegetables mixed in. It had been many, many months since I had had any seafood or any fresh vegetables. Although the amount of food was huge, I ate everything down to the last grain of rice. When I was finished, I ordered another ice-cold beer and leaned back in my chair. I was full and warm and dry and safe. It was a feeling that I had not had for months. The food had been absolutely fresh and delicious and I began to realize that I had forgotten what food could be. For months my only food had been meager amounts of an unpleasant, cold, unappetizing substance and a constant feeling of hunger and galling emptiness had become just a normal part of life.

I got back to the main road somehow and stopped in a bar for a drink. I was about the only person in that bar and one of the girls who worked there came over to talk. She was from Cambodia, was extremely beautiful and could speak English well. She was much different from the other Vietnamese women that I had seen in town because she had very, very dark skin, almost black.

I sat down at a side table and the Cambodian girl brought me a cold beer and then sat down to chat a bit. I probably had not even spoken to a woman in many months and the conversation, although she was cheerful and upbeat, seemed to me to be some sort of surrealistic experience. I didn't know what to say, I was completely at a loss as to what people talk about. She made a lot of little jokes and I laughed but I could not fathom how to reply to or engage in idle chatter. She was a civilian and lived in a safe area and had a normal life, I was an Infantryman just back from life in the bush. We had nothing in common I thought but I was vaguely aware that I had lost my ability to interact with people. I had become de-civilized and I couldn't remember how civilized people conversed or acted. Even if I remembered it, I realized that, for some reason, I was incapable of being part of it.

After about five minutes, I looked out of the window and saw a large pile of sand about ten feet in diameter and five feet tall. I could see an old woman working with a hoe, working very vigorously, trying to spread out that tall pile of sand. The afternoon sun was murderously hot and she was working directly in the sun, doing very hard physical work. I thought that she was working like she had been promised a thousand dollar bonus if she finished in the next hour, or if she didn't finish it quickly her family would be killed. I thought that you would never see such a sight in the US, but here, there it was, and it wouldn't be the last time I saw something like that. The fact is that that womans family probably would die of starvation and/or disease if she couldn't keep that source of livelihood. I asked the Cambodian girl how much money a woman like that would be paid for a days work. She said about three dollars. It was just another of many culture shocks.

After a few hours of drinking, I left the bar. It was dark now and I decided to head back to base camp but ran into a guy from my squad named Pierce while walking up the road. We decided to get something to eat and drink some more. The little three wheel busses were all about and this guy told me that they could do a wheely, like a thousand horsepower dragster with its front wheels lifted off of the ground when it suddenly accelerated. I told him that was impossible and he said, "OK, Watch". He ran into the middle of the street, into the middle of fast moving traffic, chasing after one of these little busses with about five people in the back of it. He then jumped onto the back of it, grabbed the luggage rack on top of the roof and leaned backwards.The front wheel of the bus came off the ground by about two feet while the driver gunned his engine and tried to steer left and right with nothing under the wheel but air.The passengers seemed completely unfazed as to those antics although the vehicle was completely out of the control of the driver and still proceeding at full speed down the road. After about ten seconds he leapt off and the bus crashed back to earth and continued on as if nothing had happened. I thought that that was very funny but wondered how we were doing to win the hearts and minds of the civilian populace. After a bit of encouragement, I jumped on a similar bus and did the same thing but I jumped off after a few seconds, having managed to make it to do a wheely. Obviously I had drank too much, my judgment was impaired.

We went down a little side street, to explore the area a little and maybe find a restaurant. It was very dark and the further we walked down the street it became even darker. There were two Vietnamese girls standing off to one side, obviously prostitutes. I was getting a little antsy about going too far off the main street and the area there was very decrepit with shacks made of cardboard and mud and sticks. I was only going to go another hundred feet or so, trying to find a place to eat, thinking that we had pushed our luck seriously a hundred yards ago. As we walked by the girls they were saying something to us in Vietnamese but I just brushed by them, almost physically pushing them out of my way and generally ignoring them, getting more and more antsy about that place. From behind, I heard the girls shout out to us "Doom on you!, doom on you!" I thought that that was an unusual curse. Doom on me. Yes, you are probably exactly right, I am doomed. I'm going back out into the bush soon, I don't really need any more doom from you, I'm already doomed. It was much later that I learned that the Vietnamese vernacular for the phrase "F—You" seemed very close to the ear of an English speaking person to be "doom on you".

We didn't see anyplace to get some food so we reversed course and walked back to the main road. Pierce decided to go in one direction and I went the opposite way. I continued walking about a quarter of a mile back towards the Air Force main gate but then suddenly decided to walk down a side road that was very dark for two hundred meters but seemed to have some small buildings with bright lights at the end.

The road seemed to me to be a very good place to walk if someone wanted to be robbed, assaulted and then killed but the alcohol kept me pushing forward. I stopped at a building and went inside to see if they served drinks or food, but quickly realized that there were various illegal activities taking place.

I saw an old woman lying on a table, or maybe it was some sort of stretcher with wheels like that used by ambulances in the States. Her body was covered with hundreds of large lumps all over her skin, obviously the victim of some sort of terrible disease. She was sweating profusely in an extremely high fever and I thought that she was in imminent danger of dying. There were two American medics there, moving her out. I don't know exactly what was wrong with the woman but it seemed to be very serious and I hoped that it wasn't contagious. Obviously the American medics were conducting some sort of "outreach" program to the Vietnamese civilian population. They didn't have any weapons. Obviously, I thought, they should be armed and with an armed escort in this section of town.

There had not been a combat jump since the Korean War and no one expected to jump in Viet Nam but the next day we were told that we were going to jump school. It was nothing like the jump school at Fort Benning, Georgia. This one had some sand pits and harnesses at the end of ropes to practice PLF's (Parachute Landing Falls) and a 34-foot tower to practice actually jumping out of an aircraft but they certainly did not have the huge 250 foot towers used at the Armys Jump School back in the US. None of us had made a parachute jump for at least six months and I suppose we could use a little refresher course.

All paratroopers are required to make at least one jump every three months to collect their special hazardous duty pay ($55 a month). Since we were on combat operations all the time we didn't have the luxury of making training jumps. Congress had passed a law that specifically exempted Airborne units in Viet Nam from having to make jumps wherein they would still get their hazardous duty pay. In Viet Nam every person also collected "combat pay" of $55 a month. Of course there was only a small percentage of actual combat soldiers doing all of the fighting and dying. So, as a Private First Class, Airborne Infantryman, on full on combat status I was being paid $210 a month.

To practice parachute landing falls, you don a parachute harness that is attached to a rope that leads to a pulley on the roof above you and is held by one or two other men. You stand on a platform about six feet tall and jump forward and off of it. That caused you to swing outwards whereupon the men at the other end of the rope will release it causing you to fall. You may swing around in a full circle or any part of it before the rope is released so that you can hit the ground either swinging forwards or backwards or to the left or right or any combination of directions. There is a standard body position to assume when landing on the ground which is feet and knees together, legs slightly bent, chin tucked in and arms extended upwards grasping the risers. When you hit there is a certain technique to be mastered so as to minimize injuries (the Parachute Landing Fall, PLF).

The thirty-four foot tower has a platform at the top of several flights of stairs that is exactly thirty-four feet above the ground. That height was chosen after serious scientific studies. Thirty-four feet is exactly the height that a human being instinctively realizes that if he jumps off and falls straight to the ground, that he will most certainly be terribly injured and will probably be killed. Many men reported to the scientists that it was less scary to jump out of a plane than it was to jump out of that tower, at that precise height.

You put on a parachute harness that is attached to a wire. You stand at the edge of the platform and the "Jump Master" takes the wire attached to your harness and attaches it to a two hundred foot long wire. The idea is that you face the long wire while standing in a mock-up of an aircraft door. It feels as if nothing is holding you up or back and that nothing is attached to you to break your fall. The two hundred foot wire is leading perpendicularly to the left. The effect is that you practice exiting an aircraft while in flight, jumping out into nothingness.

You stand at the edge, looking down exactly at the ground forty feet below you if you're six feet tall. Then, you put your hands on the side of the "door" and, with all of your might, pull yourself forward while at the same time leaping as strongly as you can out into thin air. You only fall straight downwards for about eight feet (if the wire or parachute harness doesn't break) and then with a jolt you slide down the wire to the end, suspended about twenty five feet from the ground for the two hundred foot slide.

At the Jump School at Fort Benning, Georgia a large number of washouts (people who change their minds or fail the course) will occur at the thirty-four foot tower. People will suddenly decide that they do not want to jump out of airplanes and many will realize that, for them, it is impossible to bring themselves to do so. Of course, if that is the way that you are, we don't want you as an Airborne troop. To even reach that point you would have had already passed a test of physical fitness which is very difficult to complete. I failed my first test. Then you would do all kinds of physical exercises during the three weeks of jump school. If you get past the thirty-four foot tower you then go to the two hundred and fifty foot tall towers. There you will be raised into the air and released with a parachute to return to earth unattached to anything else. That will usually put the fear of God into you, especially if you see men crashing into the tower on the way down, their chutes immediately deflating and then watch as men scream for their lives, two hundred feet above ground, holding onto the steel framing of the tower if they had been lucky enough to grab as their chute collapsed, which I witnessed several times.

The next step is actually exiting an aircraft while in flight and that can give one pause to think as well. As you approach the open door with the sound of a hurricane inside the aircraft and with it rocking and dipping, and you see the ground rushing past you at a hundred miles per hour while you are at twelve hundred feet high, the full gravity of what you are about to do becomes crystal clear.

They say that the first time that someone does something is the hardest because they face the fear of many unknowns. After they have done something once, they realize that the experience wasn't as bad as they feared and are willing to do it again. Sometimes the first experience, of anything, is much more scary and dangerous than they had imagined and then never want to repeat that experience. Sometimes the first time is the easiest. After some men experience the first jump, they have a keen insight into what it is really all about, and they never want to experience it again. Of course a jump at jump school would be a very, very slight indication of what an actual combat jump would really be like. They said that this exercise was just to keep our jump skills at an acceptable level. We trained at the school for a couple of hours and then went back to the base camp.

Any time in base camp was good. If we had the time and opportunity, we drank a lot but also ate our fill of the bad food at the mess hall and went to the PX to pick up some American canned food and snacks. It was a time to recuperate from the operations in the bush. Our bodies desperately needed rest and recuperation and respite from the inhuman physical demands of jungle combat operations but we usually had far too little time to accomplish what was really needed to restore our health and strength. Every man upon first joining the 173rd Airborne Brigade was in top physical health and condition but every combat operation diminished and debilitated him. Men very rapidly lost any bit of body fat reserves due to the heat and humidity and illnesses of the bush and horrible physical demands of beating the bush. They then lost muscle mass as their bodies were slowly destroyed by the extraordinary physical demands that were required every day. Every day in the bush made a man weaker and sicker than the day before. The stress of constant danger took its toll as well, on the body and the mind, injuries that no amount of time or rest or food or alcohol could ever fully repair. In retrospect, I think that it did something to your personality and to your outlook on life and to your way of thinking.

Chapter 19

OPERATION JUNCTION CITY
Feb 22-15 March WAR ZONE C

Half a league, half a league,
Half a league onward,
All in the valley of Death
Rode the six hundred.
"Forward, the Light Brigade!
Charge for the guns!" he said:
Into the valley of Death
Rode the six hundred

Alfred Lord Tennyson

Jonesy with a captured VC claymore

We got the word that we were going out on another operation soon. We were told that it would be a big operation with other Army and Marine units involved. In fact it was going to be the biggest operation of the war so far. We would be a blocking force. Other units would be pushing the enemy force into us. The other Army and Marine units would be the hammer and we would be the anvil. The other units would push the enemy towards us and we would stop them dead in their tracks, at least that was the thinking behind the operation. We would be located a mile or two from the Cambodian border.

On the last morning in base camp, as we were just about to depart for the operation, we were told that it was to be principally an Airborne operation, where the basic and principle assault into enemy territory was to be by airborne infantry. It would be the first direct assault by parachute infantry since the Korean war and that the 173rd Airborne Brigades 2nd Battalion was to be the principle participant. We were given this information only a few hours before the parachute assault was to take place, thereby precluding any chance that that information could be passed onto the enemy.

The word was that the 2nd battalion of the 173rd was to make a parachute infantry assault from north to south. Almost simultaneously, the 1st and 4th battalions would be combat landed by helicopter to provide security for them, one on the right and the other on the left of the drop zone.

We loaded up onto trucks and were transported about four miles to a location near the edge of the Bien Hoa air base. I wasn't sure whether we were still technically still within the confines of the base or somewhere just outside of it. I guess that the long convoy of trucks within and close to the base was to deceive any enemy observers into thinking that we were going out to an operation relatively close to the base camp. The last mile of the trip was over a one lane, extremely primitive and very dusty red dirt road.

We quickly, within reason, given the horribly heavy loads that all soldiers in my squad were carrying, unloaded from the back of the trucks with all of our equipment and then moved as quickly as possible off to the side of the road and about twenty feet into the surrounding bushes. That bushy vegetation was so thin that we were not effectively concealed from anyone passing by. We stayed in that spot for a while,

I fully expected to get the word to move out at any second, but the order never came.

After about five minutes I realized that I had not seen anyone traveling down that road, military or civilian, the road seemed to have been completely closed to any traffic whatsoever at some point at both ends. I guess that Command didn't want any enemy observers to see us suddenly switch from trucks to helicopters because then they could alert their more remote units to prepare for an attack.

The civilians only knew that this road was closed. That's all they knew. It was probably a major inconvenience to them but possibly a matter of life or death to us. I was a bit relieved that we didn't have to worry about any enemy disguised as civilians coming down the road and hitting us with bombs and small arms fire, but then I thought that that wasn't much of a problem. Any VC traveling down that road shooting at people would have had to run a gauntlet of about a hundred and fifty paratroopers who had nothing better to do than to test fire their weapons on an obvious enemy target. Of course, any VC attacking us from the road might well produce ten American causalities before realizing their terrible mistake.

We stayed close to the road for about another ten minutes until we started to hear the a dull roar in the air. It seemed to be far away but within fifteen seconds the level of the sound had risen a hundred fold and it was obvious that there helicopters close by. Orders were suddenly shouted for everyone to move deeper into the vegetation. Everyone close to me quickly stood up so I struggled to my feet, noting that the exertion of just arising from the ground with all of my equipment was already a difficult and painful task. Through a gap in the trees I could see a line of helicopters flying slowly ahead, about thirty feet above the ground, preparing to land.

We only traveled about fifty feet until we broke out into a very long clearing of just long lush grass. I was a bit shocked to learn that this wide open area was so close to us and we didn't realize it was there. The first five helicopters flew almost directly overhead and then past me and when I looked to the right I could see another fifteen choppers. By this time we were engulfed in the overwhelming clatter of the powerful machines. Conversation was impossible and any shouted orders wouldn't have been heard but everybody knew exactly what to do. All of soldiers were in their assigned groups, one for each helicopter and everybody was looking to their left and right, moving forward or backwards as necessary, quickly aligning themselves along an imaginary straight line, each group separated by about seventy feet.

The lead helicopters had flown past us, with each succeeding chopper being closer to the ground than the one that proceeded it. It was a surrealistic atmosphere of noise and mini hurricanes of hot air filled with a strong smell of jet fuel exhaust. The machines seemed to defy any sense of gravity and common sense, seemingly held above the ground only by their incredible clatter and the forces contained within their immensely powerful engines. It seemed as if it was an extremely vivid dream with a nightmarish touch of the helicopter door gunners slowly passing by, both hands on their machine guns, frantically scanning the ground and trees. They seemed to have a look like they expected to see King Kong come charging out of the jungle with a huge machete in his hand.

As each helicopter touched down, the group of men assigned to that airship quickly ran forward and boarded and then that chopper immediately lifted off. The choppers took off as quickly as they had landed, with an incredible roar, each one rising a few feet and then tilting so that it faced nose downwards, the pilots slanting their rotors so as to achieve maximum speed out of this area, sacrificing height for distance. I think that those pilots more than red-lined their instruments. Their cockpits were filled with screeches and horns and flashing lights indicating that their aircraft were being over-stressed and demanding attention from the pilots, but those pilots seemed to simply ignore those warnings completely.

Some of the guys called the troop carrying helicopters that we rode in "Hueys". I think that was from their technical designation as a UH-1 helicopter. Other soldiers called them "Slicks" but I don't know why. Most of us simply called them "Choppers" because of the sound that they made. When they are making drastic maneuvers, under full throttle, the blades emit a very loud and distinctive "Chop! Chop! Chop!" usually mixed amongst a very loud "Whap, Whap" sound, like the blades are slapping broadside into cardboard or water or trees or something.

Most of the helicopters flying in a hostile airspace and all of the helicopters engaged in a helicopter assault, especially the gunships, were pushed to their limits and beyond. I don't really think that those choppers are even supposed to make those sounds but all of them did from time to time in the combat zone. Under normal circumstances I don't think that they will make that whapping sound but in support of a combat operation there were no helicopters making milk runs or sight-seeing trips for tourists.

We flew for about ten minutes, gradually gaining altitude until we started flying over green rice paddies and patches of jungle. I seemed to notice something unusual out of the periphery of my vision and looked almost straight downwards at an area on the edge of the jungle almost directly below our airship. There suddenly appeared a series of big explosions on the ground. It took a few seconds for me to figure out what was happening, and then I realized that it must be our artillery, following our flight path on the ground with high explosives to suppress any possible ground fire. At least I hoped that was the situation, because otherwise some of these choppers were going to start to be blasted out of the sky. Then I also realized that the artillery might be in response to a fire mission called in by the lead chopper who may have taken enemy fire from the ground and now we were passing directly over that location. I recalled that I used to worry about being shot at while at 1500 feet but since it had never happened I had put the thought of it out of my mind. Now I realized that we could have taken fire while at a high altitude but we would be unaware of it unless a bullet actually hit the helicopter. A few minutes later we were flying considerably lower than what was customary and I wondered why we were taking unnecessary risks. So far this operation had proceeded without any extraordinary dangers and I had been relatively calm but now I could feel the effects of adrenaline being pumped into my blood at an increasing rate. I was abruptly aware that my life could end before I even stepped foot on the landing zone.

After about another fifteen minutes of flying the landing zone came into view and soon this flight of choppers set down into the middle of a large rice paddy. We pushed ourselves out of the choppers, landing directly into the paddy itself and then running towards the tree line of the surrounding jungle, avoiding the long, thin earthen dikes that divided the rice field into scores of square sections. Thankfully this paddy was essentially dry, with long, thick, lush grass growing in it. We pushed into the tree line and proceeded only another fifty feet until we came to another huge rice paddy. We stopped at the edge of the dike that bordered it. Supposedly we were waiting for the remainder of the troops in succeeding flights of choppers to land and then catch up to us.

We had only been there for a few minutes when out of nowhere there was a sound like a plane approaching us fast and low. I looked quickly to the left and suddenly saw a helicopter about a hundred yards away flying at top speed at an altitude of about eight feet. It flew from left to right, paralleling the line of soldiers, passing by about thirty feet in front of us. To my astonishment, it was spewing a huge amount of white smoke. I just stared at it in a stupefied fascination as it rushed past the line of men, expecting it to crash into the earth at any second and hoping that it wouldn't kill a platoon of soldiers with it. It continued past the end of the ground soldiers and flew another hundred yards before pulling up sharply and veering to the left. At the instant that it started to rise the immense billow of smoke suddenly stopped completely and it flew off apparently in perfect mechanical health. The dense line of smoke that it had dispensed was rising very slowly but it seemed to have actually sunk a few feet because it was now a solid wall of smoke from the ground to about twelve feet tall. I thought that it wasn't acting like most smoke but actually seemed to have a tendency to stay in a solid mass. There was very little wind but still I thought it very strange that the smoke wasn't rising much at all. Then I suddenly realized that it was so thick that it had completely blocked our view of anything to our front and that it also blocked the view of anyone on the other side of it, far off into the jungle tree line. Suddenly the explanation of that phenomenon hit me. That helicopter must have had some kind of smoke making machine on it. It had deliberately put down that barrier for some reason, perhaps to shield us from enemy fire or, perhaps I thought, to conceal the paratroopers on the ground when they land, who by now should be making their parachute assault.

We waited for ten minutes and then pushed through that extremely dense smoke for about twenty feet before breaking out into the bright sunshine and wide rice paddy on the other side and then continued onwards into the tree line on the far side. There were no parachutes or men in the paddy nor could I see any parachutes descending.

It took about half an hour to reach the edge of the jungle as we traversed a very wide area of rice paddies. I kept looking up for group of troop transport airplanes and their cargo of paratroopers who by now should be exiting their aircraft in a full balls out airborne assault, but I never saw them. The 2nd battalion did indeed make a combat parachute assault that day. I don't know whether they jumped in before we arrived on the field or whether they jumped while we were in the jungle and wouldn't have been able to see or hear them but I'm sure that, at least my Company didn't provide much close in security for their actual landing.

About four hundred meters into the jungle we came upon a VC base camp. There was a large rectangular pit about ten feet by twenty feet long and three or four feet deep. In the middle of it was a rectangular area about the size of a table where only about a foot of the earth had been removed and in the middle of it was dishes and bowls containing rice and other foods, all of it still warm. This was both good and bad to my reckoning. Good that we had disrupted the VC and bad in that they would have fled into the surrounding jungle and were probably preparing an ambush for us.

My squad stayed in the kitchen area for about five minutes while other soldiers searched the surrounding system of trenches and fighting positions but they didn't find anything of value and we got the word to move out. I thought of smashing their bowls of food just to ruin their lunch and took a few steps, reaching towards the bowls but suddenly caught myself. I realized that the VC may have had time to booby trap things and if I started to throw around bowls and stomp on pots and pans that maybe my lunch might be ruined. I was fairly apprehensive for the next hour or so, fearing that the escaped VC had regrouped and had set up a hasty ambush but we finished that day without any enemy engagements.

We beat the bush for another day or two and then came to our set up site for the night. We dug the usual fighting positions but that task seemed to require energy reserves that I had to drag up from the deepest recesses. For some reason that days hump had almost drained me utterly and completely of all of my strength. Every shovel full of earth seemed to weigh ten pounds. All I could think of was just finally finishing the job and collapsing to the ground. I was almost finished digging when my squad was also ordered to dig another hole to use as an ammo sump, to protect our mortar ammo from enemy gunfire and incoming mortar fire. I finally dragged myself over to that work which some other soldiers had already started. We eventually finished that and I just fell to the ground, too exhausted to even erect a poncho hootch. I just wanted to sleep and give my bones and muscles and brain a respite from the beating that it had taken that day. I was on the ground for less than ten seconds when a Sergeant came by and ordered all of us to dig prone shelters next to our hoochs, about a foot and a half deep with dimensions of a coffin. That was to provide some cover from enemy fire in the event that we were sleeping when an attack began.

When finished with that task we put our poncho over the prone positions, six inches off of the ground and slept in the holes which provided some protection while we were asleep. All of this extra digging must have been because they expected some very serious assaults against that location. By the time I had finished digging my legs and arms were shaking uncontrollably. I had pushed my body way beyond any remotely reasonable demands, apparently my muscles and nerves were shutting down or going into spasms. I was way beyond exhausted. I don't remember if I had to pull guard duty that night or if I did I don't know how many shifts I had to pull. I don't remember anything of that night.

Early the next morning we got the word that we would be staying at that location. Probably the line platoons sent out patrols into the surrounding jungle but at least the Mortar platoon didn't have to beat the bush that day. Later in the day some of the other guys found some VC sixty mm mortar rounds without external charges on them among the thick vegetation inside the perimeter or close by outside of it. That prompted a more through search which found some cooked rice that had been spilled onto an anthill and a VC claymore mine. It was circular and concave, about fifteen inches in diameter and two inches thick. I shuddered to think of the damage that could do to a group of men. I got out my camera and took a picture of it set up on the ground with Jonesy, one of the men who found it, half kneeling behind it and aiming it at the camera. It didn't have electrical cord attached to it or have a blasting cap stuck into it so theoretically it would not explode but I didn't like the idea of staring into a contraption that was designed to kill me and ten other men in the vicinity. Who knew how old it was or how it was stored or if it was damaged or defective not to mention booby-trapped. Usually, the older an explosive is the more unstable it becomes so that it can explode for any reason or no reason at all. But it made a good picture.

That perimeter was our base of operations for the next seven days. The mortar platoon mostly stayed at this one location and the other platoons went out on two or three day patrols into the surrounding area. They found a Company sized base camp and killed two to five VC but took some wounded themselves.

On the evening of our last day at that site, the nighttime briefing told us that the next day we would begin a new mission and operation. Military Intelligence suggested there was a large force of VC in the area. We would begin a broad front against those enemy forces, engaging them and pushing them in front of us. The Marines would be landed by sea the next day and move inland towards us. The two Allied forces were scheduled to meet about six days after we began. Our mission was to catch the enemy between us, and then squeeze, a classic hammer and anvil operation I guess. I wondered if the enemy would choose to flee from our Airborne forces or decide to fight it out with us and flee from the Marines.

We loaded onto helicopters the next day for a relatively short flight. My group was scheduled to get onto the second stick of choppers. We were standing in a dry rice paddy with an island of jungle at the end of the paddy about three hundred feet from us. The first stick of choppers arrived and were boarded by the troopers. The stick lifted off and as the lead helicopter over flew the end of the paddy they were suddenly subjected to enemy ground fire from the patch of jungle. The VC were shooting at every helicopter as each one passed over that area, all in a line. There must have happened to be a flight of jet attack aircraft close by because an air strike was quickly called in on them and within five minutes a couple of airplanes came in fast and unloaded high explosive ordinance onto the enemy area.

A few minutes later the second stick of choppers landed and my group quickly boarded. The flight of choppers wasted no time whatsoever in lifting off. The pilots pushed their machines hard, trying to achieve maximum forward acceleration out of that area. I had hoped that the air strike had taken care of the VC problem but as we flew right through that little "sniper alley" I could catch a few yellow muzzle flashes from the ground almost directly below us. Within a second my chopper had over flown the enemy, at an altitude of about a hundred feet, much too fast for me to acquire a target and fire on him. Once we were a few hundred yards past the enemy and rapidly gaining speed and altitude I settled back for the remainder of the flight. I contemplated the fact that this was the very beginning of this new operation and that ten seconds into it, we had already been subjected to enemy fire. I took it as a bad sign of things to come.

We choppered in without any problems and set off into medium jungle. The mission continued for another two days without encountering any enemy forces or base camps. By this time the Marines had assaulted from the sea and were pushing towards us. On the third day the front of the line began making contact with snipers and small groups of enemy forces. At random times throughout most of the afternoon there would suddenly be a flurry of gunfire that would quickly reach a crescendo and then just as quickly die down. The VC initiated contact only to break it off a minute later and fade into the surrounding jungle.

The next day was a repeat of the previous one but with the enemy contacts becoming more frequent throughout the Battalion. A small patrol from one of our platoons met some resistance and suffered one soldier killed and four wounded over the period of those two days. Sometime in the afternoon the line of march halted for five minutes while some of the Sergeants were called to a meeting with their platoon leaders. When they returned we were informed that the Company had received radio reports that the Marines had run into the large enemy force and inflicted heavy causalities on them. We hurried our pace for the remainder of that day and the next, trying to close the distance between us and the Marines but I don't think that my Company engaged in any more firefights.

That night we got the word that the enemy force was almost caught between the two Allied forces but that they had retreated. Rather than facing either the Marines or our Airborne force they had decided to engage neither one and had withdrawn to our left and right, squeezing out between our hammer and anvil.

The next day elements of my battalion actually met up with some of the Marines.

Early the next morning I was in my fighting position on the perimeter. There were elements of my battalion close by, riding on top of tanks. They were suddenly assailed by small groups of VC who sprang from the underbrush and ran in front of the tanks, spraying them with automatic weapons and hitting them with recoilless rifle fire. The recoilless rifle looks like a cannon barrel but actually fires a rocket, its usually used to destroy tanks. While that action was occurring I heard a noise that I took to be that of a large piece of shrapnel falling through the tree before hitting the ground about thirty feet in front of me. The engagements were very brief, lasting less than a minute with the enemy engaging in hit and run tactics but they had inflicted causalities on the American paratroopers.

When things had settled down a few soldiers came walking over towards my position. They stopped in exactly the spot that I assumed that that large piece of shrapnel had landed and they called to me to come over and take a look at what they had found. I just yelled to them "Yeah, Yeah, I know It's a big piece of shrapnel." But they said that I was very wrong about that. I got out of my hole and went over to them. Lying on the ground was an unexploded recoilless rifle round. I think that it must have traveled through a lot of brush before finally landing there, it would have had to have done so given that the enemy had been about a hundred yards away. That would have explained the noise that I had heard. It wasn't a big piece of inert shrapnel falling through the trees, it was a high explosive rocket traveling directly through the trees and aimed at me. I thought that if they had deliberately aimed it at me that they had made an almost perfect shot but I figured that in the excitement of the battle that one of the VC had missed the tank that he was aiming at and I was just in the direct line of fire. It hadn't exploded, perhaps because the brush had slowed its forward speed, or maybe it was a dud, or maybe it was just a miracle that it didn't explode and tear me into a hundred pieces.

While the medics were attending to the wounded and dying and Medevac choppers were called in the rest of us were ordered to break camp and saddle up for the days operation. The orders for this day was for us to alter our direction of travel ninety degrees from the main thrust of the operation so far and chase after the large VC force that had split in two and gone in opposite directions to avoid being caught between the two main Allied forces. All of the battalions set out on unique compass headings, each becoming separate forces.

The pace of the march was faster than normal and I was concerned that we might be running into a large ambush. I guess the Generals saw the operation as a dash to close with and destroy the enemy, I feared that we seemed to be in a big hurry to meet our deaths sooner. Luckily, we didn't hit any enemy ambushes that day and I guess the VC were in a big rush to vacate the area because they apparently didn't have time to put booby traps in our paths or maybe they did but we fortunately avoided them somehow.

We set up camp that night in an area where the ground was cleared. There was no vegetation at all, just bare earth, where we set up our fighting positions and poncho tents for the night. The land sloped very slightly away from us towards the north so we could see the surrounding jungle for miles in that direction. About an hour after sunset when it was very dark, there was suddenly a bright light about a mile or two away, followed quickly by another and another. The lights were shimmering and shaking slightly and were moving. I thought at first that the lights originated from the ground but quickly realized that they were parachute flares being dropped from an airplane. I could just barely see a hint of an airplane slowly flying in a wide circle over that area and dropping a flare or two on every revolution.

Apparently one of the other Battalions had come under attack and called for the area to be illuminated. I couldn't hear any gunfire but that was to be expected because of the distance between that Battalion and ours. Then I saw what looked like a searchlight coming down from the plane onto the ground. It was an eerie iridescent red color that seemed to shimmer along the entire length of it. I didn't know what it was at first but soon heard a low groaning sound. Then the source of the light was cut off from the plane and the light seemed to travel rather slowly towards the ground. It was something like a water hose being suddenly shut off, with the water still traveling downwards. Then I realized that the red searchlight was actually the tracers coming from a Gatling gun aboard an airplane. That was "Puff the Magic Dragon" in action, he was firing three thousand, six hundred machine gun rounds a minute into the flare lighted area about two miles from me, that's sixty rounds per <u>second</u>.

That gun shot out so many rounds so quickly that it didn't sound like a machine gun, it just made a steady loud groaning sound that was unearthily horrible, it seemed to me to somehow be the sound of death itself, which is exactly what it was for anyone caught in its beam. The "searchlight" was a death ray, as strange and deadly as anything from outer space. Obviously the boys over there were having some trouble that night, I surely hoped that they were not being overrun.

During the next days operation through the jungle we started to get reports of casualties in our battalion and other battalions. Most of the guys in my Company had known each other for a year or more and many of them were friends and acquaintances of many men in the other Companies of our Battalion and even some in other Battalions. Much closer to the action, some of the rifle platoons in my company were making contact and taking casualties.

My platoon started to take sniper fire later that day. The action was towards the front of the line but we all hit the ground. The troopers at the front started crawling towards the enemy and soon all of us were low crawling forward, bodies being dragged along the ground. I came to a dirt road and had almost crossed it when word was passed down to halt the advance, that an air strike was being called in. A few minutes later there was suddenly a very loud sound of a jet flying directly over us at about two hundred feet high and probably at five hundred mph. An instant later the shock wave of the jets passing was surpassed by the enormous explosion of a large bomb.

The noise of the explosion was huge, very impressive and it was mixed with a strong shock wave through the air, among the sound of shrapnel tearing through the leaves of the jungle all around us. That was followed seconds later by the sound of other shrapnel, a lot of it, that had been thrown high into the air and then fell through the trees and leaves and landed all around us. That plane was followed by other jets, each dropping one or two bombs. I'm not sure whether there were six jets in a line or just two that swung around in very tight circles and made successive attacks.

The shrapnel fell all around us and among us, extremely close by. I could clearly see the shrapnel hitting the ground on the bare dirt road and stirring up small clouds of light brown dust and couldn't believe that no one in my Company was getting hit by it. I thought that the first bomb had landed very close to us but each succeeding aircraft dropped their bombs closer to us than the one preceding one. Each succeeding explosion sent shrapnel ripping through the leaves and branches closer and closer to the ground until the last bomb shot a river of shrapnel that shredded the vegetation only a few feet above our heads. Each bomb in its turn also ejected more and more shrapnel upwards that

produced more of a hailstorm of shrapnel raining down upon us. I thought that surely some of the soldiers on the ground would be torn apart, subjected as they were to this maelstrom of white hot jagged metal. I was also worried that one of the planes would drop their load directly on top of us. It also occurred to me that those aircraft were being directed by controllers on the ground. That meant that there was a serious enemy force very close by.

We got the word that the next plane would be the last and when he came in fast and furiously, unloading his ordinance exactly on target, I thought that those pilots were very accurate since the bombs landed less than a hundred feet from us. About two seconds after those last two bombs exploded there was a tremendous rain of shrapnel, I could clearly see about twenty or thirty large pieces hitting just on the small dirt road so that there must have been hundreds of shards of the shrapnel landing in the jungle amongst us. I could feel the shock waves of the shrapnel as I laid on the ground as they smashed into the earth. Suddenly there was a sharp cry of pain from a soldier close by.

I spun around on the ground partially to see a guy who was in my squad about fifty feet away. He was squirming on the ground and sort of jumping around on his knees, looking like he's trying to shake something out of the leg of his pants, then falling to the ground again, grasping at his leg with both hands. He suddenly sat upright on the ground and started to tear at his pants leg. It had a ragged, torn, burned hole in it and some sort of very jagged, silver colored metallic object was protruding from it. The guy was painfully exclaiming "Ow!, Owww!, Ow!" as he tried to grab the piece of shrapnel and pull it out of his leg.

But it was extremely hot and instantly burned his hands so that he could only touch it for a split second. He then grabbed at it determinately and tried to pull it out but after just a second he involuntarily recoiled backwards so convulsively that he smacked his back onto the ground. It looked like he had received a severe electrical shock. He tried to grab it again, his face flushed with pain and panic, trying to rid his body of that white hot object that continued to sear the skin and muscles of his leg, but again, his body stiffened immediately, pulling his hands away as his body recoiled from the pain. He tried it again with the same result.

Now I was a bit panicked as I helplessly watched that soldier suffering so much and acutely aware that even if something could be done that at any moment the air might be filled with shrapnel from the next bombing run. Then suddenly an idea came to me. I reached down to my belt and unsnapped my bayonet, figuring I could dig it out with that. I yelled to him "Pierce! I'm coming!" Maybe it was a coincidence but when he saw me crawling towards him with a big knife in my hand he made a final, beyond desperate, grab at the metal, seizing it with both hands and wrenching and twisting it viciously with all of his might. After an interminable three seconds, which seemed like three minutes, of unimaginable, indescribable, way beyond nightmarish agony, he finally wrenched the large ragged piece of white hot metal from his flesh, tearing it out with such violence that it went flying upwards, his hands instantly releasing their grip of such a horror and his upper body recoiling backwards, instinctively, away from such an excruciating insult to his body and mind. He laid there on his back for a few seconds, his arms outstretched towards the sky, undoubtly in shock, probably trying to have his brain make sense of the absolute awfulness of the pain that he just went through. Then, I guess, his training kicked in and he rolled over to lie on his stomach, seemingly casually, and assumed a prone fighting, firing position. "I'm OK" he said. Obviously, obviously you are not OK I thought. That shrapnel obviously has hurt you badly. He never complained about it, he just "drove on." for the remainder of the operation.

We got the word a minute later that we were moving forwards. The aerial bombardment had ceased, as did the enemies small arms and sniper fire to the front of the line that had initiated that whole situation. Although the enemy could have easily renewed their fire, there seemed to be a sense of comfort (relative of course). Relative to the preceding minutes of violence beyond belief, things seemed to be very quiet and calm. I low-crawled over towards the injured soldier, concerned that he may not be able to walk. He was sitting on the ground, bent at the waist, examining his wound. As I approached I asked him how he was and he replied that he was OK. I said, "Let me take a look at that" but he quickly pulled his pant leg back down and said, "It's all right, Lets go."

All I could see was a very jagged hole in his pants leg, burned black around the edges. That piece of shrapnel must have caused a very nasty and deep wound indeed but apparently it didn't cut any tendons or too many important muscles. The incredible heat of it would have seared shut any cut blood veins or arteries I thought. He just pulled his pants leg back down, put on his rucksack and carried on. That's how it was. A severe injury would be ignored. If you could still walk and function, you just carried on. A bad injury that would send a man to the emergency room in the States, followed by cleansing, antibiotics, surgery and a few days in a hospital, would be ignored in the bush, as a relatively trivial wound, one that would certainly not take you out of action.

Later that day one of the Company's platoons stumbled upon a VC base camp. The word was passed down the line that that platoon had encountered VC and had taken prisoners. That was all any of us knew until later that night when I talked to some of them. They told a story of how they had somehow found themselves inside the enemy camps perimeter before they realized that they were surrounded by fighting positions and trenches. How a point platoon

had walked through a VC base camps encircling system of trenches might seem inconceivable to a civilian but to a Viet Nam Veteran it seems perfectly reasonable. The VC were masters of concealment and camouflage. The report was that the Americans had suddenly came upon a trench system with about fifteen VC in it, expertly concealed by dense vegetation. The Americans at the front of the line of march had walked right past the trench, moving parallel to it and separated from it by only a few feet.

Apparently, two soldiers almost simultaneously spotted separate Viet Cong. The enemy were inside the trench and peering up at them from below ground level, mostly obscured by heavy plants and bushes. Both of those Americans said that they were so shocked and surprised by the closeness of the enemy that, without thinking, they both just jumped into the trench, yelling in mid-air a warning to their platoon mates, knocking down the VC in the process and then just kicking and stomping them. Other guys told me that when that happened, they suddenly saw a bunch of other VC partially stand up or start moving around only feet away and those Americans jumped or dove head first onto the enemy, they were that close. All of the guys who jumped into the trench told the same story of not wanting to fire their weapons because they didn't want to accidentally shoot any Americans by accident, it was very extremely close combat. They all said that the situation in the trench was a wild scene of bodies intermingled very closely together, with rifle butts and bayonets and bare knuckles and boots flying wildly.

One guy told us that he had actually passed the end of the trench when the alarm was sounded and when he spun around he spotted a VC rise up from the trench only about five feet away who began to raise his rifle. The VC had his back to him, aiming at the American soldiers now approaching him. That trooper said that he took two steps forward, thrusting his M-16 directly into back of the enemies head, wishing that he had a bayonet on the end of his rifle so as to stop the VC's shooting of his friends inatantly. That would have been sooner that the split second that was necessary for the paratrooper to switch the safety of his rifle to full automatic and pull the trigger, unloading nineteen rounds.

Everyone involved in the action that I spoke with said that the fight was finished very quickly. In the end, there were no friendly causalities but every VC in that trench had been either killed, wounded or captured. It was also determined that of fifteen VC in the trench, only one was armed. It must have been some sort of training that they were on. The armed VC's weapon had a beautiful blond/light gold colored wooden stock. Maybe it was French. It was obviously some type of hunting rifle for a rich man, certainly too fancy and finely crafted for standard military issue. The American soldier who had killed

the owner of that rifle had put eighteen rounds into the mans head and the last bullet into the stock of the VC's rifle. A large piece of that stock was missing, torn off jaggedly by an M-16 bullet so that half of what remained was just splintered and shattered wood. Back at base camp it would be placed behind and above the bar at the enlisted mens club, now renamed "Corfman Hall" after the first American who was killed in our battalion, the guy killed by mortar fire about fifty feet from me on that large rock, six lifetimes ago.

The American casualties were mounting at an alarming rate as we encountered small bands of VC throughout the following days. At night we would get the word as to who had been killed or wounded that day. For example, one night, the word might be "Cunningham and Borch were killed today and Johnson lost both of his legs and Peters was blinded and his face shot up. The next night might be "Reynolds from 1st platoon had his arm shot off and Chuckie and Wiley were taken out by a rocket". That had a big effect because almost everyone knew each other, most of them had been friends for two years or more while serving with the 101st Airborne Division in Kentucky.

Many of the men in this unit had close friends, sometimes their best friends, in this unit. They knew those men, not as anonymous fellow soldiers but as people who had wives and children and girlfriends and brothers and sisters and parents and family and friends back in the States. Those names represented real people, men with whom they had trained and partied with. Men that they had known personally, with whom they had worked and talked and joked and listened to music with, drank beer and jumped out of airplanes with.

Men who showed pictures of their children and shared their plans and dreams for the future. The reports of those causalities were acutely and painfully felt by everyone who knew them. After many a hard days hump filled with danger and pain, those causality reports added a layer of sadness and anguish and horror to men who were already thoroughly exhausted in body and mind. The men mourned privately and quietly, most of them expressing their emotions only by sitting alone, staring at the ground in their wearied sorrow and despair, deeply immersed in their grieving and bereavement.

I was a replacement and knew almost no one outside of my platoon and even then I knew most of them only by sight. To me, those reported casualties were soldiers that happened to be on the same operation and close to my area when they were hit and that concerned me but I noticed that I really had no human sympathy for them at all. To me they were just names on a list, a list that would probably have my name on it soon enough. I had a vague realization that somewhere in my soul there was a place for compassion and sympathy but those virtues seemed to reside in a place that was now deeply hidden and calloused over.

As surely as my skin had been torn and ripped apart deeply or my kidneys damaged by dehydration or my hearing partially destroyed, I realized that my psyche had been altered and damaged. My body was not the same as it was when I first entered this country and I was saddened to now realize that my mind was not the same either. I could only hope that if I survived this ordeal that maybe my mind would revert to its previous state. I had been a young, happy, healthy human being before this war. Now, both in body and mind, I had become something else. I knew that my skin would scar over and relatively heal, that my organs might well regain most of their function and that my hearing might be OK with hearing aids but I wondered whether the mind could heal itself. Clearly, something had changed, and not for the better I feared.

That evening a helicopter delivered hot food that had been prepared in a field kitchen at a forward supply base. It was packed in aluminum, olive drab painted oval containers with some sort of thin insulation. Each component of the meal was in a separate container, that is, one container might contain mashed potatoes, another beef and gravy and another carrots. The containers were set up on the ground with a man stationed behind each one with a large spoon. A Lieutenant was in charge of the food and the serving of it. He would call for one group of men at a time and the section Sergeants would in turn call out the names of two men in their sections to go and get some food. That way there were only about six men in line for the chow at any one time and all sectors of the perimeter remained almost fully manned. Back at base camp the mess line would consist of maybe fifty men standing close to each other. This mess line consisted of six men standing ten or fifteen feet apart, still maintaining their combat intervals so that any one enemy mortar round wouldn't kill all of them, and all of them fully armed in case of attack. All of those men knew that they were not standing in line at a fast food joint back in the States to get a burger, fries and a shake. They may have suppressed it, forced it out of their minds, refused to consider it, but the fact of the matter was that they could be killed at any split second. Not that they could be, it was likely that they would be. I could just see the scenario years later as a trooper told a friend: "I just went up to try to get some mashed potatoes and I suddenly lost my left arm and right leg."

It was very good to get that food, maybe the first decent hot meal in ten days. Actually it couldn't really be described that way. It was probably hot at one time but by the time it arrived in the field it was luke warm. It was typical Army Mess hall food, bland, of inferior quality and not enough of it. I still thoroughly appreciated it though because it was much better than C-rations. I ate every speck of what I was given and wanted more but there was barely enough to serve all of the soldiers manning that night perimeter and so everyone received a closely rationed amount of food.

We all carried mess kits that consisted of two small oval shaped metal containers onto which the food could be served. One of the containers had a folding handle so that it could be used for cooking. The idea of individual mess kits and hot food cooked in large kitchens was good but there was a problem with that concept. After eating, the mess kits were still dirty with left over sauce and bits of food. I suppose the proper concept would have been to have large drums of hot soapy water available with which to clean the metal plates. I guess that someone didn't think of that or maybe the cleaning apparatus was unavailable or couldn't fit into the single chopper that delivered the food along with passengers and various other equipment and supplies. Three days later, when hot food was brought in again, when I opened my mess kit it had the rotten remains of the previously eaten food, mixed with small particles of leaves and mud, some of it washed off only by old insecticide and sweat. Everyone else's mess kit must have been in the same condition and I think it probably caused a number of men to become sick. The only way to really clean the kits was with a Brillo pad and lots of hot soapy water. No one thought to carry a Brillo pad, even if such things were available back in base camp. Everyone had a bar of soap but no one had enough heat tabs or C-4 explosive to heat water for cleaning. The most critical element though was water. A soldier would not waste the precious water in his canteens to try to get clean his kit. The choice was to try to clean the kit and go without drinking water for maybe the next thirty-six hours, or to leave the kit as it was. It was really no choice at all. We were chronically dehydrated, sometimes to an extreme degree. A dirty mess kit would probably might make a soldier very sick, a lack of any water for more than a day might well kill him with heat exhaustion.

The next day, the mortar platoon stayed in place and the other platoons went out on patrol. They encountered some VC and had become embroiled in an exchange of fire. When the U.S. troopers returned to our position in the late afternoon they were carrying one of their wounded on a makeshift stretcher made of two small tree trunks with a poncho stretched between them. The soldier on the stretcher was from my platoon, a short, wiry, little tough guy named Sgt. Sanchez. I don't know why he went on that patrol, maybe they were short a Sergeant or he was acting as the forward observer for the mortar platoon. He was lying on the stretcher, his face red and distorted in agony, but he didn't utter a sound. He was in obvious very severe pain and distress having been gut shot. A medivac chopper was called in and he was evacuated to a hospital. I never saw him again. I think that he survived but I'm not sure by any means.

The next day the mortar platoon again remained in place. We got word over the radio that one of the Company's platoons had discovered enemy hoochs and underground bunkers that contained a number of radios, a lot of documentation, papers and maps, printing machines and a large number of cameras. Towards the end of the day, we knew from radio traffic from that patrol that they were very close to our position, on their way back in. I wandered over to the area of the perimeter where they would be approaching, just to welcome them back and ask them about what they found.

From the radio transmissions, they were only about two hundred yards away but I waited for over fifteen minutes and was about to walk away and look for them, assuming that they must have entered the perimeter from another direction. The soldiers in the closest fighting positions suddenly became alert to some noise to their front and a minute later one of them called back to us and the other nearby perimeter guards that the patrol was arriving. A soldier suddenly appeared to materialize somehow from amidst the dense jungle then moved forward slowly, staring straight ahead. He was looking directly in my direction but he seemed to be watching something in the far distance. He walked right past the soldier standing in his fighting position without a glance or any acknowledgement of his presence and then walked right past me and the other two soldiers standing close by, still staring straight ahead. He looked like a zombie, totally oblivious to his surroundings. Then another soldier from the patrol appeared out of the jungle and then another, each of them looking and acting like the first man.

I reflexively stepped back a few feet to let them pass unimpeded, amazed and appalled at their condition. Then others from the patrol emerged. Some stared off into the distance, some had their heads hung low staring at their feet as they walked and some franticly looked to the sides and in front of them as they staggered back in from their patrol. Most of them appeared to be seriously dazed or brain damaged. They were far beyond the ragged edge of exhaustion, completely soaked with sweat and filthy dirty. There were vines and broken leaves caught in the buttons of their uniforms and on their equipment. Each man was breathing as if he had just finished a four hundred yard dash. I was dumbfounded, wondering what could have caused those men to be in the unbelievably wretched condition that they were in. The men just filed past me, completely ignoring my questions and my presence.

I seriously questioned for a second whether they actually were dead, they looked like they had just crawled out of their graves, with an effort that was beyond humanly possible. They couldn't even speak because of their exhaustion. I tried to imagine what they must have endured that day to be in such shape but I couldn't imagine what could possibly have done such things to those men. Then I abruptly realized that that was how every one of us looked, every day, after beating the bush. Apparently all they were thinking about was trying mightily to struggle another fifty feet and finally putting down their loads.

Although most of the men just filed past us ignoring us completely, some of the men managed to gave two or three word answers to our questions. Many of the men had cameras hanging around their necks that looked to be in new condition and of very high quality. Those men had discovered and then plundered and destroyed an extremely valuable site and disrupted an enemy unit that had been the main object of this operation. History books record it as one of the three most important defeats of the enemy during the war, the capture and destruction of the Central Office for Propaganda for Viet Nam (COSVN). I've never seen any mention in a history book about the beyond extraordinary struggles, hardships and insufferably horrible pain and suffering that those troopers endured to accomplish that goal.

* * * *

Around five o'clock two helicopters landed in a very small LZ that had been carved out of the heavy jungle that surrounded us. About six soldiers immediately went over to the choppers as soon as they touched down. To have so many men suddenly group together was highly unusual, especially around a helicopter on the ground which would be a prime target for any enemy close by. I watched as the air crewchiefs pushed some cases of C-rations to the edge of the ships that were picked up and carried away by the closest couple of troopers. The other men started unloading heavy machine parts which I slowly realized were the components of two fifty caliber machine guns, two more mortars and a big supply of ammo for those guns. I walked over in that direction to find out what was going on. I was startled for a second when I suddenly saw two black pajamaed VC five feet from the skids of the chopper, sitting on the ground among bushs that were wildly flailing about in the choppers prop blast. Their hands were tied behind their backs and they seemed to look at the chopper in terrified disbelief. Then I remembered that we had got the word down the line earlier that day that some VC had been captured. I don't know whether those prisoners were starkly frightened by the number of heavy weapons being delivered to this small unit and the overwhelming destruction it would effect on their friends if they attacked later that night or scared to death of the idea of being thrown into that hellish mechanical monstrosity shaking and roaring next to them, to be flown off into some otherworldly horror they couldn't imagine.

I felt just the slightest tinge of pity for them but then realized that they were actually very lucky. They were being removed from the battlefield and unless they fell out of the chopper or had it shot out from under them by their friends, those two soldiers would wake up the next day alive. That was most certainly not a certainty for the men on the ground within this perimeter. I learned that choppers would be landing here in the morning to evacuate those heavy weapons and we would just hump one mortar and ammo among the platoon.

Late that afternoon, close to dusk, I was in a fighting position with another soldier on perimeter guard. Other than a few faint sounds every once in a while of men in the center of the perimeter there was no sounds or noises at all. The warm air was very still so that there wasn't even the faint rustling of leaves. There was absolutely no jungle noises. No sounds from insects or birds or animals, or enemy.

For some reason, I decided to walk around the perimeter a little bit. Mostly out of boredom, but I really wanted to know the exact dimensions of our perimeter, in case we were attacked, and/or overrun at night. I walked about a hundred yards, keenly aware that I was presenting a good target for a sniper. I approached a machine gun emplacement and decided that I had pushed my luck long enough and would sit on the ground and talk to the machine gun guys for a few minutes, just to give any VC snipers a break from targeting me. But, before I reached that machine gun team, from somewhere rather close by in the surrounding jungle in front of them suddenly came the loud voice of an enemy soldier taunting us. He was yelling "Fuck you, Fuck you, Fuck yoooooou".

I ran and dived to the ground, low crawling for the next fifteen feet to the machine gun position and the sand-bagged, dug up little berm that they had dug, crashing crudely beside one of the guys in the gun team. He was quite surprised by my antics, his face registering an expression of surprise and wonder, such as "What the Heck is your problem?" I shouted to him my alarm, "Do you hear that?" This was like something out of a movie. There was still some lingering light as the sun set so that obviously the VC could see our perimeter. At night I wouldn't have fired on a sound because that would readily identified the exact location of our position because of the muzzle blast, but it wouldn't compromise anything if I fired some rounds right now.

I switched my M-16 to single fire and took aim at the jungle. I was going to let that Cong shout one more time so as to get a better idea of where he was and then light him up. I said to the guy beside me, "Lets put some fire on that little wise guy", but he just looked at me in a strange way and simply said, "That's just a "fuck you" lizard". I stated strongly and derisively, "That isn't a lizard!, its a gook!" He calmly told me "No" and then informed me that he's not sure if its a lizard or a bird because you can never see them, but for sure it isn't VC. His tranquil demeanor finally persuaded me that he was correct and I slowly slid out of my state of high alert. I had to force myself to override the insistent message of close danger from my hearing, insisting to myself that it was just an animal out there. It wasn't as if the shout was "Puck you, or Ruck you or Buck you" and it wasn't as if it sort of sounded like a human voice. I don't know how it could possibly have sounded more genuinely human. As night quickly descended the voice in the woods went silent. I thought that this is a strange jungle indeed, even the animals tell you to go f . . . yourself.

About an hour after sunrise on the next day, we had finished striking the camp. The fighting positions had been filled in with the dirt that had been shoveled out of them the day before, sandbags were emptied and packed away in our rucksacks and the thin trees that had formed a framework for the roof of the fighting positions had been broken and scattered. The ponchos had been packed and everyone was just sitting around, waiting for the line of march to begin.

Out of nowhere two attack jets swooped past us flying very low, releasing their bombs almost immediately. I caught a glimpse of their ordinance as it dropped away from the planes at an angle as its forward momentum propelled them forward at probably three hundred miles per hour. They must have hit within a half second of their release. Where they landed to earth was hidden from view by the surrounding jungle but there was no noise of an explosion or shrapnel or smoke suddenly thrown into the air. About fifteen seconds later I started to see the top of what became a huge cloud of black smoke slowly rising from the impact area and realized that the planes had dropped napalm. Their target was an area about four hundred yards from us, directly in the direction of our line of march. We hadn't received any word regarding that bombing run so I don't know if the air strike had been called in on an identified target or whether the pilots had spotted a target of opportunity or whether it was just a preventive strike to clear our line of march although the latter would have been an unusual occurrence.

We moved out directly towards the column of smoke although it was hidden from view as soon as we entered the jungle. We moved forward for about two hundred yards when we started to distinctly smell gasoline and burned wood, the smell becoming extremely strong as we pushed further into the jungle. Ten minutes later we reached the actual impact area. The bombs had landed about seventy feet apart from each other. Each of the long bombs had swooped in with tremendous force and speed, approaching the ground at about a thirty degree angle and pushing down stands of bamboo and shattering trees before they struck the earth. Every bit of vegetation within a fifty foot radius of the point of impact had been completely burned and blackened when the napalm scattered and was set aflame. A shiver went through me as I looked at that hellish scene, realizing that any living creature caught in that firestorm must have died horribly, their bodies utterly destroyed, reduced only to blackened ashes and bones.

There was raw, unburned globs of napalm stuck to trees and leaves at the edge of the burn area. Some of it slowly moving towards the ground like warm wax while other bits had formed a skin that was slowly hardening. I reached up and pulled a piece off of a bamboo leaf.

It was a milky clear substance, gasoline mixed with a bonding agent to make it sticky. I rolled it between my thumb and forefinger gradually increasing pressure until the glob popped open and revealed the contents to be a sticky glue like substance smelling strongly of gasoline. I rubbed my hand roughly on some nearby leaves to rid myself of it and walked away disgusted and dismayed at the people who invented such a weapon.

Throughout that day I had to continuously force myself be aware of my surroundings and alert for mines or booby traps or enemy soldiers because thoughts of that damnable napalm continuously intruded into my consciousness. I'd catch myself deep in thought, contemplating what it was like for anyone that had been engulfed by that napalm and, more importantly, thinking what would happen if I was ever hit by it.

We didn't encounter any enemy forces that day nor did we have any causalities. After we had dug in later in the afternoon a helicopter brought in hot food, so, all told, it was a relatively good day in the bush, of course it was a hellishly, unimaginable day of suffering and pain for a civilian. Someone had come up with the excellent idea of delivering paper plates along with the food so we wouldn't have to use our filthy mess kits. To top off the day, there was some food that was left over after everyone had been served. I was close to the chow line when one of the soldiers serving the meal said that seconds were available. I jumped up and ran the few feet to a serving container and I gorged myself on two extra plates filled with mashed potatoes, wolfing it down like a desperate animal.

We had only been humping fifteen to two thousand meters each day for the last two days but in the morning we got the word that day we would be humping eight thousand meters. We usually humped three thousand meters, about two miles per day but that was two miles in a straight line on a map. We would many times greatly meander left to right to search more ground and maybe climb up and down hills all day so that a two thousand meter hump might in reality turn into a ten thousand meter hump. That might well be up and down mountains and across many streams.

With the equivalent weight of a refrigerator packed with ice in the freezer on our backs it was beyond words what the pain and suffering these Infantrymen endured every day, in tropical heat and humidity. The information that we would hump three thousand meters really provided no information as to how long and hard that days operation would be. For this very long hump we were to leave our rucksacks and any other equipment and take only the necessities. That was the only time that we ever left our rucksacks full of equipment behind.

My platoon was told to leave the mortars behind and that alone meant that the hump would be far less backbreaking for us. All of us carried a small canvas pack inside our rucksacks. It was worn low on the back held up by an attached belt and thin suspenders. Of course we took all of our ammo and grenades and canteens and one meal but the load was considerably lighter then usual and relatively very easy to carry. We covered a lot of ground on that day, mostly through open areas but didn't encounter any enemy or enemy positions.

The next day, we were told that we would be picked up by choppers in the morning and flown to another landing zone. For this mission we would be operating very close to the Cambodian border. There were strict orders from the White House not to cross the border, not even to fire in the direction of the border even if we were fired upon. About a half hour later the Company Commander called us all together for a briefing and said that there was no clear demarcation line of the border in this area. It was marked only by a line on a map and from the ground there was nothing to indicate which side of the border we were on. He said that our line of march was supposed to be no less than a mile from it but that its entirely possible that we may cross it. Then he said that despite the White House orders, if anyone is fired upon and we return fire, or we cross the border in pursuit, he certainly would not hear it or see it. I was proud of him but I had already made up my mind that if someone shot at me on the other side of an imaginary line expecting me not to light him up it might well be the last mistake of his life.

All of us had been taught in basic training that there are lawful orders and unlawful orders. I slowly realized that in a combat situation there are orders that you follow and orders that you do not. If I had gold embossed orders directly from the White House Scotch taped to my forehead I wouldn't think twice about disobeying them if the alternative jeopardized my life or the lives of any other American soldier. The idea that someone had a free pass to try to kill the men in this Brigade so that the White House staff wouldn't be embarrassed by the cluckings of some effeminate diplomat thoroughly disgusted me.

That night a chopper came in and delivered mail. I received a package from my family that was filled with chocolate covered fudge candy bars. Those packages provided a large part of my food intake on various missions. My mother had followed my advice from a previous letter that I had sent and had gratefully wrapped each bar individually in aluminum foil. Nothing could be done to prevent the candy bars from completely melting in the daytime heat, even when they were stored deep in the middle of my rucksack, but the aluminum foil kept them intact and when they were unwrapped at night the chocolate would usually have mostly solidified.

The chopper also contained a big surprise. We were absolutely astonished to learn we were to be issued two warm cans of beers per man. I drank my beer right down no problem. Unbelievably, I thought, some soldiers complained that the beer wasn't cold and others derisively remarked that they couldn't even get a slight buzz with only two beers. Other men traded their beers for C-rations and others played cards, gambling their beer. One guy in my squad kept winning and winning until he had accumulated thirty cans of beer. He drank down six quick beers and then seemed to give it a rest for a while. I asked him what he was going to do all of the other beers and he said that he was going to hump it the next day and sure enough the next day he strapped a case of beer to his rucksack and off he went. He would drink six warm beers for each of the next four nights. We humped for another day and then set up in a very small grassy meadow.

The next day, we had moved out only about two hundred feet when we got the word down the line to stop in place for ten minutes while other units were aligned and tanks moved into place. The line of march had crossed a dirt road and when we stopped I was at the edge of it but not yet across it. There were six or seven lines of march so there were a number of soldiers located as I was at the edge of the road. I just sat down, taking it easy in the shade of the jungle at my back when I saw three tanks rumbling along the road, approaching from my left.

I thought that it wasn't a good idea for the tanks to be traveling on a road because there might be mines buried there. Then I thought that if a tank does hit an anti-tank mine its liable to kill the tank crew and also kill a bunch of nearby infantrymen. The lead tank passed by me with its treads crushing the ground about twenty four inches away from my outspread feet. I watched it travel another fifty feet and then I turned to my left to watch the tank that was following it approach and pass me by, again missing my feet by inches. I was amazed at how expert those tank drivers were, what with being so good at judging distance around their tank. Then I suddenly realized that maybe the drivers didn't even see us. Of course in civilian life anyone in their right mind would have jumped back ten feet from those threads.

A few seconds later I looked to my right again, for some unknown reason. Suddenly there was powerful but muffled explosion that sent a shock wave through the ground, seemingly emanating from the lead tank, now about 100 feet away. It abruptly stopped, literally, dead in its tracks. There was a lot of dust and smoke around it and when I went to investigate, sure enough the tank had hit a mine and the tread had been broken in half. There had been a number of soldiers who had been sitting close to that tank when it was hit but luckily the tank tread had absorbed most of the explosion and resulting shrapnel. None of the infantrymen had been wounded and the explosion hadn't penetrated the crew quarters of the tank.

Plans were changed and we remained stationary for another twenty minutes. The stricken tank crew obtained another tread, probably a spare from another tank and set about making repairs. I pulled my rucksack a few feet backwards into deeper shade and watched them as they worked. They seemed to know exactly what to do but it was very heavy work and they were sweating profusely in the full sunlight. The task seemed straightforward but the tread probably weighed more than a thousand pounds and had to be manhandled around by five or six tankmen. The damaged tread had to be removed first and then the new one attached. As they tried to fix it, the huge metal sprocket on the tank that was still usable turned the old tread but after a few feet of movement it suddenly caught in the dirt and jammed up. That shifted the entire monstrous weight and mass of the tank violently sideways, nearly smashing into the soldiers close to it.

The tank driver again engaged the drive sprocket and the tread moved a few feet but then suddenly shot out sideways nearly cutting in half some of the nearby soldiers. Now the tread was severely out of alignment and had to be manhandled back into place by several men with five foot long pry bars. They tried it again but this time, the portion of tread on the ground suddenly shot out sideways. Why and how it didn't cut off the feet of some of the workers I will never know. That terrible work continued for another twenty minutes until the old tread had been removed.

The infantry was only supposed to have waited for ten minutes. It was now well beyond that time. I didn't know if that situation was due to unknown problems or weather we were ordered to stay in place to provide security for the tanks. My guess is that it was the latter reason.

Then the tankers started to put the new tread on. It was laid out in a straight line in front of the tank and than about eight soldiers manhandled half of it so that it caught onto the front and rear sprockets. This should go well I thought. But no. Putting on that new tread was equal to or exceeded the dangers of taking off the old one. That job really required two huge big cranes, three huge tow trucks, six safety inspectors, twenty well paid workers with a death wish and a full day to do the job correctly. Those guys were obviously operating under emergency combat conditions.

I was just sat there, frightened but fascinated by the whole spectacle, calmly trying to calculate how many fingers and toes and arms and legs and lives would be required to finish the job, but also slowly realizing how thoroughly enjoyable it was to have a mini vacation from the brutal hump that I faced. I just thought, the poor buggers, they were really frightened and suffering as they went about their back breakingly dangerous job immersed in diesel smoke and brutal sunshine. But then I thought, I wish that I was one of them. Eventually they shall mount their tanks and then sit down all day. They won't have to hump my agonizing load all day and they are impervious to normal booby traps and small arms fire. Yes, I thought, they are a bunch of poor buggers and I feel sorry for them a little, but their current agonies and fears are a very small fraction of what every man in this Company will endure this day and everyday deep in the woods. I looked at them and zealously wished that I was one of them. They eventually finished their task. As the tanks moved out to the east, we started walking northwards, beginning another day of abject misery.

That evening, we set up as usual and dug in. I went to chop down some small trees to use to support sandbags as overhead cover on our fighting positions. I got our squads only machete from my squad Sergeant and walked into the jungle right outside of our perimeter. The area was thick with trees from 2 to 5 inches in diameter so I didn't have to search all around to find what was needed. A few hard smacks of the machete blade easily felled the trees. Once down, another cut had to be made so that the section of tree was about 8 feet long. Then the piece of wood was held upright in one hand and the machete was used to cut off all of the small branches, being careful not to chop off your fingers in the process. The first two trees came down easily and were quickly processed into usable pieces. The initial chop into the third tree produced a very strange sensation in my hand. That tree must have been of a different species from the first few because it required a lot more chopping to severe it. With each successive stroke a weird vibration and strange, strong pain traveled up the machete and into my hand. I examined the machete closely and noticed that the black plastic handle had a piece missing so that part of the metal tang was touching my palm as I tightly gripped the handle with each blow.

With each chop the vibration traveled painfully further up my arm and deeper into the bones of my arm. It was as painful as it was unique and after a minute I had to cease operations. I removed my shirt and wrapped it around the handle but that padding didn't reduce the shaking and pain very much at all, it just mostly made the machete handle unwieldy to grip and more dangerous to use. I thought that that machete is not going to do us any good if we have to chop through the jungle all day, and that it would probably be impossible to get a replacement for it any day soon. The wood had to be cut. I continued my work, eventually having to deal with a five inch thick tree that would be used as the main support for the smaller ones. That was an unusually tough tree and each chop of the machete sent a sharp jolt of pain into my bones like a dose of ice water on a fractured tooth. I eventually chopped it down but not without a vicious, long period of excruciating pain.

I had walked out to get that wood very much relieved that the days agonies of the march and the back-breaking labors of digging in were finished. I glumly realized now that my full ration of pain for this day had not yet been suffered. What should have been an easy task accomplished at my leisure had turned into some sort of agonizing torture session. I thought again of just how much I wanted to get out of this nightmare.

Early the next day we set about breaking camp. Every morning it was a hassle, to say the least, to shovel all of the dirt into the fighting positions hole that we had to dig out the previous evening and then untie and dump out fifty sandbags and chop up and scatter the sections of trees used for overhead cover. We were supposed to be meticulous about filling in the fighting positions. If we left them unfilled the VC would have ready-made positions available to them throughout the area of operations. Even partly filled positions would give them cover if they came under attack.

Anyways, I didn't want to make life easier for the enemy. I didn't like the idea of them coming into one of our previously dug out positions and then laying about, taking advantage of our hard dug positions. Actually, even if we filled in the holes, they would be much easier to re-excavate because the hard dirt would have been loosened by our labors. In the morning, I had the idea to throw the trees that were used for overhead cover into the fighting position, and throw in the little branches that had been cut off of them and anything else that would take up space so that I wouldn't have to shovel so much dirt. That idea seemed to work very well because the result was a hole that would be very frustrating to dig out again because of the tree trunks and branches embedded throughout the dirt, helter-skelter, at odd angles.

The night before, the resupply chopper didn't bring any food but it did bring big commercial chainsaws and five-gallon container cans full of gasoline. We had been told that the next day we would load our mortar onto a chopper and would be humping the chainsaws instead. I was very relieved to load that mortar onto a chopper that morning and watch as it was flown up and out and away from me. What an horrendous nightmare of horror and pain that piece of iron had inflicted on me. There are no words to describe it.

A few soldiers were standing around a pile of three chainsaws and some five gallon gas cans near the middle of the LZ so I walked over to check things out. Simply out of curiosity I picked up a chainsaw and was surprised at how heavy it was. That thing was obviously designed for heavy duty, continuous, commercial duty, sawing down big trees all day long. A person could easily cut down a tree eight feet in diameter with one of those. It had a handle on it running left to right, perpendicular to the long blade. The handle was located above the motor so that the machine was roughly balanced when it was carried.

That made it relatively easy to manhandle it but it was very difficult to get it through the underbrush because the jagged saw-toothed blade would get caught on everything. I figure that those saws weighed about forty pounds, about the weight of a mortar baseplate, a weight that would feel like two hundred pounds after humping it for a while. We humped those saws and gasoline cans all that day (a five gallon can of gasoline weighs about forty-five pounds, a murderously heavy burden, carried in one hand).

At night we came to an area where there were trees about twenty feet tall and six to ten inches in diameter with very heavy underbrush about three feet tall. We were told to use the saws to cut down enough trees to form a one helicopter landing zone and to clear an area that would be used for a night position.

Almost no one knew anything about operating any type chain saw, much less a machine so large and heavy and powerful at this one that obviously required a lot of training and experience. A soldier next to me fiddled with the controls of his saw and then yanked its starting rope.

The motor started instantly and the quiet of the jungle was torn apart by its extraordinarily loud racket. The soldier operating the machine involuntarily pushed it away from his body, holding it at arms length with both hands, and then swung the blade mostly above his head. By the look on his face he could have been holding off a maniac with a meat cleaver with ten times the strength of a human being, which is exactly what he had. The blade was engaged and whirring at full power. He didn't know how to shut it off or how to lower its power. He tried to push it as far away from his body as possible, apparently only more terrified of letting go and having it run around the ground and killing everyone around him than he was of holding the horror and letting it kill him in some kind of horrible way. He was probably correct. To let go of that screaming mechanical monster would have probably resulted in a group of soldiers being torn apart. He had a tiger by the tail. That monster shuttered, going fast and then slow but it didn't shut off.

A soldier standing very close to him suddenly darted his arm out towards the saws motor and hit a switch which quickly killed the engine. The guy who had killed the switch started talking to the terrified saw operator and I decided to go over and listen to what he was saying.

Apparently the second soldier knew all about chain saws and he was giving a brief but very informative lecture on its use and operation. After about ten minutes I was told to grab a saw and start cutting down the numerous relatively thin trees within the landing zone.

The powerful saw cut through them with no resistance whatsoever. After about a half hour of cutting a chopper descended into the LZ carrying a fifty caliber machine gun and three mortars and ammo to reinforce our night position.The LZ was filled with bushes about three feet high so the chopper just hovered with its floor about seven feet from the ground and the crew chief pushed and kicked the guns and ammo off of the chopper.

The next morning a chopper came in to pick up the heavy weapons and to deliver a Chaplain, a Catholic priest.We were told that he would say a very quick Mass.There was a protestant and a Catholic Chaplain that worked with our Brigade. I think that they even had a Jewish chaplain attached to our Brigade.

The Chaplains had to cover a lot of area and a lot of separate encampments so that a visit by a Chaplain to any particular platoon was a rare event. Given their limitations it was very rare for one of them to show up on a Sunday.They tried to show up on any day possible to administer to their flock, but mostly, their flock was spread out all over the jungle and engaged in killing and/or being killed day after day, Sundays not excluded.This priest first had a quick ceremony.There was no time to hear each mans confession, so a general Sacrament of Penance Rite was administered, where each man in the group silently confessed his sins and then Absolution was granted to the entire congregation.

That was a situation that was, and can only be, administered under the most extreme circumstances. I thought that this is indeed the most extreme and most necessary and immediate circumstances.Within a few minutes I would be proved to be right.This was the season of Lent. After the Mass the priest quickly told us to not even consider "giving up" anything for Lent.We were officially relieved of any Lenten duty of fasting or not eating meat on fridays. It was all too true when the priest said,"You men don't have anything to "give up". Our lot during this season, as in every season in Country, was to suffer, suffer dearly, suffer greatly, much more than I could have ever imagined.

In perspective, we had one actual doctor physician assigned to a Battalion. One actual doctor assigned to six hundred men involved in hard core combat. They had one Chaplain, of whatever faith, assigned per Battalion. One doctor, one Chaplain.

The reality was that they needed, per Battalion, of hard core infantry, during a serious operation, was twenty doctors and thirty Chaplains. This was no joke, it was not some kind of Hollywood movie. It was a situation where many men were killed or badly wounded. Their families forever effected beyond severely. Some of the soldiers so horribly scarred and mutilated and/or paralyzed and blinded that they would never return to a regular civilian life. Others so traumatized by their tour of duty would suffer brain and psychiatric injuries that are incurable. And who would care for those men?

We moved out on our mission and started to encounter groups of houses made out of sticks and straw. The word was passed down to not damage any of them. I thought, I don't know what type of games are going on at headquarters but I didn't like to leave these huts standing so that the VC could use them again. Me and two other men were taking turns carrying the chainsaw(forty pounds) and a five gal can of gasoline(about forty-five pounds). I would carry the chainsaw for while, then switch off with the gasoline can with another soldier for a while and then carry neither one for a while. I concocted a plan with the other two men. The guy with the gasoline would splash some of it onto the roof of the huts and the next man in line would light it with a match. We were at the end of the line so no one else could see what we were doing. As we marched along, we left a trail of flaming and smoking huts behind us. The fact of the matter is those huts could probably be reconstructed in a day or two out of materials that are readily available, but it seemed that we were doing our part for the war effort.

That night, after we had settled in, I realized that it was Friday. I had never really thought about it before but now I started to think about the situation that I now found myself. If I was back in the States I'd most likely be hanging around with my friends, maybe riding around looking for girls or having a beer or getting a pizza or playing pool. Maybe I'd get a submarine sandwich and a cold Coke and go home to watch the weekly horror movie on TV while a fan was blowing cool air around the room and worry only about whether the bait shop would run out of worms for the next days fishing trip.

I looked around at our night encampment site. Some men were cleaning their weapons and others were heating cans of C-rations over their makeshift little stoves. I knew that there were about forty men in this perimeter but most of them were completely hidden in the underbrush. My clothes were stiff with dried sweat and dirt and I noticed that the forest green color of our uniforms that identified us as Americans was now completely obliterated by the brownish red of dirt and dried mud, a coloring that could be seen only where our clothing was not a mottled dark brown and black color.

I was thirsty but I didn't want to take a sip of the warm foul water in my canteen because I knew that it might have to last all of the next day. I hadn't even seen a TV or a pizza or a pool table or a woman for many months, nor had I seen any of my old friends or family or even talked to them. I surely couldn't hop in a car and go for a joy ride nor could I just walk to the corner store and get a cold Coke or a bag of potato chips or an ice cream bar. The only thing I had to eat were C-rations and even they would have to be eaten cold. I wasn't going to be watching a horror movie that night but I may well be in the middle of a horror that made "The Night of the Living Dead" movie seem like a Girl Scout picnic. I began to realize that we were in an environment that none of us could have imagined. It truly was a different World I thought, another universe really, existing in another dimension. It was most certainly another reality. I could never have imagined that reality and as I looked around me I could not fully believe what I was seeing and experiencing.

Thoughts started to run through my mind, snippets of sounds and sights and smells, quick pictures life on the march and in the bush. I questioned for a second whether any of those things had really happened, whether I had actually experienced the things that suddenly flooded my mind. Maybe it was all just a dream I thought, and maybe I was now just in the middle of an incredible nightmare. I remember walking over towards the center of the perimeter thinking that I was beginning to lose it, hoping that it was all a dream but thinking that the whole thing was simply too terrible to have been a dream. I didn't think that anyone's unconscious mind could possibly conceive the reality of Viet Nam.

The next day was a repeat of the former day, humping through relatively light jungle and encountering enemy base camps and bamboo houses that we continued to set afire. In the early afternoon we came upon another small base camp with about 10 fighting positions. There were some panels on the ground made of thin sticks with leaves interwoven among them to form a shelter from the rain or sun. I picked up a couple of them to examine them more closely. Someone had done a good job with that piece of handiwork. Obviously someone had spent a considerable amount of time constructing those panels and it was remarkable that someone could have produced it using only natural materials at hand. It was probably waterproof because it was so tightly woven. It seemed that the person who made it had individually selected each leaf and placed it carefully onto the latticework because each leaf seemed to fit perfectly. I thought that it was really a work of art by a highly talented workman. Then I took my bayonet to them trying to break them apart and when that didn't work too well because they were so finely constructed, I chopped on them with my entrenching tool. My philosophy was to deny the enemy anything at all, to destroy anything that may be of use to them. It took a surprising amount of work to destroy the panels which I sullenly realized would probably only require a days work to replace.

When we reached our night encampment site I was immediately told to start cutting out an LZ, even before I could begin digging in. I lugged the chainsaw over to where a few other men with saws had gathered. A Sergeant was in charge of clearing the LZ and he pointed out to each man with a saw the exact trees that he wanted felled. I pulled the starter rope for my chainsaw many, many times but it refused to start. Another soldier walked over to me and after quite a bit of fiddling and adjusting and pulling the starter rope many more times it finally started. There was a separate lever that engaged the chain but that was in the "off" position so the chain was not moving. I picked up the blaring thing and walked over to the first tree that I was to cut. I knew enough to realize that I had to first make a "V" cut into the trunk and that the location of that cut would determine the direction that the tree would fall. The tree was about fifty feet tall. The trunk at the ground was a very irregular shape consisting of folds of wood so that its cross-section would be a rough star shape and three feet across. As the trunk rose to a height of about five feet the folds gradually diminished and the trunk was almost circular in shape and only about eighteen inches thick at eye level. I walked partly around the tree and noticed that it had a slight lean in one direction and it had some thick vines on it that were draped across other trees. All I could do was hope that those vines wouldn't alter the direction of the fall of the tree too much. It was a concern because other soldiers were in the general vicinity cutting other trees and digging in and I didn't want the tree to fall on top of then. But really, a person would need a computer and three days of study to give a rough guess as to where that tree might fall.

I flipped the lever that engaged the chain, picked up the heavy vibrating machine so that it was about at the level of my head and applied the saw to the tree. The saw bit into the wood and immediately jumped backwards as if someone had kicked it violently. I thought that that was just some sort of aberration so I just brought the blade back and swung the blade strongly into the side of the tree. That time, the saw seemed to almost explode, the blade wickedly kicked back as if it had been hit by a speeding truck, the blade thrown into a wide arc, throwing me off balance while I desperately held onto it with both hands. I thought that I don't have to worry about that tree falling and hitting someone because that machine is probably going to cut my head off before I manage to fell it. I tried the same maneuver a few more times, with exactly the same results. Finally I put the machine on the ground and stepped back a few feet, trying to understand what was happening.

A trooper close by had been watching my antics and went over to me to provide some instructions. I told him that I think that there was something wrong with the machine because I had used it the day before without any problems. He patiently explained to me simply that this tree was obviously made of a very dense, hard wood. Secondly he explained that I shouldn't be holding the saw over my head because that made it much more difficult to handle and much more likely for the machine to instantly cut off legs and generally butcher the operator of the saw. Lastly he pointed out a flattened piece of metal that was attached to the machine, running perpendicular to the blade. It was about 8 inches long and five inches wide with several very acute angular cuts made into it so that at one edge of it was the top of four or five sharp points. He picked up the saw and while demonstrating, he told me to shove the points into the tree before making the cut. The trick was to lock the machine to the tree by stabbing it with the points and then move the blade around in a circle into the tree, using the bar with the steel points as a fulcrum or a pivot point. I grabbed the saw and shoved the machine into the side of the tree points first. Then, as I brought the blade to bear into the trunk, the machine vibrated strongly and jumped around a bit, but the blade held and started to eat into the trunk. That technique changed everything. When that tree fell, I put down my saw and went over to the other soldiers struggling with their machines and demonstrated the technique. I noticed that the soldier who had instructed me was going around and giving advice which I had very strongly and imploringly had requested of him. The pace of felling the trees picked up considerably after that and no one was killed or maimed in the process.

Later that afternoon, I had set up my poncho hootch and was going through my equipment, checking that nothing had been lost on the trail and that everything was all right. I had been carrying the blasting cap that went with the claymore mine that another guy was carrying. We tried to always separate the two. The blasting cap was a little silver colored piece of hardware made of extremely thin metal about the size of a cigarette with two wires protruding from it. In side of it was an explosive that was detonated electrically I really didn't like carrying that cap because they were so prone to go off by themselves, especially if handled improperly, and I figured that falling on one if I have to hit the ground would pretty well mishandle it.

I first put it in my rucksack but there were too many things in there that could shift around and crush or crimp it and set it off. I finally decided to keep it in an ammo pouch on my lbg belt, but I really didn't like the idea of it going off next to a hand grenade that was next to my stomach.

The soldier who was carrying the claymore was sitting close by and I told him that I would gladly trade him that four-pound claymore for my one ounce blasting cap. He was more than willing to make the trade. Even after I fully apprised him of the dangers of the cap he seemed to be completely unfazed by my fears. He snatched the blasting cap out of my hand and threw it into his rucksack like it was nothing more dangerous than a can of beans. I really didn't like carrying the extra four pounds because after a few hours of humping it would feel like an extra forty pounds, but I was greatly relieved to get rid of that cap.

A resupply chopper came in with food and I ran to the line to make sure that I got some before they ran out. As I was walking away with a plate full of food in one hand and a canteen cup of liquid in the other a chopper that was about fifty feet away began to lift off, kicking up a huge dust cloud. The edge of the downblast came at me very quickly. I don't think that I could have possibly sprinted away from it but I couldn't even walk fast because I was trying to balance the plate and drink as it was. I dropped to one knee and put my cup on the ground, trying to cover it with one hand while I bent over and pushed my plate partly inside my open shirt but the prop blast grew much stronger and I was thoroughly enveloped in a dusty squall of dirt and bits of leaves and twigs. When it passed, my food was covered in a quarter inch of dirt and my drink was completely befouled. I walked back to my fighting position and tried to salvage some of the food, but it was impossible to save any of it. Another guy told me to go back and get some more, but I figured I had my chance, I would not go back because that would likely result in someone else not getting any food, or some people getting less food.

We still had another fifteen minutes to go until the full alert sunset guard and I noticed a small group of five men gathered together sitting on the ground. I knew three of them by sight, the other two soldiers I had never seen before. I walked over to the group and one of the soldiers introduced me quickly to two new Lieutenants that had just been assigned to the Company. From the tone and content of the conversation and the looks on the new officers faces, I quickly concluded that the new replacements were as green as I had been when I first arrived in this country.

A medic was trying to tell them the realities of the bush and disabuse them of some of their pre-conceived notions. One Lieutenant listened intently while the other brushed off any advice. The one attentive Lieutenant seemed to have some difficulty in grasping some of the concepts that the medic told him and in frustration, the medic started by asking him if he was stupid and rapidly escalated to calling him all manner of names. Actually the medic had been trying to give that Lieutenant a huge amount of information in a very short period of time. One of the other second Lieutenants strongly objected to that manner of speaking to an officer by an enlisted man and told the medic to hold his tongue.

The medic dropped the insults and continued speaking but after a few minutes the previous tone and content of the conversation was beginning to return and the miffed officer suddenly stood up and walked away. The medic told the attentive Lieutenant, "Listen, I don't have much time to talk to you. You must learn many things very quickly or you will be killed and you probably will get other men killed." The Lieutenant looked around at the four other men in that group who were all unconsciously nodding their agreement. The Lieutenant had a dumbfounded look which was completely understandable given the amount of advise that had been thrown at him within the last ten minutes. He just looked back at the medic through the string of curses and insults and said, "Tell me more."

We were told that night that operations would not begin the next day until after noontime, if at all. On the next morning, around ten am, men were just hanging around with nothing to do. They had already eaten what they had available for breakfast and cleaned their personal weapons and packed up their rucksacks, ready to move out.

There was one little poncho tent still remaining that had not been broken down and packed up, in fact that poncho had another poncho attached to it and set up so that it looked like a little boy scout tent. I noticed that there were a bunch of men gathered in that area so I wandered over to see what was happening.

As I approached the men standing close to that tent, I asked them what was going on. They told me that a poker game had been going on for some time and that about twenty men had lost all that they could bet and that the sum of their losses were now being wagered between just two men. I walked a bit further to look inside the little tent and couldn't believe my eyes. There was a pile of money, Military Script, about eighteen inches wide at the base and about six inches high. I couldn't believe that that amount of money was floating around among the soldiers out in the field.

I was told that that was just the tip of the iceberg, that that pile included many IOU's that were for extremely high amounts of money. The game had come down to just two people, one a Sergeant and the other a Lieutenant, each holding roughly the same amount of money. I thought that that situation was unbelievable, first, since gambling was strictly forbidden and secondly because this betting was between an NCO and an officer, both of whom should have shut down such a situation as soon as they detected it. Each hand of poker resulted in a huge pile of money being swept over by the winner. The Sergeant and the Lieutenant looked to be deadly serious. The "pot", I figured, was equal to two years salary of each participant.

I asked a few guys around me why they would continue to gamble, where both of them were so much ahead of the game. They told me that both of those men were eligible for R&R in a few weeks. One of those men would be able to buy his way into R&R in Hawaii and be able to see his wife, the loser would not be able to do so. They told me that both men had received letters from their wives that they were divorcing them and that this was the only chance that they had to try to save their marriages. I don't remember which guy won, I may have just turned around and walked away, not knowing who won. I didn't want to see who won. The winner had a <u>chance</u> to save his marriage and family life, the loser lost his family.

Later that day, my squad Sergeant told me and two other guys to go over where they had a little target set up to zero in our M-16s. I had been carrying an M-16 for quite a while now and should have asked to go to the berm in base camp to zero in, but I just hadn't thought of it. You adjust the front and rear sight by turning it with a special tool which we didn't have but it had been designed so that the tip of an M16 bullet made an excellent substitute. The target was only about fifty feet away, but after ten minutes and thirty rounds, I still couldn't really zero it in properly, but that was all the time we had so it would have to do. I don't remember what was so important as to take us away from the task at hand but I do remember thinking that sighting in my weapon properly should have been priority number one.

We went out on our search and destroy mission later in the day. The word was that this would be a hump of six to eight thousand meters, more than double a normal day and if we zig-zagged, which we usually did, or went up and down hills it would be much longer. We had humped for about two hours through medium-dense jungle, some trees about sixty feet high but mostly thin trees no more than a few inches thick amid bushes and very thin vines. I glanced to the front and saw more of the same, then looked down for a few steps when suddenly I found myself in bright sunshine and in what seemed to be some otherworldly forest.

The trees and bushes and vines were exactly the same as we had seen for the last hour except that there were no leaves on any of them. I noticed that the nature of the ground here changed drastically because it was now composed completely of loose green leaves that were so thick that it formed a very soft surface on which to walk. It looked as if a hundred men had spent all day very carefully picking every leaf off of every tree and plant without disturbing them in any other way. I picked up a leaf and noticed that it was very fresh, it must have fallen within the last day or two. But the question was, what made every living tree and bush suddenly shed every leaf that they had. What could possibly be the scientific explanation of such a phenomenon?

Then I remembered that the U.S. was spraying chemicals from aircraft to cause defoliation so that enemy activity could be more easily spotted from the air. I seemed to remember listening to a briefing that we were to avoid such areas under all circumstances. They said that the chemicals were not dangerous, but, I wondered, if that was true why were we ordered to strictly avoid such areas, and I wondered why we were going through one of those areas now. There was no obvious indication of the chemical used. I figured that it was probably a colorless liquid or powder. It was only later that I learned that the chemical was simply called "Agent Orange." They called it Agent Orange because the fifty-five gallon barrels of the chemical had an orange stripe on it. The chemical itself was light grey, almost transparent. We would hump through other such areas in the next few months. We didn't make any enemy contact on that day. It was just a typical day of utter agony humping through jungle and light forest and rice paddys except that, although we didn't know it then, on that day we had begun to have been seriously poisoned as well.

The last mile was a small trail that we followed, which is something that we never did because it was a likely place for the enemy to string trip wires for booby traps or mines. For some strange reason, the last mile wasn't too bad. The load actually felt lighter for some reason, probably because my body was shutting down and going into shock, I was actually happy and light-headed and dizzy. Obviously the pounding and punishment of the days hump on my body had been so extreme that it was now somehow affecting my brain. I was almost giddy but I realized that I couldn't maintain a hundred percent lookout, I wasn't a hundred percent alert to my surroundings and that could be fatal to me or the other soldiers nearby. I tried to gather my wits about me but I just couldn't shake the bizarre mental haze. Probably heat exhaustion I later figured. Luckily we were close to the night site and I managed to arrive at it without any enemy interference.

The next day was Sunday. I thought how completely different this was from a Sunday back in the World. A chopper brought in food and we had bacon and scrambled eggs, real eggs, for breakfast. It was extremely unusual to get hot food while in the field and that was the first time that breakfast was ever delivered to us. We stood around amongst thick bushes waiting to be told to get our food. The sun had been up for over an hour and the water from the moist ground was beginning to evaporate but it must have been slowed and caught on the leaves of the bushes because the humidity felt like it was extremely high. After about ten minutes my squad got the word to go to the chow line.

We were the last ones to be served so we just stood next to the food containers while we ate so as to be first in line if there was any food left over. The food containers had been set up in a little area, about twenty-five feet long that was devoid of any bushes, it was just bare earth. It had been a relief to get away from the sweltering atmosphere amongst the bushes but now we were standing in direct sunlight.

After about a minute the full impact of the tropical sun started to scorch us. My shirt was bone dry now and stiff with dirt and sweat so it felt like I was wearing a shirt made of cardboard. The heat of the suns direct rays seemed to go right through the shirt, it felt like my upper body was encased in an oven. The temperature of the air next to my skin started to rise very quickly and I became alarmed at its intensity. The food servers were just standing around waiting for instructions and I urged them to start passing out more food. As the minutes ticked by I began to yell at them and at anyone in the vicinity to do something, make a decision, pass out more food or decide to hold it. I became very angry because it felt like I was being cooked myself and knew that I couldn't remain out in the sun for much longer. On the other hand I was frustrated and appalled because I knew that whether we got more food or not, I would eventually have to return to the surrounding bushes and the dreadful humidity and heat on the ground among them.

I reached the point where I couldn't take another second more of the scorching sun and started to walk away when the servers suddenly started to give out some more eggs. I ran back fifteen feet, pushing my way into the line where I should have been if I hadn't just walked away. A soldier dropped a spoonful of eggs on my plate and I scampered away back to my fighting position. The environment among the bushes was miserable but not as bad as it had been ten minutes before. I guess that the sun had baked every bit of moisture out of the ground and the humidity had dropped.

A guy was putting hot sauce onto his scrambled eggs and I commented to him that I had never seen anyone put it onto eggs. He assured me that it was good and told me to put out my plate whereupon he splashed some of the red liquid onto my eggs. I had never even seen hot sauce until a few months previously and I was not used to it all. I started to eat but the sauce stung my mouth. I thought that if I was back in the World I would just throw the food away, why eat something that hurts you. But the protein and calories of eggs were too precious to waste, it didn't matter much what they were covered with, it was desperately needed nutrition. As I ate I reflected on how this situation was different from what it would be if I was home on this Sunday morning. People in the U.S. were enjoying a calm, cool sunny Sunday morning filled with good food and good wishes while we experienced a wretched, miserable existence where even the food was painful. I suddenly thought to myself that I was a very long way from home.

The next day the mortar platoon was going to carry one mortar so equipment was redistributed among the men in the platoon. My squad would not be carrying the mortar so I ended up being assigned to carry a chainsaw and a five gallon can of gasoline. Those two items alone weighed eight-eight pounds and I had probably another seventy pounds of gear, that's a hundred and forty-eight pounds of gear to hump around a tropical jungle all day. Was that really humanly possible? Before Viet Nam I would have said no. Now I realized that it was possible but the suffering and pain, all day, would be beyond anything that I could have imagined previously.

I had to carry the saw in one hand and the gasoline can in the other so I had to sling my weapon. You couldn't just carry your weapon slung over the shoulder so that a shrug would put the rifle into your hands because it would constantly fall off of your shoulder while walking or be pulled off by vines and thorns. I had to put the sling on the left side of my neck where it would continue at an angle across the front of my body and connect with the stock of the weapon near the beltline on the right hand side. Therefore, the weapon was suspended at an angle across your back. To access the weapon I would have to drop the chainsaw and gasoline can, bend over grasping the sling and try to pull it over my head, which wasn't easy since the rifle and sling had a bad tendency to get hung up on the load bearing equipment or the rucksack. I wasn't a soldier, just a pack mule. It is a fact that pack mule cannot be loaded with so much weight, they can't handle it.

This was just an unbelievable hard and horrible hump. Most of the days operation was through relatively open underbrush but every once in a while the chainsaw would catch on a tree or vine and it was just further agony and frustration to disentangle it. Everyday was just an endless torture, hard labor beyond imagination, struggling mightily with each step, using every bit of strength to just go one more foot forward, then just one more foot. The weight of the equipment relentlessly and brutally stretched muscles and tendons and ground away at joints. It felt as if my body was being torn apart.

The vines pulled us off balance, sometimes stopped us in our tracks and constantly tripped us. A simple trip wasn't just a matter of quickly shuffling our feet to maintain balance. Many times it resulted in an unexpected, desperate struggle by exhausted, extremely heavily burdened men suddenly finding themselves falling face first. They were forced to quickly contort their bodies trying to maintain their balance, torsioning their joints and muscles ultra severely under the crushing loads that they carried. If a soldier wasn't quick enough or lucky enough and landed face first onto his rifle he would shatter the bones of his face. It might also cause his WP grenades to split open or his blasting caps to explode. If a soldier fell sideways he might also fall directly onto punji stakes or a tripwire or a mine.

Thorns always catched our arms. Many times while humping I would suddenly stop abruptly and notice that an arm had been somehow pulled behind my back, almost as if someone had reached out and grabbed me. If the line wasn't moving too fast I would have time to step back a few feet and try to disengage my skin from the thorns and then drive on. Many times though the line was moving too fast and I couldn't afford to take the time to back up. In that case I would just shove my arm forcefully forward and tear the thorns loose in which case I could pull them out of my arm at my leisure. Most of the time that tactic just resulted in the thorns ripping and tearing the skin as you tear yourself free while the thorns remained firmly attached to the plant. Yes, there was blood, a lot of it.

We were beyond absolutely filthy dirty. We were wearing the same clothes that we started with fifteen days ago. Every step could be your last due to mines or booby traps or snipers or an ambush or mortars or rockets or recoilless rifle fire. Killed by friendly fire from napalm or cluster bombs or artillery or gunships was always a possibility. There would be no warning of any of those. When they came, they would come out of nowhere. Men would instantly be killed or maimed or burned or atomized or torn and shredded. But you wouldn't dwell on such things. It took every possible amount of effort, physical and mental, that one could muster, just to put one foot in front of the other and push forward with all the weight of the equipment. It would feel like my body weighed five hundred pounds and that I was carrying a thousand pounds. We were absurdly under-nourished and thoroughly de-hydrated and suffering with the effects of extreme sleep deprivation. The dysentery and malaria that some of the men had must have just added another dimension of torment to a life that was thoroughly saturated with torture and pain and misery. Words alone really cannot possibly describe our suffering.

I couldn't pay attention to the flank to watch for any sign of the enemy. All of my concentration was focused only on trying to hump this load another step. When we stopped one time, I put down my load and collapsed on the ground. I was very thirsty and went to reach for a canteen on my rucksack but I didn't have the strength to even reach around for it. I had never been so beaten down. I didn't have the strength to reach for my canteen but when the line of march resumed again, I stood up and grabbed the saw and gasoline can again and moved out.

It was like this: say you pick up a very heavy box and start to walk down the street with it. After a short while it seems to become very heavy and after another short period you realize that you cannot carry it any more, that you must put it down. Maybe at that point you decide to carry it just a few more feet, at which time you simply cannot hold it and you drop it. Well, in the bush, you cannot drop it. You must hold onto it. Now it seems like it weighs two hundred pounds but you keep going. You are amazed that you can carry it another fifty feet, but you are also amazed at the level of pain that is involved. You can carry it a lot farther than you think that you can, although you will start to have a heart rate so high that it can cause a heart attack in a young man. You will be breathing faster that you thought humanly possible, and you will have pain that you hadn't ever imagined. That's the way it was, everyday. You have to experience it to have any idea of how brutal it was. There really are no words to describe it but extreme, brutal torture is a mild description. Humping eight thousand meters with that load and in that temperature and humidity is basically humanly impossible. The fact that those soldiers accomplished the task is testament to their superhuman suffering.

Towards the end of that day we came upon a small U.S. encampment that contained three artillery pieces. Fighting positions were already dug and there were sandbags about two feet tall surrounding the entire perimeter. The guys who had done all of that work had moved out onto a mission and we would spend the next fifteen days just sitting around all day, pulling perimeter guard on and off throughout the day and night. We lived on C-rations mostly with some hot meals every three days or so but we had access to a water trailer so we could begin to get within some normal range of hydration, let our bodies heal to some degree and catch up on some sleep. This entire time was uneventful except for various fire missions for the artillery that would begin suddenly at any time day or night, depending on what the guys out in the bush needed or had run into.

Thirty days after being in the bush, trucks pulled up and we loaded our gear for a convoy back to base camp. These were big trucks that could hold about fifteen men and all of their equipment. The bed of the truck was about four feet off of the ground and there were wooden bench seats along both sides of the truck that could be folded up. The beds of the trucks were covered with two layers of filled sandbags that would provide some amount of protection if we hit a mine.

When we first started the convoy we were probably more than a hundred miles away from anything that remotely could be called a town, much less a city. After riding for about two hours we started to see more and more civilians along the road, walking from their homes to tiny villages. There weren't many people at first, maybe two people per mile but as we got closer to a main village there were maybe a hundred people per mile on both sides of the road. It occurred to me that some of these people had quite a distance to walk between villages, and I wondered what they did if they had to go to the bathroom. Just then, I noticed an old woman squat near the ground, at the closest edge to the road, two feet from the passing truck traffic and roll up one of her pant legs to her crotch to urinate. Ah, I see now how that situation is handled. Even still, it was very unusual to see such a thing, and see other people completely ignore her as they walked two feet past her.

Almost all of the civilians wore shallow conical, yellowish colored hats that were made of a kind of straw. They were quite wide which was very good for keeping the tropical sun off of the head, especially working out in the open rice paddies. The civilians all wore dingy, baggy clothing in drab browns or greens with the pallor of the color of the dust that was thrown up from the dirt highway.

After another hour or so we approached a large town and the traffic increased significantly with motor scooters and trucks. There were quite a few young women and girls walking beside the roadway wearing the traditional VietNameese outfit of a silk dress that fell to about mid-calf but was slit up the side almost to the waist. It had long billowy sleeves and sort of a Chinese collar. It was worn along with ankle length silk pants. I think they call that outfit a "bao dai". It is really was a very attractive outfit, uniquely Vietnamese. The pants were mostly either black or white but each dress was one of many different bright colors. The colors of the dresses in the bright sunshine were so vibrant it just blew me away after so many weeks of just green and brown down in my world. To me the bright colors were dazzling, startling, surprisingly strange. As astonishing as it may seem, I had actually forgotten that bright happy colors even existed.

After a long road trip we finally entered the little town of Bien Hoa that was on the edge of the big airbase and our base camp. I was on a truck towards the middle of the convoy and as the truck got closer to the main gate men started running out of the small shops and bars and restaurants. As we got even closer, there was a crowd of men running down the sidewalks and in the street, running very fast towards the middle of the town and the main gate. I became very concerned and yelled to the guys in the truck, "Hey!, Get up!, There's something going on!" Noone in the truck was concerned in the least bit. They all remained sitting on the seats, casually regarding the hoard of men who seemed to be running for their lives. I thought that there must be a major VC force approaching the town. The guys said to me, "Don't you know why they are running?" I said, "No, but they are running away from something". They said, "Yeah, they are running from us". I asked why would they be running from us and they said, "Because they know that very soon we will be back here downtown". I realized what they were saying. The mostly Air Force Airmen rear echelon people lounging around a sleepy little town don't want to be anywhere near five hundred paratroopers just back from a thirty day combat operation. I realized that there will most certainly be all kinds of trouble tonight after we change into civilian clothes, get liquored up, and go looking for some sort of diversion downtown.

Note: There was about eighty men in Alpha Company at that time. This operation resulted in fourteen men wounded and one man killed in action. The Companys platoons engaged in 6 separate firefights. They killed 6 enemy soldiers and captured one of them.

Chapter 20
BASE CAMP D

Checking for Snipers, Chainsaw in Foreground

By the time we got back to base camp, we had not had a shower for thirty days and our clothing was ripped and torn in many places and generally raggedy and filthy. The very first thing to do was to take a shower. Then we secured our gear, lined up at the supply sergeants hootch and were issued a new uniform shirt, without any insignia whatsoever and pants. Some of us took the new shirt to store in our lockers but on the side, arranged to have our old shirts cleaned by a local Vietnamese woman, if of course the shirt was salvageable at all.

We went back to our platoon tent and were ordered to clean our weapons and equipment thoroughly before anything else. A couple of soldiers suddenly struggled through the front screen door of the platoon tent carrying four cases of ice-cold beer, complements of the Captain. Almost immediately, quarts and half-gallon bottles of hard liquor suddenly appeared (probably from different peoples footlockers from our previous time in base camp) and we went at it energetically, cleaning our weapons and drinking deliberately, purposefully and thoroughly.

I went downtown, got something to eat, drank more than my fill and staggered back into base camp by myself a few hours later. Just as I had made it all the way back to the platoon hootch, just a few feet away, I reached for my cigarette lighter and discovered that it was missing. The last time I had been downtown I had bought a zippo lighter and had it engraved with a combat Infantrymans badge and parachute wings. I couldn't understand how I had lost it at first but then remembered being besieged by a group of about twenty children who swarmed all around me in Bien Hoa begging for money and food or trying to sell me things. Some of them had tugged at my clothing and generally gently jostled me. I was pretty sure that one of them must have picked my pocket. I was already stewed and should have just called it a night but I decided to go all the way back into town and find the little buggers. By the time I got back downtown I was pretty well wiped out. I walked up the street a bit but couldn't see the group that had accosted me, and then realized that I wouldn't recognize them anyways. I turned around and started walking back. Somebody must have picked me up in a truck, I don't remember. All I remember is finding myself back at the platoon hootch completely worn out from way too much booze and way too little of anything else for the last thirty days.

The next day we were ordered to stay on base. We were told that we would be moving out on a new operation at any time. In the afternoon, we were ordered out of the hoochs for physical training, otherwise known as PT. We couldn't believe it. We desperately needed rest and recuperation. We got more than enough physical activity out in the bush. That absurd idea was the brainchild of our new Company Commander. The old Company Commander spent most of his time during an operation on the ground, humping alongside his men, sweating and bleeding and suffering the ordeals of the men that he commanded. The new Company Commander almost never even set foot on the ground. He spent all day riding in a helicopter, high above the tops of the tall jungle trees in cool air with a constant breeze blowing on him while his men were tortured below. The old Company commander was well respected. We didn't know much about the new Captain but what we did know we didn't like at all. The idea of doing PT in base camp, between operations, marked him in our minds as some sort of lunatic. We did some pushups and sit-ups and ran around a bit in the full sunlight over dusty dirt roads before it was over. While running some of the senior NCOs left their position in line and ran up to have words with the Captain I think, announcing in no minced terms what they thought of this PT idea because we stopped running a few minutes later. We never again had physical training while back in base camp.

Over in the 2nd battalion area they had a sort of drive-in theatre. It was a large screen where they could show movies and bleacher type seats made of airstrip runway plates, metal plates about two feet wide perforated with many two inch holes. We had learned that a movie was going to be shown that night so myself and a few other guys went over there after the sun went down. The show had already started and since all of us had been drinking we caused a bit of a ruckus as we settled in, laughing and joking among ourselves. Everyone else sitting there seemed to be very serious and were intensely staring at the screen, seemingly fascinated at what they saw. I lit up a smoke and took a few swigs from my beer before I really looked at the movie.

I was expecting to see a Hollywood production in color but was surprised to see what seemed to be a black and white homemade movie. A guy said that these were the movies that were captured during the last operation by my Company. They were obviously propaganda films meant to be shown to new VC recruits. There were scenes of jets flying at an altitude of three thousand feet, then a VC shooting at it with an old thirty caliber machine gun, then a scene of the plane falling from the sky and crashing. Then there was a scene of some VC firing into the jungle followed by a scene of about thirty American helmets and a surprisingly amount of assorted American gear and weapons lying on the jungle ground.

Myself and other guys thought that it was very funny because it showed some situations that were highly unlikely or almost impossible although I didn't like the scenes of all of the American gear and hoped that it was just stolen and had not actually been taken from American bodies. They had two of those films and halfway through the second one I and others decided to go back to the hooch and drink. As we were leaving, laughing, we looked around and saw a bunch of men who were watching the movie with their mouths open, horrified by what they saw. They were new guys, just in country who had not as yet been out in the bush. We told them that the film was just a bunch of propaganda, but they didn't believe us. I thought to myself that yes, that film was unrealistic but the reality of the bush in fact is much more horrible. Those new guys had no idea in their wildest imaginations of the torture and agony and fear and hunger and thirst and sickness and death and maiming that awaited them. Neither, I thought, did the VC recruits being shown that film.

We went back to the hooch and started drinking and listening to music on tape recorders. About an hour later we heard gunfire coming from what sounded like inside our perimeter. Guys were running past our hooch with weapons to reinforce the perimeter. I was wearing civilian clothes with black pants and a red short sleeve shirt. Some of the guys in the hooch grabbed their weapons and ran outside. I grabbed my M-16 and ran a few steps, then backtracked and grabbed a few bandoliers of ammo and slung them over my shoulder. I almost reached the door when I realized that this might be a major fight so I ran back to my bunk and put on my load bearing gear with hand grenades and smoke grenades and ammo pouchs full of loaded magazines, turned and ran out of the door. A few steps out I suddenly stopped, ran back to my bunk and threw on my helmet and then ran out the door and down the street, in the direction of the fire. I was thinking "If only my brothers and the guys I used to hang out with could see me now".

I thought, You guys are back in the States and playing cards or bowling sitting around with your friends drinking beer or going to the drive-in with your girlfriends. This is an entirely different World, and an entirely different Existence that you really cannot imagine. You are going to get high on beer, you are going to win a few dollars playing cards, you are going to make out with your girlfriends at the drive-in movies. I am running into a full blown military operation and the killing is about to begin in seconds, if it already hasn't already. In two minutes one of you is going to loose three dollars in a game of cards, in two minutes I am going to lose my life or my arms or legs or stomach or eyes or part of my brain, not to mention that I am going to try to do the same to some poor VC recruit. But I wished that someone would take a picture of me. Dressed in civilian clothes but very much loaded down for bear with a full auto M-16 rifle, LBG, grenades, bandoliers of ammo and wearing my helmet.

I ran to the end of the street about a hundred feet away and turned left. There were about twenty men on the road, some of them heading over the 2nd battalions area, others running directly towards the berm of the perimeter. Still others suddenly appeared from my left having just left their hootchs. Several of them suddenly stopped when they hit the road, some were holding their load bearing gear in their hands having just hastily scooped them up and were looking around franticly trying to determine exactly what was happening and what they should do.

As I approached them I yelled to follow me, to go down to the perimeter section at the end of the road. While running I noticed that there was some activity in the 2nd Bat area. Some soldiers over there were on the ground and facing towards us, away from the perimeter. That really concerned me because it indicated that the enemy had already breached the outer defenses and were already among us. I continued running another ten feet, running much faster than a few soldiers in front of me, rapidly approaching them and about to pass by when three of them dropped unexpectedly to the ground. I slowed for a few seconds to observe them, suddenly shocked at the thought that they had spotted VC and were trying to avoid being shot. One man had an M-60 machine gun. He pulled down the bipod and spread it out widely then opened the top cover. His assistant gunner already had a belt of ammo inches away which he instantly placed into the weapon, pulling ammo out of his box of bullets with his left hand. The gunner slammed the cover shut and violently cocked in the first round. All the while, the ammo bearer was on the ground with his M-16 pointed outwards and calling off targets while all three men simultaneously twisted around on the ground to face the enemy and moved closer to each other. The three individual men seemingly melding into one creature. All of that happened almost instantly. As occupied as I was in trying to make sense of the chaos, trying to locate the threat and try to think of what to do, while expecting to be shot at any moment, I noted that the skill and competence of that machine gun crew was amazing, they had dropped to the ground, acquired their target and put their gun into action within two seconds.

I tried to stop running and skidded past them on the dry dirt, suddenly shocked and confused because although the machine gun crew had not yet fired they had clearly acquired targets that were near the outdoor theatre and others within the 2nd Bat area. Strangely enough, there were men near the theatre that were on the ground with their weapons pointed in our direction. I thought that the VC had over-run the 2nd battalion area and were already amongst us. I dropped to one knee and brought up my weapon, aiming at the dark shapes in the shadows but very worried because there were probably Americans over there for sure. I yelled out "What's going on?" and a few guys close by yelled back, "We're having it out with the 2nd battalion."

Apparently some guys from my battalion (the 4th Bat) had some disagreements with guys from the 2nd battalion. Fist fights had escalated into shots fired and now there was basically going to be a gang fight with military weapons. Very luckily, some Lieutenants and a Sergeant happened upon the scene and got control of the situation. I stood up and urged the soldiers close by to stand up also as a gesture that we would not be firing and then I and others slowly walked away.

The next day, they took away all of our weapons and locked them in a huge steel cargo container/trailer. We would never again be allowed to keep weapons by our bunks in base camp again.

The next day, word was that a Catholic chaplain was hearing Confessions over in the Second battalion area. I walked over towards that area, towards a tiny wooden building no more than five feet by seven feet. It was probably some sort of storage shack, but they usually used it as a Confessional. When I was almost there, I saw a Chaplain who had walked right past that building and was now approaching me. As we drew nearer he smiled and said hello. I asked him if they were still hearing Confessions and he said no, but that he would hear my Confession if I wished.

I said yes, I would like that and then took a few steps towards the wooden building but I suddenly noticed that he was not moving. In fact, he just had his head bowed towards the ground and was softly saying some prayers. I turned back, realizing that he was conducting the Sacrament right then and there with both of us standing right out in the open. I bowed my head and after confessing he gave me absolution and the Sacrament was over. By that time a few other soldiers were walking towards us, wanting to have their Confessions heard. The priest chatted with me briefly. I wish I could remember what he said but I cannot. He seemed very friendly and very kindly and very gentle and substantially older than most of the troopers in the Brigade, perhaps he was thirty years old or older.

His name was Father Watters. I would meet him again later out in the jungle. I could not have known it at that time, but about six months from that date, after he had deliberately extended his tour of duty in Viet Nam, to "Be with his boys", he would be awarded the Congressional Medal of Honor, posthumously, killed while totally disregarding his own safety to rescue wounded soldiers and then administering aid to a group of wounded and dying men in the middle of a battlefield, killed by a two hundred and fifty pound bomb dropped by an American pilot. Eternal rest grant unto him, O Lord, and let perpetual light shine upon him.

The next day we had a memorial service for the men who had been killed on the last operation. We stood in formation while someone said something while we stared at the display in front of us consisting of a pair of boots representing each man killed in the Company on the last operation. That service had a lot more boots than previous services. Commendations were read and some men were awarded purple heart medals for combat wounds and one soldier was awarded a bronze star with "V" device for valor. Then the Company Commander was awarded six air medals, each one requiring the reading of a separate commendation. I guess you get an air medal for each twenty hours spent in an aircraft, or something like that. I couldn't believe that he would accept those medals for comfortably riding in a helicopter while his men suffered so much, beating through the jungle below him.

He seemed to beam with pride as the commendations were boringly read six separate times, each a repetition of the previous except for the dates. I'm sure that it looked good on his service record but it certainly didn't look good to me. To say the least, as the British say, it was simply "bad form."

One of the men in my Company had been caught smoking marijuana. For all intents and purposes, nobody consumed alcohol or drugs during a combat operation, it would have been tantamount to suicide. This man however had been caught smoking weed while off-duty in Bien Hoa village. The Company commander made a big deal of it and gave us all a big lecture the next morning which I largely ignored. However, towards the end of his speech he emphasized, "That man will be punished!"

Two days later we began a new operation by loading up onto trucks. As we rolled away from the Company area we spotted the guy who had smoked the dope. He was standing in the shade, leaning lazily against a hooch with a cold can of Coca-Cola in his hand. Someone said that that guy was not going out to the field because part of his punishment had been to be "restricted to base" for two weeks. Someone said, "Man, that boy is getting over!" "I know what I'm going to do the next time I get back to base!" I didn't know right away what he meant by that but within a minute or so I had a mini brainstorm and hatched an evil genius of a plan. If I made it back from this operation I was going to buy some marijuana, roll it into a big cigarette, light it up and then go into the Company commanders office and ask him if he wants a puff. Hopefully my "punishment" would be not to go on any more combat operations for a while.

Chapter 21

OPERATION JUNCTION CITY II

March 20-April 13 WAR ZONE 'C'

"Oh father, why are you so sad, on this bright Easter morn?
When Irishmen are proud and glad of the land where they were born."
"Oh, son, I see sad mem'ries view of far-off distant days,
When, being just a boy like you, I joined the old Brigade.

~ An Old Irish Pub Song ~

Hot LZ, Taking Direct Enemy Fire

Just before loading onto the helicopters we were told to just look straight out from the side and do not look at the pilot or co-pilot and especially not to look at any instruments.

Of course, since my life depended on that aircraft, almost the first thing that I did was to check out the situation. I didn't see anything out of order, but I did notice an instrument with a small television screen about four inches wide that seemed to have a map displayed in green and white. As we traveled, I noticed that that map kept changing, apparently directly related to our position as we flew. It was something right out of a James Bond movie at that time and I suppose it was top secret.

The helicopter assault is always a time for apprehension. We had made many such assaults and most of them had been without problems, I expected this one to be the same. We touched down in a clearing in the middle of the jungle that had very little vegetation. The ground was mostly solid rock with little or no soil covering it. I jumped out of the right side of the chopper and ran about ten feet before dropping to one knee to search for any signs of an enemy attack. The plan was for everyone on the right hand side of the choppers to exit the aircraft, run a short ways and then when the choppers ascended to turn around and run in the opposite direction, joining the men who had exited from the left side who would be in the process of running for the tree line. The flight of choppers lifted off almost immediately. I turned around to run but suddenly stopped after two steps because the second stick of choppers were already swooping in, filing past us like a monstrous freight train and very nearly landing on top of us. The soldiers from that stick exited the aircraft and as the choppers began to lift off the whole right hand side group ran, ducking under the skids of the choppers as they charged forwards and upwards.

I ran about fifty feet when the third stick of choppers landed and for some reason I wanted to take a picture of the scene. I grabbed my camera, pulled it from its case and quickly advanced the film while lining up the shot. I knew that I had to be very quick or someone would start yelling at me to join my group. The roar of the choppers was very loud but just before I snapped the picture I heard cracking and zipping sounds as enemy bullets flew past me. A jolt of electricity seemed to go through my veins as I suddenly realized that if I could hear those bullets above the din of the choppers it meant that the VC were lighting me up personally. Instead of running forward to join my squad, I ran to my right to intersect a group of soldiers that had just exited the choppers. They wouldn't be aware of the incoming fire over the noise of the choppers unless the bullets were hitting the choppers directly. I yelled to them, "Incoming, Incoming, Hot LZ!" but with the sound of the choppers they couldn't hear me. They were moving very quickly anyways, away from the landing zone and directly into the enemy fire whether they knew it or not. I dropped my camera into the top of my shirt pocket and took off running as fast as I could to join my squad which was rapidly approaching the surrounding tree line.

We advanced towards the tree line in a wide front and just as the leading edge of the assaulting troopers had penetrated the forest by about forty feet they abruptly stopped. That left me still standing in the clearing right at the edge of the tree line with a clear view of the surrounding tree line and the sky, a few hundred feet from where the choppers had landed. The word was passed down the line that we were to halt our advance for a while. I watched as the last stick of choppers charged out of the LZ, passing the edge of the clearing and then out over the jungle. As the clatter of the choppers quickly subsided it was replaced in direct proportion by the sounds of gunfire. A few minutes later we got the word that the VC were shooting at all of the choppers as they flew out of the LZ. As close as I could estimate, the VC were about three hundred yards away from the rightmost elements of American Infantrymen. We just stayed in place for about ten minutes while I wondered what the plan was. I expected to get the word that we would shift our line of march to attack on a wide front but then the word was passed that an air strike had been called in. I scanned the sky in the direction of the shooting but I didn't see any aircraft. Then, for some reason, I turned around to look in the opposite direction.

There was no noise to warn of its advance. My head jerked back involuntarily when I suddenly saw a black object that seemed suspended amid the wide expanse of a bright blue sky. I was instantly deeply frightened by what looked to me to be the personification of death. For a moment it appeared not to move, as if deciding who to kill I imagined, then it slightly altered its bearing, aiming almost directly at me and came charging forward, seemingly hell-bent to complete its final mission to destroy mens bodies and souls. In less than two seconds it assumed a shape that had a sharp point with small triangular wings, reducing its altitude at an alarming rate and approaching at an impossible speed in total silence, passing over the LZ at treetop level at such a speed that it appeared as only a blur.

A shock wave ripped through us followed instantly by the bang and concussion of huge high explosives at close range. As it banked upwards and to the right I could finally see that the instrument of death was an airplane, it jets roaring defiance and malevolence as it streaked away from the scene of its murderous mission. Moments later I heard a roaring sound from high overhead and saw a propeller driven airplane diving directly towards the enemy, releasing two bombs at the last second and abruptly pulling up as the target area erupted in a huge cloud of flames. There were a number of aircraft on station so the attack continued for another five minutes with some of the planes attacking with long runs at tree level while others dove in from high altitudes. Some planes dropped two five hundred pound high explosive bombs while others dropped four two hundred and fifty pound bombs or groups of hundred pound bombs while others devastated the area with napalm.

As one of the first attacking aircraft passed over the target, dropping his last load of bombs, he quickly pulled up, gaining altitude quickly, turning to the right and flying in a wide circle that brought him back towards the target. Having unloaded all of his high explosive ordinance, he came back into the face of death to attack with his automatic cannons. As he came around in his last quarter turn he swooped down so abruptly that I thought he was going to crash. He pulled out hard at a hundred feet above the earth and as he came in line to the target he opened fire from almost a mile out. For the first two seconds there was no sound but suddenly what looked like a kind of silver, translucent curtain seemed to magically appear in the middle of the LZ, running down its center for its entire length.

The huge, high explosive rounds from his Gatling gun type of weapon, almost one inch thick rounds from his automatic cannons, tore through the clearing, filling the air from two to twelve feet high with hundreds of what looked like white rods of light, streaking past at a thousand miles per hour. I just stood there, mesmerized by the apparition, shocked into rigidity, staring at a supersonic river of destruction a hundred feet away, knowing that the tiniest splash of it would vaporize a man.

The blare of the cannons mixed with the outraged roar of the aircraft quickly reach a crescendo while the stream of cannon fire condensed into a tight pattern. An instant later the wall of projectiles vanished, followed micro-seconds later by the blur and shockwave of the aircraft as it screamed past us less than two hundred feet away. Then another plane attacked with rapid fire cannons and then another right after him. The stream of cannon fire seemed to become denser with each run, harder to see through, as if the air had become foggy and it remained somewhat opaque even between runs. It was as if the tremendous volume of fire had shocked the air somehow, knocking the moisture out of it, tearing apart and destroying the air itself.

Almost all of the pilots had attacked at what must have been the utmost limits of their aircraft, flying in at what seemed to be impossible speeds. The dive bombers were so close to the ground before releasing their bombs and pulling up that it seemed that they would surely crash into the ground and be killed. The low level horizontal runs were so close to the treetops and at such high speeds that it seemed humanly impossible to maneuver an aircraft within such tight restrictions. The very slightest miss-step or misjudgment surely would have killed the pilots. When they over flew the targets some were only fifty feet above the enemy, close enough to hit with a stone.

Their targeting was extraordinarily precise, the tiniest mistake would have killed whole platoons of nearby American Infantry. We all knew that the flyboys "got over". That they returned to base every night to a cozy bunk and a cold beer, but I give them the well deserved credit due them. They saved our bacon on several occasions and I have to admit that most of them probably couldn't take on a full regulation load of ordinance because they had to factor in the weight of their manhood.

When the air strikes were completed we were ordered to move out. The original direction of the march was changed so that we swept through the bombed out area. Everything there was black. Large areas were utterly devoid of any vegetation whatsoever, what had been there had been vaporized. Surrounding those areas were trees and bushs that seemed as if they had been painstakingly painted with a pitch black paint that burned through them completely. The earth itself was scorched a deep black. There was no evidence of the enemy, only smoke and shattered wood and the smell of burnt vegetation mixed with the gasolined napalm and the acrid and poisonous fumes of high explosives.

We almost immediately came upon a VC base camp about fifty to seventy-five meters from the end of the landing zone. It was the typical, roughly oval ground plan for a VC camp with a trench connecting all fighting positions but that camp also had hoochs made of sticks and bamboo. They were unusual because they had floors made of bamboo or had straw mats on the ground. Under the floors were underground rooms dug deeply into the earth. There were no VC and not much of anything else of value.

We humped for another four hours and I was getting very mad about carrying so much weight. When we stopped for a minute I threw the barrel of the mortar on the ground as hard as I could. My squad Sergeant gave me a hard look but didn't say anything. It was almost impossible to damage the barrel really, if it could survive the force of throwing a twelve pound round a mile high and five miles down range it could take a hit on the jungle floor. I wasn't really mad at the barrel. I had just allowed myself to develop a burning rage so as to pump additional adrenaline into my blood so that I could manage carrying that thing.

We moved on through relatively light jungle when I spotted something through the trees, lying on the ground, that was very unusual. The soldier in front of me had stopped so I moved off of the line of march to investigate it. It was an empty grey colored fifty-five gallon metal barrel with markings on it indicating that it was tear gas, probably powdered I guessed. I wondered how that could have possibly ended up in the jungle, out in the middle of nowhere. Obviously it had been dropped by an aircraft to make life difficult for the VC. That much CS gas would clear out a small city but I wondered what effect it would have out there deep in the bush.

We soon came upon an enormous enemy base camp. There were foxholes all over the place, each with a little solidly built overhead cover. Most of those holes were not connected by a trench to each other as all of the other previously discovered base camps had been. The fact that those fighting positions were not in any orderly arrangement indicated to me that it was just a place that the enemy had occupied for one night and had then moved on, maybe dug in for cover from American bombardment but not set up to defend from attack.

My best estimate was that it had about a five hundred meter diameter, plenty of fighting positions for plenty of enemy. I was very glad that it was unoccupied but was very concerned about running into an enemy force that was large enough to occupy such an area. That was a very bad sign because it indicated that there had been an enemy force of from five hundred to a thousand enemy soldiers in that area recently. Some American troopers were sent in amongst those fighting positions but they didn't find anything. It wasn't a through search because we only stayed there for about five minutes. Apparently the orders were to continue on with the mission at hand.

Later in the day the Company encountered some VC and one of the platoons took casualties. That platoon was ordered to stand in place and the other platoons moved forward and past them. I saw a Sergeant that I knew kneeling on the ground and crying softly because one of his long time, best friends had been killed. The thought crossed my mind that I should say to him "What are you crying about?, You're probably next!". Then I was hit with the thought that actually, I would probably be next. Anyone of us could be next, at any moment, including me, and there certainly would be more killing and horrible wounds to come. As I walked past the guy so dreadfully affected by this latest horror, I was slightly aware that I was developing an attitude that wasn't very sympathetic, not very kind, not very human. I should have felt sorry for that guy and his great loss, but I just didn't. Two weeks later that Sergeant would be killed by enemy fire. "Ask not for whom the bell tolls".

We finally came to a hard dirt road about thirty feet wide. On each side of it was an embankment sloping up until it was about ten feet higher than the road. At that point the embankment was flat for about ten feet wide ending at a solid rock wall that went up almost vertically for another fifty feet. We set up for the night there on the flat part of the embankments. We couldn't dig fighting positions because the embankments were mostly solid rock. All around were volcanic rocks about the size of watermelons or bigger, so we gathered those and arranged them into individual circular fighting positions, placing rocks upon rocks so that the walls were a few feet high. Then my squad and I were ordered to made a separate, larger circular fighting position for the mortar and then set the gun up.

The road ran to the north for about three hundred feet away, where it dropped very steeply downwards about forty feet in elevation. It continued for another fifty feet and then ran level across a rice paddy for probably another hundred yards and then entered very heavy jungle on the other side. The rice paddy extended from both sides of the road for hundreds of yards.

The next morning I wanted to check out the limits of our encampment so I walked north along the embankment until I reached the place where the road dropped down. At that point the embankments suddenly ended with a steep, twenty-foot drop. Looking north, the high walls along the road blocked my view of everything behind me and more, but I had an unobstructed view of about 150 degrees, from the northwest to the east, but it was an amazing sight. The sun brightly illuminated the near solid carpet of bright green rice plants and sparkled off the water they were planted in, a dazzling display of life itself I thought. There was nothing in front or above me of me to block the magnificent vista of a bright, cloudless, beautiful blue sky. The jungle floor on the other side of the paddy was forty feet lower than where I stood so I could see for miles over the top of the jungles canopy. The light and open space of where I stood seemed incredible, astonishing. It was as if I had lived all of my life deep in the jungle and this was the first time that I had ever seen an open expanse of land and the vastness of the heavens above.

Behind me was the road that ran at the bottom of high walls on both sides of it. Most of the men on that road were living in a monochromatic world of brown dust, rock walls and volcanic boulders with a thin ribbon of blue sky directly overhead. The surrounding area of jungle that we had staggered out of on the previous day was a world where a man was surrounded by fifty shades of green so dense that he couldn't see another man fifteen feet in front of him. Where the sky was just numerous tiny, irregularly shaped pieces of blue filtering through the thick tangle of leaves and vines and branches that seemingly threaten to smother him from above.

I was looking back up the road when the noise of a chopper caught my attention. When I turned around to face the sound I was surprised to see it only a few hundred feet away, fifty feet above the paddy and coming almost straight towards me, approaching on a flight path that was directly in line with the road. When the chopper passed over the drop-off it was about 10 feet off of the road so that when it passed me t I was at eye level with the pilot and passengers of the ship. I could see that the Brigade commander was on board. He looked directly at me and the thought crossed my mind that I should salute him, but in the bush, you never salute anyone. A salute in the field marks a valuable target for any sniper that's looking for someone important to kill. That lesson was taught to me when I first arrived at my unit. A Sergeant had told us to never salute anyone and why. Almost no one wore the insignia of their rank, neither the enlisted mens chevrons on arms of their shirts or the small collar insignias of officers. Someone asked the Sergeant how we would know what a mans rank was. The Sergeant just said, "Hey, If someone tells you to do something then just do it!"

The mortar platoon stayed in place while the line platoons went out on combat patrols into the surrounding jungle. Later that day a helicopter brought in two more mortars and crates of ammo. My squad was ordered to move our mortar to the embankment on the other side of the road so that all three guns were set up in the same area. Of course that meant that we had to set up another mortar gun fighting position out of big volcanic rocks, a difficult, hot, backbreaking task.

Early the next morning the Company sent out their line platoons to patrol the area. During the day I could hear sporadic bursts of gunfire as the platoons encountered the enemy in the surrounding jungle. Towards the end of the day, some of the patrols returned with a large amount of captured weapons and ammo and tools, pliers mostly. As evening approached I and a few other guys were ordered to load that equipment onto helicopters that were landing on the road. We were in the midst of loading the first ship when the pilot suddenly lifted off without any warning and flew off, nearly knocking some or us down. It could have very nearly been a fatal accident.

A second chopper landed and as we were piling the heavy boxes onto his ship the pilot yelled at us that we put too much weight onto his aircraft and ordered us to take some of it off. The pilot of the third chopper shouted for us to stop loading before we had even placed half of what the first chopper had been loaded down with. Those pilots were attached to some unit, not with the 173rd Airborne Brigade. There was still a lot of equipment left on the ground. While we waited to see if other choppers would arrive I looked at the equipment more closely, wondering how this equipment had gotten out here in the middle of nowhere and impressed with what seemed like the high quality of the tools. I grabbed a pair of long-nosed pliers and squeezed the handles together as hard as I could. The tool broke apart in pieces in my hand. I guess they were not as good as they looked.

A few minutes later another helicopter landed but this chopper was part of a unit that was attached to the 173rd Airborne Brigade (Separate). The Separate designation meant that the 173rd was not part of a Division or larger unit so it did not have helicopters or tanks or large artillery as part of its assigned equipment and had to borrow those resources as needed. A separate helicopter squadron was "attached" to the 173rd. They were known as the "Cowboys" and that was painted onto the nose of their choppers in large letters along with a fanciful picture depicting a cowboy riding on a helicopter. They were known as a wild bunch and generally held in very high regard by the infantrymen. The pilots were known for their reckless antics which were actually examples of extraordinary courage and extremely skillful flying.

We loaded equipment into the chopper but stopped when we the weight of the goods was roughly equal to the amount loaded onto the previous helicopter. The pilot turned around and said, "Hey, there's only two choppers behind me. If you guys want to get rid of all of that today, then throw some more on." One of the soldiers on the loading crew told the pilot, "The other choppers said they couldn't take off with a load bigger than that." The Cowboy pilot smiled and said, "Load on all you want!". We had piled in another very substantial load of tools and ammunition when the pilot yelled to us that we only had another thirty seconds to work because another chopper was approaching and he had to take off. I looked up to my right and spotted another chopper about a hundred and fifty feet away, coming in slowly about twenty feet high. I hadn't even heard it approaching over the roar of the chopper that we were loading. Then the pilot waved us off with an apologetic look, apparently sorry that he couldn't stay longer and take on more cargo. The roar of the chopper increased three-fold as the pilot demanded every possible bit of power from his ship while the loading crew instinctively backed away from the screaming machine. The chopper seemed to be bolted to the ground, it would not lift off at all. I realized that we had grossly overloaded the chopper and approached it to pull off some of the equipment but the pilot noticed me and shook his head slightly from side to side and just smiled. After another ten seconds the choppers skids started to shimmy sideways and the ship lifted off the ground about 1 inch. The tail of the ship lifted upwards with the chopper assuming a rakish angle, nose down and tore down the road at full speed making all manner of unusual sounds. I thought that it was going to shake itself apart. By the time he reached the road where it sloped downwards the skids of the chopper were still only about an inch off of the ground. He banked sharply to the right and I couldn't imagine that he had enough power to clear the trees of the jungle now two hundred feet in front of him but somehow he managed. The situation with the next two Cowboy choppers was an exact repeat of the first.

About an hour later, a few minutes before sundown, there was a little excitement from the men near the north end of the road, where it sloped steeply down through a rice paddy. They had spotted some VC in the jungle across from the rice paddy. The fire direction control(FDC) team yelled out "Fire Mission!, Guns 1, 2 and 3!" All the members of the gun crews and I ran over to the mortars to put them into action. A Sergeant in the FDC shouted, "Deflection 1250, Charge Zero, Elevation 980, Fire at will, Fire for effect!" I spotted two VC in black clothing with AK47s in their hands running along the tree line and into the rice paddy. The gunners and assistant gunners, including myself very quickly adjusted the gun while the ammo bearers furiously started to tear open mortar round canisters. I grabbed a round and was placing it into the tube when suddenly we heard "Cease Fire!". I thought, Why cease-fire now? The enemy were in plain sight. I dropped the round down the tube. The scraping metallic sound of it falling towards the firing pin galvanized the other two assistant gunners to release their rounds as well. There was a sudden "Boom ... Boom ... Boom" in quick succession as the three rounds blasted out of the tubes, temporarily drowning out the continuous shouts of "Cease Fire!" from the FDC. I ran down the road about 100 feet as fast as I could so I could see the rounds land. While I was running, the rounds were still in the air and in an extremely steep parabolic trajectory that would take them a thousand feet high before falling to earth. Just as I stopped running I heard a two second long scream of the bombs approaching the target followed immediately by three almost simultaneous, powerful explosions blasting apart the jungle ten feet away from the paddys edge. The rounds were tightly grouped and exactly on target. I was extremely pleased and proud of my skill and the proficiency of the FDC and the gun crews.

Then, as I stared at the blasted jungle and the smoke slowly rising from the impact area I was jolted by the thought of, "What have I done?!" I became aware that the smoking ruin of the jungle may well contain the bodies of men mangled and torn apart and killed by my hand. Perhaps there were men lying on the ground with horrific wounds. While I was trying to process those thoughts people suddenly started urgently shouting orders for everyone to get under cover immediately. I ran down the embankment, across the road and up the opposite slope to an unoccupied fighting position. That position was the last one along the road so I had a commanding view of the rice paddy and the jungle at its opposite edge. I knelt inside the circular wall of volcanic boulders with my M-16 resting on the top of it, pointing outwards towards the road running through the jungle that had just been mortared, expecting an overwhelming mass of attacking enemy troops to come charging across the rice paddy. After two minutes of frantically searching the tree line for any movement I yelled back to a soldier in a fighting position behind me "What's happening?" He yelled back, "Stay Down!, A gun ship is coming in."

Within the last six minutes of this action the sun had set and it was just now getting very dark, very quickly. The green of the jungles canopy had suddenly turned a dark brownish color and a blackness had swept over the rice paddy and into the woods, saturating the area among the trees with a malevolently deep darkness. A minute later a helicopter suddenly materialized from behind the high stone wall lining the road. It flew for another hundred feet, slowed for a few seconds, searching for someone to kill, then its tail reared up and it unleashed a horrifying torrent of destruction upon the land.

From the belly of the beast there was an incredible eruption of an impossibly powerful weapon, its port side gatling gun blasting forth thirty six hundred rounds per minute from its six revolving machine gun barrels. The entire area was enveloped in a deafening, dreadful, mechanical roar that excitedly vibrated the ground and seemed to turn the air itself into a dense, trembling substance. For a second, the chopper looked as if it had suddenly impaled the ground with a solid bolt of glowing red iron rods that were still attached to the airship. Then the rigid rods seemed to become flexible and limp as the gunner swept the target area. It looked like there was a long red mop-like thing hanging from the helicopter, with a hundred glowing red strands about a hundred and fifty feet long just sweeping back and forth through the jungle, originating from a ten foot long yellowish white flame attached to the helicopter. The absolutely astonishing rate of red fire belied the true avalanche of bullets because the red tracer bullets would be only about five percent of all the rounds flying from the mouth of the weapon. At sixty rounds per second you can't hear individual rounds being fired, just a truly terrifying, unearthly roar and that was just from his left gun, he had another one on the starboard side.

When the pilot released his trigger the world abruptly became stone quiet even as the red shafts of gunfire shrunk away from the ship and silently continued downwards, seeming to penetrate the earth for their full length. Then the pilot would open fire again and the strands of red reappeared and began raking across the target area. It was a terrifying, truly surrealistic sight. The sights and sounds of that unearthly spectacle were so overwhelming that I just stood there transfixed and awestruck by it all.

Somewhere in my brain an alarm was trying to make its way past the sensory overload. Suddenly I felt cold. The air was warm, my clothing was warm, but it suddenly felt as if a thick cold fluid was flowing through my veins, chilling my body from the inside out at an alarming rate. I quickly realized that if that pilot made an error and swept us, for even a split-second, we would all be killed and I was suddenly very afraid. I crouched down in my fighting position, peering through the gaps between the volcanic rocks of its sides at the terror before me, acutely aware that with no overhead cover I was utterly vulnerable, that a split-second touch from that deadly lash would instantly destroy me.

The gunship banked sharply and seemed to flee from the area, but within seconds it flared up, turned about quickly, assuming an acute, nose down rake, and the engines suddenly erupted with an outraged roar as the pilot attacked the target at full throttle. The ship lost altitude rapidly, seemingly determined to kill it victims by suicidaly crushing them with its skids, but then at its last split second, the aircraft pilot activated its death ray of mini-gun fire. The jungle beneath him was obliterated in a furious hail storm of projectiles, beyond expectation, beyond experience, indeed beyond belief. Then that scenario was repeated with the pilot attacking from another direction. The entire assault consisted of a total of about twenty seconds of fire on the target during the three separate attacks from different directions. The whole action seemed to have been from some not yet imagined science fiction movie featuring a futuristic yet prehistoric looking mechanical creature equipped with some sort of incredible death ray. Of course, I realized that that is exactly what it was, a death ray of previously unimaginable sound and strength and fury and death. I was glad that they came, but was even gladder when they left. They broke off the attack as quickly as when they had started. I watched as the chopper departed off into the night, a quickly fading muffled sound of thunder and faint red and green running lamps providing very, very faint evidence of the all-consuming slaughter and destruction that had just occurred.

The air was now very still. I had a last smoke of the day and took a few swigs of water from my canteen and then laid down to go to sleep. I could almost always very quickly fall asleep but this night I lay awake for almost an hour. It seemed as if my brain would not allow rest until the events of the previous half hour were processed and filed away. But it was impossible to fully evaluate what I had just done and witnessed.

My body was shivering although I didn't feel cold and I noticed that a sudden fit of shaking coincided exactly with my thoughts of the helicopter unleashing its maelstrom of death. And then there was another darker feeling, starkly repugnant and uncomfortable in an ugly way, as thoughts flittered across my consciousness regarding the enemy that I had fired upon. Human beings that I had just tried to take their lives away and probably did. I tried to push the thoughts away and fall asleep but I was continually brought back to full wakefulness with my body twitching fitfully, my arms and legs suddenly flailing about and my body shaken with uncontrollable shivers. I desperately just wanted to just fall asleep, to push away everything, to escape somehow from my existence. Somehow, after about an hour of that torment, I thankfully slipped into a state of semi-consciousness that had to suffice for that nights rest.

The next day started out quietly. Again we would stay put with the mortars to support the patrols if they needed us. Choppers brought in a hot breakfast. There were outbursts of gunfire all day, some of it from the patrols around us in the bush and some of it, I think, coming into our set up area on the road to the south, probably VC probing our position for weaknesses, or maybe attacks that were quickly put down by the perimeter guards. The gooks were coming in to get us but the perimeter patrols were doing a good job of keeping them at bay. It vaguely occurred to me that the gooks were damned and determined to first kill the mortar crews.

Around noon another re-supply chopper landed among us on the road with a Catholic chaplain aboard. Word was passed that there would be an Easter mass in a few minutes. I had no idea that it was Easter, I didn't even know that it was Sunday. It was a magnificent day, the sunlight seemed to have a golden tint to it. About twelve guys and myself gathered around the priest who engaged us in light banter while he diligently set up his Mass kit upon some crates of C-rations. The equatorial sun shone directly upon us but for some reason it felt benign, a soothing, life-giving heat. He withdrew a wide piece of cloth from his kit and placed it around his neck, an elaborately decorated vestment that was in stark contrast to the brown and black color of the hard road and rocks surrounding us and the dirt that stained our uniforms and gear. It represented to me kindness and compassion, civility and sanctity, gentleness and love, a stark reminder of another world far away where people lived good lives. The priest seemed to be in a bit of a hurry as he said the Mass. I guessed that he was trying to minister to as many soldiers as possible on this Easter Day and was probably trying to catch one of the very few outward bound choppers from this location to another Companys perimeter somewhere out in the vastness of the surrounding jungle.

He was at the point in the Mass where he was into a little sermon when there was suddenly a burst of gunfire coming from behind us, from somewhere out in the jungle to the southeast. There were a couple of military radios relatively close to us that had been mostly silent but now the radio traffic began to increase in frequency. They started with a few terse messages then quickly built in urgency as instructions and interrogatories and orders were relayed among a net of radio operators and commanders. The priest continued with his good words but I found it extremely difficult to pay attention because the radios were telling a desperate story, in abbreviated military jargon, the unhappy central message being that one of the platoons was coming in with dead and wounded.

The priest probably was aware of the radio traffic and what was happening because he abruptly ended his sermon and quickly continued the Mass. We were all kneeling on the dusty, solid stone floor of the outdoor church without roof or walls when someone ran past us heading towards the southern end of the road, ordering us to grab our weapons and follow him on the run. The priest had just begun the Consecration and I knew that we really shouldn't leave the Mass and the priest until that most solemn part of the Mass was completed. I went to place my hand onto my rifle but stopped just short of it, suddenly struck with the sacrilege of holding a weapon while in the direct presence of the holy Sacrament. Jesus the Christ, who had preached love and forgiveness and kindness and praying for your enemies was being celebrated and I almost picked up my weapon. The irony of it was not lost on me. On the other hand, I wanted to run off and try to save my fellow soldiers as quickly as possible. The priest began to speak very rapidly and within fifteen seconds he had completed the most solemn part of the Mass. I grabbed my weapon and jumped up, the priest yelled to the others, "Go!"

Me and about ten other men ran about a quarter of a mile. Some of the men were wearing load bearing gear so they had a number of magazines of ammo and grenades but I just had a bandolier of ammo slung around my neck. It occurred to me that I should run back and get my LBG and extra ammo but the game was on. I thought that we were heading straight out into the jungle to engage directly, that we were to join a desperate fight already in progress. I'd have to make do with the ammo that I had. I glanced at my belt, knowing full well that I had left my bayonet behind but hoping that somehow it might be there, alarmed at the thought of having to use it up close and personal but dismayed even more that I didn't have it.

We ran past the perimeter guards and the relative safety of the encampment and continued down the road, ten lightly armed Infantrymen running pell-mell, not knowing exactly when to stop or where to go, just running and listening for any gunfire or signs of the beleaguered soldiers in the bush. It occurred to me, as Hanoi Hanna of radio fame, referred to the 173rd Airborne Brigade, that we truly were a small gang of "juvenile delinquents in green t-shirts" We were a bunch of teenagers running full on into a gang fight with automatic military weapons. I yelled to some of the soldiers close to me with grenades to give me a couple but they rightfully ignored my request. They had very uncomfortably worn their LBG loaded down with ammo and grenades and I didn't, I didn't have a right to ask them to give me a grenade or two.

We ran a goodly distance and I was worried that we had passed the soldiers that we were searching for who were probably still in the jungle and even more worried that we were running right into an ambush when we suddenly spotted a few soldiers staggering out of the jungle, onto the road. Their uniforms were every inch a dark green, saturated with sweat, and a helmet full of it flooded over their faces and into their eyes and dripped onto their arms and fell to the ground. Their arms and faces and necks were covered with numerous scratches and cuts, blood and bits of leaves and caked mud covering their skin and embedded in their torn skin.

They had smooth, curved, razor-like gashes and wounds that looked like they had been snagged by a line of fishhooks that ripped the skin upwards as they were torn out. They had puncture wounds, slender ones and wide ones, some shallow, some deep and some with thorns or the ends of woody spikes still embedded in the skin. They had cuts that were still bright red and others congealed over with a mass of dark purple blood. They were cut and torn and ripped and stabbed horizontally and vertically and at every other angle, injuries that intersected other injuries like a psychotic game of tic-tac-toe.

We quickly determined that they were the platoon that we were sent out to assist. They were frightened and revulsed, horrified, forlorn and despairing, outraged and inconsolable. They looked like madmen. They had a thousand yard stare yet they twitched and fidgeted and looked all about like they expected to be stung by some enormous creature that was within feet of them yet somehow couldn't be seen. I guess I was distracted for a moment, staring as some soldiers from the patrol walked away from us on the road because when I turned around I noticed three or four men alongside a stretcher being carried at each end by two other soldiers. The stretcher was a makeshift arrangement of two long rails fashioned from thick saplings with a poncho spread between them to hold a man. An expedient devise manufactured on the spot under emergency conditions. Most of them were bearing part of the burden yet they staggered slightly from side to side and lurched forward sporadically and then backwards a little. It was almost as if the jungle itself had a grasp on the stretcher and the wounded man lying upon it andwas trying to pull him them back into its immense body of living horrors.

I ran to the stretcher along with some other soldiers from my group and grabbed one of its rails to relieve the exhausted troopers struggling with it, but they told us, in a most serious way, to get our hands off the stretcher. The wounded man was one of theirs, a member of that unique platoon, and the stretcher bearers seemed to be resolutely determined to carry the trooper to the very last step that would mark the end of the patrol. A few other soldiers emerged in single file from the bush and then another stretcher crew. Again, I and a few other soldiers ran to give aid but those soldiers were even more adamant than the first crew in insisting that we not even touch the stretcher.

The man on that stretcher had a poncho covering him from his boots to the top of his head. My first thought was that the injured man was in shock and was covered to conserve his body heat. Then I thought that the poncho was covering his face to protect him from falling debris as he was carried through the underbrush, but as I watched the stretcher go by, I could see that the poncho was wrapped around his body and another poncho seemed to be wrapped tightly around his body from the shoulders up, completely covering his face and wrapped around his head. My final rationalization was to wonder how he could breathe, but as the stretcher passed by me I had to acknowledge the terrible truth that lying wrapped on that stretcher was the dead body of an American Paratrooper. Then another group carrying the bloody body of another wounded soldier appeared from the jungle. Someone asked them if they wanted any help and one of them simply said "No" and they passed by us in total silence. I guess they wanted to personally bring back the dead and wounded in their platoon, undoubtedly their friends.

All my group of men could do was to just stand around, watching the tortured troopers file out of the woods, waiting until they we were certain that all members of their platoon were out of the bush and accounted for. Then we ran back towards the perimeter, mixing amongst the platoon, not knowing what to say or what to do other than providing reinforcement to their ranks and flank security for men who seemed worn out beyond measure physically and mentally. One of the soldiers escorting the body of the dead trooper carried a helmet in his hand. It was completely destroyed. It looked as if it was made of aluminum foil and someone had forcefully stuck their fingers into it about twenty times, from the inside outwards, bursting the metal outwards with such force that it had mushroomed back towards itself in some places while other eruptions looked like straight, jagged horns projecting from the helmet.

Shrapnel had torn through that helmet while still on a mans head, tearing through his face and brain before it went out through the other side of his helmet. I figured that that helmet belonged to the guy on the stretcher who was completely wrapped up in a poncho. There must have been little or nothing left of his head and face. The trooper carrying the helmet told us that the soldier that was killed had been the pointman on the patrol and that he had opened a gate leading to a house. The gate was booby trapped and instantaneously separated the soldiers soul from his mortal remains. Weeks later that helmet was placed at a new jungle school that was being set up in base camp for new replacements. If a picture is worth a thousand words then that helmet, knowing that a man was wearing it when it was destroyed, must be worth a thousand pictures. Just one look at that helmet must have taught those new guys lessons that could never be explained by an instructor or adequately described in the words of a book.

Throughout the day sudden outbursts of gunfire erupted at random from the jungle surrounding us, indicating that all of the patrolling platoons were being engaged by the enemy. A pandemonium of mechanical mortal combat came from all directions, from the north and then the southeast, then from west and back again towards the north and from the east the next time. There were sharp reports from engagements close by and duller noises from a mile away or distant rumblings of explosives and barely discernable clatter from machine guns off in the distance. It was as if the surrounding jungle was slowly boiling up death. Sometimes the gunfire was only a few rounds and far away, sometimes it might begin as a hundred round burst from a machine gun answered by AK-47 fire and hand grenades. Sometimes it would be all AK-47 fire as the VC sprang an ambush then immediately retreated. There were brief engagements as a lone soldier fired a few quick shots or a sixty second skirmish as small groups of men fired upon each other and longer episodes as forces engaged each other with thousands of rounds fired at close range. The reports of VC rifles and AK-47 sub-machine guns were clearly distinguishable from the sharp rap of American M-16s and M-60 automatic weapons among the explosions of hand grenades thrown in the midst of close quarters battle. Amongst the exchanges of gunfire there was sometimes an appalling babble of explosions from enemy B-40 rocket propelled grenades and mortar rounds impacting, answered with American anti-tank rockets and claymores mixed with the "thump" and "crash" as American grenadiers brought their weapons into action.

All of the engagements ended abruptly and then there were periods of quiet where I forsakenly hoped that the killing had stopped for the day but then it would start up again. On a few occasions, there wasn't any sound of gunfire but I suddenly heard a series of "thunks" that puzzled me for a few seconds until I realized that they were the dreadful sounds of VC mortar rounds leaving the tube. I could do nothing but freeze in place, holding my breath in deadly anticipation while the rounds arced high in the air and then began their plunge to earth, seeking out the bodies of American soldiers on the ground. There was a lot going on out there, all around us, and I felt very sorry for the guys out there in the action. It wasn't until I heard the thunking launch of the VCs second mortar attack that I suddenly realized that their target could be me and the men within the perimeter on the road. I don't know why I hadn't thought of it before but I rather quickly became aware that a prime military objective of the enemy would be to attack the road within the perimeter, destroy the stores of ammo and supplies, take over the helicopter landing zone and kill the mortar gun crews.

We got the word later that day that "C" company had been involved in a ferocious, widespread battle that had taken the lives of three American paratroopers. This had not been like any Easter that I had ever seen, or ever imagined for that matter. (I found out much later that in fact it was "A" company, my company, that had been involved in the action and killing.) I imagined people back in the States dressed in their best clothing and walking to Church on a sunny spring morning. I wondered if any of them had any idea of what was really happening here in this little piece of Hell.

The wounded had been brought to a central area on the road with the stretchers roughly aligned head to toe. In a world of brown rock and green uniforms the white battle dressings and bright red blood that seeped through many of them luridly marked the emergency aid station. There were about five medics working on the men so there must have been some medics stationed within the perimeter. The men on the ground came in bandaged but it looked as if the medics were checking the wounds again and replacing the battle dressings that must have been applied in the heat of combat. They also seemed to be thoroughly examining the wounded and applying more of the huge bandages to wounds that had not been immediately obvious.

Every so often there was shouting among the medics and one or two of them would rush to the side of another medic as they desperately engaged in various medical techniques. MedEvac helicopters had been called but they didn't arrive very quickly. The word was passed that the first chopper would take out wounded only, which made sense since the soldiers completely wrapped in ponchos had all the time in the world.

I had tried to write a letter to my mother and father a few days before but the envelopes were sealed shut by the humidity or rain or sweat or creek crossings. As the first chopper touched down I tore off a piece of a C-ration box, about the size of a postcard and wrote my parents address on one side and a quick note on the other to say that I was OK. We didn't need stamps, we just wrote something, I forgot what it was, in the place where a stamp would go and it would be delivered, one of the benefits of being in Viet Nam. I figured that this operation might have a mention in the newspapers back home and I wanted my parents to know that I was still alive, or, at least, was still alive on this Easter Sunday.

Another chopper came in to take out the dead, wrapped mummy style in ponchos. I ran over to the door gunner and gave him my post card and asked him to mail it. He had a camera out and began to take pictures of the dead Americans on the ground. A soldier walked over to him, took the camera from his hands, pulled out the film and threw it on the ground, then handed the camera back to him and walked away, all without saying a word. The door gunner just sat there in silence while the dead were loaded on and then the chopper took off. By the way, that postcard never arrived.

The next day was a repeat of the previous days. All during the day gunfire could be heard around our main encampment. Off to the north there seemed to be a particularly long engagement in the early afternoon. From the huge quantity ofVC fire I guessed that an American platoon had been ambushed by a full Company of VC or that an even larger enemy force had engaged the Americans and were intent on killing every one of them. The American fire, subdued at first, quickly reached a crescendo of overwhelming M-16 and M-60 and M-79 fire among the explosions of hand grenades. It sounded like the men in my Companys platoon were fighting for their lives, which was exactly what they were doing. Eventually the fire slowed and then stopped altogether. From the radio traffic that I could hear that the men in the American Platoon were coming in with one dead and several seriously wounded. I was appalled that we had taken causalities, but also surprised that a majority of them had survived such an onslaught. I think that one man in my Company was KIA and three others wounded on this day. I knew all four of those dead and wounded men. The wounded men were so grievously injured that I would never see any of them again.

The next day the choppers came in the early morning to take out two of the mortars and some of the ammo for them. The orders for the day were to continue our mission back into the jungle. My squad had to hump the mortar plus carry mortar rounds. There were plenty more of the heavy projectiles that were distributed among the other members of the heavy weapons platoon and the rest of the Company. Among all of us we carried one mortar but rounds enough for four guns. It was just even more weight to carry where our usual loads were already beyond unreasonable and unbearable. I felt very sorry for the men in the line platoons that had to carry the extra mortar rounds. They would suffer carrying equipment that they could not personally use.

We humped for the next two days, crushed and tortured by the weight of our equipment, pushed far beyond what I had thought were the limits of physical endurance and paying for it exorbitantly in agony and anguish. During the second day when the line had come to a stop for a while my legs gave out from under me. I just collapsed face down and lay there with my arms in front of me on the ground. I was beaten beyond words, way beyond exhausted, in a wretched agony from humping all of that weight. I didn't even try to maintain a lookout off to our flanks. The thought occurred to me that I would be much better off dead. Immediately a swarm of about a hundred small black mosquitoes descended upon my right arm. I had run out of insecticide days ago so I tried to swat them away but they would not be deterred. I tried to swat them against my arm, which was partly successful, but they were very quick and there were plenty of them. Then I realized that I was just squashing bugs against the skin of my arms, which were filthy dirty and covered with matted hair and blood and deep ulcers. If these mosquitoes had malaria, there was nothing that I could do to prevent an infection. I just laid there completely beyond exhaustion, watching as a hundred little bugs penetrated my skin and began to feast on my blood and or my flesh. I was genuinely surprised that they would want my blood because I felt as if I had no life left within me.

I was so completely exhausted and beaten and in such agony that I could barely believe that I was still alive. I truly expected that one of the mosquitoes would take a tiny drop of blood and that would be the very last bit of life force that my body contained. We stayed in that one spot for about five or ten minutes. When the line started to move again I attempted to stand up and was dumbfounded at the realization that my body actually managed to do what my will demanded of it. The brief respite had allowed me to gather some bit of strength and I staggered onwards, somehow, for another few hours of unbearable misery. I can't remember the rest of the afternoon. What happened that evening and night is probably buried somewhere deeply in my brain but its beyond my conscious recall.

The next day we didn't break camp because our orders for the day were to stay in place. We set up our mortar and fired some registration rounds to make the fire direction control team get some bearings and ranges and generally be faster and more accurate if a fire mission was called for later. Then it was decided to fire some H&I, a bit of Harassment and Interdiction bombardment. We fired a group of rounds into the surrounding jungle, hoping to hit someone through dumb blind luck or to at least harass the enemy and generally let them know that we were in town. The FDC called for six rounds. I had seen other guys fire them off very quickly so I decided to try to do the same myself.

Anyone standing relatively close to the gun would hear a succession of distinct sounds as the gun went into action. First there would be a metallic tinkling sound as the round is fit into the mouth of the mortar tube. When the round is released there is a scraping/tinkling sound for a second or so as the round slides down the tube. When it hits the firing pin at the bottom of the tube the primer charge explodes, instantaneously igniting any other explosive charges on the outside of the round, which will propel the round high and long into the sky. When the round blasts out of the tube, the force and noise from the resultant propellant explosion varies depending on the type of round, how many (propellant) charges are on the round, and where your head is in relation to the top of the barrel (which depends upon whether you are the gunner (sixty%), the assistant gunner (a hundred %), or the ammo bearer (twenty%). Of course those statistics can change instantly, due to hostile fire, causalities and combat contingencies. For the assistant gunner who dropped the round and is standing next to the tube, the sound can range anywhere from that of a weak, muted shotgun to an explosion that can literally knock him to his knees, an explosion so violently loud and powerful that he can feel as if he had been hit in the side of the head with a baseball bat at full power. One single round fired at charge one can result in permanent hearing loss, some of the rounds had eight charges on them, why such things didn't kill the men who fired them I'll never know, probably they did.

I dropped in the first round and quickly dropped the next one. Then turned and grabbed two more rounds from the ammo bearer before the last round left the tube and then dropped the third round in, I was getting into a rhythm. The fourth round went in an instant after the previous one blasted out of the tube and I went to drop in the fifth round but suddenly the guys standing around watching let out gasping sounds and some of them turned around and walked quickly away, like something horrible had just happened and they didn't want to see the results of it.

I had tried to load the round into the mouth of the tube a hundredth of a second after the previous round blasted off. The round in my hand had just a fraction of an inch to go across the mouth of the weapon while the previous one was still on its way up the tube, on its way out. One of the guys said, "He's lost his hand!" I looked over at my hand and it was still there, but the round that I was holding had most of its charges blasted loose from it.

There were two Sergeants standing around and they were outraged. One of them said, "That's it for sure! You'll <u>never</u> get promoted!" I cared nothing about being promoted, I was just very thankful that my hand was still there. Of course, if the two rounds had collided in my hand, they may well have exploded, killing everyone within eighty feet of the gun. I decided right then to never again try to load the rounds so quickly. Six rounds put into the air before the first one lands is good, five rounds fired even faster with the sixth one killing the gun crew is bad.

I met a new guy later that day that had just been assigned to the Company. He was a staff Sergeant and wore a Special Forces insignia on his right shoulder, which meant that he had already served in combat with the Special Forces (the Green berets). He was a lanky guy, probably in his late twenties and I guessed by his rank that he had seven or ten years in the army. He seemed rather friendly and I asked him how he came to be assigned to the 173rd Airborne Brigade. He said that he had already served a year in Viet Nam with the Special Forces and had made it back to the States alive but then he received orders to go back for a second tour of duty. He said that he immediately quit Special Forces but was then still sent to Viet Nam. I asked him why he didn't want to serve with Special Forces anymore and he said that it is about the same as a death sentence for sure. He figured that at least he had a chance with some other outfit. I liked this guy and hoped that he would be assigned to my platoon because I thought that I could learn things from him and his experience would be very valuable. He wasn't assigned to Weapons platoon although I saw him once in a while later out in the field. In three months he would be dead due to enemy hostilities.

I had been told about a month before that I would be going on R&R (Rest and Recuperation), a mini vacation, in about six weeks. I just knew that it would be very good to get out of this situation some day. I didn't start counting down the days towards that date, because I figured that there wasn't much chance of me making it out alive for another six weeks and I hadn't really given it any thought. On this day though, for some reason, I realized that I only had another fourteen days or so, and began to entertain thoughts of what I would do if I ever got the chance for R&R. The first and most important thoughts were of food and while I was contemplating what a pizza looked like, my section Sergeant came up to me and told me to get on the next chopper going out. I had no idea why he would tell me to do such a thing. When I enquired why I was to do that, he said, "To go on R&R".

I explained that I was not due for another two weeks but he just became irked and ordered me to get onto the next chopper outbound. I walked back to our mortar position and began gathering up my gear. I had no way of knowing when the next helicopter might land or even if any more choppers were due that day at all. I saw two guys in my squad and started to tell them that I'm going on R&R when a chopper suddenly came in for a landing. Sometimes the choppers stayed on the ground for half an hour and sometimes they just kicked out ammo and food and lifted off almost immediately, we never knew how long they would remain in the area. I grabbed my gear and ran out to it and jumped into it on my stomach just as it was lifting off, much to the surprise of the door gunner and much to the consternation of the pilot who suddenly and unexpectedly had three hundred pounds added to his airship. I just wanted to get out of this situation at the earliest possible moment.

The door gunners yelled something to me but I couldn't understand what was being said over the noise of the chopper. I just nodded my head "yes" a few times. The co-pilot looked off to the side and I guess when he didn't see some Sergeant yelling wildly to stop he probably decided that I hadn't just cracked up and suddenly decided to desert the Army. I figured that eventually someone would discover the mistake and I'd be sent back to the field but at least I'd "get over" for at least an hour or so. But it was to be. I was in fact due to go on R&R. Five minutes before I was thinking of the hardships and dangers of another fourteen days in the bush and suddenly I was in the air and on my way to somewhere safe. The shock was as if I had been buried underground, trapped for weeks, and suddenly and unexpectedly someone opened a hatch and let in fresh air and sunshine and escape to the world of the living.

Chapter 22

R & R

Returning Enemy Fire

After a few changes of helicopters and airplanes we finally arrived back at base camp. There was almost no one around. It was virtually deserted. I wondered if they even had guards at the berm or were just Air Force military police riding around the perimeter to provide security.

I took a shower and changed into civilian clothes then went to the Company Commanders hooch to find out what was going on. A clerk checked his records and informed me that I would be leaving the next day. As to exactly where I would be going, I would be told the next day. I only had about fifteen dollars in military script, expecting to go on R&R after payday. I tried to go to the Brigade office to get an advance on my paycheck, but they were closed and wouldn't open again for another two days. The enlisted mens club was closed so I couldn't even get a soda or candy or beer so I hitched a ride on a military truck down to the airbase and picked up a half gallon of gin ($1.65), a carton of cigarettes ($1.00), some cans of coke and some potato chips.

When I returned to our Companys area I suddenly had the urge to take another shower.The trip to the PX was hot and dusty and sweaty but I had already taken a shower two hours ago, never mind going without a shower for weeks in the field. I walked over to the shower area, amazed to think that I could take a shower with an almost endless supply of water and not sharing the area with twenty other guys.The water was certainly not hooked up to a heater but the tropical sun on the huge water tank had heated the water to a very comfortable and warm temperature. I took a long and luxuriant shower, a million miles removed from my fellow troopers still in the jungle.

The Company clerk had told me to turn in my weapon to the supply Sergeant but he wasn't around to supervise so I kept my weapon and ammo beside me in the hooch. I felt safer with my rifle close by, but was concerned that if this base was overrun, that I was one of very few people in this area to defend it.This huge base was constantly probed by enemy sappers, trying to destroy airplanes, but there was never an enemy infantry assault of any size against it while I was there.A month later enemy sappers would destroy a number of aircraft.A year and a half later, this base would come under an extremely strong attack by enemy infantry.

That night, I was packing and realized that I only had two sets of civilian clothes and they had not been washed since I last wore them months ago and in any event they were all wrinkled. I didn't have time to get them washed and ironed and so resigned myself to wearing the only uniform that I had, Army winter issue greens, that had some semblance of being clean and pressed since I had never worn it since entering this Country.

The next day I hopped onto a truck and was brought to some other area of the base. Everyone formed into a single file, enlisted men and officers together, and at the front of the line we were each given a slip of paper with our destination and length of stay. People were going to Thailand, the Philippines, Taiwan, Australia and Hawaii. I drew Hawaii, which seemed OK with me, especially since it was for ten days total, compared with only seven or eight days for the other places. People were talking about which destination they had drawn. I noticed that there was a bit of excitement regarding Hawaii and when I stated that I had Hawaii, about five men quickly approached me and asked me to change destinations with them.

Some of them were officers who seemed particularly desperate to go to Hawaii. I found out later that they were probably so because they could have their wives and children meet them there. Although it was strictly forbidden to travel to the continental United States, some men landed in Hawaii and immediately booked the next trip to the States to see their family and friends. In retrospect, I probably should have traded my ticket because some of those guys were really desperate to go to Hawaii, and with good reason. Most of the men that I knew had their girlfriends break up with them while they were in Viet Nam, and most of the married guys had their wives divorce them, or waited until they returned home to divorce them, probably because they could collect their paycheck up until then and could collect their life insurance in case they were killed in Viet Nam.

Maybe its just a co-incidence that I knew of so many men that that happened to, or maybe its just a dirty little secret that's never been investigated before. As for me, I had a girlfriend when I joined the army, but told her that three years is a long time. She used to send me letters and then began to nag me in the letters to buy her a hope chest. I thought that that would just probably give her false hope. She was consumed with the idea of a hope chest while I'm in a place and situation that I could have never imagined, in a World that neither she nor I had ever envisioned. I sent her a nasty letter and broke up with her. I found out later that she had a nervous breakdown and had to be placed in a mental hospital for a substantial amount of time, and that my actions seemed to be the chief cause of it. The problem here is that she had a nervous breakdown because I wouldn't buy her a hope chest, but these men with me seemed to go on under conditions that were thousands of times more threatening and we seemed to do OK. The problem is that we were slowly being permanently destroyed, emotionally, physically and mentally, we just didn't know it at the time.

We were taken by bus to the main civilian airport in Saigon where there was a booth, run by the US government, where we were to turn in our military script money and get greenbacks in return. The guy at the front of the line turned in seven hundred 0 dollars worth, the next guy turned in five hundred dollars worth, the guy in front of me turned in six hundred dollars worth. Then it was my turn. I pushed nine dollars in military script through the cage and said "Nine dollars". The guy in the booth looked at me in surprise and counted the money.

He said, "You need a lot more than that", in fact I had been told that you couldn't go on R&R unless you had enough money to cover your expected costs. I just forcefully said to the guy, "Just give me my money and don't say anything!!" He seemed to recognize my predicament, and that I was in no mood whatsoever to listen to bureaucratic objections to me leaving this place. He seemed to understand the gist of my message, handed me my money, and said, "Happy landings".

It was a long ride to Hawaii in a civilian plane and the time zone difference was about seven hours. We landed Sunday morning about five-thirty am. Once on the ground and into the airport, we gathered around a Sergeant who gave us some general information about Hawaii and introduced us to a number of representatives from a number of different hotels. One by one they announced the location of their hotels and their amenities and prices.

I quickly asked if they required payment in advance and all of the representatives said that they required at least a substantial down payment. One by one, men selected various hotels and were whisked away in company vehicles and taxies. Eventually, most men and representatives had left so that there was only me and about five other soldiers standing around with only two hotel representatives left. I approached one of the hotel reps and asked if I could work out a deal to pay in full for a week, but to make that payment three days from now. I didn't mention that I had only nine dollars in my pocket. He was very receptive and quickly agreed. We rode to his hotel, a second rate place far back from the main drag, without any amenities at all but it was a thousand times better than my recent accommodations.

I got a few dollars worth of quarters from the front desk in change and went to a telephone booth to call my parents. In Viet Nam, I think that there were some telephones that could reach the United States but I never saw one. Maybe there were a few in Saigon or on some large air base but no one that I knew ever had access to an overseas telephone. That was just one more small but significant part of the deprivations of a combat soldier in Viet Nam. Combat troops here spent an entire year without ever hearing the voice of their family or friends.

My mother answered the telephone call and seemed a bit shocked. I told her I was in Hawaii, and she probably thought that I had been badly wounded, but eventually I explained what was happening. My father got on the phone and I explained my financial situation and asked if he could send me a western union telegram with two hundred dollars. He said he would do so right away and the next day I had some spending money.

There didn't seem much to talk about on the phone. I guess I just really didn't want to talk much at all. What was there to say? If my parents ever had a remote idea of the nightmare that my life had become, I don't know what they would do. I never really expected to see them again. I just expected to go back, eventually, into a world of hurt, extreme deprivations, hopelessness and death. I had been released from the torture chambers for a week and I could eat and drink and be clean and see normal people, but then I would have to return. That would be very, very hard to do. It felt like I was a condemned prisoner who was eating his favorite food as his last meal. It's kind of hard to enjoy such a meal. I would have liked to hear my parents voices longer but I had the thought that at some point they might be telling their friends what my last words on Earth was to them.

I went back to my room and decided to take a shower. This was a total luxury, that I could take a shower in privacy, with hot and cold running water. I washed down thoroughly and grabbed a white towel to dry off. I then went to put the towel back onto the rack and noticed that it was a dark brown mottled color. I thought that it was white when I started, and couldn't understand why it now seemed so different. I pulled another white towel off of the rack and rubbed my arms and shoulders. Now it was a medium brown color. I had taken three showers in the two days before I left Viet Nam and could not at first understand why these towels were turning brown. Then I realized that the sweat and dust and mud of Viet Nam was imbedded in my skin. I got back into the shower and soaped and rubbed and washed down over and over again in hot water for about ten minutes. When I again dried off, the towel was a light brown. I again got into the shower and stayed there for about twenty minutes, scrubbing and washing vigorously and this time, the new white towel that I used to dry off with was only a light dusty color.

I dropped my civilian clothes off at the front desk to be sent out to a laundry but they said it would require two days. So I went out and about with my winter Army uniform on, which was completely inappropriate attire for that weather, but it was the only clothes that I had to wear.

I found a supermarket and walked into its air-conditioned confines. That air-conditioned coolness was something that I had not felt for the last six months and it felt excellent. I was flabbergasted at the aisles after aisles of food that I had not seen for a long, long time. I got snacks and candy and pastries and milk and soda and liquor and approached the cashier. There was a sign that said that the legal drinking age in Hawaii was twenty years old. I would be twenty in a few weeks, I was still a teenager, but they didn't ask for an id, something that every other place in Hawaii would demand. A cashier at a market recognized the significance of the Parachute badge and CombatInfantryMans badge and the Airborne 173rd patch on my left shoulder and excitedly told her nearby workers the significance of them. She was greatly impressed.

I went back to the hotel, laid down in bed, drank my booze and ate my snacks and watched TV (which I had not seen for many, many months) and thought to myself that life is good. Apparently the booze caught up to me and I started to get dizzy, a bad case of the "bed spins". Nauseous, I eventually I had to climb out of bed and lay down on the coolness and hardness of the carpet on the floor to then pass out into sleep.

I walked around Honolulu the next day to get the lay of the land and around evening I spotted an Italian restaurant. It looked fairly pricey and didn't have a menu with prices near the door but I decided to try it anyways. It was a very nice place, the Maitre'de was very friendly and the waitresses couldn't have been more friendly and helpful. I had on my uniform and had noticed before that although Honolulu had a large contingent of Army personnel stationed there that I almost never saw anyone wearing a uniform. I have to say that that uniform had a very good effect on everyone I met and they seemed to go out of their way to be friendly and helpful.

At the restaurant I opted for a plate of spaghetti and meatballs and the waitress brought out a huge plate of food. I looked around at the few other diners and their meals were very small. I wouldn't doubt that the cook had gotten out a big plate and gave me a double serving, no extra charge. I ordered glass after glass of red wine. I managed to get back to the hotel room somehow. I laid down upon the bed but after a few minutes it was extremely uncomfortable, I just couldn't stand it, just couldn't stand the softness and easiness of a good civilian mattress. I rolled out of bed and laid on the hard floor and then drifted off into sleep.

I went sightseeing, in a way, the next day. Stopped at a K-mart or something and ordered a cheap grilled cheese sandwich at their lunch counter. I could appreciate how cheap and poor quality the food was but realized that it was a lot better fare than I was used to. I wandered around the Honolulu tourist district for a few hours. Then went back to my hotel room to drink and plan my actions for the night.

About nine PM I went out and about, eventually sighting a night club. Again, I was wearing my Army winter uniform with full decorations. The bouncers couldn't have been nicer or easier, but my ID showed me to be two weeks less than the drinking age and they very nicely but most assuredly refused to give me admittance to the club, although they were more than apologetic about enforcing the law. Just as well. How could I possibly talk to girls, or any civilian actually. My point of view of the world was a thousand times removed, into a completely different reality, from their reality.

Walking back to my hotel room, I somehow passed by the Italian restaurant of the night before. Again, I thought that the best item on the menu was the spaghetti and meatballs and again, the waitress brought out a huge plate of food. When I had finished the meal the waitress gave me a menu and asked if I wanted desert. I couldn't imagine anyone wanting desert after such a big meal but as I examined the menu, I suddenly realized that I wanted more food. I told her that I wanted another huge plate of spaghetti and meatballs. She seemed shocked but she delivered another huge meal of which I ate every last speck. I must say that I didn't want any desert after that.

On the way out, I noticed that they had a bar at the beginning of the restaurant and decided to get a drink or two. The bartender was friendly and did not ask for an id and poured freely. After one drink, I noticed that they had a jukebox and sat down at a small table/booth to review what songs were available. I put in a coin and pressed the button for the song "blowing in the wind" and ordered another drink. I was struck by the nice melody and particularly by a line in the song that goes "where have all the soldiers gone? Gone to flowers every one". I thought that, no, <u>all</u> the soldiers have not gone, but a lot of men in my Company and Battalion and Brigade have gone to flowers and a lot more will before their tour of duty is ended. I thought, yes, I will probably "go to flowers" within the next month or so. I realized that this would probably be the last time that I would be in a civilized world, with good food and water, where every step would probably not be my last. I would be going back to another universe where deprivation and pain and maiming and starvation and thirst and slit latrines and torture and horrible suffering was a soldiers daily life.

I thought that these civilians at this bar, who seemed so happy on their vacations, could not imagine in their worst nightmares how life was in the war zone, seven time zones away. I played that song over and over and looked around at that bars patrons and bartender, anticipating their derogatory remarks about my continuous selection of particular songs, but there was no reproval. I liked listening to certain songs, over and over and the patrons of the bar looked over at me, with full insignia on my uniform and probably knew that I was here for R&R and would soon be going back to Viet Nam. I thought that it was very nice of them to force themselves to listen to my selections tonight since I would probably be gone the next day and they would thereafter not have to suffer my selection of songs. But it also occurred to me that the patrons of this bar, mostly middle-aged males, knew exactly what the decorations on my uniform meant, and that they decided to cut me a lot of slack.

Eventually I staggered out of that bar after about five more drinks and five more repeats of that song, and finally made it back to my hotel room and collapsed onto a grossly nice and comfortable bed. After a few minutes, I had to fall out onto the floor to sleep. Now I realized that I couldn't sleep on a comfortable bed. My previous life of sleeping in filth and coldness and hardness on the earthen ground had now made it impossible to sleep on something that was warm and comfortable. I wondered how long, or if ever, it would take to get adjusted to sleep on a civilian bed, that is if I ever survived my tour of duty in Viet Nam.

I began to run out of money and made another call to my father for another hundred dollars. I called him at about eleven pm, local time, forgetting that it was four am in Boston. I don't remember much about the rest of the time there, but finally it

came to the time that I was supposed to report to the airport at four am the next morning. I settled accounts with the hotel the night before and took a nap, setting the alarm on the hotel supplied clock for two am. Too soon, the alarm awakened me and I had a few shots of liquor and got my stuff together. I just walked out of the hotel with my duffel bag on my shoulder and started walking down the middle of the street, half hoping that a drunk driver might come barreling down through the darkness and kill me.

Everyone was in bed, there was no traffic at all on those side streets and it was very quiet. I could only hear my bootsteps on the street. The tropical trees on some streets arched over the roadway, forming a sort of tunnel. I knew what I was returning to and it crossed my mind to just walk away, go somewhere, anywhere, desert the Army. I could eventually make it back to the States and maybe hide out. They would probably eventually catch up with me, but at least I'd have a break from the horror and suffering that surely awaited me.

I thought that if I deserted then I would get prison time and a dishonorable discharge, but then I weighed the severity of that situation against another four months of torture and eventually probably death. The fact that a dis-honorable discharge from the military follows a person for life seemed to be a better alternative than an honorable discharge due to death or missing limbs, and/or blindness or something worse seemed more and more to me to be the better trade-off for the former alternative. I was deliberately walking back into a horrible world of pain. It was probably the most difficult thing that I would ever do. How I ever did it I will never know.

Then I thought of the guys in my squad, and thought that I should be back with them. Maybe I could help save them from being killed or help them when they were in danger some time. I think that the decision to continue towards the airport was the hardest decision that I have ever had to make in my life and somewhere in my mind a voice screamed "Don't go!! "You cannot subject yourself to that agony and torture anymore, you will be killed or maimed for sure!!" But, in true Airborne style, I decided that since I had been assigned to Viet Nam, I would go "All the Way", and I just put one foot in front of the other, hesitatingly, until I encountered a taxicab twenty minutes later and took it to the airport.

I got back to base camp at night. The next morning they told me to load onto a chopper and I was flown out to a mission already in progress. I stayed there for about a half a day. It was a real shock, mentally and physically, being back on an operation and out into the jungle again. I only spent about two hours humping the bush then four hours after I was inserted into that nightmare, we loaded into trucks to go back to base camp. I don't know why I was subjected to that. Another day of rest would have been good, and given me some time to get myself more mentally prepared for this situation but the powers that be decided to subject me to just another day of savage physical abuse and torture.

Chapter 23

OPERATION UNIONTOWN

April 17-26

If you can keep your head when all about you Are losing theirs and blaming it on you;

Rudyard Kipling "If"

Arrellano with Full Color Patch

Back in base camp we cleaned our weapons and took a shower. We were all anticipating a few days of rest and respite from the jungle.

After a while some of the guys said that they would be going downtown later if we got the word that it was OK. We started talking a bit and arranging who's going to go where and do what. I asked the soldiers who were around me, who could hear me, a general question of "Hey, where's that Sergeant that we went downtown with last time?" "He was a really good guy, lets make sure that he goes with us this time".

From my general audience they said, "Who are you talking about?" After a few seconds of confusion and abject un-memory, I suddenly remembered his name, which I recalled. "Sergeant Anderson". I told them, "You know, that chubby Sergeant named Anderson." Suddenly the entire platoon tent went deadly quiet. It seemed to me to be a "Twilight Zone" moment. I had no idea of what was going on. I thought to my self "why has everyone here suddenly decided to stare at me in what seemed to be horrible disregard and ill contempt? Then, one guy spoke to me softly, with a concern and reverence in his voice, that I found shocking and amazing in its delicacy and humanness amid this world of horrible harshness. It was a civilized, gentle response, a hundred and eighty degrees opposite the looks of hate that surrounded me.

In the presence of seemingly outraged anger from his fellow troopers, in a low tone of voice, he demanded, gently but firmly, to know, what I was talking about. As smooth and soft as his voice was, it indicated that a very violent fist-fight or maybe something very much more extreme and deadly was about to occur without the right response from me. "Didn't you hear about Sergeant Anderson?" He said. I said "No". There was a sudden quiet for ten seconds throughout the platoon tent. Everyone seemed to freeze in place instantly and I surveyed this scene with all of these guys staring intently at me with what seemed to be either acute hate or shock or both. Then one of the guys quietly said: "Man . . . . , didn't you know? Sgt Anderson got blown away about two weeks ago". I said, "What are you talking about?" "What do you mean blown away?" Then another guy said, very softly, "He's dead, Man . . . ." (note: many years later I found out that he had been killed on Easter Sunday. He had been the FO (Forward Observer) for the mortar platoon, which explained why I almost never saw him with my platoon out in the field because he would have usually been with the platoon that was on point.) I had no idea.

I didn't answer. I was just in shock and horrified as to what he said. "It couldn't possibly be true what he said" I thought. About ten seconds later the noise level picked up and everyone went back to what they were doing but most of the conversation had ended. Someone turned up the volume significantly on their tape recorder and, it seemed, everyone, at the same time, started to refresh their drinks with more liquor. "No one tells me anything." I softly muttered.

That's how it was in the bush most of the time, you only saw three or four guys during the whole operation. Sometimes you got information, most of the time you did not. Sometimes you went Downtown on leave after an operation and sometimes you went home in a body bag and sometimes your friends had gone home in a body bag weeks after you ever heard about it.

There seemed to suddenly be some kind of unconscious group decision to go downtown. We had been waiting for authorization to do so but we hadn't heard anything so far. There seemed to be some kind of group decision that happened quickly. A group of us just decided to go, regardless of any administrative consequences. Many of us just dropped what we were doing and moved out in a group, headed into town. A sizable proportion of soldiers did not go into town but just stayed in the platoon hootch. Those men were mostly older career soldiers and married men. They would procure huge quantities of liquor and get involved in some serious card gambling. Others would sit on their cots and listen to music on expensive tape players that they had purchased in country at a huge discount, most of the men remaining faithful to their wives.

We stayed in base camp for eighteen hours and moved out again on another mission. It was not nearly by any imagination enough time to let our bodies recuperate from the damage done on the previous operations. This would be a search and destroy operation not far from our base camp, in the region around Long Binh. We loaded onto trucks in the morning, not by any reasonable estimate capable of pursuing a combat operation due to our physical limitations and injuries. We were driven for about an hour, finally arriving at an area that we were to secure for a civilian construction site. We stayed there for a couple of days while patrols were sent out, but those patrols stayed very close to our little base of operations. My platoon stayed with the mortar but didn't have any fire missions. At least my platoon didn't have to engage in daily combat patrols so we actually did have some rest from the horrors of a combat hump.

Each day a number of VietNamese construction worker civilians would arrive early in the morning. I wondered what they thought of going to work every day and needing men with rifles and machine guns and mortars surrounding them to maybe somehow protect them somewhat from being killed or maimed. And for what? So they could very luckily work at their work for eighty cents per hour? Of course, I then thought, we are not even getting that much in salary. Maybe we were just protecting the site, maybe some of those guys would be back at night as VC. Some of them were very friendly, some of them had some strange expressions on their faces. Who knows what the situation was. A guy who looked at me with a strange expression might be the guy that I might save at the expense of my own life. On the other hand, he might be a VC who, knowing the layout of our compound, might sneak up that night and kill me and four other soldiers with an explosive. I really didn't know whether to wave hello to him or to shoot him. We stayed there for another few days. It was dangerous duty I

thought but literally a thousand times less dangerous and difficult than a hump through the woods.

We got the word that we would be loading into helicopters the next day for another mission. This new mission would take us into an area that had not contained soldiers other than North VietNamese or Viet Cong soldiers since the end of World War Two. They had had plenty of time to build tunnels and base camps and fortifications and to plan and set up ambush sites and map the area and plan for defending it and practice fighting in it and mark and register every little landmark for mortars and artillery. They had probably last fought the Japanese in this area twenty years before and therefore had twenty years to improve their defenses even more.

We rode on the choppers for quite a while and landed without incident. We walked into medium dense jungle until about one pm then came out of the jungle where I could see the blue sky again. There was an immense area with no trees at all, just elephant grass about twelve to fifteen feet tall. It was so dense that you had to maintain a distance of only about three feet between men in the line in front and in back of you or you would lose sight of the line of march. Overhead the sky was wide open but inside you could only see a foot or two in front of you and a very small patch of blue above you. The only way to follow the line of march was to take notice of the slightly tramped down and pushed aside grass in front of you. In the open sunlight it was very hot and the humidity must have been close to a hundred percent.The ground was saturated with water but at least it wasn't mud, at least we weren't sinking into it.

It felt like being in a sauna and I don't think that a man would last very long in that environment, especially with our loads of military gear. It was just murderously humid and extremely hot walking through that ridiculously tall grass in that location.The tall grass didn't permit any wind to blow by us.The grass was about an inch thick and was stiff enough to support its height of fifteen feet or so.The edges of the grass were so thick and incredibly sharp that it could easily cut any person or animal walking through it I thought.

We certainly cannot walk through this I thought, our clothes and bodies will be cut to ribbons before we got out of it but it wasn't too bad at all, I guess because the men in front of you did most of the pushing aside of the grass. It would be impossible to stomp it down, it was just too tall and dense. It was a very strange sensation walking through that grass, only being able to see two feet all around you, everywhere you looked it was just dense green grass.You couldn't see where you were going, the only thing that could be seen was a small portion of blue sky above but the grass was so dense that most of the time you couldn't even see the sky, just very dense grass all around and above you, sort of like an ant walking on the bottom of a very high quality rug that is six inches thick. I had a distinctive sensation of drowning.

After about an hour we exited that situation and again entered jungle. Eventually the jungle became relatively dense with medium sized trees spaced closely and heavy bushes and ground vegetation and a lot of thin long vines growing everywhere.The word was passed down the line for me to take the right flank position.There was always a pointman, the first guy in the line, a very dangerous position because he would usually be the first one to encounter an enemy ambush or trip a tripwire or get killed or injured by a mine or booby trap or sniper.At the end of the line was the rear-guard man. His situation was especially dangerous because if the enemy was following us he would be the first to encounter a situation and he had no one in back of him to help him out.The left and right flank men were not put out very often, they particularly were out by themselves, very dangerous and exposed to ambushes with no backup whatsoever.

Crossing an open rice paddy did not require flankers, heavy jungle or vegetation precluded their use because they would have to stay within five feet of the men in the main line, just to maintain visual contact. Plus, the pointman and people behind him might be hacking away at bushes and vines just to be able to advance and the flankers in that situation would fall behind the group if they had to make their own trails with machetes. I moved out about twenty feet to the side of the main column as the right flanker. My job was to detect any enemy that might approach us or lie in wait to hit the main columns flank. Actually, the flankers had the most dangerous positions. They were essentially out there on their own, a pointman and a rear-guardsman all in one, with no one close by to support you. You are on your own, making your own way through the jungle. If the enemy sprang an ambush, sometimes you would be caught between the fire of the enemy and your own men and then be murdered by both sides.

In that position, you had to be constantly aware of where the main line of march was. It was very easy to get too close to friendly troops and even easier to get too far away from them and become lost out there, all by yourself, in the middle of a dark jungle where if the animals won't kill you the enemy or your own friendly troops will. At the same time, you had to concentrate on every bush and tree and listen closely for any sign of enemy activity and, of course, had to try to watch for booby trap trip wires, mines, punji pits, signs of enemy troops and a hundred other very deadly dangers which had a decidedly serious probability of killing you and/or your fellow soldiers at any second.

After about ten minutes of flanking, I called out that I was coming back in. I shouted loudly that I was coming in because I didn't want anyone on the main line of march to mistake me for an enemy and kill me. When I reached the main line of march I put out the word up the line and down the line that I needed a machete. After a few minutes a Sergeant came walking back down the line. He had a machete and was mad that I had come back in, that I should have stayed out there on flank. I told him that

the pointman and others at the front must be using machetes, actually you could see that they were because we were passing small trees and vines that had been chopped down and hacked at. I told the sergeant that I needed a machete to cut my way through or I could never keep up with the main line. The thin long vines were catching my equipment at every step and I had to go through continuous bushes, trying to bull my way through by viciously kicking the vines and breaking them but I could not possibly keep up with the line of march without a machete, the vines just simply slowed me down too much.

He gave me the machete and I went back out, reminding everyone within earshot not to forget that I am out there. After about an hour I was relieved and another guy took my place while I resumed walking in the main line. An hour later I went out on flank again, but this time on the left. After about thirty minutes they called me in because we had come to an area where the jungle was much less dense. It was scary out there on flank.

We settled in for the night after each two man teams dug their fighting positions about four feet deep, cut down thin trees to make an overhead cover and filled up about thirty sandbags to put onto the roof. It was a horrendously difficult task. The end of a day long murderous hump was a back-breaking task of making a fighting position. We set up the mortar and ran out the aiming stakes. Then we got a fire mission to shoot a white phosphorus round about two hundred meters out. The forward air observer wanted a registration round to mark on his map in case we needed air support later and a "Willie Peter" out into the bush should shake up any VC who might be planning an attack.

The WP rounds were about the largest rounds that we carried. We had high explosive rounds and parachute flare rounds also, they ranged in weight from about nine to fifteen pounds each. I dropped the WP round in, it slid down and blasted off but it didn't sound right at all. The round went up into the air about a hundred feet and then came right back down, landing about ten feet from the gun. It did not explode, either because it was a dud or it was not ejected from the tube with enough energy to dis-engage the internal safety pin, which would have been due to a defective round or because it landed on relatively soft earth so that it didn't mechanically split open.

I just stood there staring at that round on the ground, wondering why it hadn't just split open upon impact, where the mere exposure of its contents to air would have caused an explosion of that hellish chemical and horribly killed the entire gun crew. Then I realized that I should get away from it because it could still go off at any time. After about five minutes a guy picked it up very, very gingerly and slowly and gently carried it off into the jungle about a hundred feet from our position. That thing was truly something that I wouldn't want to touch with a ten-foot pole, actually, I'd hate to touch it with a hundred foot pole.

The next day we began our search and destroy mission again. Now it was very sparse jungle. The trees were thin and spread out, the ground was covered with grass about fifteen inches tall. After a while we got the word that the pointman was encountering trip wires. We did not stop to disarm them, it was just another situation where the pointman pointed at the wire to the man behind him, and that man then stepped over the wire and turned to the man in back of him and pointed and so on down every soldier in the line. We were encountering a tripwire about every five or ten minutes for the next half-hour. For some reason, word was then passed down the line that I, personally, was to come to the front of the line and be the pointman.

In all the time that I had been in Viet Nam I don't think that I had ever been the pointman and I thought that this was not a good time to become one. I walked quickly up to the front of the line and started to walk relatively slowly, looking for the black trip wires that might be hidden in the grass in front of me. At the same time, I had to search the jungle far ahead and the grass to the left and right out for a distance for anyone waiting in ambush. Plus, I had to look closely downwards directly in front of me for any trip wires. After about ten minutes I started thinking that the VC probably put those trip wires up deliberately in this area so that when we tripped one, the VC would launch an ambush or hit us with mortars and when we tried to move out to seek cover we would be hit with consecutive tripwire claymores or grenades.

The immediate area was wide open and I feared that snipers in the far off tree line would commence fire on us at any second. So, I decided to speed up the pace of the march, our best bet would be to get into the tree line of the jungle ahead because we were fairly exposed to fire from the heavy jungle all around us about two hundred yards away. I really hated to go faster and make everyone behind me that much more burdened and abused by their loads but I figured that the immediate dangers called for that.

After about five minutes there was some shouting from behind me which I took to be something very significant because, as exposed as we were, if we were not spotted by the enemy there's no reason at all to advertise our presence with yelling. Word was passed up to me to stop. After a few minutes a guy came up to me and said that I had walked over a trip wire, and the next two guys in line had done the same. I found that hard to believe and walked back about sixty feet to see for myself. A guy pointed it out to me but I still could not see it. Eventually, he pointed his finger and said, "See, its right here, an inch from my finger". When I looked closely and squinted my eyes I could finally barely see it. The wire was black and extremely thin, the others had been much thicker. I resumed being pointman after some various comments and criticisms from the other guys.

I decided to slow down and look very, very carefully down in front of me but after about five minutes there was again a low shout from behind me. The same situation

had occurred. I had somehow managed to step over a trip wire without tripping it off. I had been extremely diligent in my search but had still missed it. Again I took the point, resolving to be extraordinarily watchful but after another hundred feet the same thing happened. I walked back to examine it, to maybe determine how I had possibly missed seeing it. The wire was black but very thick, two stranded like an electrical lamp cord. Maybe it was a communication wire, or a trip wire, or both. It was stretched very taut and attached to a grenade about ten feet away. I don't know why or how I had missed seeing that one. I had again somehow not spotted the trip wire and somehow not tripped it but had stepped over it, or maybe I did trip it and the trap malfunctioned. Anyways, the Sergeant was outraged by my performance and I was ordered to resume my original place near the back of the line and someone else became the pointman. The screaming Sergeant told me that I would never, ever, be on point again. That was more than fine with me. I don't think that we encountered any more tripwires that day.

The next day we were humping through relatively heavy jungle when the word was passed to hold up the line for about ten minutes. We got the word that they were calling in a medivac chopper for a guy who just joined the unit in the field about two days ago. Word was that he was in very bad shape due to heat stroke. I could see this humping killing someone and began to wonder why most of us never succumbed to it. This guy being evacuated must be a raw recruit straight over from the States, but in retrospect, it might well have been a heart attack or stroke. I wondered many times how I could push myself more than two more steps before I had a heart attack or stroke at nineteen years old.

We almost never had enough food or especially water. I cannot explain why I never heard of anyone else in my company falling victim to heat stroke or heat exhaustion. One explanation is that many of us probably did suffer from those maladies to some degree, but you just had to drive on, one foot in front of the other, in a hotter and more humid environment than most people have ever encountered or imagined and with an impossible load of equipment on your back. In retrospect, I think that some of the times that we were told to stay in place for five minutes was probably due to a trooper being medi-evacked due to heat stroke somewhere along the line of march.

One of the rules was that if someone dropped out, the other men in his squad had to hump his equipment. That kept you going and going. You didn't want to ever make life even more miserable, if that was possible, for your brothers in arms. Myself and probably everyone in my Company would rather die than to do that. The problem was that was not a sentiment uttered by a philosopher in an ivory tower. It was a very real possibility that a trooper might well lose his life to heat stroke but would do it rather than cause further misery and torture to his brothers. The suffering was unimaginable.

After a few hours we encountered terrain as we had the day before, relatively open space. I sat down as the line stopped for a few minutes and then noticed behind me and to the left there was wire on the ground. This one looked like ordinary black lamp cord. It wasn't stretched tightly so I figured it was probably not a trip wire, but it could be attached to a claymore mine or it could be commo cord for an enemy landline telephone. I stood up and began to slowly follow its course, it was well hidden in the grass but every five feet or so I could make out a bit of it. I followed it for about seventy feet, where it entered a tangle of bushes. I really didn't want to pursue its course any further. I thought that it might well be attached to a telephone and if so it might well be protected by a trip wire explosive in front of it or be manned by a team of VC that could just be waiting to kill a curious American. So I returned to my previous position, sat down and dug my feet into the earth. I took up the slack of it and then with both hands I pulled on that wire as hard as I could. It was attached securely somewhere. I jerked it violently a few more times with all of my strength but it didn't move.

OK. Now its time to investigate what was going on. I stood up with the wire in my hands and followed it. After about a hundred feet it was wrapped around a small tree a few times and then trailed off into the jungle again. I walked another twenty feet but didn't want to get into the jungle too far, I was already way too far from the main line and was risking being shot by other guys in the line who wouldn't know that I was rummaging around out there. I pulled on the line very violently but it was attached to something again, further into the jungle. I tried as hard as I could to break the line but it was too strong to break.

I cut it with my bayonet and coiled it up as I walked back to my original position. I gathered it all up into a jumble and began to stab it over and over again with my bayonet, chipping insulation off of it and shorting out the dual wires so that hopefully that wire couldn't be used again. I must have appeared to be a total maniac to other guys around me who couldn't realize what I was doing.

The next day we were given the daily briefing in the morning. We would be humping four thousand meters. Of course that was four thousand meters on a straight line on a map. That did not include any small mountains that we might have to climb or any streams that we might have to cross and it certainly did not include any zig-zagging that was necessary due to the terrain or done just to search more territory or for other tactical reasons. We humped through relatively light jungle until about two O'clock when word was passed down to me to begin to estimate how far we are traveling. I knew approximately how many steps I needed to take to cover a hundred yards on flat land, so now I began to count my steps, realizing that it would just be an approximation.

I had discovered in Advanced Infantry Training how many steps I needed to cover a hundred yards, but realized that I couldn't know for sure how many steps it takes to cover a hundred yards walking through the jungle with all of the heavy weight that we carried, stepping over vines and walking around trees and bushes. I figured that we had already humped about twenty five hundred meters so we should only have about fifteen hundred meters more to go. I passed the word up the line after I estimated that we had covered another five hundred meters. Then the word came back down the line to me to send up the count every two hundred meters. And so it went for the next two hours when the word came down to stop passing up the count. I figured that we must be very close now, in fact I estimated that we had humped five thousand meters altogether.

About an hour later word came down to pass up the count. I passed up the word that I had stopped counting. I thought that they wanted me to stop counting, but they wanted just for me to stop passing up the word every two hundred meters. I don't think that that situation went over very well with the Company commander. Word came down to me to estimate the distance since the last count. I really didn't know with any accuracy at all, but passed up that my best guess was fifteen hundred meters. Now I began to suspect that we were either lost, or the Captain had received orders on the radio to proceed to a location that was different from what we had been told in the morning.

We proceeded further and I noticed that the sun was getting low in the sky. We needed about an hour to dig our night positions and it looked like we had less than that until sunset and we were not even at the proper location yet. After humping another twenty minutes we encountered a rice paddy and we began to cross it. After I was into the paddy for about fur feet, the line stopped. I couldn't see any reason to stop, because I could see the pointman a hundred yards ahead and there were no obstructions. We never stopped in a paddy because we were completely exposed out there. I saw a spot nearby where a mud dike had crumbled and sloped down into the water. I moved over to there and sat down, resting my pack on the dike and managing to only have my lower legs in the water. The other guys were just sitting in the water, with their backs against a dike, with water nearly up to their necks.

Then I noticed a little island of sorts in the paddy. It had a number of medium sized trees on it and it rose up four feet above the water level of the paddy. There were a group of men over there taking off their packs. Then the word came down that we would spend the night exactly where we were. That was just beyond imagination. Why would we possibly spend the night without benefit of digging night fighting positions and completely exposed to enemy attack in the middle of a rice paddy? Men would have to sleep sitting in filthy water up to their necks. At night they would be

very cold and they would have quarts of blood sucked out by leechs before the sun came up after a particularly agonizingly long night of misery.

Most of us were still in a line of march formation. We didn't have a perimeter of any kind. Whatever the reason, that is what we did. I was very lucky at having grabbed the spot where the dike had crumbled because I could lay down, although at a sloping angle. Plus, I had brought my air mattress. After blowing it up half of it was on the sloping dike and the other half floated in the water so it would keep my entire body out of the water. I took out my poncho liner and wrapped it around me. I realized that I was "golden" as they said and quickly fell asleep, feeling very sorry for the misery that most of the other men in the Company would have to endure that night.

The next day immediately after dawn we began to move out. The men who had been on that island must have slept well, being completely out of the water on relatively flat land. Those men were the Company Commander and his entourage. What an absolute outrage that he had gotten us lost and subjected his men to a night of absolute misery in a very exposed position while he had remained dry and warm. We humped out of the paddy and into the jungle for about three hours when word came down the line asking if anyone had seen the Company Commanders personal weapon, a mini M-16. No one had and the next thing we knew, we did an about face and humped another three hours back to our previous nights position. The Captain went over to his little island and looked all around but couldn't find his weapon.

Now, we started the mission again. Now we would never have time to achieve our objective for the day and that Captain had subjected his entire Company to an unnecessary six hours of humping because he forgot to take his weapon with him in the morning. Our first Captain, for the first six months, was a good guy who was always on the ground humping with his men. He was brave and extremely competent, this new Captain was something else.

We started humping again but this time we seemed to take a slightly different route, maybe we were to set up a night position in a different place than the one planned earlier that day. We came out of the jungle into a more open territory. I was about fifteen men back from the pointman when I spotted something about a hundred feet to my front left. There were two thin trees about ten feet tall and about ten feet apart. Between those trees was a spider web about four feet tall and ten feet wide, with the strands about two inches apart. In the middle was the biggest spider I had ever seen, or could have imagined. It must be some kind of unknown species I thought. It was pitch black and had two red fangs that were so big that I could easily see them from a hundred feet away. The body was probably about six inches in diameter and its length from the tip of one leg to the tip of an opposite leg was probably two feet. I thought that it would take a lot of flies for that thing to feed every day. Then I thought,

obviously it was catching birds or snakes or something in that huge web. Its prey had to be more than three inches thick to be even caught between any strands of its web. I thought that if I had been the pointman and we had to go through that area I would have shot that thing. It would have been bad to shoot it because the gunshot would have alerted any enemy in the area, but I hated to think of the idea of that thing jumping on someone with its huge poisonous fangs. We passed by it about fifteen feet away. I had my weapon pointed directly at it for as long as I could see it.

Eventually we arrived at a place to set up our night position. They used to refer to it as a "lager" site, I never knew what the word "lager" meant. I had brought a hammock with me on this operation that had a built-in tent and mosquito netting. It was extra weight and I had not had an opportunity to use it until this night where I found two trees of appropriate thickness and distance between them to be able to set it up. It seemed to be a good idea to bring that piece of equipment. I wouldn't have to sleep on the ground and I could adjust the netting so that it would be completely impenetrable and it would provide shelter from the rain. After an hour of trying to sleep, it was really very uncomfortable, lying in a long "U" shape, plus, it was off the ground and if we took fire or an attack at night I would wish to be as close to the ground as possible.

I finally got up and disconnected it from the tree. It was too late to set up a poncho tent and I had no sticks to make stakes for it anyways, plus this was no time to be making noise hammering in the stakes. So, I put the hammock on the ground and pulled the netting around me, which wouldn't help too much because it was now touching my clothing and skin and just fell asleep with that arrangement. I never carried that hammock on any further operations. I suppose that that hammock/tent was the result of a considerable amount of research and development. The concept looked excellent on paper but in this environment it just didn't work. Every man in my Company had been issued that piece of equipment but almost no one ever brought it out on an operation.

I had obtained a large plastic bag from someone and had placed my 35mm half-frame camera in it the night before, hoping to keep any rain off of it. Now in the morning, I noticed the bag was filled with condensation. The inside of the bag was soaking wet, as was the camera. It didn't work properly and forever afterwards the shutter would lock up at low light levels. This environment was so damp and humid that you couldn't even keep something dry inside of a sealed up plastic bag.

A soldier in my platoon had a motion picture camera for making home movies. I think that he was the only person with that because they were so expensive. Every once in a while, if he could, he would take some quick shots of his surroundings. He would catch glimpses of jets dropping high-explosives or napalm or get a shot of the

helicopters going in for an assault landing or maybe the mortar being fired or "dust-off" choppers coming in to pick up the wounded. He then sent the reels of film home to his family. After a few months the local television station heard of those tapes and began broadcasting them. The guy said that he was from a small town.

About an hour into our hump through the jungle on the next morning, I noticed about forty pieces of paper on the jungle floor, most of them were brightly colored yellow. I was trying to decide how that paper came to be way out here. As I examined one that hadn't been too damaged by rain, it seemed to be some sort of propaganda leaflet from the US. I think that it implored the enemy to surrender, that they would be treated well, and to use that leaflet as their "ticket", to be presented to Allied forces. On other operations I would see many of these leaflets, in very many varieties of different colors and pictures and wording. Aircraft dropped them over areas of suspected enemy infiltration or along their supply routes.

We were on patrol for about four hours, humping through heavy jungle when I heard a half-scream behind me. A new Lieutenant vigorously wriggled around standing, like he was having some sort of epileptic fit. He slapped hard at his neck and face and then grabbed his rucksack and tore it off of his body. He had a look of horror and shock and I had no idea what had happened to him until he tore off his lbg and then his shirt. Then I could see hundreds of red fire ants swarming over his back and neck and head and face. Directly above him was a number of large green leaves that had been stuck together into roughly the shape of a bee hive, that was the ants nest. jmm

Half of it had been torn open, probably by the Lieutenants gear. A couple of guys near him just started laughing at the Lieutenants antics, knowing full well what was happening, and finally one guy rushed a few steps forward and started to brush off the Lieutenants back. Other nearby soldiers stepped back smartly, knowing full well that they certainly didn't want an army of stinging ants to bite them. The Lieutenant looked around at the laughing men, wide-eyed with shock, and pathetically beseeched those soldiers to tell him what was happening to him. He was being stung by hundreds of fire ants, a situation that he had probably never before encountered or even heard of, back in the World. One of the laughing guys said "Lieutenant!, you've just been "baptized!", Welcome to the jungle!".

It was a nest of fire ants. They were not in every area of Viet Nam but they were very prevalent in some areas. Almost every man had already encountered them the hard way or had seen someone else get it and everyone knew to be very careful around them. A soldier had to be on the alert for many enemy and explosive dangers but we all knew, from previous bad experiences, to look out for fire ant nests in the trees.

Bumping into one was like breaking open a nest of bees. The ants were medium-sized and a brownish-red in color with outsized little pincers on their head. While sitting during a break in the hump one day, I picked up one of them and put it on my

hand in an experiment to determine just how something that small could inflict such a painful little bite. I noticed that the ant would not bite the palm or back of my hand, the skin was too tough. The ant would run directly to the web of tender skin between my fingers and bite down. Then he would shake his head vigorously, trying to dig in his pincers deeper or to try to rip out a bit of skin. I also noticed that he extruded an unusually large amount of some kind of clear liquid from his mouth. It must have been that liquid that put the "fire" into fire ants. The pain was something less than a bee sting, but if you hit a nest they would instantly drop upon you and you might have a hundred or more of them start biting you. The fact is that they are venomous and tend to attack in swarms of up to five thousand, they are extremely aggressive if disturbed. It was something to be avoided. The nests were fairly easy to spot if you were really looking for them, but during heavy humping they were easily missed, especially in heavy undergrowth.

At the beginning of this operation we were all issued flak jackets, as some sort of experiment. These are rather heavy vests actually. They would not stop an enemy bullet but were supposed to provide some protection against shrapnel, say from a grenade. I think that the Marines wore them all the time while on bush operations but they seemed to me to be much more trouble than they were worth. They probably weighed ten pounds or so, which just added a thousand pounds of agony to our already absurdly heavy loads. They were also about an inch and a half thick which did not allow any sweat to evaporate from the part of the body that they covered. The end of this operation would mark the end of this experiment and we would never use them in the jungle again.

Towards late afternoon, while pushing through the bush, as usual with every ounce of strength, just trying to keep up, looking downwards mostly. I looked up and saw a big animal on the trail, about five feet from me. I was shocked and dismayed because I had been struggling so mightily, I didn't even see that animal until it was so close. I was dismayed that I didn't have the psychological bearing to have not thrown down the barrel of the mortar and bring my M-16 to bear on it instantly. The other guys, some only ten feet from me, had obviously seen it and seemed to ignore it, but I thought that it was very strange, with its long hair in that jungle scene.

It took a few more seconds for me to finally realize that it was a dog, a German Shepard. I didn't recognize it immediately because it was hanging its head so low that I couldn't even see its face. That dog was so exhausted that it didn't even know what it was doing anymore. Then I spotted a soldier who was walking in the opposite direction to our line of march. He was an MP, a Military Policeman, and it was his dog. The dog had been walking all day and was now just walking around aimlessly and oblivious to its trainers voice. The MP stopped the dog and checked him out, then picked him up and started to carry him. We brought MPs with us on some operations, they were supposed to handle civilians or prisoners and their dogs were supposed to

detect booby traps and go down tunnels. I don't know, I never saw the MPs or their dogs do any of those things but on most operations there could have been a dinosaur a hundred feet in front of me for the entire mission and I would have never seen it.

An infantrymans world in the bush usually consisted of only perhaps the two or three people in front of him and the two or three men behind him. A country boy told me about five minutes later that, "A man can never outrun a dog but he can easily out walk one". I saw MPs on several other occasions carrying their dogs, especially towards the end of the day. The heat and humidity must have been very hard on the dogs, especially with their fur, but at least they didn't have to carry any very heavy equipment like the soldiers I thought.

As the day progressed, I noticed again that it was getting late, very late. We were still humping when the sun finally set. Obviously we were lost again. We never went on patrol at night, it was just too dangerous. A person couldn't see any booby traps and the noise of a hundred men bulling through the undergrowth would be loud enough for any enemy to hear us coming with plenty of warning and plenty of time to throw up a hasty ambush.

The line started to bunch up because of the darkness. The combat interval between soldiers of thirty feet reduced down to three feet away from the man in front and in back of you. At any more distance a soldier would loose track of the line of march of men. I knew that within a few minutes a soldier would literally not be able to see his hand in front of his face. The word came down the line to stop in place. Then a few minutes later the word came down that we would spend the night exactly in the spots that each of us occupied at that moment. This again was an absurd situation. There would be no fighting positions, no time for that. We were completely vulnerable to attack and we didn't even have room to set up the mortar. We were probably lost, I thought, and if that was so we couldn't call in any artillery or air support or resupply or medivac. Because of the extremely dense vegetation we couldn't even set up poncho covers for the night. That situation was not only extremely dangerous but it was also an extremely cold and uncomfortable situation. Luckily it didn't rain that night nor did the VC in the area know exactly where we were and hit us with mortar fire.

Early in the morning, before the sun came up, all of us were awake and in any type of defensive position or behind any type of cover that we could find, anticipating a dawn attack. About fifteen minutes after dawn, we got the word that we would move out immediately, we wouldn't have time to eat or make a cup of coffee. I guess that someone finally realized the vulnerability of our situation and there would be no delay in getting out of that location as soon as possible. We humped out, eventually coming upon an area in the jungle where there were two or three large tents set up around noon time. It was some sort of BSOP, a battalion forward resupply base. A BSOP is usually a very little affair with five or fewer men, with boxes of ammo and food and some clothes and equipment. This one was very different. It was obviously very secure because they had set up some pipes for showers. They actually had barrels of hot water heated by gasoline and pumped upwards to the showerheads. It was a setup where maybe ten men at a time could take a shower. Someone had the excellent idea to just walk into the showers with their clothes on and try to get some of the dirt and sweat off of them but that didn't work too well. So then we took off our clothes and took a shower, then put on the soaking wet, still filthy clothes. They actually had some warm soda and beer there. Most people didn't bring money out on an operation because there would be no place to spend it, but I always brought some along on the rare chance that there may be something to buy.

I bought a beer for myself and a few other guys in my squad, then a few of us got another. My squad Sergeant looked at me with some sort of disgust or distain. I don't know whether that was because we were drinking beer or because no one offered to lend him any money to get one. He never asked and I never offered.

We went back on patrol after about a two hour rest and humped for another four hours to reach our night site. Whatever filth that we had managed to wipe off with the shower had mostly come upon us again. We humped for another day and on the morning of the next day about ten trucks came to our site and we loaded up for the return convoy to base camp. The backs of the trucks had a wooden framework over which there was canvas to serve as an overhead and sideways enclosure. On those trucks the sides were rolled up so that we could see what was going on as we went down the road. There were a number of flak jackets in the back of the truck so all of us put our rucksacks on the sandbagged floor and put on the jackets.

There were about fifteen men in each truck and four men, one in each corner, had to stand up for the duration of the ride. They were guards and had to be especially vigilant. I was ordered to be one of them so I stood at the left rear of the truck bed with my weapon and a few bandoliers and lbg but at least I could leave my rucksack on the floor. We started going through small villages with simple dirt-floored huts made of cardboard and recycled tin. Someone had a radio and the occupants were listening to rock and roll. Some guy was talking about a good recipe that he had with grape juice and vodka. I asked him if I could get some of that when we got back. He said no problem. We would be back in base camp within two hours if we weren't ambushed or blown up with a mine and I was really looking forward to getting some food and then get some booze and go downtown and then get some sleep.

The sun was blazing in a cloudless sky but the canvas roof of the truck provided excellent shade. As we rode there was a strong breeze and it felt good, it felt comfortable, something that I had not felt at all during this operation. I looked ahead a hundred yards and spotted about five men in civilian clothes carrying weapons and packs. They were mixed among the civilians, walking on the very edge of the road, our trucks passing them by only a foot or so away. I think that they came from behind a house and were going to cross the road when they noticed at the last minute the MP jeep with a machine gun on it leading the convoy of trucks behind it.

The moment I spotted them I leaned over the side of the truck and casually let the muzzle of my weapon come to bear upon them but withheld my fire. We usually had strict orders not to fire unless fired upon and there were other civilians around anyways. The first three trucks passed them, then ours. I figured they must not be VC if they are not running or firing. I thought that they must be the local civilian defense force. Just as I passed them, I gave them a little wave and some of them were clearly surprised but after a few seconds some of them waved back and as I continued on, I could see them waving to the following trucks. About two minutes later we heard on the radio that those supposed civilians had fired on the last truck in the convoy and there were American casualties. I thought that the guys in that last truck were probably like me, happy and comfortable a minute ago, and now suddenly their world changed and they were shot up. The word was that the Americans had replied devastatingly upon that little enemy group.

We finally arrived at the base camp. When we got off of the trucks, we were ordered to stand in formation on the Company street, with all of our equipment. We had to wait around for about thirty minutes in the full sun while all of the trucks arrived. The Company commander came out and told us if we needed ammo or supplies or clothes to go directly to the supply hooch before going back to our platoon hoochs. He said that we would be going out on another operation in five hours. We all looked at each other, wondering if we had heard him correctly. There was a brief consultation with some senior NCOs and then the Captain repeated his remark, we would be going out again, in five hours. What a nightmare, beyond a nightmare.

Chapter 24

OPERATION NEWARK
April 26-30 WAR ZONE "D"

Will yearly on the vigil feast his neighbours,
And say 'To-morrow is Saint Crispian:'
Then will he strip his sleeve and show his scars.
And say 'These wounds I had on Crispin's day.'
Old men forget: yet all shall be forgot,
But he'll remember with advantages
What feats he did that day:

Shakespeare

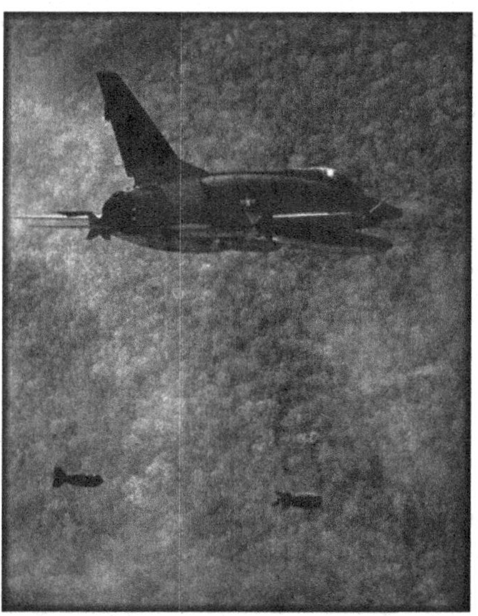

Jet Aircraft Dropping High Explosive Ordinance

We made our assault by helicopter. When I landed on the second flight of choppers into the landing zone, I could see a low-lying bank of smoke in the middle of a large rice paddy next to where we landed. Obviously a chopper had come in low to lay down a smoke screen to cover our landing to some extent. As the choppers lifted off and their noise lessened, I could barely make out the sound of gunfire about a hundred yards ahead of me. I looked over in that general direction and then saw as the smoke dissipated on the rice paddy that there were VC in the open, carrying a small mortar.

The lead Company was firing on them and, I think, other VC in the jungle at the edge of the paddy. I couldn't stay around to watch because my platoon was already moving out, in the opposite direction from the enemy. We had a predetermined plan and direction and order of march.

We were carrying extra mortar rounds and walking through light vegetation for a while and were sweating profusely. Some guys carried a green towel around their necks to keep the fire ants off and to wipe the perspiration from their eyes but I never did that. I figured that the discomfort of a bunch of ants possibly biting was less than the added, constant discomfort of not having as much of your skin exposed as possible, to help cool you down. The river of sweat sometimes ran into my eyes but then I just rubbed it away with my hand. Anyways, once the sweat started, it would run in little rivers away from your eyes if you drew a line on your face with your fingers so as to direct the river of sweat to follow a line away from your eyes.

The sweat started on your forehead and then there would be some sweat under your arms. Then the front of your shirt would be soaked with sweat and soon thereafter your back as well, I would imagine, but could not see because of the rucksacks. Then you might notice that the rolled up sleeves of your shirt were completely saturated with sweat at about the time you notice that there is a large amount of sweat around your belt. Then, the top of your pants and pockets would be wet and then your knees for some strange reason. Eventually all of your pants would be thoroughly saturated and there would be a swishing sensation in your boots as the sweat pooled in your boots. The boots each had two small brass fittings in them, something like small screens, to allow drainage if you crossed a stream, which didn't quite work very well but was good for draining out most of the water after a creek crossing. A man in this environment and under such heavy loads sweated more than could have been imagined in civilian life, a lot more than I had ever seen anywhere. This was not a situation where a person might be a bit embarrassed by some perspiration under their arms. This was a situation where a man was thoroughly soaked from the top of his head to the bottom of his boots with quarts of sweat.

Eventually we came to a creek with steep banks. The head of the line had some combat engineers with them and they had knocked down a large tree with explosives to form a bridge for us to cross. Other men before me had already crossed but I thought it looked rather chancy because although the tree was probably three feet in diameter, it was perfectly round and the area on top of it on which your boot would make contact was very small. I would not have tried to cross over it in civilian life but now we had to negotiate it with full gear and equipment. As soon as I crossed with the barrel of the mortar, someone told me to stay there near a particular tree and then continued ordering other men out of the line to stand with me. Eventually I could see that he was pulling out the men of my squad, the men with the three parts of the mortar and other guys with extra ammo. We just waited there for about ten minutes as the other guys in the line of march crossed the tree bridge. Some of them noticed our little group and they started laughing and pointing at us. We eventually asked them what was so funny, and they said, obviously you are the guys who fell off of the bridge. I asked them why they thought that and they said its obvious, you guys are all soaking wet, from head to toe.

Someone said, "Hey, we're the mortar platoon" and the expression on their faces changed instantly. They said, "You mean you didn't fall off the bridge?" but they suddenly knew the answer and suddenly realized why it looked like we fell into the creek. Actually, I think that they at first laughed mostly out of anxiety. They must have known that if someone fell off of that bridge into that creek that it would be extremely difficult to get them out and that the weight of the equipment on a man in a fast deep creek might very well drown him before he could try to shrug out of all of his equipment. Every step a trooper took could be the last one of his life in this world and men were taking that last step almost every day.

The next morning we got our daily briefing and daily password. Most of the time I could never remember the password. This morning, we were told, curiously, that we had a chance to make out or modify our last will and testament and that a resupply chopper would carry them out today to headquarters. We had already made out our official last wills and I couldn't think of any reason that a man would find it suddenly urgent to make an amendment to his will. We were in the thick of it now, we were all lucky to still be alive and no one could be certain that he would be alive for another five minutes. There were many, many ways to die in Viet Nam and a lot of men who would survive this experience would see every one of them up close and personal, if not to themselves than to their friends.

We humped around for another few days when we got the word over the radio that some guys in part of our Battalion had found part of a .50 caliber machine gun. That was the main purpose of this mission. The VC had been shooting at helicopters with that .50 and that could not be allowed to stand. A .50 would blow a chopper out of the air very easily. The guys did not actually find the machine gun itself but they found an apparatus that the machine-gun attaches to. It was a regulation Anti-Aircraft device that mounted on a tripod and had large semi-circular pieces into which the operator fit his shoulders, specifically made for bringing down aircraft. Capturing that would make it much more difficult for the enemy to bring down a chopper. With a slight smile of satisfaction and sympathy, I thought of those VC trying to run away with that big machine gun. The weight and substance of that weapon alone could be enough to kill them, trying to hump that thing at full retreat through the jungle I thought.

Later that afternoon we arrived at our night position and dug in. We were on the edge of a rice paddy, in heavy jungle. About a hundred yards from me was a little circular island maybe fifty feet wide with some tall trees on it out in the paddy. It looked like it was connected to land by a narrow spit of dry earth. I decided that if I had time after setting up that I would walk over there and check it out. I was just about finished digging in and setting up a poncho tent when there was a loud noise for about a quarter of a second followed immediately by a powerful shock wave of an explosion emanating it seemed directly from that little island.

I knew right away that it was artillery, our artillery. There was some commotion and after a few minutes we got the word that it was a short round. When a round is fired from a mortar or cannon, it can fail in certain ways such that it will fall short of its target. If they are firing at the enemy, over the heads of friendly forces, a short round can then easily kill or maim the very soldiers that it was designed to protect.

After they seemed to get the situation sorted out via the radio, someone said "Where's Pauley?" That question went up and down the line around the perimeter. Someone said that they thought that he had walked over to that island and a few guys went running out to it. There was a bit of some kind of commotion on the island for a few minutes, I couldn't make out what was happening. Then I could see the guys carrying back a body. Pauley had decided to do what I was going to do and that short artillery round had killed him.

The next morning the officers had been given paper copies of new orders from headquarters, I don't know whether it was from Brigade headquarters or higher up. They instructed the officers not to take unnecessary chances. That they should not be at the front of the line of march and in case of contact with the enemy that they should seek cover immediately. The reasoning was that the men would need their leaders alive to effectively mount a defense or assault. There were four Lieutenants all sitting around me and a few other low level Enlisted men. They read those instructions aloud and started discussing it amongst themselves. One of the Lieutenants asked us what we thought of it. I didn't much like it at all for some reason, even though the reasoning seemed sound. I just said that I didn't really know.

As they continued to discuss the orders they reasoned that since they were leaders, their motto is "follow me". (actually that is the motto of Infantry leaders) They said that they would not ask their men to do anything that they themselves would not do.

They said that their job was to lead by example and their place was where it was most dangerous. One of them rolled up his paper and threw it away. One of the others told him to keep it, that they shouldn't be allowing any official orders or instructions to be found by the enemy. One of them suggested that they tear them up or burn them when another said that he was keeping his in his pocket. When asked why, he replied that he was low on toilet paper anyways. Of course that was not the real reason. He was so contemptuous of the order that he was literally going to wipe his ass with it. They all thought that that was an excellent idea and they walked away to join their respective platoons, all with their orders in their pockets. A splendid group of men I thought. A magnificent group of human beings and Officers. I was proud of them. True American heros in the finest traditions of Airborne Infantry.

Later that day, while humping past some tall bamboo and tall trees with vines on them, out of nowhere there was a huge roar extremely close overhead followed immediately by extremely loud machine gun fire and "Pit, Pit, Pit" sounds all around. The "Pit" sounds were exactly like that made by bullets hitting the trees and ground very close by. There was also something actually falling from the sky, hundreds of heavy things, crashing through the foliage and landing all around us and on top of us.

I was very confused at first until I finally figured it out. A jet plane had come out of nowhere, flying at top speed about a hundred feet high directly over us while firing his 20mm Gatling gun cannon. The "Pit" sounds were the very large brass shells being ejected that rained down through the trees and directly upon us, each one easily capable of inflicting bad causalities if not death due to their velocity and weight. I wondered what he was firing at, what ever it was it was obviously extremely close to us. I really hoped that he wasn't targeting Americans by accident.

When everything had happened so unexpectedly and violently it had startled me badly and I thought that that was very unusual because I seemed to have lost my startle response. Most people develop a hyperactive startle response after duty like this I am told, but my reaction was becoming just the opposite I had thought. Of course, a plane flying 100 feet over you at 400 mph, firing its huge automatic cannons, with no warning whatsoever, might give almost anyone a jolt, the noise of the jet engine alone was like an explosion followed immediately by a rain of death and destruction.

We humped on for another two hours or so, each man keeping his interval. You could go all day without talking to anyone, you could go for many days, even weeks, without saying much at all to anyone. Each man was an island unto himself. I don't know what used to keep my mind occupied or much of what I used to think about. Most of my mind was occupied in searching the flanks for enemy activity and struggling with my pack and equipment, thinking, "Just a bit further, just a bit further, just put one foot in front of the other, keep up, keep up, don't have a heart attack, maybe we'll stop in a minute or so". It was without exaggeration just pure agony.

We were walking through medium jungle now, with vines on the trees and very heavy undergrowth. Suddenly I realized that we were walking on a dry creek bed. There were relatively steep banks on both sides, the creek bed being about twenty feet wide. There was a concentration of big bushes growing just in the creek bed, about eight feet tall and ten feet wide and we had to walk in a ziz-zag fashion around them as we moved upstream.

Out of nowhere there was a huge roar and I caught a glimpse of something white or metallic flash by about eighty feet directly overhead at an incredible speed and a split second later the entire area was saturated with very heavy things falling all around us, directly on top of us. I noticed some strange objects on the ground, obviously some of the things that had just fallen on top of us. I picked up one of them that was near my feet. It was green and weighed about two or three pounds. It was about the size of a grapefruit. On the top of it was a strange silver device that looked like four flattened little windmill blades. I asked, to no one in particular, what those things were. One of the guys said it was a butterfly bomb. A large number of them are placed in a canister. The canister opens and fifty or a hundred bombs are dropped. Under the right conditions one master canister could destroy a battalion.

That pilot had spotted our line of march, mistook us for the enemy and directly and expertly and accurately hit us with a load of cluster bombs. Every one of the hundred or so men in the line of march should have been blasted to pieces. That pilot had made a perfect attack on us but, for some reason, none of the bomblets had exploded.

The little blades flutter and spin while they are falling. It's a safety device so that if the pilot unloads his ordinance too close to the ground then the bombs won't explode and bring down his own aircraft with their shrapnel. When they are released, they have to fall a certain distance, with the little blades whirring in the air for a certain number of revolutions until they are fully armed. I thought that they didn't explode because they had landed on the heavy bushes but some of them must have struck the ground directly. Either they were defective, or, more likely, the pilot had dropped them at such a low altitude that the safety devices didn't have time to arm. I'm very surprised that some of them didn't directly hit soldiers because at least four of them landed within twenty feet of me. I don't know for sure why they did not explode, but if they had there would not have been even one man who was not at least terribly wounded or blasted apart.

Apparently every radioman in the Company called in an emergency "cease fire". Another plane flew very close to us thirty seconds later but apparently he had gotten the word to break off the attack at the last possible moment and didn't release his ordinance onto us.

The word was passed down the line for someone to throw a smoke grenade to mark our position. Immediately there were about forty grenades thrown all up and down the line, of all colors, with a resulting massive cloud of white and green and yellow and red and purple smoke. The word was then passed that there was just too much smoke, that the pilots couldn't determine for certain what color it was supposed to be. I think the Air Force was told not to attack anywhere there is any kind of smoke. The word came down that every tenth man was to pop green smoke. After a while in place, things were sorted out with the Air Force and we continued our march. I wonder what that pilot dreams about these days, knowing that he tried his best to kill a hundred U.S. ground troops but due only to altitude or bad bomblets or bushes or him attacking at too low an altitude or, probably more likely, an act of God, he was unsuccessful.

We carried different colored smoke grenades. Americans used to carry just green smoke but the VC started to make their own so that when the Americans would throw green smoke to mark a target, the VC would throw their own green smoke grenade to confuse the situation. So we eventually got different colors, white, green, red, yellow and purple. We might be instructed to pop green smoke on our position and throw red smoke grenades towards the enemy, or on a large open space that we are using for a night site, we might be instructed to pop yellow smoke for a helicopter coming with supplies and pop purple smoke where we wanted a medivac chopper to land. These grenades had about the same dimensions as a can of soup, about five inches long and three inches in diameter. They had a ring on a cotter pin that held the silver spoon in place. They worked just like a hand grenade except that they did not explode. The pin could be pulled and the grenade dropped a few feet away without any problems.

Unlike a hand grenade, they only had a two second fuse. When they went off, there was a "pop" sound then a sizzling sound as the fuse set the contents on fire. First there would be just a little smoke for the first few seconds but you could see the paint on the outside start to sizzle and burn. It must have been white-hot inside. Then there would be a surprisingly large amount of smoke ejected from the top of the grenade. It would burn for about two or three minutes.

Later that night as we moved into our night position, there was a lot of small open spaces among the trees, we all would be able to find a good place to sleep tonight on the flat grass in those places. I noticed that there were coconut trees very close by with coconuts still on them and some on the ground. Next to them were banana trees with ripe fruit and next to that was a little plot of pineapples. I thought that I would eat well tonight.

A resupply chopper came in to drop off a few guys and some mail. I got a letter from my mother, who usually included a package of Kool-Aid and in this letter was a small 3x5 inch filing card with something printed on it. My father had written that his secretary had found a prayer and had typed it up for me.

It read:

"Prayer to St. Joseph".

> **Oh, St. Joseph, whose protection is so great, so strong, so prompt before the throne of God, I place in your hands all my interests and desires. Oh, St. Joseph, do assist me by your powerful intercession and obtain for me from your divine son all spiritual blessings, through Jesus Christ, our Lord, so that having engaged here below your heavenly power I may offer homage and thanksgiving to you the most loving of fathers. Oh St. Joseph, I never weary of contemplating you and Jesus asleep in your arms. I dare not approach while He reposes near your heart. Press Him in my name and kiss His fine head for me and ask Him to return the kiss when I draw my dying breath. St. Joseph, patron of departing souls, pray for me"**

On the back of the card was these words:

"Whosoever shall read this prayer or hear it or keep it about themselves shall never die a sudden death or be drowned nor shall poison take effect on them, neither shall they fall into the hands of the enemy or shall be burned in any fire or shall be over powered in battle. Say nine mornings for anything you desire. It has never been known to fail".

My mother had already given me a cloth religious medal enclosed in plastic. On one side of it was a picture and the words "Sacred Heart of Jesus I love you. Sacred Heart of Jesus thy kingdom come".

I wore that on my dog tag chain, between my two dog tags.

I couldn't send back a letter because I had left my envelopes back at base camp. I had obtained a new type of envelope that had two flaps that sealed when they were pressed together. Regular envelopes wouldn't work because just the humidity made them useless, they would not seal. Anyways, my writing paper was saturated with water and sweat and I couldn't find my pen.

After I finished my duties I wandered over to the coconut trees and picked up some of the nuts that were on the ground. They were covered with a tough fibrous material and after many unsuccessful attempts to cut it open with my bayonet, I hacked it in half with my entrenching tool. I didn't want to lose any of the coconut milk, but there was none in that nut anyways. The meat was extremely hard and dry. After much trouble I pried a piece out with my knife and put it in my mouth but it had no taste and was very hard, it was inedible.

But the bananas looked good, they were yellow and ripe and there were several large bunches. The fruit was smaller than I was used to but I peeled one and bit into it. It was filled with little tough strings that were impossible to bite through with the remainder of the fruit being soft and mushy and of a strange taste. It was like trying to eat banana flavored Popsicle sticks. Next I tried the pineapples. I had to dig them out of the ground. I cut one open and cut off a slice. I don't think that it was quite ripe because the flesh was very tough and also had a strange taste. The feast of fruit that my body had eagerly anticipated turned out to be thoroughly no good.

We continued the operation the next day or so and then came to a wide-open space with no vegetation at all, just brown-red dirt. It was very close to a small landing strip and we would stay there for an hour and then load up onto a cargo plane. While hanging around there, a guy came over to us and asked if we had any salt. The C-rations usually included a small packet of salt. He said he needed it for his ear. I asked what was wrong with his ear and he said "no, not my ear, this ear" whereupon he pulled some disgusting black dried up object out of his pocket. It was the ear of a killed VC. I think he said that he had a collection of them. He put the ear on the ground in the bright sunlight and sprinkled salt onto it. He said it was to dry it out and to preserve it. It was said that some of the enemy believed that a person could not enter Heaven if his body was not intact. When the enemy found one of their dead with an ear missing the message was not only did we kill your guy, we sent him to Hell as well.

We picked up our gear and moved a few hundred yards towards the landing zone and stayed for a while out in the open under a very hot sun, waiting for the order to get onto the airplane. A guy approached a medic pulled off his equipment and his shirt and had a quick conversation with him. The medic pulled a bottle of something out of his kit bag and began to spread a liberal amount of it on the guys back. Just then, other guys approached the medic and stripped off their shirts and the medic applied the same solution to their bodies. I asked what was going on and the medic pointed to one guy whose back was a bright red, covered with hundreds of little pimples. He said it was prickly heat. I thought that it was very unusual, I had never seen anyone with that ailment before.

Then, suddenly, I felt in intense itchiness and burning on my back, and tore off my equipment and asked a guy behind me to check me out, to see if he sees anything on my back. He said, "Yeah, you have it for sure. Your back is as red as can be". I went over to the medic and as soon as he applied his substance onto my back there was substantial relief from the ailment. I put my equipment back on and started to move out. I thought it a great coincidence that so many people came down with the malady at the same time. I guess it was just the exact combination of sun and temperature and humidity and dirt on our bodies. Maybe it was the sun hitting our backs because we had our rucksacks on the ground. Maybe we all had a bad case of it already, but the sweat and humidity kept it under control. I'm not sure what the answer is but it never happened to me again.

We loaded onto a small cargo plane that had a bulldozer already inside it. It was strapped down well with chains and I guess we were an afterthought. I figured that that aircraft was supposed to only carry that bulldozer on a strictly cargo run and we were added at the last minute. We filed in, and were slowly packed together as tightly as possible, like riding in a crowded subway train. We would all take this ride while standing up, there wasn't enough room for any of us to sit. The aircraft took off and I kept my eye on the hold down chains attached to that bulldozer. That was a very heavy piece of machinery and if those straps broke a lot of us were going to be crushed, in fact, if those straps broke and that bulldozer started to shift it would probably knock the tail of the plane off or crash through the side of the aircraft. It was hot and uncomfortable in that plane with no windows open and no air circulation at all. After a while I started to feel sick, and then sicker. If I had to heave, I would have to do so into my helmet, one of the little tricks they taught us in jump school. At the last possible moment, I could not have held it in for another minute, we suddenly felt a jolt and realized that we were finally on the ground.

We had landed on some dirt runway, some type of little base camp for use mostly by the Air Force. We unloaded and sat in the open for about an hour and then started to move out. After humping our gear a ways on that very primitive airbase, it was getting late so I guessed that we would be spending the night here. We came upon a large tent that was padlocked shut but we could see around the edges that it contained cases of soda and beer. Someone managed to climb under the edge of the tent or cut it open in the back and reported back that it was some kind of PX(Post eXchange) with a counter and a cash register and loaded with many good things. We were told to stay out of it for now and someone contacted the Air Force and asked them to open it for business. The reply was that it was closed for the day and that they didn't want us to buy anything anyways because they only had enough for themselves.

That answer did not go over well with me at all. I cared little for a bunch of flyboys hanging around this little airbase all day. We hadn't had a soda or beer or candy bar in a long time, and we could use the extra nutrition. I told a few guys that I'm going shopping and worked my way under the tent while a couple of guys held up the edge, with great difficulty, while I climbed underneath it. I grabbed some warm cans of Coke and started throwing them outside. Some other guy just walked over to the front of the tent where it was locked up and started working on it with his entrenching tool and soon the front door was open and about six guys went inside. A Lieutenant came along and ordered us out so I grabbed a few packs of cigarettes and candy and cokes and came out and distributed them among my squad. The Lieutenant said there would be hell to pay for this. I thought, the CO can send them a check from the company fund, and what were they going to do to me? Put me in the brig for taking some rear echelon clerks warm cokes and candy bars? Anyways, jail would be far better than this situation, I could really use a few weeks of laying around. The Lieutenant wrote down my name and the name of others involved. We never heard another word about it.

We moved another four hundred yards and set up near the edge of this little air base. There were fighting positions already dug so that would save us some time and trouble. We were told that we would have the next day off, that we would just stay at this place and that we would have a barbeque with steaks and beer. We sat around all day, which was a real luxury. I realized that I had no idea of what day of the week it was. About two hours after dark the stuff arrived and they started up the barbeque, which was supposed to have started much earlier in the day. They asked for volunteers to man some empty positions on the perimeter but no one was game for that. We ate our steaks, which we had to cut with our mess knives, which were filthy, and drank freely from a trailer full of iced soda and beer. None of us drank much beer because we knew that the next day we would be on another mission. I don't know who was on guard duty that night, or if anyone was. We were promised a night of respite and we were all going to insist that we got it.

We moved out the next day, and loaded onto Chinook helicopters to be dropped off on another part of this operation. These were very large helicopters that had a drop down loading ramp at the end of the aircraft and two doors on each side. It had two very large propeller blades that drooped down when there were not spinning. In flight, the blades actually interlocked like a blender. I really did not like riding in a contraption like that because I didn't like the idea of two huge propellers intersecting at high speed. What would happen if they got out of sync? Anyways, they presented a large target and were regarded as unreliable. They could carry heavy payloads and probably up to forty men at a time, but because the aircraft was completely enclosed, we couldn't fire out or get a good view of the landing zone as we assaulted.

We landed without incident and humped for a few days. It looked like it was going to rain at night. I set up a poncho tent with another guy. One poncho was enough to cover two men, and usually one of the men was on perimeter guard anyways. I stretched out the poncho as tightly as possible because the wind was picking up. If the wind became stronger it might blow down the poncho or cause it to flap noisily in the middle of the night so I pounded the makeshift stakes deeper into the ground than I normally would. The ground under the tent was mostly flat but it sloped downwards towards one end. I got my entrenching tool and dug a trench all around the edge of the tent connecting it to another trench that led downwards. The guy with me had never seen that and I explained that the rain would run off of the edge of the tent, go into the trench and hopefully drain away from us. Then I took his poncho and put in on the ground to keep the naturally damp ground off of our skin and clothes. It rained very hard that night and the wind was very strong and gusty but the trench system worked very well. The poncho on the ground was a good idea as well. Not everyone was to be on guard duty that night, so I talked someone into using their poncho so that my partner and I would have one to wear while sitting in a fighting position, in heavy rain in the middle of the night while on guard duty.

The next day we humped all morning through relatively open ground and then came to a jungley area that sloped upwards. We stopped about a hundred and fifty yards into the tree line. There was a cleared out space about twenty feet wide, probably produced by seasonal monsoon rains. At the edge of it was a ledge, sort of like a long bench in a way about three feet tall, with the slope of a little hill going upwards that supported our backs as we sat upon it. There was some small vegetation where we sat and I reached down to examine it because it looked strange for some reason. Then I discovered that there were punji stakes imbedded everywhere, sharpened bamboo pieces about six inches long. But most of them looked old and had fallen down mostly so that their angle out of the ground was not as sharp as it should be. I warned the other guys to be careful. Then a guy said "ow", then "ow!, OW, OW!!" louder and louder until he finally jumped up. He had sat on a stake and it had started to work its way into his buttock. We all thought that that was funny, but I told him he ought to check with the medic because the VC were known to smear feces on those points, just to cause a particularly nasty infection days later.

A small tank moved into our area and a number of civilians jumped off of it. Many of them had cameras, some still and some motion picture types. It was a South Korean news team and they took pictures and movies of various things for about ten minutes. Some of them came up to where I and my little group were sitting and started chatting with us. One guy seemed to be very friendly and happy. He spoke English very well as opposed to his associates. He and I talked for about ten minutes, an upbeat conversation and then he was called back to the tank, his group was moving out.

They all got on top of the tank and I waved goodbye to them from a hundred and fifty feet away. The guy I had been talking to was smiling broadly and waving to me. They went down a little road for about fifty feet and I turned around and walked over towards my fighting position. A few seconds later there was a big burst of gunfire from directly behind me. I spun around and looked towards the tank. There was a group of black pajamaed enemy soldiers running perpendicularly directly in front of the tank, twenty feet in front of it, spraying it with AK-47 fire. There was a lot of smoke and dust in the area. Men were jumping off of the tank, but most of them I thought were just falling off of it, landing heavily on their heads and shoulders and then not getting up.

My first instinct was to run down to the point of enemy contact. But then I thought that the VC might be launching an all points attack. Better, I thought, to run away from the action to my front and take up a position in case the enemies plan was to divert our attention to the front while they mounted their main attack from our rear.

Anyways, the main attention of the soldiers on our very hastily arranged perimeter was to the front. I had had an almost overwhelming desire to help the wounded men on the ground. Anyways, I thought, there was a lot of American firepower pointed down to that area so what was really needed was for all soldiers to be on full alert from all directions of a further enemy assault.

I spotted a rectangular hole and jumped into it. Nice of the VC to have dug a hole that I can use I thought. Then it occurred to me that I hope they haven't booby trapped it. I had been in my fighting position for less than a minute when out of nowhere I saw a brilliantly bright flash from somewhere close to the tank, in front of it. Something flew within feet of the tank and directly at me. Something white that looked like the size of a telephone pole streaked about five feet overhead and a few feet to the left, traveling so fast that I didn't even have time to think about ducking down in the split second that it came directly at me. I felt the heat from its flame and an incredible roar from it that seemed to fill every molecule of the air and every bit of my body. A split second later there was a crashing sound close behind me and an instant later the rockets' noise suddenly stopped.

The tank had been ambushed a hundred feet beyond our position. The Americans closest to the tank instantly returned fire but the VC immediately broke contact. A guy close by me went down to the tank to investigate while those of us on the perimeter peered intently into the surrounding jungle for any sign of movement. That guy returned from the tank and reported that all of the men from that news crew were either dead or very badly wounded. He said to me: "Hey, you know that guy you were talking to, the real friendly guy?" I said "Yeah, did you see him?" He said, "Yeah, He's dead for sure".

Then he said, "Did you see that big rocket? I think it landed right behind you."

We took a little walk around and spotted a rocket lying on the ground. It was about nine and about six inches thick. I wondered where the VC ever got their hands on that thing, and how could they have carried it around. I thought that maybe the rocket that we were looking at on the ground might have been from an American aircraft, a dud that just happened to be in that location from months ago. But that would be too much of a co-incidence because it was exactly in the place that I figured the rocket had been shot at me would have landed. It didn't explode, I don't know why, but if it had I certainly would have been killed. I don't know what they did with the dead and wounded or with the tank or with that rocket because we moved out after a little while. It was only then that I began to ponder what had just happened. I was just talking to a happy human being a few minutes ago, he had waved goodbye to me, and twenty seconds later his life had been instantly terminated from this Earth.

We continued our mission, humping through the jungle for about two hours, walking past splindly trees about fifteen feet tall and three inches wide dripping water and pushing through wet underbrush. The interval between men was about ten feet which meant that that was the limit of visibility into the jungle all around us. In some s rare places a person could see farther. Without any warning a soldier about thirty feet in front of me suddenly dropped prone to the ground and the next two soldiers in line dropped in quick succession. I quickly and silently fell to the earth and turned around to look at the man behind me. He had instantly detected what was happening and he was already on the ground and the soldier behind him was quickly doing the same. There was no word coming down the line but obviously something was happening up front. I laid there for a couple of minutes trying to detect anything happening close by when the word came down the line, hoarsely whispered from man to man: "There's gooks nearby!"

Now I could hear some noises very distinctly in the jungle to the right of the line of march. It sounded like a deer crashing through the underbrush, then there were sounds of more and more things running by about thirty feet away, running parallel to the line of troopers lying on the ground. Then I spotted them. I thought at first that they must be deer because human beings cannot run that fast but then could barely discern that they had only two legs each. I quickly acquired them as targets and swept my rifle to the right, following them. I was ready to spray them when suddenly I was very concerned. Who are they? Are they civilians?, ARVN?, Americans? Within very few seconds they were obscured by the jungle and I had lost my targets.

A few moments later there was an outburst of gunfire from the front of the line. I figured that the VC were surrounding us with a Company of enemy soldiers and that they would be making their assault at any second. I flipped over on my back and shrugged off the rucksack, then quickly assumed a prone position on the ground facing directly to our flank. I unlocked the snaps to two ammo pouchs on my bandolier and flipped the safety on the M-16 to full automatic, at this range I wouldn't have to worry about being very accurate nor would I have time for single shots, this was going to be all over in a matter of seconds.

I wondered why we didn't just fire but then I thought that we should let them get closer so we could get more of them. Of course letting them get closer would have been more dangerous. Then I thought that it might be friendly forces out there. Maybe another line of men had ventured off of their predetermined course, so we shouldn't open fire until we are sure of who they were. After all, most of the time our standing orders were "Don't fire unless fired upon". That made it much more dangerous for us, but at least it helps to prevent friendly casualties.

Some of the troopers at the front of the line made contact and opened fire and there was a brief exchange of automatic and machinegun fire but the VC broke off the contact after a minute or so. About a minute later I could hear the whine of mortar shells coming in but they were landing about three or four hundred yards away as near as I could estimate. Then other rounds came in. The length of time between when you can begin to hear the whine and the explosion indicates how far away the round had landed. That time interval kept decreasing while the loudness of the explosions kept increasing, the rounds were being "walked in", closer and closer to their intended target or at least closer to me.

An enemy forward observer was watching where the rounds landed and then communicated with the gun crew how close they were to their target so that the gun crew could make corrections to bring their explosives onto target. The word came down the line that they were not American mortar rounds. The VC that had made contact were now calling in their mortars onto us. There's not much you can do in such a situation. You could seek cover behind a big tree except that there was no way to hide from a mortar. If you were against gunfire, it would be coming from a certain direction. A mortar drops down upon you. You can get a round directly in front of you and the next could be directly behind or to the left or right or directly on top of you.

The rounds came closer and closer. I had a picture of a huge prehistoric monster stomping through the jungle, coming to kill us. Within a minute the rounds found us and started to explode among the line American Infantrymen, yellowish-white flashes and explosions tearing up the earth and trees, walking right through our line of march and then mercifully continuing on past the men lying helplessly on the damp dark jungle floor. They continued their bombardment but it seem that now their rounds were hitting a hundred feet or so away from us. That situation would be temporary, until the enemy FO acquired us more accurately and called in a correction to the gun crew. Actually, I thought that he was doing a pretty good job, technically. We could hear the mortar rounds blasting out of their tubes, probably five hundred meters away.

After about ten minutes, the front of the line decided to move out. They might have been hesitant to do so at first, anticipating a VC ambush set up ahead. That was our choice, to stay there and die or to move out and probably die in an ambush. I think what happened is that someone called in an air strike to our front onto anything that might be out there and that caused the VC to break off their attack. For most of the rest of the day, we could hear mortars being fired at us, that is you could hear the blast as they left the tube. Some of the rounds landed close to us and some landed relatively far away but the VC could not quite zero in on us as we continuously moved through the jungle.

The next day we had walked for only a few hundred meters when we came upon a dirt road. As I stepped out of the jungle I could see all of the soldiers that were in front of me in the line walking along the right hand side of the road. I couldn't believe that we were staying on the road because we almost never traveled on so much as an animal path because that is where the VC would likely set up trip wires or mines but I was glad because we could travel much faster and the days torments would be finished sooner. Then we stopped, on the road for some unknown reason. After five minutes we resumed our march along the road. About five minutes later I noticed that the first two platoons had vanished from the road and realized that the pointman had veered off at an angle, undoubtedly following a compass heading and I soon found myself following the man in front of me into the jungle and further and further away from the road.

After the last few days I expected to make contact with the enemy at any minute and was extra vigilant and on high alert, ready to react instantly. The minutes ticked by slowly, second by second, while I thought that every heartbeat increased the already very high probability of imminent combat but the minutes eventually turned into hours and each step gradually turned into hundreds of meters but still there was no contact.

I had visions of the enemy massing somewhere in front of our line of march, waiting to spring an ambush that would engulf the entire Company or VC mortarmen standing by, waiting for us to walk by some type of landmark that had already been marked on their plotting charts so that they could hit us with extremely accurate fire from a mile away. But after a while I found myself distracted, my vigilance mis-directed by the beating that my body was taking from the murderously heavy equipment that I was humping and the heat and humidity.

After the time camped on the road I was relatively well rested but the humidity and heat and the weight of my equipment bore down upon my body brutally. Each minute and each step became more painful than the one before it. Eventually, my mind came to be filled with harsh commands to keep going. It was as if my brain was shot through with iron rods, with incessant, unwanted, screaming and yelling commands, almost auditory hallucinations, to **maintain the line**, to **drive on**, to **go forward at all costs**, each message measured by a cry of torment of pain and abuse from all over my body. It became very difficult to think at all.

The finer concepts of searching the surroundings for signs of the enemy or watching where I was stepping for mines or trip wires or searching the trees for snipers or being alert to the sounds of sudden gunfire were beyond my mental grasp and eventually the concept of danger was no longer a consideration. When the line stopped I could fall to the ground and momentarily relieve some of the suffering. If the line remained stopped for a few minutes I could begin to collect my thoughts, remind myself to be observant and vigilant, maybe look around for signs of the enemy, maybe

remember to check my grenades and weapon. But soon, as the line in front of me moved out again and I struggled to my feet and drove on, after ten or twenty feet the torment and suffering would return with a vengeance and drive most reason from my mind so that I was something less than human. After what seemed like twenty days instead of ten hours we reached the place where we would stay for the night.

Late that afternoon we reached our night site but this time the first thing that we did, even before digging in, was to set up our mortar. We had been taking it all afternoon, now we were going to give it. The fire direction control started giving its directions and we started dropping rounds on three or four suspected VC mortar positions. A re-supply chopper brought in a number of boxes of mortar ammo. With the extra ammo, we started to bring our fire close to our perimeter, and around it, not necessarily dropping it on close in possible VC infiltrators but mainly to register it in, in case we were attacked that night. We knew for a fact that VC were out there so we took mortar rounds out of their canisters so that they would be ready for instant action and sustained fire if our encampments perimeter was assaulted during the night.

Previously, I had painfully discovered the technique of dropping a round into the mortar and to then instantly stoop down as far as I could on bended knee and place the palm of my hand over my right ear because if we were using five or six charges on a round, firing at a far distance, the pain from the explosion when the round left the tube would literally knock a man to the ground.

As we fired close to the perimeter, just using charge zero or charge one, I realized that now even that produced pain that was extreme. I realized that something was wrong with me if a relatively mild blast could knock me to the ground. It would be impossible to just stand there and quickly drop round after round into the tube as might be required. I then realized that the rate of fire from our gun was seriously compromised. It didn't worry me greatly at that time, I just figured that firing the mortar over all of those months had damaged my eardrum and that it would probably get better with time. I was very wrong. The fact of the matter was that probably my eardrum was ruptured, the tiny bones inside the ear were dislocated or broken and it would result in permanent, lifelong serious hearing loss.

The next morning we loaded the mortar and the mortar ammo onto a chopper. They would fly it back out to us that night and thankfully, we wouldn't have to hump that gun and ammo that day. Very soon after beginning that days mission, early in the morning , I think that there was some enemy contact because we could hear gunfire off in the jungle sporadically but it was probably some other American Company's making contact, not us, or at least not my platoon.

At one point when the line stopped, I sat on the ground and then noticed that I was beside a fire ant nest that was located in the middle of a bush. I pulled out my insecticide and slapped some onto my neck. Chances were they wouldn't bite my face because its skin was tough and flooded with sweat and dirt and if they die, I could brush them off. Still, I didn't want to use insecticide unless if I absolutely had to. I then checked the drawstrings of my pants around my boots and checked the cloth flap covering the inside of the fly of my pants. Everything seemed ok so I just relaxed and lit up a smoke.

Then I had the thought to put some insecticide on the small branches around the circumference of the bush, so that the ants would stay away from the edge of the bush near our trail and not jump onto the troopers that were following me. There were hundreds of ants, all of them going in all directions, looking for food I guess. But then I thought, if there are hundreds of ants about, how many thousands of them were within the nest, waiting to come swarming out and biting the troopers in back of me? I applied the insecticide to about five little branches and noticed that ants would approach it but then turn away suddenly and go back. It was working very well. That insect repellent was some sort of extremely heavy-duty military strength oily substance. If someone was to get it into their eyes it would sharply sting. If someone accidentally got some on their lips, it would actually turn their lips numb like some sort of biological novocaine.

The ants then started to use other branches so I put a drop of the insect repellant on every branch that I could see, but the ants continuously found new branches and I ended up eventually putting it on over a hundred small branches (and using up my meager supply).

I figured that those ants must be very angry now and since they are extremely aggressive by nature anyways, that if they figured a way to get out of that bush that they would attack every man behind me. Eventually, I could see that the ants only had one remaining branch to use and as soon as I applied the final drop, the ants should be locked into the bush for a while, or so I thought. As soon as that final drop touched that branch, the nest erupted with a thousand ants that came out of the nest and immediately dropped to the ground. Now I had made the situation much worse. Just then we moved out again, leaving me amazed at the communication and organization and intelligence of those insects. I hoped that the enraged little buggers wouldn't bite too many of the guys in back of me too many times.

I eventually came upon a large, dark green metallic object that was stuck into the ground about ten feet away from the line of march. Suddenly I realized that it was a five hundred or thousand pound bomb that had been dropped by our planes. It was obviously a dud, I thought, until I remembered that some of those bombs had timers on them to explode hours or even days after it had been dropped. That was to kill or injure any enemy who came upon them and began to dismantle them to recover the explosive. Even if it did not have a timer and failed to explode when it hit the ground,

it could easily explode unexpectedly, at any time and for any reason or for no reason. I didn't like being anywhere near it, and near it meant anything closer than a thousand yards. If that bomb goes off it is going to kill half of the Company I thought. Oh, this is a good one I thought. Some genius back in the States had figured out a way to kill a few VC who tried to harvest the explosives, through trickery, but the end result is in the death and destruction of fifty hard core American infantrymen who had to patrol through the swath of death that the Air Force had laid down and through the naive assumptions of scientists who had no idea whatsoever of the realities of combat.

As we walked further we encountered an area where an air strike had been successful, at least there was no unexploded ordinance. The area was torn to pieces and most of the ground was black. There were large holes where the bombs had landed and the vegetation and trees around them were raggedly cut off at about a forty-five degree angle away from the center of the explosion. I thought for a moment that, maybe, if someone was five feet away from the center of the explosion then they might survive, because no shrapnel would have hit them if they were prone on the ground. Then I realized that anyone that close would of course be killed by the concussion, in fact, persons lying on the ground a hundred feet away or more would be killed by the concussion.

The next morning, we were told that we would be humping about fifteen-hundred meters, stopping for a while, and then hump another fifteen-hundred meters. A usual day was a three thousand meter hump, but I wondered why we would be stopping for a while. Around one pm, we arrived at an area that would make an excellent night site. I think that some people had already used it that previous night. We sat down and after about ten minutes were told that we would spend the night there. That was excellent news to me because it meant that we didn't have to hump another mile (and three hours) or so.

My squad Sergeant told us to dig in. Myself and another guy started to take turns digging a two man fighting position but then after about thirty minutes the Sergeant returned. A helicopter had previously brought in a small water trailer, something that is usually towed behind a jeep. It carried perhaps three or five hundred gallons of purified water. The Sergeant told Pierce, a guy in my squad, to take over my digging and told me to gather up the canteens of everyone in the squad and fill them from that water tanker.

I gathered up about ten canteens, holding them with all of my fingers through the loops of their tops and in my arms and approached the tanker which was near the top of a little hill about two hundred meters away in a very exposed position, There was absolutely no vegetation around it at all which I thought to be extremely unusual but cannot explain. I decided to keep my canteen separate because all of the other guys canteens would be mixed up, it would be impossible to figure out which canteens

belonged to whom. I filled up my canteens and a few others when I decided that I might as well drink my fill right now, I could certainly use it.

I drank from my canteen, the water was not hot and it was not cold but it did not taste of severe purification iodine chemical smells and tastes which I fully expected, which was an extremely welcome change. I downed my first quart and refilled the canteen from the brass spigot and drank down another quart as well. Then I filled the canteens of two other men and was about to fill up the remainder when I realized that the longer I spent filling up canteens, the less time I would have to spend digging.

I still could use some more water so I drank two more quarts. Then I filled all of the canteens. I didn't at all feel full or fully hydrated after having drank four quarts of water. I thought that that was unusual.

A guy came by and pointed further up the hill, about a hundred and fifty feet away from the water and told me that there was a woman up there. I thought that that is impossible, why would a woman be out here, in the middle of an operation. He said that she was a reporter or something. I couldn't believe my ears, but he was very sincere and told me to go up there, that she was wearing ordinary army jungle fatigues. I walked up there and sure enough, there was someone with a long ponytail in jungle fatigues. There was a guy beside her dressed the same way but for some reason I thought that he was not a soldier. They both wore green army fatigues but there was something about their uniforms that didn't seem right. They were not American uniforms, as close as they were to our uniforms there seemed to be something out of the ordinary, maybe it was the slightly different color, or location of pockets, or buttons. They were sitting on the ground and the woman had a long loaf of French bread and the man pulled a bottle of wine out of his backpack. I thought that that was completely unbelievable. We were in the middle of an operation, an extremely dangerous operation, and here was a woman and her boyfriend having a picnic?

We almost never saw reporters out in the bush, certainly not American reporters and certainly not a woman. I learned later that this woman was, I think, Catherine Leroy, a French free-lance journalist, the guy with her I think was her photographer. She had made the parachute jump with the 173rd and would later be shot in the chest with the Marines and later taken prisoner by the VC and go on to become world famous reporter covering other wars.

I walked back to the water trailer to pick up my canteens. I thought that that was an excellent opportunity to hydrate. I picked out my canteen and downed it, then refilled it and drank down that too. Then refilled the canteen with a quart of water and drank that, then refilled the canteen and downed that water. I refilled my canteen and was about to drink it down but something told me that that was a bad idea. I had

consumed seven quarts of water within the last fifteen minutes. I filled my canteen and began to gather up all of the other canteens when I noticed a flash far away.

I spotted an aircraft that had just dropped some bombs. Behind him, another plane came in and dropped napalm just as the faint noise of the first explosions reached me. They were about a mile and a half away. I stood there for a few minutes watching the air attack. Another plane swooped in and unloaded its bombs, two long bright slivery canisters, napalm probably or maybe a canister of butterfly bombs that had dropped off of the plane inappropriately I thought, but as I followed the path of the bombs, as they penetrated the jungle, there was not any fire, obviously they had failed to explode.

Then, a split second later, as the plane flew past where they should have exploded, the bombs shot out of the jungle and bounced steeply upwards. They had not only failed to explode, but now were bouncing, much higher than I would have expected. One of them landed and that was the last that I saw of it, but the other returned to earth and immediately bounced upwards again, in a very high arc at least a hundred feet high. It fell down and crashed onto the earth but then bounced up and then down again and again, perhaps five times, in a parabolic arc. I couldn't understand why it wasn't being smashed flat each time it hit the earth but obviously it wasn't.

Then I suddenly did some mental calculations and figured that if it bounced two more times it would land in the area of my platoon. After one more bounce, I tried to yell out to my squad, but they were too far away to hear me. I waved my arms and shouted at the top of my lungs but it was of no use. Then it bounced again and I calculated that the next bounce would be very close to my squad which was about 200 feet from me. I quickly looked around for some cover, fully expecting it to explode and kill me. It would be like a mortar round, it would be coming down on us from above and there was no place to hide from that. I just dropped to my knee as it appeared to go through the trees exactly where I estimated it would land, exactly where my squad was digging in, and then it bounced sharply off to the left and disappeared from my sight around the side of the hill.

I immediately tried to grab up the canteens, but a second later I heard a very strange sound of something coming through the jungle and towards us at a very high rate of speed. It sounded like a propeller or piece of metal or something, making a very distinct "whirring" sound, becoming louder as it approached our position and cutting through trees and vegetation seemingly without slowing down at all. I ducked down on one knee again, searching the jungle but not seeing anything. The noise suddenly stopped at what appeared to be close to my fighting position. I picked up the canteens, they were much more unwieldy to carry now that they were full, and ran down to my squad.

I went directly to the two guys who were digging my fighting position. One guys name was Smitty and the other guy, the one taking my place while I fetched the water, was a guy named Pierce. They were quite nonchalant, not excited at all, in fact if anything they seemed to be bored. Pierce was digging the fighting position as Smitty was resting, sitting on the ground.

I excitedly began to tell them what I had seen, quickly describing the large object bouncing through the jungle. Smitty said: "Yeah, I just heard something crashing into the jungle every two seconds or so and I asked Pierce, if he heard it". He said that Pierce didn't quite make out what he had said, so Pierce stopped digging for a second, straightened up from his back-breaking labor, and turned to his left 90 degrees, to face Smitty and ask him what he had said. Then Smitty told me that he saw "something", it was much too fast for him to determine what it was, he wasn't even really sure if he had actually even seen anything, but he was sure that something very big had crashed into the earth, almost directly in the hole for a split-second and then seemingly vanished instantaneously.

While Smitty was recounting events from his perspective, Pierce had turned around and returned to digging as if nothing had happened but I noticed that Pierce was bleeding profusely from his chin and asked him about it. Pierce hesitated for a second, choosing his words, I guess, when Smitty suddenly started to speak very excitedly. He said, "Hey, it was unbelievable, did you hear that whirring sound?" I said, 'Yeah, for sure. Do you have any idea of what that was?' Smitty answered, "Pierce had stopped digging and walked about 8 feet away from the hole to take a break" "Pierce was just standing there by himself when suddenly his body rose straight up off of the ground, very quickly, did a summersault in mid-air about 8 feet up then he fell down on his back. He really landed hard.". Smitty said that he couldn't believe his eyes. Pierce just levitating off of the ground like that. I asked Smitty what that had to do with the "whirring" sound. Smitty just said to me, "Come over here, I'll show you something." I followed Smitty for about 15 feet where he showed me a piece of silvery metal laying on the ground. It was about 2 feet long and rectangular in dimension, maybe two and a half inches wide and an inch in thickness, with a sort of round eye at the end. Maybe it was something that held bombs onto a plane. The end opposite from the eye had obviously been torn apart from other part. It had obviously been torn, raggedly, from what it was supposedly to have been attached to. It seemed to be some kind of thing that you would expect from an aircraft. I still couldn't quite fathom what he was saying, and I asked Smitty what that object had to do with anything. He said, "that's the thing that hit Pierce!, That's the thing that was making the "whirring sound!". Smitty continued, "When Pierce landed on the ground, I saw that piece of metal over there, it kicked up a bunch of dirt!". I couldn't believe that Pierce was still alive. Why that thing didn't take his head off is beyond my explanation and how he could continue on as if nothing had happened just flabbergasted me.

The story of the big silvery thing had not yet been fully explored. I told them what I had seen and of its bouncing. I have to admit that I would not have believed my description myself if I hadn't seen it with my own eyes. They didn't believe that such a thing could happen, that something like that could bounce for a mile and a half, but that story suddenly made sense to Smitty, who thought that he had seen something "appear" in the fighting position, crushing down the earth and then vanish.

Pierce then said something about the hole that he was digging and we could see that one edge of it had been collapsed and compressed. That thing had landed almost right in the fighting position that they were digging. It had missed Pierce by an inch or less and only because he had turned 90 degrees, at the last possible millisecond, to ask Smitty what he had said. At that very instant, that bomb had landed right at the edge and partly into the hole that Pierce had been digging. Pierce was now only concerned about doing additional work to dig the hole. That thing had landed with such force that it had profoundly compacted the dirt. Now Pierce had to use the pick portion of the entrenching tool on it because the earth had become much harder and the digging much more difficult. Shrapnel had already wounded Pierce 3 times and now he had missed a napalm bomb by an inch and had been struck by that whirring metal piece directly. Pierce had just missed being killed two times, within 10 seconds, and hit with an uppercut that no human could ever possibly deliver of white hot metal that for any expectation should have knocked his head off. He was totally unfazed by it.

I was very impressed with his demeanor but then, later, realized what the situation was. Pierce had almost been killed, twice, but in the scheme of things out here that was of little consequence. He still had to finish digging that hole. He still had to carry on. He still had six months to go until the end of his tour of duty over here. I guess from his perspective, he was still alive and that's all that really mattered.

Whether he would ever get back to the United States alive and with most body parts undamaged was another question and the fact that he was almost killed had nothing to do to the answer to that question, therefore, that experience was of no consequence to him at all. I began to call him "the human magnet" after that. Before his tour of duty was finished he would be wounded by shrapnel four more times.

We stayed there for the remainder of the afternoon and took our time digging positions, which was a nice break from the routine. After a while, I decided to take a walk around, hoping to see that woman again and checking out what equipment, if any, had been brought in by chopper and generally scopeing out the perimeter to get an idea of the layout of our encampment in case we were attacked or overrun at night.

I walked by a machine gun crew when I heard a familiar, loud cry of "fuck you!" sound out in the jungle. I fell to the ground, pointing my weapon outwards and trying to acquire s target on the wise guy enemy in the jungle in front of us. I wasn't going to kill him because he was a wise guy, I was going to kill him because he was too close to us. The machine gun crew assured me that it was a lizard and pointed out its position to me, but I couldn't see it because of the heavy undergrowth. I couldn't tell for sure if it was on the ground, in the bushes or on the trees or the vines hanging from the trees or in the trees. It was, I guess, in plain sight but I couldn't quite see it because it blended in very well with the surrounding vegetation.

The machine gun crew had been listening to it for the last five minutes and had eventually determined its position exactly. It was emitting its call frequently and it was annoying the guys in the machine gun crew. I made a few comments about it. I commented that I would kill it if I ever had a clear shot at it, when the gunner allowed a simmering rage to get the best of him and he suddenly cocked the lever of his gun and let loose a burst of about twenty rounds at the creature. Suddenly, I could see the lizard running for its life perpendicular to our point of view, with bullets following his trail and tail very closely. It was pretty big really. What looked like a storm of dirt and leaves stirred up by its tail as it ran was actually the machinegun bullets perfectly following him, about a foot behind its tail as the gunner tried to bring his fire directly onto the creature as it ran for its life. The last I saw of it, it was running for its life deeper into the jungle, with ten rounds per second of machine gun fire very accurately following a foot behind it, all the while loudly hollering "fuck you, fuck you, fuck yoooou."

The next day was the end of the operation. They brought in trucks and armored personnel carriers (APC's) to bring us back to base camp. They arrived twenty minutes prior to our scheduled departure. Among the arrangement of vehicles was a contraption that I had never seen before and I walked over to investigate it. I spoke to the crew and they said it was an 8-inch self-propelled gun. It was something like a bulldozer or tank with an enormous cannon barrel on it. They told me that the convoy would be headed by a few Military Police jeeps with mounted machine guns, followed by this 8 inch gun, followed by us on trucks and APC's.

I and a few other men were ordered to ride on top of one of the APC's. We could have ridden inside but that would have been very hot, all closed up within there but it would have been safer than riding on top of it as we did. Anyways, on top we could provide fire if there was an ambush and although the direct sun was hot, the breeze as we went down the road felt good.

The convoy was very long and as we proceeded down the road for a few miles we frequently stopped, I guessed so that the vehicles could try to maintain some combat related distance between them selves. At one stop I noticed a man standing on the corner where the main road (a dirt road barely wide enough to let two modern vehicles past each other) intersected a little village road. Actually the main road was only two lanes wide, sometimes coated with asphalt but mostly just a hard-packed dirt road. That man looked about five feet tall and ninety pounds. His skin was dark brown and in his hand he had a spear made out of wood with a metal tip. He was natively naked save for only a loincloth and he was transfixed by the spectacle of jeeps and trucks and

self-propelled artillery and APCs going by with men with weapons and equipment from the 20th century. That guy looked like he was from the Stone Age, which is just about right. Probably he was a Montenard (Mountain Person) and, yes, they did live in the Stone Age.

There was a tank parked nearby and there were a bunch of little kids on top of it. I almost yelled for those kids to get off of it before they got hurt when I realized that they were ARVN troops, Army of the Republic of VietNam. They were all adults but they were so small that they looked like children.

We went through some small villages alongside the main road. There was tens of miles between villages. Those small villages were composed of houses made of crooked sticks and cardboard. Most of the very young children were naked, others wore only torn and filthy t-shirts. There was a lot of smoke from the cooking fires inside the hootches. That smoke mixed with the diesel fumes of the convoy made the air feel oily. There were a few dogs tied to stakes. In Viet Nam you never saw them running free, they were always tied to a tree or a stake. In that country they were not pets, they were livestock and used for food. There were little shops that reminded me of what an abandoned garage in the middle of a rundown American city might look like. People were walking around buying food at little stalls and others were just waiting, stooped down with their backsides an inch above the ground.

It occurred to me that the price of the weapon that I was carrying would probably improve the lives of these groups of those people drastically. Those people looked like they were on the edge of existence. Their only worldly possessions seemed to be worn out and torn clothing, sandals made of old automobile tires and maybe an ancient iron cooking pot. Their houses were made of crooked sticks and cardboard and pressed beer cans and leaves and bamboo. There were no radios or televisions, no refrigerators or stoves or running water or electricity. The floor was just dirt with chickens running around inside the houses.

After a few hours, our armored personnel carrier broke down. We were stranded there for about an hour until another APC pulled in front of us and hooked up chains to tow our vehicle. As we proceeded down the main dirt highway, there was just exactly the right distance between the two vehicles so that the clouds of dust turned up by the APC in front of us blew upwards and over us and into our faces and completely covered our equipment and us. It wasn't an enjoyable ride at all, breathing diesel smoke and dirt. The dust covered every inch of our skin so that our perspiration was not cooling us at all. We just had to sit there, in the hot sun, and breathe in huge amounts of dust and exhaust smoke and continuously wipe our eyes with the sleeves of our shirts just to be able to see anything at all.

By the time that we got back to the base camp, all of us on top of that APC were completely covered in reddish brown dust about a half an inch deep. It looked as if we had been dropped into a bucket of paint, submerged for minutes into a huge pot of dirt and clay and paint. Just our open eyes showed that we might be human.

Chapter 25

April 31-May 3

It is not the critic who counts; nor the man who points out how the strong man stumbles, or where the doer of deeds could have done them better.
The credit belongs to the man who is actually in the arena, whose face is marred by dust and sweat and blood; who strives valiantly;

Theodore Roosevelt

Helicopter Assault

When we first arrived in camp, we were told to get food and ammo from the supply Sergeants hooch and then to clean our weapons before we did anything else. We were told that we were staying there for a very short time and then would be moving out on an operation. We were to be here for such a short time that no one would be allowed to even take a shower. I started to clean my rifle in the platoons hooch but the dust from my face and uniform continuously fell onto my weapon as it dried. As much as I tried to clean my weapon, the falling dirt from my face made that impossible. I dropped my gear inside our platoon hootch, grabbed a bar of soap, and walked directly outside, towards the shower.

Some Sergeants yelled for me to get back. Ten feet outside of our hooch tent I encountered a couple of Lieutenants walking past. They saw me, heard the loud commands emanating from our tent and they suddenly and loudly ordered me to get back to my hooch. I just looked at them harshly and continued onwards, their commands having no effect on me whatsoever. I didn't care a bit about their orders. I was going to take a shower and if that meant that I would have to spend a month in the brig then so be it. That was of no consequence to me. I had been ordered to clean my weapon and I had been ordered not to take a shower or clean off my face. They were totally opposing orders. It was impossible to comply with both. If those Lieutenants had decided to physically restrain me from my goal, then I would have fought them, I would have thrown punches if necessary. For some reason they left me alone and continued along their own way. I was going to take a shower, or at least wash off my face and head, and anyone in my way was going to pay a very serious price.

If I didn't take a shower, or at least clean off somewhat, it would have been impossible to clean my weapon, and then maybe I'd have to face an article fifteen action. If I did clean off somewhat then I could have cleaned my weapon but then had to face administrative action for disobeying orders not to take a shower. My decision was to wash off my face and head and neck and then go back to clean my weapon which might well save my life and the lives of my friends. If that decision led to me losing a rank in pay, but saving my fellow troopers, not to mention that I might enjoy being free of a huge amount of dust and dirt, then so be it. I thought, a good Commanding Officer would have let me go, a bad CO would have strung me up. I think what happened was that our Platoon Sergeant walked into the hooch while I was washing off, learned of what the commotion was and then reamed out any and all NCO's who had anything to do with yelling at me. I walked back to the hooch, soaking wet but relatively cleaned of a quarter inch of solid, dried, flaking mud on my face. No one mentioned anything involving the incident at all. Obviously my platoon Sergeant had earlier noticed the incredibly dirty condition that I and the others on that APC had been in. The platoon Sergeant was Sergeant Winfrey. A good guy.

The rest of the Company was going on its operation but me and about four other guys were taken by truck to a separate helicopter for our own little mission. Our job would be to provide security for an outpost that was on top of an almost impossibly steep mountain. It was probably three thousand feet tall and was really like a narrow piece of solid rock sticking straight out of the ground.

We landed directly on the top of that mountain by helicopter. The terrain at the top was mostly flat. They didn't have much security and I didn't think that they would need much because it would take the enemy weeks to climb to the top and they would have to use specialized mountain climbing equipment and be expert with its use.

We brought our mortar and an hour after arriving, we fired off a number of rounds to get our bearings more or less. The rounds landed in the jungle thousands of feet below us, close to the mountains sheer walls. We could just barely determine where they were hitting because of the very heavy vegetation. There was no use in getting a registration in close, because the entire top of the mountain was only about 200 feet wide and filled with men and equipment. I suppose the mortar would come in handy for any Americans patrolling the jungle around the mountain. But was essentially useless for defending this position. We just put our equipment in fighting positions that had already been dug and just took turns pulling guard duty all day and night.

At the top of the mountain were perhaps forty soldiers, most of them signalmen manning some very large pieces of radio equipment. There was a small barracks that was located in the center of an array of about ten antennas of very large and very different looking configurations. Off to one side was a little mess hall and small wooden buildings used for offices and equipment shacks.

During the next evening, I was walking around and heard someone playing rock and roll music. I wandered over to that area and expected to see a tape player but the music was coming out of a military radio. It was similar in general appearance to what the radiomen in my company carried but it was slightly bigger, something like what would be carried on a jeep. It was hooked up to an antenna that was about ten feet long but only an inch wide and extremely thin. That radio played continuous advertisements for products, which the U.S. Military station never had.

It seemed not to be a VC radio station because the only thing that the Viet Cong radio ever advertised was our impending deaths (along with good rock and roll music).

The guys operating that radio informed me that they were listening to WABC in New York. I couldn't believe it, but they told me that, especially at night, being so high up, it was a phenomenon that is known to occur. I stayed there for about 15 minutes until the disk jockey gave his station identification: WABC, New York. These guys obviously had a life that was far different from that of the men in my Company. They stayed up there, where it was cool, they got three meals a day and were not subject to attack. They never did any hard work and were probably rotated back to base camp frequently. They were cool, had an easy life, ate well and were safe. Yes, that was a completely different life from the soldiers beating the bush three thousand feet below them and out into the steaming green expanse of jungle surrounding that mountain.

We stayed there for about four days until we were told to pack up. A few hours later a chopper landed to drop off supplies and to pick us up. The pilot asked us if we wanted a good ride (whatever that meant), and we all said sure. The pilot told us to hold on tightly and he lifted off. He flew forward for about a hundred feet until he just barely cleared the edge of the mountain and then dipped the nose of the aircraft downwards at an angle that I thought was impossible for this chopper or any aircraft save a dive bomber.

We went virtually straight down, about twenty feet away from the face of the mountain, with the pilot pouring on the gas to the engine to go faster than what was already a powered freefall. About two hundred feet from the ground, he pulled up with what looked like all of his strength or maybe it was with all of his concentration and we quickly found ourselves traveling horizontally with the skids of the aircraft about two feet off the ground over mostly rice paddies. We, as usual, were not strapped in to the aircraft at all and were sitting on the floor with our legs dangling into empty space. The pilot must have been pushing his chopper to the limit because I had never been in a chopper with the engine roaring so loudly. Our speed quickly ramped up to its absolute maximum within ten seconds. I had never been in a helicopter that traveled at anything close to that speed, I didn't know that it was possible. Every three seconds or so, the pilot would quickly "bump" the helicopter, making it jump up about a foot and then immediately drop down a foot as he hopped over the little dikes on the rice paddy and then sped over the main portion of the paddy at an altitude of less than two feet.

We went for a few miles like that when I noticed that we were approaching a tiny village that was built on a little hill about fifteen feet tall with large trees surrounding it and mixed among the hootchs. As we approached, the pilot pulled up at the very last split second and we flew over the roofs of the village, missing them by about two feet, roaring over the village at top speed and then dropped down immediately to another stretch of rice paddy. Then we encountered jungle with trees of varying sizes, most of them very tall and the pilot abruptly gained altitude and flew over that area, missing the tallest trees by about three feet and finally came into a landing zone at base camp at full speed. It was about a fifteen minute ride in a chopper with the pilot pushing every mph out of the engine and using every bit of his considerable skill. Yeah, that was really a good ride. It was an incredible demonstration of absolute mastery of an aircraft and of absolute fearlessness and courage. Yes, I do think that that pilot was deranged. But he had all of the finest attributes of a combat helicopter pilot.

Chapter 26

OPERATION DAYTON

May 4-May 17 QUAN LOC

APC with Men Dismounting

The other five men and I stayed overnight in base camp in Bien Hoa. Early the next day we loaded into a chopper to join the rest of the Company still out in the field on an operation. We were flying at about fifteen-hundred feet for a while, then dropped to about a thousand feet and I could hear the pilot and flight crew talking, saying that we should be very close to the landing zone. I looked down onto the jungle and could not see any place where we could land. We flew in a wide circle twice, searching the jungle below, then the pilot radioed to the soldiers on the ground to throw a smoke grenade to mark their position. A minute later the pilot radioed that he had spotted red smoke and we began to descend. I leaned backwards to look through the windshield but could only see jungle, so I leaned forwards and outwards searching the jungle in the direction of our decent. There was nothing to be seen except green jungle, then, as we were about a thousand feet away, I could barely make out a tiny hint of pinkish color. The pilot had spotted it right away. On the ground, that smoke grenade would be pouring out huge amounts of dark red smoke and I was amazed that at a thousand feet away, it would look so subtle and insignificant. The landing zone must have been enlarged from a very small area, there was only enough room for one helicopter to land, and the pilot would have to do it very carefully.

We met up with another platoon and humped the bush for four hours, patrolling around the landing zone until we encountered a dirt road and loaded onto trucks for a two hour convoy back to base camp. I don't know why my little group couldn't have just stayed in base camp, but it was our duty to hump the bush and get filthy dirty again, and maybe wounded or killed, if only for four hours. "Ours is not to question why" When we arrived at base camp, we stayed for less than sixty minutes, just long enough to get some ammo, not even enough time to get some mess hall food or a cold soda. We were taken to the airfield and loaded onto helicopters and began another search and destroy phase of that operation.

We beat the bush for about three days. On the fourth day the mortar platoon was ordered to stay in place to provide fire support to the line platoons that went out on patrols. We stayed there for three days. We just hung around for those days, not having to go out onto patrol. I suddenly realized on one of those days that it was my birthday. I was sitting on a little mound of earth, trying to place myself where I could get some shade from the small, sparse trees that were prevalent in that area. I contemplated that now I was no longer a teenager. I had been nineteen years old but today I was twenty. I got my camera, and started to draw things on the ground between my feet. It said something like "May 11, 1967", and then I improved that by adding pieces of twigs to make that message more prominent, and then took a picture of it. I thought that that picture would remind me of that day, if it ever got developed and if worse came to worst that if my family ever got my effects, they might see that at least I made it to my twentieth birthday.

During that time a chopper brought in a few guys as replacements, most of them were right out of jump school but one guy had been in the Army for over a year. A guy approached me and told me he had just flown in. He would be part of my platoon, in fact he was assigned to my squad. His name was James Biernacki. We spoke for a while and he told me that he had come from Fort Benning but had volunteered for Viet Nam. I incredulously asked why he had done such a thing and he said, "I didn't like the chicken shit associated with stateside Army life". I said he had been very lucky to have not been ordered over here before anyways. That's when he said that he was exempt from combat and from Viet Nam because he was the only child of his mother. Sons who were the sole support of their mothers were exempt from posting in Viet Nam. I told him to fill out forms to get back to the States, that it was an absolute horror show over here, but he would have none of it. He was a friendly guy and I liked him right away and made a mental note to try to take him under my wing and teach him everything that I knew. I couldn't have known then that nine months later he would be killed in action by an enemy soldier.

We were talking one time and Biernacki said that he was from Chula Vista, California which is next to San Diego. For some reason he hated the city of Chula Vista and I couldn't understand it because it was my impression that San Diego was beautiful. He said that yes, San Diego was beautiful but he had grown up in Chula Vista and hated it. I told him that he shouldn't hate a city. I said, "Hey, Maybe you'll be killed over here and they will name a street after you in Chula Vista" He said, they could name a street after him in San Diego, that would be OK, but not in Chula Vista. *

*note: There is now a beautiful little street of new homes in Chula Vista named Biernacki Way. At the top of the street sign it says "deceased war veteran".

Later in the day, it was decided to fire a few registration rounds at pre-determined co-ordinates. The new guys gathered around to watch our techniques. Some of the guys had never fired a mortar before and were not trained in their use. We got directions from the fire control team, and aimed the gun appropriately. I took a round in my hand, and explained to the men that the round had three safety pins that had to be removed before it could be dropped into the tube. I carefully removed all safetys and told the guys that the round was fully loaded and primed and ready to go. I walked over to the barrel and raised the round to put it into the tube, but dropped it. I caught it in my left hand and juggled it, trying to desperately prevent it from hitting the ground but it did. The new guys watching were horrified. Then I told them that, you shouldn't ever really do that, then I got another round and was playing around with it and dropped that deliberately and directly onto its nose onto the ground. The new guys were beside themselves in panic, thinking that they were going to be killed at any second. Then I told them that even with the three safetys removed, the round had an internal safety that would automatically be activated if the round left the tube with a certain minimum amount of force and velocity. I had just been joking around. I thought that it was a novel way to show them that the rounds were pretty safe, especially since they would be humping the extra rounds, but they seemed very disturbed by my demonstration. Actually the round could have possibly been defective and dropping it on its nose could have caused it to detonate. If that was the case then the internal safety would have been defective and the round would have exploded when it hit the firing pin at the bottom of the tube. That scenario would probably kill the gun crew anyways.

We had three guns set up and a pretty good amount of ammo. About an hour later, we could hear some gunfire out in the jungle. There was some radio chatter that seemed urgent by its tone. I moved closer to the radio and could hear one of our very small patrols calling in a fire mission for our mortars. The fire direction control team seemed very nonchalant and seemed to be casually making their calculations, seemingly in no hurry at all. The radio chatter became more and more urgent and we could hear an increase of gunfire somewhere out in the jungle. A Sergeant yelled "fire mission!", Number one gun!" and that crew sprang into action. They set up the mortar according to the fire direction control parameters and fired one round. The radioman in the bush called in a correction to "drop four hundred, right two hundred", which meant that the round had landed four hundred feet in front of and two hundred feet to the left of where he wanted the rounds to drop.

I guess someone decided that this might be a good time for all three guns to get some experience and the order was given: "Fire mission!, Number two gun!" The radio message from the small patrol engaged with the enemy became desperate and said that the enemy was much closer now. Number two gun was given new parameters and fired off a round. The men in the jungle called back "drop three hundred, right one fifty!". Obviously the fire direction control team was being very careful, bringing in the rounds in small increments so as to not hit friendly troops. There was another adjustment and number two gun fired another round that brought the round two hundred yards away in front of the troops and a hundred and twenty-five yards to the left of where the men being attacked wanted it.

Now, the radioman in the bush was screaming into the radio, more than over the edge in panic. He screamed that they were being overrun. Then, in a forsaken cry he yelled, "Put the fire on us. Put the fire directly on top of us!!" The tone of his voice sent a cold chill through me. This was obviously an extremely desperate situation. The fire direction control yelled, "Fire mission!, Number three gun!". That was my squads gun.

They gave the parameters of elevation and deflection and charge number and ordered us to fire only one round but I realized that it was a very small adjustment from what was

given for number two gun and would result in bringing in the fire that was a hundred yards from where the men under attack needed it. My gunner and I adjusted the mortar to correspond with the firing coordinates. We were ordered to fire only one round, I strongly whispered to the ammo bearer to get as many rounds ready as he could. We were set up to fire and the fire direction team yelled "one round, fire at will!" I jumped in front of the gun and turned up the elevation then reached over and turned the horizontal aim of the mortar, just guessing, what the appropriate adjustments should be.

The gunner looked at me with huge eyes, in shock, as if to ask what in the world I was doing. What I was doing was completely against regulations, against proper procedure, against common sense and defying and taking over his tasks and responsibilities. I looked him in the eye and strongly whispered, "Don't say a word. Just shut up!".

The ammo bearer had noticed what I had done and I just looked at him and said, "Shut up and give me rounds until I tell you to stop!." I grabbed the first round and shoved it down the tube, followed by another and another and another while the fire direction control team screamed "Cease fire, Cease fire!, Cease fire!!". I had to stop anyways because I had expended all of the ammo that was immediately available. I was only supposed to have fired one round. I was also supposed to let the gunner set up the aim. Obviously I had exceeded my tasks. In the States I would have faced a serious court martial, if someone was injured or killed by my mortar fire, imprisoned for many years or faced a firing squad, due to intentional homicide. But this wasn't the States and we were certainly not playing war games.

I walked closer to the radio and could hear someone on the other end screaming for his life amid a roar of gunfire. The mortar rounds were in the air. Ten seconds later we could hear through the radio the sound of my first mortar round exploding then suddenly the communication stopped completely in mid sentence. A few seconds later we heard the explosions of the mortar rounds through the jungle, which would have taken a few seconds to travel from the besieged soldiers position to ours.

Our radio operator tried to reestablish contact but could not get a reply. Everyone in my group was absolutely still. The radio operator seemingly trying to make contact with a bunch of dead men. "Oh no" I thought. "I've killed the American troopers." I looked over at the FDC team, expecting to see them pointing their rifles at me. I thought that perhaps I had killed some Americans by deliberately putting the fire directly upon them.

Everyone just stood dead still hoping to hear some radio report from the troops under attack. After a couple of minutes there was suddenly a voice from the radioman in the jungle saying very weakly, "Cease fire, cease fire". Our radioman asked for a situation report but there was no answer for another minute, just dead silence. Then a slightly stronger voice from the patrol just said "Cease fire!, Cease fire!, Enemy contact broken off!". That patrol had taken casualties from enemy fire and probably from my fire. A few minutes later the patrol radioed in that they were returning to our location with their dead and wounded. Someone asked them on the radio if they needed assistance but they strongly just said: "No!!" A few minutes later they reported a very abbreviated Sit Rep, a Situation Report. They specifically mentioned that at least one enemy was killed due to our mortar fire. I jumped up and down yelling "number three gun!, number three gun!" (my gun) but everyone else was very somber, very somber indeed. I was acting like our high school football team had just won a game, the others seemed to have a very different view of it. We, I thought, should be happy, they realized that we had just killed a man. Eventually, I would see their point of view and it would haunt me for the rest of my life.

I expected to hear someone tell me that I would be court-martialed for recklessly disobeying orders but no one said anything. We all sat down on the ground to shake off some of the adrenaline. That patrol came into the Company's perimeter after about an hour and a medivac chopper was called in to take out their casualties. We didn't see them come in, we just knew of it by listening to the radio traffic. One man had been killed and others wounded.

After about a half an hour, three guys approached my group who were sitting around the mortar tubes. One of them asked, "Who fired the last three rounds at us?!" I figured that my rounds had wounded, or maybe killed, some of his friends and there was going to be some fisticuffs or gunfire at any moment. The soldiers seemed to be much more than deadly serious. Their uniforms were dark green, soaked with sweat and covered in detritus, thousands of tiny parts of torn apart leaves and twigs. I ran over closer to them and said, "Yeah, that was me!, You said to put it on top of you and the fire direction control team was bringing it into you too slowly so I took matters into my own hands"

By their demeanor I really fully expected them to shoot me and I tried to move my hand nonchalantly down to the fire selection switch on my rifle. One of them looked at me hard, very hard and then extended his hand for a handshake. He hung his head downwards, looking at the ground, and softly said "Thank you man. You saved our lives". His other two friends very very solemnly shook my hand without saying another word and then they walked slowly away without another word being said. I think that two men in their little squad of six soldiers men had been wounded and another killed in that little battle. I surely hoped that I was not responsible for any of those friendly casualties.

We were picked up by helicopter the next day and choppered into a huge meadow. At one end of it was an artillery base with about six guns. The artillery men had probably been there for a while because they had made little houses out of sandbags and lumber, they probably got the lumber from the boxes that the ammo was delivered in. They probably had hot food flown in every day and they certainly did not have to hump the bush. They also had a trailer that probably contained a thousand gallons of water when it was full.

We had not had much access to water lately and myself and a group of infantrymen walked over to the water trailer to fill some of our canteens. The artillerymen took great exception to that and claimed that they didn't have enough for themselves. We argued that we needed the water much more than they did and that they could call in for another trailer, but the artillerymen were adamant in their argument. The Infantrymen simply ignored them and we started to fill our canteens. A few artillerymen ran to their shelters and returned with their M-16s to reinforce their argument. Some of the Infantrymen, I thought, would just prefer to be shot right there, in fact, it might be a good thing if the artillerymen shot them and they could be airlifted out and not have to go on this mission. In the end, a few officers intervened and the taking of the water was stopped, but not before most of the Infantrymen had loaded up.

We walked a short distance and entered the jungle on the patrol. After a while we stopped for a minute and I noticed a little land leach inching his way towards me as fast as he could. I spotted a spider web on the ground and picked up the leach and put him into the web. Almost instantly the spider who had been hiding from sight in a hole made of web material, stomped out, reminding me of Jackie Gleason on a rampage. He hesitated for a second then grabbed the leach in his fangs and dragged it back down his hole instantly. I thought that that was a horrible punishment for that leech for just trying to get some lunch at my expense.

Later in the day, about two o'clock, we came to a small stream and it was decided that we would set up a night position there. We dug in and then, by small groups, were allowed to go back to the stream to get some water and to wash up. There was a little waterfall of sorts, falling from a large rock about fifteen feet tall into a little pool about fifteen feet wide. We jumped in with all of our clothes on and scrubbed with soap to wash our clothes as well as our bodies. I noticed a Sergeant sitting on the large rock with a fishing pole that he had fashioned out of a stick. I don't know what he was using for string or for a hook or for bait but he looked very relaxed. He looked like I would expect someone to look who was fishing at the old fishing hole down on the farm. I thought that this is not the old fishin' hole in Mississippi at all. This is another State, another Country, another Continent, really another World. The troops in Viet Nam referred to the United States as the World, such as "Man, I can't wait to get back to the World" or "I got a package from the World." Viet Nam, from the perspective of an Infantryman was not part of Planet Earth, not ever close to what everyone had ever seen or experienced in the United States.

After the second group of men were finished washing, there was some soap suds in the slowly flowing water, and then, within a few minutes, there were fifteen small fish floating belly up on the surface, I don't know whether it was the soap, or the dirt and insecticide from the men, that killed them. It occurred to me that in this land and condition that we couldn't even take a bath without something dying.

We humped out the next day. We were still humping long after we should have stopped for the afternoon to dig in defensive positions for the night and were still humping when the sun went down and it was getting extremely dark. We came to a large clearing and got the word to stop there and we would be picked up by armored personnel carriers (APC).

The platoon Sergeants and Platoon leaders had obviously gotten the word as to what we were going to do, but they most certainly did not pass that word down the line, so that most men had no idea of what was going on. We arranged ourselves into groups of about ten men and about ten minutes later I could hear heavy machinery moving in the distance, seemingly moving towards us. A convoy of APC's pulled in and the crew of the APC that was closest to my group whispered, desperately it seemed, for us to board the APC. The crew of the APC seemed to be very frightened and wanted to leave this area as soon as humanly possible. Some of the APC's had extremely small lights, not for seeing in front of the vehicle but mostly so that the vehicle in front of it could determine its position. Most of the men in my group quickly loaded through the main door at the back of the vehicle and quickly settled inside the APC but I and a few others rode on top of it.

It was tricky to decide where to locate yourself on that APC. Inside provided protection from small arms fire but on top you were farther away from an explosion if the APC hit a tank mine. Inside was cramped and airless while on top provided a breeze. If we were attacked the men on top could quickly dismount and return fire but the men inside would be spared the first few seconds of enemy action. I thought that if we are ambushed and the lead vehicle was disabled, I and the men riding atop the vehicles would instantly jump down and return fire, but if that happened, I wondered what the APCs would do, they might just shoot their way out and keep going leaving men on the ground. All of that should have been decided before we even met up with the APCs but I guess it wasn't. This whole idea of riding on the APCs seemed to have been hatched at the last minute. I'm pretty sure that the crew of the APC that I was riding on didn't like the idea of riding around in the darkness at all. Maybe we got lost or couldn't make it to our destination and the Cavalry was called out to save us.

They started to go very quickly and I wondered how the driver could see anything in front of him. Maybe he had a nightscope or maybe he was just driving blindly, following the tiny lights on the APC in front of him. We seemed to be driving at an insane speed given the almost total darkness all around and in front of us. We eventually came to a large clearing, stopped and unloaded. The APC crews seemed to be very shaken up about their little mission to pick us up out of the bush at night. They seemed to be very agitated and their agitation was not relieved even when we arrived at our destination. For the most part, most of us had no idea of what had just happened, or why it happened.

We found out later that this was the Blackhorse armored unit base camp in Quan Loc and we stayed there for a number of days. The next day I could evaluate that base camp a lot better than the night before. There were very few trees, the ground was mostly bare red clay/dirt. This was obviously a major forward supply base, very rudimentary but it had some large tents that contained a regular doctor and a dentist. That base camp was nothing more than a sprawling forward supply base with extra supplies laying around on the ground and a few buildings.

The next day we were told that we could see a doctor or dentist who had set up tents in that area. Some of the guys went to the doctors' tent to get some treatment that was beyond the scope of the medics. Most of them had health issues that should have been addressed by a qualified physician days or weeks ago but hadn't been. Out in the bush, as an Infantryman, basically, if you could still walk then you obviously didn't need a doctor. A lot of the soldiers really desperately needed the care of a physician. I had been having a bad toothache, on and off for the last two months and went to see the dentist.

He was in a big dark green tent and his dentist chair was some sort of collapsible contraption sitting on the bare dirt floor inside. Really not much more than a lounge chair that someone might bring to the beach. He had green wooden boxes of instruments and supplies. It really looked primitive, it didn't look good at all. I don't think that he even had a bright light. I was really dreading a filling because I don't think that he even had electricity. I imagined that he had some sort of hand-powered drill or he would chisel out the cavity by hand.

He took one look at my tooth and decided to pull it out. It wasn't bad at all, I thought, it didn't really hurt at all at that moment. I also asked him if he could fix a temporary crown on my front tooth. That had been on for over a year. It was just a very temporary contraption that had turned brown and black, it looked disgusting and horrible and was falling apart, but he told me that he couldn't do anything for it under those conditions.

The painful tooth was bad and he decided to just extract it. It probably didn't need to be extracted and would not have been under ordinary circumstances, but I was an Infantryman. This was not a situation where he would do his work under the medical standards and accruements of a professional setting in the civilized world. This wasn't a case where he would take x-rays and do some work and then I would set up another appointment with his secretary. I was an Infantryman and as such, why would he be much interested in my dental health or appearance? I was an Infantryman and as such I would probably be killed in action very soon. Why should he work to maintain my dental health and appearance when it would probably be destroyed within a few weeks? He gave me an injection of novocane and pulled the tooth out. It really didn't hurt at all. When he was finished, I looked him in the eye and said "Thank you." I thanked him for saving me from some dental pain, and he seemed to be genuinely thankful to me for not changing my rifles selector switch from "safe" to "full auto" and didn't kill him where he stood. I knew full well that if he was working on a big Air Force Base and I was some rear echelon Air Force type that he would have gone to extraordinary measures to save that tooth.

When I was in basic training I was returning one Saturday night from the local beer hall and tripped over a wire, crashing face first onto the sidewalk. That had resulted in a few of my front teeth being shattered. The dentist at the emergency room just put on an extremely flimsily clear plastic cap on one of my front teeth and told me to carry on. Now, fourteen months later, that cap had turned dark brown. I asked the dentist if he could correct that problem and he replied that that was cosmetic dentistry and that he didn't practice that in the field. Actually, he probably wasn't equipped for that. He told me that there was nothing he could do for me.

Actually, I wasn't too concerned about my physical appearance. It would be a major problem if I returned to the World, but I didn't think that I ever would. Still, I was a bit irked that that dentist couldn't have done something to make my corpse look good at the funeral parlor.

I went back to my squad and my squad Sergeant seemed to already know that I had had a tooth extracted. He asked me how I was, which I thought was extremely unusual, and he asked if I needed the rest of the day off from usual duties. I said that I was perfectly fit.

We stayed in that position for a few days, providing security for a number of artillery pieces and for the platoon sized patrols that were sent out from my Company. I noticed, eventually, that there was a very large hole, rectangular in shape, about a hundred feet long and about eight feet deep, that looked like it had been dug by a bulldozer. It was located about two hundred yards from our position and used for trash, mostly lumber from wooden artillery and mortar shell boxes, but also old food and C-ration cardboard boxes and anything else.

The camp was being broken down and they broke down the wooden latrine that had been set up and dumped that and the barrels of human waste into the trash hole and we threw in any bad ammo or grenades or dud rounds. A bulldozer was brought in to cover the entire mess with four feet of dirt. We loaded onto trucks and moved about five hundred feet and then stopped for about ten minutes while the convoy got into their pre-ordained positions, the troop transports lined up correctly. The MP jeeps dashed around and APCs rolled up and down the line, trying to find their assigned positions among the convoyed trucks of troops.

Before we left, just waiting in one spot so that the convoy could arrange itself properly, a crowd of about twenty-five 25 Vietnameese civilians descended onto that trash pit and started to dig it up. We yelled to them, eventually at the top of our lungs, to stop. I think that they heard us yelling but even if they did, they certainly didn't understand English. I thought that they might understand the urgency and warning in our voices but apparently they did not. If they did, they were completely oblivious to our warnings.

By that time, the civilians must have uncovered the human waste and ordinance yet they kept digging, I think, for the chance that there might be some C-ration cans in there, which there were. I thought to myself "How desperate must these people be?, To go through that, to dig through human waste, to risk being killed or maimed by the duds and grenades, for the off chance that maybe they might get the chance to get a can of old food that the Americans had rejected. Obviously these were people at the very edge of existence.

We rode on the trucks in the convoy all the way back to our base camp. It took about six hours.

Chapter 27
SECRET OPERATION

We stayed in base camp for fifteen hours_and then went out on another operation. The word came down that this new operation would be a search and destroy mission. We would move out on trucks and be transported for fifty miles and then load onto helicopters. We would be doing this to try to fool the enemy. Try to deceive them that we were going on a local operation by truck convoy. We were told that this was a secret operation into an area where no friendly troops had ever operated.

In an attempt to mask our operation we were told that once that we were deployed, there would be no artillery that we could call in. We would not be resupplied at all. There would be no Medivac helicopters available and we would receive air support only under the most dire circumstances. We could not rely on any outside help whatsoever. This was supposed to be some secret operation. Immediately before moving out we were ordered to remove our 173rd patchs from our shirts, just cut them off. That didn't go over well at all with the troops. It was a point of pride for us to wear our 173rd patchs, in full color, on our shirts. A defiant statement against the enemy. On a dark night the white wing of the patch would be a clear target for an enemy approach but that was why we didn't wear a camouflage version of the patch. It was just an in your face defiance and bold statement to the enemy. Higher command required that we cut off those patchs. I guess they didn't want the enemy to know what unit they were dealing with. Actually, we were very far away from our usual area of operations. Perhaps they didn't want to alert the enemy that we had suddenly been moved that far north, I don't know for sure.

Enemy strength was estimated at two Divisions so that was about twenty to one odds against us. The enemy was reported to be dug in well, they had been digging in since WW2. That didn't sound like a good plan to me at all, but what did I know? We were given four days worth of C-rations each, which everyone immediately sorted through and threw away what was not absolutely essential, basically leaving each soldier with one days worth of food, one days worth of calories to be consumed over four days.

We loaded onto the trucks and rode for several hours when suddenly the trucks stopped and within seconds a flight of about twelve helicopters swooped down and landed. We instantly jumped off of the trucks and ran to board the aircraft. It was all very well coordinated. As I was lifting off, I could see that the second string of men, who were to load onto the next flight of helicopters, had already jumped off of their trucks and moved off of the road, concealing themselves in the underbrush and the trucks had already started moving away.

I could see that we were now flying over a very jungley area, the color of the foliage was a dark green and it looked as if there were mostly very tall trees, probably with vines, but we had no idea of how the area would be at the landing zone or how the terrain would be as the operation progressed.

Our landing zone was the only place in the general vicinity where a chopper could set down. In fact it was only big enough for two or three choppers to land at a time. It looked like a large tree had fallen and knocked another old one down with it, so that the landing zone just consisted of two enormous, fallen tree trunks on the ground and a lot of shrubbery about five feet tall. The insertion of the men went very quickly with us jumping out of the choppers before they even actually landed and the choppers taking off immediately. We didn't wait to secure the landing zone but moved out in platoon size lines immediately.

I don't think that we were humping the mortar or its ammo on that operation. The mortar platoon would be straight light infantry. That meant that we were relieved of a lot of weight but we were still carrying a substantial load. We crossed a creek and then another and another, all within about a fifteen minute interval of time. I didn't know if we were following a zig-zag course or if there were a number of meandering creeks in that vicinity. Most of the creeks were about the five feet wide and three feet deep with light brown, slippery, slimy sides moderately steep about eight feet high. We didn't have to use the "gun in your face" technique to climb up the sides, but those creeks were a substantial obstacle and they slowed us down a lot.

We were now taking large, white malaria pills once a week. We had also been issued a handful of medium sized salt pills and told to take one or two a day, I guess to replenish the salt that we lost through sweating. We just went on and on and on and on for days, each day being like the one before it, just simply hot and horrible. Every minute of humping over that terrain, in that jungle was brutally painful. Every step jolted around the rucksack which strained your backbone and shoulders. It was, I imagined, like being on a medieval rack all day, constantly being slowly pulled apart. Just constant serious pain and misery. And at any moment you could be killed or maimed by any one of a hundred possibilities, all of them likely to occur to you or someone in your Company. An absolutely horrible and desperate and painful condition, all day, minute after minute, hour after hour, day after day.

By that time I had acclimated myself to the fear, just pushed it down deep into my psyche. I couldn't function well if I was constantly worried about the likely dangers so I just simply didn't worry about it anymore. The absolute brutality of the hump required me to use all of my concentration upon willing myself to just keep driving on, willing my body to continue beyond what I had considered to be human limits, enduring suffering beyond what I had ever thought humanly possible. Day after day after day. The day to day life of an American Infantryman in Viet Nam was beyond the comprehension or imagination of most civilians back in the United States. Truly, "When a Country declares war, it declares war on its own soldiers."

We crossed many streams each day which meant that we had plenty to drink, plenty of filthy, dirty, muddy, disease ridden water. I wishfully thought that since the streams were running so fully and fast that maybe it wasn't so filthy. I had acclimated myself to getting by with a very minimum amount of food, but I had exhausted my very meager supplies after three days. Essentially I had eaten one days worth of food spread over the last four days and even I was getting very hungry. At a nightly briefing we were again reminded that we would not be re-supplied on this operation. I think what might have happened was that we were supposed to go a certain distance each day but couldn't maintain our daily goal because the terrain was not as expected or maybe we were diverted to a new locations. Throughout the day we encountered many creeks that had to be crossed, maybe thirty or so each day.

The next day we were told that we would be intersecting the night position of another Company on this days mission. There were reports that some American units were not picking up after themselves and leaving things that could be of use by the enemy. They were supposedly told that another American unit would be coming through that day so to be sure to police up their equipment and dispose of their trash properly, which meant burying it and camouflaging any indication of the burial places.

After humping half of the day, we finally came upon the night encampment of the other Company. Most of the vegetation within the perimeter had been chopped down by machete and then removed so that the area was mostly barren dirt with many weeds and vines and leaves strewn about and stomped into the soil from the soldiers boots. Many of the fighting positions had not been completely filled in, there was trash all over the place including C-ration cans that the VC use for booby traps by putting grenades into them.

There were loose M-16 and M-60 machine gun rounds, maybe even some M-79 ammo and loose hand grenades and smoke grenades. That situation was outrageous. Some of the men who had been there the night before, supposedly knowing that we would be through the next day, had set up C-ration/grenade/tripwire booby traps although they were crudely emplaced and could be easily seen for what they were. What really concerned me was that some of those guys might have set up some good booby traps that cannot be seen. We stayed there for a few minutes, probably while the Company commander gave his report on the situation to Battalion headquarters over the radio. We started to follow the path of the men who had been there on the previous night and at first, it looked like elephants had made a path, the soldiers had beaten down the jungle with just their feet and bodies. After a short while we set a new course following a new compass heading.

Eventually we came to day eight of the operation and we had run out of food four days previous to that. No one really said anything in complaint but even I was extremely hungry now. We were told that a plain troop transport helicopter, a slick, would attempt to fly over and kick out some C-rations, but they would not stop so as to give away our position.

The word came down the line of march to be on the lookout for a helicopter. We humped through the bush for the next hour while, I guess, the Company commander tried to contact the helicopter and bring him to our location. We couldn't pop a smoke grenade to mark our position since that would surely alert the enemy to our presence. The chopper couldn't just fly over to our general vicinity and circle around looking for us because that would surely catch the attention of any enemy in the area. So I guess, we kept moving until the Company commander could see some mountains from which he could determine our position exactly. Eventually I reached a little clearing on the top of a hill where part of the surrounding countryside could be seen.

The line of march stopped and after a few minutes a helicopter suddenly appeared almost directly over me. It slowed very rapidly then hovered about fifty feet from where I was standing. The aircrew kicked out four cases of C-rations, and then the chopper quickly continued onwards. Most of the C-ration cases split open upon impact and some of the men searched diligently for any meals that may have been scattered in the underbrush. Four cases of C-rations equals forty-eight individual C-ration meals. That was distributed to over a hundred men, who hadn't eaten for four days.

I think that I got a piece of candy or maybe it was a muffin-sized piece of bread in a can. That's what I had to eat after eating nothing for the last four days and I considered myself lucky. We humped for another full day and maintained our night position for another night and on the next day the operation ended. I never heard one complaint from the men about the food situation. I think that in the scheme of things, only one piece of bread was my only nutrition over a six day hump. In the scheme of things it was just a minor inconvenience.

Chapter 28

WAR ZONE "D"
May 16-May 17

but who does actually strive to do the deeds;
who knows great enthusiasms, the great devotions;
who spends himself in a worthy cause;
who at the best knows in the end
the triumph of high achievement,
and who at the worst, if he fails,
at least fails while daring greatly,
so that his place shall never be
with those cold and timid souls
who neither know victory nor defeat.

Theodore Roosevelt

Helicopter assault, Flying Over Jungle

I don't remember how we returned from the previous operation. A number of men in my platoon didn't feel very well at all. If I remember correctly, some of them felt very hot and others felt very cold but all of them felt very weak and sick. We got the word a few days later that more that a very large percentage of the soldiers in the Battalion had come down with malaria. There was a big investigation. I guess that the malaria pills that we were taking once a week were the wrong kind of medication for the particular strain of Malaria that was in that area of the country where we had just conducted our previous operation. Now we would be issued small white malaria pills that were to be taken every day plus large malaria pills that were to be taken once a week.

Everyone in my squad, and most of the people in my platoon, did not have malaria, for some unexplained reason. We stayed in base camp for about twelve days while most of the men in my Company writhed in their bunks, suffering the horrible effects of that disease. A fully staffed Company has slightly less than three hundred men. For the entire time of my tour of duty in Viet Nam, I think that our company only had about hundred men.

We were going to go out on a new operation and the men suffering from malaria were not fit for that, or anything for that matter. For this new operation, my Company would field nineteen men. Not three hundred or even one hundred, just nineteen soldiers were now the full combat capability of Alpha Company. Those of us who were not seriously ill were issued C-rations. Everybody went through the packs and threw away anything that they were not going to eat. Scrambled eggs in a can was a particularly disgusting meal and everyone who got one of those threw them into an empty box in case anyone else wanted them. Every man was given his C-rations, there was no choice whatsoever as to what a man was given. Once a case of C-rations was opened, men were thrown their meals without regard to what he might desire. The choices were beefsteak, ham & eggs, ham slices, turkey loaf, spaghetti & meatballs, ham & lima beans, meatballs & beans and the combination of beefsteak, potatoes & gravy.

Each of those meals were disgusting. The meatballs tasted and felt like chewy rubber, the ham slices were full of gristle as was the beefsteak. About the only thing that I could stand was the ham & lima beans. I would open the can so that the lima beans were on the top. Then start to heat it up and when it was warm I would add to it a can of cheese spread on top and then a liberal amount of hot sauce.

Usually I would just eat the beans and cheese. You didn't have a choice in what you got. The best that you could hope for was to trade some of your C-rations to another man for some of his C-rations. You could only hope that someone would take your scrambled eggs in trade for peanut butter, but I never found anyone to make a trade like that.

In every C-ration box was a brown plastic bag that was sealed. Inside of it was a book of matches, a couple pieces of Chicklets type chewing gum, a packet of coffee and a packet each of sugar and salt and pepper. There was a plastic spoon and an amount of toilet paper about the size of half a package of cigarettes. There was also a box containing four cigarettes. The principle C-rations also contained things like bread in a can, crackers, fruitcake, pecan roll, pound cake, a very small can, less than half the height of a tuna fish can, containing cheese spread or peanut butter. And there was a can that contained a candy disc and a package of cocoa. People would try to trade the items that they had received with other men. I would usually trade my main food item for cheese spread or peanut butter or candy or bread. It was well known that peanut butter and cheese spread would alleviate, somewhat, the effects of dysentery.

I don't remember how we got into the bush for this operation, but we were humping along on the first day and I noticed that one of my hard plastic canteens seemed to be swelling up. I had had a brainstorm while in base camp and decided that I would fill one of my canteens with Coca-Cola and bourbon. The pressure of the soda in the heat and continuous shaking caused by walking caused that canteen to distort very noticeably and I decided that this would be a good time to start drinking it. When I loosened the cap, the gas rushed out with a loud noise and the guy in front of me swung his head around and I just whispered to him that "Its all right". He asked me what that noise was but I just said that I knew what it was and not to worry about it.

We were not humping the mortar on this operation so that I was probably only carrying about seventy-five pounds total, which was a terrible load but lighter that what I usually carried. At this time we were moving slowly through the jungle on level ground and were stopping frequently so it was, relatively speaking, not such a back-breaking ordeal as our other operations. We had made no enemy contact so far. In retrospect, drinking on duty was completely reckless but it seemed like a good idea at the time. While in base camp and particularly downtown most of the guys would drink or smoke marijuana but in the bush that was completely forbidden. I never saw anyone do it while on an operation, except for the one mentioned previously, and noone would ever allow anyone to do it anyways. The middle of an operation in the bush was not the time or place to be anything but completely alert.

Anyways, after drinking down a few heavy swallows, I started to get a little buzz and thought that, yeah, this is a good idea. Of course the booze made me feel as if I was more alert but the opposite situation was the case. After about an hour of that drinking, while I felt a good little buzz, I noticed that I had become much weaker. The weight of my load, that had been tolerable, now seemed to be extremely heavy. Also, whereas before, I could use reserves of adrenaline and determination and will power to push on, now I found that I could barely keep up with the men in front of me. Then, eventually the effects of the booze started to wear off. As my buzz decreased, my strength came back to me but my stomach was upset and I was probably even more dehydrated than before. Overall that idea of drinking while on an operation turned out to be a very bad idea.

Immediately prior to this operation we had been issued new equipment, which consisted of basically a collapsible, translucent plastic bag with a cap, a new type of canteen. It had a green, nylon cloth carrier, which protected it to some extent from punctures and a strap for carrying. It was a major improvement because we could now carry an additional two and a half quarts of water and that made a tremendous difference. Now we would have two and half quarts of water in additional to our two, one quart canteens. So now we could live on four and a half quarts of water a day and have some left over for the next day in case we couldn't find water on that particular day. Carrying the extra water was extra weight of course, but it was well worth it.

We came to an area where there were trees spaced out almost evenly from each other. The trees didn't seem to be in a straight line like a plantation would be but I thought that it was odd how those trees seemed to maintain a certain distance from each other. There had been some scrawny bushes on the ground but all of them seemed to be straw-colored, like they were dead, maybe it was a seasonal thing. The line of march had stopped and as usual, most soldiers couldn't know if we would be stopped for five seconds or five minutes or anything in between. I didn't want to remain standing up with the incredible weight of the my load on me and I didn't want to sit down because if we were only to stop for a few seconds, the strain just to get back onto your feet wouldn't be worth the momentary respite from sitting on the ground.

I decided to just kneel down on one knee. I brushed my forehead of sweat and hoped that we were getting close to our night position. I was trying to estimate how far we had come that day and looked off to my right and towards the front of the line of march for any signs of enemy activity in the forest. I lowered my head for a moment, in utter fatigue and pain. A few moments later as I brought my head up to look around there was suddenly an explosion about thirty feet to my left. I had barely seen it out of the corner of my eye. The explosion was an inverted cone of exploding plant material and dirt and shrapnel. I thought that it might have been a grenade thrown by the VC or maybe thrown by an American but there was nothing around that might be a target, except maybe me.

I went to swing my weapon to my direct left, all of that occurring in one second, when suddenly there was another explosion, about thirty-five feet from me and a second later another explosion that was about forty feet from me. There was absolutely no warning from the first two rounds but the third round had a whining sound that lasted a hundredth of a second before it exploded. I only then knew that it was enemy sixty millimeter mortars and they had us zeroed in. They had us a good one. There was some yelling but I couldn't make out what they were saying. I should have been flat on the ground but I remained on my knees and peered around a tree in front of me to try to hear what was being shouted. I still could not understand what was being said, but I saw men suddenly stand up and begin to move forward. The enemy mortar rounds now seemed to be about a hundred feet in front of me and eighty feet to my left. I hoped that the VC were shelling the general area and maybe did not know for certain that they were almost dead on target. If that was so, the rounds should be moving away from me as I pushed forward.

The line of march was moving at a strong pace now and the rate of shelling started to slow down. I thought that I could hear some muffled sounds a mile or so away and thought that those explosions had a strange quality to them. Then I realized that those sounds were probably the sounds of the mortar rounds leaving the tubes. I hoped that other people heard them too and that maybe they could call on the radio and get some artillery or air support onto those positions. After a few minutes the mortar fire stopped. Word came down the line that we had casualties from gunfire at the front of the line. I had not even heard any gunfire. Probably, a firefight broke out at the same time that the mortaring started.

I began to think about a strange phenomenon. When the mortar rounds had landed right next to me, I didn't flinch. I realized that in the case of a mortar or grenade, if you hear it explode, it is already too late to seek cover. If you hear it, the shrapnel has already gone past you. I thought that I should remember that lesson. Of course after the first explosion it would be a good idea to seek some kind of cover. I also realized that I did not react instantly. The first two rounds had hit while I was trying to figure out what they were. I thought that I should start planning my actions so that the first few seconds of an action won't be filled with the thoughts of "What is it?" and "What should I do?" The problem was that there are many ways to die in combat and for many of them there is little or nothing that you can do to protect yourself. Death and disfigurement came out of nowhere in this country and mostly, there was never any warning whatsoever.

We met up with other units in a large area that was shared by several Companies and settled in for the night. The next day the mortar platoon was going to stay in the night position. I was assigned to help out some combat engineers who were going to blow up some defective munitions. On the ground, all laid out in a row, was a very long line of VC munitions along with US artillery and mortar rounds, defective claymore mines, hand grenades, booby trap devices and two 55-gallon drums that were filled with all manner of small arms bullets.

My job was to take some detonation cord, which is like a thin rope that is made out of an explosive material, and wrap it around the artillery and mortar rounds. I didn't like that job at all since these were defective rounds and duds and could theoretically explode at any time, for any reason or for no reason at all. I wrapped the cord around one and then continued the cord to the next round and wrapped that and so forth. We probably had over a hundred rounds rigged like that and then they were all detonated simultaneously. I was prepared for quite a show but it was disappointing. It wasn't nearly as loud or explosive as I imagined it would be. I think that the det cord mostly broke the rounds into pieces without actually setting off the explosive inside them. After that someone poured gasoline into the fifty-five gallon barrels of small arms rounds and set them alight.

They sounded like popcorn sort of when they exploded, very loud and dangerous popcorn. The projectiles did not go very far at all because they were not contained in the barrel of a gun and all of the projectile energy was dissipated in three hundred and sixty degrees. I got very close to those barrels to throw in more rounds. There were many rounds going off simultaneously. Other guys were doing it too, but I thought that it was very dangerous. It could certainly put someone's eye out, to say the least.

We moved out the next day, I don't think that we were carrying the mortar so it would have just been a horrible hump through the woods and arrived at our a night position about an hour before sunset. We set about digging in immediately and went at it strongly and quickly to get it done before the sun had set completely.

When I went out into the surrounding jungle to chop down some trees for our overhead cover, I noticed a number of old, small, dead branches on the ground which produced quite a loud "snap" sound when I stepped on them. After setting up the overhead cover on our fighting position and covering it with sandbags that we had filled, I went back into the jungle and gathered up large numbers of those snapping branches. I broke them into foot long pieces and scattered them all over a hundred feet in front of my fighting position. My thinking was that if the VC probed the position at night then I could easily hear them coming, I'd have some advance warning.

That night, sitting on the ground with my feet dangling into the fighting position, I was glad that I had hit upon the snapping branch technique. It was absolutely pitch black dark. I literally could not see my hand in front of my face. Sometimes when it was as dark as that and I had perimeter guard, I would hold my eyelids open with my thumbs and index fingers to make sure that my eyelids were actually open. There was absolutely no light whatsoever. There was absolutely dead silence. In such an absolute absence of input to ones senses, a person could not be sure that he was even awake, especially if he was beyond thoroughly tired, fatigued well beyond any civilians knowledge or imagination.

In the jungle, with a hundred men around, I think that all of the animals sense them, or smell them, and get as far away from them as possible. Most of the time, even the insects would be quiet, except for the incessant buzz of mosquitoes seeking human blood as a meal, holding off a quarter of an inch from a soldiers skin and eardrums only because of the toxicity of the commercial/industrial/military grade insecticide that we were issued. So you sit there, all alone, completely alone in total blackness and silence for two hours at a time, trying to hear the stealthy approach of a human beings intent upon murdering you.

The nearest American soldier might be twenty feet away but you could certainly not talk to him. That could alert an enemy sneaking up to kill you. In many ways, you were completely alone, many times seemingly the only human alive on the planet, save for the enemy out in the bush who are intent upon killing you or your friends that very night. In that scenario, I would usually be wearing my load-bearing gear so that I had ready access to extra magazines of ammo and grenades. I would probably have had my entrenching tool in one specific corner of the rectangular hole so I would know exactly where it was if the situation deteriorated where that would be my only weapon. I would have committed to memory the approximate distances and directions to the closest fighting positions to my left and right. Then I would just sit there, listening intently for any noise and trying to prepare myself mentally for an enemy assault that might begin with me being shot in the face, or, more likely, with a huge roar and flames. The most difficult thing to do was to stay awake. The daily physical tasks completely exhausted us after one day and we would be on operations for fourteen straight days sometimes. We were chronically dehydrated and the constant vigilance while on the march and enemy contacts probably exhausted us mentally.

My platoon had it easy compared to the line platoons since many times we might only have to pull one or two guard shifts during the night. The line platoons would pull three shifts per night. That is, everyone would be on guard for hour beginning at six pm. Then the regular guard duties began, with each pair of men who had dug a fighting position together taking turns. So, if I was paired with a guy name Arrellano then maybe I would continue on duty until nine pm. Then I would sleep from nine pm until eleven pm at which time Arrellano would awaken me.

Then I would be on guard duty from eleven pm until one am, at which time I would awaken Arrellano and sleep for two hours until three am and stay awake for the rest of the day. Then, at five am everybody was awake and on guard duty until about fifteen minutes after the sun came up. That means that I got four hours of sleep during the night and that was broken into two two hour sessions. It was a regimen that civilians could never possibly imagine humanly possible. The pain and suffering was absolutely beyond the imagination of civilians.

Sometimes I held my eyelids open even if it wasn't pitch black dark. I admit that I did fall asleep on several occasions, it was impossible to do otherwise. I used certain tricks such as holding a lighted cigarette close to my skin and burning myself, hoping that the pain would jolt me back to complete consciousness. Sometimes I would push a stick into my body to produce a sharp pain to try to keep myself awake. Sometimes I would put a stone between two fingers and crush them together with my other hand to produce pain. Sometimes even that would not prevent your brain from just shutting down in utter and complete exhaustion.

If you smoked, the smoke could give away your position to the enemy, but I smoked anyways, especially if the smoke was being blown into our perimeter rather than outwards where an enemy could detect it. I would get down into the fighting position and fire up a match and light my cigarette. It took quite a bit of practice to be able to do that without allowing any light to escape at all, in any direction. Sometimes I would take a poncho and drape it over my head and back and light up under it. Other times I would drape my shirt over my head. After a few weeks of developing the technique, I could get into a tight crouch, bent over, in the corner of the fighting position, down very low, and by cupping my hands could light a cigarette without showing any light whatsoever. Of course, while taking a puff, you had to cup your hands so as to not allow any light from the cigarette to be seen, and, not to allow the cigarettes reflected glow off of your face to be detectable. That took a bit of practice but after a while I could do it perfectly. When it was so perfectly dark as it was sometimes in the jungle even the slightest light could easily be seen.

So every once in a while, you could take a smoke break, or maybe grab a drink of water. The point was not to move at all if you could avoid it because even the rustling of your clothing while you made a slow movement could easily be heard in an environment where there was absolute silence. I had to listen for the sounds of anyone trying to infiltrate the perimeter of the night site, and sometimes depend on sound alone if there was absolutely no light whatsoever. It could be extremely boring, especially if you were very tired. Sometimes I would say prayers.

I would never think about what I was going to do when I got out of the Army, I didn't think I would make it out of there alive. I wouldn't think of my friends back home or think back fondly on my childhood memories. This was very real and very dramatic. I was responsible for my little piece of the perimeter and out in the jungle were people intent upon killing me and the men in my platoon. I didn't think of anything other than just trying to stay awake, and, I have to admit, somewhere deep inside me, I hoped that someone would just shoot me in the face and end this nightmare.

Earlier that night, a helicopter had brought in the makings of a "firecracker". It was a metal, five-gallon can of gasoline. A special powder was poured into that can and that turned the gasoline into something like a weak jelly. Then, there was a metal tube that contained an explosive that was inserted into the can and screwed on where the cans cap normally would be. That explosive had two wires attached to it and they were attached to a long length of wire. At the end of the wire a "clacker" was attached, which is a device normally used to detonate a claymore mine.

That can was then placed about a hundred feet in front of the perimeter. The "firecracker" was to be used primarily as a sort of last ditch defense against a major attack, but sometimes, we would detonate them at random, just to give the VC an idea of what they might encounter if they try to sneak up upon us or attack us. That night they said that it would be detonated at two forty am, during my shift at guard. I kept looking at the watch so as to be prepared for it, but I guess the watch that I was using was not in sync with the guy with the "clacker" because, suddenly, without any warning, there was a sharp explosion of red flames shooting upwards and yellow horizontal flames of jellied gasoline going in all directions. It was quite a show. The flames burned for about fifteen seconds.

No, it would not be a good idea to be anywhere near that thing when it was detonated. It was really a psychological weapon. A good

Claymore mine would do more damage to an enemy attack but no one likes the idea of being covered in gasoline, especially when it is sticky, and on fire.

It had been my turn at guard duty on the perimeter. I was seriously tired but managed to somehow stay awake for at least most of the time. Finally, my watch indicated that I had finished my tour, so I slowly extricated myself from the foxhole, so as to make as little noise as possible and then started walking towards the interior of the perimeter, in the direction that my squad had set up in. But, I was extremely tired, way beyond description, on the brink of just falling to the ground and instantly going to sleep and I wasn't exactly sure where my squad was located. Also, it was almost pitch black dark so I couldn't see more than five feet in front of me, I was just going on sense of smell or some kind of sixth sense, pure guesswork.

I walked up about a hundred feet and expected to see hootchs but there were none to be seen. I wasn't sure whether that was because I was in the wrong place or simply because the visibility was so poor. I kept walking in a straight line because I figured that even if I couldn't see their hootchs that I would eventually find them by tripping over their hold down stakes or falling onto one of the ponchos. But obviously my sense of direction was wrong because I kept walking and walking, way past where they should have been. I was beginning to be afraid that I had over walked the perimeter on the other side and find myself outside of the opposite side of the perimeter where I would probably be blown away, no questions asked by our own guards.

Then, out of the blackness and silence, I heard a command: "Who goes there?" I thought to myself, "What kind of perimeter guard would ask who goes there from someone coming from within the friendly perimeter? But then I thought it was obviously a perimeter guard who had the courage to risk his own life in an attempt to avoid a friendly fire situation, to challenge someone who he probably suspected to be a VC sapper.

Technically, he should have "challenged" me with something like "34" (the days password) to which I should have replied something like "Eisenhower", but luckily, the guy realized that most people do not remember the daily changing "password/response". The answer to his challenge of "34" provoked my generic response of "censored Me!! Lower your weapon!, I'm 173rd Airborne!". He probably realized that my pea soup thick Bostonian accent could not be have been achieved by a Viet Cong infiltrator. I briefly spoke with him and he told me that I had been on the eastern end of the perimeter and had walked all of the way through to the western perimeter. Luckily I had just missed going out beyond the perimeter.

He gave me directions to my squads encampment, but it was so dark that I thought that his instructions couldn't really help me, but, by fumbling around in the dark, and awakening a number of persons, I finally found my squad area. Of course, that detour took many minutes, during which time our part of the perimeter was undefended. I finally found the designated soldier to take over guard duty. After I woke him up and was sure that he was fully awake and on his way to guard duty, I immediately climbed under the rain shelter of my poncho hooch and instantly fell into a deep sleep.

Although, the probability of attack was extremely high, my body was completely exhausted and my mind and emotions were beyond, by far, any normal limits of endurance. Surely, since I was Airborne Infantry, I could, and would, go far beyond what most civilians would regard as possible. However, little did I recognize at that time that I had already far, far exceeded those limits. I would later learn that such demands upon a human being can prove to be impossible to sustain regardless of superhuman willpower and determination. I wanted and needed and required, and my body and mind demanded, some type of rest, if only for a most very minimal amount of time.

We humped for a couple of more days. That operation was another fifteen to one odds, with us being outnumbered, but this time we were told that we could depend upon air support and maybe artillery. I figured that we were not really put in there to fight and win. We were put in there for bait. The VC would see that we were badly outnumbered, would group together to attack, and then air support and artillery could decimate them. Of course that was during and after they would inflict a lot of casualties on us. Anyways that was my hypothesis. We were Airborne but we weren't Supermen. I think that that would be good for the Generals in the Pentagon and the politicians who could say that a thousand VC were killed today and we only lost seventy-five American Paratroopers.

We had been humping mostly through light to medium jungle when we suddenly came to a large area that was mostly just wide-open green grass. There was a large stand of jungle with very large trees sort of in the middle of this wide area, sort of like an island in a sea of green six-inch high grass. We walked over towards it and as we got closer we could see that the area had been heavily bombed, by air I would guess, because there were many very large, thick trees maybe four or five feet in diameter that had been blasted down and laying on the ground, on top of each other, facing every which way, sort of like enormous "pick up sticks". The explosions had been so powerful that most of the leaves had been blown off of the branches and were lying on the ground in a thick carpet. That was much too much destruction for artillery, there must have been at least five hundred pound aerial bombs dropped there to have done so much damage.

There was an overpowering smell of chlorophyll from a million leaves being blasted into a billion pieces. I remembered that smell from back in Boston after a big hurricane when many leaves were ripped off of trees and other big trees uprooted. All of that destruction was done in an area of about a hundred meters square. We climbed over and under the blown down trunks and through the tangled branches searching for bodies or equipment or trenches or tunnels but didn't find anything. Obviously, there must have been some substantial enemy activity there a few days ago and the VC must have been caught, out in the open so to speak, by a flight of Air Force fighter/bomber jets.

We set up for the night and I was on guard duty at about ten pm. It was very dark but there was some light filtering through the jungle top so that here and there I could make out part of a bush or very barely make out a corner of a tent a foot off of the ground. In front of me was almost pitch black dark, but within the perimeter there was a small amount of moonlight scattered about, penetrating the jungle canopy far above.

As usual, there was no sound whatsoever. Then, I thought that I heard a faint sound very close by. I pointed my M-16 towards the sound, or where I thought the sound was coming from. It suddenly seemed to be coming from my left side and slightly behind me. That was a bad situation because if I fired to my side and missed, the shot may hit the guy in the fighting position next to me. The sound repeated about every thirty seconds, lasting for a few seconds at a time. Then it seemed to be closer to my back, towards the center of the perimeter so I turned my body to face inwards.

Then I really didn't want to fire because the round would pass through our night area. If I didn't hit it, or if the round went through it, the fired round might hit someone sleeping within the perimeter or hit a perimeter guard in back of me. I was listening very intently now and it seemed that the Thing, what it was I could not determine, was within a few feet of me. I put down the M-16 very slowly and quietly and slowly and carefully pulled out my bayonet. When I undid the snap of the strap that held the bayonet into its sheath, the extremely slight sound of the snap being pulled apart seemed to me to be very loud. For some reason I was not wearing my helmet. I bent down, finding it by feel alone and put it on, I really don't know why I thought of doing that, maybe because I figured that if this thing was going to shoot me in the forehead that maybe the helmet might afford some protection.

Something was very, very close now, within two feet or less. There was some slight moonlight there and I should have been able to see it, but I could see nothing out of the ordinary. There was more than a bit of panic welling up. I kept commanding myself: "Maintain, Maintain!" I could hear something like deep breathing sounds, sounds that occurred very, very slowly. I thought that I could feel its warm breath directly on my face. My best guess now was that it was a very large animal. "What the Heck!!" I thought. It had actually reached over and pressed down on top of my helmet. "Where is this thing!?" I thought. Its obviously right in front of me but I can't see it at all. It had actually reached out and pressed down on my helmet, pushing down three times, I guess to see if I was edible. Luckily I had put on my helmet and it probably now thought that I would be a hard meal to digest.

I stood there, in the blackness and silence of the middle of the jungle, fully expecting something or someone to grab me by the throat and tear it out or plunge a bayonet into my heart or shoot me in the face or jump into my position and start killing me. I wasn't sure if it was a large animal or a man but I realized that it was certainly some kind of monster in the almost total darkness that would probably take my life in a horrible manner within seconds. "No, maybe I'm overreacting, maybe I'm hallucinating" I thought. But then I realized that I had been pulling this perimeter guard duty for many, many months. This was a new and unique experience.

I didn't want to strongly whisper a warning to the soldier in the fighting position fifteen feet away to my left because I thought that

that might cause an infiltrating enemy soldier to just let loose a burst of automatic fire at him or at me or at both of us. I didn't want my platoon mate to be suddenly killed by something that he was probably completely unaware of.

I told myself that I would deal with this thing, up close and personal. It was my problem and I would deal with it, but that I would cry out a warning as soon as it struck me. I tried to prepare myself for an extremely vicious fight against something that I could not see. I steeled myself for a fight with bayonet and fists, and forced myself to think of stabbing and hitting the creature or man as many times as possible before he or it took my life from me. Then, suddenly, there was a muffled "whoosh" sound, like something jumping, scraping his body against vegetation and scruffing his feet upon the ground and it was all over.

That sound had come from my left rear and I had been expecting it from my right. I was shaken up quite a bit, and disconcerted by the fact that, whatever that was, it could have easily gotten me. I did not hear it land from its jump and thought that whatever it was, it must have jumped a huge distance. How it ever got from my right side to my left side I'll never know. What is was, I'll never know. But I was just left standing there, bayonet in hand with my heart pumping very fast and my blood filled with more adrenaline than it had ever seen while I tried as hard as I could to muffle the sounds of my hyperventilating breathing.

In retrospect, I came to an explanation. I didn't realize at that time how damaged my hearing was due to firing the mortar. When I thought that the danger was to my direct front, I was off by forty-five degrees because the hearing in my right ear was, and is, permanently damaged. It was probably a tiger. If he had grabbed me by the head or the throat to drag me off and eaten me, I wouldn't have been the first or the last soldier in Viet Nam to have been killed in the middle of the night that way.

When my two hours of guard duty was up, I awakened the soldier who was scheduled to take over. Although the incident had occurred an hour and a half earlier, I told him in no uncertain terms that there was something out there, something very serious. He seemed to completely disregard my warnings, just dismiss it out of hand. Now I can see his perspective. I told him that there was something around there that was extremely dangerous. Of course he knew that, that was the reality. There were creatures out in that jungle that would come in and kill you for supper. There were also enemy soldiers out there that were intent upon coming in and killing you and as many friends of yours that they could. That was the reality of a combat situation, every night.

We humped for another two days and hadn't crossed any streams. Therefore I had been without any drinking water. I was extremely thirsty to say the least. Finally we came to a small stream, about an inch deep and began to cross it. The water was filthy and muddy but I quickly took out a canteen and began to fill it. The water was so shallow that I had to dig a little hole, stirring up more mud, so that I could put the canteen in on its side deep enough to try to mostly fill it. I only had time to partially fill two canteens then had to hurry to catch up with the line of march, realizing that I was holding up the troopers behind me in the line of march and that they would have to hurry up.

I took out my little bottle of iodine pills and placed a tab in one canteen, knowing that the water would not be purified for another hour at least. I opened the other canteen. I just had to have a drink, right then, being overpowered by the desire to get some liquid into my body. I knew it was wrong but I was way beyond thirsty. I took an iodine pill and swallowed it, then drank from the raw water in my canteen. My thinking was that maybe it could purify the water while it was in my stomach, or at least that's what I irrationally hoped would happen. Due to extreme luck I did not get sick.

That night we set up in a small clearing. There were some very large trees but just grass on the ground, no bushes at all which was unusual. As dusk approached, everyone took up a guard position. At my fighting position I evaluated the situation. To my right and to my rear was the principle encampment area. To my left, about twenty feet away was very heavy jungle with huge trees and hanging vines with very heavy undergrowth. To my front was a very long area of mostly open grass. After dark, it was my turn to pull guard duty for the first two hours. A soldier came up to me at the beginning of my shift and gave me a strange device that looked like a very compact telescope with a rather large lens. It was a Starlight scope. There was a lens through which the operator looked at one end, but light from the front did not go straight through as in a telescope. The theory of its operation was as follows:

light enters the front lens and is picked up by a miniature television camera and displayed on a miniature television screen, after the light had been magnified a hundred times. That light was in turn viewed by another miniature tv camera and displayed on another miniature TV screen, further magnifying the light 100 times. That was repeated by another camera and screen so that when a person looked into the end of it, he was actually viewing a miniature TV screen where the light intensity read from the front lens was a million brighter.

Basically, that Starlight scope could see in the dark. It could easily see things illuminated by the moon and if the moon was not out, it could see things illuminated just by starlight, in fact, it could see things that were illuminated by the miniscule phosphorescence given off by worms or vegetation. The guy told me not to use it unless it was a real emergency because its battery life was very short. He also told me that it takes five or ten minutes to "warm up", after it is first turned on to get a good picture. About an hour later, I decided to turn it on, just to see how it worked. At first all I could see was a blank screen, then, after a few minutes, I could make out the shape of the bushes in front of me and to my left. The picture was very much like looking at a black and white tv, except that this picture was black and green, a rather eerie effect because everything seemed to shimmy slightly. After a few more minutes the picture was clearer but not of much value and I decided to turn it off, to save the battery.

The next day, the guy who was had been on guard duty after me asked me how I liked that Starlight scope and I simply told him that it was better than nothing but not by much. He told me that he had turned it on for half an hour and that the picture was as clear as bright daylight, objects could be very easily discerned, except that everything was in shades of black or green. I thought that it was a very excellent device, if only we were issued enough batteries to be able to use it all night, every night, which we never were.

On this operation we had been issued C-rations and also some B-rations, otherwise known as "LURP" rations (Long Range Reconnaissance Patrol) rations. They consisted mostly of a big bag of dehydrated food. You had to heat up about a quart of water and then pour that into the bag and wait five minutes before you could enjoy rehydrated vegetables with bits and pieces of what was supposed to be beef but tasted like and felt like bits of rubber. Those rations were much lighter than C-rations but a big problem with those rations was that you needed a spare quart of water, which we usually did not have. Plus to boil a quart of water really required a lot of heating tabs which we never nearly had enough of or C-4 explosives which we never had enough of. The result of this plan, that must have looked good on paper, was that now we went even more hungry a lot of times.

While humping through the bush, I began to fantasize that maybe I might make it out of there alive. If that happened, what would I do with the rest of my life? I thought that maybe I could be a mercenary, maybe even end up in Viet Nam with a lot more pay than I was making as a soldier. I thought how much would I charge, to be a soldier again in Viet Nam. I thought maybe twenty thousand dollars a year, enough to buy a good house and a new car at that time. Then I thought that I would never do another full year of this, so maybe I'd charge five thousand dollars for a month. As I humped along through the jungle, tortured by each step and facing death or maiming from a hundred threats, I finally realized that I would not do this again for even one day, not even for a million dollars. I was really in this country because the Army had ordered me to go. I hoped that my actions might help some VietNameese people in some ways and if that is so then I am glad that I could help. But, for money alone, for any amount, I would never do this again.

Chapter 29

WAR ZONE "D"

May 18-May 24

It doesn't require any particular bravery to stand on the floor of the Senate and urge our boys in Viet Nam to fight harder

George Mc Govern

Giant Foliage

We returned to base camp at eight thirty at night. Early the next morning one of the soldiers in my platoon was showing others some

VC equipment that he had acquired during the last operation. He had some pistols that looked to be in serviceable shape and one that looked as if it could not be salvaged. Pieces were missing from the grip of the weapon and it seemed to be frozen with rust. I asked him if I could have it and he grudgingly said that I could keep it. I looked all around the platoon hootch and finally found a shallow metal pan. I put the pistol into that pan and poured out two full cans of gun oil onto it and placed it up high on top of a stand-alone closet.

I hoped that by the time I returned from the next operation that it would be loosened up enough to take apart and made operable. I specifically did not put it into my personal footlocker because I figured that if I was killed that some rear-echelon clerk would probably slap a shipping tag on it and send it to my parents. If that happened, I didn't want them to get a box full of oily goo. Around ten am on the next day we moved out again on another operation, only fourteen hours since our return to base camp.

We assaulted by helicopter without incident and humped all day until we came to a medium sized clearing where there were some American artillery and four point two inch mortars (known as "four deuce") already in place. Just after my squad was assigned a place for the night and I had dropped my gear, without any warning whatsoever there was suddenly a huge roar. A jet had come in, about a hundred feet high and at full speed, and dropped a load of butterfly bombs about two hundred feet from me. There was an almost instantaneous explosion of a hundred rather large explosions of red flame and white light as the grapefruit sized bombs smashed into rubber trees at about eight feet off the ground mostly or onto the ground. If anyone had been in or near those rubber trees their bodies would have been ripped apart by hundreds of jagged pieces of white-hot shrapnel.

I was shaken and disturbed because it took place so close to the perimeter. If the pilot had been off by a slight amount he would have killed thirty or so Americans. I don't know why they ever made that air strike or why they made it so close to us and we certainly had no warning of the attack. If I was a VC close to that attack, I would have abandoned any plans of attacking that perimeter and withdrawn miles away or maybe made new plans to get out of the Country. That explosive air attack with the butterfly bombs was utterly devastating.

My mortar platoon and the three other mortar platoons in the battalion stayed at that site for three days while straight out light infantry platoon patrols from the four Companies were sent out in different directions. During that time our new platoon Sergeant got it into his head for some reason that he would go out at night on an ambush mission. That new platoon Sergeant probably had fifteen years or more in the Army but he had never been to Viet Nam and had never been in combat. He seemed to have the attitude that it was his platoon now and he was going to change around everything. Of course, as far as I and the other guys in the platoon were concerned, he was just a "f—new guy".

He went out with the ambush patrol just as the sun was going down. I don't know how far they went into the jungle but about twenty minutes later we received a message on the radio for a fire mission. We were going to fire a round and the ambush patrol would notice exactly where it landed and report back. It would be what's called a registration round. The Fire Direction Control team (FDC) team would then mark where it landed onto a map and plotting board so that if that patrol required mortar support later in the night then we could provide more accurate fire and provide it faster.

I guess that the new Platoon Sergeant, with the ambush team, called in his location and then called for a round to be dropped a hundred and fifty feet away from him. The FDC team argued with him over the radio at length and suggested that the first round should land five hundred feet from his position, in case he was inaccurate as to his location. The Platoon Sergeant, I guess, argued that he knew exactly where he was. I thought that it was extremely foolish of him to call for a round so close to where he thought that he was on a map, the slightest mistake could be disastrous.

The Platoon Sergeant won the argument, he had authority over the FDC anyways. I helped set up the gun, with the directions that we received, and then dropped a round down the tube. We could barely make out the sound of the of the round as it exploded in the distance about thirty seconds after being shot out of the tube. There was no reply over the radio for about a minute, which was worrisome because we should have received an immediate radio response regarding where the round landed with respect to the location of the ambush patrol.

Then the Platoon Sergeant called by radio and instructed us to not touch the mortar at all until we heard further from him. About fifteen minutes later the Platoon Sergeant came crashing through the bush, without notifying anyone that he was getting closer to our perimeter. Why he wasn't shot immediately by the perimeter guards I don't know, he rightfully should have been. He was outraged and went directly over to my gun and started yelling that the gun was not set up properly, according to the directions given by the FDC. I and others pointed out to him that he said not to touch the gun, that of course it was not exactly set up right because every round knocks around the mortar and it has to be readjusted after each round, if possible under the circumstances.

He said to set it up again, and he listened to the directions from the FDC and watched as we adjusted the gun to their exact specifications. Then he inspected the mortar round to make sure that it was the right type and that it had the proper number of charges on it and looked through the sight on the mortar to make sure that the gun was aimed properly, deflection and elevation properly adjusted. He checked everything, which was perfect, then told us not to touch that gun again until we heard from him again. Then he stormed off into the bush, by himself, to rejoin the ambush patrol, begging, I thought, to get shot by any VC in the area. That was completely outrageous behavior. Storming through the bush, at night, by himself, would be a very good way to get himself killed and he put the ambush patrol in jeopardy by pointing out their position to any enemy in the area.

Finally, we received his radio message to fire a round. I very gingerly put the round into the tube so as to not move the gun at all from its set up from its set up position that the Platoon Sergeant had so meticulously scrutinized and we fired off a round. We expected a report over the radio within two minutes, reporting where the round landed and expecting a correction to our fire. This time there was no resultant radio message at all. That situation was very unusual and bad. Our radio operator tried repeatedly to establish contact with the ambush patrol but received no answer. That indicated that everyone on the ambush patrol had been killed or the radio had been destroyed. About fifteen minutes later, in the full darkness of night, the Platoon Sergeant again came crashing through the bush at full speed. Again I couldn't understand why he wasn't immediately challenged or lit up by the guys on the perimeter, or for that matter shot by the VC in the bush.

This time, the Sergeant was completely disheveled. He was covered with dirt and leaves and I figured that he had the round dropped extremely close to him and the patrol. Again he was outraged and inspected the gun carefully. This time, we had automatically reset the gun and it was in perfect form. This time he got the directions and set up the gun himself, ordered us not to touch it, and stormed off back into the bush. I went over to the gun and checked it myself.

That Platoon Sergeant had done a good job of setting it up, not perfect, not as good as my team would have done, but it was OK. Fifteen minutes later, he called in to fire another round. From the radio traffic I knew that that was not some kind of immediate fire, it was just a registration round. I placed a round half way into the tube holding it with the web of my hand. I should have dropped it immediately but then got another idea. I pulled the round out of the tube and placed it on the ground. Then I slowly walked over and talked to the FDC and said, "Look, that idiot is going to get himself and half of the ambush team killed. Why don't you give me new co-ordinates so we can drop the round a hundred feet away from the co-ordinates that he gave you?"

The FDC team smiled slightly and told me that they had already taken that into consideration. The present adjustments should put the next round a hundred feet <u>away</u> from the exact coordinates given and demanded by the Sergeant. I dropped in the round. The Platoon Sergeant radioed back that yes, it was a perfect round, a hundred feet from his position. I looked over at the FDC team with a big smile, the FDC team seemed quite pleased with themselves. Of course, if the FDC had followed his orders the round would have landed directly on top of the Sergeant and killed him and his team.

The next day, my platoon stayed put and the other platoons went out on patrol. For some reason, one of the guys in the mortar platoon went out on patrol and ended up being shot in the leg by one of our own men. I don't know the full details of it.

Later that evening, I was near a radio that was tuned in to the frequency of a radio with an ambush patrol that was lying in wait out in the bush beyond our perimeter. The radio near me was turned on full time. When a radio is tuned to a certain frequency but noone is broadcasting a message there is the noise of static. Of course, when someone else broadcasts a message then we could hear it. Actually, when the other radio operator presses the "talk" button but doesn't speak, there is a noticeable change in the noise of the static, usually most of the static would stop, it was a distinctly noticeable change to anyone listening.

Especially on ambush patrols, there may be a situation where the enemy is so close that broadcasting a message on a radio would give away the location of the ambush patrol. In such cases, they used coded pushes of the talk button to send a message. For example, to initiate a message, the ambush radio operator might push the talk button three times very quickly. That would be picked up on the listening radios as three very quick changes in the noise of the static. On this night, there seemed to be a bit of commotion by the radio operator near me by a radio operator named Brown and a few other guys nearby.

They were picking up the three quick button pushes which meant that the radio operator in the field had an urgent message. Brown whispered into the microphone "Are you in close with the VC?" The reply was two quick pushes, which meant, "yes". He then whispered into the microphone "Do you request a mortar fire mission at the registered location?" The reply was one push, which meant "no". Brown then whispered into the mike "What do you need?" The response was five clicks, which meant an air strike was requested. He then whispered "We cannot give you an air strike at night. Can you talk at all?" The reply was eight pushes, which did not have any meaning. That went on for about ten minutes, where we couldn't understand what was trying to be said, and codes that contradicted each other or that had no corresponding meaning. After a while there was no coded messages being sent and we didn't know what was happening. Was the ambush team wiped out? Was the RTO terribly wounded? We didn't know, it weighed on our minds. Was there some terrible problem with the ambush patrol? We didn't know but due to the coded pushes of the radio we suspected the worse. For thirty minutes there was no communication, verbal or the coded pressing of the talk button. Then the whole scenario started up again.

The next day I found out that the radio operator on the ambush patrol was a new guy who did not know any codes whatsoever and was completely unaware of the significance of pressing the "talk" button. He was not even listening for incoming messages. The entire scenario of the night before was just him just nervously pressing the "talk" button on his radio as he laid in ambush, completely unaware of our side of the conversation.

We hung around all day and dug in deeper and filled in more sandbags. There was straight infantry manning the perimeter while we were located about thirty feet in from the perimeter. The guys on the mortar, or the inside perimeter only had to pull guard duty for two hours a night, which was much better than the soldiers on the perimeter.

I was just lying down under my poncho tent at night when there was suddenly a flash of light and a large explosion from outside the perimeter but very close to it. Dirt and shrapnel with two hurricanes of wind flew all around me but I wasn't hit. The VC had infiltrated close to our perimeter and set up their own claymore mines and then detonated one of them, hoping to kill guys on the perimeter and anyone else close by. We then went on high alert, and I climbed into the gun pit with sandbags around it about two feet tall and laid down with my weapon and LBG but after a while I just fell asleep and about an hour later I awoke and just crawled back to my hooch and fell back asleep. The next day, the guys found two more VC claymores outside of the perimeter, aimed inwards to our positions. I don't know why the VC didn't set them off.

The next day the patrols went out again but they started taking casualties. As they were brought in, there weren't enough medi-vac helicopters available to evacuate all of the wounded so the Brigade Commander brought in his personal command chopper and picked up two wounded men and evacuated them himself, under enemy fire.

We had been firing a lot of mortar rounds during those days in support of the patrols in the bush and for harassing fire. Each mortar round had six to nine charges and if we were not firing at maximum distance then a lot of spare explosive charges were not used. We had quite a large pile of those unused charges and had no use for them but they could be used by the enemy for their own mortars or to make booby traps. We were told to destroy those charges so we spread them out in a big pile about three feet tall and six feet in diameter. Inside the mortar tube they will explode with the micro, micro micro tight tolerances of the gun and produce a very huge explosive force but out in the open they will just burn rather quickly but not explode. Someone just put a match to the charges at the edge of the pile and within thirty seconds the entire pile was burning furiously like some sort of giant blowtorch, reaching up about eight feet tall, then eventually burning out after about ten minutes, completely burning up the entire supply of excess charges.

That evening my platoon got the word that we would be going on a new operation the next day. We would be picked up by helicopter and meet up with Army of Republic of Viet Nam (ARVN) troops to search the area. We were told that this would be an area where no allied soldiers had ever been, not even ARVN. We were picked up and landed by helicopter without incident. About noon we met up with ARVN troops who were riding on Armored Personnel Carriers (APC).

We walked on the ground while the ARVNs slowly proceeded forward and generally close to their American Infantry assault troops who also served as their personal bodyguards in a way. I really didn't like the whole idea of that operation. No allied troops in that area for the last thirty years? They have probably been digging in for the last thirty years. About one pm we got the word that we would stop for thirty minutes for lunch. Stopping for lunch was almost unheard of, it almost never happened. Based on what had been said about that area, I thought that it was very dangerous and we had no idea of what we would run into or the size of the enemy force in this area. I thought that it was a very stupid idea to stop for lunch, but for whatever reason, I was glad to get the tortuously painful weight of my equipment off of me for half an hour.

I looked over at the ARVNs and expected them to be on full alert, I didn't think that they would be so stupid as to stop for lunch but I was wrong. Several of the ARVN APCs had live chickens tied up among their equipment and the ARVNs started to make a small campfire out of branches and then killed and plucked the chickens and started cooking them. I guess we had stopped because the ARVNs insisted on their chicken lunch. Maybe they thought that it was safe with our infantry all around them. I really didn't like the idea of providing security in such a dangerous area while they cooked up a Viet Nameese version of gourmet chicken. We, of course, ate warm or cold C-rations. They took their sweet time in preparing the meal, probably well over an hour. Anyways, I thought, I could really use the respite from destroying my body with the horrendous loads that we carried. Then it struck me that we should put our rucksacks on the APCs. I approached my platoon Seargent and platoon leader with that brilliant idea but after ten minutes of negotiating with the VietNameese, that idea was nixed. I think that it was because of a total gap in language communication between VietNameese and English.

We humped for another hour or so and then we met up with some trucks that took us to our night sight. It was still very early, about three pm and we dug in very quickly, the dirt being soft. The next day, patrols were sent out but my mortar platoon stayed behind, set up beside a 4.2-inch mortar. I didn't have much to do because other men were assigned to be on duty to man our mortar for a few hours so I began to walk around the area. I think that there was another Army Company, not 173rd Airborne, set up in the area so the perimeter encompassed a very large area.

In one place was a large open field and in it was a little tent, just a standard poncho set up flat, about two feet off of the ground, out in the open sun. Inside that tent was a guy who looked extremely ill and he was sweating more than profusely. Someone told me that that guy had malaria and was waiting to be medi-evaced by helicopter. The temperature under that poncho must have been a hundred and thirty degrees, at least, but I guess the malarial fever was even more brutal. I have no idea of what happened to that guy who was suffering from malaria under that little poncho hootch. I still sometimes wonder weather that soldier survived his ordeal, I doubt it.

There was some sort of building that had mostly fallen down. It looked as if it was made out of some sort of solid stone, it looked as if, at one time, it must have been of some sort of major significance because it was so fancy, with stone carvings. I thought that maybe it was an old church or maybe the entrance to a graveyard. It had mostly been destroyed by bombs or just fallen apart due to age. I walked around it, studying it for a while, then walked only about a hundred feet and noticed that a rubber plantation bordered the north side of that perimeter. I walked to the northwest a bit because I could see a nice little house, like a ranch house, something that you might see in the U.S. That was extremely unusual and I never saw anything like it in Viet Nam.

There was a man just coming out of the door of that house, dressed in civilian clothes, with brown pants and a nice white cleaned and pressed short-sleeved shirt. He waved to me and then walked down a dirt path about a hundred feet long and said "Hello". He was obviously French and could speak English just barely enough for me to understand him. I asked him about the situation and he told me that he owned the rubber plantation and that the house was his, in which his wife and children lived. This situation was extremely unusual because we almost never operated around civilian houses but this house was all by itself, out in the middle of nowhere.

The Frenchman was probably about thirty years old and invited me to join him in his house for a meal and some wine. That was an almost irresistible offer, but I begged off, pointing to my clothes, which were beyond filthy dirty. I probably had not taken a shower for a week or more and my clothes probably looked as if they hadn't been washed in six months. He insisted that it was OK and really wanted to express his thanks to the soldiers around his house.

I thought that he would probably really like to have two Companys of American infantry around his house at all times. He insisted that his wife would not mind my appearance but I couldn't imagine myself, in my present filthy condition, to be in someone's house. I realized that the condition of myself and the other men in my Company was far from any definition of what is a minimal standard required by Western civilization. I thanked the guy and slowly walked away. I dearly wanted to partake of his supper and wine but I couldn't bring myself to go into his house in my present condition. He was probably the only non-Vietnamese civilian that I had spoken with for the last ten months.

I think that we were loaded onto trucks later that day and were brought to a very large clearing in the forest. There were already many other men from other units there and some large tents had been set up. We got the word that we would be there for two or three days. The word also was that a number of generals and legislators and other VIPs and reporters would be visiting the area on the next day.

I thought that that whole thing was absurd. We were pulled off of an ongoing operation that was producing all kinds of captured food and equipment and destruction of enemy tunnels and base camps and making lots of roads. Now we were ordered to go to this location so that a bunch of rear echelon generals and congressmen could go back and tell everyone that they were in the thick of it in Viet Nam, making sure that the boys were taken care of. That entire general area had been completely cleared of any and all enemy. There was a hundred times more men and equipment than was necessary to secure that area for anyone. But it was OK with me because it meant that we didn't have to beat the bush all day. We even had hot meals flown in and had water trailers nearby.

At mid-morning of the next day we got the word that the generals and the legislators would be flying in by helicopter in an hour or so. We were told that we were to just fire our weapons into the surrounding jungle at a given signal, just to make sure that not even a squirrel was within thousand yards of that position was alive, I guess. They also said to fire off as many rounds as you want because they were bringing in huge supplies of ammo and we could then get brand new ammo. All of my ammo was old and dirty and had been saturated with sweat and swamp water and had seen many creek crossings so I was determined to fire off a goodly portion of my ammo. Of course, I would keep at least half of it, just in case that we were attacked or the new ammo never arrived.

When you fire a single round, the M-16s recoil, while light, is still enough to throw the rifle to the right and upwards slightly. You can almost instantly recover, aim and fire another single round but the recoil will again throw off your aim. On full automatic, you don't have that split second to bring the rifle slightly back to the left and downwards so that when you fire on full auto, the rifle lifts to the right and upwards a little with every round so that after one second of firing, which is about ten rounds, the rifle is pointing very much upwards and to the right, very far from the original target. My squad Sergeant fired off a few magazines on full auto, firing from the hip, and he controlled the weapon very well, obviously he had practiced that many times and had finally gotten the knack of it, I had to give him credit.

We got the word that firing would commence within two minutes. When the command was finally given the perimeter erupted with hundreds of men firing simultaneously. There was enough ordinance being thrown out to stop a division in its tracks. The previously peaceful area was suddenly transformed into a place that seemed to have suddenly descended from a hitherto unknown dimension. There was a truly terrible roar of hundreds of men firing every weapon from M16s to M60 machine guns, along with M79 grenade launchers and LAWs (Light Anti-tank Weapons). Men were firing from prone positions and standing up firing from the waist while machine gun crews fed belts of ammo into their guns. It seemed as if hundreds of men had been dropped into a sea of muzzle flashes and rocket flames, mixed in with a huge amount of white smoke and the distinctly acrid smell of gunpowder.

There was a small tree about a hundred feet from me, about fifteen feet tall with a trunk about six inches in diameter. I thought that I would try firing my M-16 on full automatic, just to get some practice firing it that way. When we got the word to fire, I fired off ten magazines, about a hundred and ninety rounds, most of them on full automatic, some of them single shot. After a few minutes we got the word to cease fire. There was suddenly a deep silence, with a huge amount of smoke wafting through our ranks with the very acrid, nostril burning smell of gunpowder in the air. I thought that that must have chased away any enemy within ten miles of us.

I went over to the tree that I had fired so many rounds at and noticed that I had nicked it once about six feet high and put one round into it about eight feet high. That was pretty bad shooting, much worse than I had expected, but under actual combat, I would have fired single shots or would have been on the ground with the M-16 bipod attached, which would have resulted in very much better accuracy on full automatic.

After about a half an hour, three very large helicopters flew in, not big Chinooks but maybe some kind of Navy or Marine choppers that probably held thirteen or so passengers. Those visitors exited their aircraft and walked around shaking hands, mostly amongst themselves. They quickly separated into six or eight groups. There were about four three star generals, four major generals and a slew of one star generals, along with a bunch of self-important looking civilians that I imagined had never so much in their life had gotten mud on their shoes. There were also about six photographers.

Each group seemed to have their own "flunky". From the way that the "flunkys" were acting, I surmised that their job was to run errands, to take notes and to generally look approvingly upon their leader and constantly nod their heads up and down, in a gesture indicating "Yes, I couldn't agree more", whenever the leader spoke. I thought that it was very funny to note that those "flunkys" were mostly full bird Colonels. There were probably twelve congressmen and they and the generals all stayed pretty much in one very small area. Some Brigadier general came over to my small group since we were very close to where they had landed. He asked some sort of lame questions and his "flunky" took many notes about something, I do not know what, but he seemed very interested that my buddy Pierce had two rifle slings, connected together, on his M-79. He asked him about it and Pierce simply said that he liked to carry the M-79 down low while on an operation.

The photographers took all manner of pictures, mostly of the VIPs next to the helicopters, with the jungle tree line a thousand feet away. I noticed that they were taking few, if any, pictures of the troops. Maybe because the infantrymen were dirty and unkempt and beaten up after two weeks in the field. I suppose, to this day, those people tell of their dangerous journey to be among the soldiers in the field in Viet Nam. Most people in America had zero credits for danger regarding Viet Nam, those VIPs did take some chances so I'd give them ten credits for facing danger. I'd give two hundred credits to the go-go girls in base camp who came over here to entertain the troops but that's on a scale from zero to a million where the average infantryman gets two million credits.

I realized that the American People had no idea of the dangers and pain and suffering and disease and filth and fear and maiming and killing that was the average infantryman's life there. It really cannot be expressed in words, there are no words for it. If you haven't experienced it, it is beyond your imagination, it certainly was beyond mine, even while it was happening. Many things exceeded my wildest expectations, I never knew that such hardship existed in the world or could be suffered day after day after day without simply killing a person. The suffering and agony of a usual days hump was beyond, way beyond, my previous imagining. Carrying a full load of military equipment all day long through the jungle was like being on a Medieval torturing device, the weight of it pulling and tearing at your joints and muscles, the pain, just horrible. In civilian life most of those soldiers would have been hospitalized after a few days. I was constantly amazed at how much endurance a human being had in him, but it was directly related to the pain. There simply are no words to describe it.

Things there were very strange and exotic, the jungle with Tarzan vines and "wait a minute" vines and leaves ten feet long and eight feet wide and wild peanuts and hot peppers and banana trees and coconut trees and pineapples. The searing sun and monsoon rains and a hundred percent humidity with a temperature of a hundred and ten and clouds below you while you are on top of a mountain and jungle above so thick that you can walk for days in total shade and pitch black dark nights in total silence. The heavy weapons and frightening massive explosions of four deuce mortars being fired and mini tanks with six tank killing rocket launchers on it, the death rays from "puff the magic dragon" and the roar of a gun ship firing a hundred and twenty rounds a second and the clank of tanks five seconds before one runs over a mine. Stone age people with spears and little people with weapons, driving tanks. People living in unimaginable squalor and people intent upon killing or maiming you and trying to do so in every possible way. Dogs tied up as livestock, huge water buffalos, elephants, black and white monkeys, deer the size of house cats and eight-foot snakes and hooded cobras and spiders that eat birds. Death and traumatic amputations and third degree burns on the face, gut shot soldiers and permanent injuries, four days without food and constant disease and filth and disease filled drinking water. Physical demands beyond imagination, turning quickly into day after day of extreme torture, pushing on, foot after foot when you think that each step will be your last step of your life, if not from a mine or a sniper that from a heart attack or stroke even though you are nineteen years old. There were horrors and hardships there that cannot be imagined and cannot be believed even when they were happening to you.

We went over to where all of the ammo had been brought in and I picked up two hundred rounds of brand new clean ammo. I walked back to my area and spent most of the afternoon cleaning my old ammo, one bullet at a time, very carefully and completely. The next day we moved out on foot to continue our operation. After about thirty minutes I decided to check my ammo in the ammo pouches on my belt. I was going to check them every thirty minutes because I wanted to try to figure out how the ammo got so filthy dirty after a few days. I opened an ammo pouch and couldn't believe what I saw. The top few bullets in their magazines that I could see, the brand new ammo, was filthy dirty, mostly with tiny pieces of leaves and stems, all over the top bullets and mixed down in the magazine with the lower rounds. I guess just beating through the bush, bulling through the vegetation, maybe with vines or thin branches catching on the lid to the ammo pouch resulted in the ammo being basically unusable after just thirty minutes.

It may have been usable actually but would be very prone to jam the weapon after not too many rounds being fired. I checked the other ammo pouches and some of them were not as bad as the first but all of them had a leaf/vegetation litter inside. I was glad that I had another hundred and fifty loose rounds in my rucksack, in a sandbag, but in an emergency they would require time to load into magazines, time that could kill a man. They should have been all ready in magazines but I couldn't get extra magazines from the supply Sergeant, not authorized you know.

We beat the bush all day but ended up almost back at where we had started at the big open area. This time, we camped for the night in the jungle very close to the open area. The next day about ten choppers came in to land on the wide-open area and we loaded on to be air assaulted into a new mission. We flew for about twenty minutes and came into a landing onto a rice paddy. I was on the first stick of three choppers that would land first. The chopper descended over a rice paddy and hovered there to unload us, about fifty feet from the edge of the jungle.

It was not a good idea to walk on the dikes of the paddies if you could avoid it because that is where the VC usually planted a booby trap or mine. We only had to go about twenty feet on the dike and I couldn't see anything out of the ordinary on it. I was about the third or fourth guy to exit the helicopter. Everyone else jumped down onto the dike and started to run into the tree line but I decided to just jump into the paddy itself. I knew it was chancy and hoped that the paddy wasn't too deep. I pushed myself out with my arms forcefully, sliding my body off of the chopper with all of my equipment and the mortar barrel in my hands. There was a distance of about five feet from the floor of the helicopter to the top of the water in the dike.

I suddenly found myself half way up to my chest in water. I had sunk into the mud almost up to my knees and was deathly afraid that I would sink deeper and drown. My mind was racing in a panic and I suddenly realized that I still had the twenty-eight pound mortar barrel on my shoulder so I threw that onto the paddy dike. That maneuver should slow down my sinking into the mud and water of the paddy I thought but also if I drowned the rest of the squad would have a critical component of the gun.

I tried to take just one step closer to the dike but I couldn't move forward and the attempt just seemed to drag me down deeper into the filthy paddy water and mud. I wanted to throw off my rucksack but was afraid that any further movement would make me sink deeper into the mud and water of the paddy. I reached out desperately to try to grab onto the dike but could barely touch it with the tips of my fingers. In near panic I looked to my right for the other guys in my squad, hoping that they might see my situation but their backs were turned to me, running as fast as they could, intent on reaching the tree line. I yelled and yelled for help but my voice couldn't be heard over the roar of the helicopters.

In the back of my mind I imagined just being stuck there, the other soldiers proceeding on with their mission me stuck there like a duck in a shooting gallery, slowly sinking deeper until I drowned in that filthy paddy water. My friend Pierce happened to shoot a quick look behind him, just to make sure that I was following him. He couldn't hear me because of the noise of the choppers taking off, and he couldn't really see me because my head was almost below the level of the dike.

I bent forward, desperately grasping with my arms stretched out as far as possible, trying to grab onto a part of the dike, with my fingernails if necessary and yelled out for someone to please save me, I was up to my neck in water and slowly sinking. I noticed that my voice was weak, I was panicking. I could see the back of one of the men in my squad, running as fast as possible under his load. I yelled again, "Help me! Please!". I didn't want to expend any more energy whatsoever because I realized that I was all alone and needed every speck of energy to try to save myself from drowning in that filthy paddy water and mud.

It looked as if Pierce saw no one behind him and probably figured that I must be in front of him. As he turned to go back towards the jungle, I yelled again and he saw the mortar barrel on the dike and knew subconsciously there was something terribly wrong since I was not carrying that barrel. He knew immediately that that situation was not right at all. He expected to see the assistant gunner, who was me, holding onto to that barrel and when he saw only the barrel, with no one next to it he instantly dropped his mortar baseplate and threw off his rucksack and ran back towards the dike, knowing that the assistant gunner should have had that barrel in his arms. I was up to my neck in rice paddy water and the bottom of my helmet was about six inches away from the level of the paddy dike. My mouth was only six inches from the top of the water and I was sinking further into the mud at every minute. He went into the jaws of Hell, at great risk to himself, to try to save me, even though he couldn't see me, on the off chance that he might be able to save me.

From his position, he could not see me or hear me yelling for my life, but he determined that I was close to that barrel and since he couldn't see me, he realized that something terrible had happened. Pierce realized that since there was just the barrel of the mortar lying on the dike and I did not have my hands on it that something very wrong was happening.

He ran back to my position, in a complete disregard for his own safety and in complete disregard for his assigned orders and mission. When he finally spotted me, neck deep in mud and water, his expression was one of suddenly recognizing something, but it was something and a situation where he couldn't believe his eyes. He shouted at me, "What happened!?" I just yelled back to him at the top of my voice, over the roar of the helicopters, "Please help me!, Help me!!, Please help me!!" He stooped down then laid down on the paddy dike and grabbed me by the back of my shirt and started to pull hard.

I yelled to pull with everything he had. I was stuck in the mud up to my knees. He pulled me out a bit and I could feel the suction break off of my boots and I grabbed the dike and put my arms over it, like a drowning man would grab a floating log. With Pierce pulling in a manner that was beyond desperate and me pulling with every ounce of energy and then some, I finally hauled myself out, flat out on my belly, onto the dike and perpendicular to the it. Now I had broken the suction of the mud and could maybe move forward, away from that sucking death by drowning. He asked if I was all right and I just replied by yelling, "Go! Go! Get the hell off of this paddy!"

That was no time to give sincere thanks and handshakes all around for saving my life from a horrible end. He ran back to his gear and scooped it up in one hand, not waiting to put it on correctly and quickly ran into the surrounding jungle. He knew that during the time that he used up in going back to save my life that the line of march had moved out and that he was way behind and that alone endangered his life. I grabbed the barrel of the mortar and quickly followed him, crouched down, into the jungle. As far as I was concerned, that soldier named Pierce had saved my life, at a total disregard to his own life and safety, and should get the Congressional Medal of Honor. But in the scheme of things, his heroism was not even acknowledged.

It took a few minutes to catch up to the other guys in the line of march and then we continued on as if nothing had happened but I was very shaken up by that episode. The rest of the men in my platoon were completely unaware of what had just occurred.

We humped for most of the day but stopped about four o'clock, which would leave us plenty of time to set up for the night. Our location was in medium jungle but there were some bare spots where we could set up our tent/hootches.

I was assigned to dig a fighting position close to a lone tree that was about ten feet tall but very thin. I started to dig and after about fifteen minutes I stopped to take a quick break. I noticed that in that tree was an ant nest made out of leaves. It didn't quite look like a fire ant nest (there is a reason that they call them "fire" ants. As small as they are they have a nasty little venomous sting which is especially bad when a hundred of them sting you within seconds)

I reminded myself to be very, very careful not to hit that nest or that tree. I could have chopped it down but then we would have thousands of angry ants running all over and into our fighting position. After a few minutes I started digging again for a while and again decided to take a break and let my fox hole buddy take over, digging his half. I climbed out of the hole and swung around with the entrenching tool in my hand and accidentally hit that small tree and the nest dropped directly onto my back near my neck.

I had stripped off my shirt in the heat and exertion of digging that hole and I could instantly feel hundreds of ants all over my shirtless back and ran directly over to Pierce and a few other guys yelling," Get them off of me!, Get them off me!" The guys didn't know what I was talking about and I turned around to show my back and continued yelling. The guys just stared at me, not knowing what was going on, when suddenly Pierce noticed the ants all over me and jumped over to me and started swatting the ants off and then he picked up a shirt to swipe them off of my back. At any second, I expected hundreds of fire ants to start biting me all at once and couldn't understand why they had not already started to tear my skin off bit by bit and inject me with their poison but Pierce swiped all of them off. I was totally unbitten. I picked up one of the ants and could see that they were reddish brown but didn't have the big pincers of the fire ants. If they were fire ants, it would have been a completely different story.

An hour later a Sergeant told me that a chopper was coming in and told me to go out there and "bring it in." I had no idea of what any of the commands meant but had seen other guys bringing in a chopper so I went to a small clearing just as the chopper was coming in. There was very little clearance between the blades of the chopper and the surrounding branches of the trees on the landing zone. I raised my arms straight up above me, then moved my arms downwards, then to the left or right to try to indicate to the pilot how to fly to avoid the trees. He looked down at me and then, I guess, decided to pay no attention to me at all, he would bring in his ship by himself, personally evaluating the clearances. He brought his ship in perfectly.

After the chopper landed I noticed that it was loaded with supplies, mostly wooden boxes filled with mortar rounds. A few other guys ran over and we started to pull out the ammo boxes and stack them up. Each wooden box was loaded with four mortar rounds, each contained in a heavy, sealed, black cardboard tube. The boxes had loops of manila rope on both sides to use as handles. Depending on the type of rounds, e.g. high explosive, parachute flare, white phosphorous or long range, the boxes probably weighed between fifty to seventy pounds. After they were unloaded, we had to move them to a new location about a hundred feet away. They were awkward to carry and the edge of the wooden boxes dug into my thigh with each step. Sometimes each soldier carried two boxes at a time, that was hard, awkward and painful labor.

The mortar platoon was going to stay here for the next day and it was decided that we would set up the mortar along a different compass heading from the one that we had already lined up onto, so we had to move the aiming stakes. It was decided that we would get some practice setting up the aiming stakes in new locations. One of the guys in my squad went running out to pick up the stakes and move them, depending on hand signals from the gunner, who was looking through the aiming sight on the mortar. It went fairly slowly but the guys got some practice. Then I decided that I would get some practice and ran out to get the stakes. I followed the hand signals from the gunner and eventually placed it in the right place, but I noticed that when the stake was placed in the exact right spot, that I could see the reflection from the aiming sight.

A few inches to either side, being two hundred feet away from the gun, I realized that I could not see the reflection from the sight. So the next time that they moved the mortar and I received directions from the gunner, I just picked up the aiming stake and ran to the left until I could see the reflection and planted the stake in the ground right there. I looked up and out towards the gunner, who was waving his arm greatly, towards his left, indicating that I should move the stake a far distance to the left. In other words, that where the stake was now, was very far from where it should be. I tried to gesture for him to look into the sight but he and the Sgt started yelling for me to move the stake far to the left. I refused. They just got more and more aggravated.

After a while, the gunner looked into the sight and was shocked to see that the stake was exactly where it should be. He just had to give me minor signals so that the stake was perfectly straight up, in other words the stake was perfectly positioned and just had to be moved so that it was perfectly perpendicular to the ground. I walked back in to the mortar position and the Sgt started to yell at me for not following their directions. I told them that they were wrong, weren't they? and that I could now set out that stake in five seconds instead of thirty or forty seconds. They told me to do it again. I started to run out and they changed the position of the mortar and therefore the aiming sight. I grabbed the stake, got a rough idea that the mortar had been moved to point off to the left, and ran in that direction and planted the stake before the gunner could even look through his sight. I even straightened out the stake so that it was perfectly perpendicular. The gunner looked through the sight, ready to give directions to move it, but it was perfectly set up. I saw the gunner tell the squad Sergeant to look through the aiming sight on the mortar. They signaled me to come in. I said to the gunner "was the stake set up right?" He said "I wouldn't believe it if I hadn't seen it with my own eyes. That stake couldn't have been more perfect if we had spent sixty seconds doing it".

That was a little trick that I had discovered, out here in the jungle, during combat operations, which we were never taught in mortar school. During basic and advanced infantry school a person could get a badge for rifle and other things in the rank of marksman, sharpshooter or expert. I got an expert badge for mortar during infantry training by setting up the gun within a certain time. My squad and I could now set that gun up ten times faster than anyone could ever do during training and qualification for an expert badge.

The next day we were picked up by trucks for the long ride back to base camp. We would be traveling in a convoy of perhaps fifteen trucks. We had been told the night before that we would be practicing ambush tactics on the way back. We would be given a signal, at a certain time, and then we were to jump off of the trucks and fire our weapons. We were going to practice that maneuver at a place where there had been several ambushes in the past. So we rode along for about two hours when all of the trucks suddenly stopped and the order was given to get off and start firing to our flanks. I jumped off and aligned myself with the other men about ten feet into the jungle from the road.

The trucks at the front of the line had already stopped and their cargo of troops had immediately disembarked and were already firing wildly at nothing and everything, which was a good response to an ambush. In the place where my truck stopped, the area parallel to our direction consisted of tall and heavy jungle vegetation about twenty feet wide, paralleling the road. Beyond that was a dry rice paddy about four hundred yards wide that ended with solid jungle. I clicked the safety off on my M-16, aimed to hit about three feet high into the far jungle and squeezed off a round. The report from my weapon caused an astonishingly unbearable pain on my right eardrum. I ignored that pain and fired off three more rounds very quickly. The pain was instantaneous and shockingly severe. Just the noise of firing my own M-16 was unbearable and although I was in a kneeling position, the sound felt as if it was a wall of pressure that hit my head so hard that I was violently thrown off balance.

Every round that I had fired resulted in my body feeling as if someone was hitting the side of my head with a baseball bat. I couldn't understand what the problem was exactly but obviously there had been some very substantial damage to my eardrum and inner ear from firing the mortar. Of course, if someone had actually hit me violently on the side of my head, right on my ear canal, it would have knocked me out and caused permanent damage. But that was almost exactly what happened to me. It most definitely caused me permanent and severe hearing loss, or, more likely, the mortar fire had already caused the problem. It most certainly knocked me to my knees and sent my brain and consciousness reeling. It basically knocked me into unconsciousness for a few seconds. It was unbelievably and overwhelmingly violent and tortuous, indescribably and horribly painful and disabling.

I recovered rather quickly from that beating and was determined to find a way to fire that weapon. I tried to cover my ear with my shoulder but that made aiming the rifle accurately impossible to achieve. I fired off another round, sighting with my left eye, trying to get the muzzle on the other side of my head. That shot was extremely off of the mark and the pain and pressure was only relieved in the slightest. It wasn't an airtight seal and just reduced the effects slightly. Plus, the recoil pushed the weapon backwards, over my shoulder so it took valuable seconds just to get back on target. Slowly, I began to realize that if this was a real ambush, I wouldn't be of very much use to anyone. At most I could fire one round every fifteen seconds while recovering from the staggering pain and loss of balance from each round fired.

I pulled the trigger once more but there was no sound. I pulled back on the bar of the weapon, to eject what I thought was a dud, but nothing happened, no round ejected. I pulled out the magazine and noticed that I still had ammo. Now I had to break the weapon apart and check for the problem. The problem was that the last round fired off all right but was mostly still stuck in the breech having not been automatically ejected. I tried to pull out the spent cartridge with my fingers but couldn't get a good grip on it. I tore my rucksack off and searched inside of it, retrieving the cleaning rod. That rod was in two pieces that screwed together, with a cylindrical, brass wire brush that screwed into the top for cleaning the barrel of the rifle. I took just one piece of that rod and threw it down the barrel but the cartridge didn't move because it was stuck so tightly. Finally, I had to screw the two pieces together and jammed it down the barrel very forcefully about three times until the cartridge was dislodged.

That misfire was probably due to ammo that was dirty but it was impossible to keep ammo clean for more than twenty minutes in the bush. Luckily this was just a practice run but the fact that my weapon malfunctioned upset me. If that had happened in combat it could have had disastrous effects on my platoon and me. Thereafter, I kept the cleaning rod taped to the rifle so that if that ever happened again I could get back into action relatively quickly.

I thought that that might be a good thing. When we returned to base camp I would go to the medics and then insist on seeing a doctor. The doctor, I thought, would certainly confirm that I really wasn't fit for duty and I could take it easy for the rest of my tour and maybe even begin to heal from the damage to my hearing. I probably could have been assigned to the base camp where I would be safe, where I wouldn't have to live a life of misery and torture, where I could "get over" and drink cold soda and beer and eat good food every day. Anyways, I might be a liability to those guys if I couldn't effectively fire my weapon.

Then, I thought, I don't want to leave those guys. I want to do my full tour. I want to be there when they encounter their next dangers. I want to be with them if I can help them out. I felt about protecting them as I would feel if they were my brothers. I really didn't know these guys very well at all, but we had been through a lot together. I wanted to do my part to try to help them make it home alive.

Its a strange phenomenon, I cannot explain why I thought that way. I guess I thought that if I was assigned to base camp that there would not be any new men immediately available as replacements and even if there were, they would have had no experience in Viet Nam.

Chapter 30

PLEIKU
May 26-May 30

Biernacki and Arrellano

I don't remember how we got back to base camp in Bien Hoa, or much of what occurred during the two or so days that we stayed there, but within sixty hours of returning we were off on another mission. I remember that there were five new replacement guys in our platoon tent when we arrived and things were rearranged a bit inside that hootch. Sleeping cots and standup storage lockers had been moved around. I initially blamed the new guys for rearranging our "furniture" but they told me that they had nothing to do with it.

I searched the top of the closet where I had left the VC pistol, that a guy had given to me just prior to our last operation, soaking in gun oil but it was not there. I asked the new replacements if they knew where it was now located but none of them knew anything about it.

I remember that we were finally told to load onto trucks that would pull up right outside of our tent. We lugged our gear outside about half an hour before the trucks arrived and I took a picture of all of our gear lying on the ground. Each mans load looked heavier than the one seen before it. This new operation would, for everyone carrying those loads, again, be another merciless, merciless horrible physical torture replete with more danger of being horribly mangled or killed than any civilian could be subjected to in a hundred lifetimes.

Eventually the trucks arrived. We put on our load bearing gear with suspenders, bandoliers of ammo and helmets, threw our loaded, tortuously overloaded rucksacks into the trucks, picked up our individual weapons and gear and boarded. We got the word then, at the last possible minute, that we would only be going about fifteen miles away from our base camp, to an area for which our Brigade had responsibility for providing security. It probably took almost two hours to reach our objective. The only reason we did so was that we were traveling in military trucks, probably with six wheel drive. Still it was a serious struggle to continue onwards through the deep mud of a dirt road.

It started to rain heavily while we were traveling in the open back of the trucks, drenching us utterly. We finally arrived at our destination which was a large cleared area containing no vegetation at all. Obviously that cleared area, about three hundred yards long and two hundred yards wide, had been recently bulldozed down to bare dirt. It was now medium-brown colored mud. Completely surrounding that cleared area was medium to heavy jungle.

My mortar platoon was assigned to a particular area and told to dig in. We were already completely soaked to the skin by the rain and our gear was thoroughly saturated with rainwater as well. About two minutes after beginning to dig fighting

positions we were all covered in mud. I took turns with another guy in digging the fighting position. When I had a break I tried to do something to set up a sleeping shelter so that some of the equipment could be protected from the rain, but I realized that all of the gear was thoroughly soaked and by the look of the dark sky and the unrelenting rain, nothing would be dry for days.

Through the downpour, I picked up a machete and walked into the edge of the jungle. I chopped down a few small saplings, about seven feet tall, about two and a half inches in diameter, then cut off the branches from the trunk. Then I chopped the main trunk into three foot sections to use as tent pegs. Each tent peg had to be chopped like a sharpened pencil with each machete stroke making the point of the strake more and more like a sharpened pencil. The tent was soon set up but the ground under it was just saturated mud about an inch deep and I realized that sleeping that night would be particularly miserable. I made a mental note to always bring the air mattress no matter how much it weighs. There was no sense in trying to wear a poncho to protect yourself from rain because we were already completely soaked with rain and wet mud. Even if we were dry and put on a poncho, with the extreme humidity, a person wearing a poncho might remain completely free from rain but would still be soaked with sweat from digging the fighting position because the poncho would not allow much air to circulate under it. We hadn't even finished digging in and we were already in a wretched situation.

During the day a large tent was trucked in and set up. That would be used as a mess tent to cook and serve hot food and as a meeting hall for the officers. I think a few officers set up their night (day) position inside that large tent, probably the company commander and the executive officer but I'm not sure. I am pretty sure that they spent a nice dry night inside there, probably sleeping on cots off of the ground.

My section had to man the perimeter even though we had the mortar with us. When it was my turn to stand guard duty the guy I was relieving went running over to me, awakened me and handed me a poncho. It was raining very heavily and with him just taking off the poncho, handing it to me and then running over to his hooch ten seconds away he must have gotten very wet, totally saturated with a truly monsoon rain. I put on the poncho and climbed out of my hooch and walked over to the fighting position. There was about two inches of water and two inches of mud at the bottom of the rectangular hole. There was an overhead cover roof of thick sticks and filled sandbags over the position. That would provide some protection from shrapnel or snipers in trees but it provided no protection from the rain. The full amount of rain falling on the roof leaked heavily between the sandbags and fell onto the guard and into the pit.

The poncho had a hood on it which covered your head and part of your face. I positioned the poncho so that I could sit on the back side of it and keep my backside out of the mud. I wasn't sitting directly in the mud and I was staying out of the direct rain with the poncho but I was already soaked and covered in mud from the work of a few hours before. This situation was unusual because of the large cleared area behind the perimeter. The moon was half full and the open area was fairly well illuminated. I thought that with me sitting between the jungle and the moon lighted area behind me that I might be a very well silhouetted target so I jumped down into the pit, into four inches of cold water and mud. After a few seconds my boots were filled with it. After a few minutes I really didn't like how that felt so I jumped up a bit and sat on the ground, with my legs dangling into the hole. I decided to lay my upper body down so as to present less of a silhouette but I had to hold my upper body and head out of the two inch mud and cold rain with my arm on the ground with my palm holding my head up, sleeping on my arm. That position quickly became very uncomfortable so I spent the next two hours alternating between standing in four inches of cold water and mud on my feet partially exposed to enemy fire, or uncomfortably lying sideways in two inches of mud and water, or sitting upright fully exposed to enemy gunfire with the wind that slowly lowered down my body temperature.

Of course, the main point was to guard the perimeter and when it was raining it was particularly dangerous. The noise of the rain falling on the leaves of the bushes and trees and vines in the jungle and the noise of rain falling on the overhead cover and onto poncho covers completely hid any noises that would be made by an approaching enemy. So you just had to be exceptionally alert to any noise or movement but it was really impossible to detect an attack or approach of the enemy until he was immediately on top of you. The guard would also have to continuously look to each side of him, sometimes you could see the fighting positions to both sides, most of the time you could not because of heavy vegetation between the fighting positions. You also had to look behind you incase the enemy had infiltrated the perimeter and was now amongst your fellow soldiers. If a sleeping man got up to go to the bathroom and you spotted him, you never knew if it was in fact one of your men going to relieve himself in the middle of the night or a VC who had just killed a man in that sleeping position and was now coming for you.

The jungle, about ten feet in front of me, was almost absolutely black. With the moonlight you could make out some of the tops of the trees or the spaces in the high foliage where the leaves let in some light and there were extremely faint light of some kind and of different colors in some places down deeper in the trees. Those eerie lights were so slight that sometimes I wasn't sure if I was just imagining them. In other places in the bush, closer to the ground, or actually on the ground, it was impossible to determine, was a dim light from reflected moonlight

bouncing off of leaves from higher above so you couldn't see anything clearly at all. It was mostly extremely dark in that jungle with various amounts of slight light shining in various places, variously illuminating parts of trees and bushes.

You basically just sat there in the cold rain, waiting to take a bullet in the face or waiting for a VC claymore mine to tear your body to pieces or waiting to hear gunfire or screaming from another section of the perimeter, or listening for any unusual sounds from the fighting position beside you which might be an American fighting for his life with his throat already sliced by a VC infiltrator. They never covered that aspect quite fully in basic training at all, to say the least. This may very well be your last night on earth, your last five minutes, and if you survived this night the next day would usually be filled with absolute torture and pain and hunger and thirst and the very real possibility of horrible disfigurement and dismemberment. My brain played with the possibility of hopelessness. Sometimes I would wonder if this was what I was put onto the Earth for?

The next morning when I awoke it was just raining lightly but it didn't much matter because I was still soaking wet from the previous day. We heated up some coffee under the poncho tent, trying to prevent the rain from distinguishing our heating tabs, but there was no sense in seeking shelter from the rain ourselves. We were already soaking wet and unless the sun came out strongly, we would remain that way for quite a long time, maybe all day, or more. Actually, we would stay completely soaking wet, our clothing thoroughly saturated with mud and rain and sweat for the next four days with really no relief whatsoever.

We were ordered to dig another fighting position inside the perimeter and two other guys started to dig a place big enough for four people. We would eventually surround it with sandbags about three feet high and make a roof out of lumber salvaged from mortar ammo boxes and then place filled sandbags on top of it. It would be a place to sleep while being somewhat protected from enemy mortar attacks.

Another guy and I were filling sandbags with one of us holding the bag open while the other shoveled mud into it and then switching tasks after a while. It was heavily raining and there were hundreds of very swiftly running rivulets of water everywhere, three inches deep. The ground on the previous day had been flat but now it was very scoured with hundreds of those little rivers digging through the ground as we watched. In fact the open ground was now mostly open water, it was mostly a field of running water. I didn't know that it could rain so hard and long anywhere on Earth.

The weather had turned cool, even cold, which added another dimension of misery to our existence. The sky was a continuous overcast of slowly moving streaks of varying degrees of blackness, The scene was of such seemingly otherworldly desolation that I could scarcely believe it. I had never seen such a seemingly malevolent display of nature in the sky.

I got out my camera to try to record it. I knew of course that the picture could never, ever record the impact of the sights and sounds and misery that we were living. The new guy had joined our little group filling sandbags. I told them that I was going to take a picture. There was six inches of mud everywhere. Everyone was beyond totally drenched from the rain. As I raised the camera to take the picture the new guy held his shovel in front of him at an angle and smiled broadly. I thought that that was funny because it was really so miserable and the new guys smile made it look like he was having fun. Actually, the guy who was smiling really meant it. He was a very friendly guy. I couldn't have known it then but he would be killed later by an enemy soldier springing out of a hidden "spider hole" and the other trooper would be permanently and severely deafened by a rocket landing next to him, but those things would happen after my tour of duty.

The mostly dug-in underground hooch was almost completed by now and some guys had already moved some of their equipment into it. A guy in my squad came up to us and insisted that we go over to the nearly completed, mostly underground house and check out something. From the tone of his voice, it was going to be something very interesting, disturbing and disgusting. My best guess was that it was a giant centipede giving birth to hundreds of babies or something.

We had constructed some stairs going down made of old wooden artillery bomb containers and there was a piece of lumber about 6 inches wide and 4 feet long that was part of the support for the bottom of the ceiling and another board running part of the way along the edge of the ceiling perpendicular to it.

There were a few large nails sticking out of the main ceiling support. Someone had seemingly hung his load bearing gear onto one of the nails so that it wouldn't take up floor space and it would be handy to grab if he needed it quickly while exiting. I noticed that and decided that it was a good idea and decided that I would do the same later. The soldier that insisted that we follow him told us to look at it. I thought: "This is why he insisted that we go over to see it?" "What is there to see?" I said: "Yeah, that's a good idea. What is the big deal?" and turned to leave. The other soldier strongly protested. "Look at what its hanging by!" he shouted. I looked closer and remarked that it was hanging by one of the large nails on the main ceiling beam. He told me to look much closer.

That was when I noticed that the LBG was not supported from falling at all by the main beam, its entire weight was hung up by a nail on the side, a nail through the pull ring of a high-explosive grenade. Still, twenty pounds of canteens, ammo and grenades held up by a bent over cotter pin was amazing. I quickly looked to see how much the cotter pin had been distorted. My head involuntarily jerked my head back a foot when I saw that the cotter pin had never been bent over, it was as straight as it was when it came out of the factory. Of course when it comes out of the factory its put into a heavy cardboard cylinder so that its impossible for the cotter pin to come out.

Apparently, the new guy had entered the hooch and hung up his gear, apparently from the canvas web gearing of his LBG but actually hanging on the pull pin of an HE fragmentation grenade, and then decided to go off somewhere. Worse still, the guy had not bent the cotter pin of the grenade over, so that at any moment, I don't know why it hadn't already happened, the gear would fall, the pin would be pulled out, the grenades' primer would ignite, and five seconds later everyone in the hooch at that time would be killed or horribly wounded.

I had a mini heart attack and turned immediately to jump out but a soldier behind me was blocking my way, whereupon I most violently pushed him out of the way, up the stairs and outside, to escape a quick and violent end. Once out of the blast area I had second thoughts and a few seconds to evaluate the situation. I decided to go back in and try to fix it. Should I go down and correct the situation? NO! I thought. I am not going to go down into that situation that can be set off for any reason or no reason and blow up in my face at any second.

I learned that the guy who was responsible for it would return soon. I decided that <u>he</u> would have to take care of it. I thought that that would be a very good idea. After about ten minutes that soldier who was responsible for that situation returned, whereupon he was advised of the situation. He went back down, seemingly unconcerned, and rearranged his LBG so that it was hanging by the suspender strap instead of the pull-pin of a hand grenade. We very strongly expressed to him our opinion of everything from his carelessness, his un-soldierly conduct, his complete disregard of such simple precautions, his character and our opinions of what sort of family he had come from. It was a brutal verbal attack upon him but a million times less brutal than the catastrophic physical damage than his carelessness could have and probably would have caused us when the weight of the LBG silently slipped out the cotter pin of his grenades in the middle of the night and set off four pounds of high explosives within a confined space while we all slept.

I pointed out to him that the grenade cotter pin wasn't even bent over and he said that he was completely unaware that he should have them bent over. So for the last week or so we had been humping the bush with this guy whose grenades could have easily been set off by having the pin catch in a big thorn or spike. I guess it was our fault for not telling the guy things like that, things that were never taught in basic or advanced infantry training back in the states. There were a number of things that we learned as we went, sometimes the lessons were learned after people were killed and sometimes after people should have been killed but through the grace of God they

were spared, just like this situation. Then I realized that when I first arrived in country that I didn't know to do that and an experienced trooper had told me about it.

The next day it stopped raining early in the morning although the sky was filled with huge dark clouds. Around noon some hot food was brought in by helicopter and a serving line was set up in the big tent and we lined up. My clothes were actually almost dry. I had just entered the tent when there was a sudden very strong wind that violently rattled the entire tent, especially the sides and a few minutes later the monsoon began again at full deluge.

Many men had already brought their food back to their little underground houses but there was probably twenty men standing inside the tent, eating their lunch off of paper plates. The men still standing in line outside pushed forward to get out of the rain but there were still about twenty men standing outside. An order was loudly shouted for everyone, except officers, who had already been served food to vacate the tent. Many men went running from the tent, food on paper plates in hand, over towards their separate hoochs, which allowed the men standing in line to get in under the protection of the large tent and get served some food.

I lifted one section of the side of the tent (closest to my hooch) and took one step into the downpour then immediately jumped back inside, letting the flap of the tent fall so as to keep out the monsoon outside. I calculated that it was raining so hard, that by the time I made it to my shelter the food would be soup or, more likely, just be washed of my plate completely.

After about five minutes all of the men that had been standing in line had been served their food and all of the enlisted men had left, but the tent was still packed with bodies standing bolt upright like sardines, all of them officers. I didn't like the idea of that at all. Some field grade officer again jumped up onto a table and started yelling very loudly for all enlisted men to leave, demandingly stating that only officers could stay. By that time all of the enlisted men had already left except for me. I was trying to shovel the food into my mouth as fast as I could but knew I couldn't finish it before that Major started screaming again. I glanced at a few officers standing directly next and around me, who were keenly aware that I was a private first class, and I lifted the edge of the tent, ready to run. My plan was to just force feed myself a few more mouthfuls and then bolt out of the tent, shoveling my food as I ran and then just throw to the ground any soup that was left after five seconds and realizing that I would most certainly be thoroughly soaked before I could arrive under my shelter.

I lifted the side of the tent with one hand and was just about to step out into that torrential, monsoonal downpour with a plate of food in my hand when an officer looked directly at me and said, "Stay here!" Even though everyone was packed extremely uncomfortably close together and my presence just added to that problem, this officer, in direct disobedience to the senior officer, told me to stay. Another officer next to him looked at me, then shifted his position to shield me from the view of the screaming Major, and said softly "Take all the time that you want. Stay here as long as you want". None of those officers knew me, I had never seen them before, but I guess they did know something that the screaming rear echelon Major did not know, about leading combat soldiers, and about human decency in general. I was extremely impressed. Three days later, after constant very heavy rainfall, one morning it finally stopped and the sun came out. A few hours later we loaded up onto trucks and went back to base camp.

Chapter 31

PLEIKU
Approx. June 1-June 8

And gentlemen in England now a-bed
Shall think themselves accursed they were not here,
And hold their manhoods cheap whiles any speaks
That fought with us upon Saint Crispin's day.

Shakespeare

Purple Haze

The very next day we moved out on a new operation. We loaded onto trucks, which took us to an area where there were big Chinook helicopters. We loaded onto the choppers and rode for about an hour. I hated those Chinooks and started to feel sick to my stomach from riding in that cramped, hot aircraft with no air circulation and not being able to look out of a window.

Our mission was to guard the area around a Prisoner of War (POW) compound. We set up in an area that had heavy jungle but also a large amount of cleared land. We were at an elevation that was higher than the POW compound and could see it clearly although it was about a mile away.

We were going to stay in this area for a while so we dug the fighting positions, as usual, and then dug a gun pit for the mortar, then a sleeping position about a foot deep and then had to dig trenches that connected the fighting positions to the sleeping positions. All of that digging took place over a period of two days and when it was finished this position was the best-fortified situation that we had ever set up.

About a quarter of a mile away was a Montegnard village. It was located in what looked like an island of jungle and surrounded by a large meadow of brightly sunlit dark-green long grass. I never got closer to that village, but from what I could make out, it was just a little congregation of houses made of leaves and branches, some of them on stilts, out in the middle of nowhere and a hundred miles from electricity or running water and two thousand five hundred years away from modern civilization.

Around noon on the second day we were going to fire a few rounds from the mortar to get it sighted in. The Companys platoons were in the jungle on combat patrols. One of the Forward Observers (FO's) that was with those platoons called in where he wanted the round to land. That FO most likely would have spotted some sort of landmark like a big rock or the intersection of two creeks or maybe a big tree at the edge of a rice paddy and would call in a mortar round and then notice onto the map co-ordinates where it actually landed.

Firing the mortar produces a significant kickback even at charge zero and at a maximum charge the kickback is unbelievably and frighteningly powerful. The firing of the first few rounds can be a very dangerous situation. If the ground is very hard or rocky, the recoil of the mortar can send the gun sideways or backwards instead of directly down into the ground. If things go wrong then the soldiers in the gun crew can easily be badly wounded or killed. You can never know for certain exactly how the gun will behave during any firing but the first few rounds are exceptionally unpredictable. With each round fired, the baseplate of the mortar is usually driven further into the ground which makes the gun more stable.

Sometimes the ground can be too soft, especially during the rainy season. In that case, repeated firing of the mortar can drive the baseplate so deeply into the ground that the guns range of direction is affected. Of course, if the gun is pounded into the ground for just about two feet then it will be impossible for the crew to get their heads below the level of the barrel and every round fired will be a fearful and violent and painful experience just from the blast of the round as it leaves the tube.

The weather for this operation was cold and rainy but we actually got three hot meals a day, which was almost unheard of. I have no explanation of why or how that was done but maybe part of it was that most of the men in my battalion, who had all come over to Viet Nam together, were now only about two weeks or less away from going home. Those men were getting very "short", that is, they had very little time left to finish their tour of duty. Some of these guys were starting to get fairly nervous. No one wanted to be killed or wounded so close to being sent back to the World. While my platoon did not go out on patrols, the straight infantry platoons did. They did not encounter very much in the way of enemy, relatively speaking, but there were always the dangers from booby traps, mines, friendly fire, accidents, etc., etc,

As is always the case, I was just minding my own business, sitting in the shade when there was suddenly a burst of gunfire, probably less than a half a mile away, somewhere off in the jungle. That initial burst was followed by other gunfire and then it slowly died away, to suddenly flare up again ten minutes later but from another direction. Obviously some of the different platoons were engaged with the enemy. I could hear a radio and it was determined after about an hour that there were very minor injuries and the enemy had broken contact. It was getting late in the day and the platoons were called in to our night position. This could possibly be their last operation.

Suddenly, there was a burst of machine gun fire close by and a little firefight broke out. The radio was filled with excited and urgent talk and it quickly became apparent that one of the platoons might be engaged with our own people who were manning the perimeter of our area. I don't know exactly how that happened. Maybe the platoon was closer to the perimeter than they realized, maybe the perimeter guards shouted a challenge and it was not heard, maybe the perimeter guards or men in the platoon were just a bit too nervous and started shooting when they saw some movement in the bush. I don't know exactly what the problem was but from the radio reports, they had taken some injured, some very seriously.

Just as that situation was getting under control out in the woods, a helicopter flew in and a Lieutenant jumped off and directly approached my little group.That guy was obviously right from Brigade headquarters or even higher. His clothes were spotlessly clean and starched and his boots were highly shined. He was clean-shaven and his hair was combed. He didn't even have load-bearing gear, I'm not sure if he even had a weapon. He asked us if we knew where Sgt. Muldoon was and some men close to me said that he was in the Second platoon, out in the bush, but that they should be back very shortly. That situation was extremely irregular. Why, I thought, would this Lieutenant come all the way out into this operation to see a particular person? The Lieutenant quickly told us that that Sergeant was married with two children, but that his youngest daughter, age three, had been killed by an automobile back in the US and that that Sergeant was authorized seven days of emergency leave. We told the Lieutenant that that Sergeant was due to go home in about five days anyways.

About ten minutes later, one of the platoons started to come through the line of the perimeter.The looked pretty well beaten up, just from the humping, but now they all seemed to have a look of, I don't know what. Three of their men had been shot up by the friendly fire, two of them badly. I looked down at the first wounded person, being carried on a makeshift stretcher of ponchos and macheteed down branches. He had been shot twice in the buttocks by an American M-60 machine gun and was in obvious distress. He didn't say anything or make any sounds, but just moved around on the poncho in extreme pain. I thought to myself that two machine gun rounds to the buttocks would destroy pounds of muscle, he'd probably be crippled for the rest of his life and that was if he survived the wounds because those rounds could have torn apart his spinal cord and ricocheted into his organs. I quickly recognized the guy as Sgt. Muldoon. The Lieutenant approached me and again asked where he could find that Sergeant and

I pointed to him writhing on the ground. The Lieutenant walked over to him and bent over to speak. I had to turn around and walk away. I couldn't bear to hear what might be said, or see the expression on the face of that Sergeant when he heard the news of his dead daughter, especially under such circumstances. When people speak of having a bad day, I think of that Sergeant. That's what I call a bad day.

Chapter 32

BASE CAMP
approx June 10 Bien Hoa

And now, my boy, I've told you why on Easter morn I sigh
For I recall my comrades all from dark old days gone by,
I think of men who fought in glens with rifles and grenade
May Heaven keep the men who sleep from the ranks
of the old Brigade

Where are the lads who stood with me when history
was made?
Oh, gra mo chree I long to see the boys of the old Brigade.*

<u>An Old Irish Pub Song</u>

*** roughly translated from Gaelic: love of my live**

The next day we moved back to base camp by truck. Now it was very close to when most of the men would go back to the United States. We hung around for another day when the word came down that it was all over. All of those men who had arrived as a unit a year ago would not have to go back out into the jungle. They would all be going home in two days or so. That was a huge relief, I think, for most of those men. It must have been. But they had all been keyed up for orders to go out for a final mission to be killed or permanently injured or maimed. When they got the word, there was not some sort of collective "sigh of relief", maybe because they realized that such orders could be changed instantly.

That was good for most of the men, but I realized that I still had another six weeks to go in the bush. I suspect that most of them realized that as well. The men were just hanging around, waiting for orders to go home. They were all packed up, like they were going to go on vacation, but with the thought in the back of their mind, that at any moment, those orders could be rescinded and that they could find themselves back in the bush or mortared that night or have the base camp perimeter overrun the next day.

I went up to the latrine and as I walked back to the platoon hooch, I thought that at any minute, and out of nowhere, the hopes and dreams of those guys could be ruined. Maybe that's why they were in a subdued state, not happy and not sad, not anything really, just emotionally numbed by the entire ordeal. I also realized that there were no specific orders that forbad me from going to the little town of Bien Hoa. It certainly it would be good to see those guys finally load up onto trucks and ride away into the sunset, to wave good by to those true soldiers, and to wish them well. The thought occurred to me that maybe it would be better if I went in amongst them right then and said goodbye. I just couldn't bring myself to do it. What would they say to me? What would I say to them? What could be said?

Those were guys that I had served with for the last eleven months. We had survived many very dangerous situations. Thoughts quickly went through my mind, split-second remembrances of shouting and smoke and blood, of helicopter hurricanes and shrapnel flying and incoming tracers and grenades and a hundred other bloody, filthy horrible things. We had survived troubles and tortures, deprivations and agonies beyond imagination. What the hell would I say to them, and what the hell would they say to me. They had survived their tour of duty, as yet I had not. I had another month and a half to go, out in the woods. They knew of the dangers and would have known, in their heart of hearts, that my chances of survival were very slim. I knew that they very well may get orders to move out and load onto planes to go back to the World at any moment, and I knew very well that I had no idea of what to say to them. I did note that the soldier who had been shot in the head was carrying his helmet. The helmet that had a hole in one side of it

and another on the other side, both holes made by one bullet, while he was wearing it. I smiled slightly. Somehow I thought that that was a fitting symbol.

Instead of walking another fifty feet and into the platoon tent, I suddenly walked off ninety degrees to my left, down a red dusty road and just stuck out my thumb, to get a ride. Actually, I had learned from past experience to just wait for a truck that looked like it was going close to the main gate,(you could sometimes tell by the markings on the bumpers of the trucks as to where they were authorized to go) and then just jump out in front of it and make it stop (or have them run me over).

Then I would tell them that I was 173rd Airborne and that they must drive me to the main gate. That worked all of the time, not because of my personal intimidation, but, I think, because of the deeds of my fellow soldiers in the 173rd who had previously insisted upon a ride.The alternative for those drivers was either the threat of a severe beating or just being dragged out of the trucks with the troopers driving it themselves. I have to say that on some occasions, a truck would pull over without any work on our part and were more than happy to give us a ride.They probably knew what thirty days in the bush really meant.

On that huge airbase, where ninety percent of the population was Air Force and the other ten percent was 173rd airborne, who was usually always out in the bush, the Air Force knew not to hinder in any way the boys when they got back from being tortured, dehydrated, starved, threatened, bombed, blown up, terrorized by booby traps, snipers,VC machine guns, claymores, friendly fire from Air Force, eaten and infected by mosquitoes and leaches and others insects, poisoned by chemicals, burned alive and generally beaten far beyond what most people could ever imagine.

Most 173rd troopers had little regard for people that lived every day on a base camp, and they had no regard whatsoever for orders from some Air Force Military Policeman.Truth be told, the Air Force MPs cut us all kinds of slack, I think that they knew who they were dealing with, and that many of those guys from the 173rd Airborne that they were dealing with, would never show up again to bother them because many of them would be killed or seriously wounded before they ever had a chance to go downtown again.

I noticed that the MP's would come down very hard on Air Force men for the slightest infraction, but allow 173rd troopers who were late in coming back to the Main gate to pass through without problems. Maybe because the 173rd troopers realized that damn near killing a gate guard could, at best, result in a highly desired rest in a military prison. Actually, what possible punishment could be delved out that would be worse than humping a hundred and forty pounds through the bush where every moment could be your last, in fact, when every moment could result in

you being permanently and horribly wounded. I think that those Air Force MP's at the gate realized the our lot in life was to run the Gauntlet every day, while in the bush, and that to arrest us for a curfew violation would not, and probably never did, result in anything other than less pain for the accused.

I made it back to base camp about nine pm. The tents were empty. All of the original men were gone. I asked around and was told that they shipped out at about five pm. I realized that I had not been there when they left, I wasn't there to wish them well, or to shake hands or to see them one last time. On the other hand, what was there to say? Maybe we could laugh at a joke that was told the last time we went downtown, but that time was tempered with the realization that we would be going back into the bush on the next day. Maybe we could reminisce about how stupid it was for that guy to put the M-79 round into a tree directly above our own forces, or maybe talk about how big that snake was at Da Nang. But the fact of the matter was that there seemed to be a distinct lack of joviality. Most men were very somber. They couldn't wait to go back home but realized that they would not be safe until they had finally actually left this country. Maybe they thought of the guys who had already gone home, but in caskets or wheelchairs. What do you say to men with whom you had endured so much? Anyways, I still had another month and more to go in country. I really didn't know if I would make it home alive or in one piece. I wished all the best for the men who left but realized that I very well may not live long enough to share their joy in returning home.

Chapter 33

CENTRAL HIGHLANDS

Cannon to right of them, Cannon to left of them,
Cannon behind them, Volleyed and thundered;
Stormed at with shot and shell,
While horse and hero fell,
They that had fought so well
Came through the jaws of Death
Back from the mouth of Hell,
All that was left of them,
Left of six hundred

Alfred Tenneyson

Air Mattress inside poncho tent

We moved out on the next day or so. The Company was very under strength but we had picked up about forty men over the last ten months as replacements for men who left the Company, sometimes due to other assignments but mostly to replace the dead and wounded of the original Company. There were a few soldiers from the original unit who had extended their tours of duty so as to eventually get out of the Army earlier and others who extended for a bonus of maybe a thousand dollars. There was also a group of about fifteen men who had just recently arrived in country and this would be their first mission.

At base camp we had loaded onto trucks that brought us to another part of the base camp/airbase and then loaded onto airplanes, flying for more than an hour to another much smaller airbase. From there we loaded onto helicopters for an insertion, all of which happened without any problems. We began with a hump of five thousand meters which was substantially more than was usual but it felt like only about two thousand meters. Part of the reason for that, I think, was that my platoon was only humping one mortar and we had fourteen men to do it with and we switched the parts of the gun around all fourteen men so no one had to hump any one part of it all day. That made our combat loads lighter than what they usually were.

The next day, the platoon Sergeant assigned the mortar to my squad and that changed things completely. The gunner, Arrellano, was back in the States on a thirty day leave. He had signed up for another three months in Viet Nam because he would get a thousand dollar bonus and, at the end of that time, he would be discharged from the Army three months early. I had argued with him about that decision very strongly, but, for some reason, he needed the thousand dollars desperately.

Two months later he would be permanently and profoundly deafened and injured by an enemy rocket that landed next to him. While he was gone, I would be the gunner and would have to carry the bipod. There was talk that I would be promoted to Specialist 4th class and moved into the position of gunner. I let it be known that they can keep their stripes and additional fourteen dollars a month. It wasn't worth it to me to carry an additional eight pounds every day.

Now I did have to carry the bipod. Arrellano knew how to carry it but I did not. I humped it for about two hours, it shouldn't have made much difference in weight, compared to the barrel that I usually carried, but it was a completely different piece of equipment and I couldn't find a way to carry it properly. I tried to carry it on top of my shoulder, like the mortar tube, but that just didn't work out, it wobbled all around because it was very asymetrical. Then I tried to carry it in front of me,

holding it up with my arms, but that was much too difficult, trying to hold forty-two pounds in front of you as you walked. I was just struggling mightily with that piece of equipment, on the ragged edge of desperation, utterly exhausted and in very serious pain. But, like everyone else, all of my thoughts and will demanding that my body deliver what is really an impossible demand on it.

The line of march stopped for a few minutes. I hit upon a new idea. When the line of march resumed I tried to sort of hang the bipod on my collarbone, in front. I took one and a half steps and I heard a "crack". My brain screamed: "Get it off of me!!". I uncontrollably fell face first towards the ground, tearing at that piece of metal, trying to get it off of me. As I fell, I realized that it was now off of me but I was falling heavily and in a hundredth of a second I would smash my face onto it.

Somehow, in absolute desperation, I turned my head and pushed the bipod very slightly to one side. I smashed my face into the ground, almost directly on top of that iron but somehow avoided smashing my face directly into it by a quarter of an inch.

The pain in my collarbone was beyond unbearable. It was a sensation that I had never felt before, like a white hot sword was slicing through my bones. I think that my collarbone was cracked under the weight. I guess my body was telling me that it would not allow me to destroy any bones. That was it. I knew that I had to figure out some way to carry that bipod, but for the time being it felt as if my body had been destroyed. I was paralyzed, my body refused to work any more. I laid on the ground, face down, and told the guy in back of me to "Drive on!", that I would catch up later.

That situation was unheard of, everyone pulled their weight, everyone kept up with the line of march. Soldiers filed past me and told me in no uncertain terms to pick up my load and carry on. Most of their comments were harsh, to say the least. I, really being the senior man in experience in that small group, told them to shut up and keep going. A very few of the troopers, seeing me facedown in obvious distress, expressed comments of concern and sympathy. In my paralyzing agony all I could manage to mutter was: "Drive on!".

I knew that that was unheard of, but finally, after eleven months I had to admit that I had met my match. I just could not go on. I wanted to go on, my mind demanded that I go on regardless of the agonizingly serious pain but apparently my body would not allow itself to be destroyed. As much as I demanded that my body stand up, it simply would not obey my commands. I was utterly destroyed. I didn't know how or what happened or why but obviously my body simply did not respond to my commands or wishes.

I guess, the word went up the line that a guy had dropped out, and some of the guys in front of me got the word, and turned around to cuss me out and/or to threaten to kick my ass on the spot.

Pierce was the first to reach me. He came running back down the line, apparently to kick the ass of a mortar trooper who had dropped out. But when he saw that it was me who had dropped out, his bearing changed instantly and completely. I was just lying on the ground, beyond played out, physically destroyed and when he saw me, and the distress and pain that I was in, he didn't say one word. He just picked up that bipod, even though he was carrying the barrel as well, and moved out with it. I wondered why he didn't say a word. I think because, he decided to pick up my load, and that, along with the barrel, it would be a superhuman load, and there was no sense in wasting energy with words. That, was the most, I don't know what, thing that I had ever seen. He must have already been under horrible duress, yet he picked up my load to add to his. I cannot fathom how a human being could do such a thing.

I immediately tried to get up and get that bipod back, but there was a horrible pain and discomfort in my collarbone and it was extremely painful and more than difficult just to walk. I finally managed to reach Pierce and told him to put that bipod down, that I would manage to hump it somehow, but he ignored me completely and carried it for another thirty minutes. After that time, I convinced Pierce to give me the barrel of the mortar, I knew that I could carry that, and he reluctantly agreed. My point here is that, here was a man under extreme duress and pain, and for a friend, picked up an additional load that by all logic should have eventually killed him.

Note: many years later, I had a routine chest X-ray. The technician took one look at the picture and stated: "motorcycle accident Right?" I asked him what he meant. He said that he sees it all of the time.

Before I could reply, he said that the doctor that reset the bone did the worst job that he had ever seen. Moreover he said that he would very willingly testify in court and that I should sue that doctor. I told him that I had never broken my collarbone whereupon he pointed it out to me on the X-ray. I'm not an expert but even I could see that something was horribly amiss. My mind flashed back immediately to that bipod incident.

After that day, the platoon Sergeant decided that all fourteen men in my platoon would take turns carrying the parts of the mortar and the extra rounds. My responsibility was to be the primary gunner. If we had to put the gun into action, I would be the gunner and as such, was primarily responsible for carrying the bipod. However, the men in my platoon allowed me to carry it for only an hour or so, at which point I was in horrible pain, and then they, without a word from me, would take that horror from me and carry it amongst themselves. That was an act of kindness that I have never seen before or after that. Those men picked up a horribly heavy load of torture and pain and humped it for a friend. I wasn't even their friend, I barely knew most of them. They humped it for a fellow soldier, but I guarantee they would not have done that for a "cherry". They realized that I had much more experience than they did. Maybe they decided that I had suffered enough during the last eleven months. I don't really know, and I still don't. But I know for certain, that they picked up a load of pain that most people cannot imagine in their worst nightmares. Most people have no idea of the pain and suffering that soldiers endure in combat.

The weather was substantially cooler. The air felt very thick actually, maybe because of the humidity, but the lower temperature made the weather very much cooler that what we were accustomed to. I didn't realize it at the time, but we were in or very close to the Central Highlands and were actually at a relatively high elevation. It was mostly open forest, I guess because of the elevation. We encountered several open meadows, or they would be meadows except that they were filled with marijuana plants. Those plants had not been deliberately farmed, I don't think, they were just growing wild and had completely taken over those cleared areas.

As far as I know, no one stopped to pick any of that marijuana. There was something about that whole area that just did not feel right at all. There was a deep sense of danger all around, at least there was for me. I guess that others felt the same thing and realized that that was not a place where a man could light up a joint tonight and be able to enjoy it in peace or, more precisely, not a place where a man would venture to dull his senses to any extent whatsoever.

The next day we began at a high altitude but worked our way down lower, down to an area of streams and jungley vegetation although there were a lot of open areas where the sun would brutally beat down upon a man. In that situation it was almost unbearable with the combination of heat and humidity and direct sun. I thought that I was going to pass out on many occasions and just barely avoided doing so by somehow reaching an area that had some shade before my body gave out completely. We patrolled at a relatively horizontal altitude for an hour or so and then started to work our way up a very large hill, or small mountain. It was very steep and our line of march was to work our way to the top by walking spirally around the mountain many, many times. Now, I thought, this was truly the worst humping of all times. The weight of my pack wasn't the heaviest of my tour of duty although it was close to it. But the major problem was that one foot was continuously lower than the other and therefore most of the weight was on one leg.

It was a situation of walking two or three steps horizontally while at the same time moving one step vertically upwards. It was almost murderous. I couldn't believe that men could tolerate that level of exertion and pain, it was far beyond anything that I considered a human being was capable of sustaining. We pushed on like that, up and around the mountain for about two hours, two hours of unimaginably tortuous pain and suffering.

I had stopped walking now, as always happened in the line to allow other men to catch up, or because we were bunching up too tightly. I was standing there, with one foot substantially below the other, bent over, trying to guess whether I should fall to the ground to take the weight off, or to remain standing. To sit on the ground would relieve the weight but then the exertion of standing up again was substantial.

There was an eerie, absolute silence all about. No one was moving. I thought only of how absolutely and horribly painful that torture was. How could I have ended up at that time and at that place under such pain and danger, when suddenly, it seemed as if all of the weight had been taken off of me. Here, in that place of horrible pain, I felt light and unburdened and at peace. I felt that way for the next five or ten minutes. It was some sort of miracle, I have no explanation for it whatsoever except that I thought that maybe my father was praying for me at that very moment. After a few minutes, we began our march again, but the burden felt very light indeed.

My squad was not taking any direct fire but all around me I could hear almost continuous gunfire. Apparently my Company and the other Companys in the area were encountering serious military armed resistance and ambushes. All throughout the rest of the day the sounds of firefights continuously surrounded us, popping up randomly in front of us, in back of us, to the left and the right, sometimes a few shots, perhaps random or perhaps by well trained snipers, sometimes a significant, almost coordinated burst, by two to five enemy automatic weapons, either effecting an ambush upon Americans or, perhaps, a defense against American soldiers who had suddenly discovered their hiding place.

The line of march would stop for a while and then my squad or section of my platoon would get the word to move up the line or back down the line to reinforce a group of soldiers who were under direct attack, to provide additional fire support and security to them while the medics tried to attend to the wounded or dying.

Eerily, amongst all of the noise and danger and shouting and suffering and confusion and fear, I suddenly became aware of a certain smell in the air that had been building up to conscious level for the last five minutes, a distinct smell of iron, like an old cast iron skillet that has just been washed and is still soaking wet.

With everything else occurring, for some reason, I became preoccupied with that now powerful smell that seemed to saturate the air. For some reason, with everything else going on, I decided to concentrate my thoughts and reasoning to try to figure out what that smell was and where it was coming from. I thought that perhaps it was due to the men firing their weapons, heating up the barrels of their weapons, but no, I had seen that before and had almost never noticed that particular smell. I thought perhaps it was due to the communist weapons, maybe firing small arms and cannons that were very wet due to rain or condensation, but again, I couldn't remember smelling that smell under previous similar circumstances, at least not so strongly as I smelled it now.

Perhaps the strong, strange smell was due to some type of rare tropical plant or tree or fruit that grows only in that location I thought. But the smell was distinctly not that of some sort of vegetable matter. Perhaps, I thought, there was a long-ago crashed aircraft somewhere in the valley below, but then ruled that out since most aircraft are made of aluminum. Perhaps it was due to old, destroyed artillery pieces from world war II, lying directly below us or across from us on the next mountain, but the wind was blowing away from us, that couldn't be the problem. Anyways, I decided, whatever it was, the smell would soon be gone as we moved away from that immediate area.

Very frequently during the rest of the day, we got the word, down the line, many times, for my platoon to rush towards the front or the back of the line of march, to reinforce soldiers caught in an ambush or under direct attack and/or aid or provide security to those wounded or killed. The second time that my squad moved towards the front of the line we came upon two or three paratroopers lying on their backs on the ground, dead or dying.

A fellow trooper was kneeling on the ground, next to one of the dead or dying, trying to hold the wounded soldiers back and head a bit off of the cold and wet dampness and rancidness of the tropical leaf litter, ten thousand miles away from home, while a medic worked frantically to try to save the injured troopers life. One wounded trooper seemed to have some sort of very weak ability to hold his head up a bit although with the help of another trooper, The other wounded soldiers heads just hung limply backwards, either already dead or close to it.

The exchange of gunfire had stopped a few minutes before my section had arrived. From the sound of the gunfire, I guessed that the enemy was on the mountain that was next to us and separated from us by an extremely steep valley. There were VC or NVA two hundred yards away, as the crow flies or as an AK47 round flies, but to get from where we were to where they were would require traversing a gully that was extremely steep, perhaps requiring a person to travel five hundred yards down a very steep mountain incline downwards and then climb another five hundred yards up and even with such equipment, it probably would have been impossible to achieve given the enormous combat loads and weights that we were required to carry. I figured that if I got away from the very edge of the path, away from the extreme decline of the side of the mountain, that the enemy would not be able to get a shot at me so I decided to get back about ten or fifteen feet from the ledge and lay down there. A medic was working on shot up troopers near the edge of the incline, I couldn't do anything to help other than to stay out of their way.

The vegetation was very unusual with large trees with very dark, glossy leaves that looked to be very hard, maybe they were unique to that environment and mountainous elevation. I noticed that on some of them there were large spots of some dark red material so I decided to walk over about thirty feet to see it closer. The smell of old iron was strong in the air. I thought that we had passed that area but obviously whatever was causing that smell was very close to where we were now as well.

On some of the leaves were spots of varying sizes from about a dime size to a silver dollar size. I reached over to touch it. It was a liquid although it seemed to be drying very quickly. It was slightly slimy and I rubbed it between my fingers to try to figure out what it was. I thought that maybe it was dripping from another, higher up tree, and I looked up but couldn't see anything red. The splatter of drops seemed to get denser as it got closer to the edge of the cliff. In the back of my mind I knew what it was but just couldn't recall what it was. Then, as I followed the path of the splatter, I noticed one of the wounded men on the ground, holding onto his stomach. The area all around him, especially his hands and shirt were covered with blood. I quickly wiped my fingers on my pants to get rid of the substance, suddenly realizing that it was blood that had come from those men. The enemy bullets had torn through their bodies, splattering their blood and flesh and pieces of organs onto the trees eighty feet away. The smell of old iron, I suddenly realized, was the smell of human blood.

Several times during the day I and the guys in my immediate vicinity came under attack and some of the guys could return fire, but it was almost impossible to determine exactly where the fire was coming from. For my part, I didn't have the opportunity to return fire. I could have fired off some rounds, but the other Companies were out there and I didn't just want to fire blindly. So that was the situation, the enemy hid out there, trying very hard to kill us, and placing accurate fire onto our position, but for the most part, we had to hold our fire unless we could exactly determine their position, which was almost impossible to do. That enemy was very good at what they were doing and most of the time they would put fire on us from positions that we expertly concealed.

One might think that a person could see their muzzle flashes but that was almost never the case. In some cases though we could see muzzle flashes, and I thought that that enemy soldier was either very inexperienced or very sure of themselves, sure that they could easily kill us without themselves being jeopardized because of superior firing positions and cover. I think that the story was that they realized that they outnumbered us by a huge number and that the muzzle flashes that we could see represented only five percent of the weapons firing at us.

Even if we could have determined where they were, there was always the urgent messages, passed up and down the line of march, to move out to help the guys within our Company. On several occasions, my section of the line reached the front of the line and set up there, falling into prone positions to face incoming small arms fire. On several occasions, when contact was broken, or sometimes when the firefight was still ongoing, we were ordered to pick up and move forward, to take up the positions of dead and wounded and bloody men lying on the ground

I and my comrades moved past the dead and dying, wondering how they were going to evacuate those men under those conditions, I don't think that they could bring in a helicopter because of the steep terrain, with us being on the edge of the mountain. So the situation was, basically, to take fire directly, and then to move to the front or towards the end of the line of march where most of the casualties had occurred and then to take their place. Then part of our group would be ambushed and shot up and then me and the men close to me would take their place. It was something like, keep moving up and down the line of march until you are killed.

Me and my immediate associates continually did that all afternoon, about six times altogether, taking fire every hour or less, moving up to support those taking fire and finding when we got there men dead and dying. The blood on the ground was something to see. I was both fascinated and horrified by it, large and small scattered about pools of blood on the bright green leaves on the ground. Usually, the leaf litter on the ground consisted of dead brown leaves, but in those places, for quite an area all around, the blood was on a blanket of green leaves, which meant that the incoming fire had been so intense that it had knocked thousands of leaves off of the still living trees.

Because of the steepness of the mountains, I thought that at least the enemy wouldn't be able to put accurate mortar fire on us, but I was wrong. Although most of their mortar rounds missed us, because of the steep terrain, they still managed to do us harm.

There was a big problem. I thought that since we were taking casualties all of the time as we humped on and on, that it might be a good idea to just stay in one place and fight it out, rather than continuously moving on and encountering more ambushes. The problem, I think, was that once we were ambushed, the enemy quickly reinforced their ambush. So the longer we stayed in one place, exchanging fire with the enemy, the more enemy there were to fight and the more likely we were to start taking mortar fire, as the enemy mortar crews could zero in on us. It wasn't a situation where we could stay and battle it out with one group of enemy, it was a situation where the longer we stayed in one place and fought it out with the enemy, the more the enemy brought up reinforcements to join the battle to kill us.

It was, I think, a situation where we were terribly outnumbered and the only thing that we could do was to try to get out of that situation. It sure as hell didn't help that we had no air support and no artillery support against an enemy that probably outnumbered us by a factor of twenty to one, who were dug in, and had been operating in this area for the last five if not thirty-five years.

The big problem was that, as we tried to push forward, to get out of this area of killing, that we might very well be going into an area of even more enemy troops or into more carefully planned and manned ambushes. I have to confess, that as I write this, I don't really remember the details very well. It was a balls out hump, with the Company just being taken apart like a fine watch, American Paratroopers killed and wounded in groups of two or three all afternoon.

The enemy had us on their own turf and they knew that turf well. They had prepared that area for just this situation and had prepared it to defend against an opposing force that was fifty times what we had. We had walked into a miles long ambush and they just turned it into a meat grinder. Everyone of us who survived that day can only thank God for a miracle and there were very many men who never got out of that area, I was going to say except in a body bags, but we didn't carry body bags, those came in from the "dust off" choppers, who picked up the dead and wounded. I don't know how it was managed to evacuate the dead and wounded because there were no landing zones within miles of that area. Maybe they were loaded onto makeshift stretchers of jungle branches and ponchos and brought along with the main line of march or maybe they were taken back down the line of march. I don't know. I was just an infantryman, and my lot was to just keep going on, and going on and going on, suffering horribly from the pain of my insufferable load, distracted momentarily by dead bodies and screaming and moaning men and blood and guts lying on the ground so that I could take the place of those wounded and dead men, to face my fate.

Eventually we got out of the area of heavy enemy contact. We had called in airstrikes onto the area and the Air Force or Marines showed up in jet fighters and I

think that their bombing did a lot to break off the contact but I didn't see any helicopter gunships. I figured that we were basically out in the middle of nowhere and beyond the range of helicopters reaching us in any reasonable time. Yeah, this was bad. I only had less than a month to go in country, and we were running into a lot of trouble, there were all kinds of casualties. I found out later that the second battalion had seventy two men killed in action in one day. That was very bad, especially considering that the second battalion probably only had three hundred and fifty men in the field, if even that, to begin with.

Later that night, word started filtering down to us of our own casualties in our Company and Battalion, names of men with missing arms and legs, names of men blinded and deafened and faces torn off, and names of men killed. Most of the names were not familiar to me, since about ninety percent of the men I knew had returned to the United States a week ago, but many of the names were familiar to the other guys in the Company. Then I realized, that those guys who recognized the names were men relatively new in country. Those were men with less than thirty days experience, learning that their friends had been killed and torn up.

I felt sorry for them and realized that that situation must bother them greatly to lose so many friends so quickly and so hideously. They must think that they will never survive a full year on the ground in Viet Nam. I felt very sorry for them that it must make them feel very hopeless and helpless. But then I thought, that that is exactly what the future holds for them. Seemingly endless days of extreme pain and torture and deprivation and fear, only to be ended in death or permanent disabilities of blindness or deafness or lost limbs or burned flesh. What a horrible outlook laid out for them. The same outlook that I had faced for almost the last year.

The last day of the operation we humped over very flat terrain. It was mostly very open forest, in fact I had never seen an area in Viet Nam that was so wide open for such a long and wide distance. It was good because the enemy couldn't hide very well in such a situation, or could they? Also, the weather was overcast and relatively cool. Sometime during the day the word was passed that we were now to move towards a destination that was different from our original orders that we had received earlier that morning. We ended up humping eight thousand meters, which was a long distance record for sure, but because of the temperature and the relatively light loads that we were carrying, it didn't seem too bad. Actually, that relatively easy day would have resulted in criminal charges if anyone in the States tried to subject troopers to such extreme maneuvers in training. Compared to actual combat conditions, the worst day in training was like an easy picnic hike. The training that we had, especially me since I went through Advanced Airborne Infantry Training, not AIT, but AAIT) (which was discontinued after two classes because it resulted in so many injuries) was extremely difficult, but it was absolutely nothing compared to what was required under combat conditions.

Chapter 34

NEAR THE CENTRAL HIGHLANDS

When can their glory fade?
O the wild charge they made!
All the world wondered.
Honour the charge they made!
Honour the Light Brigade,
Noble six hundred!
The Charge of the Light Brigade

Alfred Lord Tennyson

Central Highlands in the Distance, view from a fighting position

We dug in for the night, it was the 4th of July. We set up a mortar and my squad was assigned to man it for the night. Just after dark, we were told to prepare some rounds for H&I fire (harassment and interdiction). We were going to fire a few rounds into the surrounding countryside just to shake up the enemy. I thought that maybe we shouldn't just fire at random into the surrounding area because we might hit civilians, but then realized that there were no civilians in this area. There was only enemy soldiers in the surrounding countryside and there were plenty of them.

We were given the firing coordinates by the fire direction control team and me and the gunner sighted in the mortar. Someone had a transistor radio and was playing it, and just as the ammo bearer handed me a mortar round, the Star Spangled Banner came on the radio. The fire direction control team issued the order "fire at will!" and I hung the round in the tube. All I had to do was to relax my grip on the round with my thumb and other three fingers and the round would drop in the tube and explode outwards. I was listening to the radio, to the song, and decided to hold fire until the appropriate time, to coincide with a line of the National Anthem. Some men yelled "let go!", or "fire!" but I held onto the round until the song on the radio played "and the rockets red glare, the bombs ..." at which instant I let loose of the round and it slid down the tube with a metallic sound, to explode out of the tube at just the exact right moment to accentuate the songs lyrics, "bursting in air", boom!.

I thought that it sounded excellent, but to most of the other guys around, apparently, they were flustered that I didn't drop the round exactly when I should have. In retrospect, they were probably very flustered because they probably thought that I dropped the round when I should have, and that the round didn't go off, so they probably thought that I was standing over a round, like a rank rookie, with a round that could be "cooking" in the tube. That would have been an extremely dangerous situation for me and them.

The next day was the end of that part of the operation. I'm not sure how that operation ended, but I think that we were picked up by trucks and then moved to a new area. There would be no more trips back to downtown Bien Hoa for me. We were going to stay in that general area for quite a while, and it was an extremely dangerous area.

At our new location was a sea of green grass almost as far as the eye could see. It was a very flat place, maybe a huge farm at one time,

I don't know. It was just a huge meadow now, with the grass about five inches tall. I wondered why the grass wasn't any taller, but I don't know. Far in the distance, was a range of mountains colored a very dark blue and grey and black.

When I saw them for the first time I had a very strong sense of foreboding. Those mountains were the Central Highlands, where many, very, very, bad things had

happened to thousands of American soldiers and would be a place where thousands of American lives would end before this war was over. From the distance where we were, that mountainous terrain didn't contain any green color at all and I thought that that was extremely unusual. Of course that area was covered with jungle and other vegetation, but it just didn't look green and that was almost an impossibility in Viet Nam.

I was very "short" now, only another two weeks to go to the end of my tour of duty. I now had some hope that I might survive, maybe even get out of this place without being blinded or losing arms or legs, or being horribly wounded so I was sort of on edge and maybe that affected my senses or state of mind. However, those mountains looked to me like some sort of real life mountains of Transylvania, and I thought that there were horrors on those mountains that were much worse than any Dracula movie could depict, and, indeed, that was the case.

We stayed in this area for quite a long time. Of course, each day, everyone expected the order to "ruck up" and move out for an operation, but after the second or third day we were still there, which to me seemed almost unbelievable. Large tents were brought in and set up. That was a highly unusual situation but we were not given any information about how long we would stay there or where our next operation was going to be.

It was cold there. During the day it seemed cool but at night it seemed downright cold. Of course, during the day it might have been eighty-five degrees and during the night it might have dropped to sixty degrees, but after the temperatures that we were used to, it seemed cold. I remember actually shivering during a couple of nights while lying down, trying to sleep.

A number of trucks came up the highway and dropped off supplies of ammo and food and one of them had some hundred pound cakes of ice. I walked up to one of those trucks and came away with a cracked off hunk of ice that weighed about ten pounds. I brought it back to a medium sized tent that we had for my platoon, and I placed it into a wooden mortar ammo box so that we could put some Cokes or water into it, like some sort of cooler. That hunk of ice stayed frozen for four days. We actually had some Cokes from the previous days that had been brought into that area by trucks. In the States, someone can just walk across the street and get a cold Coke. As an infantryman in Viet Nam, a cold Coke was almost an impossibility to obtain during their entire tour of duty in the field. Now, finally, we had access to a cold Coke but the problem was that a cold drink was the last thing that we needed. It was decidedly cold.

One day, I decided to walk around, following along a small stream that had carved a little meandering gully, about six feet wide and three feet deep through this huge wide

area of grass. I hoped to find some small pieces of driftwood so that I could make a little campfire to heat up some coffee and maybe get warm, from that cold, damp, dank weather. The nearest trees were miles away. After about thirty minutes I was a substantial distance from any other soldiers when I was suddenly startled by a voice behind me. I was wearing my helmet and lbg and carrying my M-16 over my shoulder and wasn't expecting any troubles because you could see for miles. I was alarmed that someone had more or less sneaked up behind me, or had jumped out of a concealed position.

The sudden voice yelling "Hello", startled me and I tore the M-16 off of my shoulder and turned around quickly, crouching down at the same time and bringing the weapon immediately and directly on target. I could immediately see that it was an American soldier, and was embarrassed to suddenly find myself pointing my weapon at him. I reminded myself that I was getting very, very short. It was my fault of course. I should have been aware of any potential problems and should have maintained a constant vigilance all around me.

That paratrooper was a black guy and kind of short in stature. He struck me right away as probably an FNG (F—New Guy), He seemed to have been shocked and horrified when I had suddenly pointed my weapon at him, (I guess I couldn't blame him), but I quickly lowered my weapon and he seemed to be very much relieved at that. He asked me what I was doing. I didn't respond directly to his question but asked him, very pointedly, what the hell he was doing. He seemed to again suddenly become very anxious and concerned, as if he thought that I was going to shoot him instantly if he didn't come up with the right answer right away. He said that he was a new replacement and decided to just take a walk and had seen me in the distance and decided to catch up with me to see what I was doing. I told him that it was not a good idea to get away from his main group, that this was not really a good place to just go off for a walk, that this was not his hometown and that this was not some kind of picnic area, and that he could easily be killed if he didn't stay close to his group and wasn't extremely aware of his surroundings.

I then told him that I was searching for little pieces of wood to make a campfire. He asked if he could join me and I told him that that would be a good idea. I told him that I would look for wood, and he could look around for any enemy, that he could provide security for me, but that any wood that I found would be mine to keep. I told him that if and when I had gathered enough, that I would probably return to my unit, but if he wanted to continue on this enterprise, that, after I had gathered my fill, then maybe I might provide security for his wood gathering efforts.

I basically told him that I was here before him, so that any wood that was to be found was mine, and he quickly agreed that that was OK with him. We established an understanding, and we started to work our way further up the creek. There was very little to be found in the way of driftwood and so we had to walk quite a ways before I could gather an amount of any significance.

We started to talk, and he told me that he had just recently arrived in country. He had been in Bien Hoa, our base camp, when most of the original members of the 4th battalion were returning to the United States. I had been back there at that time, but I guess that he had remained in base camp, while I moved out onto this operation, while he remained in base camp while they processed his paperwork. Now, weeks later, he had finally been assigned a Company and platoon. Eventually he told me that he was assigned to my unit, Alpha Company, heavy weapons platoon. I really felt sorry for that guy, he had eleven months and two weeks to go to finish his tour or duty, and I only had less than two weeks to go, but I didn't tell him that I was very "short".

As we walked along the streambed, we started to talk, and he asked me if I had ever heard of a guy named "Mallen". I asked him to spell the name and he spelled it "M A L L E N". I said that, maybe, I had heard of that name, because the sound of his voice as that he asked the question seemed very strange. I wanted to know how the hell he ever knew of my name. I asked him why he was interested in that guy named "Mallen". He said that when he was in our platoon hooch, back in base camp in Bien Hoa, when everyone from the original 4th battalion was going home, he said that he had heard those guys talking about a guy named "Mallen". He said that he heard that some guy named "Mallen" had gone "balls out" against three machine gun nests and that he had gone down many tunnels etc, etc.

He said that they spoke of him at great length and that that guy had asked them, "Who is this guy Mallen?", Is he some kind of Paul Bunyon of Viet Nam?, Some kind of folk-hero legend?. He said that they told him "No, Mallen is not some kind of Paul Bunyon, Paul Bunyon is a fable, Mallen is the real thing. The things that Mallen did make Paul Bunyon look like some kind of sissy". He told me that he didn't really believe them, but they told him: "Try to get assigned to A company, and if you can, try to get assigned to the Weapons platoon, because if you do, Mallen will take care of you, Mallen will cover your ass".

At first I started to laugh to myself, but then realized that I did not have a nametag on my fatigue shirt, so that guy could not know who I was. But the thing that convinced me that that guy was not fooling was when he looked at me seriously and asked, "Is there really a guy named Mallen?" I looked at him and said, "Yeah, you're looking at him." That really seemed to confuse him, I guess he expected to see a guy about seven feet tall, then I said to him, "Hey, don't believe everything you hear". He looked me in the eye, and said, seemingly very sadly: "If only ten percent of what those guys said is true, you are unbelievable." He then told me that he said to those guys back in base camp "Who is this guy Mallen really? Is he like some sort of legend in Viet Nam?". He said that, for a few moments they were at a loss of words and then one of them said: "Yeah, Mallen is a legend. He's a legend in his own time."

I just considered myself a common man. To know that the men in my Platoon held me in regard seemed to me to be the equivalent of receiving ten Medals of Honor. Those guys had suffered indescribable hardships and horrors and deprivations and dangers and sufferings, and they thought that I was special. To me that was unbelievable.

About two nights later we got the word that we would finally be moving out on the next morning. We would be going into the heart of the Central Highlands, but would start out at its foothills. That was not good news at all. I really had a foreboding about that whole place, whether it was just the look of it from afar, or the casualties that we taken close to that area, or the lay of the land or the fact that the North VietNameese had years to lay out ambush sites or just the fact that I was getting very short, ie: had very little time to go to finish my tour of duty, I don't know. Probably it was all of those reasons.

The next morning, everybody was loading up, putting on their equipment, ready to walk down a ways to be loaded onto helicopters. The platoon Sergeant walked up to me and Keating, both of us having the same day to depart Viet Nam, and told us to go up to the supply tent and help the supply Sergeant to load up trucks with the extra gear. We were to load up the trucks and then get onto the next chopper out, to join up with our Company.

We helped knock down the supply tent and started to load the excess gear onto trucks when Keating began to talk to the supply Sergeant, telling him that when he gets back to base camp that he will need people to help him unload the trucks and put away the equipment. The supply Sergeant seemed to suddenly realize the wisdom of those words, and Keating pushed him further, enjoining the Sergeant to take him back to base camp with him, to help him back there.

The supply Sergeant, out of worry about how much he would be stressed by off loading all of that equipment himself, or by mercy towards Keating, who only had another week to go to the end of his tour of duty, told Keating that he was right and that he would take him along to help him(and keep Keating out of the combat zone). When I heard that, I begged the Sergeant to take me along as well. The Sergeant knew that he was putting himself in the position of taking all kinds of heat from the Company Commander by taking men out of the combat zone. I pleaded with the Sergeant to take me along as well. I told him that it was going to be a lot of work unloading that equipment back at base camp. I told him that I was to go back to the USA on the same day as Keating. I told him that I needed some serious dental work done on my front tooth. I don't know which of those arguments were persuasive but the Sergeant finally relented and told me that I could go back to base camp with him as

well. We loaded everything onto the trucks, which was hard work but nothing like humping the bush with full packs, and then jumped into the back of a truck which took us to a dirt airstrip about an hour and a half away.

At the airport, I read a letter that I had received from a girlfriend of my best friend back in the states. I started to believe that, maybe, I would actually make it out of this place alive and in one piece. I had a pen or pencil and started to write on the back of that letter what I would like to eat when and if I ever made it back. That list included things like: a six pack of ice cold Coca-Colas, a tuna fish sandwich on rye bread with mayonnaise and lettuce, a good hamburger with cheese, American cheese, a cold glass of milk, maybe even chocolate milk, fried clams and fried haddock, a bag of roasted peanuts, tomatoes, and onions and cooked green beans and kidney beans. Cold, clean water and spaghetti and meatballs with Italian sauce and a pizza with pepperoni and potato chips and pears in sugar sauce etc., etc. All things that I had not been able to have for the last whole year. Things that I needed desperately for nutrition and vitamins. For the last year those things had been unattainable luxuries. I really looked forward to have such things. I came up with a long list of things that I had not had for the whole year so far. Things that are readily obtainable in the USA but were unheard of in this part of the world.

Well, maybe there were soldiers who had free access to such things, but I can assure you that in my Company and Brigade, no man even came close to having the possibility of getting such things in that country. Things like watching TV, riding in a car, wearing clean clothes, taking a hot shower, wearing civilian clothes, swimming, going to a drive-in theatre, maybe with a girlfriend, eating hot or cold food, drinking tea or coffee with real milk, going into an air-conditioned building or sitting in the shade whenever you wanted to, getting eight hours of sleep, etc., etc., etc., and not subjected to constant danger and not brutally tortured everyday.

We waited for a few hours until an airplane was available, a small troop carrier/cargo plane, and the trucks were driven on to it. We roared down the red dirt airstrip, putting up a huge cloud of dust behind us. About an hour later we set down at Bien Hoa airbase and an hour later were back at base camp, Company headquarters.

Keating and I put on our gear and started to walk over to the platoon hooch, but the supply Sergeant insisted that we start to unload the truck and put the gear away immediately. I didn't much like that idea as I wanted to get out of my filthy clothes and take a shower and get a cold coke but the Sergeant convinced me that it was a good idea because when we got most of it inside, we'd be done for the day. Then we would be free to get cleaned up and go to the px and the mess hall and then maybe downtown.

When we were finished, the Sergeant told us to turn in our weapons, but I told him that they needed cleaning and I'm sure that he didn't want to wait around any longer while we cleaned them. That Sergeant knew very well that there was strict orders for us to not possess weapons in base camp, after previous problems. But I think that he, very much like I, would feel much better if we all had weapons, since we were about the only people in the Company or Battalion area now. I knew that I would sleep better that night. I told the Sergeant that we might as well keep all of our gear and weapons overnight and clean them thoroughly tomorrow, so Keating and I went back to our platoon hooch with all of our weapons and grenades etc.

Its not too clear what I did for the next two days. I'm sure it involved getting or trying to get cold drinks. Anyways, I got over for sure but I was concerned about the guys in my Company and how their operation was going. On the second day, I ran into the supply Sergeant and he told us that from what he had heard, the day before, the Battalion had run into some very major problems and the word was that an entire Company had been wiped out. He said that he was getting all kinds of trouble for letting me and Keating go back to base camp with him, and he was getting demands to put us onto the next aircraft and send us back.

I'll always be grateful to that Sergeant. He said that he told the Commander that that was probably a bad idea and that anyways, it would probably take three days for us to get a plane back to that area and then have to find a way to meet up with a chopper that was going to our exact Companys position in the woods. That much was mostly true, but I suspect that the supply Sergeant and the Company Commander realized that Keating and I had done our duty. We had put in a full tour (minus three days), and it was time to let us get out of the country alive or at least in one piece. In any event, that supply Sergeant who had denied me extra magazines for my weapon many months earlier, had put his career directly on the line to protect me, someone that he didn't even know. It must have cost him and his career dearly. May God bless him.

The next day, a truck pulled up to our platoon hooch and a solitary soldier jumped off the back of the truck, landing very heavily under the weight of his load. He slowly rose to his feet and walked down towards me, towards the supply Sergeants hooch. He was only five feet from me when I suddenly realized that it might possibly be McGrath. McGrath was the guy that was supposed to go back to the US on the same day as Keating and myself. I said to him "McGrath!" but he didn't even slow down and I had to almost step in front of him and yell "McGrath!" He took a few more steps past me before he finally stopped. I could see that it was McGrath, or at least was kind of sure that it was him and I was very glad to see him, very glad to see that he was still alive and was finally back to base camp. He looked at me as if he was in a fog, like he was looking past me a mile down the road, a thousand yard stare. He spoke very softly and acknowledged my presence, telling me that he had to report to the supply Sergeant that he was back.

I stepped out of his way. Something was very wrong here for sure. I wondered why he was acting the way that he was. Maybe, I thought, he was very tired and exhausted, he certainly looked it, but, after all, he had just gotten off of that truck. Before the truck he would have been sitting down on an airplane for an hour. So why, I thought, did he look so bad, in such extremely bad shape? He had been in the bush for 3 or 4 days and that explained why he was so absolutely filthy dirty. He was probably extremely dehydrated and very hungry as well, but he looked utterly exhausted, as if he would walk just a few more feet and then fall dead from the exertion. There was more though. Mentally, he seemed to be on another planet, as if everything that he saw was foreign to him. The answer, I think, is that he had just endured three days more of an operation than me Keating and I had and that his condition was probably exactly like the condition of every infantryman on that operation. But that operation also had already resulted in more than a hundred men in our Battalion killed or wounded. That had done something to him, something bad, and even then, I had a bad feeling that he might not get over it soon.

The next day, Keating, McGrath and I went down to Brigade headquarters to get our orders to return to the US the next day, find out which airplane we would get on and at what time and to draw our pay (in US currency). We then went back to the Company area and hung around all day, packing up our gear, listening to the radio, and trying to fit into our minds that, maybe, we would get out of here alive, just maybe. That night I didn't sleep very well at all.

I found out later that many men stationed in the rear had a chart or picture that was divided into three hundred and sixty five pieces, one piece for every day in a year. Each day the man would cross off or color in one piece of that puzzle and would then know how many days he had left of his tour of duty in Viet Nam. I think that every man in my Company knew exactly how many days he had left but I never saw any of those charts or pictures. Frankly, I wouldn't have bothered with one if I had it. It would just remind me of how many days I had left, <u>in theory</u>. In practice, I never thought that I would make it out alive or in one piece. There were just too many things going on, all of them horribly brutal and viciously deadly.

The next day, we loaded onto a truck, then another truck, then a bus. Suddenly we were at the airport but the three of us somehow got separated. I was to board the plane in the first group and found myself being ordered to go somewhere and give someone my duffel bag and have it inspected for any contraband or weapons etc. Then, the next thing I knew, I was walking up the gangplank of the aircraft, looking around for Keating and McGrath but not seeing them anywhere, and scanning the horizon, my final glimpse of Viet Nam, deeply sucking in the diesel fumes and junglely, humid air of Viet Nam, getting my last breath of this entire experience.

Now I was on the plane, sitting next to the maniac who was telling everyone that we were all going to be killed at any minute. The thought occurred to me that maybe I should just beat this guy, give him the beating of his life then tell him, "Hey, that is one one-millionth of what me and my friends just went through". But, I decided against it, for several reasons. First, it wasn't his fault that he had gotten an easy job. Two, I had had enough death and killing and beating and suffering and starving and agony and blood and tearing and burning of flesh and blinding and breaking of bones and danger and fear to last me a lifetime. Visiting a tiny, tiny bit of that on that guy would still never give him an idea of what life in the bush for an Infantryman inViet Nam was really like.

The wigged out guy beside me would finally regain some sort of consciousness about an hour away from Hawaii. At that time he would turn to me, seemingly calm and rational, and quietly ask: "Are you going to kill me?" I would simply tell him: "No" and then, in a flash of brilliance, tell him: "And I won't allow anyone else to hurt you". That would change everything for him. He would sit, alert yet calm and relaxed for the remainder of the eighteen hour flight but wouldn't utter another word.

I settled back in my chair for the takeoff, and when the planes wheels finally left the ground I felt a huge sense of relief. I stared out of the window, fully appreciating the magnificent view of the bright green foliage below, shimmering in bright sunshine and a perfectly clear light blue sky. After a few minutes the ocean came into view, a deep blue framed by golden sand and the pilot suddenly announced, just at we were about to fly over the beach below that we were leaving Vietnameese airspace. It was a moment that I couldn't believe. How, after all of this, was it possible that I got out of this alive? I spent the next ten minutes thanking God that I had been spared, and would thank Him many, many more times later. It was not just a matter of luck by any means, it was a miracle, a series of miracles. Thank you Lord Jesus. All honor and glory to God the Father.

<u>Glory be to God in the Highest</u>